CW01524522

THE FABER LETTERS

Books by
Sir William Golding
1911–1993
Nobel Prize in Literature

Fiction
LORD OF THE FLIES
THE INHERITORS
PINCHER MARTIN
FREE FALL
THE SPIRE
THE PYRAMID
THE SCORPION GOD
THE PAPER MEN
RITES OF PASSAGE
CLOSE QUARTERS
FIRE DOWN BELOW
TO THE ENDS OF THE EARTH
(comprising *Rites of Passage*,
Close Quarters
and
Fire Down Below
in a revised text;
foreword by the author)
THE DOUBLE TONGUE

Essays
THE HOT GATES
A MOVING TARGET

Travel
AN EGYPTIAN JOURNAL

Plays
THE BRASS BUTTERFLY
LORD OF THE FLIES
adapted for the stage by Nigel Williams

WILLIAM GOLDING

The Faber Letters

Selected and edited by

TIM KENDALL

faber

First published in 2025
by Faber & Faber Ltd
The Bindery, 51 Hatton Garden
London EC1N 8HN

Typeset by Sam Matthews
Printed and bound by Gomer Press, Llandysul, Wales

A CIP record for this book is available from the British Library

ISBN 978-0-571-37442-7

10 9 8 7 6 5 4 3 2 1

Contents

Illustrations

Introduction

After William Golding won the Booker Prize in 1980 for *Rites of Passage*, he wrote to his editor at Faber & Faber, Charles Monteith. This was no ordinary thank-you letter. Looking back over a relationship that had already lasted twenty-seven years, Golding finally came out with the 'embarrassing and unEnglish' sentences: 'Three people have been of major importance and influence in my life and you are one of them. There is a way in which I am as a writer at least partly your creation.' In Golding's personal pantheon, Monteith completed a Trinity with his father Alec and his wife Ann.

The reasons for Golding's gratitude are not hard to find. During the war he had decided to abandon poetry in favour of prose, but two completed novels and one work of non-fiction later, he seemed no closer to finding a publisher. Off went the typescript to the next firm on the list, and soon enough it came back – with few, if any, words of encouragement. He remembered after one rejection 'shouting furiously – "It's Good! I know it's good!"', but no one seemed to be listening. Golding's next novel, 'Strangers from Within', looked set to suffer the same ignominious fate as its predecessors when he started sending it out on New Year's Day, 1953. By the time it landed on the slush pile at Faber in September, it had done the rounds and collected at least seven (and probably more) rejections on the way. The typescript bore the telltale signs. Only the first few pages were badly dog-eared: it was possible to pinpoint where everyone had given up reading. In case that evidence wasn't already inauspicious enough, Faber paid a freelancer to vet their unsolicited typescripts, and she gave her brutal opinion of 'Strangers from Within' in the top left-hand corner of Golding's cover letter: 'Absurd & uninteresting fantasy [. . .]. Rubbish and dull. Pointless.' Her verdict was rounded off with a large encircled 'R' for 'Reject'.

The man who picked up this unprepossessing document – later remembering it as 'a large yellowing manuscript [. . .] bound in rather depressing hairy-brown cardboard' – would become the finest talent-spotting editor of his generation. Charles Monteith had been employed to take over editorial duties from T. S. Eliot, who had recently bought shares at Faber to help keep the firm afloat in the midst of a serious financial crisis. The stakes could hardly have been higher; Eliot privately feared that Faber might not last another two or three years. It was Monteith's urgent job to set about refreshing and rejuvenating the list, and the extent of his success is demonstrated by the writers he recruited: Samuel Beckett, P. D. James, Ted Hughes, Sylvia Plath, Seamus Heaney, Jan Morris, Paul Muldoon and many others were published partly or wholly thanks to his scouting.

In the absence of a biography, we glimpse Monteith through other people's lives and letters: Thom Gunn in 1961 turning up for lunch with Monteith at a Pall Mall gentlemen's club wearing leathers and cowboy boots ('I had no idea at all he would arrive so bizarrely attired,' Monteith wrote in apology); Sylvia Plath lying in her hospital bed next to a bunch of flowers (tulips, perhaps?) sent by Monteith after an appendicectomy; Philip Larkin complaining that Monteith's periodic queries over the progress of the next book sounded like a Catholic priest asking if there would be another little one arriving this year. Seamus Heaney once recalled that his first letter from Monteith – who had been impressed by a batch of Heaney's poems in the *New Statesman* – felt 'like getting a letter from God the Father'. For three decades, Monteith bestrode the literary scene, and it was always surprising to find an author who hadn't met him. After lunch with the novelist Colin Wilson, Golding wrote to Monteith that Wilson must be 'the only person in England you don't know'.

In September 1953, all that glory lay ahead. Monteith was still the new boy on probation, not even a minor deity, let alone God the Father. With exquisite timing, he joined the firm just days after Golding submitted his typescript. 'Strangers from Within' may well have been the first novel that Monteith championed at Faber's weekly Book Committee meeting. He needed to overcome resistance to get it accepted – the sales director declared it unpublishable – but despite their doubts no one at Faber wanted to discourage the new editor. It was an extraordinary beginning to an extraordinary career: what better way to impress his senior colleagues than to find, almost on day one, a much-rejected typescript by an obscure forty-something schoolteacher and turn it into one of the bestselling novels of the twentieth century?

The processes by which the tatty pages of 'Strangers from Within' became *Lord of the Flies* are recorded in the letters published here between Golding and Monteith, as well as in later accounts by both men. The typescript that Monteith read is lost, but Golding's earlier manuscript survives and it allows us to appreciate the challenges that Monteith helped him to address: the unfocused opening that describes a nuclear war and the hurried evacuation of a 'job lot' of boys just before the bomb drops; the jarring description of an unnamed 'other person' on the island – some sort of benevolent supernatural being who dances 'courteously' with Simon in the forest; the tendency to overstate and over-elaborate; and most conspicuously of all, the erratic spelling and punctuation that plague Golding's unpublished writing. Monteith had the patience to look beyond these fixable problems and see what others before him had failed to see: as he himself put it, 'the island was vividly, brilliantly real and the boys were real boys'. For all its abundant flaws, 'Strangers from Within' was a masterpiece in waiting.

The letters leave no doubt about the power relations between Golding and Monteith in their early exchanges. Golding was desperate and ready to agree to anything. He later regretted the toning down of Simon from an out-and-out mystic to a strange loner who may merely be suffering from epilepsy; in every other respect, he not only accepted Monteith's advice but revised the typescript even more drastically than Monteith had planned. The revisions took months and the delay before a final decision from Faber must have been agonising. (Two decades later, Golding had a nightmare in which Monteith wrote 'despondently' that the alterations had not persuaded him that the typescript could ever amount to anything.) Elated when his novel was accepted for publication, Golding called Monteith 'part-author', gladly conceding that if it 'achieves any measure of success, much will be due to your severe, but healthy pruning'.

Scholars sometimes claim that *Lord of the Flies* sold slowly at first, and certainly sales were much more modest than in the early 1960s when it spread across the United States and ousted *The Catcher in the Rye* as the campus novel of choice. Yet by any first-novel standards *Lord of the Flies* did well from the start, with a reprint ordered on the back of overwhelmingly positive reviews and, within weeks of publication, three studios interested in the film rights. American publishers, on the other hand, were less discerning: even in its final form, the novel picked up more rejections in the United States than in London. Realising their mistake, several of those same firms later made strenuous efforts to acquire Golding's novels. His muddled publication history in the States – culminating in two major publishers squabbling in court for the rights to his seventh novel, *Darkness Visible* – must have made him all the more grateful for the support and stability provided by Faber.

Golding stayed loyal to Faber throughout his life despite the suspicion, borne out several times by lucrative offers, that he could make more money elsewhere. In a journal entry from the late 1970s, he records Ann and his daughter Judy insisting that 'I dont use the clout that I have with F&F', but, he adds, 'I am still grateful and shall always be for the rescue operation they did on the middle-aged man who had written Strangers From Within. Thou shalt not muzzle the publisher that treadeth out the corn.' Golding never lost that sense of obligation. He negotiated directly with Faber over his books, accepted their offers without haggling, and allowed them to act as agents for his novels abroad. Whether his loyalty was to the firm or specifically to Monteith never needed to be put to the test: Monteith spent his entire publishing career at Faber and became chairman in 1977. When he stepped down and went into semi-retirement four years later, Faber wisely kept him on as Golding's de facto editor; he continued to read and discuss Golding's works with him right to the end. 'Without Charles' – Golding's journal again – 'we could almost say, no William Golding. Ann and Charles as literary parents!'

The story of 'Strangers from Within' and its makeover may give the impression that Golding was an inept genius and Monteith his efficient deliverer. If so, Golding learnt quickly. Never again did he require the same level of intervention. Some novels arrived out of nowhere 'like flying saucers', as he described them to Monteith, while others struggled painstakingly through multiple drafts, but in every case Golding had internalised the lessons of Monteith's editing. When he hesitantly submitted the typescript of his second novel, *The Inheritors*, no doubt expecting a similar series of extensive revisions, Golding was taken aback by Monteith's judgement that it could be published as it stood, explaining in his delighted panic that he had not intended this as the final version. Similarly, the third and fourth novels, *Pincher Martin* and *Free Fall*, required Monteith's assent more than his blue pencil. The fifth, *The Spire*, proved more recalcitrant, and Monteith's detailed suggestions helped Golding to bore a tunnel through a series of confused and conflicting drafts. Just as importantly, Monteith talked him down from calling *The Spire* 'An Erection at Barchester'. Golding had a career-long knack of causing editorial palpitations with his titles: *Pincher Martin* was known for a time as 'The Chinese Have X-ray Eyes', while his sixth novel, *The Pyramid*, narrowly avoided being published as 'Stilbourne Stories'.

Although Monteith was the chief protagonist in Golding's dealings with Faber, the supporting cast included several others who became trusted friends. There are letters in this volume to Rosemary Goad, who started as Monteith's secretary and ended up as Faber's first female director; Peter du Sautoy, the firm's general manager, responsible for overseeing Golding's financial interests abroad; Matthew Evans, who succeeded Monteith as chairman and once gave Golding a Krugerrand ('Value about two hundred and thirty pounds,' Golding noted drily) for resisting a poaching attempt from Penguin; and John Bodley, Golding's nominal editor at Faber after Monteith's departure, of whom the Goldings were sufficiently fond that they invited him to spend several weeks with them on a small boat travelling along the Nile. Ultimately, though, it was Monteith who managed the firm's relationship with Golding, a huge but volatile asset who was often fretting and in need of reassurance.

It took more than two years for their letters to replace 'Dear Monteith' and 'Dear Golding' with 'Dear Charles' and 'Dear Bill'. As an employee dictating correspondence to his secretary, Monteith was always on duty, which is one reason why he sounded more formal than Golding despite being a decade younger. Their growing friendship was founded on crucial similarities. Both were grammar school boys from the provinces (Lisburn in Monteith's case, Marlborough in Golding's), both read English at Oxford (where Golding was the only grammar school boy in his college), and both served with distinction in the war. They shared a love of Greece, science fiction and fine dining, as well as the fine drinking that accompanied it. Their careers and reputations moved in lockstep: Monteith told Ann after Golding's death that 'probably the most important event in my own life was Faber's publication of *Lord of the Flies*'. Yet, although they could eventually have been mistaken for pillars of the establishment – Monteith as Fellow of All Souls in Oxford and chairman at Faber, Golding as Nobel laureate and knight of the realm – both were outsiders doing their best to hide the fact that neither man ever quite belonged.

John Sparrow, Warden of All Souls, warned Faber in 1953 that Monteith 'lacked distinction' and suffered from a 'coarseness of fibre'.

Golding, similarly, had been labelled 'not quite a gent' by the Oxford University careers service, which judged that he lacked the necessary refinement to teach in a public school. Golding was tormented by a sense of social inferiority throughout his life, and his preoccupation with money, apparent even in his very last letter to Faber when he had long since accumulated far more than he could ever hope to spend, was a bulwark against a deep sense of inadequacy that could easily lapse into self-loathing. In his journals, Golding characterised his outward self as 'Bolonius', an imposter whom someone would sooner or later expose. As a man who kept his private life private – homosexual acts were not even partially decriminalised in the UK until 1967 – Monteith knew that fear all too well. In the 1970s he was subjected to a campaign of harassment that involved libellous letters being sent anonymously to Golding and a number of other prominent people in the arts and judiciary. The episode was so excruciatingly painful that Golding vowed not even to commit the details to his journal.

Monteith was uniquely placed to understand that Golding would always be one bad review away from a crisis. He needed regular encouragement. Golding admitted that he could 'only just' write his books, and he ascribed his barren patches to a failure of nerve. As soon as he was able to afford the expenditure, he made sure to avoid publication day for novel after novel, explaining to Monteith that he wanted to be 'out of the country when the various hatchets fall'. Unfortunately, Golding could not escape when *The Pyramid* appeared in 1967 because Judy was awaiting her degree results. Monteith's in-house memo records the consequences: 'Golding is in fact still at home although very much in hiding and Ann said he was in a very nervous state, not reading any of his reviews and refusing to speak to anybody at all on the telephone.' The reviews for *The Pyramid* were perfectly respectable, but that had long since stopped being the point. A dozen years passed before Golding published another novel, and for most of that time he doubted that he would ever dare to write one again.

Golding's correspondence with Monteith and Faber ebbed and flowed according to his own productivity: in the period 1954–67 he published six novels, a play, and a volume of essays and reviews; from 1968 to 1978 he managed one slim collection of stories, suffering as he was from the interrelated issues of depression, alcoholism and writer's block; and from 1979 until his death in 1993, there were five new novels (plus another published posthumously) as well as a travel book and a second volume of essays. The letters map onto his tripartite career, falling away in the trough of that middle period but coming back during the late 1970s as Golding broke his drought by somehow managing to write two prizewinning novels concurrently. *Darkness Visible* (1979) and *Rites of Passage* (1980) relied on Monteith's approval. Having sent Monteith the latest draft of *Darkness Visible* along with his own verdict that it was 'a mess [. . .] jumbled, inconsistent, wallowing', Golding suffered physically while waiting for a reply: 'No letter from Charles Monteith [. . .] – that makes my teeth ache'; 'Still no letter from Charles! I had a dreadful night'; 'no Charles by second post. My heart is not so much in my boots as down below them and buried.' Knowing his author, Monteith often warned Golding not to 'think gloomy thoughts' if his reply to the latest typescript did not arrive immediately. The advice never worked.

The Booker Prize in 1980 and the Nobel Prize in 1983 seem to have given Golding some small measure of peace. When John Bodley took over as his Faber editor in the mid-1980s, most of Golding's agitation was directed towards more tangential topics like cover designs, with very little discussion of the novels themselves. Retired though he was, Monteith continued to serve that purpose behind the scenes, writing blurbs and offering suggestions over plotting as late as 1988 when Golding finished the last novel that would appear in his lifetime, *Fire Down Below*. Relatively little correspondence survives from the period because discussions were usually face-to-face; Monteith would travel down to Cornwall and stay with the Goldings for days at a time as they thrashed out any problems with the latest novel over a bottle or two of wine. That these trips were not all, or even mostly, about the work is implied by one of Golding's more laconic journal entries: 'Ann and Charles are now watching Neighbours and drinking champagne.' Matthew Evans remembered calling in on the Goldings early one afternoon and finding Monteith dozing in a deckchair while Bill and Ann slept upstairs; he retreated and left them to their slumbers.

Monteith has the honour of being the only person to whom two of Golding's novels are dedicated. The dedication to his ninth novel, *The Paper Men*, reads 'For my friend and publisher CHARLES MONTEITH'. Friendship takes priority, and the preference for 'publisher' over 'editor' cannot be accidental: it serves as a reminder that Monteith *is* Faber. At various times through the 1980s, Golding felt uneasy about what he saw as Monteith's increasing marginalisation at the firm, so this was more than an act of gratitude; it was the gentlest of warnings, all the more eye-catching for coming immediately after Golding's Nobel triumph. In the event, Golding's relationship with Faber held firm until his death in June 1993. Monteith died in May 1995, not quite living long enough to see the posthumous publication of *The Double Tongue* with its dedication that honoured him as first among equals:

> The author's family
> wish to dedicate his last work
> to all those at Faber
> who helped, encouraged and cared for
> him and his writing
> over the past forty years.
> Above all, this book is for
> CHARLES

A Note on the Text

> It's a moody-making thought that some bugger will either silently
> (unobtrusively) correct my spelling, or even worse, interrupt the text
> with brackets and sic in italics. But my bad grammar and bad spelling
> was me. To correct them for ressurection is to ally yourself with the
> pusillanimous objector who said 'Lord, he stinketh!' Of course I do,
> but let me come up like I was.

Although Golding was thinking about the posthumous publication of
his journals when he wrote this entry in 1982, there is no good reason why the same principle should not apply to his correspondence.
As authors' proscriptions go, his statement may lack the severity of
Shakespeare's 'Curst be he that moves my bones', but its force is compelling enough. I have kept editorial interventions to a minimum by
correcting errors that are obvious slips of the pen or the typewriter
('7th' for '7ht', 'to' for 'ot', and so on) and leaving everything else to
stand ('ressurection') without all those prim little brackets and sics
that Golding deplored. The hair-raising thing, after all, is not that
a Nobel laureate should be unable to spell – Yeats got there first –
but that Golding spent two decades teaching English to teenagers.
Although he was sacked from his first job at Maidstone Grammar,
that seems to have been for what he later described as 'an unacademic
combination of drink, women and politics' rather than an inability to
sort out his apostrophes.

Every letter in this volume comes with contextual information. The
author and recipient are named – Golding is always abbreviated to
'WG' – and the date is given. Letters are identified as MS (manuscript),
TS (typescript), PC (postcard) or TELEGRAM. They are all found in
the Faber archive unless clearly stated: letters marked MONTEITH and
GOLDING in the top right-hand corner are in the hands of the respec-
tive families; EXETER denotes the William Golding Literary Archive at
the University of Exeter, and EMORY the Charles Monteith collection
at Emory University in Atlanta, Georgia. The abbreviation 'J' refers
to Golding's unpublished journals: running from the autumn of 1971

until the day before his death in 1993, these amount to 2.4 million words and prove invaluable in detailing his moods and movements. The journals' evidence has helped to date and annotate letters that would otherwise have remained elusive.

I have followed the same editorial standards for all correspondence, whether to or from Golding. When Golding writes with unintended irony about his 'laisser faire' spelling scheme, Monteith (or Monteith's secretary) mirrors his mistake in the reply. Both errors have been left uncorrected. Text that is underlined in the letters is here italicised and dots have been removed from acronyms for ease of reading. The only other differences come in the headers and valedictions. Golding threw away most letters from Faber and rarely made copies of his own letters. His originals survive in the Faber archive, sometimes dated, sometimes on headed paper, and sometimes with his scrawled address added in pen. (Golding was a left-hander taught to write right-handed, which can make legibility a problem; there is a word on the opening page of the *Lord of the Flies* manuscript that continues to defy all comers.) Whether honoured in the breach or in the observance, these epistolatory conventions seem worth preserving, and in my notes I have done my best to convey Golding's inconsistent approach to dates and locations. The same does not apply to letters from Faber because the vast majority exist as file copies with no header and no signature but only Monteith's initialling: 'CM' or sometimes 'CMM'. Rather than including initials that would not have been added to the version received by Golding, I have left the end of those letters blank. For the many letters that Golding has signed and then typed his name more formally, I have only included the signature.

My initial intention for this project was simply to make an edition of the correspondence between Golding and Monteith. Working in the Faber archive, and finding wonderful letters to other Faber employees, I soon realised what a weirdly self-denying ordinance that would be. The bigger problem is that an exclusive focus on Monteith would distort the last decade of Golding's career, as Monteith gradually withdrew from his official (and then his unofficial) role at Faber. John Bodley assumed many of Monteith's duties, liaising with Golding over sales, cover designs and publicity, and helping with the perennial challenge of coming up with decent titles for his novels. Books have to end somewhere, and this volume would be at least half as long again if I had included all the correspondence between Golding and

Faber. Even so, I have represented Bodley generously because he was Golding's only other Faber editor. Apart from anything else, Bodley's correspondence with Golding is often very funny. The misunderstanding over what Golding means by 'tits'; Golding's annoyance over an old acquaintance writing a novel called 'Lady of the Thighs'; the commotion when a 'landlubber' artist makes an illustration of a ship with its sails 'arse-backwards' for the cover of the sea trilogy – whatever the situation, Bodley always seems to relish both the privilege and the absurdity of his role.

Golding thought long and hard about whether his journals should ever be published. What he would have made of an edition of letters is impossible to say because, as one particular journal entry reveals, he never foresaw the possibility: 'The days when ones correspondence was published, are gone, I believe, since so much communication is done by 'phone.' The sheer heft of this volume demonstrates his misjudgement, but the telephone does undoubtedly take a toll. The sinking of Golding's yacht *Tenace* in 1967 and the winning of the Nobel Prize in 1983 – both, in their different ways, life-changing events – leave almost no trace in the letters of the period. This should not imply that Faber did not trouble itself to enquire after Golding's health when he and his family nearly drowned in the Channel, or remained unbothered when one of its authors became a Nobel laureate. Other forms of communication were, of course, available. I have added annotations and year summaries to fill these silences in the correspondence so that Golding can be tracked not only across but beyond his letters. Golding liked to think of himself as a moving target; the annotations try to keep him in sight.

Readers of edited correspondence know how annoyingly mysterious any excisions can seem: there is no way of telling whether the excised passage was deemed too dull to be suffered into print or so scandalous that lawyers would have taken an interest. This volume transcribes letters whole wherever possible. If the style is the man – even the bad spelling and bad grammar – it follows that arranging to meet in the office next Thursday at 3 p.m. is the relationship, or at least an essential part of it. I have, nevertheless, made two kinds of redaction. The first occurs only once, when Monteith quotes a racist quatrain by Philip Larkin. I doubt that this edition is any the worse for banning the N-word, but I have provided a reference for readers curious enough to hunt down Larkin's verse for themselves. The second kind of redaction seeks to protect the living. The English schoolboy who argued that Piggy's glasses could not have made fire, and about whom Golding expressed the fervent hope that he would end up drug-smuggling in Turkey, does not deserve to be outed fifty years later; nor does the reviewer who so infuriated Monteith that he joked about hiring a hit-man. In the last months of his life, Robert Browning picked up the newly published correspondence of Edward FitzGerald and was distraught after reading FitzGerald's flippant remarks from twenty-eight years previously: 'Mrs Browning's Death is rather a relief to me, I must say: no more Aurora Leighs, thank God!' I can only apologise if any FitzGeraldisms still lurk in this volume.

THE FABER LETTERS

1953

William Golding first comes into view as a schoolteacher living in a council flat in Salisbury with his wife Ann and his children David (b. 1940) and Judy (b. 1945). His only significant publication to date is a short volume, *Poems*, from Macmillan in 1934. Having decided during the war to abandon poetry and dedicate himself to prose, he has since completed at least two novels and a work of non-fiction, none of which has found a publisher. It looks like the same fate will befall his next novel. When it turns up on the slush pile at Faber & Faber, 'Strangers from Within' has already been rejected at least seven times. Luckily for Golding, Faber has recently appointed a new editor, Charles Monteith, who is keen to make an impression by finding his own authors to add to its prestigious list.

WG to Faber & Faber   MS

14 September 1953   21 Bourne Avenue, Salisbury, Wilts.

Dear Sir
    I send you the typescript of my novel
      'Strangers From Within'
which might be defined as an allegorical interpretation of a stock situation.
    I hope you will feel able to publish it.
      Yours faithfully
        William Golding

Faber routinely paid a freelance reader to provide advice on unsolicited manuscript submissions. She has written her verdict in green ink across the top left of the cover letter: '*Time: The Future* Absurd & uninteresting fantasy about the explosion of an atom bomb on the Colonies. A group of children who land in jungle-country near New Guinea. Rubbish & dull. Pointless ℞' ℞ is her abbreviation for 'Reject'.
    'Strangers from Within' is an early title for *Lord of the Flies*. See the Appendix for Charles Monteith's account of the novel's genesis.

3

Charles Monteith to WG

15 October 1953

Dear Mr Golding,

I am afraid we've kept '*Strangers from Within*' rather a long time and I am writing simply to say that we are interested in it, but have not yet reached any decision about it. I hope to let you know something more definite before long.

Yours sincerely,
Charles Monteith.

WG to Charles Monteith MS

20 October 1953   21 Bourne Avenue, Salisbury, Wilts.

Dear Sir

Thank you for your letter dated 15th October. I am glad that Messrs Faber are interested in my novel 'Strangers From Within' and hope they will decide to publish it.

Yours Sincerely
W. G. Golding.

Charles Monteith to WG TS

27 November 1953

Dear Mr Golding,

As I mentioned in my letter of 15th October, we are interested in 'STRANGERS FROM WITHIN', and I should very much like to have a talk with you about it.

Is there, I wonder, any chance of seeing you in London in the near future? I suggest tentatively next Thursday, 3rd December; alternative dates that I could manage are Monday, 7th, and Thursday, 10th. If any of these would suit you do please let me know. So far as time is concerned, I suggest 12 noon and I should be very pleased if you would lunch with me afterwards; but if an afternoon appointment would suit you better, 3 p.m. would do instead. I look forward to seeing you soon.

Yours sincerely,
Charles Monteith.

As is standard practice throughout the correspondence, the file copy has been initialled by Monteith in pen above his printed name. The original letter received by Golding would no doubt have carried Monteith's full signature.

WG to Charles Monteith

MS

28 November 1953   21 Bourne Avenue, Salisbury, Wilts

Dear Mr Monteith

Thank you for your letter of the 27th November. I will come up to town on the 3rd December, next Thursday, and be at 24 Russell Square at twelve noon.

I am very glad to accept your invitation to lunch, and look forward to meeting you

Yours Sincerely

William Golding

24 Russell Square had been the home of Faber & Faber since its founding in the 1920s.

WG to Charles Monteith

TS

6 December 1953   21 Bourne Avenue, Salisbury, Wilts.

Dear Mr Monteith

Here are some bits of the emended version of my novel – the beginning, the middle and the end. I've done away with the separate bits, Prologue, Interlude, Epilogue, and as you'll see, merged them into the body of the text. Furthermore, chapter one, now begins with the meeting of Piggy and Ralph, and I'm allowing the story of how they got there – or all that is necessary of it – to come out in conversation.

Simon is the next job, and a more difficult one. I suppose you agree that I must convey a theophany of some sort or else he wont be as big a figure as he ought. I'm going to cut down the elaborate description of it, though, and try to get the same effect by reticence. Then I'm distributing odd bits and pieces of 'Simonry' throughout the text, to build him up.

As you see, the 'commander' is now the 'officer'; Ralph's dream about his father has gone; and I'm making Piggy's speech ungrammatical but not mis-spelling it.

If these changes are satisfactory, I hope to have them completed in a very few days. Re-reading the novel as a stranger to it, I am bound to agree with almost all your criticism, and am full of enthusiasm and energy for the cleaning up process. In fact I'm right back on the island.

I hope you'll forgive the tatty and uncorrected type-script, and this formless letter, but I've worked hard and am a bit dazed. What do you think of 'A Cry Of Children' as a title? It's got at least two levels, which is more than the other had.

Thank you for our very pleasant meeting and lunch. I hope to return it some time.

yours sincerely
William Golding.

This is the first letter to Monteith that Golding types. He has added Monteith's name and his own signature by hand, as well as making several small additions and corrections.

In his essay on *Lord of Flies* (see Appendix), Monteith recalls the first meeting with Golding and his suggestions for how the typescript should be revised. That typescript is lost but an earlier manuscript also contains the passages to which Monteith objects. It opens by describing the hurried evacuation of a 'job lot' of boys in the last desperate minutes before a nuclear explosion. Their plane is then damaged in an air battle, and the boys float down onto a coral island in a detachable tube under a huge parachute. At Monteith's urging, Golding cuts these pages and the novel begins with the boys already on the island.

The manuscript portrays Simon as a mystic. He ventures alone into the forest, where he meets an unnamed divinity – the 'other person' – who dances with Simon and communicates silently. Monteith remembers concluding that 'Simon was not to me, and would not be, I suspected, to most readers wholly credible'; he asks Golding to tone down the mysticism and 'make Simon explicable in purely rational terms'.

Charles Monteith to WG   TS

14 December 1953

Dear Mr Golding,

Very many thanks for your letter and my apologies for having been so long in replying to it. My excuse is that I was very busy last week and hadn't time to get down to it properly.

As you can probably see from a quick glance at them, I have gone through these emended bits fairly carefully and I am more than pleased with the way the revision is going. The main faults to be put right were structural, – prologue, interlude and epilogue; and the 'theophany' of Simon. It seems to me that you have dealt with the first quite admirably, and I look forward very much to seeing what you have done with Simon.

The other criticisms I had to make related more to the 'surface' of the book; they were textural or superficial rather than structural, – e.g., the way Piggy talks. And, as you can see from the various tentative emendations I have pencilled in, I think the 'surface' could probably still be polished up a bit here and there. What I feel about these new bits you have sent is that you are perhaps still tending to over-emphasise; to make points rather too directly when they could be made more effectively by implication.

Instead of going through the various points in detail, I am sending these new bits back with my own suggestions pencilled in; by looking at the various alterations I have made I think you can see the sort of thing I have in mind. I do hope you don't think I am being too niggardly about all these alterations, but I feel that in this novel it is frightfully important, if possible, to get the emphasis exactly right.

I look forward to getting the rest of your amendments when they are ready; then, if I may, I'd like to go through them, and indeed through the whole novel again, in the same sort of way. Then perhaps we could have another talk about it.

'A Cry of Children' is a much better title, I think, but I am still not completely happy about it. I have a sort of feeling that the word 'island' should be there somewhere. But we can leave that until the very end. A perfect title is the sort of thing that is suddenly revealed rather than thought out.

Yours ever,
Charles Monteith.

WG to Charles Monteith   TS

18 December 1953   21 Bourne Avenue, Salisbury, Wilts.

Dear Mr Monteith

Here are some 'Simon' extracts. I hope you'll forgive my own MS scribbles lying on them thick, but they are mainly corrections of an obvious sort. I'm sorry to have been so long about them, but I've been ill since I saw you last and this has held up production.

When I got your corrections to the previous extracts I examined them carefully and I accept them in full. I recognise my own anxious tendency to overstate and propose to guard against it. I also observe an extraordinary inability to put commas and apostrophes in the right place!

I dont know how long you are taking at Christmas but I shall be at the following address from the 22nd of this month to the 8th of the next – 29 The Green Marlborough wilts, Telephone 645.

There are a number of places in the story where I feel some small additions are necessary. I've not bothered to include these as you'll see them when I put the whole thing together again.

With every good wish for Christmas and the new year
      yours sincerely
        William Golding.

29 The Green, Marlborough, was the address of Golding's parents. He grew up there; the house appears regularly in his recorded dreams and several times in his novels and essays.

Charles Monteith to WG   TS

30 December 1953

Dear Mr Golding,

Here are the 'Simon' bits back, again with my tentative emendations pencilled on. I think you have hit on the right approach to this most tricky of all the problems in the novel; and my emendations are again simply 'tonings down' of emphasis. I think the danger to be guarded against now is turning Simon into a prig, a self-righteous infant who insists on saying his prayers in the dorm while the naughty boys throw pillows at him. In the early stages I feel it is enough simply to indicate that he is in some way odd, different, withdrawn; and therefore capable of the lonely, rarified courage of facing the pig's head and climbing to the mountain top.

The allegory, the theophany, is the imaginative foundation; and like all foundations is there to be concealed and built on. As a general rule, I think, the more completely the 'gimmick' is concealed, the more effective it is. Did you notice, for example, in L. P. Hartley's recent novel *The Go-Between* how the boy's name Leo, which reoccurred again and again, helped to build up the atmosphere of feverish high summer? Leo is, of course, the appropriate Zodiacal sign and all the echoes of the word are full of lust and heat and blood.

I look forward very much to the next instalment; or to seeing the whole thing if you are now in a position to put it together again.

Best wishes for 1954.

Yours sincerely,

The Zodiac sign Leo is associated with fire and covers the period 23 July–22 August. L. P. Hartley's *The Go-Between* (1953) tells the story of twelve-year-old Leo Colston, who stays with his schoolfriend Marcus at his country home in Norfolk during the hot summer of 1900. Leo becomes the go-between delivering secret messages between Marcus's sister Marian and a local farmer, Ted. Their relationship is finally discovered, with catastrophic consequences for all concerned.

1954

This is Golding's *annus mirabilis*. The year starts with him busily revising his novel in the light of Monteith's recommendations. By the end of February, it is under contract and has acquired a memorable title: *Lord of the Flies*. The book is published to almost uniformly favourable reviews in September; within the first month, three film studios enquire about the rights. This sudden success ushers in the most prolific period of Golding's life. Dissatisfied with progress on his latest manuscript – a novel titled 'In Search of My Father' – he puts it aside and completes an initial draft in November of what will become his second published novel, *The Inheritors*. Around this time, he also writes a short story titled 'Miss Pulkinhorn' and another story, 'The Rescue', for which he soon develops grander designs.

WG to Charles Monteith   TS

10 January 1954   21 Bourne Avenue, Salisbury, Wilts.

Dear Mr Monteith

Here are the pieces put together. Perhaps you wont mind inspecting the whole thing? As you'll see I've everywhere incorporated your own suggestions. I've lost any kind of objectivity I ever had over this novel and can hardly bear to look at it. This is partly due to my nasty bout of tonsillitis and about the highest temperature ever recorded, but mostly to the effort of patching – so much more wearing than bashing straight ahead at a story!

As a title I thought of 'Nightmare Island' but abandoned it as being too crude. The current one seems all right, if a bit flat.

I will still clean up the text if you wish and you can excise what you like. Part of the trouble has been that I've felt so disinclined to cut down the total number of words. However I've got over that, and the total is now up rather than down. So if you want to throw away any more Simon, go ahead.

I havn't re-typed some pages on which your changes were confined to removing my painful commas. If you want the script for a printer I shall be only too glad to go over it again and make a 'fair copy' more or less.

    yours

      William Golding.

Charles Monteith to WG TS

12 January 1954

Dear Golding,

I feel terribly contrite at having badgered you so much about the novel, particularly when you were ill; and I am more than grateful to you for having been so patient and having worked so hard at it.

I am a bit pushed at the moment, but I'll go through it the moment I've got time and then write to you again.

I do hope you are over your tonsillitis by now.

> Yours ever,
> Charles Monteith.

Charles Monteith to WG TS

11 February 1954

Dear Golding,

I am delighted to be able at last to write and say that we've definitely decided to accept your novel. And though I can't make any promises about this, I am quite hopeful that we shall be able to publish it this autumn.

First of all, I'd better tell you the terms which I have been authorised to offer you for it. Here they are: –

Royalties: 10% to 2,000 copies, 12½% to 5,000 copies, 15% thereafter.

Advance: We shall be willing to pay you £60 as advance on royalties; £30 on signature of contract and £30 on publication.

Option: We should like to have an option on your next two novels.

If you find these terms acceptable let me know; a draft contract can then be prepared here and forwarded to you for signature.

Now about the text. I have been through it all again and let me say at once that I was delighted to find that I was just as much gripped and excited by it as I was the first time I read it. The various emendations and patchings seem to me to have been admirably worked into the original draft.

I've done a bit more editorial work on it. It's been confined as usual mostly to cleaning out commas – thousands of them, I'm afraid; I've also made one or two fresh excisions – toning down Simon to fit in with the tonings down of other parts of the story; and I've redrafted a few sentences here and there, but none of these redrafts are of more than minor importance – just part of the final polishing process. If you would like to have the manuscript back to see what I have done or to give it a final check yourself, do let me know and I'll see that it's sent to you.

In your last letter to me you said – and I was very grateful for it – that you would be willing to type a clean copy of the final version if this should be necessary. I don't in fact think that it will be necessary. It's quite true that the version I have got now is pretty well littered with corrections, but they are all minor ones and I think it should be clean enough for the printer. I'll consult one of our Production people about it and see what they say; if, as I hope, they say it's all right as it stands that will, of course, save a lot of time and will save you a lot of very tiresome labour. But if they do insist on a clean version, I am afraid I'll have to send it to you for re-typing.

Finally, the difficult matter of the title. I must confess that I'm not terribly keen on 'This Island's Mine'; but I've got to confess as well that I haven't so far been able to think of anything very exciting myself. Here are one or two ideas that occurred to me: –

> 'Beast in the Jungle'
> 'The Isle is Full of Noises'
> 'An Island of Their Own'
> 'Fun and Games'

If you get any fresh inspiration about this I hope you'll let me know.

I do hope you'll write or give me a ring next time you come to London; it would be very nice to see you again.

Looking forward to hearing from you.

> Yours sincerely,
> Charles Monteith.

Faber's standard advance for a first novel was £50. At the insistence of the firm's chairman, Geoffrey Faber, this was increased to £60 (the equivalent of £2,000 in 2025) as an acknowledgement of Golding's patience during the decision-making process.

'This Island's Mine' seems to have been Golding's suggestion. It alludes to a speech by Caliban in *The Tempest*: 'This island's mine by Sycorax my mother, / Which thou tak'st from me' (1.2.332–3). Monteith's letter to Golding dated 1 March 1954 implies that at one stage Golding had intended the same lines as the novel's epigraph. The second item in Monteith's own list of possible titles includes a reference to another of Caliban's speeches: 'Be not afeared; the isle is full of noises, / Sounds, and sweet airs, that give delight and hurt not' (3.2.127–8).

WG to Charles Monteith

MS

14 February 1954   21 Bourne Avenue, Salisbury, Wilts.

Dear Monteith

Thank you for your letter. I'm delighted that Fabers are going to publish the novel, and I accept the terms they offer.

I hope that removing commas has not been too desperately boring. As far as a title is concerned, I can only think of

'Nightmare Island'
    and

'To End An Island' – which last appears to me to have something. It has several applications and is the sort of Title which would catch the eye in Boots or Smiths. I shall be glad to know if you agree, and if you do not, how long the question can remain open.

I come to town very seldom, but shall certainly be glad to ring you when I do.

> Yours Sincerely
> William Golding

Charles Monteith to WG

TS

25 February 1954

Dear Golding,

We have now thought again about a title for your novel and the latest suggestion I have got is that it should be called LORD OF THE FLIES. This isn't my own suggestion; it occurred to someone else here; I myself am rather inclined to think that it is a good one. It comes, of course, from one of the most important and memorable episodes in the book and we all think that it's the sort of title which would make an impression and would help the book's sales. If, of course, you object to it, we shouldn't dream of pressing it on you, but if you agree we should be perfectly prepared to accept it.

One further problem has arisen. We are inclined to think that your novel might be helped if the chapters were given headings, though once again of course we won't press this suggestion if you would rather leave them as they are, simply numbered in order. I have in fact drawn up a list of tentative chapter headings which is attached to this letter, but these are purely suggestions and I should be very grateful to know: (a) if you would mind us giving headings to the chapters, and (b) if not, what chapter headings you would like. On the attached list you will find typed on the right-hand side some alternatives to my own suggestions which you might like to consider. This is a rather more urgent problem than the problem of title, since if we do adopt chapter headings they will have to be printed at the top of the pages of text; so I would be more than grateful if you could let me know about this fairly soon.

One further thing. As you may have seen from the papers, a £50 prize is being awarded this year at the Cheltenham Festival for a first novel published between October 1st, 1953 and September 30th, 1954. If we can get your book out in time, I should very much like to enter it for this, and I wonder if you would have any objection? If you haven't, it is, of course, another reason for getting ahead with the production side as quickly as possible, for page proofs of all novels entered have got to be submitted by 1st June.

I know you will be relieved to hear that our Production people say that the present manuscript can go the printers as it stands. So there will be no need for any further typing labours.

Yours sincerely,
Charles Monteith.

In an internal memo dated 19 February 1954, Monteith reports that 'A.P. has suggested LORD OF THE FLIES. I think this is very good myself and it refers to what is perhaps the central episode of the novel.' A.P. was Alan Pringle, a Faber editor with a reputation for finding the right title. Another internal memo is probably similar to the document sent to Golding with proposed chapter titles. It lists Monteith's suggestions in order, with alternatives in red ink (made by his colleague Ann Faber) next to three of them. In the event, all but one of Monteith's titles were accepted; chapter 11, which he had called 'The Fat Boy and the Twins', instead followed Ann Faber's suggestion and became 'Castle Rock'.

WG to Charles Monteith MS

28 February 1954   21 Bourne Avenue, Salisbury.

Dear Monteith

Thanks for your letter, and my apologies for this wretched pen, but I'm out of every other sort except this pedagogic pink.

I like 'Lord Of The Flies' as a title. I used the phrase in the book with malice a-forethought, since its' a translation of 'Beelzebub', or something. Let us settle for it straight away.

About Chapter headings –

My instinct is slightly against them; but I dont really care either way. In any event, I regard the question as one to which you are far more likely to know the answer than I; so if you think they are a Good Thing go ahead. I've ticked the ones in your list that I like best.

I certainly dont object to 'Lord Of The Flies' being entered for the Cheltenham Festival prize. Do I enter it myself, or do you? I hope *you* do!

I'm very glad to hear that the manuscript is good enough for production.

    With best wishes

      William Golding.

The letter is indeed in 'pedagogic pink' – presumably the same pen that Golding used to mark schoolboys' essays. 'Beelzebub' overwrites Golding's initial spelling: 'Baalzebub'.

Charles Monteith to WG   TS

1 March 1954

Dear Golding,

Very many thanks for your letter. You will be pleased to hear, I think – I certainly am – that LORD OF THE FLIES went to Production this morning and you should be getting galley proofs before very long. I've asked them to be as quick about it as they can. I am also trying to get a nice jungly jacket, designed by Anthony Gross or somebody like that: lots of creepers, palms, tall trees and small boys.

I am very glad you like LORD OF THE FLIES as a title. We are all happy about it here. And since, as I mentioned in my last letter, we think this is the sort of novel which is helped by chapter headings, we are going to use the ones which you have agreed to.

I am glad you agree to let us enter your novel for the Cheltenham prize. We will look after all the formalities; there is no need for you to worry about it. There will, of course, be dozens of novels entered, so you shouldn't be disappointed if nothing happens there. But I think it's worth trying.

By the way, if you want to dedicate the book to anyone or to insert any preliminary matter of that nature, would you please let me know as quickly as possible? I've deleted the 'Tempest' quotation (the bit about Sycorax), since that refers to a title which we have now abandoned. There is no need, of course, for any dedication or any epigraph unless you particularly want to have them.

    Yours sincerely,
    Charles Monteith.

Faber went ahead and commissioned the printmaker and painter Anthony Gross to make the 'nice jungly jacket' with tall palms and small boys. Gross also designed the jackets for Golding's next three novels: *The Inheritors* (1955), *Pincher Martin* (1956) and *Free Fall* (1959).

    For the *Tempest* quotation and the abandoned title, see Monteith's letter to Golding dated 11 February 1954.

WG to Charles Monteith   MS

2 March 1954   21 Bourne Avenue, Salisbury, Wilts.

Dear Monteith

    Thank you for your letter – all the news seems very good, and I think you have been very quick. I want this dedication put in the front of the book – on a page by itself, if the paper situation warrants it.

    'For my mother and father.'
Perhaps it could go where the Tempest quotation once was – if it had a page to itself.

    I dont build on the Cheltenham prize, though of course I should like to have it.

    Let me know if there is anything I can do to help on the good work.
    Yours Sincerely
        William Golding

Monteith confirmed in a brief note to Golding on 3 March that the dedication to Golding's parents had been added.

WG to Charles Monteith   MS/TS

27 March 1954   21 Bourne Avenue, Salisbury, Wilts

Dear Monteith

    Your publicity department wanted some facts about me, but I am ashamed to say that I lost their letter. I wonder if you would be kind enough to give them the enclosed sheet and my apologies? I take it that the few facts I have put there are sufficient.

I hope you enjoyed Rose Macaulays Pleasure Of Ruins after your Attic experiences. Living as I do in an area practically scheduled as a public monument by the National Trust, I found her outlook – antiquarian rather than archaeological – very refreshing

Yours Sincerely

William Golding.

WILLIAM GERALD GOLDING

Born St Columb Minor, Cornwall, 1911.

Attended Marlborough Grammar School and Brasenose College, Oxford.

Married 1939, two children.

Navy 1940. Served in cruisers, destroyers, mine-sweepers, and ended the war in command of a Rocket Ship. Saw action against submarines, aircraft, Bismarck, 'D' day on French coast, and island of Walcheren. Acquired a great admiration for naval traditions and spirit.

1945, schoolmaster at Bishop Wordsworths' School, Salisbury. Main interests – sailing, and quite inexplicably, classical Greek which he has taught himself and now reads avidly. Cannot understand this. Writes poetry, and has published a good deal, but believes that poetry should have a surface meaning as well as depths, and finds this a handicap.

LORD OF THE FLIES is an adult view of what might happen in real life if children were left alone on a tropical island. The book treats this situation as a modern myth to be explored, and finds that the shape of society depends on the moral nature of the individual. The author examined carefully the habits of children at play, and drew conclusions which are not flattering to humanity. The remoteness of the story was helpful; and the imaginative experience so intense that at times the author felt that he had access to the plane on which mythology comes into being as an expression of deep truth.

Golding's reference to Monteith's recent 'Attic experiences' makes this the first of many letters that the two men share about their love of Greece.

In *Pleasure of Ruins* (1953), Rose Macauley explores the reasons why so many people across the ages have found the spectacle of ruined buildings pleasurable.

Golding was born not in St Columb Minor but two miles further west at his maternal grandparents' home: 47 Mount Wise, Newquay. He spread the misinformation for many decades, as an unpublished journal entry unrepentantly explains: 'When asked which St Columb I was born in [i.e. St Columb Major or St Columb Minor] I say firmly "St Columb". Newquay shall not pass my lips' (J, 16 November 1986).

Except for a lone verse in *Poetry Review*, Golding's 1934 volume, *Poems*, was the extent of his poetry output. Macmillan turned down a second collection.

Charles Monteith to WG   TS

29 March 1954

Dear Golding,

Very many thanks for sending on the notes about yourself; they are exactly what we wanted.

The other day, by the way, I saw a couple of specimen pages of LORD OF THE FLIES which the printer sent in as a sample and they looked quite admirable to me; I am sorry there wasn't time to send them on to you, but as you know, we are pushing on with the production side of it fairly fast. You should be getting galley proofs before long.

I haven't, alas, read Rose Macaulay's book, though I certainly mean to and everybody tells me how good it is. Indeed, I've got such a frightful nostalgia for Greece at the moment that I rather doubt if I could bear to read it just now.

            Yours ever,
            Charles Monteith.

PS Have you read THE CONFIDENTIAL CLERK yet? If you haven't, do let me know and I'll send you a copy.

T. S. Eliot's verse play *The Confidential Clerk* was first performed in 1953 and published by Faber in March 1954.

WG to Charles Monteith   MS

25 April 1954   21 Bourne Avenue, Salisbury, Wilts.

Dear Monteith

Thank you for your letter of 29th March. I'm sorry not to have answered it before, but schoolmasters only have holidays to spend, and I've been away for a month.

You mention galley proofs of Lord Of The Flies – but I havnt had them yet. I thought you might like to know this, in case they've gone astray.

I havnt read 'The Confidential Clerk' and should certainly be glad to see a copy.

> Yours ever
> William Golding.

Charles Monteith to WG TS

27 April 1954

Dear Golding,

Thank you for your letter of 25th April. I may have been over optimistic about the galley proofs of LORD OF THE FLIES. The latest news is that we probably won't have them until about 10th May. When they come, by the way, I would be extremely grateful if you could deal with them as quickly as possible for I'm very anxious to get the book into page proof before the end of May; the reason is that 1st June is the closing date for Cheltenham entries and we have got to have page proofs for that.

I'm enclosing a copy of THE CONFIDENTIAL CLERK with this letter; I very much hope that you enjoy it.

> Yours sincerely,
> Charles Monteith.

WG to Charles Monteith MS

4 May 1954   21 Bourne Avenue, Salisbury, Wilts

Dear Monteith

Thank you for the letter, and for 'The Confidential Clerk' which I am reading with pleasure. I must try and see it when the theatre here gets round to it.

I note that you expect proofs at about the tenth of this month. I will certainly correct them at top speed when they come. I shall be glad to hear that they are in Cheltenham by June 1st!

> Yours ever
> William Golding.

Charles Monteith to WG

20 May 1954

Dear Golding,

I have just finished reading the galleys of LORD OF THE FLIES and this note is simply to let you know that I'm even more enthusiastic about it than I was before. Though I must have read it through four or five times by now and seen it at every stage, I still simply couldn't put the proofs down until I had finished them. And I'm delighted to find that it's had precisely the same effect on several other people here who hadn't read it before; indeed, in two cases I have had complaints that it resulted in nightmares! What a terrific book it is; I do congratulate you on it.

Don't worry, by the way, about the Cheltenham Festival. As you probably noticed, I had some short galleys prepared – which are infinitely more easy to cope with than ordinary long galleys – and the Festival authorities are quite willing to consider novels in this form. They will be submitted in a day or two.

And many thanks, too, for dealing with your own galleys so quickly. We can now get it into page proof. The only point that perhaps still needs a little attention is the question of Ralph's hair! Again, it struck me that there was a danger of over-emphasis here. The long, blinding hair is of course enormously important, but could it be that it's referred to rather too often? If you don't mind, I think I'd like to delete *some* of the references to it. By doing that I'm quite certain that the effect will be enhanced rather than diminished. But if you don't agree, do please say so.

> Yours ever,
> Charles Monteith.

Lord of the Flies did not win the Cheltenham Festival competition. In 1956 the Festival Director, John Moore, confided to Monteith that the novel had 'produced among our judges powerful enthusiasms and powerful antipathies', but that the 'strong feeling of the antis' ensured that it 'just missed getting in the first three'.

WG to Charles Monteith

21 May 1954   21 Bourne Avenue, Salisbury, Wilts

Dear Monteith

Thank you for your letter, and the kind things you say about 'Lord

Of The Flies'. I only hope that other people agree with you!

By all means cut Ralph's Hair for him – I had some doubts of it myself.

Let me know if there's anything else I can do to help on the good work.

yours
William Golding.

WG to Charles Monteith MS

23 May 1954   21 Bourne Avenue, Salisbury, Wilts

Dear Monteith

After your last letter I took 'Lord Of The Flies' and read it again, to try and find something that would give me nightmares – but what I found was a quantity of misprints that I had not corrected! I made such an effort to get the whole book back to you without delay that I'm afraid the proof-reading, particularly in the last bit of the book, was not close and accurate. Is there anything I can do about this? Or will it be sufficient if they are put right when the book is in page? – if that is the correct technicality.

Yours ever
William Golding.

Charles Monteith to WG TS

24 May 1954

Dear Golding,

Many thanks for your letters. At the moment I am going through the galleys myself and I will correct any misprints which I spot. But further corrections can certainly be made in page, so you can give it another going over then.

Many thanks for saying I can trim Ralph's hair a bit.

Yours ever,
Charles Monteith.

WG to Charles Monteith MS

17 June 1954   21 Bourne Avenue, Salisbury, Wilts

Dear Monteith

I have just received back the galleys that I returned to you as corrected. I am horrified to find what a quantity of mistakes I left in for you to deal with. My only excuse is that I thought it was such a rush job that I worked non-stop and therefore scamped it. However I'm very sorry that you had so much work to do that should have been mine.

The page proofs seem to me to be attractive, and the novel genuine, as far as I am able to judge. May I say at this point that I think you have done a very clever and helpful piece of work on it? The novel is swift, now, with a measure of subtlety, and tautness. If it achieves any measure of success, much will be due to your severe, but healthy pruning.

I see commas sprinkled over this page mechanically a nervous habit like biting the nails. when writing to you in future I shall omit all ⸜ punctuation⟨!⟩

  Yours ever
   William Golding

The copy-editing marks are Golding's.

Charles Monteith to WG TS

21 June 1954

Dear Golding,

I was delighted to receive your very nice letter of 17th June. Working on LORD OF THE FLIES was to me a very real pleasure. From the moment I first read the manuscript I was quite sure about its quality; and I *thought* I knew the sort of pruning and trimming that was needed. As the process went on it must have been rather maddening for you to see your own work being mauled about by somebody else, but I am more than pleased that you are satisfied with the final results. And may I say again how very grateful I personally am to you for having received all my criticisms so kindly.

22

We have provisionally fixed September 17th as publication date. The other day I saw the drawing which Anthony Gross has made for the jacket and thought it admirable. I do hope you like it; as soon as proofs of it are ready I'll send one to you.

When we met last year I remember you telling me about another novel you were working on. Is it too early, I wonder, to ask you how it is going? I'd be more than interested to see it when it's ready.

Yours ever,

WG to Charles Monteith   MS

25 June 1954   21 Bourne Avenue, Salisbury, Wilts

Dear Monteith

Thank you for your letter. I feel very cheerful about 'Lord Of The Flies' at the moment, and full of surprise that I could ever have written anything so interesting. At the moment it's my favourite book! I only hope reviewers dont think its' a boy's book gone wrong.

You asked after the other novel we discussed – ~~'Telegonus.'~~ 'In Search Of My Father'. Can I – may I – risk imposing on you by saying what I have about me at the moment, and asking for advice from your end? I apologise in advance for what is obviously going to be a huge letter, and hope it doesnt catch you just going off to Aleppo or Mecca or somewhere.

I started 'In Search Of My Father' about a year ago. The theme is, or rather was to be the father–son relationship. We all, (mythologically) go off to find him and end up by displacing him in the world, killing him in fact, and loving and pitying him at the same time for our mortality. I wrote about 130,000 words of this and have, perhaps 30,000 to go. The book became a picaresque, with adventures, hair-raising and smutty, but of unequal interest. The original idea sank down, but is still there, I think. Working again on 'Lord Of The Flies' came between me and the first conception and the book faltered.

Then you sent me 'The Confidential Clerk' (for which, thanks! I enjoyed it and want to see it, but honestly am floored by it – I feel a significance which escapes me. I'll send it on to you but have left it at school at the moment) and at the time I was producing a Greek Play down here, so my interest in the theatre re-awoke. I've done a good bit of amateur writing for the stage, by the way, and some semi-professional acting. I began to think of a play about the forces of nature which we have evoked, and I call it 'Dionysus' – the Bacchae of Euripides stands at the back of it. Is this of any interest to you? I hear by bush telegraph that various publishers, incensed by the sales of plays over the counter, are trying to get in first by publishing plays before they are successes instead of after, so the idea is not entirely hair-brained.

Then there is my first novel 'Short Measure' about a school boy who is killed by the preoccupation of the people who should be looking after him. That went to over twenty publishers most of whom said it was good material, and vivid but badly integrated. (I précis.) I forget what your readers said, but they must have seen it. I feel myself that the basic conception was honest and good and that some chapters are moving: but the strands arnt woven close.

What do you think? If you feel the effort is warranted, I will clean up and type out a chapter of 'In Search Of My Father' so that you can judge for yourself – my ms is quite illegible as you can see. Or is 'Short Measure' worth a re-examination? I have the battered typescript of that by me.

You are quite entitled to say 'My dear Golding you must paddle your own canoe – Fabers are not going to tow you!' and I should accept that. But I have so little critical faculty myself and feel that you know so well what you want, that these points are well worth putting forward.

However I realise that 'Lord Of The Flies' and its' part-author are a very small pebble on the seasons beach so don't hesitate to be matter-of-fact when you reply to me!

    Yours ever
     William Golding.

In Greek mythology, Telegonus is the son of Odysseus and Circe. Having killed his father by accident, he marries Penelope, his father's widow. Despite returning to 'In Search of My Father' several times – even as late as the mid-1980s – Golding never finished it, and it remains unpublished, as do his completed novel 'Short Measure' and his play 'Dionysus' based on Euripides' *The Bacchae*. The 'Greek Play' that Golding was producing at the Studio Theatre in Salisbury in May 1953 was a different work by Euripides – *Alcestis*.

'my ms is quite illegible': see Golding's letter to Monteith dated 1 December(?) 1954: 'my ordinary handwriting is illegible even to my wife'.

Charles Monteith to WG TS

28 June 1954

My dear Golding,

Many thanks for your very interesting letter of 25th June. I'm more than glad to know about all the things you have on hand at the moment.

Of course I'd be delighted to see IN SEARCH OF MY FATHER; and I'd be very grateful indeed if you would, as you suggest, type out a specimen chapter and send it to me. Though from what you tell me, I'm pretty sure it's going to be impossible to form any sort of judgment about it until I have seen the whole book.

So far as SHORT MEASURE is concerned – yes; do please send that in, too. Though I'm not expressing any verdict on it in advance, the fact that it has been turned down by so many people may very well mean that it is the unpublishable first novel which practically all successful writers have somewhere in their bottom drawer. But I would quite sincerely appreciate the opportunity of seeing it and I'll tell you quite frankly whether or not I think anything can be made of it. So do please send it in as soon as you like. And could you see that it's addressed to me personally?

I'm interested to hear about your play and again when you've finished I'd very much like to have a look at it; but the rumours which have reached you about publishers nowadays being interested in plays before they're produced haven't, I must confess, reached me. Alas – apart from verse dramas by established poets and the collected works of major West End luminaries like Terence Rattigan – plays are almost invariably pretty hopeless publishing propositions from a commercial point of view. There are very occasional exceptions, but these nearly always follow on an outstanding stage success. So though I really do want to read the play and hope you'll send it to me, I rather anticipate that my advice about it will be that you should simply start sending it round to the various theatrical producers.

I am surprised, by the way, that you are 'completely floored' by THE CONFIDENTIAL CLERK. I should have thought quite an appropriate sub-title for that would have been 'In Search of my Father'. Helpful hint – Euripides Ion. Please don't, by the way, bother to send it back; it's a present from your publishers.

So glad you're feeling cheerful about LORD OF THE FLIES; I am, too. It won't, of course, be everybody's cuppa, but I'm very much hoping that it may take the fancy of at any rate some of the reviewers. If they think about it even half as well as I do, they ought to review it well.

> Yours ever,
> Charles Monteith.

Eliot modelled the plot of *The Confidential Clerk* on Euripides' *Ion*: both plays are driven by a confusion over parentage. Golding's simultaneous reworking of the Odysseus–Telegonus myth, his staging of *Alcestis* in Salisbury, and his attempt to write a play based on *The Bacchae* show him engaging with similar sources and subjects.

WG to Charles Monteith   MS

12 July 1954   21 Bourne Avenue, Salisbury

Dear Monteith

I'm sorry not to have sent off those chunks of writing I told you about – exams and what not have caught up with me. I'll push them off to you as soon as I can put them together and have a moment to look through them.

> Dont bother to acknowledge this.

>> In haste
>> Yours ever
>> William Golding.

This letter is written on Bishop Wordsworth's School headed paper. The school's address and telephone number have been crossed out in red pen, as has the printed information in the left-hand corner: 'J. MCN. MILNE, BA, BMUS, ARAM. VICE-MASTER AND DIRECTOR OF MUSIC.' John Milne was one of Golding's closest friends; the two men shared a love of sailing and of music.

WG to Charles Monteith   MS

18 July 1954   21 Bourne Avenue, Salisbury, Wilts

Dear Monteith.

I thank my publishers for their gift of 'The Confidential Clerk' which I have read again, and enjoyed. I still prefer 'The Cocktail Party' which I think is a greater play but this is certainly a most extraordinary and fascinating one. Perhaps our local rep. will do it and then I shall have a more accurate means of comparison.

Here is 'Short Measure'. I hav'nt re-read it, and feel that perhaps I'm inflicting on you something that ought to be burnt – but the intention was honest in the beginning.

I'm also including a lump of 'In Search Of My Father' – a random lump, more or less. This is the first raw writing with all its new crudity. If you can tell me whether or not you detect any energy latent under the pages that could later be expressed more fully I'd be very grateful. The nasty customs and so forth came from a mélange of classical and anthropological reading. You may detect some Zenophon here and there – the bits missing from the school editions.

I hope this doesnt catch you on the wing for the Mediterranean. I shall understand a very long pause before your reply.

> Yours ever
> William Golding.

T. S. Eliot's verse play *The Cocktail Party*, published in 1950, is based on Euripides' *Alcestis*. Golding's admiration for it may have prompted, or been prompted by, his own staging of *Alcestis* in 1953.

Xenophon (or Zenophon, as Golding consistently misspelt it) was a Greek general, historian and philosopher born in 430 BC. Golding considered Xenophon's war memoirs to be among the best of their genre.

Charles Monteith to WG   TS

20 July 1954

Dear Golding,

Many thanks for sending me SHORT MEASURE and the chunk of IN SEARCH OF MY FATHER. There may, as you anticipate, be a fairly long pause before I am able to write to you about them. I'll be away for virtually the whole of August and I'm not sure if I'll have time to do more than glance at them rather quickly before I leave. But I'm very grateful to you for sending them and I look forward very much to having a look at them.

It won't be very long now till LORD OF THE FLIES makes its début. Publication date, I think, is 17th September. I sent it in to the Book Society, by the way, and though they are not, alas, going to give it an official 'recommendation', they are going to mention it in *The Bookman*

– which means, if they follow their usual practice, that they will proba-
bly print a short extract from it in either the September or October issue.
Yours ever,
Charles Monteith.

Charles Monteith to WG TS

23 July 1954

Dear Golding,

Are you really 'Balaam'? That pencilled note on the cover of SHORT
MEASURE has excited my curiosity enormously. I do hope you don't
mind my asking.

Yours ever,

Balaam is an Old Testament prophet who appears in the Book of Numbers.

WG to Charles Monteith MS

26 July 1954   21 Bourne Avenue, Salisbury

Dear Monteith

No, I am not Balaam nor his ox nor his ass –

The explanation of the scribble is obscure. The last reader, I imagine,
wrote it in, and as I did'nt send the book out again I didn't bother to
rub it out. Then I shoved the book off to you without looking at the
title and forgot that it would certainly give you a shock. I'm sorry – no,
I'm not that prophet. What a pity!

Yours ever

William Golding

PS I'm also sorry about the Book Society, and inclined to get a bit
up stage – or rather having seen some of their recommendations, I'm
inclined to curl a lip under my whiskers and say 'thank heavens!'.
Couldn't we overprint the cover 'Not Recommended by the Book
Society'? I'm sure that would draw the public in their – dozens.

Or shall I jump off the top of Salisbury Spire with a parachute?
Excuse this frivolity where a sober subject like sales is concerned; but
I've just been sailing and am still feeling rather bluff and seaman like.

WG.

Summoned by the king of Moab to curse Israel, Balaam begins the journey on his donkey (in some translations, ass). A sword-wielding angel descends to block his path; only the donkey can see the angel, and it refuses to move forward. After Balaam beats it, the donkey is given the power of speech, at which point Balaam is permitted to see the angel.

Charles Monteith to WG

TS

28 July 1954

Dear Golding,

I read the sample of IN SEARCH OF MY FATHER the other day and I thought I would let you know at once that I'm enormously interested by it and look forward very much to seeing the whole thing when it's ready. Indeed, I had rather a bad dream last night about pale, tattooed fat boys. I don't think there's any point in saying much more about it now. But once it's finished and I've had a chance to read it all, there will doubtless be lots to say.

I've also read SHORT MEASURE and though it's a readable and promising novel, I do honestly think it would on the whole be better not to try to do anything with it. The promise has, after all, been fulfilled in LORD OF THE FLIES and will go on being fulfilled in IN SEARCH OF MY FATHER. At this stage, I think, it wouldn't be worthwhile to revive an early effort. What SHORT MEASURE lacks, I feel, is that imaginative fire, compulsion or whatever it is, that keeps LORD OF THE FLIES alive and moving and exciting. I found that I never got really frightfully interested in it. I do hope this doesn't sound too harsh and unsympathetic; it's certainly very crudely expressed.

Many thanks for clearing up the Balaam mystery. I didn't *think* you were Balaam, but I was enormously puzzled by that pencilled note.

I'm disappointed, too, about the Book Society not recommending LORD OF THE FLIES. The principles on which they choose and recommend pass all comprehension, but I don't think we need worry about it. Now the book has got into nice, manageable bound proofs quite a number of people here have read it who hadn't read it before and they are all, I'm delighted to find, as enthusiastic about it as I am.

> Yours ever,
> Charles Monteith.

The 'pale, tattooed fat boys' of Monteith's nightmare feature in the passage from 'In Search of My Father' that Golding had sent him. Telegonus, captured in battle, is taken to a king who keeps boys in cages – 'naked and painted, and hideously fat'. They are stuffed with food until they eventually drown in their own obesity.

Charles Monteith to WG   TS

6 August 1954

Dear Golding,

A piece of very good news. I have been dropping proof copies of LORD OF THE FLIES at various strategic points and the first reaction came today: – a very enthusiastic telephone call from the editor of 'John O'London's Weekly' – 'The best thing of its kind since A HIGH WIND IN JAMAICA'. And LORD OF THE FLIES is to be 'John O'London's' Book Choice for September. There will be a big splash about it, and I trust about you, too, in their issue of September 17th. Very many congratulations. I am enormously pleased about it myself.

I am just off to France for a holiday and won't be back until September 1st. I will certainly try to remember to send you a postcard.

Yours ever,

Founded in 1919, *John O'London's Weekly* was a literary magazine with a circulation of 80,000 at its peak.

Charles Monteith to WG   TS

3 September 1954

Dear Golding,

The most unexpected piece of bad luck. We just heard this morning that *John O' London's Weekly* is ceasing publication with their issue of September 10th; and so by one week we are going to miss their big splash about LORD OF THE FLIES. Alas, alas! Nothing could have been more completely unexpected. What makes it even more bitter is that the Editor writes to say that Richard Church has done a very good and very enthusiastic review, – and there will be no *John O' London's Weekly* to print it in. All we can do, I am afraid, is to ask Church's permission to quote him in our early advertising. I imagine he will be willing to do that, and it will be some help in getting the book off to a good start.

I have just seen some of the advance copies, and I think they look extremely nice; I don't know if your copies have reached you yet – probably not, but they certainly will before long.

I had a very agreeable holiday in France – in the South it was sunny most of the time.

Any more news about how IN SEARCH OF MY FATHER is going? I am looking forward enormously to reading the completed manuscript.

Yours ever,

Richard Church's unpublished 1,500-word review finds that *Lord of the Flies* carries 'a weight and authority that compel attention, and finally stamp it with the seal of truth'; it is, Church concludes, 'a most significant novel worthy of survival as a work of art both concrete and authoritative'.

WG to Charles Monteith   MS

7 September 1954   21 Bourne Avenue, Salisbury, Wilts

Dear Monteith

– I suppose you are back from the south now. Thank you for your postcard. I'd have sent you one from Devonshire, but didn't know where to send it. I've seen the book-cover which seems admirably suitable.

What about 'John O' London'? Do we save anything from the wreck? I've written to the editor to say how sorry I am about the whole business, as seemed only proper; but dont know whether anything positive can be done. Do editors ever say to each other – 'take this, it's no good to me now, and you may as well have it!'

Yours
William Golding

The Goldings had spent their summer holiday in Paignton.

Charles Monteith to WG   TS

8 September 1954

Dear Golding,

As you will see from the enclosed copy of our own Faber Bulletin – which goes to newspapers and magazines all over the country

– we are doing what we can ourselves to save something from the *John O' London's* wreck. And we have also had Richard Church's permission to quote from this review in our early advertising. But *what* a pity that this notice isn't going to be printed as it stands, – though Church may, of course, manage to get something into some other paper about the book. Let's hope that he does. In any event, I thought you would be interested in reading what he was going to say.

By the way, Webster Evans, *John O' London's* editor, would very much like a signed copy of the novel – he has collected signed copies of all the *John O' London's* choices. I am enclosing an extra one with this letter and if you would be good enough to sign it and send it back to me so that I can forward it to him, both he and I would be very grateful. Incidentally, I'd very much like a signed copy for myself, but perhaps we can leave that until we have a chance to meet again which won't, I hope, be in the too distant future.

One other piece of encouraging news. John Connell – *Time & Tide* and *The Evening News* – wrote yesterday: 'LORD OF THE FLIES has kept me from my work; it is brilliant and formidable.' And so indeed it is. I'm so glad that you like the book jacket; I thought it admirable myself.

Yours ever,

John Connell reviewed *Lord of the Flies* in *The Evening News*, judging it to be 'vivid and enthralling; it stirs your blood and it touches your heart'.

WG to Charles Monteith   MS

10 September 1954   21 Bourne Avenue, Salisbury, Wilts.

Dear Monteith

Here is the returned and signed copy for Webster Evans. You seem to have salved a great deal from John O' London, though of course full publication would have been better. I'm glad John Connell likes the book. If many people like him are in favour we shall have a success of esteem on our hands – you note my reserve as to £.s.d. – which will be difficult to cap. I've written more of 'In Search Of My Father' but it's going slowly. I've had another idea which will push in. Never mind, though – the principal thing is that I feel the urge and will get something done. The Lord defend me from getting too cocky! My wife and children have agreed to keep my ego under.

> Yours ever
> William Golding

Charles Monteith to WG   TS

13 September 1954

Dear Golding,

Many thanks for sending me the signed copy of LORD OF THE FLIES. I have sent it off to Webster Evans who will, I know, be very grateful for it. It won't be long now till it's out. Like you, I'm looking forward very much to hearing what the great world thinks of it; and again like you, I'm feeling pretty confident.

So glad that IN SEARCH OF MY FATHER's going well.

> Yours ever,

Charles Monteith to WG   TS

20 September 1954

Dear Golding,

Very many congratulations on the wonderful notices that LORD OF THE FLIES has been getting so far. Doubtless you have seen yesterday's *Observer* and *The Times* on Saturday; but did you see Friday's *Time & Tide* and *Daily Mail*? Now I'm looking forward enormously to reading this week's bunch.

> Yours ever,

Lord of the Flies had been published on 17 September in an edition of 3,000 copies. Stevie Smith in the *Observer* praised it as a 'beautiful and desperate book – something quite out of the ordinary'. *The Times* described it as 'a most absorbing and instructive tale', while *Time and Tide* called the novel 'an example of how a truly imaginative writer who is also a deep thinker [. . .] can produce a work of universal significance'. Pat Murphy, the *Daily Mail* reviewer, reported, 'I fell under the terrible spell of this book and so will many besides'; that comment seems to have particularly pleased Golding, who quotes it in his letter to Monteith of 22 September. Monteith was also contacted directly by enthusiastic readers, among them C. S. Lewis, who called the book 'a brilliant success' and judged that 'the island is better conveyed to one's senses than any I can remember'.

WG to Charles Monteith MS

22 September 1954   21 Bourne Avenue, Salisbury, Wilts

Dear Monteith

Thanks very much for your congratulations. We are very pleased down here – I have been signing copies already, but unfortunately only friends; but I calculate that at least sales have reached double figures! I'm also touching wood and keeping my fingers crossed for next week-ends' reviews – surely this is too good to last.

I've seen the reviews – friends phone them in, like an unofficial press cutting agency. I particularly liked 'The terrible spell of this book' and the 'many besides'. You may know my headmaster, F. C. Happold, another Faber client? I've now given him nightmares – not, I'm afraid for the first time.

Did you notice the compliment to the title 'apt and poetic'? And Churche's stuff about economy of effort? I feel these are properly addressed to you, and your pruning hook. I wont repeat thanks, but you know how conscious I am of your help.

> Yours ever
> William Golding.

Golding's headteacher at Bishop Wordsworth's School, F. C. Happold, published several books with Faber about education and religion, including *Towards a New Aristocracy: A Contribution to Educational Planning* (1943), *Everyone's Book about the English Church* (1953) and *Adventure in Search of a Creed* (1957).

Charles Monteith to WG TS

30 September 1954

Dear Golding,

I thought I would let you know that we have just heard that Arthur Calder Marshall will be reviewing LORD OF THE FLIES in the Home Service at 4.45 on October 17th. I'll certainly be listening in myself.

Did you see that splendid review in the *Manchester Guardian*? The only one so far, I think, to get the point of the title.

> Yours ever,

PS

Latest flash! A telephone call from Ealing Studios. They are 'interested' in the possibility of filming it. No decision yet, but hope to let us know in a few days. Don't bank too much on this as the chances are that nothing will come of it; but I needn't say how much I hope that something *does* come of it – what a super film it would make! As soon as we hear anything more I'll let you know.

'The point of the title' prompted what was almost the only reservation expressed by Douglas Hewitt in his otherwise laudatory review for the *Manchester Guardian*: 'Perhaps, too, the slaughtered pig's head adopts Beelzebub's name of Lord of the Flies too easily in the mind of the delirious little boy and tells him too dogmatically that the Beast which they all fear is a part of themselves.'

In a letter of 6 October to Faber's general manager, Peter du Sautoy, who was away on business in the United States, Monteith was able to report that *Lord of the Flies* was 'under consideration by Ealing Studios, Pinewood and Columbia', but he remained pessimistic about the prospects: 'I can't see it for a moment being made into a film, – just think of the casting problems! But what a super film it would make.'

WG to Charles Monteith MS

17 October 1954   21 Bourne Avenue, Salisbury, Wilts.

Dear Monteith

Thank you for your letter. I have delayed replying because I wanted to hear Marshall first. I think he must have done 'Lord Of The Flies' a bit of good judging from my own flattered feelings. The other reviews seem to me pretty good too, though of course I cant really judge their impact, if any, on other people. Nobody has used the word 'mythology' yet, however. When they do that, my cup will be full.

May I say too, that the good bits in the reviews have scared me stiff? How on earth am I ever to earn such remarks again? This seems to me to put 'In search of my Father' right out of court. It would only turn out to be an inferior 'Sinuhe The Egyptian' or 'Long Ships'! It needs recreating mentally. After *three* breakdowns and a marked distaste, I've put it – two thirds written – on one side. The other idea which has been working in my mind, (and I've written nearly a quarter of it) seems more immediately fruitful. I'm really writing it at a tremendous lick. Its about H. Sapiens and H. Neanderthal. I'll say no more about it, till I can send you a copy for you to decide whether Fabers might like it.

I'm dreadfully busy – I've got to lecture to live, as well as teach, what with school fees and the rest of it. So the amount of time I can put about number two 'The Inheritors' (title provisional only) is conditioned by the need to lecture bored army types on music or an earnest WEA class on the history of the seventeenth century, or the modern novel, about which I know nothing. Am I going to make any money out of L of F? If so I will let the army and RAF go and get down to it. Also I should like Fabers to cover their expenses!

One other thing – Agents, shady and otherwise have been after me to pick up the crumbs from a table that as far as I can see will be bare for a long time. One and all they inquire about American rights and so forth. This has put proud ideas in my head. *Is* Fabers going to publish in America and so on? Of course what you tell me will be in confidence – tho' I dont know the etiquette of these things (I've told Curtis Brown that I'll let them have short stories and anything else apart from novels that I may happen to write or have by me, but they dont know how little they'll get.)

Have you heard any more from Ealing Studios? Funnily enough I had been thinking about the camera eye when I got your – may I say 'jubilant' – letter. I keep reminding myself that billions of books are published every minute; but you certainly contrive to convey personal interest. Believe me, I'm grateful for it

Yours ever

William Golding

Amidst a generally positive account of *Lord of the Flies*, Arthur Calder-Marshall had particularly praised Golding's expertise in 'build[ing] up his suspense' and reaching 'a dizzy climax of terror'.

The Egyptian and *The Long Ships* are historical novels by Mika Waltari and Frans G. Bengtsson respectively. *The Egyptian* (*Sinuhe egyptiläinen* in the original Finnish) was translated into English in 1949 and turned into a Hollywood film in 1954. Its ancient Egyptian setting would have grabbed the attention of a fervent Egyptologist like Golding. *The Long Ships*, a story of Viking adventure set in the tenth century, is a 1954 translation from the Swedish *Röde Orm*.

'school fees and the rest': Judy had joined the Godolphin School in Salisbury as a day girl the previous year and it was an ongoing challenge for the Goldings to afford the fees and uniform.

WEA stands for Workers' Educational Association, a voluntary body providing adult education courses. To generate supplementary income, Golding regularly gave talks and classes for the WEA, the Women's Institute and similar organisations.

Charles Monteith to WG

21 October 1954

Dear Golding,

Thank you very much for your letter of 17th October. Yes; Arthur Calder-Marshall's broadcast was very good; and there's a frightfully good review in this morning's *Listener*. I'm delighted to be able to tell you that we decided yesterday to reprint, – which is the best of all indications that the book's really selling very nicely.

I'm a bit sorry, I confess, to hear that IN SEARCH OF MY FATHER has been laid to one side, – I can still remember those fat boys – but since the new one's really moving at the moment, I'm sure you're absolutely right to get ahead with that. I look forward more than I can say to reading it when it's ready.

I'm not at all surprised that agents have been swarming round; indeed, one or two of them told me that they were going to have a shot. It's perhaps a little difficult for me even to try to advise you about this particular problem – since the theory is that agents exist to protect defenceless authors from the inhuman rapacity of publishers – but if you do feel like leaving it to one side for the moment, I really would like to have a talk with you about it the next time you manage to get to London. And perhaps I ought to say now that in my own view it *is* often very useful for an author to have an agent; it's really a matter of deciding whether or not what he can do for you is worth the 10% cut he takes. And then there's the question of which agent to choose.

So far as an American edition is concerned, we have been doing our level best to place it in the States ever since page proofs were ready. My colleague, Peter du Sautoy, is over there at the moment and he is very keen indeed on getting it taken by one of the big American firms. To date he hasn't, alas, been successful, – not a reflection on LORD OF THE FLIES, but on the very odd fact that English novels which have done well here have been tending recently rather to fizzle out in the States. Knopfs have it under consideration at the moment; and even if they don't take it I have high hopes that someone else will. We're also trying to place it in France and Germany and if anything happens there I'll certainly keep you informed. If it's taken in the US or abroad that will, of course, mean an extra royalty for you.

About film rights. In this country Ealing and Pinewood were both interested and I've also succeeded in arousing the interest of Columbia and MGM. The only decision we have had so far is from Pinewood – I enclose a copy of their letter. As I mentioned to you in my last letter, I really shouldn't build too much on the possibility of having LORD OF THE FLIES filmed, – it certainly would be a splendid film, but I should have thought the subject would give an ordinary film company a very bad attack of cold feet.

Do let me know if you ever plan to come up to London. It would be very nice to see you again. And don't hesitate to keep in touch about problems arising out of either LORD OF THE FLIES or the new book.

Yours ever,

The reviewer in *The Listener* was George D. Painter, who called *Lord of the Flies* 'a powerful first novel' and predicted that 'Mr Golding's future work will be worth watching for'.

Although Monteith spared Golding the details, at least ten American publishers rejected *Lord of the Flies*.

The Pinewood Studios verdict came from the director, producer and screenwriter Sergei Nolbandov, who wrote that the novel was 'most exciting' but that he could not see 'how one could make a film of it'. Nolbandov ended with a request to be sent Golding's future novels as they appeared.

WG to Charles Monteith   MS

27 October 1954   21 Bourne Avenue, Salisbury, Wilts.

Dear Monteith

Thanks for your letter. I'm sorry again to delay in answering it, but I'm writing hard at the Inheritors. I want to get at least a first draft done straight away, to avoid the flop of 'In Search Of My Father'. I've got half done already and am scribbling madly. I think in the end it might do.

I'm glad to hear that you are reprinting; guesses vary from a pessimistic 1000 to an optimistic 5000. My wife thinks that the first dozen are out and you're printing another dozen! Opinions down here, even from close friends is that the book is quite out of the ordinary. More nightmares!

About agents – I told Curtis Brown that I wanted to sell any short stories or articles I could, and would send them any I could find in cupboards. I left them in absolutely no doubt as to my feelings of loyalty to Fabers for this big start I've been given. I certainly shouldn't hand myself over to any agent lock stock and barrel, but if, I thought, they take a cut of odd things that are no good to Fabers, and which wouldn't get published without them, everybody is a penny or so better off. What do you think of this? In any case I've *signed* nothing! I should certainly like to hear your advice on the whole subject. Perhaps I could get up to London sometime soon and we could meet if you're not too busy.

I was very glad to hear of the tentacles you have stretched out over the world. They tell me Australia is a cinch for a new book. I like to think of somebody reading it upside down. As far as films are concerned – believe me I've never built on it. I have a rough idea of what the film public wants and it isn't what I've got.

If it gets going ever in France we ought to call it 'Roi des Mouches' – very subtle.

> Yours ever
> William Golding.

A month after publication, Faber decided to supplement their initial print run of 3,000 copies with a further 2,000.

The literary agency Curtis Brown had turned down 'Strangers from Within' before Faber accepted it. Golding stayed loyal to Faber throughout his career, and in turn Faber acted as agents for his novels internationally. Curtis Brown helped Golding to place reviews and stories.

Charles Monteith to WG   TS

28 October 1954

Dear Golding,

We've just had an offer for the film rights of LORD OF THE FLIES which I must pass on to you at once. I'd be more than grateful if you could let me know your reactions as quickly as possible.

I'd better explain at the start that the film rights of a novel are very seldom bought outright at once by a film company. What the film company usually does is to buy an option for a definite period; and at the time they buy the option they also agree the figure they will pay for the story if they do eventually decide to take it. I do hope this is clear.

I'd better say, too, that as I think you know, both Columbia and MGM (USA) have it under consideration at the moment; and if either of these should take an option they would almost certainly be able to pay more for it than a British company; and, again, if either of these should eventually decide to buy the story, they would pay more for it. But my own feeling is that since LORD OF THE FLIES is such an unusual book, it would frighten off the average film producer. In this country it has already, I'm sorry to say, frightened off Sir Michael Balcon.

Now for the offer we've had. It comes jointly from a British director, Mr Phil Leacock, and a British producer, Mr Michael Hankenson. You may remember Leacock's film THE KIDNAPPERS, which was a great success about a year ago, – all about two small boys in Nova Scotia who kidnapped a baby as a pet. Hankenson came to see me the other day and both he and Leacock are clearly very keen indeed to try and make a film out of the book. They both read it and were fascinated by it, thought at first the idea of a film was quite impossible and then found they couldn't get it out of their minds. They both feel now that it could be done. They still haven't, however, put the idea up to a film company and what they want is two months' option which they would buy personally to work on the idea so that they have something definite to put up to Pinewood, the studios to which Leacock is under contract.

The figures Hankenson mentioned to me were for the option £100; and for the story, if they persuade Pinewood to take it, 'about £700 to £800'. My own advice in principle is that you should accept this, since I think the personal enthusiasm of these two men offers the best chance – still of course only a chance – of getting LORD OF THE FLIES onto the screen. The £100 for the option is, I think, fair enough; but, subject to your agreement, I propose to ask £1,000 for the story (you do realise, don't you, that of all these sums you get 90% and we get 10%). Hankenson wants a word pretty quickly, so, as I say, I'd be much indebted to you for a very early reply.

Thanks for your letter which arrived this morning. Sales at the moment – it's been out now not much over a month – are a bit over the 2,000 mark which for a first novel is really very satisfactory; and it keeps on selling pretty comfortably.

Many thanks for all you tell me about Curtis Brown, etc. If you manage to get up to London I'll be more than glad to have a chat with you about it.

The book's on offer now in a considerable number of European countries, but it's too early to expect any response as yet. In Australia we'll of course be selling our own edition, but since shipping takes several weeks, I don't expect they're on the Antipodean market yet. Like you, I've a feeling it will do pretty well there.

By the way, have you heard yet from *Vogue*? I gather they want to photograph you for one of their features.

So glad THE INHERITORS is going well. When it's ready I look forward more than I can say to reading it.

Yours ever,

Michael Balcon was a renowned film producer who ran Ealing Studios. As director of *The Kidnappers* (1953), Philip Leacock had recently enjoyed box-office success with a film that cast children in significant roles. Michael Hankinson (not Hankenson) had directed a number of films in the 1930s; he continued to make short films into the 1960s.

WG to Charles Monteith   MS

31 October 1954   21 Bourne Avenue, Salisbury, Wilts

Dear Monteith

Confirming our phone conversation, please go ahead with the negotiations for Filming Lord of the Flies with Mr Hankenson and Mr Leacock. I will be guided by you in this matter and leave the whole thing in your hands.

I'm coming to London on Tuesday, 2nd November and will ring you from Waterloo. Dont bother to write if you wont be available – I'll arrange to see you some other time.

Yours ever
William Golding

PS Really good news about sales I think. 2000 is more than I should have expected from a book of that sort.
W.G.G.

Golding had phoned to find out whether there was any chance of negotiating a percentage of gross income if the film went ahead.

Charles Monteith to WG   TS

8 November 1954

Dear Golding,

Prospects of LORD OF THE FLIES being filmed have momentarily got rather dimmer. Hankinson rang me up on Friday to say that Pinewood have another film about small boys on the stocks and don't therefore feel at all hopeful about the chances of taking on LORD OF THE FLIES. In the circumstances he and Leacock – understandably, I think – feel they wouldn't be justified in buying an option. But they are still very keen indeed on the idea of filming the book; and still have high hopes that they will be able to persuade some other Studio to take it on. They are both prepared and anxious to work on a draft scenario, or at any rate to think in a detailed and concrete way about its presentation; and they would very much like to meet you and have a talk about it. If you are agreeable to this idea they would like to arrange it soon; indeed, if possible sometime this week. Leacock has got to go away before very long for a short time and would like to see you before he goes. They would both be quite willing to go down to Salisbury and meet you there.

My own view is that if you feel like seeing them about it, it would be an admirable thing to do. They are both quite obviously and sincerely enthusiastic; and my hunch is that this personal enthusiasm of theirs provides the best chance there is of getting LORD OF THE FLIES onto the screen. I haven't, of course, given them your address, since I don't know whether you would like to see them or not. Hankinson's address is: –

    1, Powis Villas,
    Brighton,
    Sussex.

I know he would be more than grateful if you would write to him or – better still – send him a wire. I have a feeling that once he's heard from you he and Leacock will be in the next train to Salisbury.

So terribly sorry that the day you were in London last week happened to be the day when I have to go into purdah for our weekly Book Committee. Do keep in touch and let me know when you will be here again.

    Yours ever,

WG to Charles Monteith MS

9 November 1954   21 Bourne Avenue, Salisbury, Wilts.

Dear Monteith

Thanks for your letter. I was sorry not to see you on tuesday but quite understand that purdah is purdah.

I've written Hankinson to arrange a meeting since it seems the nearest way to getting somewhere with Lord Of The Flies. Being photographed for Vogue was the most frightening experience I've had since D. day.

I hope Lord Of The Flies continues to sell and that Fabers have got their money back.

Yours

William Golding.

Charles Monteith to WG TS

18 November 1954

Dear Golding,

Another news flash about LORD OF THE FLIES. It is the November choice of the Comite Litteraire Franco-Britannique. This is a Book Club operating in France which chooses one English book a month for circulation to its members. I haven't any idea so far how many copies they will want, but it's certainly a distinguished organisation and I do congratulate you most sincerely on having been chosen.

Do let me know, by the way, how you got on with Hankinson and Leacock. I'd be interested to hear.

Yours ever,

WG to Charles Monteith MS

21 November 1954   21 Bourne Avenue, Salisbury, Wilts.

Dear Monteith

Thanks for your letter. I was delighted to hear about the French Book Club. Perhaps it may even lead to a translation, in time.

I wrote to Hankinson offering to see him down here; but at that time he was unable to come. Now I am inviting him down for a meal and talk on Wednesday next; and if he cant manage that I might get up and see them both in London the week after. He sounds keen enough.

I am now in a bit of bother over Curtis Brown – I said – would they care to see a thing I wrote about seven years ago, a dilatory formless thing about sailing with a view to cutting it up into articles or essays or what have you? To my astonishment they leapt at the idea, saying that publication of such a thing (they havnt yet seen it!) was very profitable. Of course if I'd known that, I'd have pushed it off to you. Now

I dont know what to do. Shall I let them see it, and say, if its any use it must go to you? Or what? I should hate Fabers to feel that I was incapable of playing as fair a game with them as they with me – . The book – 'Seahorse' – was turned down by a number of publishers and I regarded it as a dead loss and forgot it. You may even have seen it.

I finished a first short draft of 'The Inheritors' about a week ago and it came out at 46,000 words. It needs much reorganisation and so on. At the moment I'm twiddling my thumbs. Supposing you ever agree to publish another novel by me, what sort of interval is best? A year? Eighteen months?

    Yours ever
     William Golding.

'Seahorse' is an unpublished account of the Golding family's adventures on a rickety boat of that name during the summer of 1947. It was probably completed the following year.

The manuscript of Golding's 'short draft' of *The Inheritors* still survives. He has written at the end of it, 'First draft finished 1315 on the 11th November in 29 days'.

Charles Monteith to WG   TS

26 November 1954

Dear Golding,

Many thanks for your letter of November 21st. I do appreciate very much that you should let me know about SEAHORSE, Curtis Brown and all that. If you do send it to Curtis Brown I'd be more than grateful if you would, as you suggest, tell them to send it to us first. I'd certainly be more than glad to look at it and let you know what we feel about it. Am I right in thinking, by the way, that when you mentioned it first to Curtis Brown your idea was not so much publication as a book but rather a possible conversion into a series of articles or essays? You will not, I hope, mind me saying – and of course this is not in any way a pre-judgment of SEAHORSE which I haven't seen yet – that you ought to be pretty careful about your second book, after all the superb things that were said about LORD OF THE FLIES.

It is very good news that the first draft of THE INHERITORS is finished. Would you like me to have a look at it now? If you would, I'd be very glad to. But if you would rather keep it for shaping and re-organising of course I'll understand. It is impossible to say definitely when the second novel should come out, but an interval of a year or eighteen months would be quite all right, I think.

I needn't say that if you do come to London to see Hankinson the week after next I'd be delighted if we could meet. Do please let me know in advance what your plans are.

Yours ever,

WG to Charles Monteith MS

1 December(?) 1954   21 Bourne Avenue, Salisbury, Wilts

Dear Monteith

Thank you for your letter. After some correspondence, Hankinson and Leacock came down here, refused my offer of lunch but gave me one in the town instead. We went to my flat for tea, and talked all the afternoon. The upshot is that they declare themselves even keener to make a film of Lord Of The Flies than before. I explained the symbolic roots of the book and apparently the film has to lay these bare. Hankinson estimates the chances of a film being made at 'slightly less than 50% – lets be optimistic and call it 50–50.'

I am making (have made and sent) a précis or synopsis of the book, playing down horrors for the men with the money. H and L will work on this and finally when we have agreed on the right shape, put it up to the seat of judgement. Like you, I dont feel very confident, but the thing is worth trying. My wife and I enjoyed meeting Hankinson and Leacock, although we havn't seen a film for years – they were very unpretentious and amiable. I hope it was mutual.

With regard to Seahorse – *if* I were persuaded to publish it as a book which is most unlikely, I should certainly show it to you first. I dont think it will make a book anyway; articles are what I intended. In any case it oughtn't to be published for years, until you succeed in making a name for me. I'm quite alive to the dangers of letting Lord Of The Flies down by following it with a load of trash. The only danger of course is the lure of quick money.

I should like you to see the short draft of The Inheritors, but dont see how I can manage it. Its in longhand and my ordinary handwriting is illegible even to my wife – this is a very clear specimen by my standards. Unless you were willing to toil like Hunt and Mahaffey on the

Christian Logia I dont think you would make anything of it. Better, I think, to let me rewrite, reorganise and type over Christmas and then have a look at the first legible version. Then I suppose I shall have to go back to 'In Search Of My Father.'!

One other point – Does the press cutting agency engage to send *all* cutting? I've had several from friends and not from the agency – havn't heard from them for getting on for two months. Has the organisation slipped, or is this in order?

I shall certainly give you a ring if I get up to London any time – I should like to have another talk

    Yours ever
      William Golding.

Golding has written the impossible date of 31 November. It could be 30 November or 1 December, but the latter seems marginally more likely: Golding may have known that the previous day had been 30 November, hence his mistake. Monteith – usually a prompt correspondent – replies on 2 December.

Golding seems also to have muddled up his papyrologists. Bernard Grenfell and Arthur Hunt discovered and excavated the Oxyrhynchus Papyri at an ancient rubbish dump in Egypt between 1896 and 1907; among the manuscripts were many Christian logia that Grenfell and Hunt edited for publication. Golding has accidentally substituted another eminent papyrologist, John Mahaffy, for Grenfell.

Charles Monteith to WG   TS

2 December 1954

Dear Golding,

Thank you very much for your letter of 31st November. I'm so glad that all seems to be going well with Hankinson and Leacock. I'm enormously excited by the possibility of LORD OF THE FLIES being filmed and I needn't say how much I hope something comes of it. I haven't met Leacock myself but, like you, I took to Hankinson when he called on me; as you say, unpretentious and aimable and, I thought, full of the most genuine – and intelligent – enthusiasm for the book.

Do keep in touch about SEAHORSE; it might, as you say, be turned into articles. If you are pushing articles round it might, I think, be worth trying one on Siriol Hughes Jones, Feature Editor at 'Vogue'. I know she has been enormously impressed by LORD OF THE FLIES; I had a most enthusiastic conversation with her some time ago and she's given it a good write-up in her Books for Christmas article in the current number. And of course if you do think of publishing SEAHORSE as a book, I'd like to see it first.

Yes; I'd much rather wait for a *legible* version of THE INHERITORS, but I do look forward very much to seeing it when it's ready.

So sorry about the press cuttings. It isn't the agency's fault, for they come first to us and we send them on. I'm afraid we have got a bit behind, but as I think you'll appreciate it's a frightful job trying to keep abreast with the torrent of autumn reviews. But I gather yours went off a day or two ago and I very much hope they've arrived safely. I notice that the *Manchester Guardian* in its survey of autumn novels calls LORD OF THE FLIES 'a dark legend' – which is nearest yet to 'mythological'!

Yours ever,

'Siriol Hughes Jones': Siriol Hugh Jones.

WG to Charles Monteith   MS

5 December 1954   21 Bourne Avenue, Salisbury, Wilts.

Dear Monteith

Thank you very much for your letter about press cuttings – they crossed my last to you in the post. I'm sorry to have been so importunate and hope to goodness I havn't got someone a rocket.

We saw 'The Confidential Clerk' done very competently by the local rep. this week. I pour dust on my head – the most shattering thing about it is the shining clarity of the dialogue, but why I ever thought it inferior to the Cocktail Party I cant think – but I once told you I've no critical sense whatever. Anyway 'The Confidential Clerk' is another good reason for putting by 'In Search Of My Father'.

Yours ever

William Golding.

'I pour dust on my head': a Persian expression indicating deep shame at having made a mistake.

Charles Monteith to WG TS

10 December 1954

Dear Golding,

I thought you might be interested to know that the BBC are doing a programme about LORD OF THE FLIES on their German service. It is being broadcast on January 30th at 8 p.m.; and – in case you know German (which I personally don't) and would like to listen – the wavelengths are 232 metres, 75, 89 metres and 49.98 metres (short wave). We'll certainly let German publishers know about it and it may help to get the book placed there.

I am enclosing, incidentally, a copy of the reprint jacket and the band which goes with it, which I thought you might be interested to see. The collection of 'quotes' on the flaps is quite superb, I think.

I am so glad that you and your wife enjoyed THE CONFIDENTIAL CLERK. Like you, I think myself it's completely successful on the stage.

Yours ever,

At the end of the letter, Monteith has added a note in pencil explaining that the programme will be 'a review of the book with reading of extracts'. The programme seems to have been broadcast earlier than originally planned, sometime around mid-January.

1955

Having completed *The Inheritors* to Monteith's satisfaction, in late February Golding moves with his family from their council flat to a privately owned flat just a short walk away. Worries about the increased rent are partly allayed by the continuing success of *Lord of the Flies*: in August, the BBC Third Programme broadcasts its audio adaptation of the novel, and it finally appears in the United States with Coward-McCann in September. That same month, *The Inheritors* is published by Faber to positive reviews. Meanwhile, Golding decides that 'The Rescue', originally intended as his contribution to Eyre & Spottiswoode's anthology of fantasy literature, should be revised and expanded to become his third novel, *Pincher Martin*. In its place, he gives Eyre & Spottiswoode a novella that he has written over the summer, 'Envoy Extraordinary'.

WG to Charles Monteith   MS

21 January 1955   21 Bourne Avenue, Salisbury, Wilts.

Dear Monteith

Thanks (delayed) for forwarding the French Broadcast to me. May I keep it or do you want it back? Reviews – notices, you call them I see – seem to go on trickling in and being good, and E. M. Forster tickled me pink.

You may have heard from Hankinson that the film of 'Lord Of The Flies' is off. The censors will only grant an 'X' certificate so the idea is now dropped. A pity.

My monitors tell me that the German Broadcast kept fading and they only heard bits. Perhaps we shall see the script, eventually. I go on bashing out the 'Inheritors', which you shall have as soon as I dare show it to anybody.

> Yours ever
> William Golding ⟶

Eyre and Spottiswood want me to collaborate in a fantasy book. They said that Fabers had agreed to allow them to approach me or words to that effect. Over Christmas I wrote a thing 20,000–25,000 words which I'll type one day and that *might* do. Its the story of a sailor who manages to reach Rockall in mid atlantic after his ship has gone down. The point is – *if* I can get round to typing it and *if* it's any good, will you like to see it before E. and S. do? Its called 'The Rescue,' and too short to be called a novel and too long to be called a short story. Very trying.

What a good book 'Lord of the Flies' is! I've just reread it and am quite convinced I never wrote it. Its much bigger than I am: perhaps it was done in committee like the authorised version. I know I shall finish this second cooking of 'Inheritors', but feel sadly inept.

Yours ever
WG.

The 'French Broadcast' may have been the script of a review of *Lord of the Flies* that Monteith's secretary Rosemary Goad had forwarded to Golding on 4 January. It had been broadcast in November on the BBC European Service.

E. M. Forster included *Lord of the Flies* among his books of the year in the *Observer*, calling it 'beautifully written'.

Golding's postscript about the publishers Eyre & Spottiswoode contains the first mention of what will eventually become his third novel, *Pincher Martin* (1956).

'done in committee like the authorised version': the Authorized Version of the Bible (1611) was the work of six committees of scholars.

Charles Monteith to WG   TS

28 January 1955

Dear Golding,

Thank you very much indeed for your letter; very nice to hear from you again. As I think you've heard from Peter du Sautoy, the Italian rights of LORD OF THE FLIES have been sold; and he's just rung me up to say that the German rights have been sold as well, – you'll be getting full particulars of that from him very soon. So that's a start; I'm delighted about it. It's still, alas, unplaced in America, but it's going the rounds.

It was tremendously good about E. M. Forster, wasn't it? And did I ever tell you, by the way, that T.S.E. read it some time ago and admired it very much. I'm enclosing with this letter an extract from Arthur Calder Marshall's review of the year's novels broadcast in the BBC's European Service on December 29th, which I thought you might like to see, – he's nice about publishers, too!

About the short story for Eyre & Spottiswoode. Yes; they did approach us about this and we said it was all right. It strikes me that a story of 20,000 to 25,000 words is pretty long for a short story, & if you *would* let me see it first, I'd certainly be more than grateful; even if it's destined eventually for Eyre & Spottiswoode, I should be enormously interested to read it.

I entirely agree with you about LORD OF THE FLIES. It's a frightfully good book. And I'm looking forward enormously to reading THE INHERITORS. I'm very pleased to say, incidentally, that LORD OF THE FLIES goes on selling very steadily. Indeed, we decided this week to put in hand another reprint which I'm very pleased about.

I hadn't heard from Hankinson about the film being off and, needless to say, am very sorry at the news but not altogether surprised. These days censors are being extremely troublesome in more directions than one.

   Yours ever,

PS

I enclose with this letter an anthology of science fiction stories we are bringing out on February 11th, which I'd be very pleased if you would accept with our compliments. I don't know if you are addicted to the SF vice, – I must confess that I am myself, but am proud to add that I was a great one for Outer Space long before it became fashionable. Anyway, I hope you enjoy some of these tales.

Reprising his earlier compliments, Arthur Calder-Marshall called Golding 'the most exciting new author I have struck this year'. He went on to congratulate 'the vast majority' of British publishers for resisting the economic argument to favour the mediocre over the original.

 The book that Monteith enclosed was *Best SF: Science Fiction Stories*, edited by Edmund Crispin. This was the first of a Faber series that ran for seven volumes until 1970. Monteith was largely responsible for creating the science fiction list at Faber; Brian Aldiss, one of his authors, later credited him with having been the only editor interested in science fiction at a mainstream publisher during the 1950s.

WG to Charles Monteith   TS

30 January 1955   21 Bourne Avenue, Salisbury, Wilts

Dear Monteith,

Thank you for your letter and the SF Anthology. I certainly am an addict. I first attained escape velocity with Jules Verne in that shell of his. Those were pioneering days and I must confess that the plush and alloy anti-gravity and over-drive of the inter-galactic companies sometimes make me yearn for the days when we set about our journeys into the unknown with little science but a kind of innocent intrepidity. However adventures like 'Out of the Silent Planet', Bradbory's 'The House' and your own 'A case of conscience' make me realise that younger men have more than we had. Like all genres work can be on any level, so what are They worried about?

I'm delighted about
Germany
Italy
T. S. Eliot.
Forster.

I wont send the short long (that I have already written) to Eyre and Spottiswoode. My thought was that you wouldnt want to publish anything as short on it's own and I've nothing to go with it at the moment except a short story which Curtis Brown cant sell because it's about the Sacrament. It's the best thing I've ever written.

About the Inheritors –

This draft is coming on fast and should be finished by the end of February. I've learnt to compose at the typewriter which is a help but I have so many doubts of myself that the horribly complimentary things people say about Lord of the Flies 'Sit on my shoulder and gibber in my ear like an ape'. So dont expect anything good – unusual it is but I cant think it'll be as successful. I'll send it off to you as soon as it's finished and then keep both fingers crossed.

I was enormously impressed by Ezra Pounds translation of the Women Of Trachis. He kept all the energy of the original, a thing hardly anyone else does. Has it been published? I'm supposed to be producing a Greek play down here in May (in a converted loft) and am wondering if I could get hold of that one.

It's very good news about the re-reprint.

> yours legibly at last
> William Golding.

The science fiction 'adventures' that Golding names or misnames are C. S. Lewis's *Out of the Silent Planet* (1938), Ray Bradbury's story 'There Will Come Soft Rains' (1950) and (included in the Faber anthology) James Blish's novella 'A Case of Conscience' (1953).

'Miss Pulkinhorn' was the 'short story which Curtis Brown cant sell because it's about the Sacrament'. The story treats a favourite Golding theme: the credibility of mystical experience. Set in a cathedral, it is an important precursor of Golding's fifth novel, *The Spire* (1964). It was adapted for radio and broadcast on the BBC Third Programme in 1960 before being published in *Encounter* the same year.

Golding's report that the compliments paid to *Lord of the Flies* 'sit on my shoulder and gibber in my ear like an ape' remembers the novel's description of Jack: 'Authority sat on his shoulder and chattered in his ear like an ape.'

Ezra Pound's translation of Sophocles' *Women of Trachis* was broadcast on BBC radio in April 1954.

Charles Monteith to WG   TS

31 January 1955

Dear Golding,

Thank you very much for your letter of the 30th; and many congratulations on having mastered the typewriter, – something I've never managed to do myself. And I'm very glad that you like BEST SF, – I thought you were probably a fellow addict.

About Ezra Pound's WOMEN OF TRACHIS. I enclose with this letter a copy of the Winter 1954 *Hudson Review* where it's printed; this is the only form in which it's been published so far either in England or America, though I've no doubt that we will be publishing it some day along with some further translations. Do keep this as long as you like, but I'd be very grateful if I could have it back when you've finished with it. If you are thinking of performing it, you ought to get in touch with Mr A. V. Moore, Messrs Shakespear and Parkyn, 8, John Street, Bedford Row, London, WC1. Moore is a solicitor and friend of Pound's, who acts for him in this country.

Thank you very much for saying that I can see the short-long about Rockall. It's a frightfully awkward length from a publishing point of view; if it could be very severely pruned then perhaps you might be able to send it to Eyre and Spottiswoode after all for their anthology. If it remains in its present form it would certainly have to be supported by two more of the same length or something like that; and do you think I could – as a Golding fan rather than a publisher – see the short story about the Sacrament? I'd certainly very much like to read it.

It's very good news that THE INHERITORS is coming on so fast.

Yours ever,

WG to Charles Monteith   TS

2 February 1955   21 Bourne Avenue, Salisbury, Wilts

Dear Monteith,

thanks for your letter and for the WOMEN OF TRACHIS. Reading confirms my enthusiasm for it. I'll keep it and try out ways and means of producing and let you have it back safely. I've asked Curtis Brown to let you see 'Miss Pulkinhorn' next time it homes.

I dont think I'll try 'The Rescue' on Eyre and Spottiswoode. It's got limitless possibilities in it – the subject, I mean – just as Lord of the Flies had. I'll leave it and occasionally brood and see if it creates itself. What curious things subjects are.

Vogue photographed me in every position and light till I felt like a national monument. They appear to have examined the proofs carefully and to have produced a travel number instead. I can see a connection. My children are very indignant about this, to be published, to have notices, to have producers and directors to tea, is one thing: but to appear in Vogue!

I'm really showing off my typing. Dont bother to reply.

    yours ever,
      William Golding.

PS

I'm pretty dull-witted. The other night I sat up in bed and realised what a thing it is that Mr Eliot likes Lord of the Flies and presumably said so. I cant wish for anything more in the way of opinion. At an appropriate moment could you convey how moved and inadequate I feel?

Charles Monteith to WG   TS

2 February 1955

Dear Golding,

Here at last is a copy of the German Service broadcast. I can't read German myself, but from the odd bits I can make out here and there it looks admirable. HERR DER FLIEGEN sounds rather well, I think.

As I think you know, Hans Flesch who wrote this talk, is going to do the translation for Fischer (your German publishers) and I gather that he hopes very much to meet you one of these days and to discuss with you some of the problems of translation. I imagine he'll be writing to you about it himself, but if you don't hear from him soon do let me know and I'll be only too pleased to get in touch with him on your behalf.

Barry Sullivan of the BBC German Service, who produced this talk and sent it on to me, says in his letter 'If Flesch's enthusiasm and usually very sound judgement is any indication, LORD OF THE FLIES will do very well in Germany.' And I'm confident that he's right.

Yours ever,

PS

Please don't bother to send the talk back.

WG to Charles Monteith   TS

7 February 1955   21 Bourne Avenue, Salisbury, Wilts

Dear Monteith

Thank you very much for the copy of Lysistrata. It was a welcome surprise. I very much enjoy being given books. Usually I have to borrow them or buy them from the tupenny box outside second hand book shops. Now, however they have begun to drop from heaven upon the place beneath. My small daughter says – 'Arn't F&F books pretty?'

yours sincerely

William Golding

PS I havn't heard from Hans Flesch yet. The bits I could disentangle from the BBC script seemed to be very accurate – and the other bits are very complimentary. Did you see that Lord of the Flies had 'Reshaped the primitive mythology of Gods, mountains and heroes?' At last!

Faber had just published Aristophanes' *Lysistrata* in Dudley Fitts's translation.

'At last!': see Golding's letter to Monteith of 17 October 1954: 'Nobody has used the word "mythology" yet, however. When they do that, my cup will be full.'

Charles Monteith to WG   TS

11 February 1955

Dear Golding,

Two more pieces of news about LORD OF THE FLIES. The first is that we had a letter yesterday from the BBC saying that they 'hope to do a radio adaptation of LORD OF THE FLIES for the Third Programme'. No details yet, of course; this was simply a preliminary enquiry to ask for our permission, – which, needless to say, has been given. As soon as I hear anything more I'll let you know at once. I'm beginning to look forward to it already. (And if it's done then'll come of course a fee for you at standard BBC rates – which are rather good.)

The second is that the Authors' Club – a highly reputable organisation – announced last June that they proposed to institute an annual House Dinner in honour of the most promising first novel of the year. LORD OF THE FLIES was, of course, submitted at once; and the Secretary of the Club rang yesterday to say that it's on the short list of three. Final decision will be made by Sir Compton Mackenzie; and the Secretary hopes to let me know what it is by the end of the month, though that date isn't at all definite. So let's keep our fingers crossed and think hopefully of Sir C.M.'s much publicised penchant for islands. When I hear the verdict I'll let you know immediately. The dinner itself will take place on May 18th.

So glad you liked LYSISTRATA. There's a chance of that being done on the Third, too. (By the way, can I interest you in my favourite idea for radio, – a Third Programme Mrs Dale? Though I doubt if even that would make me as regular a radio addict as Journey Into Space did. How empty life seems without it.)

     Yours ever,

Monteith has added by hand the sentence in brackets at the end of the first paragraph, going off the edge of the page in the process. The letter reads 'then'll course a fee'; the version printed here – 'then'll come of course a fee' – is a guess.

  Compton Mackenzie was so closely associated with islands, he threatened to take legal action against the publishers of D. H. Lawrence's story 'The Man Who Loved Islands' because readers would assume that the main character was based on him.

  Mrs Dale's Diary was a serial on the BBC Light Programme. *Journey into Space* was the BBC Light Programme's hugely popular science fiction offering; it had just finished its second series several weeks before Monteith's letter.

WG to Charles Monteith   TS

13 February 1955   21 Bourne Avenue, Salisbury, Wilts

Dear Monteith,

  I'm delighted and rather terrified at the possible expansion of Lord of the Flies. 'Keep running Rastus – Dem's not flies; dem's buckshot!'

I'm moving house – force majeur, this present house is being de-requisitioned and I shall have to pay loads of rent like a real rate-payer – so I'm hard up. Is there any chance of the advances on foreign editions being paid when the contracts are signed, or must I wait for Fabers bi-annual share-out? If so I shall have to ask my bank manager to cash my notices.

The Inheritors creeps on, not assisted by this house changing business.

yours ever

William Golding

Please turn over

About journey into space – too right!

About Mrs Dale's Diary for the third –

I am willing to colaborate anytime. 'At Home with the Huxleys'? My wife suggests 'Diary of a Brothel Keeper' as being within that area of boyish emancipation which we now expect of the third and enjoy so much.

WG

Golding's 'Rastus' comment quotes the punchline to an offensive joke in which two black men steal chickens from a henhouse and are shot at as they run away.

The Goldings had been living in a council flat, hence the cheap rent.

'the third': the BBC Third Programme.

WG to Charles Monteith

TS

15 February 1955   21 Bourne Avenue, Salisbury, Wilts

Dear Monteith,

Here is the first legible draft of The Inheritors. I'd better explain. Usually I write two drafts, then type a third draft, then muck about with that. This time I wrote a sketch, then typed a reorganised version which I hoped would bore a tunnel through the story. I havn't bothered about style, spelling, punctuation but driven in a mad and uninspired rush to get the thing into a shape where I can leave it for a bit and then go back to it. It's a roughly shaped bit of marble or gritstone or putty but it's nowhere near final – hardly begun in fact.

I wondered whether I dared send you such a mess and began pulling a sentence or two about; but that led to one thing and another; and I realise that there's going to be no point at my end where I could say 'This is a completed draft'. It would just go on altering.

If you can bear it, would you skip through it from the beginning? I know the last two chapters are supposed to reveal all; but not in this draft they dont – so much the worse, I suppose. Unless the reader gets on my side of the fence, though, he might as well stay away. You may see why if you can decipher my spelling.

Am I being unethical? Do publishers have to put up with this sort of thing? Be prepared for the flop of the season. But an objective criticism of the whole thing would be of enormous value to me.

I've got on to Arthur Moore and I think we shall do the Pound translation in our closet drama. It'll be fun to produce, anyway.

Thank the lord I finished this thing before we started moving. Four and a half weeks of slave labour. I've still got my fingers crossed for the third programme.

By the way – this is the only copy of The Inheritors in existence. But not the last I hope.

> yours disjointedly
> William Golding

I should explain that this opus rises out of a thesis in H. G. Wells' Outline of History where he suggests that we get our bogeys from Neanderthal man or his equivalent skulking round the camp and snatching up unconsidered children. Hence all these tears. We might have a quotation on the title page, if and when.

'Hence all these tears' comes from Terence's *Andria*: '*hinc illae lacrimae*' (126).
    H. G. Wells's *The Outline of History* (1920) describes the history of the world from its creation to the First World War. An entire chapter is devoted to Neanderthal man.

Charles Monteith to WG   TS

16 February 1955

Dear Golding,

Thank you very much for your letter. Peter du Sautoy tells me that in the case of foreign editions advances are certainly payable on signature and we'll send them to you as soon as they arrive. But they haven't, I fear, arrived yet. So I've arranged with our accountant to send you a cheque for £100 on account of accrued royalties and I do very much hope that this will be some help. House moving must be a frightful business.

No further word yet from either the Authors' Club or the BBC, but I'll certainly keep you posted.

Yours ever,

Charles Monteith to WG TS

17 February 1955

Dear Golding,

Very many thanks for sending me THE INHERITORS. This is simply to acknowledge it; and to say that of *course* I'll be delighted to read it through and let you know what I think of it. I'm a bit pushed at the moment, so pleased don't be disappointed if you don't hear for some little time. I want to wait until I really have time to settle down and read it carefully.

It's very good news that you are probably going to do the Pound WOMEN OF TRACHIS. It should be enormous fun to produce.

By the way, don't forget to let me know your new address once the house moving's over.

Yours ever,

WG to Charles Monteith TS

19 February 1955   21 Bourne Avenue, Salisbury, Wilts

Dear Monteith,

Thank you for your letters and for the kind thought about the accrued royalties which have now arrived and been swallowed by my three-headed bank manager.

It's good to know that you dont mind toiling through the draft of THE INHERITORS. I shall be quite glad not to get it back immediately, partly as I may be able to satisfy Eyre & Spottiswoode in the meantime and partly because I can now stand back and think about it as a whole. I'm conscious of innumerable faults in it myself and can only hope that you'll think it might be worth publishing in the long run. I can also see more clearly latent symbolisms and significances which ought to be built up.

We shall do THE WOMEN OF TRACHIS in our cupboard. If you ever hear of anyone who has staged it I should be interested to know.

I'll give you my new address when we move in.

yours ever

William Golding

With a pencil at the top left of the letter, Monteith has listed the names of all the Neanderthals in *The Inheritors*.

There is no evidence that the production of *Women of Trachis* took place; Golding's daughter Judy recalls that her father's intense preoccupation with Greek tragedy was not shared by everyone in the theatre company.

WG to Charles Monteith TS

28 February 1955   Flat 2, St Mark's House, St Mark's
                                 Avenue, Salisbury.

Dear Monteith,

Thanks for your letter which was very warming. I must own to being a bit startled to find that THE INHERITORS is finished! But such a generous assessment would persuade anyone much more doubtful than I was.

Here is the situation as I see it.

(1) I hoped that all major work was finished. I hoped I shouldn't have to do any drastic re-organisation.

(2) As I worked at a fantastic speed to get it done before the dreadful business of moving house caught up with us, I expected the texture to be patchy at least – threadbare English and sentences that I let pass in order to catch up with the next one. I accepted that as the price of seeing the thing in the round.

(3) There are certain omissions that ought to be filled in. e.g. The hunters should shoot their arrows into the painting of a stag; Tuami should be seen at least once before we get inside him scraping at the knife with which he will kill Marlan; the manes of the hunters, Pinetree, Bush, etc. didn't seem to me to come off.

All of which boils down to this; how much alteration to the text, in that sense of current change rather than general re-hash is possible or desirable? If it can be done in your first galleys (if that's the right word

– I mean those suspiciously long sheets of novel which you first send –)
I agree that pressing on is the thing. But if you have to have a clear text
for that then I ought to do a bit more work on the MS. I should like
not to of course.

The upshot is that I'm in your hands as usual. I've no particular feeling of possession over the book. I mean that I'm wide open to advice
or that deft and pruning pencil of yours. And finally if your judgement
says that October is worth rushing for, let us rush.

Terms – aren't they more than the contract says? They seem very
generous to me and of course I'm very glad to accept them.

I can't finish without saying how pleased I was to get such an appre-
ciative letter from you – and All Souls of all places!

> Yours Ever
> William Golding.

Golding's address is so new that he has forgotten to include 'Flat 2' and adds it in
pen afterwards. In later letters, he often omits 'Flat 2' altogether.

In an internal memo, Monteith reports that he had written to Golding
from All Souls on 26 February, telling him 'how delighted we were' with *The
Inheritors* and urging him to allow the book to move straight to production
after 'a little superficial editing' by Monteith himself. That, he assured Golding,
would allow an autumn publication date. He proposed an advance of £120 –
double the amount given for *Lord of the Flies* – and much improved royalties:
12.5 per cent on the first 4,000 copies and 15 per cent thereafter. (As Golding
noted, these terms were more generous than Faber was contractually obliged to
offer.) The letter has not survived, but Monteith also records his first reaction to
The Inheritors in his essay 'Strangers from Within' (see Appendix): '"O God", I
said to myself, "first it was schoolboys, now it's cavemen. Bloody *cavemen*."' On
closer inspection, Monteith seems to have concluded that *The Inheritors* was an
even greater novel than *Lord of the Flies*.

'the manes of the hunters': this is likely to be a slip for 'the names of the
hunters', but as several of them are named after the style of their hair ('Pine-tree',
'Chestnut-head', 'Bush'), the mistake has a suggestive logic.

Charles Monteith to WG   TS

1 March 1955

Dear Golding,

Thank you very much for your letter of February 28th. Of course
I agree that the various points you mention should be dealt with; and
I think the best thing to do would be for you to deal with them in the

manuscript. We can then put it straight into page proof – skipping the galley proof stage – which will save some time.

I'm returning the manuscript therefore with this letter and I'd be very grateful if you would: –

(a) Attach any insertions to the blank page facing the page where they are to be inserted; and mark clearly, preferably in coloured ink, precisely where they are to go.

(b) Complete now any final tidying up of style, etc., that you'd like to do.

I'm still keen to make THE INHERITORS an October book if possible; and though I don't want to rush you after all the very fast and concentrated hard work you've put into it recently, I wonder if I could dare to ask you to let me have it back in its final form in, say, a week or ten days' time? My profoundest apologies for setting what may seem an impossible deadline. And, of course, if it *is* impossible, we'll quite understand and fix a later publication date.

So glad you find the terms acceptable. I'll see that a draft contract is drawn up and forwarded to you. Yes; they are a bit of an improvement on what was laid down in the first contract, but we are all quite sure that it's a very well deserved one.

Needless to say, if you are ever likely to be in the Oxford area at a week-end, I'd be more than delighted if you'd come and see me at All Souls.

Yours ever,

WG to Charles Monteith

TS

2 March 1955   Flat 2, St Mark's House, St Mark's
                      Avenue, Salisbury, Wilts

Dear Monteith,

Thank you for the MS, letter and telegram. I'm sorry about the panic – it was my fault really as I should have put a ring round this address or something.

I'll do my very best to get THE INHERITORS back to you within ten days. I see you have done an enormous amount of work on it already. I like the idea of next October as a publication date.

I should certainly make a point of contacting you were I to find myself in Oxford at the weekend. You reveal yourself slowly, as a publisher, hard-headed business man (see yours of the twenty-sixth) and now Fellow of All Souls till you begin to tower like a cave-bear.

Ought a palaeontologist, anthropologist, archaeologist, hard-headed scientist to read the MS of THE INHERITORS? I haven't done any research for the book at all – just brooded over what I know myself and left it at that. I should hate to be hit over the head by a reviewer who knows his antiquity better than I do. I suppose though, that's an occupational hazard.

yours ever
   William Golding.

Monteith had sent an urgent telegram to Golding in the afternoon of 1 March: 'INHERITORS MANUSCRIPT SENT TODAY TO OLD ADDRESS VERY SORRY. MONTEITH.' As that was the only copy, the panic was justified.

Charles Monteith to WG   TS

3 March 1955

Dear Golding,

So glad the manuscript arrived safely; and it's very good indeed of you to say that you think you may be able to get it back within ten days.

No; I don't on the whole think it would be a good idea to have THE INHERITORS vetted by an expert. If he had any suggestions to make they would be the wrong sort of suggestions; and I am sure there would be very few reviewers who know much more about pre-history than the people who have already read it here, – and to us, as ordinary non-expert readers, it carried complete conviction.

   Yours ever,

WG to Charles Monteith   TS/MS

7 March 1955   St Mark's House, Salisbury

Dear Monteith,

Here is the MS of THE INHERITORS, corrected at least in some ways – I hope now it will do.

You must have thought me very fussy or mock-modest when I sent it to you first. I owe you an explanation over that. You see I have a streak of imagination in me which makes it fairly easy for me to sink into a story completely. That means that after a prolonged immersion the circumstances of the story seem ordinary and I am tired of them. It's only when I read the story again as though it were written by someone else that I find it differs from my ordinary, every-day life. Hence my wails of misery when I sent the MS to you. The alterations were ones I thought you were going to find necessary yourself! And I am so slow witted that I protested when you said none was needed.

However I've made a lot of surface corrections, re-typed several pages that were almost all inset and added a few typed insets for good measure. Really when I read the MS again (I'd not read it straight through before you had it) I was very pleased with it indeed. I felt some of the same pleased and puzzled astonishment as when I re-read LORD OF THE FLIES. However did I do a thing like that? Stories float in the air and settle in these parts like flying saucers.

I hope you'll help with this one and make any adjustments you think are necessary to the text. As for me I shall now return to reading the Odyssey in my wonderful eighteenth century edition. Sing hey day, freedom! Freedom!

> Yours ever
> William Golding   PTO

Ignore this if you like.

Possible objections I *had* that might be of use.
(1) Are the first chapters too slow? Have they enough intrinsic interest to hold a reader?
(2) Terrain – I've left it confused. Not deliberately I'm afraid – I just started off without a geological basis and now I cant clean it up. I attempted to make a virtue of the confusion by the inset to page 28, but I dont suppose anyone will notice.
(3) The graph of excitement in chapter 10 rises and falls instead of going straight up. It seems to me to have virtues nevertheless but are they sufficient to compensate?
(4) Chapters generally dont seem to me to be littered with the usual prehistoric impedimenta. 'He listened intently. Beyond the sparse growth of tree-ferns an aurochs bellowed deafeningly while a flight of pterodactyls creaked towards the steaming swamp. Glub lifted his eolith—' Perhaps no. But all the same I have the feeling that the forest is a bit twentieth century. I hope it doesnt matter.

(5) Names?

(6) A most important visual image seems to me to be the fall. I've only just understood why – no that's not true. I've just formulated the reason. Is it clear enough?

The first page of the letter is typed, and the second (beginning 'Ignore this if you like') handwritten.

'Sing hey day, freedom! Freedom!': this phrase, with variations, crops up occasionally in Golding's letters when he finishes a novel or abandons a burdensome job. He is quoting *The Tempest*, when Caliban is in his cups: 'Freedom, high-day, high-day freedom, freedom high-day, freedom' (2.2.162).

'A most important visual image seems to me to be the fall.' In a note at the end of the *Inheritors* manuscript, Golding has written, 'The centre *symbol* is the waterfall, the timestream, the fall, the second law of thermodynamics. It must be vivid.'

Charles Monteith to WG TS

n.d. [between 8 and 11 March 1955]

Dear Golding,

I cannot thank you enough for having been so wonderfully prompt with The Inheritors. It has gone off to production this morning.

Of course I can understand just how you feel about it when you have worked so close up to it for so long. I am immensely pleased that you now realise yourself how very good it is!

So far as the various subsequent points you raise are concerned, I am perfectly happy to leave everything as it is. I am quite certain it is far better *not* to be too precise about terrain; and *not* to be too Wardour Street about pre-history, in both respects I think the book as it stands precisely right at the moment. Though I know you are worried about the names, I have always thought myself that they are perfectly all right; and I have consulted several people here who have read The Inheritors and find they all agree.

The first two chapters are, perhaps, a little slow but I doubt if it matters, – certainly I did'nt myself find my interest slackened.

One small disappointment. A ring from the Secretary of the Authors' Club to say that Compton Mackenzie did not after all pick 'Lord of the Flies' as the 1954 first novel to be feted. I do not know yet which book was in fact chosen but I gather a press announcement will be made before long. Needless to say I am personally certain Sir Compton was wrong! but the fact that Lord Of The Flies was in the last three is pretty splendid anyway.

Yours ever,

Charles Monteith.

This letter has been typed by someone other than Monteith's secretary, Rosemary Goad, which explains the unusual layout and the absence of a date.

Wardour Street runs through Soho in central London. It gives its name to 'Wardour Street English' – the tendency, especially in historical fiction, to adopt a pseudo-archaic vocabulary and style.

The Authors' Club Best First Novel Award went to David Unwin for *The Governor's Wife*.

A scrawled note at the bottom of the letter implies that the original version, sent to Golding, contained a handwritten question about H. G. Wells's *The Outline of History*. Golding's response on 12 March seems to corroborate that assumption.

WG to Charles Monteith TS

12 March 1955   St Mark's House, Salisbury, Wilts

Dear Monteith,

I'm glad THE INHERITORS has gone off to production. I suppose that means a carefree month for me and I'm very willing to enjoy it.

About the Wells quote – I havn't a copy of the original Two volume edition by me, but I'll get across to Marlborough next week and look it up. As soon as I have it, I'll send it on. I think it's essential, either as an epigraph – right? – or for the blurb. Or for both.

I am very disappointed over the Author's Club. Much more than I anticipated. It just confirms that the appetite grows with what it feeds on. I repeat to myself that such a succession of near-misses is good for the soul if not for the reputation and pocket. I hope it won't jam any chance we have of radio presentation.

Yours ever

William Golding.

The copy of *The Outline of History* belonged to Golding's father – a huge admirer of H. G. Wells – so a trip to Marlborough was required.

Golding's allusion in the third paragraph is to *Hamlet*: 'why, she would hang on him / As if increase of appetite had grown / By what it fed on' (1.2.143–5). His reaction to the disappointing news prompted Monteith to write a note on the top left corner of the letter before filing it: 'We shouldn't have told him about either the Authors' Club or the BBC.'

66

WG to Charles Monteith   TS

16 March 1955   St Mark's House, Salisbury, Wilts.

Dear Monteith,

   Here is the reference from Wells, and a copy of what I consider to be the relevant part. As you can see it's a quote within a quote.

'Outline of History' (subscription edition) page 55.

'The truly human post glacial Palaeolithic people was an enormous leap forward in the history of mankind. They had a human fore-brain, a human hand, an intelligence very like our own.'

'We know very little of the appearance of *Neanderthal man*, but the absence of admixture seems to suggest *an extreme hairiness, an ugliness, or a repulsive strangeness in his appearance over and above his low forehead, his beetle brows, his ape neck, and his inferior stature. Or he – or she – may have been too fierce to tame. Says Sir Harry Johnston, in a survey of the rise of modern man in his "Views and Reviews"; "The dim racial resemblance of such gorilla-like monsters, with cunning brains, shambling gait, hairy bodies, strong teeth, and possibly cannibalistic tendencies, may be the germ of the ogre in folklore."'*

   I still find that quote as uproariously funny today as I did many years ago when I first read it.

   Relevant stuff about teeth occurs on page 52 (chapter ten). I'll only send that if you think more necessary.

   Diffidently I suggest that page 55 should be used with care. The phrase about admixture is dynamite since even I know that for twenty years we've been discovering the new one's descendants – Neanderthaloids. I've marked in red a possible epigraph.

   Sorry about the moaning in my last letter. I've got 'flu, I think and am incapable of counting my astonishing blessings.

>   yours ever
>   William Golding

Golding has added his unchanged telephone number under the address alongside 'please note'.

   Golding marks his emphasis here by underlining in red ink (shown here as italics), picking out the passage to be used for the epigraph of *The Inheritors*.

'Neanderthaloids': a series of hominid fossil discoveries, particularly those made at Skhul in Israel between 1929 and 1935, led to speculation that they were either hybrids of *Homo neanderthalensis* and *Homo sapiens* or a transitional form in the development of modern humans. *The Inheritors* leaves open the possibility of future interbreeding when the 'new one' – a Neanderthal baby – is adopted by *Homo sapiens* towards the end of the novel.

Charles Monteith to WG   TS

18 March 1955

Dear Golding,

Thank you very much indeed for the quotation from Wells. I think the bit you have underlined in red should serve admirably as an epigraph. I have ordered 'Outline of History' from the London Library and when it arrives I'll read through the whole of the pages to which you refer me before finally sending a note about it to our Production Department. It is a *very* good quote; and should set the note admirably.

I am filled with most sincere remorse at having raised your hopes – about the Authors' Club – only to dash them. I really do wish now I hadn't said anything until I'd known what the result was. Do please forgive me (I still, by the way, haven't heard who finally was chosen). Nor is there any further news about the Third Programme. One of the regular producers, Peter Duval Smith, is very keen indeed to do a radio adaptation but so far as I know nothing has yet been finally decided. It's just possible I suppose that he might run up against the same sort of obstacles encountered by Hankinson and Leacock.

But please don't be disheartened by any of this. 'Lord of the Flies' by any reckoning was one of the most outstandingly successful first novels not only of 1954 but of recent years. And people are still reading it, still talking about it, still recommending it to their friends. Hardly a week passes without someone saying to me how impressed they have been by it. And now of course we have got 'The Inheritors' to look forward to.

How are you finding your new house? It must be a great relief to have all your moving troubles over, though there is probably a fair amount of settling in to do yet.

Yours ever,
Charles Monteith.

WG to Charles Monteith
T S

20 March 1955 St Mark's House, Salisbury, Wilts

Dear Monteith,

thanks for your letter of consolation and more, though final, apologies for the squeal of pain that occasioned it. Really it *was* 'flu which I've now had officially. I'm only now aware of how low I've been feeling during these past weeks – thank heavens the Inheritors got by when it did.

Yes, moving was hell and we still live in an atmosphere of bare boards and lino that won't fit.

About the BBC. Duval Smith wrote saying that a colleague of his was 'trying to adapt' Lord of the Flies for radio. So what will be will be.

I ought to have said this before; but if you are ever in striking distance of Salisbury we shall be very glad to put you up. We have a very fine view which is relatively free of jet aircraft.

yours ever
William Golding.

Peter Duval Smith's BBC colleague was the playwright Giles Cooper, who adapted many works for radio and television.

WG to Peter du Sautoy
M S

20 April 1955 St Marks House, Salisbury, Wilts

Dear Mr du Sautoy,

I am delighted to hear that you have succeeded in placing Lord of the Flies in USA. A thousand dollars sounds an enormous sum, relatively.

I've filled in the form, but not very completely I'm afraid.

Yours Sincerely
William Golding

Peter du Sautoy had written to Golding on 18 April with the news that Coward-McCann had offered a $1,000 advance against a 10 per cent royalty to publish *Lord of the Flies* in the United States. Du Sautoy apologised to Golding for the delay in securing a deal, explaining that the book had been rejected by 'a large number of the leading American publishers'. Among the firms who turned it down were Doubleday, Knopf (twice), Macmillan, Scribner's, Harper, Criterion, Dutton, Viking, Lippincott, Harcourt, Brace, and Duell, Sloan & Pearce. Replying to Robert Giroux at Harcourt, Brace, du Sautoy admitted that Giroux's rejection was 'disappointing, but not altogether perhaps surprising; we had many doubts about the book ourselves'. To Dutton he acknowledged that the book was 'a bit of an oddity'.

Coward-McCann published *Lord of the Flies* in September; their publicity information sheet was the form that Golding filled in. A page of extracts from the form, preserved in the Faber archive, includes Golding's description of the theme of *Lord of the Flies*: 'Theme is an attempt to trace the defects of society back to the defects of human nature. Moral is that the shape of a society must depend on the ethical nature of the individual, and not on any political system however apparently logical or respectable. The whole book is symbolic in nature, except the rescue at the end where adult life appears, dignified and capable, but in reality enmeshed in the same evil as was the symbolic life of the children on the island. The officer having interrupted a man-hunt proposes to take the children off the island in a cruiser, which will presently be hunting its enemy in the same implacable way. And who will rescue the adult and his cruiser?'

Charles Monteith to WG   TS

21 April 1955

Dear Golding,

May I send you a brief personal note to say how delighted I am to know that LORD OF THE FLIES is to be published in America by Coward-McCann. They are an excellent firm who should, I think, look after the book very well. Please forgive me for not having written before, – I've just come back from a short and very agreeable holiday in Ireland and didn't hear the good news until I got back.

I don't think, by the way, I ever thanked you and your wife for your extremely hospitable offer to entertain me if I should ever be in Salisbury. I'm very grateful indeed for it. And, needless to say, if I *am* ever near Salisbury, I shall be only too delighted to accept it.

Yours ever,

WG to Charles Monteith   TS

24 April 1955   St Mark's House, Salisbury, Wilts

Dear Monteith,

It is good to hear from you again. Yes, I was also delighted to hear that Lord of the Flies is appearing in America. I've always wanted to see the Grand Canyon – and who knows?

A point has occurred to me about the epigraph for THE INHERITORS. Ought I to write to Well's publishers and ask their permission and then acknowledge it in the book? Sorry to be so ignorant and pestering.

Yours ever,
William Golding

Charles Monteith to WG   TS

25 April 1955

Dear Golding,

Thank you very much for your letter. There's no need to worry about the epigraph for THE INHERITORS. I've already cleared that up with Wells' agents and his executors. They have given full permission for it to be included, provided some acknowledgment is made, – and I'll see that something suitable is included in the prelims.

Yours ever,

Charles Monteith to WG   TS

14 July 1955

Dear Golding,

News has just reached me from the BBC – perhaps it reached you long ago – that they are planning to do an adaptation of LORD OF THE FLIES in the Third Programme on Sunday, August 28th, with a recorded repeat on Friday, September 2nd. Times haven't been announced yet; and the dates, I gather, aren't completely definite, though they very much hope they will be able to stick to the ones they plan. We are promised 'atmospheric music' composed by Christopher Wheelan of the Old Vic; and the parts are to be distributed between real small boys and grown-ups imitating them (I hope that will be all right!). I needn't say how enormously I'm looking forward to it – but as I shall be in Ireland then, and possibly in the West of Ireland, I'll have to keep my fingers firmly crossed. In those parts Third Programme reception isn't always as good as it might be! But I'm quite delighted that it's going to be done and if I get any more details of course I'll let you know at once.

I'm so glad you like Anthony Gross's jacket for THE INHERITORS, – I thought it absolutely admirable myself.

May I send, by the way, my best wishes for the holidays to you and to your family.

Yours ever,

Christopher Whelen composed music at the Old Vic for at least ten Shakespeare plays and for Eliot's *Murder in the Cathedral* during the 1950s.

WG to Charles Monteith   TS

19 July 1955   St Mark's House, Salisbury, Wilts.

Dear Monteith,

It was good to get a letter from you again. The bush telegraph had been beating steadily and I was infuriatedly aware that the BBC were going to do LORD OF THE FLIES sooner or later. On one occasion a man swam up to me, said intensely 'Congratulations on the Third Programme' and swam away again. But I could find out nothing definite. Now you put me out of my frustration.

Grown-ups imitating children sounds a bit like the Goon Show – but after all, why not? During the broadcast we shall be somewhere in the neighbourhood of the Scillies, I hope, so perhaps neither of us will hear the Pig's gruesome accents clearly.

I've finished and sent off the story for Eyre and Spottiswoode and they seem quite excited about it. Now I havn't a ghost of a notion in my head for anything else.

The West of Ireland should be a wonderful place to recover from the rigours of London and Oxford. I hope you enjoy yourself there.

yours ever,

William Golding.

Golding was a fan of *The Goon Show* on the BBC Home Service; he even wrote what he called 'Goon verses'.

Having decided not to submit 'The Rescue' for Eyre & Spottiswoode's volume of fantasy writing, Golding instead sent them his new novella, 'Envoy Extraordinary'.

Charles Monteith to WG

20 July 1955

Dear Golding,

Thanks very much for your letter. Yes; the Scillies sounds almost as difficult as the West of Ireland. What a ghastly bore they should decide to do it just then. But I've a vague – a very vague – notion that it might be possible to persuade the BBC to play over the recording privately at one of their studios. And if both or either of us miss it, would you like me to have a shot? It would be very nice indeed if you and your wife could come up to London for it. That reminds me, by the way, that we'll be having a cocktail party here some time in the early autumn – October 6th has been fixed provisionally – and it would be very nice if you could both come to that. A proper invitation will certainly be going to you later and I needn't say how much we all hope you'll be able to accept.

Yours ever,

WG to Charles Monteith

26 July 1955   St Mark's House, Salisbury, Wilts.

Dear Monteith,

To hear Lord Of The Flies in a BBC studio would be great fun, I think. Certainly if we miss the broadcast I should like you to try and arrange a private session – audition? – if it is at all possible. I agree that the end of August and the beginning of September is a tactless time to choose but after all something has to be ground out to fill up the silly season.

The cocktail party sounds most exciting and we should certainly like to come. I hope when the date is finally settled that we shall be able to accept.

Yours ever,
William Golding

PS
How impressive Fabers' note paper is getting!

Charles Monteith to WG   TS

16 August 1955

Dear Golding,

The BBC have just changed their mind about the date of the repeat broadcast of LORD OF THE FLIES. It's to be on Wednesday, August 31st instead of Friday, September 2nd. But the original broadcast still remains fixed for Sunday, August 28th. That, by the way, is going to be an all-Faber day on the wireless, for the Critics – enterprising creatures – are going to talk about Larry Durrell's new book of poems, THE TREE OF IDLENESS, which we published recently.

I've just seen an advance copy of THE INHERITORS – your copies should be reaching you very shortly – and I think it looks very nice indeed.

        Yours ever,

Charles Monteith to WG   TS

9 September 1955

Dear Golding,

I do hope you heard the LORD OF THE FLIES broadcast – I sent you a post-card about it the next morning from a remote post office in County Galway. By a wonderful fluke Wednesday, 31st, was one of the rare nights when the Third Programme was not only audible, but completely clear; and listened to with the Atlantic booming dramatically outside, L. of the F. terrified and impressed me as much as ever. If by any chance you didn't hear it – I seem to remember you thought you might be sailing off the Scillies on the crucial dates – do please let me know and I'll see if there's any possibility of fixing up a private hearing at the BBC. Perhaps it could be fitted in with a trip to London for our party. The date of that, by the way, has been changed to October 13th; and may I say again how very much I hope you and your wife will be able to come.

Have you heard from *Vogue*, incidentally, that the photograph is going to appear at last in their October issue? That will coincide beautifully with the publication of THE INHERITORS. I can't tell you how much I envy you having a photograph in *Vogue* – that, I think, is real glory.

        Yours ever,

WG to Charles Monteith   TS

10(?) September 1955   St Mark's House, Salisbury, Wilts

Dear Monteith,

Thank you for your card and letter. I'm glad that the Third
Programme penetrated to Ireland – it skipped Cornwall on the way. I
heard some odd bits of what sounded like very distinguished incidental
music and some impressive flies but the rest was worse than silence –
morse, Moscow, and an occasional wail which may have been either a
littlun or the Heaviside Layer. So if you can possibly persuade the BBC
to put on a performance (or a repeat!) I shall be very glad to hear it. Of
course I understand that this may not be possible.

Owing to the sinister threat of the Inland Revenue we did not go
sailing round the Scillies. We ended by sailing a minute and battered
dinghy on the South Coast of Cornwall – day sailing of the humblest
type.

I'm glad to hear about Vogue. As you say, there's glory for you!

I think we can manage the 13th. What an excitement.

I hope Vogue will help The Inheritors. My thumbs are already
pricking.

> yours ever,
>
> William Golding

WG has dated the letter '18th September', which is obviously wrong. Monteith
sends a short acknowledgement on Monday 12th, so the most likely date is
Saturday 10th.

The Heaviside layer (sometimes known as the Kennelly–Heaviside layer or the
E region) is a layer in the Earth's ionosphere that reflects radio waves.

'There's glory for you' is a verbatim quotation from Humpty Dumpty in Lewis
Carroll's *Through the Looking-Glass*. 'My thumbs are already pricking' alludes
to the Second Witch's reaction as Macbeth approaches: 'By the pricking of my
thumbs, / Something wicked this way comes' (4.1.44–5).

Charles Monteith to WG   TS

12 September 1955

Dear Golding,

Very many thanks for your letter which arrived this morning. I look forward very much to seeing you on 13th October. I've just spoken to the BBC about LORD OF THE FLIES; and they assure me that there will definitely be a repeat; and that it will probably – though not certainly – be some time early in October. They promised to let me know as soon as a definite date has been fixed and of course when I hear from them I'll pass it on to you at once. It could hardly be better, could it?

> Yours ever,

WG to Charles Monteith   MS

20 September 1955   St Mark's House, Salisbury.

Dear Monteith,

I uncross my finger just for a moment to thank you for your enthusiastic note. Yes, I cant imagine a much better write-up than John Davenport's. My spies tell me too that The Inheritors has appeared in shops that had never risked their money on the 'Lord of the Flies' – a material point.

We very much look forward to seeing you in London this autumn.

Yours ever
> William Golding.

The Inheritors was published on 16 September in an edition of 5,000 copies. Monteith's 'enthusiastic note' has not survived; it may have been sent to Golding from All Souls in response to John Davenport's review of *The Inheritors* in the *Observer* on 18 September. Davenport had called the novel 'a *tour de force*' and, detecting 'Wellsian powers of creative imagination' in Golding, concluded that he was 'the most purely original English novelist of the last decade'.

Charles Monteith to WG   TS

26 September 1955

Dear Golding,

I'm delighted to know that you and your wife can come to our party on the 13th October and I wonder if by any chance you'll be in London in time for lunch? If you are, I'd be quite delighted if you'd both lunch with me. Do please let me know if you can and I'll suggest a time and place.

Don't miss the *Spectator* next Friday!

> Yours ever,

WG to Charles Monteith

29 September 1955   St Mark's House, Salisbury, Wilts.

Dear Monteith,

Thank you for your invitation to lunch. I am afraid though, that we can't get to London early enough to meet you for it, so we must ask to be excused, with much regret. Perhaps there may be an opportunity at a later date.

The papers seem favourably disposed to the INHERITORS but O tempora! O mores! (My own translation is Oh Times, what manners!) You probably dont see the provincial press so I must inform you that a Grantham paper describes THE LORD OF THE FLIES as an educational experiment on an island. THE SOUTHERN DAILY ECHO however describes the two books as an 'Exciting contribution to English literature'! I have no shares in this paper.

As I write this I receive three copies of the American edition of L of F. Most encouraging.

Could you give (when possible and convenient) some idea of how people are buying THE INHERITORS as compared with the other? The notices are most respectful on the whole but I feel the touch of the Higher Criticism like a cold wind and see myself spiralling up towards being a third programme novelist, universally admired, but unread. I shant change because I cant – but I'd like to know. Four times a tour de force! Don't look round now but I think we are being followed.

Could you possibly forward the enclosed letter to Fischer Verlag? They had queries which I answered but got the letter back from the dead letter office so I must have mucked up the address somehow.

By the way, several people have commented on the jacket of the INHERITORS, saying how striking it is. I dont know Anthony Gross personally but he might like to know this.

One of the boys at my school has defined empathy as 'the power to move both ears at once'.

We are both looking forward to the party.

     yours ever

      William Golding.

Fischer Verlag was the German publisher of *Lord of the Flies*.

30 September 1955

Dear Golding,

Terribly sorry that you and your wife won't be here in time for lunch on the 13th. Will you, I wonder, be staying the night and still in London at lunchtime the next day? If you are perhaps we could lunch together then. It would be most delightful. In any event I'm looking forward very much to seeing you at the party. (A great many other people have told me how they are looking forward to meeting you then.) By the way, could you give me any idea what time you hope to arrive in London? Eliot has said that he would much like to meet you and I thought that possibly a good time for that would be Thursday afternoon. He will be at the party, of course, but there will probably be rather a scrum and he feels he mightn't have an opportunity to have a proper conversation with you then.

I'm so glad your three copies of the American edition of LORD OF THE FLIES have arrived safely. I've got one, too. It looks rather good, I think, though I prefer our own jacket. Anthony Gross did that, as well as the jacket for THE INHERITORS. He'll certainly be very pleased indeed to know how much you like them.

I'll certainly send on your letter to Fischer Verlag.

I've just heard from the BBC, by the way, that the repeat of LORD OF THE FLIES will take place not in October but on Tuesday, 22nd November in the Third Programme at 9.5 p.m. The date seems to be quite definite, but the BBC say that the time is liable to alteration almost up to the last minute and that it would be as well to keep an eye on the *Radio Times*.

Tour de force. Yes indeed. You can't imagine how pleased I am that I *didn't* use that phrase in the blurb. And Isabel Quigly doesn't, I think, use it in that admirable notice in today's *Spectator*. (The photograph in *Vogue*, I suppose, should be out by now, though I haven't seen it yet myself.)

About sales. THE INHERITORS is selling very steadily, I think, but I'll certainly try to get some definite information about figures from our Sales Department. As soon as I have it, of course I'll write to you again and let you know.

Looking forward very much to seeing you on the 13th.

      Yours ever,

Isabel Quigly in *The Spectator* called *The Inheritors* an 'astonishing book' and considered Golding 'the most original and imaginatively exciting novelist we have today'.

WG to Charles Monteith TS

1 October 1955   St Mark's House, Salisbury, Wilts

Dear Monteith,

Yes, I think the notice in the Spectator was a smash hit. Dont bother to look at VOGUE, please. It makes me look as though I were seated in the police station trying ingratiatingly to explain away my possession of a packet of dirty postcards.

You are pressingly hospitable and I feel rather conscience-stricken. I may as well confess that we had thought we would dash up to London and dash down eating both ways in a dining-car and perhaps cramming a show or improving exhibition in during the afternoon. If you are now booked for lunch on the 13th we will still do that – only I will first see Ann into a seat and then come along to Russell square for a conversation with Eliot (since I assume that will be of at least a semi-professional nature.)

However since we cant possibly make lunch on the next day and if you are still free for the 13th may we change our minds? In that case we will re-organise down here and get up to London in time for a bite with you. The rest of 'plan 1' could still stand. I hope we havnt seemed too ungracious, but we both felt you were going to have a heavy day anyway on the 13th. You see we both teach, and I have tried to effect a complete dichotomy between what is due to the school and what is due to the career of an author now blooming like a Christmas rose. However we can scrap school on the morning of the 13th without difficulty.

Yours ever,
William Golding.

Charles Monteith to William Golding TS

3 October 1955

Dear Golding,

Need I say how delighted I am that on the 13th you and your wife *can* arrive in time for lunch after all. Yes indeed I am still free and am looking forward very much to you both lunching with me then. I suggest that we go to a small restaurant in Charlotte Street called The Etoile where they usually produce rather good food and have a quiet meal there. Would it be convenient if we met there at one o'clock? (Charlotte Street, by the way, is in north Soho and runs parallel to Tottenham Court Road.) I hope that this is OK. We can arrange then for some convenient time for you to come and meet Eliot here; I think he will be in all that afternoon.

About sales of THE INHERITORS. Up to the end of last week – that is to say a fortnight after publication – the sales were approximately 1800; and I am told that it is selling 'strongly'. This is really a very good figure indeed to have reached in such a short time, – certainly well in advance of where LORD OF THE FLIES was at the same distance after publication. We ourselves are very satisfied with it. LORD OF THE FLIES too is still selling steadily though of course it is now over a year since it was published, – the sales of that have been far far better than the sales of an average first novel, but since LORD OF THE FLIES *is* so far far better than the average first novel that doesn't I must confess surprise me. What is very encouraging about it is that it remains so strongly alive, – people are still buying it, reading it, talking about it. And of course you will now have the American sales as well, – and the French, German, and Italian sales once the translations are ready.

I will certainly keep in touch with our sales department about how THE INHERITORS is going and if there are any really striking developments I will let you know straight away.

Yours ever,

Peter du Sautoy had sent a note to Monteith on 30 September reporting sales for *The Inheritors* of 1,800 copies; he added that, as of 16 September, *Lord of the Flies* had sold 4,662 copies.

WG to Charles Monteith   MS

9 October 1955   St Marks House, Salisbury, Wilts.

Sunday

Dear Monteith
    Just a scrawl to let you know that we shall be delighted to meet you at one oclock on Thursday at the Etoile.

I'm very gratified, by the way, at Fabers magnificent advertising spread. Few people find themselves the largest of type on a Sunday page unless they've been in the dock

    Yours ever
        William Golding

WG to Charles Monteith   MS

15 October 1955   St Mark's House, Salisbury, Wilts

Dear Charles

I cant tell you how much we enjoyed our day in London – we only hope that you weren't too exhausted by the end of it. We caught our train with a moment or two to spare, having dived from the 'bus into a taxi when it became clear that the bus had no intention of going anywhere near Waterloo! It was a great privilege to meet Mr Eliot and to be illuminated subsequently by your galactic party. In fact, thank you very much.

I hope you have managed to read the Eyre & Spottiswoode story to the end. I should have said it is called 'Envoy Extraordinary' and is not to be read too solemnly.

    Yours ever
        Bill Golding

After two years of correspondence, at last Monteith is 'Charles' and Golding 'Bill'.
    Golding's memory of meeting T. S. Eliot, as recorded in an unpublished journal entry from 1972, sounds rather less deferential: 'Eliot was fairly impressive in a Donnish sort of way but not excessively so. Charles led Ann and me to see him as to a god. We sat fairly mum, while he talked of umbrellas and rubber trees. Later he informed me that Simon in Lord Of the Flies must be cut to the bone. "We cannot portray a saint, Mr Ah. But for evil we need only look into our own hearts." The silly old twit. As if I hadn't known that' (J, 10 April 1972). The memory suggests not only that Eliot could not bring to mind Golding's name, but also that at some point he had discussed revisions to Golding's typescript with Monteith.

Charles Monteith to WG   TS

18 October 1955

Dear Bill,

I'm delighted to know that you and Ann caught your train after all.

It sounds as though it was a near thing and if I put you on a wrong bus – I'm horribly afraid I must have – I do apologise most sincerely. I was certain it was the Waterloo bus, but of course it *was* after the party! So glad you both enjoyed it; we were all delighted that you could come.

ENVOY EXTRAORDINARY has been despatched to Eyre & Spottiswoode, – lucky people! It is superbly good, I thought, and it really did make me laugh like anything. Some day, I hope, it will be republished under the Faber imprint. Along with three or four more of the same length it would make up a most admirable book.

Many thanks, too, for the Audience Research report from the BBC, – a most interesting document. And please don't forget, by the way, that you promised to pander to my baser instincts by sending me some-time a full list of the firms who turned down LORD OF THE FLIES. I should hate to miss that.

No proofs yet from Howard Coster, but they should be here any day now.

          Yours ever,

In his letter of 18 October to Monteith, Golding had included the BBC Audience Research Department's report on their broadcast of *Lord of the Flies*. It had 'made a far greater impression on audiences than the Appreciation Indices (65 and 62) might suggest' because 'a good many listeners were at the same time fascinated and utterly appalled by the tale'. A minority had condemned it as unrealistically 'nasty', but the majority praised it as a 'remarkable allegory, full of terrifying implications'.
Howard Coster had photographed Golding for *Vogue*.

WG to Charles Monteith   TS/MS

22 October 1955   St Mark's House, Salisbury, Wilts.

Dear Charles,

Herewith Coster's prints. He says will I tell you that he's put them on shiny paper in case you want them immediately for blocks but that they are available on matt texture also. I hope this means something.

Number 'F' is what I really look like but number 'A' is what I should like to look like. So will you publish 'A' if the sitter's opinion carries any weight?

I'm very cheered that you liked ENVOY EXTRAORDINARY so much. It is a 'made' story written to a definite date in an indefinite panic. I'm also very sad that F&F arn't doing it. I've had little pipedreams of a Christmas Book á la 'Gallico' with illustrations in the Corinthian manner; the sort of thing to send to Auntie in the nursing home. You may be interested to know that I havn't succeeded in selling it anywhere in England or America among the Glossies.

> Yours ever
> Bill

PTO

Can Fabers send me two more copies of 'The Inheritors?' I've tried to preserve a uniform mean-ness in the matter of complimentary copies – but it's become impossible.

> Yours
> B

The letter is typed until the first valediction, then handwritten in red ink.

Paul Gallico, journalist and writer of fiction, published booklets of his newspaper columns every year. Illustrations in 'the Corinthian manner' would suit 'Envoy Extraordinary', which is set in ancient Rome and features a Greek inventor.

Charles Monteith to WG   TS

26 October 1955

Dear Bill,

Thank you very much indeed for your letter of 22nd October and for sending on Coster's prints. They are frightfully good, I think, and I entirely agree with your choice of A. That's certainly the one we'll use. Most impressive it is.

About ENVOY EXTRAORDINARY. Yes indeed; if it had been free for us to consider I'd have thought about the possibility of turning it into a 'little gift book' a la Gallico, – though how well those sort of books actually do always tends to be pretty chancy. But since, alas, it was committed to Eyre & Spottiswoode – the fruit of their inspired invitation to you to contribute to their anthology (which I shall *certainly* buy) – I could only admire and enjoy; and, I must admit, begin to form plans – which I think I mentioned in my last latter – for its eventual republication under the F&F imprint. Didn't you once mention to me a long short about a sailor marooned on Rockall? I wonder if you ever finished it? It could certainly be just the sort of thing to go into a book with ENVOY EXTRAORDINARY.

I'll certainly see that two more copies of THE INHERITORS go off to you. In fact, I believe they've already gone.

Monday night I missed – for the first time since it restarted – *Journey into Space*. And I live hourly for the repeat on Sunday evening.

Yours ever,

Eyre & Spottiswoode published its anthology *Sometime, Never: Three Tales of Imagination* in 1956. The other tales were John Wyndham's 'Consider Her Ways' and 'Boy in Darkness' by Mervyn Peake.

Having never thought that he had the option to consider 'Envoy Extraordinary', Monteith was troubled by Golding's remark in his letter of 22 October that he was 'very sad that F&F arn't doing it', and his reply was an attempt to clarify and reassure. Monteith was already plotting behind the scenes. He enquired directly to Eyre & Spottiswoode about their rights and discovered that they lasted for two years after publication.

WG to Charles Monteith TS

26 October 1955　　　　　　St Mark's House, Salisbury, Wilts.

Wednesday

Dear Charles,

This is an interim report – I havn't forgotten that I am to pander to your self-regarding instinct by producing a list of the publishers who turned down Lord Of The Flies. But the fact is the list of names is hard to find! I shall go on looking however until it turns up.

I'm also doing an arrangement of ENVOY EXTRAORDINARY for the Third Programme. You see that after all the Light isn't the only programme to produce Science Fiction. What an austere scream. (But don't say I said so!)

I hope people continue to buy THE INHERITORS. I'm really feeling rather moody about novels because the general idea seems to be that now I've demonstrated a certain clever eccentricity I should set too and produce a tea-cup novel, a twentieth century story. But I couldn't care less. I've got an idea and a good one about the present cosmic mess but I find myself sneering at it unconsciously. I'm much happier with a less promising idea about pre-dynastic Egypt.

Yours ever
Bill.

Golding has written 'Wednesday' in place of a date. The 'less promising idea about pre-dynastic Egypt' is the seed of 'The Scorpion God', a story that Golding finishes in 1964 and, after further revisions, publishes in 1971.

WG to Charles Monteith   TS

28 October 1955   St Mark's House, Salisbury, Wilts

Dear Charles,

Here at last is the list of the rejections for STRANGERS FROM WITHIN as it then was. I find it very sobering. At the same time two other books of mine were going the rounds – SHORT MEASURE which you have seen and an Arthur Ransome for grownups CIRCLE UNDER THE SEA which I had forgotten till I turned up this list of 'Old unhappy far-off things'. So you see I have now just about covered my outlay on postage! (By the way, I regard CIRCLE UNDER THE SEA in its present form as quite impossible.)

Two copies of THE INHERITORS have now turned up. Thank you for attending to this.

>   yours ever
>   *Bill.*

STRANGERS FROM WITHIN. (LORD OF THE FLIES.)

	Sent	Returned
Jonathan Cape.	1st January 1953	5th February
Andre Deutsch	5th February	17th February
Putnam & Co.	19th February	12th May.
Chapman & Hall	13th May	11th June.
Hutchinson	12th June	24th June.
An Agent	24th June	19th July
John Lane	24th July	20th August
Faber & Faber	20th September	

Accepted for publication 12th February 1954.

The speaker of Wordsworth's 'The Solitary Reaper' observes a 'Highland Lass' reaping and singing by herself. He speculates that she is singing of 'old, unhappy, far-off things'.

Golding's joke about having barely covered the cost of postage was one of a series of comments that might have been construed as expressing his general dissatisfaction with sales and income. In an internal memo to Peter du Sautoy dated 3 November, Monteith warns about Golding's unhappiness, 'though I'm not clear whether he blames us or the eccentric nature of his talent. But he certainly seems obsessed by the idea that he's never going to make any money by writing. The answer to this seems to be that he has and is. Perhaps he has no idea at all about the average earnings of novelists.'

The list of publishers is annotated in pencil with a question mark next to 'An Agent' and an X to the right of the Putnam & Co. return date. The agent was Curtis Brown. Underneath the list, in Monteith's hand, are more possibilities about which Golding seems not to have been certain: Gollancz, Eyre & Spottiswoode, and Macmillan. If these publishers were approached, it must have been during the lengthy period listed for Putnam.

Charles Monteith to WG   TS

2 November 1955

Dear Bill,

Very many thanks for the list! It certainly increases the gratified glow of my baser instincts. How *could* all those people have been such chumps?

THE INHERITORS, you'll be glad to hear, continues to sell very steadily – the 3,000 mark is now well in sight and our Sales people are very pleased with it. I'm having a band printed to go over the dust jacket with all those nice quotes on it. It should go well with the band we put on LORD OF THE FLIES, – which still goes on selling very steadily; and it's now well over a year since publication.

It's extremely good news that you are arranging ENVOY EXTRAORDINARY for the Third. That should be superbly good. And of course in the more immediate future there is the repeat of LORD OF THE FLIES on the 22nd.

Yes, I noticed too that some reviewer had suggested you should have a shot at the twentieth century; and I remember my only feeling about it was a profound hope that you wouldn't feel in the least bit tempted to accept the idea unless you wanted to do it anyway and felt entirely happy about it. I'm all for pre-dynastic Egypt myself. And *please* don't forget those fat boys. They still haunt my dreams occasionally.

Yours ever,

PS

Copies of THE INHERITORS went off some time ago both to *Antiquity* and to Jacquetta Hawkes. I met Jacquetta H. (or P.) recently and she told me how very much she was looking forward to reading it.

86

The 'fat boys' feature in the extract from 'In Search of My Father'. See Monteith's letters of 28 July 1954 and 21 October 1954.

Jacquetta Hawkes was a writer and archaeologist with a particular expertise in Neanderthal remains. She had married J. B. Priestley in 1953 and now went by her new married name, hence Monteith's second thoughts.

Charles Monteith to WG   TS

23 November 1955

Dear Bill,

Now at last I've heard LORD OF THE FLIES on the Third without hundreds of miles of Irish static between me and it, – and how *very* good it was. I was as enthralled as ever.

I thought you might perhaps like to have this, – it's James Blish's SF novel which we'll be publishing sometime next spring. Since it's an uncorrected proof copy, and since it's full of ODD WORDS, it may be a bit haywire here and there. I do hope you enjoy it.

My regards to Anne.

Yours ever,

PS

The Sunday Times Book Exhibition at the Festival Hall has been a great success. Many enquiries about you from enthusiastic readers.

The SF novel in question was Blish's *Earthman, Come Home*.

Ann is occasionally spelt Anne in the letters from Monteith. This is probably his secretary's mistake rather than his own. The same slip is made in his letter dated 18 October, but there the extraneous 'e' has been deleted in pen, presumably by Monteith himself.

WG to Charles Monteith   TS

30 November 1955   St Mark's House, Salisbury

Dear Charles –

This is a hasty note to thank you for your letter and gift of SF. I havn't read it yet I'm afraid because the family grabbed it and I havn't been able to have a turn. A glance at the first few pages however forwarns me that an exact understanding of the scientific principles involved will tax me to the uttermost.

In fact it made me spindizzy.

I agree that Lord Of The Flies made terrifying radio. (A bit on the long side between you and me but we should worry.) I've written nice thank you for having me letters to the people involved. If only the ripples of The Inheritors would spread a bit wider! I have an uneasy feeling that it's flopped though I still think it was good.

Yours ever

Bill Golding

PS Ann exchanges regards with you.

In Blish's novel, a 'spindizzy' is an anti-gravity device.

Charles Monteith to WG   TS

2 December 1955

Dear Bill,

So glad EARTHMAN, COME HOME arrived safely. If you get a chance to read it, do let me know what you think of it. An interesting piece of Blish juvenilia, by the way, JACK OF EAGLES, has just been published here in 'soft covers' by Nova Publications – a new concern related to *New Worlds Science Fiction* as the Greyfriars Library was related to *The Magnet*.

THE INHERITORS continues to sell very steadily. Indeed, though it's now nearly three months after publication, more than a hundred copies a week are being taken regularly; and the total sales, I believe, are well over the three thousand mark. With it, of course, we started off with a much bigger initial printing than we did with LORD OF THE FLIES, – if we hadn't we would certainly have had to reprint long ago.

Yours ever,

WG to Charles Monteith   MS

11 December 1955   St Mark's House, Salisbury, Wilts

Dear Charles

Thank you for your letter: I've managed to borrow back 'Earthman Come Home' from my children and have enjoyed it. His universe is credible while one reads and his main character clear enough. I suppose his strength is in Titanic engineering conceptions rather than fantasy.

I got torn between two novels and ended by writing neither – so far. I'm very distressed about this. I returned to Rockall ('The Chinese Have X-ray Eyes') and it ran out at 37 thousand, an impossible length. I'm going to take a couple of weeks off and think.

I might get over to Blackwells for some book-buying this Christmas. I suppose you'll be recuperating from London in Ireland – I seem to remember du Sautoy saying so.

I'm sorry about this scrawl but my typewriter hasn't recovered from Rockall – overheating I think.

> Yours ever
> Bill

'The Chinese Have X-ray Eyes', a working title for what becomes *Pincher Martin*, survives as a sentence in the published version of the novel.

Charles Monteith to WG   TS

13 December 1955

Dear Bill,

Thank you very much indeed for your letter of December 11th. I'm delighted to know that you enjoyed EARTHMAN, COME HOME. Yes indeed; 'titanic engineering conceptions' is what Blish is supremely good at. His new one, which we've just had in, is part of the 'Earthman' saga, but precedes it in time, – and deals principally with the building of the Great Bridge on Jupiter. A project which has haunted my imagination most persistently for the last week or two.

And I'm quite delighted, too, to know that Rockall has been returned to and the story finished. I long to read it. Do please send it up and let me see it.

Alas, I won't, I fear, be in Oxford until some time in January – as you guessed, I'm going home to Ireland for a few days at Christmas – and I really am most terribly sorry if this means an opportunity missed of meeting you there. But perhaps we can manage something in the New Year. Peter and Molly du Sautoy, I know, very much hope that you and Ann will be able to manage – though they know it's difficult – a week-end with them at Datchet some time during term when the boys are at Bryanston; and if you *can* manage it, I do very much hope it can be combined with a trip to Oxford. Peter will, I know, be writing to you about this shortly.

Looking forward very much to seeing you again before too long, I hope.

Yours ever,

The Blish novel dealing with 'the building of the Great Bridge on Jupiter' is *They Shall Have Stars*, published by Faber in 1956.

Peter du Sautoy's wife was Mollie, not Molly. As with the misspelling of Ann, this is probably a secretarial error.

Charles Monteith to WG   TS

28 December 1955

Dear Bill,

Just a line to congratulate you on Arthur Koestler's wonderful bit about THE INHERITORS in Christmas Day's *Sunday Times*. Need I say how deeply I agree with every word? Incidentally, I was dining with Stephen Spender the other night and was delighted to find that he, too, is a tremendous Golding fan.

Do please let me know when I'm going to see the Rockall story. I'm looking forward to it enormously.

All best wishes for the New Year.

Yours ever,

Considering it to be the outstanding novel of 1955, Arthur Koestler had called *The Inheritors* 'an earthquake in the petrified forests of the English novel'.

WG to Charles Monteith   MS

29 December 1955   29 The Green, Marlborough, Wilts.

Dear Charles

Yes Koestler's write-up was very good. I quote the earthquake bit to myself at regular intervals. I'm glad to hear that Stephen Spender likes the books – its mutual; or is that ambiguous? Let it stand.

About Rockall.

I've had violent second thoughts. It really *could* be a full length novel because there is one there, only hidden. Sorry to sound obscure.

Anyway, let me have another go in January/February as I did at the Inheritors and that *might* be good. At the moment its a rather un-splendid torso. Its typed but only because I did the first draft that way instead of in longhand. And it petered out at about 37 thousand from sheer exhaustion. I wrote the lot in seven days. Silly.

I took my son David (15) to Oxford yesterday to give him a preview. He was interested in the Proctorial administration more than in any-thing else – dreadfully significant, I feel. I'd also forgotten that Thursday was early closing and only had about half an hour in Blackwells.

I hope you enjoy Ireland – and the New Year.

     Yours ever
      Bill
              PS
Sorry for the scrawl – typewriter still in dock.

Golding and his family were spending Christmas at his parents' house in Marlborough.

1956

Before Easter, Golding invests £300 of his royalties in *Wild Rose*, a thirty-seven-foot ketch that occupies his family on sailing holidays for years to come. Later that summer, they make national headlines when *Wild Rose* gets caught in a Channel storm; after three days adrift they limp into Le Havre with damaged sails and a flooded engine. *Pincher Martin* is published in October, Golding's third novel in two years. Although the reviews are mostly favourable, amidst the praise can be heard, for the first time, outright hostility. Golding is already working on another novel but gets distracted by the opportunity to turn his novella, 'Envoy Extraordinary', into a play starring Alastair Sim.

Charles Monteith to WG   TS

2 January 1956

Dear Bill,

Thank you very much indeed for your letter of December 29th. It's very exciting news that Rockall is going to turn into a full-length novel and I look forward enormously to seeing it when you've had another go at it.

So terribly sorry that I wasn't in Oxford for your expedition there last week and I do hope we can meet there before very long.

I had a very agreeable domestic sort of Christmas in Ireland, – though the weather was a bit damp and drizzly as Irish weather usually is.

Very best wishes for 1956.
          Yours ever,

WG to Charles Monteith   TS

24(?) February 1956   St Mark's House, Salisbury, Wilts

Dear Charles –

I've just finished the second draft of the sailor & rock story. I think it's pretty bad but there is a certain amount that is worth saving. This will mean a good month's work.

Assuming without prejudice (which I believe is the correct legal phrase) that you're interested could you tell me some things about dates? If you were to accept the story at the end of March is this still too late for the autumn book tide? Because if it would be, then I'll put the draft away and come back to it later, since a few months would make no difference. This is all very confused but I hope you can see what I mean. The name of the story at present, for reference, is: PINCHER MARTIN. The 'without prejudice' by the way refers to F&F accepting this third book. My reason for putting it away would be first, because I'd see what was essential in it better and second, because I've got a couple of commissions hanging over my head which I could perhaps work off in between.

You probably know that Lord Of The Flies is a financial flop in USA. Never mind – so is GODOT; which I've now seen and enjoyed immensely. I only hope it doesn't touch off a whole salvo of literary enigmas.

Yours ever
Bill

Here, and in many later letters, Golding signs 'Bill' and types his full name beneath.

Golding may have got the date wrong. See Monteith's reply, also dated 24 February.

Explaining in a letter to Peter du Sautoy why Coward-McCann would not publish *The Inheritors* in the United States ('it will get nowhere'), T. R. Coward added that only half of the firm's initial 5,000 print run of *Lord of the Flies* had been sold so far.

Monteith saw *Waiting for Godot* in London during August or early September 1955 and found it 'a very odd and remarkable piece of work'. He contacted Beckett's agent and acquired the print rights for Faber.

Charles Monteith to WG   TS

24(?) February 1956

My dear Bill,

Thank you very much indeed for your letter. I'm delighted to know that the second draft of the sailor and rock story is finished and I'm looking forward more than I can say to reading it. I've just consulted Dick de la Mare about the dates query. He tells me that if we have the story at the end of March we could most certainly publish it this autumn; and I must confess that I *would* rather like it for the autumn if that's at all possible. But of course if you'd prefer to keep it for a few more months I shan't press you about it; I'd rather leave it entirely to you. PINCHER MARTIN sounds admirable. I like it enormously.

So glad you enjoyed GODOT, – I enclose a copy of our edition in case you haven't read it yet. Did you see, by the way, the middle page article on it in the TLS last week? Very good indeed, I thought.

Yours ever,

This replies to Golding's letter of the same date, so one of the letters must be wrong. In the absence of proof, the best evidence comes from one of Golding's journal entries: 'But how often is the letter writer certain of the date or careful of it, if he is? My own circumstances are such that a day or so either way can always be allowed for carelessness & insouciance. Dates don't really matter' (J, 20 August 1978).

Dick (Richard) de la Mare, son of the poet Walter de la Mare, rose through the ranks to become chairman of Faber in 1960. His area of expertise was book design and production; T. S. Eliot considered him 'the greatest living producer of books'.

Faber had published *Waiting for Godot* a fortnight earlier, on 10 February. That same day, the *Times Literary Supplement* ran a long article by G. S. Fraser declaring *Godot* 'a modern morality play, on permanent Christian themes'.

WG to Charles Monteith   TS

26 February 1956   Flat 2, St Mark's House, Salisbury, Wilts.

Dear Charles,

Thank you for your letter and the present of your neat edition of GODOT. I'm delighted to have it. Yes, I *did* read the article in the TLS and knew after that what I ought to have thought. Anyway, understood or not, it was most impressive and moving. I dont see that intellectual comprehension is necessarily the most valuable experience that one gets from the stage.

I'll go ahead with PINCHER MARTIN and try to get it to you by the end of March or early April.

I heard that the first impression of Lord Of The Flies is now unobtainable but being searched for by those who know. This makes me feel very distinguished – rather like a piece of chippendale.

Yours ever,
Bill

'chippendale': the much sought-after furniture named after the eighteenth-century cabinetmaker, Thomas Chippendale.

Charles Monteith to WG TS

28 February 1956

Dear Bill,

Very many thanks for your letter. I'm looking forward more than I can say to PINCHER MARTIN.

Yes; the article in the TLS was quite an eye-opener to me, too, – though I think that what it says is probably right. When I saw GODOT, though, I didn't speculate much about its 'symbolism'; like you, I simply found it an extraordinarily moving and extraordinarily entertaining piece of theatre, – a sort of sublime apotheosis of a cross-talk act.

The first impression of LORD OF THE FLIES is indeed a collector's piece, – I hoard my own two copies of it most jealously.

Yours ever,

WG to Charles Monteith TS

19 March 1956   Flat 2, St Mark's House, Salisbury,
                                 Wilts.

Dear Charles,

I'm sending you the MS of Pincher Martin a bit early. I've got into a hopeless state over it and now the only resource I have is to ask you to read it through for counsel's opinion. Perhaps if you can spot the essential weaknesses there might be time to clear them up in a couple of weeks work. However I shant be surprised if you see no future for this sanguinary mess.

I believe we are meeting in a months time. I personally look forward to seeing you again very much. What I *ought* to do, though, is to go into purdah or retreat for a few months to do some heavy re-thinking.

Do you know anyone with a four berth cabin cruiser for sale at £500 or less? No, I thought not. My family are goading me into buying one to take the place of our old wreck. It's been terribly difficult to concentrate on anything as flippant as a novel when contemplating anything as serious as buying a boat.

Yours ever
    Bill.

The question about the cabin cruiser has been underlined in pencil by Monteith, who has added a note in his own hand: 'Any suggestions?'

Charles Monteith to WG TS

21(?) March 1956

My dear Bill,

Very many thanks for PINCHER MARTIN. This is simply to acknowledge its safe arrival and to say how enormously I'm looking forward to reading it. When I have, of course I'll write again straight away. (It may be a few days, I fear, since I seem to be horribly bunged up at the moment.)

I'm much looking forward to meeting you and Ann again, – on April 21st, isn't it? Minsted and the South Downs should be quite wonderful then.

I don't, alas, know of anybody with a suitable or, indeed, any sort of boat for sale; but I'll most certainly spread the word around and let you know any results that occur.

> Yours ever,

Golding's reply, also dated 21 March, means that one or the other must be wrong.

Minsted, near Midhurst, was the home of Geoffrey Faber, so the event on 21 April was probably a social gathering for a small number of Faber employees and authors.

WG to Charles Monteith MS

21(?) March 1956   Flat 2, St Mark's House, Salisbury.

Dear Charles

Just a line to let you know the remark about your helping to find us a boat was meant to be funny! In fact the South of England swarms with brokers who will sell you anything from an RAF rubber dinghy, to the Queens – the difficulty lies in the choice.

I keep my fingers crossed over Pincher Martin

> Yours ever
> > Bill

Charles Monteith to WG TS

26 March 1956

My dear Bill,

PINCHER MARTIN is absolutely tremendous. I can't even begin to tell you how impressed I am by it, – I'm still getting nightmares! And *of course* we want to publish it this autumn. So far as terms are concerned, would the same royalties as for THE INHERITORS be OK, i.e., 12½% to 4,000 copies, and 15% thereafter? And an advance of £200, half payable on signature, half on publication? Do please let me know and then Peter du Sautoy will send off a draft contract straight away.

————

I do hope the boat buying goes well. I'm in the same sort of tizzy myself! After a lot of mad hunting I've at last succeeded in getting a flat, – and now of course my mind is in the most tremendous whirl about distemper and furniture and paint and wallpaper and all that.

Looking forward very much indeed to seeing you and Ann at Minsted.

Yours ever,

WG to Charles Monteith MS

27 March 1956   St Mark's House, Salisbury, Wilts.

Tuesday

Dear Charles

I'm delighted that Pincher Martin will get by! Yes, the terms are OK.

We shall be dashing off to our boat which we have almost bought on Friday and perhaps not reappearing till the nineteenth – How formal is this week-end? Do we dress for dinner and so forth? Your reply will affect the speed of our return!

Yours ever, and very seamanlike

Bill

Charles Monteith to WG   TS

29 March 1956

Dear Bill,

Very many thanks for your letter. PINCHER MARTIN is with our Production Department now; and, all being well, should be out in the fairly early autumn. By the way, have you by any chance got a carbon copy of it? And if you have, could you possibly lend it to me for a short time? It would be very useful if I could send it off now to Anthony Gross so that he can get to work at once on the jacket. But if you haven't, please don't worry about it; he'll be able to work from a proof copy, – though if he had a typescript now that would, of course, give him rather more time.

It would be as well, I think, to pack a dinner jacket for the Minsted week-end. Sometimes – though not always – there's dressing for dinner and so on.

     Best of luck for your holidays.

        Yours ever,

WG to Charles Monteith   MS

4 April 1956   St Mark's House, Salisbury, Wilts

Dear Charles

Just a note to say that no I havn't got a carbon copy of Pincher Martin. Is this a frightful breach of etiquette between publisher and author?

Thanks for your letter by the way. I'm very glad you like Pincher – I've already thought of one or two extra sentences that ought to be inserted.

I've bought a boat, a huge one, fourteen tons now lying in Rochester and I'm terrified of her. Somehow I've got to get her to Southampton and if I could afford it, I'd take her by road.

     Yours ever

       Bill

PS

I'm back here till next Tuesday when I return to Rochester and take the awful plunge.

The new boat, *Wild Rose*, was a ketch built in 1896.

Charles Monteith to WG TS

9 April 1956

Dear Bill,

Many thanks for your letter. It's perfectly OK about there being no carbon copy of PINCHER MARTIN. Gross will certainly be able to do it in time from a set of proofs.

Could you let me have the extra sentences; and let me know where they are to go in? I'll pass them on to the printer and he may be able to deal with them straight away.

The boat sounds enormously exciting. Best wishes for its maiden voyage.

Yours ever,

Charles Monteith to WG TS

24 April 1956

My dear Bill,

Here is the manuscript of PINCHER MARTIN. Could you please let me have it back with the new bits added as soon as you can manage it? It will be OK if we have it within a week or ten days.

I enjoyed more than I can say meeting with you and Ann at the week-end; and I look forward to seeing you again before long. I do hope we can manage that Oxford trip.

Do let me know sometime how all went with 'Wild Rose'. I enclose a couple of books for her library!

Yours ever,

WG to Charles Monteith MS

1 May 1956   St Mark's House, Salisbury, Wilts.

Tuesday

Dear Charles

Just a line to let you know that I have your two letters and the MS of Pincher Martin. I am sweating at this at the moment and will forward it to the printers the instant it is finished. Thank you for the additions to Wild Rose's library. They are useful and entertaining and decorative!

We left last tuesday and got to Southampton on Friday afternoon without a single panic. Good weather except on the last day and even then the gale was in the right quarter and simply blew us home. Wild Rose now sits demurely among a lot of flashy and expensive yachts – like a Salvation Army lassie who has strayed into an expensive joint by mistake.

It was good to see you at Minstead. We both enjoyed ourselves thoroughly.

Yours ever
Bill.

In a change of plans, Monteith had written a short letter to Golding on 30 April, asking him to make any additions to the typescript and send it directly to the printer.

Charles Monteith to WG   TS

28 August 1956

My dear Bill,

What a turn we all got this morning – headlines in every paper we picked up!

It must have been an absolutely appalling experience. I do hope you and Ann and the children really *are* all right – and 'Wild Rose', too.

Some time – when you feel like recollecting it in tranquillity – I do hope you'll tell me the whole story. It must still, I imagine, seem a bit of a nightmare.

Anyway, I'm more delighted than I can say to know that you're all safe and, I hope, well.

Regards to Ann.
Yours ever,

PS

We've just heard that PINCHER MARTIN is to be Recommended by the Book Society. We'll put a nice band on the jacket!

No doubt Monteith saw the report in *The Times* headlined 'FAMILY'S ORDEAL IN CHANNEL STORM: YACHT THREE DAYS ADRIFT'. The article stated that 'A Salisbury schoolmaster, Mr William Golding, and his family brought their 33ft. yacht Wild

Rose into Le Havre this evening after drifting helplessly in a Channel storm for nearly three days.' They had been attempting to cross from Yarmouth to Cherbourg. Caught in a storm, the boat's foresail split and its mainsail was damaged. They eventually limped into port with a flooded engine and a broken radio.

'recollecting it in tranquillity': Monteith alludes to Wordsworth's famous statement in his Preface to the second edition of *Lyrical Ballads* (1800): 'Poetry is the spontaneous overflow of powerful feelings: it takes its origin from emotion recollected in tranquillity.'

WG to Charles Monteith MS

10 September 1956 St Mark's House, Salisbury, Wilts.

Dear Charles

Thank you for your letter of the 28th August, which I found waiting for me when I got back last night. It's good to hear about the Book Society.

We are all quite fit I think, since the Wild Rose affair was not half as perilous as the papers made out. However it was quite bad enough.

Thanks too for 'They Shall Have Stars' which I hope to enjoy when I can get it back from young David.

Excuse the scrawl – a hurried acknowledgement is all I can manage at the moment.

> Yours ever
> Bill.

James Blish's *They Shall Have Stars*, first mentioned by Monteith in his letter of 13 December 1955, was published by Faber in 1956.

WG to Charles Monteith MS

23 September 1956 Flat 2, St Mark's House, Salisbury, Wilts.

Sunday

Dear Charles

Could I have twelve copies of 'Pincher Martin' instead of just six? I think this is provided for in the contract at 2/3 published price. And it will swell the sales!

I'm amused that Pincher is to be recommended – it's probably the bad language that did it; any book that uses four letter words must be good.

I see that you are going to have The High all to yourself, bar pedestrians and bicyclists.

Yours ever

Bill Golding

Someone (not Golding) has drawn a line from the word 'Sunday' and added '23.9.56'.

The entrance to All Souls in Oxford is off High Street, known locally as 'The High'.

The 'bad language' is scattered through the novel, most conspicuously towards the end when Pincher shouts at God, 'I shit on your heaven!'

WG to Peter du Sautoy

MS

2 October 1956   Flat 2, St Mark's House, Salisbury,
                                  Wilts

Dear Peter

Many thanks for your long and judicious letter. I'm glad to hear that *Pincher Martin* stands some chance of getting done in America.

About what to do – dont wait till we come up next week unless you yourself want to. I've complete confidence in your wisdom and so forth – settle the business how you like and we shall agree amiably this end.

Ann and I are looking forward to seeing you on the eleventh: – and Mollie too, we hope.

Excuse the scrawl. I'm changing a tyre.

Yours ever

Bill

Du Sautoy had sent Golding a long letter setting out the (already labyrinthine) publication history of his novels in the United States and reporting the interest of Harcourt, Brace in acquiring the rights for *Pincher Martin*. The contractual complications around Golding's work would continue for the next twenty-three years and would finally be settled in the American law courts.

Charles Monteith to WG

TS

18 October 1956

Dear Bill,

We've just heard that the Critics are going to talk about PINCHER

MARTIN on Sunday, October 28th. The book critic will be Walter Allen.

It was very nice indeed to see you and Ann again last week. Do let me know when you're next going to be in London.

And I long to know, of course, what the next novel's going to be; and how it's progressing. IN SEARCH OF MY FATHER? Or something quite different?

      Love to Ann.
        Yours ever,

The Critics was the BBC Home Service's weekly arts show.

WG to Charles Monteith MS

20 October 1956   Flat 2, St Mark's House, Salisbury,
                         Wilts

Dear Charles

How exciting and terrifying – the critics! Please bribe everybody immediately.

I believe I told you that the Arts' + the Arts' Council have drawn me into trying to write a play for them. That isnt done yet but I'm trying to work it off by Christmas.

Then I *think* – after a couple of weeks walking round the Marlborough Downs – I ought to be able to finish off a novel I started called (for reference) The Horizontal Man. I'll try and get it to you in time for the Autumn list '57 if you decide to accept it.

I'm finding doing two full time jobs a strain and both suffer. I do neither.

About visits to London – I'll certainly let you know next time I'm going to be present and at liberty for an hour or two but it doesn't happen very often. Salisbury is right in the sticks.

      Yours ever
        Bill.

The play was to be based on 'Envoy Extraordinary', and despite Golding's garbled reference to 'the Arts' + the Arts' Council', it had been commissioned by the actor Alastair Sim.

    'The Horizontal Man' is probably a working title for *Free Fall* (1959).

Charles Monteith to WG
TS

22 October 1956

Dear Bill,

Many thanks for your letter. I look forward enormously to THE HORIZONTAL MAN. I do hope it – and the play – go well.

Delighted to know that the prospects are so bright for a Harcourt, Brace edition of PINCHER MARTIN. They are first-class publishers and I think they would look after the book extremely well.

> Regards to you all,
> Yours ever,

WG to Charles Monteith
MS

30 October 1956   Flat 2, St Mark's House, Salisbury, Wilts.

Dear Charles

Thank you very much for your note. The reviews certainly havn't been pleasant (though Richard Ward is about to broadcast a solitary 'rave' on the West!) but after all that's an occupational hazard like silicosis. I hope it doesn't have an adverse effect on sales. As far as I'm concerned personally it's reducing my head to reasonable proportions: so the only loser is that absurd figure one sets up on a rock to stand for oneself in a sea of circumstances. If you meet C. A. Lejeune will you tell her that my small daughter wants to play 'chopsticks' to her ten thousand times running?

> with best wishes
> *Bill.*

PS

Times Lit: Sup: and New Statesman go a little way towards restoring a balance. But no one seems to realise that Martin is torturing himself, and that he was a murderer – at least in intention!

'Nothing burns in hell but the self.'

Pincher Martin had been published on Friday 26 October in an edition of 5,000 copies and was (by and large) unfavourably reviewed in the Sunday papers two days later. Monteith's note has not survived in the Faber archive, probably because he sent it from All Souls to commiserate with Golding. Both men would also have heard *The Critics* on the BBC Home Service that same day, in which the *Observer* film critic C. A. Lejeune deplored the novel for seeing 'nothing but the nasty side' of the human body.

The anonymous *Times Literary Supplement* reviewer praised Golding's 'remarkably sustained imaginative intensity'; Richard Mayne in the *New Statesman* called *Pincher Martin* 'a first-rate novel, shaking and compelling'.

The 'West' was probably the BBC's West of England Home Service.

'Nothing burns in hell but the self' is translated from the fourteenth-century mystical treatise *Theologia Germanica*. Aldous Huxley quotes the phrase in *The Perennial Philosophy* (1945), which is likely to have been where Golding first encountered it.

WG to Charles Monteith   MS

6 November 1956   Flat 2, St Mark's House, Salisbury,
                               Wilts

Dear Charles

Forgive this paper for being what it is. Yes – I heard Frank Kermode and it turned all my adrenalin into glucose or what ever happens. I'm writing him a fan letter straight away. (Its great fun rubbing shoulders with Coleridge and Wordsworth. But how incredibly penetrating he is!) And how incredibly dependent I find myself on praise or blame – quite revoltingly so. My dear Charles, I am beginning to *believe* all the good reviews and forget all the bad ones.

I'm going to be in London on the 15th of November. Is there any chance of our meeting? My programme is BBC 4–5, Garrick Club 5–7 – early train back to the sticks.

Ann sends her regards and would like to know how Ann Faber is – doesn't like to write and ask, but felt it is all very worrying.

I should like to write a funny.

    Yours
      Bill.

PS

    Ann said she sent love, *not* regards – I expect you have them too.

Golding is evidently replying to another lost note from Monteith. The apologetic opening is odd because the writing paper is his usual sort.

Frank Kermode's 1 November broadcast on the BBC Third Programme had praised Golding in the same terms as Coleridge praised Wordsworth: he achieves a 'union of deep feeling with profound thought [. . .]. This is the character and privilege of genius, and one of the marks which distinguish genius from talents.'

Charles Monteith to WG TS

8 November 1956

Dear Bill,

What very good news that you're going to be in London on November 15th. I do hope you'll be here in time to lunch with me. If you are, could you meet me at the Travellers Club about 12.45? (The Travellers is in Pall Mall, a modest building tucked between the Athenaeum and the Reform.) If by any unhappy chance you won't be here in time for lunch, do please – if you can manage it – call in to see me during the afternoon.

Lots of good reviews coming in now. I think the latest batch has just been sent off to you.

Looking forward very much to seeing you on the 15th.

Love to Ann.

Yours,

WG to Charles Monteith MS

9 November 1956   Flat 2, St Mark's House, Salisbury, Wilts

Dear Charles

I can get to the Travellers Club by 12.45, I think; provided I can find Pall Mall. It is kind of you to offer me lunch and I look forward to it.

The reviews seem pretty good, by and large and are full of desirable quotes. Now all people have to do is buy the book!

Yours ever

Bill

Charles Monteith to WG TS

16 November 1956

Dear Bill,

Here's a copy of Frank Kermode's broadcast, – I thought you might like to have it. I'll enclose, too, a couple more clippings that have come in.

It was very nice indeed seeing you yesterday. I long to know how the Alistair Sim rencontre went.

By the way, I enquired about the Japanese prints book which David's interested in. I think it probably must be a forthcoming volume, JAPANESE LANDSCAPE PRINTS OF THE NINETEENTH CENTURY, in the Faber Gallery of Oriental Art. It won't be out, I'm afraid, until some time in the spring. Has David got, I wonder, the other Faber Gallery Japanese prints book, – JAPANESE COLOUR PRINTS edited by Wilfred Blunt? If he hasn't, I'd be very pleased indeed to send him a copy as a present.

    Yours ever,

WG to Charles Monteith MS

18 November 1956   Flat 2, St Mark's House, Salisbury

Sunday

Dear Charles

Thank you very much for the pleasant, though brief, encounter on Thursday. It's so pleasant to have a sort of civilised interlude between these perfectly disgusting train journeys.

The Alistair Sim rencontre went swimmingly. He is – you probably know him – a most charming man to meet. I sat and allowed myself to be entertained with a series of splendid portraits – man, between heaven and hell – a baby discovering its personal identity – 'I know who I am! I'm the little bugger who doesn't like porridge!' And so on. At times I had the fabulous feeling of one who is elevated to the throne of all the Russias and has the Imperial Ballet to dance for him in exalted privacy. He is very easy to like and I think, laid himself out to please. Why, later, in the chattering crawling train, did I realise that I had been told exactly the sort of play he would like written for him and the limits he would accept. Perhaps I'm slow-witted. Anyway that realisation did nothing to damp my enthusiasm for him as a raconteur, host and amiable character.

Pause.

I like Frank Kermode's broadcast. Thank you very much.

About David – he has qualms about accepting a present, but I'm sure he'd love to have the book! Yes please.

    Yours ever
     Bill.

Charles Monteith to WG TS

20 November 1956

Dear Bill,

Delighted to know that the Alistair Sim meeting went so well. He sounds an absolute charmer. I do hope, too, that a play comes of it. I enclose a copy of JAPANESE COLOUR PRINTS – and also a rather nice recent one on JAPANESE SCREEN PAINTING – for David, with our very best wishes. I do hope he likes them.

Have you seen the current *London Magazine*? Nice review of PINCHER by Francis Wyndham.

Love to Ann,
Yours ever,

Francis Wyndham found that *Pincher Martin* 'shows imaginative gifts of astonishing quality' and, looking ahead, that Golding's 'potential achievements seem to be unlimited'.

WG to Peter du Sautoy MS

22 November 1956

Dear Peter

Thank you very much for your letter – it's good to hear from you again.

Yes – Sunday was a day of wrath, sackcloth, and penitential psalms, but as you say the outlook now seems a little brighter. I'm glad that Harcourt Brace have now done the decent thing.

Love to you and Mollie from us both
Bill

The Sunday in question was 28 October, two days after publication of *Pincher Martin*, when the reviews were mostly negative. Du Sautoy wrote to Golding on 20 November that 'there have been some excellent reviews, after that miserable Sunday', and that 'I have the impression that the book has not only consolidated your reputation but taken it an important stage further'. He was also able at last to confirm that 'we have now fixed up with Harcourt Brace [. . .] for the American edition of PINCHER MARTIN'.

WG to Charles Monteith   MS

12 December 1956   Flat 2, St Mark's House, Salisbury,
                                    Wilts.

Dear Charles

Thank you for the London Magazine. Its good to see that the reviews
are improving – Listener, Spectator etc – since Black Sunday.

Yours ever
    Bill

Charles Monteith to WG   TS

13 December 1956

Dear Bill,

News of a Boxing Day treat. The BBC have just rung to say that
PINCHER MARTIN will be discussed in a broadcast to be given on
December 26th in the Third Programme from 6.0 to 6.40 p.m. The
speakers will be Graham Hough, Anthony Quinton and Alan Pryce-
Jones. No further details so far. I've a sort of feeling it'll be a general
discussion on Novels of the Year.

            Yours ever,

1957

Golding's profile receives a significant boost in January when he makes his debut on the BBC television panel show *The Brains Trust* – the first of six appearances before the programme ends in 1961. There is no new novel for Faber this year, but *Pincher Martin* is published by Harcourt, Brace in the USA as *The Two Deaths of Christopher Martin*. Although Golding has started work on a manuscript that eventually becomes his fourth novel, *Free Fall*, he directs most of his energies towards adapting 'Envoy Extraordinary' for the stage. The resulting play, *The Brass Butterfly*, is finished by the end of the year.

Charles Monteith to WG   TS

8 February 1957

Dear Bill,

Do please forgive a pestering letter. It's only to ask whether or not there will be another novel in time for the autumn. If so – and need I say how very much I hope there is? – could you possibly give me an idea of when it will be ready? If it's to go safely into the autumn list we should have it fairly soon, since production nowadays seems to take such an appallingly long time.

Many congratulations on your début as a Brains Truster. I much admired and enjoyed it.

Love to Ann.

Yours,

Golding had made his debut as a panellist on *The Brains Trust* – a BBC television show answering questions sent in by the audience – on 20 January.

WG to Charles Monteith   MS

9 February 1957   St Mark's House, Salisbury, Wilts

Dear Charles

Many thanks for your letter and *The Stones of Troy*. This slim volume I enjoyed very much indeed: I must admit however that a major part of that enjoyment was the snob value of having read the same books and recognising the allusions. But what are PAXOI? Or is it a locative? Joking apart I think this is the highest kind of verse, even if it never takes off and becomes something else.

About the novel – I cant give a solidly firm date at the moment because I've been too-ing and froming between the novel and my perfectly lousy play. If you can give me any time I will certainly kill myself; working. Is it possible for you to give me the last date *firmly* by which the novel would have to be finished so that you would have a chance to accept or reject?

The Brains' Trust was most amusing and exciting. Its' I should think the easiest way of earning money in the world – no nervous strain, interesting people, and all you have to do is to talk. I hope I get asked again, some time, but of course all that's problematical.

Ann sends her love
    Bill.

The most extraordinary thing about the telly is that it *works*! Its not a fake – the performers are really there, doing what they seem to do. All sorts of odd people mention the performance to you, and they all saw the same thing and you remember doing it. Is that impossibly banal? I suppose I'm trying to convey the difference between intellectual aware-ness and an astonished physical acceptance of the fact – or something.

How is the anthology of good/bad verse going?
    Bill

The Stones of Troy was a volume of poems by C. A. Trypanis, published by Faber in early 1957. Golding's joking comment about 'PAXOI' refers to Trypanis's poem of that title, in which the typography makes it uncertain whether the word begins with an English capital 'p' or a Greek capital 'rho'. If the former, then 'PAXOI' could be locative: 'to Paxos'. If the latter, the word means 'thorns'. In reality – as Golding probably knew – both readings are wrong. 'Paxoi' is the plural of 'Paxos' and an alternative name for it, referring not only to the main island but to the smaller islands dotted around.

Charles Monteith to WG   TS

14 February 1957

Dear Bill,
    Many thanks for your letter of 9th February.

About the deadline for the novel. Could you possibly let us have it by March 31st? Our production people tell me that if you could they can get it into the Autumn list, – barring of course such disasters as strikes in the printing trade or earth tremors in Russell Square! But March 31st really *is* a deadline; book production does take an appallingly long time nowadays.

Love to Ann and the family,

Yours ever,

WG to Charles Monteith MS

21 February 1957   St Mark's House, Salisbury, Wilts.

Dear Charles,

a hurried scribble to let you know that I dont see much chance of getting an MS to you in March. I'll do what I can; but the hope I have is almost nil.

I'm sorry about this – is there any chance of publication round about Christmas?

In haste

Bill

Someone has written 'NO' – with what looks like a red crayon – next to Golding's question.

Charles Monteith to WG TS

28 February 1957

Dear Bill,

It wouldn't be wise, I think, to publish any later than mid-November – I've consulted our Sales Department about this. Books published after that very often don't reach the remoter bookshops until too late for the Christmas buying, – which starts about the end of November – and fall desolately into the trough which follows. It would be much wiser, I think, not to rush it – I know what a fearful time you're having with the play – and we'd be very happy indeed to have it for our spring list next year.

Love to Ann.

Yours ever,

WG to Peter du Sautoy

26 March 1957   St Mark's House, Salisbury, Wilts.

Dear Peter

Thank you for your letter. I'm completely foxed for titles. Here are some.

1   Crustacean.
2   Aftermath.
3   Epilogue.
4   The Chinese Have X-ray Eyes.
5   Perchance To Dream.
6   What Dreams May Come.

(For in that sleep of death, what dreams may come
When we have shuffled off this mortal coil
Must give us pause.)

I suggest 4 or 6 as the best of this poor bunch. But really I'd rather it kept its' original title, if necessary with an explanatory paragraph as a foreword. But I'm not sticking my chin out on this one.

> In haste
> *Bill*

John McCallum had written to du Sautoy from Harcourt, Brace on 13 March requesting to change the title of *Pincher Martin* for publication in the United States. He explained that the name carried no meaning there and would hurt sales; in its place, he proposed 'The Rock' or (from *Paradise Lost*) 'Where Time and Place are Lost'. Golding and du Sautoy countered with the manuscript's original title, 'The Chinese Have X-ray Eyes'. They finally – and reluctantly – accepted McCallum's next suggestion: *The Two Deaths of Christopher Martin*. As far as American readers were concerned, this was Golding's second novel: *The Inheritors* remained unpublished in the United States until 1962.

Charles Monteith to WG

16 April 1957

Dear Bill,

I thought that David and Judith might perhaps like to have PLAIN SAILING, – though I imagine they're far too experienced sailors by now to learn much from it. And I thought you might perhaps enjoy, too, this new collection of SF stories we published the other day.

You'll be impressed by Beckett's FIN DE PARTIE, I think. Absolutely terrifying! He hopes to have the translation finished by the end of August and I imagine we'll be publishing it early next year.

Much enjoyed your bit in the London Magazine. Best of the lot, I thought.

Love to Ann.

Yours ever,

The Faber books that Monteith was giving away were *Plain Sailing* by Gabor Denes and *Best SF Two: Science Fiction Stories*, edited by Edmund Crispin. It sounds like Monteith also sent Golding a first edition of Samuel Beckett's play *Fin de Partie*, published by Les Éditions de Minuit in January 1957. Faber published it in Beckett's translation as *Endgame* in 1958.

Judith: the given name of Golding's daughter; she preferred Judy.

Golding was one of nine authors who had contributed to a debate in the latest issue of *London Magazine* about the proper relationship of writers to 'the fundamental political and social issues of their time'. His article insisted that 'current affairs are only expressions of the basic human condition where [the writer's] true business lies' and he aligned himself with what he called the 'Aeschylean outlook' that involved 'looking for the root of the disease instead of describing the symptoms'.

WG to Charles Monteith   MS

25 April 1957   St Mark's House, Salisbury, Wilts

Dear Charles –

Thank you for the books which we are all enjoying. I dont know about the children but the sailing book is just my cup of tea – particularly at this season.

I've had a searing time with the drama and now have a deep admiration for anyone who can write even a bad play. I'm coming rapidly to the conclusion that the only play I shall ever write which is any good, will have no contrivance about it at all – free fantasy, or something. Enter a goldfish bowl bleating gently. 'Mend me! Mend me!'

I'm glad you'll be doing Fin de Partie – Godot knocked me. There's no other news – I wrote some of a thing about Euripides and some of a thing about the H. bomb and then stopped. The truth is I've overworked these last three years and need to slack. Have you a small Greek or Italian island for sale?

Yours ever

Bill

Thanks from the children and love from Ann.

The writings about Euripides and the 'H. bomb' have disappeared without trace.

Charles Monteith to WG   TS

6 September 1957

Dear Bill,

Any chance of seeing you at the Science Fiction lunch on Tuesday? I gather that LORD OF THE FLIES features among the prize winners for something called the International Fantasy Award! Not alas the first prize winner, – that has gone to Tolkien's LORD OF THE RINGS.

Delighted to hear from Peter about ENVOY EXTRAORDINARY and Alistair Sim, – and delighted, too, that the world of the novel is about to be re-entered! I'm looking forward to the new one enormously.

Love to Ann.

　　　Yours ever,

The International Fantasy Award, an annual prize for the best science fiction or fantasy book, became defunct after 1957.

WG to Charles Monteith   TS

11 September 1957　　　　St Mark's House, Salisbury

Dear Charles,

Thank you for your letter. I'm a very casual answerer but have an excuse this time as we've been worried about Ann; but she's all right now and full of life.

No, I wasn't invited to the Science Fiction Lunch but couldn't have made it anyway. The menu could have been fun. Having said that and tried to think of an example I own myself stumped for one.

I didn't know there were prizes for fantasy. Are they momentous? Return tickets? A small disintegrator? Something silver mounted for putting back tooth paste? Should Professor Tolkien, self and Another have stood on those little stands they have in swimming baths on the telly?

It will be a relief getting back to a novel after floundering in the shallow waters of the drama. I dont say there arn't deep waters – God forbid – but they dont seem to be for me. Envoy Extraordinary makes the basis for what might be a gently amusing comedy but I dont think it will set the West End on fire.

I've entered young David for King's Cambridge, because he wants to read mathematics and philosophy; but that's two years off and they may not take him. So if you meet the relevant people please say what an intelligent boy he must be!

Yours ever
Bill

Ann had been suffering from depression.

Charles Monteith to WG   TS

13 September 1957

Dear Bill,

I'm more sorry than I can say to hear that Ann hasn't been well, – but relieved and delighted to know that she's now so much better. Do please give her my love.

You missed nothing by missing the Science Fiction lunch. I shall long remember the look on Tolkien's face when there was pressed into his hand by Miss Clemence Dane a chronium plated object representing a space rocket, a chronium plated cigarette lighter nestling at the foot! No prizes – fortunately I think – for runners-up. The imagination boggles at the thought of the same idea executed in some baser metal.

I'm looking forward more than I can say to the play of ENVOY EXTRAORDINARY. Is that the one for Alistair Sim? And, of course, looking forward enormously too to the new novel.

If you plan to be in London any time in the future do please let me know. It would be nice if we could meet again.

Yours ever,

'chronium': chromium.

1958

A year that ends in disaster begins positively, with *The Brass Butterfly* performing well on its provincial tour before moving to the West End in April. Faber publishes the play in July. The chances of *Lord of the Flies* being filmed increase when the young theatre director Peter Brook interests Sam Spiegel in the project. Spiegel is fresh from the Oscar-sweeping success of *The Bridge on the River Kwai*, but his vision for a film with girls as well as boys – and American rather than English – scuppers the plans. Golding all but finishes his fourth novel, *Free Fall*, by the end of the year. In the autumn, the family moves out of rental accommodation to their own house in Bowerchalke, nine miles south-west of Salisbury. There Golding meets and befriends the politician Wayland Young, the historian and biographer David Cecil, and the society photographer Cecil Beaton. Golding's father, Alec, dies of heart failure in December. Golding is devastated, and, years later, recalls that he shed 'the most of tears I have ever had'.

WG to Charles Monteith

MS

13 January 1958   Flat 2, St Mark's House, Salisbury,
                                  Wilts.

Dear Charles

Here is a belated thank you for HAWK IN THE RAIN by the W.G. of poetry – oh savage irony! I enjoyed them, sitting sadly on a pile of my own threadbare verses. Prose feels like the ground floor, somehow – stuff written by poor fellows who cant climb the stairs.

Here is a – for me – important Query. I've written – or am just finishing – a chaotic draft of Novel No 4 which will run out at 65,000, I think. Its only when I reflect on the general shapelessness of it that I realise that I have driven a furrow through what *might* be more than one volume. i.e. I could *either* condense and condense and re-write until the lot packs in small and terse; *or* I could divide it in four parts and expand in each to say what I want – except that I dont know what I want to say. Practically, it means this – am I to believe that you would be willing to publish a volume, say in the autumn, knowing that three others would follow at intervals? Or is the four decker out?

This is all agin my own theory of the novel – and hell what is a theory anyway? I must own the fact that I gave Ann 12 vols of Proust for Christmas has had some influence on my judgement. I'm both worried and idiotically elated by the idea. I'm asking you, rather than Peter, because after all, you are my literary godfather – a degree of Lat: Lit:

     Yours ever   Bill Golding

Sometime, Never. has 'achieved a SF breakthrough' in America!

Monteith had sent Golding a copy of Ted Hughes's first volume, *The Hawk in the Rain*, along with the *Glasgow Herald*'s review which called Hughes 'the William Golding of poetry'.

    'Lat: Lit:' may be an abbreviation for 'Latin Literature', although the reasons for the reference are unclear.

Charles Monteith to WG TS

16 January 1958

Dear Bill,

Very many thanks for your letter of January 13th. We'd have no qualms at all about a four-decker; indeed, we're in the middle of one at the moment by Lawrence Durrell. JUSTINE, which we published in the spring of 1957, was Part One; Part Two, BALTHAZAR, is coming out in April of this year; and Durrell plans two more before it's all complete.

I'm looking forward enormously to your Part One. Could you please let me have it by March 31st *at the latest*? That, I think, would be more or less a deadline for getting it into the autumn list, – and I *would* very much like to publish it in the autumn of this year. Of course it would be tremendously helpful if you could let me have it before that.

I do hope we manage to meet soon. Do please let me know when you plan your next trip to London. How are things going with THE BRASS BUTTERFLY? Our own *very* tentative publication date is May 23rd. How would that fit in with the West End production? I'm much excited, too, by the increasing flow of cuttings about the LORD OF THE FLIES film.

     Love to Ann,

      Yours ever,

Lawrence Durrell's *Alexandria Quartet* was completed with *Mountolive* (1958) and *Clea* (1960).

    The Brass Butterfly was the title of the play for Alastair Sim based on 'Envoy

Extraordinary'. The script was published by Faber in July.

Rumours were starting to grow that *Lord of the Flies* might be filmed as a collaboration between the English theatre director Peter Brook and the Hollywood producer Sam Spiegel.

WG to Charles Monteith   MS

26 January 1958   Flat 2, St Mark's House, Salisbury.

Dear Charles

Thank you for your letter. I'll get you an MS before 31st March; but whether it'll be part I or the whole thing condensed, I dont know. I dont seem very capable.

Brass Butterfly opens at Oxford on 24th of February; so please use your influence with the Hebdomadal, abdominal or whatever council it is, and the Mayor and corporation. It will wander North perhaps as far as Edinburgh, casting side glances towards London and nipping into the right theatre as soon as it becomes available – we hope. I'll let you know if I am coming up to London.

> Yours ever in haste
> Bill

Someone at Faber has corrected Golding's date in pencil, crossing out 'Feb.' and replacing it with 'Jan.' The same person has added a note in the left margin of the paragraph about *The Brass Butterfly*: 'Circulated to all directors, etc. 27/1/58'.

The Hebdomadal Council was the University of Oxford's governing body from 1854 until its dissolution in 2000.

Charles Monteith to WG   TS

27 January 1958

Dear Bill,

Very many thanks for your letter of February 26th. Already I'm looking forward enormously to the manuscript. And I'm looking forward very much, too, to THE BRASS BUTTERFLY. Peter, Molly and I will, God willing, be at the New Theatre on March 1st. Is there any chance of you and Ann getting up to Oxford then? Though perhaps you'll be going to the opening on the 24th.

> Yours ever,

Monteith is referring to the date given in Golding's letter (26 February) rather than the actual date it was written (26 January).

WG to Charles Monteith

MS

3 February 1958   Flat 2, St Mark's House, Salisbury, Wilts

Dear Charles

Ann and I are bidden fairly firmly by the cast to turn up to the first night of the *Brass Butterfly*. It would be great fun to see you on Saturday, but I feel for an author to see his own play twice in one week is shameless self-indulgence. I might take my parents and children over from Marlborough on Saturday, but should attempt to spend the playtime in the bookshops. Mollie and Peter will be seeing us on the Monday – I suppose there's no chance of your changing to then? In any case we must meet soon – its' very provoking as that Saturday is slap in the middle of my half term and really a *much* better time for us to get up to you than the Monday before. However there it is.

Spare a thought on Monday, and cross your fingers
        Yours
         Bill.

Charles Monteith to WG

TS

5 February 1958

Dear Bill,

Thank you very much for your letter of February 3rd. I had a word with Peter; and we *will* go to the first night (i.e., on the Monday rather than on the following Saturday). It should be enormous fun and we're looking forward to it very much indeed. It's wonderful to have an excuse to go down to Oxford on a week day! If you and Ann haven't fixed something else up, I'd be delighted if you'd come round to my rooms in All Souls at about 6.30 for a pre-theatre drink with me and the du Sautoys. I imagine that afterwards you'll be going to some sort of celebration with the cast; but if by any chance not, do come back for a cold supper with Molly and Peter in my rooms.

Much looking forward to seeing you then.
         Yours ever,

WG to Charles Monteith MS

11 February 1958   Flat 2, St Mark's House, Salisbury,
                                    Wilts.

Dear Charles,

I'm getting six tickets for You, Peter & Myself. Will pick them up at the theatre.

We shall be delighted to come to you at All Souls – lost souls to All Souls – after six oclock, and then go on with you all to the theatre.

I'm afraid tho' we're expected afterwards at the Randolph for the Sims and the Coles – this seems reasonable in the circumstances; but actors take so long to get out of costume and makeup that perhaps we can meet for a bit after the theatre performance. It seems such a pity not to be able to relax for a bit with you in academic calm; but I dont see quite what I can do about it. Ann says I must add thank you from her; it is very sweet of you to go to all this trouble to make the ordeal fun for us.

> Yours ever
> > Bill

Alastair Sim starred as the Roman Emperor, and his protégé George Cole as the young inventor Phanocles.

Charles Monteith to WG TS

25 February 1958

Dear Bill,

What a wonderful evening it was – torrential congratulations! It went superbly well – a most tremendous success.

Very much thanks for getting us the tickets. Rosemary and I enjoyed ourselves enormously. How very nice it was to see you and Ann again!

> > Yours ever,

Rosemary Goad had joined Faber not long before Monteith. Working initially as his secretary, she ascended the ranks to become Faber's first female director in 1970.

The PR benefits of Faber's attendance are apparent in a letter from Ann to Monteith, written the same day, in which she thanked him for his support ('we were enclosed in a tight little group of well wishers') and for a telegram sent from Faber that 'more than compensated for the absence of one from Eyre & Spottiswoode'.

Charles Monteith to WG
TS

28 March 1958

My dear Bill,

A brief note to say how enormously impressed I was by the wireless adaptation of PINCHER MARTIN. It really was superbly good, I thought.

So sorry to hear you've been ill; and I do hope you're completely restored by now.

Love to Ann.
Yours,

Pincher Martin had been adapted for the Third Programme by Archie Campbell and broadcast on 23 March. Golding's daughter Judy recalls walking in on her father listening to the radio, which was producing 'strange, rather strangled dialogue and a generous display of BBC sound effects'. 'Oh good,' she said. 'Is it *The Goon Show?*'

WG to Charles Monteith
TS

30 March 1958   St Mark's House, Salisbury

Dear Charles,

I thought PINCHER MARTIN was good too. Now we have only to sell the idea of THE INHERITORS to the third to establish an all-time record. Or telly, do you think?

The BRASS BUTTERFLY continues to do enormous business – see how rapidly I have mastered the essential technical terms of the theatre!

About novel number four (FREE FALL, for reference) I have a complete draft written which has some fairly good bits here and there; but I'm afraid the draft needs re-writing and re-organising. But what is *really* the matter is me: I seem to have exhausted myself and dont really care whether it's a good book or not. It seems to me that I must put it by and forget it for a bit, as I did Pincher.

This is all the more trying when I seem to have reached a point where people expect sombre mandates from me, if they expect anything. But in a better world, I should like to write a funny or poetry, or perhaps both. And then again, I cant go on doing two jobs for ever. Etcetera.

We shall see you on the 17th April for a bit, at least. Sorry to be so incompetent.

Yours ever
Bill

Isn't FREE FALL just what everyone would have expected?!

The Brass Butterfly was enjoying a week-long run at each of its venues: Oxford, Liverpool, Leeds, Newcastle, Edinburgh, Glasgow and Manchester. It then opened on 17 April at the Strand Theatre in the West End and ran for a month.

Charles Monteith to WG   TS

2 April 1958

Dear Bill,

Very many thanks for your letter of March 30th. Please don't worry about FREE FALL – admirable title! – not yet being in final draft. Do hang on to it until you're completely satisfied with it. It'll almost certainly mean that we'll have to postpone publication until the spring of 1959; but I don't think that matters a bit. THE BRASS BUTTERFLY will be a splendid 'Golding item' for 1958! Delighted to know that it's doing so well. Is there any news yet, by the way, about when it's to open in London?

Looking forward very much to seeing you and Ann on the 17th. Would you, I wonder, like to have dinner with Molly, Peter and me afterwards? We'd be absolutely delighted if you would.

Yours ever,

WG to Charles Monteith   MS

8 April 1958   29 The Green, Marlborough, Wilts

Dear Charles

Thank you for the letter and invitation to dinner. Unfortunately since we accepted for the cocktail party on the 17th we have been informed that 17th April is first night for the *Brass Butterfly* in London. It looks therefore as though we shall have to make our bows and courtseys at 6 p.m. sharp and then be whistled to the theatre – the Strand, I think. We envisage staying up for the night; but dont know whether we are supposed to dine with the cast late or retire to some modest hostel and consume biscuits and milk until the shudders abate. But which ever it is – alas we cant have dinner with you, much as we should like to. But it's all ridiculously exciting, however absurd.

Yours
Bill.

Charles Monteith to WG TS

9 April 1958

Dear Bill,

Many thanks for your letter. Alas that you won't be able to dine with us on the 17th, but of course you can't! My very warmest good wishes for a successful first night – most exciting! I'm looking forward to seeing you beforehand.

Love to Ann.
Yours ever,

Charles Monteith to WG TS

24 June 1958

My dear Bill,

I was most terribly sorry to hear from Peter about your operation; but delighted to know that you're up and about again now. Operations can, I know, be most appallingly weakening and lowering affairs.

Many congratulations on the offer of the travelling scholarship which John Lehmann told me about on Friday. Peter tells me that – for reasons which I can well understand – you're still not decided about whether or not to accept it. I do hope, though, that you'll feel able to; and it means a pleasant month or two abroad.

I'll enclose with this a few books which may help to while the hours of convalescence! Three of them – NON-STOP, STRANGERS IN THE UNIVERSE and BEST SF THREE – are our own most recent SF offerings. And I'll send you, too, an historical novel about Theseus, THE KING

MUST DIE, which Peter and I were given in New York and which both of us read with very great pleasure on the boat coming home. I do hope you enjoy them.

Our American trip was the greatest fun. Though we were both pretty tired by the end of it, we had a superb voyage back – pure Mediterranean cruise weather. And that set us both up most wonderfully!

Love to Ann,
Yours ever,

PS

I'll put into the parcel, too, David Stacton's ON A BALCONY – Ancient Egypt!

The operation was an emergency appendicectomy, from which it took Golding several months to recover. To help fill the 'hours of convalescence', Monteith sent him *Non-Stop* by Brian Aldiss, the story collection *Strangers in the Universe* by Clifford D. Simak, and the latest anthology by Edmund Crispin in Faber's *Best SF* series. *The King Must Die* was Mary Renault's novel about the early life of Theseus. David Stacton's *On a Balcony* is set in the fourteenth century BC and focuses on the reign of Pharoah Ikhnaton (Akhenaton).

John Lehmann chaired the Scholarship Committee of the Society of Authors which awarded Golding a £200 travel grant. Its purpose was to foster contact between creative writers and colleagues abroad.

WG to Charles Monteith

TS

28 June 1958   St Mark's House, Salisbury, Wilts

Dear Charles

Thank you for the positive pile of books to cheer my convales-cence. My head is a drunken riot of bull baiting and Esef ankhamon. Delightful too, this reading of books with the dust jackets still on them and still without dust.

I wonder how you found New York? I saw it mostly from sealevel so to speak and there wasn't any UNO building eheu fugaces and no telly. I am finding it more and more essential not to be hurried; so USA wouldnt do at all.

Next Easter we had proposed a family outing in the direction of Italy; and I now have an extra £200 to spend, so we *might* duck into Yugo-Slavia. As time draws near I shall be terribly glad to get addresses of 'colleagues abroad' – also some instruction in the use of sign language when contacting the natives. What trade goods do you advise? Have you any old copies of the BOP?

What a pretty little book you have made of BRASS BUTTERFLY! I should like to see it produced some time.

Bill

'a drunken riot of bull baiting and Esef ankhamon': Golding is collapsing together the ancient Greece of Renault's novel with the ancient Egypt of Stacton's.

Golding had been stationed in New York for three months during the first half of 1943 while waiting to collect an American-built minesweeper and take it back across the Atlantic. The United Nations Headquarters in Manhattan was finished in 1952.

'eheu fugaces': the first two words of Horace's Ode 2.14. The phrase expresses regret that time passes so quickly.

'BOP': balance of payments. Yugoslavia persistently struggled with a balance of payments deficit after the war.

1959

In April, Golding faces another emergency as Ann is taken ill after a family holiday in Italy. She undergoes surgery to remove a cyst from her breast. Golding worries about the *Free Fall* manuscript during these months. He is never entirely satisfied with it, and when the book is published to mixed and occasionally savage reviews in October, he agrees with some of the criticism. There is no negative impact on sales; boosted by a feature on the BBC television arts programme, *Monitor*, they are stronger than for previous novels. In the summer Golding joins the panel of the Book Society, welcoming the steady income but regretful about having to read so much new fiction. The extra money helps fund a trip to the Netherlands in August on *Wild Rose*; Golding goes back to Walcheren attempting to exorcise the trauma of his wartime experiences there. At the end of the year, his short story 'The Anglo-Saxon' is published in *Queen*. There is also a glimpse of Golding's next novel: *The Spire* is still five years away, but he has already begun mulling over a story about 'Barchester Spire'.

Charles Monteith to WG   TS

29 January 1959

Dear Bill,

In your letter to Peter you asked for advice about FREE FALL; and the only advice we can both give you is that you should let us publish it straight away. It really is absolutely superb. We're enormously impressed and we send you our most enthusiastic congratulations.

I've a feeling from all those fascinating notes on the back of some of the pages that you have been wondering about whether or not to do some further work on it; but, quite honestly, I don't think it needs it. We both think that the working out of the book is completely clear – as well as enormously powerful – and really doesn't need any more elaboration; but of course if you yourself should feel that you'd like to do some more to it, please do. But we haven't, I fear, any suggestions about what could be done. As it stands, I'm sure it's first-rate.

One or two minor points. Of the various titles you suggest, we all think – not only Peter and I but the entire Board – that FREE FALL is easily the best; and I wonder if we might settle for that? We hesitated for a moment – as I think all publishers still would – over the words 'fuck' and 'fucking'; but we *don't* raise any objection to them and we don't advise you to delete them. The silly little genteelism of f–k would, in the context, look foolish. It's just possible, though – and I feel I ought to mention this now – that the retention of these words might possibly militate against the book in some quarters – the Book Society, for instance. I don't feel that – at this time of day – this risk is a very serious one; but of course if the Book Society should raise objections after they've seen proof copies with the words printed in extenso we could all think again. But at the moment I'm all for going ahead and letting them stand. Lastly, we wonder if you'd mind simply running through the typescript again for spelling mistakes, punctuation and small things like that? Places, for example, where your typewriter has run on at the end of a line and hasn't quite finished a word! If it would be of any help to you, we could certainly have a fair copy made by a copy typist – at our expense, of course – for you to do a final revision on. If you'd like us to, please let me know; and I'll hang on to the typescript until I hear from you.

That leaves only the question of terms. Would the same royalty as for PINCHER MARTIN be all right, i.e., 12½% to 4,000 copies sold and 15% after? And on that royalty an advance of £400, payable half on signature and half on publication? If you agree, we'll send you a contract straight away.

FREE FALL really is wonderful!

     Love to Ann.

     Yours ever,

PS

One small pedantic point. On page 54 there is a pre-1939 Communist meeting going on at which the speaker makes a reference to the Russo-Finnish war. I'm speaking entirely from memory, but I'm pretty certain that that war didn't, in fact, happen until after the second world war broke out. I think it was late 1939 or early 1940. (Indeed, I know I'm right, for I've just remembered that it was because of the Russo-Finnish war that I gave up taking the Daily Worker when I was up at Oxford!)

Golding's letter to du Sautoy does not seem to have survived in the Faber archive.

'those fascinating notes on the back of some of the pages': several typescript pages have Golding's own handwritten comments on the back; most have been crossed out, perhaps indicating that he has dealt with them in the following draft.

'the various titles you suggest': the typescript seen by Monteith has on its title page 'FREE FALL alias THE TASTE OF POTATOES alias NOTES TOWARDS A RESOLUTION alias ON CREDIT'.

The words 'fuck' and 'fucking' appear in the first three pages but disappear from subsequent typescripts and from the published novel. 'You know I'm a fucking liar dear dont you' is revised by hand in a second typescript to 'You know I'm a sodding liar, dear, don't you?', while the other example is part of a sentence that is cut altogether.

Monteith's comment about the *Daily Worker* – a Communist newspaper that later became the *Morning Star* – points to an inglorious episode in its history when it was unsure of Moscow's official attitude to events in Finland and reversed its editorial position several times between morning and evening editions as it tried desperately to fall into line.

WG to Charles Monteith   TS

31 January 1959   [Headed Paper: Ebble Thatch]

Dear Charles,

Thank you for your letter of the 29th January which was very heartening. There always seems to me a measureless gap between the image in my eye and the word on the page; what dishonesties there are in the book come from that gap – incompetencies rather than dishonesties. I meant the book as a bit of imagery for a whole baffled generation, meant to convey planlessness, chaos and impotence but I seem to have ended the book less certain of what it is about than when I started. But thank you – both – for your kind words. You allow me to hope that there's enough left to get by the SBP.

Terms seem generous to me – as ever. Of course I accept them. With grateful thanks.

FREE FALL be it.

About a fair copy – Thank you, but is one necessary? Of course I'll have another go at the TS. It was never meant, I repeat, as more than notes towards the novel I was going to write! Perhaps a bit more than that, but not final, certainly. Hence the gay abandon in the use of swear words. Like you, I should think twice about 'fuck' and 'fucking' for publication. The only trouble is that I felt them as right in the context. However let's leave them for now. If I can keep the power of the speeches without using them (F&F) I certainly will.

Russo-Finnish war noted. I'll clean up the history generally.

A personal point – When you are next at All Souls and you hear of an Oxford College which has difficulty in finding enough commoners to fill next years lists up remember me! As far as I can find myself, you cant even get an entry, unless you have a scholarship. This is not only very bad for my son, but also very bad for Oxford!

  Yours ever

   Bill

Ann sends her love.

The Goldings had moved house in the autumn, returning to Ebble Thatch in Bowerchalke where they had lived briefly in 1940. The headed paper is embossed as follows:

EBBLE THATCH,
BOWER CHALKE,
N^R SALISBURY, WILTSHIRE.
BROADCHALKE 275.

 SBP: Serious Book Police – a private joke between Golding and Monteith.

 (F&F): possibly a joke, because Golding sometimes uses the same abbreviation for Faber & Faber.

Charles Monteith to WG TS

2 February 1959

Dear Bill,

 Thank you very much indeed for your letter of January 31st. I am absolutely certain about the quality of FREE FALL – as is everybody else who's read it here (three more over the week-end). We are looking forward enormously to publishing it.

 Very glad that the terms are all right. Peter is drawing up a draft contract now, and you should have it in a day or two.

 I'll send back the manuscript with this letter, and I'd be most grateful if you'd run through it again for the various small points I mentioned in my last letter etc. When it comes back I'll show it to David Bland, our Production Manager, and ask him if he thinks the printers will need a fair copy.

 I'll certainly do what I can about David and Oxford. I imagine that you yourself have already written to BNC about him; but I'll certainly – if you'd like me to – have a word with the new Principal, Maurice Platnaeur, whom I know slightly. I'll also mention him to the authorities at Magdalen and Pembroke, where there might just possibly be a vacancy going. Have you, I wonder, tried Wadham? I know that they have been expanding quite a bit in recent years and are taking far more undergraduates than they used to. If you haven't, I think it might well be a good idea for you to write personally to Maurice Bowra – do mention my name if you'd like to. I rather think, by the way, that he's a Golding fan!

> Yours ever,

Golding's alma mater was Brasenose College ('BNC'); the classicist Maurice Platnauer was Principal from 1956 – and therefore not all that 'new' – until 1960. Maurice Bowra, literary scholar and friend of countless writers, was Warden of Wadham College from 1938 to 1970.

WG to Charles Monteith   TS

11 March 1959   [Headed Paper: Ebble Thatch]

Dear Charles,

Herewith the amended typescript of FREE FALL. The last few pages are new and so forth. Tell me you dont like them and I'll rewrite.

Peter murmured sweet words about having the whole thing typed for me again – would this be too much of a bore? I've dazed myself with this confounded book and shall be very glad to get it off the stocks.

Peter also said how much you would enjoy our present house. He and Mollie seemed to like it. You know, my dear Charles how delighted we should be if you could see your way to abandoning Oxford for Bower Chalke one week end.

I'm going to set too and write a play of some sort; and then return to novels in the Autumn. How would you like a large historical novel? Or has Alfred Duggan cornered the market?

> Yours
>> Bill

The English historian and novelist Alfred Duggan became successful in the 1950s with a string of novels set in the distant past. His favourite subjects were the Roman Empire, the Crusades, and England before the Norman Conquest. Golding knew him slightly because they were both members of the Savile Club. Reading him again in 1974, Golding recorded in his journal that 'his novels are low-keyed and seem scholarly but I am not historian enough to be certain about that' (J, 2 April 1974).

Charles Monteith to WG TS

17 March 1959

Dear Bill,

I read FREE FALL again last night – and was even more completely bowled over by it than I was when I read it first. My sincerest congratulations again on a most superb book. And I think that the new pages at the end are wonderful.

Yes, of course we'll have the whole thing retyped before we send it to the printers. I'll send it off today to a girl called Wendy Jackson, who used to be Morley Kennerley's secretary and who's very good at this sort of work. I'll ask her to do two copies, so that we've one for ourselves and one for Harcourt, Brace. When she's produced the fair copies, I'll send them off to you so that you can check quickly through them.

How very kind of you to invite me down for a week-end at Bower Chalke. I'll most certainly take you up on that; and I'm looking forward to it enormously. Molly and Peter have both told me how much they like your house.

Yes indeed; I think there would be room for a large historical novel. Despite Alfred Duggan the market isn't yet cornered.

Yours ever,

PS

I've just realised that you're off to Italy very soon – before Wendy will have finished doing the fair copies. So when they come, we'll send one straight to the printers and send you with the proofs both the original typescript and her fair copy. I don't in fact think there'll be many – if any – slips, for she really is extremely careful.

Best wishes for a wonderful time in Italy to you all.

Morley Kennerley was a director at Faber, where Wendy Jackson had worked for him.

WG to Charles Monteith MS

25 March 1959   Ebble Thatch, Bower Chalke,
Salisbury, Wilts

Wednesday.

Dear Charles

A hasty note to thank you, and say that we are now leaving for Italy on 30th of this month – flu knocked us out. So if the MS of *Free Fall* can be here by teatime on Monday next I could take it with me and let you have it back in the course of the next ten days.

Mr McCallum (Harcourt Brace) wrote a few days ago asking for the MS of *Free Fall* for their Autumn list. I thought you ought to know this if he hasn't contacted you already.

    Yours
      Bill

Harcourt, Brace had still not published *The Inheritors* in the United States, so *Free Fall* was Golding's third novel to appear there.

Charles Monteith to WG TS

1 May 1959

My dear Bill,

Just a very brief note to say how terribly sorry I am to hear about Ann – Peter told me about it yesterday. When you see her, do please give her my love and my very warmest good wishes for a quick recovery.

      Yours ever,

PS

I'd be delighted to send Ann some books to read in hospital if she feels up to it. Do please tell me if she does; and if there's anything particular you think she would like.

Golding reported to Rosemary Goad on 23 April that they had 'had a wonderful time in Italy. All superlatives exhausted.' Soon after they arrived home, Ann found a small lump in her breast. An operation revealed it to be a benign cyst.

WG to Charles Monteith   TS

6 May 1959   [Headed Paper: Ebble Thatch]

Wednesday

Dear Charles,

Thank you for your kind note about Ann. Peter may have told you that she has been very lucky and is – as we say in our veiled way – in the clear. Your offer of books was much appreciated; one day we might take you up on it! Anyway our thanks and Ann's love to you.

I'm returning the MS of FREE FALL herewith. It was good of you to get it typed so clearly and thus allow me at once a breathing space and a fair copy to work on. Would you thank Mrs Bland for me? Really, one way and another I'm being thoroughly spoilt.

There's not much to say about this corrected copy; with the exception of one or two insets its mostly details of grammar I'm afraid. I always have great plans for a completely new version but never seem to be able to do more than niggle.

Yours ever
Bill

David Bland was the production manager at Faber. His wife Mary had prepared the new typescript of *Free Fall*.

Charles Monteith to WG   TS

6 May 1959

My dear Bill,

I'm absolutely delighted to hear from Peter that Ann's so much better. Do please give her my love. I'll also enclose with this a couple of books which she might like to read while convalescing – Edmund Crispin's new anthology, BEST DETECTIVE STORIES, and Codrington's CRICKET IN THE GRASS, which really is, I think, rather a delightful book. I'll also pop in – for you – James Blish's A CASE OF CONSCIENCE. I remember you liked it when it was a short story in BEST SF, and I wonder what you'll think of it as a full-length novel? It's had a remarkably good – and wide – reception from the critics here. Usually they ignore science fiction altogether or relegate it to small, humble boxes at the bottom of their literary pages.

Do please forgive me for pestering you about the typescript of FREE FALL; but time really is getting pretty short now and we would like to have it as soon as you possibly can manage it. Peter tells me that you're still a little worried about the last chapter. Can I assure you that I myself think it's absolutely first-rate as it stands – and so, I know, does Peter. This really is a perfectly honest opinion – not just the anguished cry of an editor who's being chivvied by his Production Department!

Hope to see you soon.

Yours ever,

The success of the *Best SF* series had encouraged Monteith and Edmund Crispin to repeat the trick with the genre for which Crispin was himself well known: detective fiction. K. de B. Codrington's *Cricket in the Grass* was a memoir of his childhood in the years leading up to the First World War. James Blish's *A Case of Conscience* had just been published by Faber.

Charles Monteith to WG   TS

8 May 1959

My dear Bill,

Our letters crossed! The manuscript of FREE FALL has just arrived and I'm most grateful. It'll go straight off to our Production Department as soon as we've copied your corrections into the duplicate manuscript which Peter will be sending to Harcourt, Brace.

All being well, we hope to have it out in September or October, but – as you'll probably have gathered from the papers – there's a threatened printers' strike hanging over our heads, and over the heads of all publishers, like a dark cloud at the moment. About that we'll simply have to keep our fingers crossed.

I'm terribly glad – more glad than I can say – to know that Ann really is all right. Do please give her my love.

Yours ever,

WG to Charles Monteith   TS

10 May 1959   [Headed Paper: Ebble Thatch]

Dear Charles,

It was most kind of you to take such trouble over books for Ann and me. She is rearing up out of convalescence by the way and consuming books at her accustomed furious pace. If there weren't any novelists it would be necessary to invent them for her. She sends her love and thanks.

A question of conscience is an extraordinary work. SF seems to me to stand or fall by its coherence and intensity of sense impression; and I'm haunted by his ceramics. Does this say most about Blish or about Golding? Isn't there some awful Freudian, coprological significance here? Anyway I'm enjoying the book and refuse to take out my sensations and examine them.

I've been a bit authorlike and difficult in the grand manner over FREE FALL and now feel apologetic. I suppose I couldn't really believe that if you start out to write a shapeless book that's what you'll end up with. I hope I havn't strung you along too far, that's all.

Strikes are terrible. One can *see* how necessary they are in the case of miners shipwrights bus drivers bakers candlestick makers and all the downtrodden and exploited ninetyfive per cent of humanity – but printers! They're different somehow.

Yours ever
Bill

Blish's *A Case of Conscience* describes life on the planet Lithia. The Lithians are portrayed as extremely skilled ceramicists; even their buildings are ceramic.

A six-week printers' strike, beginning in late June, shut down provincial newspapers and disrupted publishing firms.

WG to Peter du Sautoy   TS

7 June 1959   [Headed Paper: Ebble Thatch]

Dear Peter,

I hope you both had a wonderful time in Vienna and Venice. We've tried to picture you in the Italian sunshine and found it difficult to believe that the place really exists!

Before you left you had a query for me about novels and The Book Society. I passed this on to Godwin and got a ruling from him. He has written a new rule into the constitution. There is now nothing to prevent a novelist sitting on the panel and submitting his own book! He will merely withdraw from the discussion of that item!

So there you are. We meet to settle the September choice on June 17th – or maybe it's the 19th. But anyway I can be considered provided the proofs are through in time.

Yours   Bill

At Peter du Sautoy's recommendation, Golding had been appointed as a panel member for the Book Society. Tony Godwin was its director.

Charles Monteith to WG   TS

12 June 1959

Dear Bill,

Peter has passed over to me your letter of June 7th about the Book Society. We're all delighted to know about the new ruling and that FREE FALL will be eligible. At the moment our plans are to publish it on October 9th – but of course if the Book Society should make it their September Choice, we would be able to push it forward. And I hope, too, that we'll have proofs in time to send it in to the Selectors' meeting in mid-June. But all these plans, of course, are liable to be thrown completely out of gear if the printers' strike comes off; and, alas, it looks at the moment as if it's going to.

Peter and Molly much enjoyed Vienna and Venice, apart from one horror incident on their first night in Venice, when somebody apparently climbed into their bedroom while they were asleep and stole quite a lot of their money and some things of Molly's. It hasn't all worked out as badly as such things can do, but poor Peter has been chasing round insurance brokers, his Bank, etc., all this week – and now he has gone off to Edinburgh for some PA meeting!

Missed you last Sunday on the Brains Trust, unfortunately; but everyone tells me you were a wow!

Love to Ann,
            Yours,

Charles Monteith to WG TS

26 October 1959

My dear Bill,

I should have written to you yesterday; but I'm afraid I was slightly incoherent after reading those bloody stupid reviews. They really were quite unspeakable – wildly off the point and, I suspect, infected with jealousy. This note is just to send you my sympathy. Don't take them to heart – they'll all be kicking themselves in twenty-five years time, if retribution hasn't struck before then!

Anyway, *Monitor* made up for it. Absolutely excellent, I thought, and you 'came over' wonderfully. One of the girls here told me this morning that she thought you were 'simply dreamy'!

> Love to Ann.
> Yours ever,

Free Fall had been published to mixed reviews in an edition of 7,500 copies on 23 October. Two days later, Golding was the subject of the BBC television arts programme, *Monitor*. The eighteen-minute piece included an interview with Golding by Peter Newington. It covered Golding's writing processes, his natural optimism, and his relationship with the sea, as well as discussing *Pincher Martin* and *Free Fall*.

WG to Charles Monteith TS

31 October 1959   [Headed Paper: Ebble Thatch]

Dear Charles,

It is good of you to be so concerned and indignant on my account. Two of the reviews have certainly been a bit scratchy and inflicted some of the wounds I suspect they were meant to. God knows why. Peter Duval Smith accepted such hospitality as we had and cheerfully put us to considerable trouble in a casual, Bohemian manner – but other than finding us dull, I dont know what he had to complain of. I dont know Toynbee at all. So I am driven to conclude there is some-thing in my manner of writing which enrages.

But detachment works, up to a point. The scratches are scratches, nothing more: and, you know, the antis are *right*. FREE FALL remains magnificent in places, inflated and anxious in others – and so, in the end, less than the sum of its parts, where it should be the multiplication of them.

After long, profound, philosophical argument, the German publishers have at last settled on a title for PINCHER MARTIN: PINCHER MARTIN.

I'm trying to write a play and shall spend a few weeks finding out if I can or not – then it's HO! for Barchester Spire or Miss Dodo.

I'm glad you liked MONITOR. I've spent a little time finding out the significance of 'Simply dreamy.' The answer sent a quick flush of blood to his cheeks.

    Yours
     Bill

Peter Duval Smith in the *New Statesman* argued that Golding 'pitches his voice too stridently': 'Some of the congregation are staring curiously at the preacher . . . Why is he shouting?' Philip Toynbee in the *Observer* concluded that *Free Fall* was 'a failure in almost every direction', and that the book was 'dull in the most disturbing way', namely that the language was disproportionately 'large and noisy'. Nearly twenty years later, while summoning the energy to redraft *Darkness Visible*, Golding reminds himself that 'Free Fall failed because I did not have the willpower to fuse the whole thing properly' (J, 2 April 1978).

'Barchester Spire' is the first mention of what becomes Golding's fifth novel, *The Spire* (1964), although it changes in fundamental ways through multiple drafts. Golding firmly believed that Anthony Trollope's fictional Barchester was based on Salisbury (not Winchester, the other main contender).

If 'Miss Dodo' is a new writing project, it does not survive among Golding's papers.

Monteith has added an asterisk in red ink after 'Simply dreamy.' and written at the bottom 'Jane Tate's description of him on Monitor!'

1960

Golding makes little progress on a novel this year but writes many reviews and essays, several of which will be collected in his first volume of occasional prose, *The Hot Gates* (1965). As well as becoming a fixture in *The Bookman* and *The Spectator*, he turns up regularly on BBC radio: in January, *Free Fall* is adapted for the Third Programme, followed by his childhood memoir 'The Ladder and the Tree' in March and 'Miss Pulkinhorn' in April. In November, *The Spectator* publishes 'Billy the Kid', his warm and wry tribute to his mother, Mildred, who had died in August after months of ill health. Looking forward, Golding decides that he will resign his position at Bishop Wordsworth's School in 1961 and accept an invitation to take up a writer-in-residence post for a year at Hollins College in Virginia.

WG to Peter du Sautoy   TS

6 January 1960   [Headed Paper: Ebble Thatch]

Dear Peter,

Sorry to have sent you on a wildgoose chase about the film rights. It was just that I saw a glimpse of hope that we might be able to stop a travesty being put out. I havn't seen the script but gather that it's wholly different from the book. I dont mind this and of course it has every chance of being a good film – but why call it Lord Of The Flies? I prefer it if they forget the book altogether. However, there it is.

I don't know what MCA are up to about FREE FALL. I got a stopped cheque from them in December and have heard nothing since. Perhaps Macallum has had second thoughts, though he sounded enthusiastic enough when he was over here.

I found the Dutch Version of Lord of the Flies amusing in its cuts. It's OK by me, however.

Dr Happold created a certain amount of fuss about letting me off to go to Manchester next week. I'm a school master after all. Which reminds me that we still havn't got David into a University. Bowra was very nice, and thank you very much – but I'd left things too late as usual. For two pins I'd go and live on sixpence in Greece like your other Monitor author.

A happy new year to you both.

Bill

PS I may have to fly to Manchester next week, in which case your expense account will have to find £7-10-0. Sorry.

PPS Could you forward a copy of *The Inheritors* to Yvonne Mitchell, 70 Audley Street with my compliments? I havnt got a copy here.

Sam Spiegel had planned to have a mixed group of boys and girls for the film of *Lord of the Flies* and wanted them to be American. Golding was unenthusiastic on both counts. Interviewed by the New York *Herald Tribune* in May 1962, he recalled that 'The book was, for a time, in the hands of an American producer who wanted to put girls on the island and make it "univoisal". My response was "Over my dead body!"'

MCA Artists Ltd was a New York-based agency that Faber had commissioned to handle some of its negotiations with American publishers. The situation regarding *Free Fall* was soon resolved: the novel was published by John McCallum at Harcourt, Brace in February.

Notwithstanding the disapproval of his headteacher Frederick Happold, Golding travelled to Manchester to give a lunchtime lecture about the origins of *Lord of the Flies* and the challenges of finding a publisher for it.

Yvonne Mitchell was an actor and author. Golding got her address slightly wrong: it was 70 South Audley Street.

Faber's 'other Monitor author' was Lawrence Durrell.

WG to Peter du Sautoy   TS

20 January 1960   [Headed Paper: Ebble Thatch]

Wednesday

Dear Peter,

Manchester mission completed; some flak on the way back and serious enemy opposition to the car on the Salisbury road. I'll send you an account of expenses when I can get round to it.

Lucky you to be flitting off to Paris in this gay way. I hope Stephen will find Paris as friendly as Germany – your contacts ought to help. Have a good time and dont do any work!

I'm coming up (Book Society) next Tuesday, 26th January. Normally I catch the five oclock back, but there's a good train at six and one or two later ones – though nothing convenient, as you know. Would Mrs Fischer like to meet me over a cup of tea? Would that do? If it's at your flat, please tell Mollie I dont eat anything and would be very willing to wash up my cup and saucer, if not Mrs Fischers: but my experience of

Germans is that they loathe tea, unless it's that horrible stuff that tastes like dish-water. But at any rate, Barkis is willing.

Yours
Bill

Stephen: one of Peter du Sautoy's sons.

Brigitte Fischer of S. Fischer was Golding's German publisher.

'Barkis is willing': an idiomatic expression with its source in Charles Dickens's *David Copperfield*. Mr Barkis indicates his desire to marry Clara Peggotty with 'Barkis is willin'', and he repeats the phrase often.

WG to Peter du Sautoy MS

31 January 1960   [Headed Paper: Ebble Thatch]

Dear Peter

What an awful time you must both be having! We know something about this, having been through almost exactly similar circumstances only a few months ago.

Will you pass our love and sympathy on to Mollie at a suitable moment? I dont suppose there is anything we can do – unless at some time you should both need a country bolthole, in which case you know where to come.

I'd have replied sooner but I'm shakily recovering from some 'flu bug or other. The spring is just about not getting under way down here; and the thought of not going to Italy this Easter is like a pain in the neck.

I hope you have good news of Stephen. David is cheerful. It's something, when they arnt suicidal.

Dont bother to answer this.

Bill

'We know something about this': sympathising with du Sautoy over Mollie's health scare, Golding is remembering Ann's operation in the spring of 1959.

Charles Monteith to WG TS

26 February 1960

My dear Bill,

I expect you've seen this article on page 115 already; but I enclose it just in case you haven't. Admirable, I think.

I was terribly sorry not to be able to go to Peter Green's lecture about you last night at the Royal Society of Literature; but I was lunching with Peter and his wife today, and he told me that he thought it went well.

How's the new book getting on?

My love to Ann. Hoping to see you both again soon.

Yours ever,

Monteith forwarded to Golding an article titled 'The Strange Case of Mr Golding and his Critics', recently published in the journal *Twentieth Century*. Its authors were two young scholars, Mark Kinkead-Weekes and Ian Gregor, who defended *Free Fall* against its detractors. Over time, the pair became friendly with Monteith and Golding, and their Faber book *William Golding: A Critical Study* (1967) was the standard critical text for several decades.

The novelist and historian Peter Green was another friend in the making. His wife was the novelist Lalage Pulvertaft. The families spent time together in Greece during the 1960s.

WG to Charles Monteith   TS

27 February 1960   [Headed Paper: Ebble Thatch]

Dear Charles,

Thank you for your letter and the enclosure. I found the article very devoted, and am grateful for that. But you know, when you look at the quotes at the end from the critics, they arn't all that far off the mark; but the article omits any aesthetic judgement and a novel stands or falls by that. Sorry. Confused.

I'm glad Peter Green did in fact give his paper and I should be grateful for a look at it. But I find in myself a quite unexpected – not indifference but – detachment from this whole business of being assessed. Sales, now, that's a different matter; and I wish I could say that 'Westward, see, the sky is bright' but alas it isn't.

The book bumbles on.

The International Literary Annual (Pamela Lyon) is publishing an article on William Golding by Frank Kermode and want to include work in progress. I dont know what I feel about this; and it seems to me very much a decision for my Publishers as to whether such a thing is desirable. At the moment I'm stalling. I should be glad to know what you think.

My apologies to Peter, if he felt I forced him to go to the RSL – I didn't mean to – but he is very duteous.

Yours
Bill

Golding alludes to Arthur Hugh Clough's 'Say Not the Struggle Nought Availeth': 'But westward, look, the land is bright.'

Golding has written a full signature – 'William Golding' – and scribbled it out and replaced it with 'Bill' above his typed name. He has also circled 'Peter' and added a marginal note: 'Perhaps you meant P. Green.'

Charles Monteith to WG   TS

1 March 1960

Dear Bill,

Very many thanks for your letter. It *was* Peter Green, not Peter du Sautoy, I talked to about the lecture! Peter du S, like me, wasn't able to get there.

About the International Literary Annual. Peter (*not* Green!) and I both think it would be a mistake to say anything at all specific about work in progress, since it might tend to lessen the impact of the book when it actually comes out. I'd be inclined to advise, I think, some pretty cagey statement – that you're at work on a new novel and that you hope it will be finished in time for publication this year, next year or whenever it is.

I do hope American sales go well this time. I'm not sure when FREE FALL is due out there; but just about now, I think. Like you, I'll be looking forward very much to seeing what happens.

My love to Ann.
Yours ever,

Monteith's justified anxiety about American sales was based on the poor performance of *Pincher Martin* (or, rather, *The Two Deaths of Christopher Martin*). Harcourt, Brace still owned the American rights to *The Inheritors*, but contractually they were not obliged to publish it until they had sold 7,500 copies of *Pincher Martin*. That figure had not yet been reached.

WG to Peter du Sautoy TS

6 April 1960   [Headed Paper: Ebble Thatch]

Dear Peter,

I'm glad you liked the broadcast. Lots of people seemed to with the exception of a dear old lady who, I am informed, thought it was horrible. You'll probably catch sight of my name in a number of strange places in the future; I'm having to accept anything with money attached, for a number of reasons.

One of them, and the best, is that David has been accepted as a commoner at Brasenose for next October. He keeps saying that it is the *last* place in the world he really wants to go to – but I think he'll go; and I shall have to write funny jokes to go on the back of match boxes to keep up with batels.

We shall be coming up on 21st April to F&F for cocktails and hope to see you both then.

You ought to see the garden! Why dont you?

    Yours
      Bill

Golding's essay about his childhood, 'The Ladder and the Tree', had been broadcast on the Third Programme on 13 March.

    At Oxford, a 'commoner' is a student without a scholarship or exhibition to support them, and 'batels' is the account run up by students for board and provisions. The usual spelling is 'battels'; 'batels' is peculiar to Brasenose.

WG to Mollie and Peter du Sautoy TS

18 April 1960   [Headed Paper: Ebble Thatch]

Dear Mollie and Peter,

Sorry not to have written before – but life is a bit mixed up down here. The essential difficulty is that my ancient mother now wants to come and live with us; and as she has to live on a ground floor and more or less be nursed, you can imagine what a difference that is going to make. In fact we have to cry off the party on thursday. I dont like doing this so late – but could you accept this as an official change of mind? What with getting another room furnished and rushing about, we simply havn't time to come up to London. So together with the party we must turn down, refuse, decline, what ever the right word is, your offer of rest before and bed after.

We are both a bit dashed at this; but there it is. You know all about families anyway and dont need much telling.

I dont know, quite, how much difference this is really going to make to writing; perhaps it will give me more time, in an odd way!

We both hope Mollie is recovering a bit from her awful time – Ann sends her love.

Yours ever
Bill

So sorry, Mollie, not to reply myself, but to leave it to Bill – I am bogged down in household duties. love A.

The postscript is handwritten by Ann.

Golding's mother, Mildred, did move in briefly to Ebble Thatch. She then went to be nursed at the home of Golding's adopted sister, Eileen (his cousin by birth). Mildred died in August, a couple of months short of her ninetieth birthday.

WG to Peter du Sautoy   TS

10 May 1960   [Headed Paper: Ebble Thatch]

Dear Peter,

Sorry not to have answered your nice letter before; and even now, I'm really wanting something, as usual.

Curtis Brown, who are my agents for various odd jobs, have an American enquiry. They want to know about the television rights of Lord Of The Flies. There could be *gold* in them thar hills. I expect the film contract would prevent it but I thought you ought to know. Could you ring them?

The garden looks very fine, we think. Things Ann puts in, actually come up; and I can kill greenfly. I'm their lord, in fact.

Our love to you and Molly
Yours
Bill

As du Sautoy was away in Ireland, his assistant Giles de la Mare replied on his behalf, explaining that 'the television rights are controlled by Ealing Studios and will continue to be for some time to come'. Giles de la Mare, son of Richard, later became an editorial director and oversaw several of the firm's non-fiction lists.

'*gold* in them thar hills': Golding also uses the expression in two letters to Monteith dated 12 September 1960 and 2 February 1965. Often wrongly attributed to Mark Twain, it became a catchphrase partly thanks to the cartoon character Yosemite Sam.

Charles Monteith to WG   TS

26 August 1960

Dear Bill,

Just a brief note of enquiry about how the new book progresses? *Please* don't think I'm pestering you about it – there are no undertones of impatience in this letter at all! – but we are just about to close our list for spring 1961 and we are wondering if we ought to keep a place for you, or if the book is more likely to come in the autumn? The autumn would be perfectly all right, but if it's to be spring, do please let me know as soon as possible. No need to say how enormously I'm looking forward to reading it!

Incidentally, a rumour reached me via Tony Godwin that you might be going to America for a year. That sounds enormously exciting, and I long to hear more about it.

I'm just back from a short – but marvellous – holiday in Sardinia, where I took to a snorkel and flippers for the first time in my life and enjoyed myself hugely, although I was only too well aware that I looked exactly like one of the more sub-human sorts of sf monster! Have you been away yet, I wonder? It seems ages since I've seen you; and do get in touch when you are next planning to come to London.

My love to Ann. I do hope you all flourish.

Yours ever,

Tony Godwin's information was correct: Golding had been invited to spend the academic year from September 1961 at Hollins College, Virginia.

sf: science fiction.

WG to Charles Monteith TS

12 September 1960   [Headed Paper: Ebble Thatch]

Dear Charles,

If all goes well I shall have a novel for you to decide about for next autumn – not spring.

Ann and I go to America (resident writer at Hollin's College) in the autumn of sixty-one for eight or nine months. David will be at BNC and Judith boarding at Godolphin. It'll make a break and there seems to be gold in them thar hills.

There's not much to add. I'm working dashed hard but mostly at odd jobs (reviewing and suchlike) which bring in ready money. I suppose it holds up novel writing a bit, but there it is.

Yes Oh God Oh Montreal is by Samuel Butler. The anthology was just out of arms reach and I didn't bother to look it up. Since then about a dozen people have written to tell me all about it – some in great detail.

Apart from Book Society meetings I keep away from London these days – cant afford the time to gallivant. But I'll certainly get in touch if and when I happen to break out. David goes up this October and if I'm up at any weekend, I'll invoke All Souls.

        Yours ever

         Bill

Ann and I invite you here whenever it should be your pleasure to come.

    B

Golding had misattributed Samuel Butler's 'A Psalm of Montreal' (the chorus is 'Oh God! Oh Montreal!') when he reviewed Brian Moore's *The Luck of Ginger Coffey* in the July/August edition of *The Bookman*.

Charles Monteith to WG TS

13 September 1960

Dear Bill,

Excellent news about the novel. Looking forward to that enormously already. And how very exciting about the trip to America – I expect you and Ann will thoroughly enjoy it. Where *is* Hollin's College?

I'd be absolutely delighted to put you up at All Souls any time you want – so do let me know if ever you want a bed on one of your visits to see David. (This term the only week-ends that are out are the last one in October and the first in November – at both of which we've college meetings, and the place tends to be chocful.) And I'll most certainly take you up on your invitation to come down to Ebble Thatch – tell Ann to expect a letter any day!

Yours ever,

WG to Charles Monteith   TS

29 September 1960   [Headed Paper: Ebble Thatch]

Dear Charles

I enclose an agreement I ought to have sent back to Peter weeks ago. So sorry.

I also enclose a letter from Curtis Brown which may amuse you. I dont know who the publishers are, or what I am alleged to have said. It's all news to me. Ann says, 'Exactly who are the pirates supposed to be?' Please let me have the letter back when you've seen it. I have a fragrant bunch of fiorituri(?) of the same sort.

No news otherwise.

Yours ever
Bill

PS

Professor L.D. Rubin, Hollins College Virginia is writing round to the American Universities asking them whether they want me to lecture. He Says 'Why dont you ask Faber and Faber to send me a little "Publicity" about you and your work, so that I can use a few quotations, etc in my letter to English Dept chairmen?'

Over to you.

The letter from Juliet O'Hea at Curtis Brown has disappeared, but Monteith's reply to Golding on 4 October implies that agents and publishers were interested in luring Golding away from Faber.

'fiorituri': blossomings, flourishings, embellishments. Golding was right to doubt the spelling: the Italian plural form should be *fioriture*.

Louis Rubin was head of English at Hollins College.

Charles Monteith to WG TS

4 October 1960

Dear Bill,

Thank you very much for your letter of 29th September and for sending me back the agreement for the paperback of THE INHERITORS. I've passed that straight on to Peter's department – as I expect you know, he and Molly are on holiday in Switzerland at the moment. I had a card from them this morning, and they sounded very cheerful.

Thank you very much too for letting me see that interesting letter from Juliet O'Hea. (I'll return it with this one.) I do hope you don't feel beguiled by this siren voice – or by the possibility of running up the Jolly Roger!

Incidentally, Rosemary Goad and a friend of hers, Elizabeth Oxley, are driving down to spend the weekend near Dorchester on Friday, October 14th; and I gather will be practically passing your door! I just wondered if I could have possibly taken you and Ann up on your very kind invitation and asked myself to stay that weekend? It would be the greatest fun to see you all, but *please* don't hesitate to say if it's no good for you – I really should simply hate to think that you felt you had to say yes. (I understand they plan to leave London about 6-ish, and we would certainly eat on the way down – so I suppose I should be with you about 9.30. They say they could pick me up again some time on Sunday afternoon!)

Love to Ann.
Yours,

PTO

PS

I've asked Ann Faber to send on publicity details about you and your work to Professor Rubin at Hollins.

CM.

WG to Peter du Sautoy TS

9 November 1960   [Headed Paper: Ebble Thatch]

Dear Peter,

Sorry to have been so slow about the Ms. It's mainly my fault. I've simply allowed myself to take on too much journalism, and am chasing desperately towards a moment when I can free my arm for a novel.

We both feel ourselves not competent in this matter, and certainly can't accept a fee. I've simply put down our reactions here as a matter of conscience, disregard them and send the books to somebody else.

Chemistry Book.

Ann says it seems simple and straightforward as it ought to be. She likes the early introduction of atomics, but doubts whether it makes a significant difference in the long run. She finds the style deliberately colloquial, and thinks this is the modern manner at that level.

In other words, difficult to distinguish between this and any other textbook, at the same level.

SCHOOL MASTER INTO FARMER

No, no, no. Books like this just arn't any good nowadays. It's like The Idle Jottings Of An Idle Fellow and nobody has any time for it. Despite the apparent humility of the writer on the surface, I cant help feeling an enormous egotism beneath, which thinks his opinion on any and every subject is worth having. If I try to pinpoint this, I should adduce his indifference to construction. The reader ought to be grateful, he implies, for anything said anyhow. But writing today is strictly professional. You *cant* pile a heap like this and call it a book.

If I found this on the shelf in a bookshop, I should read, perhaps as much as a chapter of it. But I shouldn't buy it . . . There are good things, of course; but these very scattered swallows don't make a summer.

The autobiographical introduction is fair; but a man who cant write entertainingly about his childhood isn't even literate. This childhood certainly isn't above average interest. The schoolmastering bits are better, but lack detail and shape. They're desultory. The farming I find dull; but this is probably a personal limitation. The letter to his son, and all the random thoughts (I'm not sure how much is letter and how much random thoughts) seems to me to be undigested. If he's got a Universal Mind, then he ought to write a Universal Book, not a ragbag.

So there.

We very much enjoyed having Charles here. Are we ever going to see you and Mollie?

Yours
Bill

Ann (halfway through the Heckstall-Smith) says she agrees in the main; but so far, finds a lot of it awfully sensible.

So where are we?

MSS returning under separate cover.

Du Sautoy had written on 25 October asking the Goldings to read two manuscripts that were under consideration at Faber: Hugh Heckstall-Smith's 'Schoolmaster into Farmer' and a study guide, 'Chemistry for Beginners'. (Before her marriage, Ann had worked as an analytic chemist at Reed Paper Mill in Kent.) Heckstall-Smith's book was eventually published by Peter Davies as *Doubtful Schoolmaster* in 1962.

'The Idle Jottings Of An Idle Fellow' is a near miss for Jerome K. Jerome's *Idle Thoughts of an Idle Fellow* (1886).

Charles Monteith to WG   TS

18 November 1960

Dear Bill,

We've a guest night at All Souls on Saturday, December 3rd; and since that's the last week-end of term, I thought that you might possibly be driving over to Oxford to collect David. If by any chance you are and are free on Saturday evening, I should be delighted if you would have dinner with me in College. And of course I could easily put you up for the night.

Much hoping that you can manage it. Love to you, Ann and Judy.

WG to Charles Monteith   MS

22 November 1960   Ebble Thatch, Bowerchalke, Salisbury

Dear Charles,

Dinner at All Souls on 3rd December sounds delightful. Yes, please.

I should want to cart David off home on Sunday morning, so if I could indeed have a bed in your distinguished haunt I should be most grateful. Black tie of course – and let me know sometime when to come to you.

Yours
Bill

Charles Monteith to WG TS

23 November 1960

Dear Bill,

Delighted to know you can dine with me in All Souls on December 3rd. And of course I can put you up for the night.

We dine at 7.30 p.m. but I will certainly be in my rooms from, say, 5.30 on; and I suggest that if you can manage it, you come about then so that there's plenty of time to get installed in your room, change, etc., and have a drink before dinner. Yes – black tie but no gown.

Very much looking forward to seeing you.

Yours ever,

WG to Peter du Sautoy MS

30 November 1960   Ebble Thatch, Bowerchalke, Salisbury

Dear Peter,

Alas and alack no – 1st December is out as far as I'm concerned. My nearest is 7th December (Wednesday) when I come up for the Daily Mirror lunch and children's comp: Is that any good? I'd be available for a cup of tea.

What a subtle character you are! You must have known that neither Ann nor I could resist the offer of buckshee books. I'll send a list and you can cut it down if you dare.

I nearly cadged a bed off you the other night – but couldn't find your number in the book, so I went home after all, which was more sensible perhaps. We seem to get terribly busy these days; and I need a firm hand to keep me down to work. Glad you liked the Spectator pieces – but journalism is getting in the way!

Yours
Bill

PS I should send you an agreement (signed) but cant lay my hand on it. I'll go through the filing system – it's OK anyway.

After some back and forth over a fee, the 'buckshee books' were settled on as suitable payment for the reports provided by Golding and Ann in the letter to du Sautoy of 9 November. Sending in their list of book choices on 16 December, the Goldings also offered 'timid congratulations' on du Sautoy's 'elevation' to the role of vice chairman of the firm: 'We feel we have a friend at court.'

Golding had published two pieces in the latest issue of *The Spectator* (25 November): a review of *Eton* by Christopher Hollis and his own childhood memoir 'Billy the Kid'.

WG to Charles Monteith MS

8 December 1960   Ebble Thatch, Bowerchalke, Salisbury, Wilts.

Dear Charles,

Peter has sent me a copy of the buried agreement, so thats' all right.

Thank you for my most enjoyable glimpse of the sweets of scholarship. I shall probably dine out in America on Lord Mallard and his centennial night on the tiles!

         Yours

          Bill.

You know we shall be delighted to see you down here when ever you can come.

The reference to a 'buried agreement' is mysterious.

Once every century at All Souls, the 'Lord Mallard' is carried on a chair across the college roofs. He sings the Mallard song and the other members of the college sing the chorus. Golding would not have witnessed the event, which took place in 1901 and again in 2001, but he may have heard the song performed.

1961

The year starts inauspiciously: in late January, Ann is rushed to hospital for an emergency appendicectomy. Golding's mood is gloomy enough already, and he still has no news to report about the next book. Some relief comes courtesy of the American mass-circulation magazine *Holiday*, which funds an April trip to Greece in return for a number of travel articles. An even bigger adventure begins in September when Golding and Ann arrive at Hollins College for his writer-in-residence post. With perfect timing, *Lord of the Flies* is becoming established as a bestselling campus novel, so Golding is treated as a literary celebrity. When not teaching at Hollins, he lectures to large audiences across the United States. During this period, he changes tack with his 'Barchester Spire' project: what he had originally intended as a comic 'long-short' turns into something much larger and more ambitious.

Charles Monteith to WG   TS

13 January 1961

Dear Bill,

We've just had sent to us a typescript called THE LYRICAL EXISTENTIALISTS – all about Kierkegaard, Nietsche and Camus – by Dr Thomas Hanna, who is of all things Professor of Philosophy at Hollins College. Would you, I wonder, like to take a three guinea look at it for us? If nothing else it would afford a sneak preview of one of your future colleagues! Do please let me know; and if you'd like to read it, I'll see that it's sent straight off to you.

Something quite different. John Bowen rang me up the other day to say that he'd been in touch with you about the possibility of turning FREE FALL into a television play and that you weren't altogether averse to the idea. He wonders if you'd like to lunch with him and talk about it further the next time you're in London – and he's been kind enough to invite me along as well. So if you could let me know a day you could manage, I'd be most grateful – and we could have an agreeable lunch à trois at the expense of H. M. Tennant's Productions Ltd.

What's the latest news about the new novel, by the way? I needn't tell you how much I'm longing to read it.

Love to Ann and everyone,

Yours ever,

Thomas Hanna's book was not published by Faber, and John Bowen did not turn *Free Fall* into a television play.

WG to Peter du Sautoy TS

1 February 1961   Ebble Thatch, Bowerchalke

Dear Peter,

Thanks for your letter. I've accepted the cheque for On The Crest Of The Wave without a murmur. Thank you for forwarding it.

We should like to meet too. (We now have a piano that even Mollie might consent to play on!) But alas, Ann was carried into Salisbury Infirmary on Monday morning and operated on for acute appendicitis. She's now looking very transparent and fragile, but convalescing and the surgeon is satisfied with her. I suppose she'll be there for another ten days or so.

So as you can see, our movements are a bit problematical at the moment – I dont suppose Ann will be good for much before a month is out though she's cheerful enough. My dashes to London tend to be a quick up and down.

But we *must* all meet as soon as we can   yours ever
Bill

Golding's jeremiad about education and its direction of travel, 'On the Crest of the Wave', was published in the *Times Literary Supplement* the previous June. If he were only now getting paid, that would explain why it was noteworthy to have accepted the cheque 'without a murmur'.

Ann had emergency surgery for acute appendicitis in late January. She wrote to Monteith from Salisbury Infirmary on 6 February to thank him for a gift of 'beautiful spring flowers'.

Mollie du Sautoy was a music teacher and a gifted musician in her own right. Golding had recently bought a Bechstein grand piano and he played it regularly for the rest of his life; the day before he died, he was trying to master some Chopin preludes on it.

Charles Monteith to WG TS

16 February 1961

Dear Bill,

The Headmaster of a large Scottish school has just written to us suggesting that we publish a school edition of LORD OF THE FLIES! The original hard-cover edition is too expensive and the Penguin edition falls to pieces! In principle I think we'd certainly like to do this, and what we'd very much like to know is whether or not you'd be prepared to agree – in principle. If you do, I'm sure we could have an estimate made very quickly and work out some financial arrangement.

The Headmaster suggested in his letter that the school edition ought to have a preface or perhaps some explanatory notes. This, of course, is entirely subject to your approval; but – if you do approve – I think it might be worth asking Ian Gregor of Edinburgh University (one of the co-authors of that essay on FREE FALL that appeared in *Twentieth Century*). Do let me know how this strikes you – and any other names whom you might like to suggest as possible introducers.

This is a very hurried letter, I'm afraid. The reason is that if we do decide to publish this edition we ought to have it ready in time for the autumn and we'd have to get things moving fairly quickly.

I do hope Ann is well on the way to recovery by now. If she's not at home already, I expect she will be before long. Do please give her my love, and let me know, too, when you are next coming to Oxford.

Yours ever,

Faber did not start publishing paperbacks until 1958, and that year it released the first paperback edition of *Lord of the Flies*. Under licence from Faber, Penguin started issuing the paperback edition of *Lord of the Flies* in 1960.

WG to Charles Monteith TS

17 February 1961   [Headed Paper: Ebble Thatch]

Dear Charles,

I cant see anything wrong in principle with a school edition of *Lord Of The Flies*. Introducers are various. As well as Ian Gregor, there's Frank Kermode; and then there's C.B. Cox, editor of the Critical

Quarterly. I cant think that notes are *necessary* but for a school edition they are probably *obligatory*. We could have some fun there –

It occurs to me that as a better idea for introducers and proposers one might employ some enormous great literary Gun? Someone whose name would cast a glow over the volume? Or would they come too expensive? Of course I quite understand that eminences like E.M.F. or T.S.E. are out; but I *did* meet Prichett the other night at an Anglo-French occasion. My point is that English children are well enough able to follow this simple, overt story without notes; and an introduction would be ample. Children wont read it anyway but it would impress the teachers.

Reading this letter through, I find it nasty in a subtle way. I'm getting proud, that's what the matter.

Ann is very nearly well again – a tiny scar and as far as we can see, no prolonged shock. Sends her love.

> Yours
> Bill

PS Had a 'phone conversation with Peter Brook the other day. He's got L of F away from Spiegel and is going to make the film himself in mexico. I agree'd to be consulted over the script. There have been three written and now he's doing the fourth, sticking close to the book.

> Bill

'E.M.F. or T.S.E.': E. M. Forster or T. S. Eliot. As for V. S. Pritchett, he had reviewed *Free Fall* favourably, calling Golding 'the most original of our contemporaries'.

Charles Monteith to WG   TS

24 February 1961

Dear Bill,

Thank you very much indeed for your letter of 17th February and for giving your blessing to a school edition of LORD OF THE FLIES. I'm writing today to Ian Gregor to see whether or not he'd be interested in doing the introduction, etc. And if he should say no I'll certainly try Kermode and/or Cox. Notes, I fear, probably are obligatory for a school edition – particularly if it is to be sold abroad in places like Ghana and Nigeria! In my mind's eye I can see this question in some future paper in the Lagos Higher School Cert: – 'The fair boy stopped and jerked his stockings with an automatic gesture that made the jungle seem for a moment like the Home Counties.'

    (a)   What is meant here by the 'Home Counties'?

    (b)   Why should this gesture make the jungle seem like the Home Counties?

I don't really think the Big Gun idea would really work. I rather doubt if the B.G. – if we got hold of one – would write the sort of introduction which we'd want for this sort of thing. And I feel very doubtful indeed about whether he'd be willing to tackle the notes!

Delighted to hear that the film really is underway again at last – and particularly delighted to know that you're going to be consulted over the script. Some of the rumours that drifted back about the earlier versions were absolutely hair-raising.

Incidentally, have you any news at all, I wonder, about when the novel will be in? Please don't think that I'm *pestering* you about it – I'm just passing on an enquiry from our Production department! In any case, I can certainly assure you that we're keeping a place warm for it in the autumn list.

Delighted to hear that Ann's convalescence is going so well. Do please give her my love. David came in and had a drink with me a week or so ago and I was absolutely delighted to meet him. We talked solid SF, and I've sent him a proofs copy of BEST SF FOUR.

            Yours ever,

            Charles Monteith

Best SF Four, edited as usual by Edmund Crispin, maintained the streak: Monteith had sent every book in the series to the Goldings.

WG to Charles Monteith TS

6(?) March 1961   [Headed Paper: Ebble Thatch]

Dear Charles,

I'm glad the school edition of Flies is ok. I'm beginning to feel like a blankeyed bust already.

About next Sunday – this is complex. My guess is that David will flee Oxford by train at the earliest possible moment. I believe his exams will be over by the end of term and I cant see him sitting around for the love of it. He'll probably leave on Friday, wearing seaboots and with his lip curled.

I should love to lunch with you but think that this time we shall all have to give it a miss. Sorry.

Novel – there is still a chance. For several weeks I havn't touched it but can get back tomorrow. Chance only.

Yours ever
Bill

Monteith's reply is also dated 6 March, so this may be misdated.

Charles Monteith to WG TS

6(?) March 1961

Dear Bill,

Thank you very much for your letter of March 6th. So sorry that you can't manage lunch next Sunday – but of course I understand. I do hope David's Prelims go well.

About the school edition of LORD OF THE FLIES. I've just heard from Gregor who says that he will be delighted to do it in collaboration with Mark Kinkead-Weekes who collaborated with him over the FREE FALL article in *Twentieth Century*. I think that between them they should do a satisfactory job. They're both at Edinburgh but they're coming down South for some conference at Cambridge for the week-end April 7th–9th, and after that they'll be in London for a day or two. They wonder if there's any chance at all of meeting you and talking the whole project over? I don't imagine that you'll be in London on the 10th or 11th but would you, I wonder, be willing to see them if they went down to Salisbury? So sorry if this is a frightful bore, and of course if you can't manage it I'm sure they could clear up any troublesome points in correspondence.

Delighted to know there's still a chance that we'll have the novel for the autumn.

Do please give my love to Ann; I do hope her convalescence is going well.

Yours ever,
Charles Monteith

WG to Charles Monteith

15 March 1961

A hurried note – sorry cant meet Gregor – we shall be in Greece, or tooing and froming 29th March–24th April. Would be delighted any other time if it's possible.

Yours
Bill

Charles Monteith to WG

17 March 1961

Dear Bill,

Thank you very much for your card of 15th March. So sorry to have forgotten about the Greek expedition. 'Need I say how enormously I envy you that?'

I'll most certainly let Gregor know; and if he can't manage another trip south I'm sure he could clear up any outstanding points by writing to you.

I do hope Ann's completely recovered by now. The Greek sun should really set her on her feet again.

Yours ever,

The quotation marks around 'Need I say how enormously I envy you that?' indicate that it may be an allusion. Monteith ends his next letter on 30 March with a similar phrase, almost word for word, but without the quotation marks.

Charles Monteith to WG

30 March 1961

Dear Bill,

I've just heard on the grapevine – an entirely reliable piece of grapevine I think – that you've been short-listed for a new literary prize called the Prix des Editeurs, which is to be awarded by an international jury in Maiorca at the end of this month or the beginning of May. There are quite a number of countries taking part; and each country is represented by a 'jury'. My informant tells me that William Golding is the top choice of the British jury. He is also apparently the top foreign choice of the French jury – though they themselves are putting forward, of course, one of their own compatriots as their top contender.

Don't – please! – build too many hopes on this. I don't honestly think it's likely that a selection committee on which there is a large predominance of Continentals would willingly let a prize like this go to an Englishman. But apparently there's going to be a great deal of publicity for all the finalists – which will be of some help anyway.

I wouldn't have written to you about this at all if I hadn't known that in fact there is going to be publicity in which your name is bound to be mentioned. So all will be out officially after the Maiorca jamboree is over.

I do hope you and Ann have an absolutely marvellous time in Greece. I needn't tell you how very much I envy you that.

Yours ever,

The Prix des Éditeurs was better known as the Prix International. The British jury included Iris Murdoch and her husband John Bayley.

'at the end of this month': the end of April.

WG to Charles Monteith TS

24 April 1961   [Headed Paper: Ebble Thatch]

Dear Charles,

We are back, and fairly sunsoaked. Greece as you might suppose was out of this world – another planet almost, in which the odd broken column (even with sunlight on it) was more or less irrelevant. We might buy a summer shack in the Peloponnese one of these days. At Delphi we found the chasm of the oracle closed by an earthquake – an old one! but got some sort of an answer to our queries. We were waylaid by an excited Greek having one word of English two of French and three of German who finally managed to convey her message to us. The Russians had put a man in orbit.

It was *fun* driving into Salonika, asking a policeman 'Pou estin he thalassa?' and being understood – but a long line of semi-educated tourists must have asked him exactly the same question. YugoSlavia was full of proper Gypsies holding fairs; and there were a few women in turkish trousers and veils, carrying plastic buckets to the well.

Your grapevine – it sounds wonderfully good news even if I get no more than a place or honourable mention. Has anymore transpired? I promise not to build any castles in Maiorca – or at least only prefabricated ones which can be rapidly taken down and reerected elsewhere.

And now back to work.

Yours
Bill

Golding has misdated this letter 24 March.

Golding started writing for the mass-circulation American magazine *Holiday* in 1961; they paid well and occasionally sent him to exotic locations. This three-week trip with his family across Greece and Yugoslavia produced the essay 'The Hot Gates', which was eventually collected in 1965 as the title piece of his first book of non-fiction. The holiday fulfilled a long-standing desire to visit Greece, a country to which, over the next few years, Golding and Ann returned at any opportunity.

The Russians 'put a man in orbit' – the man being Yuri Gagarin – on 12 April.

'Pou estin he thalassa?': 'Where is the sea?' Golding's point is that he can make himself understood by using ancient Greek. The phrase ἔστιν θάλασσα is found in (for example) *Agamemnon* by Aeschylus.

Charles Monteith to WG   TS

25 April 1961

Dear Bill,

Delighted to get your Greek communiqué and to hear that it all went so splendidly. I was sure it would. I'm half thinking of trying to go to Greece myself this summer. I've only spent about three days there in the whole of my life but it infected me with an insatiable itch to go back.

Nothing more has come through on the grapevine about Maiorca, I fear; but if anything does I will of course let you know.

Love to Ann,
Yours ever,

Charles Monteith to WG   TS

10 May 1961

Dear Bill,

As you will probably have heard by now, the Prix des Editeurs which I wrote to you about last month, was in fact divided equally between Samuel Beckett and some Spanish writer whom I've never heard of before called J. Borges. I really am sorry; but I'm afraid it only bears out my prediction that there'd be strong continental resistance to giving a prize like that to an English writer.

Gregor and Kinkead Weekes called in here to see me the other day and I gather that they had a long and very enjoyable day with you talking over the school edition of LORD OF THE FLIES. I'm extremely grateful to you for all the help you're giving them over this, and I've a feeling they're going to do it very well.

Love to Ann,
Yours ever,

'Some Spanish writer' was in fact the great Argentinian poet and short story writer Jorge Luis Borges, who rose to international prominence as a result of winning the prize. As Monteith's ignorance suggests, until then Borges had been virtually unknown across the English-speaking world.

According to Mark Kinkead-Weekes, Golding had expected a pair of 'Scotch moralists'. Meeting Kinkead-Weekes and Gregor for the first time at Salisbury Station, his reaction was 'My God, I'd better get some more beer in.'

WG to Peter du Sautoy TS

14 May 1961   [Headed Paper: Ebble Thatch]

Dear Peter,

Nice to hear from you – it seems ages since we met. Alas I'm not in London that week at all – not until June, in fact. If you like to tell your chaps, though that I'll be lecturing round in the States, and they'll probably come across me somewhere, for what that's worth.

We hope everything is all right your end – we have the partially fragmented feeling of people who know they havn't got much longer before taking the plunge. I personally dont think I'll come back to teaching – I've worked too hard, and now a sort of built-in safety valve is refusing to let me go on doing it.

Greece was gorgeous.

Ann sends her love to you both.
Bill

Du Sautoy had invited Golding and Ann for a drink and dinner on the evening of 17 May. Among the party was to be 'a couple of young American academics' – the 'chaps' to whom Golding refers.

Charles Monteith to WG TS

22 June 1961

Dear Bill,

Just a brief line to put into writing, as it were, the suggestion I made at Peter's the other evening about ENVOY EXTRAORDINARY. We'd be absolutely delighted to republish this – if necessary by itself; but we do rather feel – as I think you do too – that it would be a good thing, if possible, to add to it either a few short stories or another one, or better still two, long-shorts. Could you, I wonder, give me an idea of what you've got available and what you think would go with it best? We'd like to publish the book in the Spring of 1962; which means that it should go off to the printer in August or September.

Rosemary Goad, Eliza Oxley and I are looking forward enormously to seeing you all the weekend after next, en route to or from Dorset. We'll be calling in either on Friday evening on our way down, or on Sunday evening on our way back. But of course we'll give you some advance warning about which it's to be – probably by telephone!

Love to you all,
Yours ever,

WG to Charles Monteith TS

24 June 1961   [Headed Paper: Ebble Thatch]

Saturday

Dear Charles

How nice to see you the other night – and I'm sorry you still cant report on minicabs. We shall be dilighted to have you all three here. There may be other people about, but we know you wont mind that.

Yes. Please republish ENVOY EXTRAORDINARY. I still think it amusing. About other items, I'm not sure. I've only two short stories extant. One, THE ANGLO-SAXON published in QUEEN, which is all right, I think, and MISS PULKINHORN which was published in ENCOUNTER and then done as a radio script. They'd total eight to ten thousand words.

As you have guessed, I'm bogged down in – or passing through – a state of creative impotence, as far as the sort of savage/tragic stuff is

165

concerned; and most unhappy about it. It's partly sheer lack of time, and partly sheer funk at being subjected, inevitably to a close, critical examination. I need oceans of time and more, simplification of circumstances. I'll get them one day, if it's not too late. My study is littered with unfinished novels, I'm practically knee-deep in them.

How about doing BARCHESTER SPIRE as a long-short? It's meant to be funny, but wouldn't carry to book length by itself. I have it (or most of it) in longhand, and the rest in my head. And like the radio things I do it wouldn't aim high; and so I shouldn't be frightened of it. I'm pretty certain I could give you an MS before we go to America – end of August.

Ever   Bill

PS I refused the other day to be televised for Columbia Network on principle; but have had sordid thoughts since, that perhaps I wasn't so wise after all.

PPS Rights in *Envoy* may have reverted to me, but I'm not sure. Curtis Brown would know.

'minicabs': a private joke. See Monteith's postscript to his letter dated 26 June.

Golding's story 'The Anglo-Saxon' had been published in *Queen* in December 1959; 'Miss Pulkinhorn' was adapted as a Third Programme play in April 1960 and appeared in *Encounter* the following August.

'the radio things I do': Golding's radio play *Break My Heart* had been broadcast on the BBC Home Service on 19 March. Taken together with the adaptations of *Free Fall* and 'Miss Pulkinhorn' (both broadcast in 1960), and his writing of an autobiographical story, 'The Ladder and the Tree' (also 1960), for the Third Programme, his output adds up to a fairly regular contribution to BBC radio in one form or another.

Golding was increasingly reluctant to give interviews to broadcast and print media. His turning down of the Columbia Broadcasting System (CBS) was an early sign of what would become a long-standing refusal to speak about his own books.

Charles Monteith to WG TS

26 June 1961

Dear Bill,

Thank you very much indeed for your letter. Looking forward enormously to seeing you at the weekend; I think it will be Sunday – but I'll let you know definitely as soon as I'm quite sure.

What an excellent idea to include BARCHESTER SPIRE with ENVOY EXTRAORDINARY. Do please go ahead and finish it; and if we can have it by the end of August we can certainly get the book out in the spring.

I remember both THE ANGLO-SAXON and MISS PULKINHORN; and if we need them to make up the length, we can certainly include either or both.

Leave it to me to sort out the question of whether rights have reverted in ENVOY EXTRAORDINARY. I can easily clear that up and, when I have, I'll let you know what the answer is.

Most terribly sorry to hear you feel so bogged down at the moment – though, as you rightly guessed, I had guessed! I have a feeling that a long sea voyage and a change of scene will work wonders.

Much looking forward to seeing you,

Yours ever,

PS And I will be able to report on Minicabs. Though I couldn't get one that evening we all met at Peter's, I was transported back from Richmond to London in one the following evening in reasonable comfort, at admirable speed, and very cheaply.

Monteith checked directly with Eyre & Spottiswoode, who confirmed that rights for 'Envoy Extraordinary' had indeed reverted to Golding.

Charles Monteith to WG TS

31 August 1961

Dear Bill,

I imagine you'll be leaving for Hollins before very long, and – as you've probably guessed – I'm writing to enquire whether or not you'll be able to let me have BARCHESTER SPIRE before you go? Do please forgive me for pestering you about it; but, as you know, I'd dearly like to have a Golding book in the spring list, and the deadline is approaching with implacable rapidity. I wonder if you could possibly let me have, too, copies of the other stories that are to go with it. I have somewhere a copy of ENVOY EXTRAORDINARY, but I'm pretty certain that I haven't got the others.

I do hope you have had a good summer – I expect you've all been sailing. If there's any chance of it at all, it would be very nice to see you and Ann again before you go, and if either or both of you are in London with a few moments to spare, do please give me a ring. I'm just back from a fortnight in Greece – mostly on Corfu and Rhodes. Heavenly.

Love to Ann,
Yours,

WG to Charles Monteith   TS

3 September 1961   [Headed Paper: Ebble Thatch]

Dear Charles,

We leave England on 14th September by Queen Elizabeth – a different sort of boat to have in the Channel!

About a book –

I havn't got copies of MISS PULKINHORN and THE ANGLO-SAXON. I *had* copies but they've gone. They were the presentation(?) copies of Encounter and Queen – hold everything; Ann has found Encounter which I enclose, but Queen has gone for good.

BARCHESTER SPIRE.

It will ultimately be two short-longs and possibly three, even four. I've done two drafts of the first and it must have another. I dont anticipate being able to *finish* that before the 14th – but I shall have four days aboard QE. The best bet, I think would be to give me an ultimate, absolute deadline. Then I'll try to catch it – I'm already feeling the benefit of no longer being a dominee. Freedom, heyday! Freedom! Oh brave new world!

And I faithfully promise to work just as hard as if I were still a school master, dammit.

Yours ever
Bill

After much agonizing, Golding had finally thrown over his teaching job at Bishop Wordsworth's School. He combines his customary allusion to Caliban's drunken excitement – 'Freedom, heyday! Freedom!' – with another quotation from *The Tempest*: Miranda's 'O brave new world / That has such people in 't!' (5.1.183–4).

'dominee': a schoolmaster (usually spelt domine or dominie).

Charles Monteith to WG TS

6 September 1961

Dear Bill,

It was very nice indeed hearing your voice on the telephone yester-day and to know that you're all so well. This letter's simply to confirm what I told you on the telephone. If we have the stories by 31st October 1961, we should, D.V., be able to get them out in the spring of next year, but that really is an absolute deadline.

One other, very tiresome, matter on which I would be enormously grateful for your help. Our spring catalogue will be going to press shortly and I wonder if you could possibly let me have some sort of brief description of the book – or brief details of what its contents are likely to be. The blurb of course – the one that will be printed on the jacket – can certainly wait until the typescript arrives. I'll cope with that then.

My very best wishes again to you and Ann for an absolutely won-derful time in America.

Yours ever,

'D.V.': Deo volente (God willing).

WG to Charles Monteith TS

10 September 1961   [Headed Paper: Ebble Thatch]

Sunday

Dear Charles,

I may have misled you unintentionally about Barchester Spire. The *completed* set will contain as many as four short-longs. But what I've written is the first one, about the building – may run out at a little less than 20,000 words. That's what I hope you'll get by the end of October.

Our address – did I tell you? –
> Hollins College
> Virginia
> USA

Could you do a menial job for me? I want to keep my Salisbury account in credit because of school fees and what-not. It would therefore be of help if any monies due to me from F&F (between now and next June) could be paid by banker's order or whatever the technique is, straight into the account of:

W.G. & M.A. Golding
Barclay's Bank
Salisbury
Wilts.

Could you pass that instruction to the appropriate office deep in the bowels of 24 Russell Square?

Odd. I already have the feeling coming over me that days of hubris are past – and I shall write a book eventually out of myself rather than out of a gigantic persona projected by a small section of the avant garde.

All our best wishes and most cordial thoughts – our next will reach you by short wave from the planet Mars.

Journey into SPACE!
Bill

Charles Monteith to WG   TS

12 September 1961

Dear Bill,

Thank you very much indeed for your letter and for clearing up the position about Barchester Spire. You're quite right in thinking that your last letter had confused me a little! But all's clear now and I look forward to both books enormously – 'BARCHESTER SPIRE and Other Stories' and 'BARCHESTER SPIRE COMPLETE'.

I'll certainly pass on the necessary note to our accountant about paying money into your bank in Salisbury; and I'll circulate your American address to all concerned.

Bon Voyage for the journey into Space.   Love to all,
        Yours ever,
    i.e. *BARCHESTER SPIRE and Other Stories* will contain, BARCHESTER SPIRE, ENVOY EXTRAORDINARY, MISS PULKINHORN and THE ANGLO-SAXON. That's right, isn't it? If you have any special views about the order you'd like them to appear in, do please let me know.

'Barchester Spire and Other Stories' never materialised, but Faber did produce some advance publicity that promised a volume comprising 'Miss Pulkinhorn', 'The Anglo-Saxon', and 'two short novels ['Barchester Spire' and 'Envoy Extraordinary'] which show Mr Golding in a more lighthearted mood than usual'.

WG to Charles Monteith TS

28 October 1961   Hollins College, Virginia, USA

Dear Charles,

You are going to hate this letter. I've now written Barchester Spire, part one, three times and at last seen what the proper scope of it is. If I were to send you what I have done at the moment it would be probably an acceptable story – but nothing like what I'm going to write. There is a book there – a proper book, which needs time, concentration, discovery and even love; all of which I mean to give it. Call this integrity if you like – an odd word to use about a broken promise! But the book is there, waiting to be hacked out, and I'd be a fool, an inopportunist, if I wasted it.

The only thing I can suggest for the spring book is Break My Heart, which the BBC would pass to you.

I'm aware that I may be damaging myself by stopping so long away from the novel-reading public; but this seems *right* to me – I mean not snatching at quick returns, as I did with the Brass Butterfly. But I'm very sorry to have strung you along like this. I'd sooner give you the whole Barchester Spire for the Autumn.

Sorry, sorry, sorry.

Ann sends her love

Bill

WG to Peter and Mollie du Sautoy TS

1 November 1961   Hollins College, Virginia

Dear Peter and Mollie,

Welcome to these fertile shores. When is your week on the hoof? Ann and I leave Hollins next Saturday, lecture at Union College Schenectady N.Y. on 6–7th, Holyoke college South Hadley Mass 8th, Dartmouth College Hanover, 9–10th.

These would seem to imply that we shall be somewhere near New York between 5–10th November.

That being so, we will give you a ring at the Grosvenor Hotel, when we get into your area, and if the moment seems propitious, arrange to meet. The trouble is, of course, that we havn't yet got used to the scale of things, and at the moment just have an idea that we shall be in the top right hand corner of America.

Everything down here is very friendly and peaceful, not an Indian in sight. We have learned to drink bourbon, smoke cigarettes with filters, say 'you all', and accept an attitude which is surely as near as nothing to pernicious anglophilia. We have so much time! Two lectures a week on the modern British novel (hard going) and the rest of the time for writing if it wern't for the parties, the mountain climbs, the trips to Williams Burg, the parties, the skyline drive, the parties, the local customs, the parties – but we have really settled down, I think. BARCHESTER SPIRE, my next book looms and dislimns and then looms again; but I have the kind of settled feeling that I am writing it.

Ann cant find anything to do – is stunned by the siestas, and the general feeling that there are forty eight hours in any one day – and then another forty eight tomorrow.

We miss David and Judith – have restless thoughts of flying them out for Christmas.

Andrew Sinclair sicked the Atlantic Monthly people on to me and I dont know what to do. He wants the Inheritors, I believe, but it seems a bit hard on John Mc Callum. I havn't answered yet – shall tell him that my novels are in your hands and MCA's.

      Ann sends her love
       Bill

Andrew Sinclair, novelist and historian, was a Faber author and a friend of the Goldings. The Atlantic Monthly Press was making a determined effort to prise Golding away from Harcourt, Brace with an offer to publish *The Inheritors* and his next novel.

Charles Monteith to WG TS

3 November 1961

Dear Bill,

Thank you very much for your letter of October 28th. I didn't – I honestly mean this – hate it at all. Indeed I'm absolutely delighted that BARCHESTER SPIRE is going to turn into a real book. Far, far better to do it properly than to allow it to go off at half cock as a long short story. Don't worry, please, about the fact that there's going to be no Golding in the Spring List. The thought of the SPIRE towering over the Autumn one more than makes up for it!

I do hope that you and Ann are having a wonderful time in Virginia. When you've got a moment do please drop me a line and tell me all about it. As you probably know, Peter and Mollie are over in New York at the moment. Will you, I wonder, get a chance to see them? I know how much they hoped it might be possible – it depends, I suppose, on how plans can be fitted in. I've had a couple of letters from Peter and he's obviously tremendously busy dashing round publishers' offices all over the place.

Love to you both,

1962

Golding's new-found fame sits oddly alongside his patchy – and increasingly confused – publication history in the United States. By the end of the year, *Lord of the Flies* is estimated to have sold half a million copies, yet people still complain about struggling to find his books, and publishers seem hesitant to invest. *The Inheritors* finally appears from Harcourt, Brace in July, the month after Golding's return to England. He brings back with him a new draft of the 'Barchester Spire' novel, but deadlines come and go with no sign of the finished typescript. After his American experience, Golding finds re-entry into domestic life difficult, and towards the end of the year he is distracted by deepening worries about his children.

WG to Giles de la Mare   TS

3 January 1962   Hollins College, VA, USA

Dear Mr de la Mare,

Thank you for your letter. As regards a French digest of Lord Of The Flies, my feelings are mixed. I dont like digests normally; but Lord Of The Flies appears to have done so badly in France anyway, that I dont see that a digest could do any harm. Since your interests and mine seem to coincide in this matter I believe the most sensible thing for me to do would be to leave a decision to you, with this letter as an assurance that I will accept that decision whatever it may be.

The New York Times said in December that paperback sales (presumably in USA) of Lord Of The Flies had reached 48000. I forget what our percentage ought to be, but surely there ought to be some dollar due from that? On the other hand I've heard nothing. Moreover Pincher Martin seems to be sold out – or did Harcourt Brace pulp what they had left six months after publication? It's all very mysterious. Where ever I go on Campuses sales seem good and everybody very interested, but to the best of my belief I've never had more than my share of the £350 odd advance. But bookshops are even importing English copies of The Inheritors, and Free Fall seems unobtainable. It's not that I am critical in these matters; I just dont understand them. After all, there are eighteen hundred campuses in

174

America, and even minimal sales round them ought to be significant.

One other thing. I am now a limited company; so would you ask your accounts department to send all future monies to William Golding Limited, Barclays Bank Salisbury?

Yours sincerely

William Golding

Someone at Faber has corrected Golding's misdating in pencil, crossing out 'December' and writing 'January' below. At the end of the letter, Golding has signed in pen and then typed his name.

Founded on 14 December 1961, William Golding Limited held its first meeting of the four directors (Golding, Ann, David and Judy) in San Francisco in April 1962.

Having seen this letter, du Sautoy wrote to Golding on 15 January to remind him that he had, in fact, received royalties for the American paperback edition of *Lord of the Flies*. He agreed, though, that it was 'ridiculous' that 'everyone should be talking about you in the United States [. . .] and nothing was available except the paperback of LORD OF THE FLIES and a few copies of FREE FALL'.

WG to Peter du Sautoy   TS

21 January 1962   [Headed paper: Hollins College]

Dear Peter,

Thanks for your long, careful letter. As I read it, you think we should stick with Harcourt Brace; and if you *do* think that, then I'm sure it's the right thing to do. However I wouldn't worry about their stretching the advance a bit from the commercial point of view. Granted I dont – and perhaps shant – have significant sales in America, they know perfectly well that moving my name would be a loss of prestige in those very circles where they sell their textbooks. What they are really asking is that I should agree to continue to be a bit of academic prestige for them; and at the same time agree that prestige is not a thing you pay money for. I dont think they can have it both ways. They've just bought Rupert Hart Davis (or is that a secret?) and if they can do that, they can certainly match the Atlantic Monthly offer; a point I would have been less insistent on, had they not been very casual so far with pushing my books, so that those books have had to make their own way. In a word; accept their offer, if you think we should – but dont let them think it generous except in the limited sense that they arnt likely to get all of it back from me directly.

Sorry to sound so sordid; but wherever I've been, people have complained of not being able to get my books – and that wasn't *all* soothing an author.

I'm sorry, by the way, we never met here; the real reason is that I'm living the sort of life I've never lived before – lectures, travel, parties, more travel – I can see my ego getting monstrous – must settle down somehow – yes, of course I got money from Lord Of The Flies paperback, our letters crossed, more or less; thank God I'll be a normal, cottagedwelling, pen-pushing, respectable citizen in no more than five months.

Ann sends her love.

Bill

The letter is typed on headed paper:
HOLLINS COLLEGE
HOLLINS COLLEGE, VIRGINIA
In his letter to Golding of 15 January, du Sautoy had argued that although Harcourt, Brace had not been especially proactive in promoting his work and were only offering an advance of $3,500 against the Atlantic Monthly's $5,000 for *The Inheritors* and the next novel, the risk of changing publisher was too great.

'moving my name': possibly a slip for 'losing my name'.

'and that wasn't *all* soothing an author': perhaps Golding meant 'and that wasn't *at all* soothing to an author'.

WG to Peter du Sautoy   TS

11 February 1962   [Headed paper: Hollins College]

Dear Peter,

Thanks for your letter of 30th January with enclosure. I didnt know there'd been postal trouble at home. It explains a kind of random element in my correspondence.

You're taking a lot of trouble on my behalf, as always, and I'm grateful. I saw John McCallum in New England last week and he was amiable – so much so that I felt a bit of a swine; but mastered my impulse to offer him something for nothing. He came to the lecture I gave at Yale and it did him a bit of good, I think – place crowded, boys sitting in the aisles and a crowd outside who couldn't get in. Lecturing goes well, all things considered.

When I got home yesterday, to find your letter, I also got a phone call which I will explain. Apparently Coward McCann have heard that

Eliot wont do an introduction for them (LORD OF THE FLIES) and cast round. They've asked John W. Aldridge (PARTY AT CRANTON? THE LOST GENERATION) to do one for them. He wanted to know what I thought, but I put him off, rightly pleading exhaustion. So I'm asking you.

He's got a pretty good reputation here, but he's ten years or more younger than me. I should have thought Forster (who probably would) or Aldous Huxley (who probably wouldn't) would have been more appropriate to give me the critical accolade – take my sword, my son! Or Koestler? It's all very difficult. I like Jack Aldridge (know him well), but the thing he did on me for the N.Y. Times amused me and made me squirm. Anyway, damn it, cant I write my own introduction? What do you think? Have you or I any control? Or must we let the whole thing go ahead – a ropey business, embalm-ment – saying nothing? I suppose to state the case fairly, I cant see Jack giving this particular devil his due.

You'll have detected a more masterful note in my correspondence of late. The fact is, I'm being spoilt, lionised, made much of, entertained pleasantly to death, listened to, looked at, photographed, recorded, finger-printed, blood-grouped, analysed, diagnosed, admired, adulated, questioned, cross-examined, interviewed, dollarised, sagifyed, and I've still got four months of it to go. The worst is that I can admit those books were good, very good, but no one but Ann and I know how helplessly I stand in front of the next one. Period.

There's not much else to say. BARCHESTER SPIRE goes on and I've ideas – but they've got to be brought under one hat and I'm fumbling. I'll still catch the Autumn tide but it'll be a close run thing.

To return to Lord Of The Flies – Is it true to say that Coward McCann can do what they like? Supposing I dont like the illustrations can I turn them down? If I dont like the introduction, can I turn it down?

We were more than sorry not to see you and Mollie in New York. I suppose there's no chance of a return? This is such an enormous country. We'd reckoned on driving between some colleges to lecture, until we turned up an atlas; but each college was one thousand miles from the next.

Roll on May and the English countryside.

   Yours ever
    Bill

In any event if I *do* prise Jack Aldridge off the job I'd like to do it without hurting his feelings because outside the printed page he's a good friend. So perhaps he'd better not know about this letter! How complicated can publishing get?

      B

Ann sends her love.

Du Sautoy had enclosed a copy of a letter he had written to John McCallum at Harcourt, Brace, in which he made an ultimatum: Harcourt, Brace should offer a $5,000 advance for *The Inheritors* and Golding's next book or they would lose him to another firm. McCallum acquiesced with what du Sautoy characterised to Golding as 'ill grace'.

Although the postal strike in January 1962 was not a complete shutdown, the postal workers were working to rule by refusing to go beyond the terms of their contract. As a result, deliveries were late and intermittent.

John W. Aldridge was Golding's predecessor as writer-in-residence at Hollins and had stayed on as Visiting Professor. His article about Golding – the best and funniest profile to that point – appeared in the *New York Times* on 10 December; it described its subject as 'an astute well-feasted Viking in full beard'.

WG to Charles Monteith

TS

28 February 1962   HOLLINS COLLEGE, VA

Dear Charles,

Here is a hasty note of at least partial reassurance. After shilly-shallying and mucking about, I got down to the book and wrote it (between fifty and sixty thousand words) in a fortnight and am properly flaked out. Of course I shall have to reconsider and rewrite and so forth; but this is a tunnel bored through the book more or less as it will be. Therefore you *will* get an MS to examine in time for the autumn tide. Even with this draft, Ann thinks some of it is good enough to stay put and at times I agree with her. I thought up a gorgeous title, though Ann says she doesnt see how you can use it. What do you think?

AN
ERECTION
AT
BARCHESTER.

Antony Gross ought to do a dustjacket of Salisbury spire only reflected in water so that it's all jazzed up. Then, at last, I could have my name written in it, just like Keats. Do you feel I'm a reliable enough person to be given the ultimate date for getting the MS to you? We leave NY in a Dutch boat on 1st June and I suppose get to England about a week later. It would be good to bring the MS home with me and even do some work on it there. (Folksy, Wiltswimsy W.G.).

I am being very distinguished out here and only talk to top people. Had a passage with a multimillionaire who had decorated the cover of Time and Tide or something.

MM: And do you propose to give up teaching and live by writing?
Me: (Raising right hand) I do.
MM: How will you discharge your responsibilities?
Me: With money.

If you see Durrell, tell him I've been lecturing on the Alexandria Quartet and think it's the most *generous* set (Head over heels in, enthusiasm, no holds barred, copious) thing since D.H.L. was in these parts.

      Yours in haste
        Bill

PS Think how AN ERECTION AT BARCHESTER would pack them in!
PPS Ann sends her love.

John Keats's gravestone in Rome's Cimitero Acattolico carries the epigraph that he had stipulated on his death bed: 'Here lies One Whose Name was writ in Water.'
D.H.L.: D. H. Lawrence.

WG to Peter du Sautoy TS

1 March 1962   HOLLINS COLLEGE, VA, USA

Dear Peter,

Thank you for your letter of 23rd February. I agree wholly with what you have said to John McCallum, and think that in the long run you will win the argument.

About John Aldridge, I'm not quite so certain. He has an enormous influence on the young over here as a critic and the young seems to be where I have a following. It's solely, as I said, that I should like one of a past generation to do it. As far as writing an introduction myself, this would be fine; but I dont see when I am to do it. I'm tied up with writing for the next four months and couldn't give them anything in time for the autumn tide. On the other hand, please note that if at any time Faber want to bring out a collector's edition – as it seems Coward McCann intend – it would be a horse of a different colour!

Jack Aldridge has never shown the slightest critical interest in my writing; and as an American, interested in new American writers, there's no reason why he should have. But of course, people like E. M. Forster, Koestler, Richard Church have been on my side very much for the last eight or is it nine years and if anybody is going to introduce the book, one of them ought at least to have the opportunity to say no; or if you want Jack Aldridge's generation in England, there are Frank Kermode, Peter Green, Ian Gregor and half-a-dozen others.

As far as the pictures are concerned I agree that we ought to be consulted – whose book is it, anyway? But I shall be leaving USA by 1st June at the latest and dont suppose anything will have been done by then.

I've heard nothing from the Edinburgh Festival people. If I *did* hear I should probably accept, since we could all four then see something of the festival possibly with free tickets or whatever; but I'd also want to see what I was letting myself in for – over here you can get yourself thoroughly exploited and exhausted unnecessarily on that sort of jaunt. England *may* be a bit easier and offer a less scarifying schedule.

Ann sends her love. We both look forward to seeing you when we get home.

    Yours
    Bill

PS Encl: letter, dont know what. Has he a publisher in his pocket? PTO. Had a long talk with Jack Aldridge last night – he agrees with me. i.e. Forster is the right man for this edition. So go ahead!

Golding has drawn a line from the word 'exhausted' to the bottom of the page, where he has added a handwritten note in large brackets: 'Only happens sometimes, of course. Some visits very easy and cordial.'

Golding did not end up attending the Edinburgh Festival. See the postscript to Monteith's letter of 14 September.

Whatever Golding's enclosure was, it has not been preserved in the Faber archive.

E. M. Forster did indeed accept the invitation; Coward-McCann's new hardback edition of *Lord of the Flies* was prefaced with Forster's essay, which begins: 'It is a pleasure and an honour to write an introduction to this remarkable book.' Coward-McCann's original plan to commission Leonard Baskin to illustrate the novel came to nothing, and the book was published without illustrations.

Charles Monteith to WG

7 March 1962

Dear Bill,

Absolutely wonderful news that the book is written – though of course I realise that you've still got a good deal of final chiselling and polishing to do.

The autumn deadline is almost on us, I'm afraid; and I think it would probably be much more sensible to save the book up for the spring rather than try to rush it through for November or early December. If we did that, you could certainly keep it till you get back in June – and even for sometime after that if you wanted to. Do please let me know if this strikes you as OK.

About the title. AN ERECTION AT BARCHESTER rolls us in the aisles – but . . . but . . .

David had a drink with me in Oxford the weekend before last. He seemed in excellent form. I had Brian Aldiss in at the same time and they talked SF to each other like mad.

Much love to you and to Ann. Looking forward enormously to seeing you both in June.

Yours ever,

WG to Peter du Sautoy

5 May 1962   HOLLINS COLLEGE, VA

Dear Peter,

I'm so sorry to hear about your father – as you say, I know what it's like. May you and I fall like sparrows when the time comes and be unnoticed. I wouldn't wish the grieving business on my worst enemy. Our very real sympathy.

We left Hollins on March 28th, I think it was and have been incommunicado ever since – a lecture tour to the far west, lecturing and sight-seeing; scandalous inattention to duty, but there it is.

I gave the Harcourt Brace lecture in New York the other day and saw John McCallum meanwhile. He seemed to want December for the MS and I agreed because a six month period in quiet waters is what I need for it. So if you agree with John for December '62 (and if possible the end) that's OK by me.

About the option – I leave it to you, in other words yes.

A point: wherever I go, people *still* say they cant get my books. Yet John admits there's no call for them. So it must be paper backs that people want; and I suppose this does not concern H B and World. Cant Putnam do Free Fall? Sorry, I now remember they're doing Pincher Martin and presumably will do The Inheritors finally.

Now you know what you want over the first two points dont bother to answer this – we shall be home on 1st June anyway.

By the way, John said his firm in UK (the one he bought – cant remember the name) would agree readily to do a photostat of the MS when you've seen it, thus saving me either the bother or the expense of duplication. I hope this is all right with you.

P Brook is pleased with the rough cut of LORD OF THE FLIES. I saw some stills the other day and they seem very much to the point.

   All our love
    William Golding

Du Sautoy's father had died just before Easter. Golding's daughter Judy recounts a conversation with her octogenarian father in her memoir, *The Children of Lovers*, in which Golding reassures her that '*eventually* you do get over the death of your parents', but that 'it takes a long time'. As he walks away, he adds, 'It has taken me thirty years.'

'fall like sparrows': see Matthew 10:29–31: 'Are not two sparrows sold for a farthing? and one of them shall not fall on the ground without your Father. But the very hairs of your head are all numbered. Fear ye not therefore, ye are of more value than many sparrows.' Given his propensity to quote from Shakespeare, Golding may also have in mind Hamlet's comment that 'There is special providence in the fall of a sparrow' (5.2.192–3).

The letter clarifies two issues that were holding up the contract with Harcourt, Brace: they needed a delivery date for the new novel (still known as 'Barchester Spire') and Golding had to give explicit consent to an option for Harcourt, Brace on the following book.

WG to Charles Monteith and Peter du Sautoy   TS

9 June 1962   [Headed Paper: Ebble Thatch]

Dear Peter/ and or Charles
   Charles/ and or Peter,
 I am now back, we are now back, all of us, after having crawled

all over USA, a large, rather barren plot, inhabited by astonishingly gentle people. John MacCallum saw us off with full brass band at the Algonquin and we now feel thoroughly international, and stand about with a slight air of profile. There really *is* an enormous interest in my books in the States and we were dead right to stick out for more money. But we all had a very good, exhausting time.

When I've got my income tax straight – if ever – and done at least a hundred and one jobs I shall be able to rewrite BARCHESTER, which definitely will be on hand when you want it; I get an immense feeling of freedom out of having given up teaching, feel a new man, in fact, which may be a bad thing.

I'll come up to London for a day soon, and will contact you a bit before that. At the moment I'm hazy because there seems so much in every direction; but the main thing is can we pursuade Peter Brook to let an off-Broadway group do Lord Of The Flies, of course after the film is out? I dont imagine either party expect to make any money; but the play would be interesting to do, good advertisement, and perhaps even an excuse for me to nip quickly over to New York where the streets are paved with gold, believe you me. Or is this all off your beat? You see, I keep getting me and you and Curtis Brown and *MCA* mixed up. A further tiny ploy I have in mind is to pursuade Peter Brook to let at least me, and Ann if possible, attend the film premier – which I gather will be in Venice, where we have never been, not being strictly in the book trade like Peter.

I liked the F&F edition of LORD OF THE FLIES (hereinafter referred to in all correspondence as FLIES) for schools. Though sometimes it *does* make me feel a bit embalmed if not mummified. A comfortable feeling on the whole. John McCallum (this ought to be in confidence, I suppose) is meditating yet another edition of FLIES if he can prise it off McCann, complete with critical apparatus, essays, bibliography, the full treatment so that no student need think for himself. A considerable saving to many.

> I'm a valuable man
> To McCallum and McCann:
> Your agreements taste like alum
> To McCann and to McCallum.

Would you care to submit my collected verse to a vet?

> Ever
> Bill

The Algonquin is a hotel in Manhattan well known for literary gatherings.

Peter Brook's film of *Lord of the Flies* had been in production during 1961. It premiered in 1963, not in Venice but in Cannes. There is no record of the off-Broadway stage play of *Lord of the Flies* taking place.

The school edition of *Lord of the Flies*, introduced by Ian Gregor and Mark Kinkead-Weekes, was published by Faber in 1962. The novel was, by then, a set text for the Cambridge Certificate of Proficiency and the Joint Matriculation Board for A-level English, among others.

The status and availability of Golding's novels in the United States had been an ongoing headache but by the end of 1962 *Lord of the Flies* had become a sensation, with sales of around half a million copies. Its success prompted John McCallum at Harcourt, Brace finally to publish *The Inheritors* in the summer of 1962.

Charles Monteith to WG TS

15 June 1962

Dear Bill,

Peter and I were absolutely delighted to get your letter and to know that you and Ann both arrived back safely. I'm replying to you since Peter is more or less mewed up with lawyers these days as in a couple of weeks we – that's to say the publishers and book sellers of this country – have got to defend the Net Book Agreement before the Restrictive Practices Court; and Peter's going to be one of our star witnesses. Whether we win or not is very much in the lap of the gods. Not very likely – but there's a chance.

Delighted that the visit to the States was such a success; and longing to hear all about it. Do get in touch before your trip to London and we must meet for a meal or a drink.

About the play. This one's for MCA so do please get in touch with them about it and what a splendid idea of trying to get to Venice for the premiere of the film. Don't forget that all of us want tickets for the London premiere!

Delighted you like the school edition of FLIES (OK we'll stick to that) Greggor's introduction is rather good isn't it?

Peter and I've both got various things we'd like to talk to you about but all that can wait till we meet. Do please give my love to Ann and say how much I hope she comes to London with you.

Yours ever,

The Restrictive Practices Court ruled in favour of the retention of the Net Book Agreement, which stayed in place until 1997. The agreement ensured that retailers were prohibited from reducing the price of books.

Charles Monteith to WG   TS

29 June 1962

Dear Bill,

Since you have just thrown off the shackles of school mastering I have probably chosen the worst possible moment to try you with two very pedagogic suggestions. If you simply can't bear the thought of them, just say so and I promise that they will never be mentioned again.

The first concerns THE BRASS BUTTERFLY which, as you know, is controlled by Curtis Brown. Juliet O'Hea wrote to me some time ago to say that Heinemanns wanted to bring it out as a school edition and was this OK by us? We have thought about it here and we can't see any reason why we should let THE BB go to Heinemanns. We have, after all, just started off our Faber School Editions with a very famous modern novel; and wouldn't a very distinguished modern play by the same author make an admirable Number Two? So I have made an offer to Curtis Brown and I expect you will be hearing from them soon – if you haven't heard from them already.

Now for the pedagogery. Most school editions of plays seem to have an Introduction at the beginning and sometimes Notes at the end – and it would probably be a Good Thing if the BB followed suit. By hunting around, I could probably find somebody able to provide all this class room material with reasonable competence – but I am perfectly certain that I would never find anybody able to do it half as well as you would yourself. Is there any chance at all of persuading you? Do please think about it and let me know. It shouldn't be a Very big or Very long job.

The second suggestion is, I confess, for a much bigger and a much longer job. It occurred to us some time ago that it might be a good idea to publish a Faber Poetry Anthology, designed primarily for use in schools; and it occurred to us too – you have guessed! – that nobody would be able to do it better than W.G. How does *that* one strike you? If you don't shrink from the idea in horror I'd be only too pleased to discuss details with you – length, period to be covered, age group, type of school to be aimed at, etc., etc. There would be no particular hurry about it, and it occurred to me that you might perhaps be able to take it on as a sort of 'spare time' job which could be done concurrently with your writing.

I am looking forward to seeing you soon. Please don't forget to get in touch before your next visit to London.

As you have probably seen from the Law Reports in the Times Peter has had a couple of gruelling days in the Witness Box in the Net Book case and though his evidence is over now he is still down at the Law Courts. (One of his answers, incidentally, was flagrantly misreported in this morning's Times.) This Net Book case really has been most exhausting and quite a business for him. I am urging Molly to take him off on holiday the moment it is over – which it won't be for another four or five weeks.

Love to Ann and family,
Yours ever,

WG to Charles Monteith TS

1 July 1962   [Headed Paper: Ebble Thatch]

Dear Charles,

Peter Campion is getting a good press isn't he? I dont know what it's all about; but it seems to be conducted in a most polite manner. I imagine if you lose you'll suffer no penalty – merely be asked to withdraw to the anteroom with a bottle of whisky and a loaded revolver.

About the anthology of poetry:

I have to confess that I am not up to this. I have never made the bold step from a classic (which other people assure me I must like) to a modern where I have to decide for myself. I had a crise de tete over imagism in the thirties and never recovered. Now, I dont care about poetry any more unless it's Greek, or a friend sends me his slim volume. The only possibility here is that you should employ a pro like Alvarez, or Frazer to supply quantities of poetry and that I should be employed as an ex-schoolmaster, sieving out what verse would be likely to appeal to schoolchildren. Is that possible? I havn't really thought; and perhaps you arn't really very serious about it all. If you *are* and are going to be in Oxford soon, I could drive over quite easily and spend an afternoon or evening with you discussing it. Or you could come here? You see I'm no longer on the BK Soc Comm (sacked in absentia) so I have no standard reason for coming to London; and if I or we do, my heart faints and a drowsy numbness comes over me at the thought of catching the nine thirty.

About Brass Butterfly:

I cant believe that *anybody* would want to do BB for schools. Oughtn't we to face the fact squarely that this play was a flop which when produced bored even the author? Moreover it has faults sticking out of it too gross to be borne. I know, because after I got your letter I read the play from cover to cover, and regard it as the one occasion on which I've been amateurish about writing and not cared about value for money. This makes the fact poignant that one Burto in America has, alas with my consent – but I hadn't reread the play – put it in an anthology of comedies for colleges from Aristoph to your repentant servant, fortunately and thoughtfully omitting the commonwealth of nations from the sales area. If you are proposing to do a schools edition, merely to keep my work with F&F, then I will string along by making some sort of agreement to rewrite the play sometime in the future, or at least try to correct its grosser faults; and we could go on from there. And the future is a long, long time.

I or we *might* come up for a bit, a day or two, perhaps that would be better and then I could see everybody. But *will* you be in Oxford? Or I could fetch you from there to here in our newly acquired status symbol which is a gross piece of self-indulgence, and purrs when driven.

    Bill

Peter Campion's 'good press' has not left any traces in the archives of the major daily newspapers, so it is a fair assumption that Golding is punningly championing du Sautoy.

The Genius of the Later English Theater (1962), edited with an introduction by Sylvan Barnet, Morton Berman and William Burto, included plays by Goldsmith, Congreve, Byron, Wilde and Shaw, as well as Golding's *The Brass Butterfly*. There was no Aristophanes. (Golding's habit of typing right up to the edge of the paper often results in misjudgements; here he can only fit 'Aristoph' on the line.) This curious anthology marked the first appearance of *The Brass Butterfly* in the United States.

G. S. Fraser's anthology *Poetry Now* had been published by Faber in 1956 and Al Alvarez's *The New Poetry* by Penguin in 1962.

'my heart faints and a drowsy numbness comes over me': compare the opening of John Keats's 'Ode to a Nightingale': 'My heart aches, and a drowsy numbness pains / My sense'.

Charles Monteith to WG

10 July 1962

Dear Bill,

Thank you very much for your letter. Of course I understand your feelings about the Anthology – and about THE BRASS BUTTERFLY as well. So far as the Anthology is concerned I will hunt round for another editor; and I will tell him that you might perhaps be willing to advise, in your capacity as ex-school master, once he has made his provisional selection.

I have a feeling that you may be judging THE BB a bit too harshly; and I have a feeling too that if we were to publish it as it stands as a school edition it might do reasonably well. Heinemanns, as you know, have made a definite offer for it; and our spies at the Cambridge Examination Board tell us that there is every chance of it being set, provided that a suitable play can be found to be set with it. Plays apparently are set in pairs. Do please think this one over again. We really would like to go ahead with it and feel pretty confident about its chances. It would be helped, I think, by the fact that the school edition of LORD OF THE FLIES has made an extremely promising start.

I'd love to see you again and to hear all your American news. Here is a suggestion. I am spending August Bank Holiday with the Oxleys in Dorset; and I wondered if I might perhaps come down to Salisbury on a morning or an early afternoon train on Friday, August 3rd, spend the day with you and be picked up by Eliza and Rosemary at Ebble Thatch in the evening. Do please let me know if that would suit you. But of course if it doesn't we must meet either here or in Oxford.

Yours ever,

Charles Monteith to WG

27 July 1962

Dear Bill,

Here's a copy of THE BRASS BUTTERFLY. When you have had a chance to go through it and make the corrections you mentioned when we talked about it, do please let me have it back. And of course I'd be grateful too if you could let me have your Introduction fairly soon. I wonder if I could have it say by the end of September? About 2,000 words should be the sort of length to aim at – though it doesn't really matter very much if you want to make it a bit shorter or a bit longer.

Most terribly sorry about the muddle about dates – I do apologize again if it was my fault. I'll most certainly give you a ring early next week to fix up some firm arrangement for next weekend.

Much looking forward to seeing you.

> Yours ever,

WG to Peter du Sautoy TS

30 August 1962 [Headed Paper: Ebble Thatch]

Dear Peter,

Thanks for your letter of 29th August. I got a letter from Schwartz passed on by Richard de la Mare and forgot to answer it. My apologies to all concerned.

In fact I'd be quite interested to make some sort of record; but there are two things to say. First, as you mention, I dont know what P. Brooke would say to it – 'Yes' I should imagine, because it doesnt hurt him or the film. Second if it took any appreciable time or thought I couldn't do it because of the novel I'm writing. First things first.

The setup sounds highly unprofessional to me, though eager. It's conceivable that they might have a future; but if there's any doubt of their competence – Harcourt Brace might know – I'd sooner leave the question until some firm with all the fixings turns up. Am I too cruel, or out of order, in suggesting that I leave that to your good judgement?

I've certainly got a reputation in USA *at the moment*, which would probably stand a record, to be sold mainly on campus. But why must it be buttoned so firmly to Lord Of The Flies? I've written other things!

> Yours ever
> Bill

Harry Schwartz of Calliope Records, Boston, had contacted Golding and Faber to enquire about the possibility of recording parts of *Lord of the Flies*. He later elaborated that he would also be interested in *The Inheritors* and *Pincher Martin*. After this letter from Golding, du Sautoy turned down the offer, explaining that Golding was busy with a new novel but that he might be interested in recording *The Inheritors* and *Pincher Martin* in due course.

14 September 1962

Dear Bill,

In a recent letter to Auden I mentioned that idea which I discussed with you some time ago of a school anthology to be edited jointly by W.G. and W.H.A., and in reply here's what he says: –

> 'Your idea of an Anthology of Modern Poetry for Schools and the prospect of collaborating with William Golding (whom I've never met but would like to) intrigues me. We shall, of course, have many things to settle, before we can begin, such as the age-group or groups, and in any case, I'm pretty booked up with jobs for the coming year, but we can discuss this, all three of us, I hope, when I come to England for the last week in October.'

All of which looks very promising and I'd be absolutely delighted to fix up the meeting a trois which he suggests. I do hope that you still feel favourably disposed towards the project – even if only as a sort of pedagogic adviser. You will see that when writing to Auden I stated specifically that it was to be an anthology of Modern poetry. From the various enquiries we have made it seems that such a book would stand a better chance than a general anthology – of which there are far too many already.

All this talk about school books reminds me, too, to enquire about the Introduction for the school edition of THE BRASS BUTTERFLY. No absolutely frantic hurry for it – and of course the last thing in the world I want to do is to interrupt the final facing of BARCHESTER SPIRE – but I'd be grateful if I could have it *fairly* soon.

I did enormously enjoy lunch at Ebble Thatch in August; and I've got a horrid feeling that I never wrote to Ann to say so. Do please give her my apologies – and my best, if somewhat belated, thanks.

Rosemary is in America at the moment on a really hectic three weeks' trip. So far she has managed to fit in Quebec, Montreal, Ottawa, New York, Denver and Salt Lake City – and indeed I rather think that she gets to San Francisco today – which is pretty good going you will agree!

I am off myself to Morocco on the 24th for two or three weeks and I'm looking forward to that tremendously. So far I haven't been away at all this summer and I am beginning to feel a bit frayed at the edges.

Love to you all,

PS I gather you didn't go to Edinburgh after all. To judge from the press reports of what happened there I haven't any doubt that you made an eminently prudent decision!

The 1962 International Writers' Conference in Edinburgh had attracted garish headlines because of its frank discussion of drug use, homosexuality and pornography. There were ferocious arguments between generations of writers, as epitomised by Hugh MacDiarmid's much-reported denunciation of Alexander Trocchi as 'cosmopolitan scum' and Trocchi's description of the 'whole atmosphere' of the conference as 'turgid, petty, provincial, the stale-porridge, Bible-class nonsense'.

WG to Charles Monteith   TS

30 September 1962   [Headed Paper: Ebble Thatch]

Dear Charles,

If you're back may I drop this little job in your lap? I personally dont in the least mind Canada doing a marathon performance of Flies but I think they ought to pay more than 150 for it – and dollars too!

I saw the roughcut (Technicality) of P. Brook's film the other day and I must read the book some day which quite clearly is a terrifying piece of work. It wont be ready for release until Spring, and may be held until Cannes, where I *insist* we all go to see it.

Barchester builds slowly, but advances nevertheless.

By the way Brook told me – probably in confidence, I forget – that Sam Spiegel sold the rights to Brook's company for one hundred and fifty thousand pounds!

De profundis clamavi et cetera. All that lovely, *lovely* money! It's not just for myself, you understand; think how much F&F would have made.

      Ever
      Bill

Monteith was still holidaying in Morocco, so du Sautoy replied to Golding on 8 October. He agreed that the Canadians should pay more for a 'marathon' broadcast of *Lord of the Flies* but doubted that permission could be granted anyway now that film rights had been sold. As for Golding's revelation about the £150,000, du Sautoy pointed out that it did also include 'a fairly complete film treatment'. He lamented that MCA had sold the rights so cheaply in the first place and wished that they had waited until Golding's reputation had grown:

'I feel very regretful about it myself, but I don't see how we could have acted otherwise at the time.' Golding had received £1,000 for the rights, and as Ann pointed out to him later, he was grateful for it.

'De profundis clamavi': 'from the depths I have cried out'. The phrase comes from Psalm 130.

Charles Monteith to WG   TS

15 October 1962

Dear Bill,

I wonder if you have had a chance yet to think about Auden's very favourable reaction to the idea of a School Anthology to be edited jointly by him and by you? I only ask because I expect he will be here either next week or the week after and – if the idea does appeal to you – I'd be absolutely delighted to arrange a meeting between you so that things could be gone into in rather more detail.

And – while I am writing about pedagogic projects – I wonder if you could give me some idea of when you think you could let me have the Introduction to the school edition of THE BRASS BUTTERFLY? *Fearfully* sorry to pester you about all this – but, as you can guess, I am being pestered a bit by our production people.

Peter has been telling me all the latest news about the film, etc. I gather that the £150,000 is probably a bit exaggerated!

We must meet soon – either with or without Auden!

Love to Ann,

yours ever,

WG to Charles Monteith   TS

17 October 1962   Ebble Thatch, Bowerchalke

Dear Charles,

So you are back – sunbronzed, probably, and with sand in your hair. I shall be glad to meet you and Auden. How when where? London or Bowerchalke, those mighty hearts are possible – but Oxford (city of screaming tires) would be most convenient because at some point I could move off and give David a square meal, which judging by his ghastly digs the poor chap will probably need. And think what it would do to my morale to be seen in public with a fellow of AS and an ex-poetry-prof! BNC would probably put up a plaque (next to Haig's, war not whisky) straight away. But the end is – find somewhere convenient for Auden and yourself and I'll be there.

Will *try* and get the intro to BRASS BUTTERFLY by the end of the month. I still have a chapter and a half – or one chapter at least to write of this draft of the erection. Then a complete rethink and rewrite. It's pretty bad, by the way. Improving minimally and I'm very gloomy. But you'll get it and make up your own mind.

£150,000 *is* right. I feel just like my goldmining grandfather – in other words, feel I *ought* to mind but dont really. In fact it makes me feel rather distinguished, like a woman who just missed making Charles II. Or a man who would have won the Monte Carlo Rally if his car had started. Or a boy who would have been captain of the school if he hadnt got measles.

Holiday wants an essay from me on Irish poets. Got any ideas?

                    Ever,
                    Bill

On second thoughts pay no attention. It will have to be all mists and lakes and twilight and what the beer is like in Ballyhooley.

'those mighty hearts': Golding is jokily alluding to William Wordsworth's 'Composed upon Westminster Bridge, September 3, 1802', in which Wordsworth describes the early-morning tranquillity: 'Dear God! the very houses seem asleep; / And all that mighty heart is lying still!' Matthew Arnold famously called Oxford 'that sweet city with her dreaming spires!' in 'Thyrsis'; Golding's 'city of screaming tires' updates Arnold for the automobile age.

Auden had been Oxford's Professor of Poetry from 1956 to 1961.

General Haig had studied at Brasenose. His plaque was conveniently removed in the late 1960s when his reputation as First World War Commander-in-Chief was at its lowest ebb.

Golding's maternal grandfather, Thomas Curnoe, had gone to California in the gold rush but failed to strike it rich.

Charles Monteith to WG   TS

19 October 1962

Dear Bill,

What an excellent idea that our meeting should be in Oxford. If I can fix that up I most certainly will. Perhaps we could do it at the party on Thursday – I do hope you and Ann are coming. Auden, I know, will be there.

Many thanks for the news about THE BRASS BUTTERFLY introduction and about the Erection. Looking forward to both enormously.

Irish poets. We've got a new one coming, Richard Murphy – we'll be publishing him in January next year. What he writes might appeal to you – all very nautical. I'll enclose with this a copy of a long poem he wrote about the Galway Hooker which he now sails between Inishbofin and the coast of County Galway.

Looking forward to seeing you soon.

     Yours ever,

Richard Murphy's 'The Last Galway Hooker' was collected in his second volume, *Sailing to an Island*, published by Faber in January 1963.

WG to Charles Monteith   TS

22 October 1962   [Headed Paper: Ebble Thatch]

               Monday

Dear Charles,

Herewith the introduction to Brass Butterfly. Please say so if it's not what you want.

I imagine we shall be up with you on Thursday – arriving early to get business done here and there; then coming on to Russell Square.

No news of the book. I'm between drafts and knocking off odd jobs, since it's likely to be my only time between now and Christmas. I enjoyed the Irish boat poem – reminds me of Wild Rose.

I shall be interested to meet Auden – met Forster in Kings the other day, so it's rather like one of those American literary pilgrimages. Ask Auden to watch out, though – Forster fell down stairs twenty minutes before I got there; and you remember what happened to *John O'London's Weekly*, and *Truth* when I was going to appear in their columns.

'This man is armed.'

   We'll see you, I think, on Thursday.

       Ever

       Bill

E. M. Forster had been an undergraduate at King's College, Cambridge. In 1953, he returned as an Honorary Fellow and took up residence in college.

Truth was a British periodical that stopped publishing in December 1957. The source of 'This man is armed' has not been traced.

WG to Peter du Sautoy TS

6 November 1962   [Headed Paper: Ebble Thatch]

Dear Peter,

Thank you for your letter of the 5th. It's good to know people are showing an interest in PINCHER MARTIN, if only a tentative one. For information; Alan Badel once discussed a film of Pincher with me, when he was part of Furndel Productions. Recently some one – I forget who – told me he was still interested. Peter Brook also wants a film script from me when we are both free; and might be deflected in the direction of Pincher. There's nothing to be done about this since it's no more than just tentative – but I thought you'd like to know.

About prices: I dont know what run-of-the-mill prices are. What seems important to me is that (1) we should try and retain some degree of control over the film treatment (if Spiegel had gone with girls in LORD OF THE FLIES we could have done nothing) and (2) we should try for a percentage, the first payment being on account of it, perhaps, just as in your agreements with me over book rights. This means we should have an interest in the success or not of the final film, as far as I can see. (3) I should like to examine (or exploit) the possibilities of being employed on the script. (4) It also seems important to me that we should get a cut on any resale of the rights between firms.

You probably think all this impossible and ridiculous; and I've no doubt that faced with a – to me – enormous cashdown offer like £25000 I should back down. It certainly seems a good sum to try for.

Could we keep in touch over an offer if it comes, and the subsequent negotiations? As far as I'm concerned I dont anticipate being hard up for the next couple of years and could afford therefore to look closely at what goes on.

It was good to see you both the other day. Our love to Mollie.

Bill

There is no copy of du Sautoy's letter in the Faber archive, but other correspondence suggests that Golding may have made a mistake. The enquiry about film rights came from lawyers working on behalf of the American director Frank Perry and his screenwriter wife, Eleanor. They were interested in *Free Fall*, not *Pincher Martin*.

The actor Alan Badel set up Furndel Productions with William Furness; their base was the Westminster Theatre. Badel was a friend of Golding, having starred as Pincher in the BBC radio adaptation of *Pincher Martin*.

WG to Peter du Sautoy   TS

14 November 1962   [Headed Paper: Ebble Thatch]

Dear Peter,

I wonder whether I've made a bloomer. You see, when I was in the States, John McCallum raised the question of a scholarly work on *Flies* about which I said little – except to treat it as something of a joke. After Putnam's letter from you, I wrote him, saying what they wanted and asking if he was still interested in the idea. Of course I now realise I had no business to do this and please disown me in every direction if it'll help. But I've not heard from him since – except to get a splendid spread sent from him in the Herald Tribune which was most flattering.

It *would* be rather fun to be treated as a defunct immortal (do you remember Armada Phillip used to have requiems sung for him while he lay in a coffin?) but not if I have to write all the stuff about me myself.

If you want the honest truth, I *like* reading about myself provided the verdict is good or at least respectful; but I dont want to have to write the definitive *Flies* setup. Let them or John McCallum go ahead if they want to – but dont implicate living me in the way of writing.

One small thing: for budgeting purposes it would help if I could know the exact percentage of sale price W. Golding Ltd gets on an American paperback. Sales are enormous at the moment; and my income will determine whether I have to raid the colleges again for money.

       Ever
       Bill.

In reply on 19 November, du Sautoy reassured Golding that Putnam's and Harcourt, Brace were planning two different kinds of book. *William Golding, Lord of the Flies: Text, Notes, Criticism*, edited by James R. Baker and Arthur P. Ziegler, was published by Putnam's in 1964; *The Art of William Golding* by Bernard Oldsey and Stanley Weintraub appeared from Harcourt, Brace in 1965.

The *Herald Tribune* spread was published on 20 May 1962 as an interview by Maurice Dolbier: 'Running J. D. Salinger a Close Second'. The title quotes Golding's remark on the success of *Lord of the Flies* across American campuses.

'Armada Phillip': Philip II of Spain, who sent an ill-fated Armada to invade England in 1588.

Du Sautoy was able to inform Golding that he received 45 per cent of the gross paperback royalties for *Lord of the Flies* and *Pincher Martin* in the United States, along with 4.5 cents per copy sold of *Free Fall*.

WG to Peter du Sautoy   T S

23 November 1962   [Headed Paper: Ebble Thatch]

Dear Peter,

At last I can write a letter to you which doesnt call for a reply! Thank's very much for clearing up these points for me. It's all very flattering of course to be snowed under from America; but it *does* mean a lot of worrying and writing on my part at a time when I'd sooner not.

Twice a week I get seaboot or spectacles letters from some eager fault-hunter; twice a week I am invited by a highschool child to write its next essay for it; and so on. This, I suppose, is a moderate sort of fame, and much drearier than I once thought – 'But not the praise, Phoebus replied, and touched my trembling ears.'

Positively no answer required.

     ever

     Bill

'seaboot or spectacles letters': Golding was plagued by correspondents – mostly young boys – pointing out that spectacles for myopia, such as Piggy's in *Lord of the Flies*, cannot make fire. See Golding's letter to Monteith of 19 April 1974 for the belated solution. The seaboots appear in *Pincher Martin*: struggling to survive after being thrown into the sea, Pincher apparently kicks them off on page 2 of the novel, and yet at the end his body is recovered with the seaboots still on. Any reader who thinks that Golding has made a mistake misses the novel's metaphysical point completely.

'But not the Praise, Phoebus replied and touched my trembling ears': in John Milton's 'Lycidas', Phoebus Apollo reassures the poet that praise and fame survive death: 'Comes the blind Fury with th' abhorred shears, / And slits the thin-spun life. But not the praise, / Phoebus replied, and touch'd my trembling ears' (75–7). Golding quotes this passage several times. See his letter to Monteith of 9 January 1963 and again of 26(?) April 1985.

Charles Monteith to WG TS

15 November 1962

Dear Bill,

THE BRASS BUTTERFLY – *school edition*

Everybody we consulted seemed to think that some annotation would help the school edition of THE BRASS BUTTERFLY. As you know we have got to think not only of schools in this country but also of places like Nigeria, Malaya and Hong Kong! We took it for granted – I do hope we were right about this – that you wouldn't want to do this rather dreary little chore yourself so we have approached a Mr Michael Davis who is an English Master at Marlborough – the senior one, I think – and he says he would be very willing to do it – particularly as he's a great admirer of W.G. So don't be surprised if you get a line from him before long.

I have taken the liberty of deleting one sentence from your introduction – the one about 'A crush on the games mistress'. This just might, I am told, cause some eye brows to be raised in some of our more stuffy educational establishments. I hope you don't mind.

. . . .

What about that dinner at All Souls? I'd be absolutely delighted if you would come over one Saturday and spend the night in College. Name any Saturday you like between November 24th and December 8th – but December 1st might be the best one since it's an official guest night.

Yours ever,

The ellipses are Monteith's.

WG to Charles Monteith TS

19 November 1962   [Headed Paper: Ebble Thatch]

Dear Charles,

By all means delete the game's mistress. One cant be too careful with them. Perhaps if it's not too late I ought to have another look at the whole thing? I wrote it during interstices and it's probably pretty lousy, like the play.

198

Yes, please let Mr Davis do the notes; he'll find all the inventions were actually invented if he looks closely enough. There was a chap who invented what is now thought to be lithography, but I cant remember his name.

I am now in a state of misery over the novel and have a fog between it and myself; but I've sworn some sort of oath not to let up on it until it's there, no matter what. Could I accept your offer, take the day off and come to All Souls for the night of Saturday, 1st? That would be fun. I'll find a hole somewhere for the car and turn up at your rooms between tea and dinner unless I hear to the contrary.

Yours ever,
Bill

Golding's published introduction makes no mention of games mistresses. Michael Davis may well have written the notes, but he is not acknowledged anywhere in the edition.

'All the inventions were actually invented': various inventions are presented to the Roman Emperor in the course of *The Brass Butterfly*, including the steam engine and gunpowder. These were invented in China at an indeterminate date; the play's final joke is that the Emperor sends Phanocles to be ambassador to China, with the implication that he is responsible for the technological advances that lie ahead. The Greeks invented a form of lithography involving a process of covering stone in wax and etching with a stencil.

Charles Monteith to WG   TS

20 November 1962

Dear Bill,

Absolutely delighted that you can come to All Souls on December 1st. Do turn up any time between tea and dinner. We dine at 7.30 p.m. – so if you arrive about 6.0 there will be plenty of time to change and have a drink beforehand. (Black tie) Looking forward enormously to seeing you then.

Here's THE BRASS BUTTERFLY introduction back. There's plenty of time to play about with it if you would like to make some alterations – but I'm sure it's OK as it stands. Thank you, too, for giving the OK to Davis doing the notes. I know he will be getting in touch with you – if, indeed, you haven't heard from him already.

Yours ever,

23 November 1962   [Headed Paper: Ebble Thatch]

Dear Charles,

Six o'clock be it, with a black tie and a decently respectful attitude to your stupendous society.

I'm returning the introduction to BB slightly emended. I'm suffering from a strong suspicion at the moment that this piece was originally written by G.B.S. as a preface to one of his plays – Ceasar and Cleopatra, perhaps. It ought to be good, therefore; but do you think one of Davis' subsidiary jobs should be checking the authorship? My mind reels at the prospect of rewriting it. Anyway I remember being struck by the uncanny likeness one of G.B.S.'s essays bears to Swift's Modest Proposal; so unless you think everybody will notice, let's leave things as they are.

I have an interior picture of what Barchester Spire (Peter insists on that title, not by saying anything directly but by always referring to the book that way) of what it should be, and am facing the task of making it that way, reduced to a whimpering, cringing, moaning thing, ninety percent convinced of its own incapacity.

If only someone could write a novel about the inside of the Rome Congress (RC) – like Advise and Consent, what a best, best seller it would be! I strongly advise you to see about that if you have a pliable RC novelist up your sleeve. All he would have to have would be Latin and the entree.

Would you like a book of essays and criticism? Putnam's Sons would; and I'm only very, very slightly serious.

Would you like a book of verse? No, I thought not. Nobody would, not even Putnam.

We are all slightly hysterical here because we are having the cottage altered and workmen march through everywhere like the kings in Macbeth.

It looks as though I shall be going to the States for a month in February; and when I know the dates for sure I'll get in touch with you about seeing Auden.

     ever
      Bill

G.B.S.: George Bernard Shaw.

The Rome Congress was the Second Vatican Council (1962–5), called by Pope John XXIII in order to update and renew the Roman Catholic Church. Allen Drury's *Advise and Consent* (1959), filmed in 1962, is a fictional account of the machinations of the US Senate in response to the president's attempt to appoint a prominent liberal politician as Secretary of State. Golding had been sent a copy by the Book Society along with a forlorn note requesting its return; the book and the note are still in the Golding family's library.

Charles Monteith to WG   TS

26 November 1962

My dear Bill,

Absolutely delighted that everything is fixed up about next Saturday. Looking forward enormously to seeing you about 6 o'clock.

And of course you are right about the introduction to BB. As I told you when I last wrote it's absolutely splendid!

All I can do about BARCHESTER SPIRE, I fear (Peter says, plaintively, that he's not trying to force that title on you and that it's entirely up to you, etc., etc., etc!) is to send you my sympathy. I know what I feel like when I'm trying to write a blurb – but what it must be like with a full length novel I simply can't imagine!

Advise and Consent about the Rome Congress – what an absolute world beater of an idea. My mind is buzzing with possible titles already.

A book of essays and criticism? Any time you would like one published push it straight at me. About the poetry though I would counsel caution!

The trip to the States sounds very exciting; and I've got a feeling that the Golding/Auden anthology is going to be quite something.

Until Saturday.

Yours ever,

Despite his denials, du Sautoy seems to have been resolute in his preference: after reading a draft, he writes to Golding on 17 May 1963 congratulating him on 'BARCHESTER SPIRE' and adds in parentheses, 'I think that should really be the title'. His commitment may have been a subtle way of ruling out 'An Erection at Barchester'.

WG to Charles Monteith

TS

6 December 1962

Dear Charles,

At last I have braced myself to write to you and thank you for your hospitality. It was very nearly an utterly wholesome occasion, a happy one, and I am now almost completely recovered from it. Perhaps, if I reach the age of eighty – which doesnt seem very likely – you will ask me again so that I can prove my hardwon ability to act like a civilised person.

My cracked nose and ribs I have passed off by airy references to the fog, ice, and the nearness to me of the steering wheel; an explanation which has been received on all sides with cynical reserve. It is all very humiliating. I beg that we may never refer to the actual circumstances again. To quote a contemporary. 'There is no owl.'

Yours apologetically and at the same time savagely,

Bill

The letter is written on unheaded paper.

Quite what transpired at All Souls that evening is, as Golding evidently wished, lost to time. The contemporary whom Golding quotes is T. H. White: 'There is no owl' comes from the third chapter of *The Sword in the Stone* (1938), as Archimedes the talking owl steadfastly denies the undeniable. Golding taught *The Sword in the Stone* at Hollins.

WG to Peter du Sautoy

TS

13 December 1962   [Headed Paper: Ebble Thatch]

Thursday

Dear Peter,

Thanks for your letter and the enclosure. Peter Brook certainly seems to have employed a complex setup. I dont know when the film will be out, and to tell the truth, I'm not particularly interested. What will be, will be, et cetera.

It seems OK to me to let Curtis Brown handle the serial rights of my novels in USA since that is apparently OK with you.

We are having the *devil* of a time here, what with having the house altered and difficulties with the children – or young people as I suppose I should now call them.

Ever

Bill

Du Sautoy had sent Golding a *Guardian* article by Maurice Hatton and Richard de la Mare (the latter being 'not our Chairman but his homonymous son') about Peter Brook's films and working practices.

Adding to the confusion over the status of Golding's American publications, MCA had been closed down by the United States government in July for breaching antitrust laws. Golding's agents, Curtis Brown, requested permission to take over the handling of North American serial rights for his novels, to which du Sautoy and Golding readily agreed.

1963

Now a full-time writer free from routine teaching commitments, Golding takes the opportunity to travel. The year is bookended with lecture trips to the United States. During the first, Golding falls ill and suffers a breakdown. Alcohol is becoming a problem; he is drinking heavily again while at Cannes for the premiere of Peter Brook's *Lord of the Flies* in June. Summer brings a conference in Leningrad and a visit to Nikita Khrushchev at his Black Sea dacha, followed by a September holiday staying on Lesbos with his friend Peter Green. The new novel refuses to come easily, but after several rewrites *The Spire* is ready in November. The year ends with a far more successful trip to the United States, during which Putnam's repeats its proposal to publish a collection of essays and reviews. This becomes *The Hot Gates* (1965).

Charles Monteith to WG   TS

2 January 1963

Dear Bill,

I enclose a copy of a letter I have just had from Gerald Pollinger of Laurence Pollinger Limited. Could you possibly bear to autograph a LORD OF THE FLIES for young Mr Wallace? If so do let me know and I'll send you a copy down.

Are you completely snowed up at Ebble Thatch? Things are fairly nasty here – but they seem to be worse the further South and West one goes. Any way, all the best to all of you for 1963 – let's hope it warms up a bit.

> Yours ever,

The novelist Irving Wallace had been in touch with Gerald Pollinger, looking to acquire a signed copy of *Lord of the Flies* for his fourteen-year-old son. *Lord of the Flies*, Wallace explained, had become 'the Holy Writ in this house as it is in the houses of my son's companions'.

The Big Freeze of 1962–3 was one of the coldest winters on record in Britain.

WG to Charles Monteith

5 January 1963   [Headed Paper: Ebble Thatch]

Dear Charles,

Yes of course I'll send a copy of Flies for young Mr Wallace. Unfortunately though I dont know his father's books and cant remember meeting him. If twere done twere well twere done quickly because I leave for USA on the 30th January – leaving work still to be done on Barchester when I get back in early March.

We have been thoroughly snowed up. I had two very near misses in the car and since then have refused to drive until the roads are clear – which should be any day now.

What about W. H. Auden and the anthology?

> Yours ever
> Bill

Golding alludes to Macbeth's plotting of the murder of Duncan: 'If it were done when 'tis done, then 'twere well / It were done quickly' (1.7.1–2).

WG to Peter du Sautoy

8 January 1963   [Headed Paper: Ebble Thatch]

Dear Peter,

Thanks for your letter – which alas, I've lost somewhere in the awful wreckage of house alterations and general uproar. It's pleasant and comforting to have your sympathy; but I dont deserve it – am just going through a black period and can only hope to come out the other end.

I leave for USA (singing for a bite of supper) on 30th Jan; and shall be back, I think on 5th March. Barchester Spire stands there, remote and mocking. I *must* do what amounts to a half-rewrite heaven help me. I may be in London before the 30th and if so, will let you know.

When the alterations are done, you must both come and stay with us, and if she feels inclined, Mollie can play Paderewski's piano.

> Yours ever
> Bill

Du Sautoy had written to sympathise over the 'troubles and difficulties' that Golding had outlined in his letter of 12 December. The Bechstein grand that Golding had bought was said to have been one of Ignacy Jan Paderewski's practice pianos.

Charles Monteith to WG   TS

8 January 1963

Dear Bill,

Thank you very much for saying you will sign a copy of FLIES for Mr Wallace junior. Here it is – together with a label, etc., for return to me. I'll pass it on to Wallace via Pollinger. Like you, I don't know anything about Wallace senior's books – but his new novel, THE PRIZE, has had a lot of advance advertising in THE BOOKSELLER and Cassells, who are publishing it, evidently think they have a big seller on their hands – I think it's all about the Nobel Prize intrigues.

Oh goodness! A horrid thought has *just* struck me. I have a horrid suspicion that Mr Wallace wrote THE CHAPMAN REPORT! But even if I'm right about this I'm sure you wouldn't wish to visit the sins of the fathers on the children.

Not at all surprised to hear about the snowing up. Things are getting much better here – but it was still snowing slightly when I came in this morning. And now of course there's this threatened power cut. Lucky you to be getting away to America.

I'll be writing again in a day or two about Auden and the Anthology.
                    Yours ever,

PS I have just heard from Professor Baker of San Diego State College who is about to start work on the first full scale biography and critical study of W.G. I've told him of course that he may see all the biographical notes, etc., which we have. This is real fame at last!

Irving Wallace's *The Chapman Report* (1960) was filmed in 1962. Both novel and film follow a team of psychologists as they interview women for a study of their sexual attitudes and behaviour.

James Baker's *William Golding: A Critical Study*, was published in New York by St Martin's Press in 1965.

WG to Charles Monteith TS

9 January 1963   [Headed Paper: Ebble Thatch]

Dear Charles,

Herewith FLIES for young Wallace. I'm *pawing* at B Spire; but maybe something is happening.

Yes, I knew about Baker and his book on W.G. He asked my permission to write it, more or less; and I just wasnt strong-minded enough to pass up the chance of reading 250 pages about myself. That has led to a sort of landslide of questionnaires and what have you. It's best to agree to this sort of thing when you're dead. I dont know anything about Baker, but suspect he'd have written the book anyway because he's got a contract for it. But I agree it's fame at last, and Phoebus is touching my trembling ears. The other aspect of this is a steady trickle of letters from High School students who want me to write their essays for them.

I'd be glad of a copy of the intro to BRASS BUTTERFLY if it's not *too* inconvenient. An off-Broadway theatre is doing it and I'd like the producer to read what I have to say about it. I might be able to persuade him to be fast and astringent rather than cosy.

> Yours ever
> Bill

'fame at last, and Phoebus is touching my trembling ears': Golding also quotes these lines from John Milton's 'Lycidas' in the letter to du Sautoy of 23 November 1962, and to Monteith in the letter of 26(?) April 1985.

Although trailed in the *New York Times*, the off-Broadway production of *The Brass Butterfly* does not seem to have taken place.

Charles Monteith to WG TS

14 January 1963

Dear Bill,

Just a brief line to thank you very much indeed for that signed copy of FLIES for young Wallace, which went off to him today.

The only copy of the introduction to BRASS BUTTERFLY is with Michael Davies at Marlborough. We have written to him today asking him to send it on to you – and I do hope it reaches you safely.

Will you, I wonder, be up in London before you leave for America? Do please let me know if you are. Perhaps we could meet and talk, among other things, about the Auden/Golding anthology.

Yours ever,

PS I needn't tell you how delighted I am to hear that something may be happening about BARCHESTER SPIRE!

Charles Monteith to WG   TS

22 January 1963

Dear Bill,

Forgive me please for not having written before now with the memorandum which I promised you dealing with the various points we covered in our talk about the school anthology last week. But here it is now.

In the first place do please let me emphasize again what I said when we met – that all these suggestions are simply suggestions and nothing more. We would be delighted with *any* anthology which you and Wystan Auden produced for us; and if you don't like any of these ideas do please just discard them. But here, subject to all that, is the sort of book we have in mind:

i CONTENTS. The anthology should be confined to Modern Poetry. The definition of that ambiguous but useful phrase we are happy to leave to the editors.

ii LENGTH. About 200 pages. I think this should be treated as a maximum.

iii INTRODUCTION. About 3,000 words.

iv NOTES. From various enquiries we have made from schools, educational authorities, etc., it seems that Notes on the poems selected would in fact increase the book's chances of being adopted by examination Boards and becoming a 'set book'. So if you feel you can provide Notes we would be delighted. At the same time we fully realise that this sort of annotation could be the most ghastly chore; and we certainly wouldn't dream of insisting – or seeming to insist – on Notes. This is entirely up to the editors.

v READERSHIP AIMED AT. Subject very much to your advice we feel that it would be desirable to aim the book at an O Level audience i.e., roughly speaking, fifteen year olds.

That I think about covers it; but do please let me know if I've missed anything out or if there are any other points we ought to talk about.

Here, by the way, is Auden's New York address –

77 St Mark's Place,

NEW YORK CITY 3.

I needn't say how much I look forward to hearing how it all works out.

I don't suppose I shall see you again until you are back from America so bon voyage. I do hope everything goes very well indeed. I much enjoyed seeing you again the other day.

Love to Ann and the family.

> Yours ever,

WG to Charles Monteith   TS

19 March 1963   [Headed Paper: Ebble Thatch]

Dear Charles,

Well I'm back after a hell of a trip. I got Asian flu the day I landed and it knocked out the first week or more of the visit. So I didnt get in touch with Auden until too late – he was leaving on a lecture tour next morning. We agreed to meet in England when he's here in late April. I'm sorry about the delay but it was disease and nothing else.

A point has arisen about a volume of occasional pieces. Harcourt Brace and Putnam's sons both want to do one from me, and I seem to remember you saying you were willing. Normally I would arrange this directly with you in simple faith; but having these other two firms angling makes the situation more complex. So I shall have to put it in the hands of Dudley Barker at Curtis Brown who will get in touch with you. But if I may do him an infinitisimal bit of dirt in advance, I dont imagine any other British publishers are interested! I'm using him solely to stand between me and the pressures of the NY gang.

My hands are still shaking slightly from the terrors of an unwived journey through the eastern states. I long to get down to the novel and reconstitute the butt end of it.

> Ever
> Bill

Golding's lecture tour had been calamitous: he was lonely, lost, ill and barely functional for much of the time. He described the episode as a 'sheer terrible fantasy, a Pincher-ish fantasy'.

Charles Monteith to WG

TS

21 March 1963

Dear Bill,

Delighted you are back – but sorry the trip was hell. There must have been a few bright spots, surely! I was very impressed when I saw your picture on display in the Cunard Offices in Lower Regent Street – distinguished people just arriving in New York via Cunard.

The volume of occasional pieces. Yes of course; we would be absolutely delighted to take this – and we would have no objection at all to dealing with it via Dudley Barker. But I wonder if there is really any need for him to cope with the British rights? I can quite see the reason for putting the American rights in his hands; but, if you would like us to, we would be very willing indeed to make an ordinary direct contract with you for the Commonwealth. Do please let me know what you feel about this. I'd be only too pleased to make you an offer of terms straightaway and get everything tied up.

Too bad about the Auden business – but of course I realise that it was impossible. As you say, he will be here in about a months time and I'd be tremendously grateful to both of you if you would talk the anthology idea over then. Of course there's no hurry – we would be very happy indeed to accept any completion date which fitted in with your other plans, and his.

And of course I'm looking forward, more than to anything else, to Barchester Spire – if that's what it *is* going to be called.

Love to you all,

Charles Monteith to WG

TS

26 April 1963

Dear Bill,

I wonder if you managed to make contact with Auden when he was in London last week? He was only here for a very short time; and I missed him myself since I was in Ireland for ten days. If, by any chance, you didn't make contact I'm sure there will be an opportunity later on when he is on his way back from Austria.

Any more news, I wonder, about the book of occasional pieces which we have been corresponding about? As you know, we'd be absolutely delighted to give you a contract for it any time you like – and it doesn't matter at all whether it's made direct with you or via Dudley Barker.

I had lunch the other day with Ian Gregor who tells me that he and Mark Kincaid-Weekes are planning to write a book on W.G.; but they feel it ought to include a discussion on Barchester Spire. I've promised them a proof copy. I've also heard – only this morning – from Professor James R. Baker of San Diego State College. His Golding book, he tells me, he has got one third finished and he expects to see it published in a year or so.

If you – or you and Ann – are planning a visit to London, do please let me know. We must arrange to have a meal together. And I imagine you are both planning a trip to Cannes for the Film Festival. The film sounds as though it's going to be very exciting.

Yours ever,

WG to Charles Monteith   TS

1 May 1963   [Headed Paper: Ebble Thatch]

Dear Charles,

Thanks for your letter. No, I didnt catch Auden. Maybe on his way back? But I dont know when that will be, or where.

Juliet O'Hea has bowed out of the essay book as far as you are concerned. It would consist I suppose of all my odd writings, some very odd; but I dont know if there's enough. In any case I'm so excruciated over this damned book I cant do anything about anything else. I've written it four times, each time getting a bit worse – now I'm writing it backwards. Looking for motives and God knows what they are. Even Ann cant help; she's as confused about it as I am, after all these drafts. I expect to finish this – rough, at least – in a week or two. Can I send it to you then for an opinion – i.e. will you tell me whether to drop it or go on? I seem to be writing in thick gloves.

I dont know about Cannes. I shall only go if the company pays for me; and I dont *really* want to see the film anyway. Might be worth it for a possible answer to an interview question; 'Mr Golding, what alterations would you like to see to this film?' Answer; 'I should like to make some money out of it.' They may make a film of FREE FALL though. That will be entertaining to watch – the American idea of pre-war Britain; a cross between CAVALCADE and MRS MINIVER I've no doubt.

Well, I must make another effort at this accursed book.

> Ever
> Bill

Hopes for an anthology edited by Golding and Auden were extinguished after these various failures to arrange a further meeting. Golding had not warmed to Auden when he met him the previous October. After watching a programme about him in 1982, Golding recorded in his journal that 'I think it's just as well I had Asian 'flu and never got round to doing with him the anthology that Charles wanted – I don't think we'd have got on. Meeting him at a party was enough' (J, 28 February 1982).

Juliet O'Hea and Dudley Barker at Curtis Brown must have concluded that there was no point in trying to negotiate on Golding's behalf in the UK when *The Hot Gates* was inevitably going to end up with Faber.

Cavalcade (1933) and *Mrs Miniver* (1942) are Hollywood representations of English society. Golding implies that they do not entirely ring true. No film of *Free Fall* was made.

Charles Monteith to WG   TS

6 May 1963

Dear Bill,

Thank you very much for your letter. Yes, of course; do please send me the book as soon as the draft you are working on now is finished. You know that I'd be more than willing to read it and to let you know what I think about it. Looking forward to it enormously.

And do send the essays as soon as you can find a moment to collect them together. Delighted that we will be dealing with you direct about them in the usual way.

What splendid news that they may be making a film of FREE FALL. It *could* be something very remarkable indeed.

Love to Ann and you all.

> Yours ever,

WG to Charles Monteith

TS

7 May 1963

Tuesday

Dear Charles,

Herewith this stuff. At the very best, it is still wildly imperfect; but perhaps there is something there; at the worst, it must be scrapped.

I've just tried this time to find a story line; and a lot is first-time cobbling.

Can you help? *Is* there anything there? How great are the irrelevances? Does a story of this sort have any right to be published at this day and age?

Ann thinks some of it is good. I hope so. God knows, I dont know myself.

I'm taking Judy down to Cannes for a few days – she's been miserable lately, poor child and I hope she'll convalesce a bit.

Sorry to push this footling job on to you

Ever
Bill

'this stuff': the typescript of 'Barchester Spire'.

Charles Monteith to WG

TS

9 May 1963

Dear Bill,

I think we have arranged – it's almost but not *quite* definite – for a private preview of the film of LORD OF THE FLIES at 5 p.m. on Thursday, May 30th. If all goes according to plan we hope to invite a number of London booksellers, etc., etc., to launch the film edition of the book. And of course we very much hope that you, Ann – and Judy and David too – will be able to come. Do please keep that date free and we'll keep in touch with you about details.

Something quite different. We have decided to follow up the school edition of LORD OF THE FLIES with the school edition of THE INHERITORS; and Gregor and Kincaid-Weekes have agreed to do the introduction and notes. It won't, I'm afraid, – and I ought to mention this now – have anything like as big a sale as LORD OF THE FLIES which, as you know, has been extremely successful as a school edition; but it should do quite reasonably well. With any luck, we ought to get it out some time early next year. May I take it that the same terms as those we agreed on for the school edition of LORD OF THE FLIES would be OK i.e. a straight 7½% royalty? If so do please let me know and Peter du Sautoy will be sending you a contract.

Looking forward enormously to reading BARCHESTER SPIRE.

Yours ever,

PS The typescript of your novel arrived just as I was signing this. Absolutely delighted to have it – and of course I'll be writing the moment I've finished reading it. That may not be for a few days – I seem to have got rather bunged up with various odd things that I've got to do – and I'd like to save your book until I can settle down to read it with reasonable prospects of tranquillity and lack of distraction ahead.

I suppose that your trip to Cannes with Judy will cancel your visit to London for the LORD OF THE FLIES preview here; and, if so, of course I'll understand, if you don't feel like having a sneak preview in London. I do hope you will though – and, even if you don't – what about Ann and David?

Monteith put a note on file reporting that he had spoken to Golding by telephone on 16 May and reassured him that he and Peter du Sautoy had formed 'the same high opinion' about the manuscript. A separate note from Rosemary Goad to Monteith, dated 23 May, argues that 'the end is terrific' but that 'the book does not really get going until about halfway through'. Faber offered terms of a straight 15 per cent royalty and an advance of £500.

WG to Peter du Sautoy   TS

1 June 1963   [Headed Paper: Ebble Thatch]

Dear Peter,

Herewith the agreements, signed, if not sealed.

It was very good of you both to let us break in with our glad rags and then take such care of us. The occasion was not really so very frightening after all, but full of flunkeys, pikemen, sheriffs, recorders, sword bearers, officers of guards, trumpeters – the lot, in fact. It wasnt beautiful, just prosperous power, and a vast accumulation of

middleclass history. I was fascinated. We stored it all up for our puta-
tive grandchildren.

As for we representatives of art, literature and science, we were
rather a ghastly crew, I thought; but we did meet Angus Wilson for the
first time, and Coco the Clown – a very worthy occasion, and one we
wouldnt have missed. So thank you again.

                    Ever
                    Bill

One of the agreements was the contract for *The Spire*.

Whatever the 'occasion' was with its pomp and flunkeys, the memory of it did
not get passed down to Golding's grandchildren.

Golding never knew the novelist Angus Wilson especially well, but the two
men enjoyed each other's company whenever they met. Golding admired Wilson's
best-known novel, *Anglo-Saxon Attitudes*, and taught it at Hollins. When Wilson
ran into financial difficulties in the 1980s, Golding contributed to a hardship
fund set up on his behalf.

Charles Monteith to WG   TS

21 June 1963

Dear Bill,

Forgive me, please, for having not written long before now about
BARCHESTER SPIRE but I wanted to try to clear a space, as it were,
during which I could really read and think about it carefully – and I
didn't manage to do that until a day or two ago.

Now that I have re-read it – and re-read it more than once – I am
even more deeply impressed by it than I was before. It really is, I'm certain, a most remarkable and distinguished novel; and I am enormously
looking forward to its publication.

I haven't, as you will see, got any suggestions at all for major changes
– simply a list of points, some very trivial, which occurred to me as I
went through the book.

In addition I have attempted two other things.
a) I have tried – but quite certainly I haven't succeeded – to do what's
called 'preparing a typescript for the printer' i.e. attended to capitalisation, commas, inverted commas, etc., etc. You will find lots of small
pencil marks of this nature – but I'm sure I haven't succeeded in catching every point that ought to have been caught. No need to worry

though. This is the sort of thing which professional proof readers are very good at – and which they will certainly keep an eye out for.

b) I've also had a shot at drawing up a suggested division into chapters. I am inclined to think that would be preferable to the book's present shape – i.e. one long continuous narrative. I'll set out this suggested chapter scheme as an appendix to this letter; and I've even, as you will see, had a shot at thinking up some chapter titles. But of course this scheme is *only* a suggestion. Don't hesitate to scrap it altogether if you don't like it; or to play about with it as much as you please.

Now for the specific points.

page 7   *The Tent*

I've got a feeling I am being stupid here but I don't, I must confess, really understand all the many references throughout the text – I think the first one comes here – to the 'tent'. There are others on pages 13, 21, 29, 30, 34, 45, 49, 50, 63, 77, 82, etc., etc. I can see – or I think I can – that the 'tent' refers to or symbolises a state of sexual attraction – either in a direct or sublimated form – between Jocelin and Goody Pangall and, later on, between Roger Mason and Goody P. But why the 'tent'? In an earlier draft was there perhaps a real tent? Or did Jocelin have some vision or hallucination evoked by Goody P. of being inside a tent. Perhaps connected with all this are the references to the 'arranged marriage' (e.g. pp 79–83)? This seems to refer to Pagnall's marriage; but, again, I get the impression that in some earlier draft more information about it was given. Perhaps I've simply missed some most fearfully obvious clue – and, if so, I can only ask you to forgive me. But I do feel that the 'tent' references and hints about the former history of Pagnall and his wife should be explained a little more explicitly. Peter du Sautoy also tells me that *he* was puzzled by the 'tent' while he was reading the novel.

page 11–13   The letter isn't really explained until a very long time later – pages 107 et seq. Perhaps that's quite deliberate though? I only wondered in rather an uncertain way about whether or not a little more explication at this point mightn't be a help.

216

page 26	I agree, I think, with your own note here i.e. that the Bishop's character should be slightly elaborated at this stage – particularly in view of Jocelin's Aunt's laughter when she hears that he has sent a nail instead of money.
page 37 *Ivo*	Again, I suspect that I am being stupid; but I must confess that I am very puzzled by Ivo who only appears – so far as I can discover – twice, once on page 37 and once on page 135. Because of the similarity between what happens to Ivo on page 37 and what, according to Anselm, had happened to Jocelin many years before (page 123) Ivo must be, I suspect, another young protégé of somebody – perhaps Jocelin himself – who, in all innocence, is being pushed up the ladder of ecclesiastical preferment with the help of a powerful friend. Again, might the answer be that Ivo played a more prominent part in an earlier draft? He can't, I think be a character of any importance – at any rate in the present version – and I wonder if it mightn't perhaps be the simplest thing to drop him altogether?
page 53	Jocelin tells the dumb stone carver that he owes his life to him. Presumably the young man helped Jocelin during the riot – but I wonder if this shouldn't be made a little more explicit in your description of the riot itself?
page 54	Am I right in having deleted the unfinished sentence at the bottom of page 54? I wonder if the transition from the end of page 54 to page 55 doesn't need a little smoothing out? Is there a connecting sentence missing?
page 60	A tiny and rather pedantic point. I've changed 'mules in foal with panniers' to 'asses in foal with panniers'. I realise, of course, that the animals are only in foal metaphorically, so to speak; but since mules can never, in reality, get into foal at all I thought this might create a little confusion!
page 70 et seq.	*The steel band* I'm sure I am raising a hare here but I do wonder if 'steel' isn't anachronistic. I asked R. W. Southern who frightened me by replying 'I'm not sure I understand what is meant by steel'!

page 74	I assumed that the purpose of the fire was to temper – or fix or do something essential to – the steel band; but, as someone woefully ignorant about these matters I'd have welcomed a little more explanation.
page 75	*The new counter*
	Here, again, I am being stupid – but I don't understand what the 'new counter' in fact is.
page 94	Was I right in supplying the word 'say' or should it have been something else?
page 106	I'm not quite clear how the last sentence on this page is meant to read.
page 138 . . .	. . . .

A lot of these, I fear, are fearfully tiresome and footling but if you could look at them I'd be enormously grateful. Then, I think, the next step is to get the whole book into galley proof rather than straight into page. In galley it would be very easy to do any additional polishing and preparing for the printer than needs to be done; and we could also get a set of galleys off Harcourt Brace.

I do hope this is of some use – but I've got a horrid suspicion that it's not.

Anyway, this is a *terribly* good book and I'm very much excited by it.

Yours ever,

PS The chapter suggestions are attached.

SUGGESTED DIVISIONS INTO CHAPTERS.

I have included, for each chapter, a number of alternative suggestions for chapter titles. My own personal preference is, in each case, the first one.

Chapter I	Dust in the Air	page 1
	Stone Bird	
	Jocelin's Folly	
Chapter II	Bishop's Move	page 18
	The Master Builder	(starting from
	Building Afloat	'There was less
	A Defended Place	dust in the air')
Chapter III	The Earth Creeps	page 35
	Creeping Earth	

....

It has just occurred to me that if you are still uncertain about the title for the book as a whole one or two of these might just perhaps be worth thinking about e.g. *Dust in the Air* or *The Earth Creeps*.

Golding incorporated many of Monteith's suggestions but he did not give titles to the chapters.

R. W. Southern was a leading medieval historian and one of Monteith's colleagues at All Souls.

'A Plumb in his Mouth': Jocelin's aunt asks the King to drop a plum in her nephew's mouth – to further his career by finding him a prestigious position. Monteith's inspired mistake shows the influence of the masons' tools. Monteith also misnames Pangall as Pagnall twice. The ellipses following 'page 138' are his own.

WG to Charles Monteith

25 June 1963   [Headed Paper: Ebble Thatch]

Dear Charles,

Thanks for your immense work and help. What you've done is give me a sort of fresh or objective look at the book. I'll certainly clear up your queries in the course of a re-do.

The title still bothers me; but we dont have to worry at the moment. Is it now *fixed* that this is for the Spring List? I ask, because if you had any ideas for September or October, I'd work like a black and get it to you in July. But if not, then I've set myself September as a kind of dead line. I hope that'll give your production side time to do the job in comfort.

I want to finish by September, because Ann and I plan to spend September – or mid-Sept/mid-Oct, with the Peter Greens in Mytilini; and I'm getting thirsty for sun and Greece.

That's it for now, then. I've just done a sort of synopsis of the whole book, using your chapter divisions. I agree with the idea of chapters and will now meditate on each as a gobbet.

Once again, my deep thanks for doing this finicky, devoted job. I only hope the book (or author rather) doesnt disappoint your expectations.

   Ever
   Bill

Golding's chapters do not quite follow Monteith's scheme: Monteith suggests ten chapters, whereas the published novel has eleven.

 Now widely recognised as racist, the expression 'work like a black' was common at the time as a variation on 'work like a slave'.

Charles Monteith to WG

27 June 1963

Dear Bill,

Thank you very much indeed for your letter of June 25th. Delighted that all those rather finicky queries may be of some use; and I needn't tell you how much I look forward to the final version. The title of course can be left – there's no immediate hurry about it, though we would like to get it settled *fairly* soon. It would be useful for preliminary announcements, etc.

It really is too late, I'm afraid, for autumn publication. Our autumn list was closed some time ago; and, indeed, the autumn catalogue is already with the printers. In any event, I'm sure it's better to wait until the spring of 1964 so that our sales and publicity people have got plenty of time to do a really thorough job in promoting the book in advance.

Mytilini in September sounds absolutely marvellous. I do envy you that enormously. Incidentally, I am going down to Dorset for the weekend 12th–14th July; and I wondered if I might invite myself down – for lunch, say, or tea – on Friday, 12th – and be picked up in the usual way later on in the evening? Of course if it's inconvenient it doesn't matter a bit – but Ann did say to let her know the next time I was likely to be near Salisbury.

Yours ever,

WG to Charles Monteith   TS

7 July 1963   [Headed Paper: Ebble Thatch]

Dear Charles,

Yes *do* come and see us – either next Friday or Sunday or both. I believe we shall have a more or less empty house over that weekend, so you wont be battered by people.

Could you drop me a card telling me what train to meet, or let me know alternatively if you propose to come by car?

Ann sends her love. We both look forward to seeing you.

Ever
Bill

PS Make it lunch if you can.

WG to Charles Monteith   TS

16 October 1963   [Headed Paper: Ebble Thatch]

Dear Charles,

Herewith yet another draft of this ghastly book. It's become a sort of Old Man of the Sea as far as I'm concerned. According to Peter du Sautoy and Dudley Barker it is now to be typed – I hope this is so; because sometime in the future (preferably the distant future) I'll have to try and exercise some sort of final judgement on the whole ludicrous thing. *If* it's not too impossible, could I have this MS back as well as the typescript? So far, Ann, I, you, Peter, Rosemary, and Peter Green have read it. P.G. said the book is *there*; but I might try it on Ian Gregor and Mark Kinkhead-Weekes. I seem to have written the whole thing with one arm tied behind my back. I will *never* try to be portentous again.

Now I'm going to try and find something to write which will amuse me. If I wrote two more long shorts, would they and ENVOY EXTRAORDINARY make a book? And I might also start thinking about that book of essays. I suppose it would need some more written?

I've had an idea at the back of my mind for a long time for a set of four long essays (might call it FOUR ENTHUSIASMS) on Greek, Sailing, Music, Archaeology. They'd be accounts of personal approaches rather than authoritative contributions; and I'd probably be scat critically by everyone who knows anything about any of them. The uninformed amateur is out, is he not? Well, it's all I am. And now I come to think of it, they'd very nearly be a biography; a thing I'd privately decided never to write.

Mark sent me the notes on THE INHERITORS; and left me feeling fraudulent and humble. Well, never mind.

All the same; between now and a final revision of THE SPIRE I've got a little time to think. My main thought at the moment is that the place I want to be is somewhere in the Nafplion–Epidavros region; but that wont do, I must write something to take this taste out of my mouth.

What do you think?

Ann came back, only to catch a cold, and is in bed nursing it; but sends her love.

> Ever
> Bill

According to an internal memo written by Monteith, one of the titles that Golding had jokingly proposed for *The Spire* was 'The Old Man and the See', punning on Hemingway's 1952 novella. Another, after John Braine's novel of 1957, was 'Room at the Top'.

'I'd probably be scat critically': reflecting his Cornish roots, Golding seems to be using 'scat' in its dialect sense: to 'scat' something is to shatter it into pieces.

Charles Monteith to WG TS

21 October 1963

Dear Bill,

Just a brief note to say that THE SPIRE – that title will do admirably – has reached me safely; and that I'll certainly arrange to have it retyped as quickly as I possibly can. Once that's done I will of course send the text back to you together with the typescript.

We are getting most fearfully and dangerously near the absolute and final deadline which makes spring publication really and literally impossible; so I do hope you will feel – when you read it afresh – that it's OK. I shan't reread it again myself until I have the new typescript.

My own personal reactions to all the other possible books you mention are simply, yes, yes, yes; but let me talk about them at our editorial committee on Wednesday and I'll be able to pass on the views of everybody else.

Terribly sorry to hear about Ann's cold – I got one myself shortly after coming back and I sympathise. I hope she's much better by the time you get this letter. You will give her my love, won't you?

Yours ever,

An internal memo from Monteith dated 18 October reports, 'It was definitely decided at the Book Committee on October 16th that the title of William Golding's new novel – which we hope to publish in the spring of next year is THE SPIRE.'

Charles Monteith to WG TS

24 October 1963

Dear Bill,

THE SPIRE

I have just had a long and tremendously enthusiastic letter from Peter Green about THE SPIRE and of course I'm delighted – though not in the least surprised – that he thinks as highly of it as Peter and Rosemary and I do. I'm looking forward enormously to reading it again when I have the retyped version – which should be here some time next week. I'll send one copy of it back to you together with the manuscript; and Peter will send one copy to Dudley Barker with the warning that it must not be treated as a final version and that nothing must be serialised from it without your approval. That's right, isn't it? And Peter wonders, too, if he could send a copy to John McCallum at the same time? Do please let me know.

We are putting THE SPIRE into our spring list though of course this doesn't absolutely commit us to publishing it then. We could, if necessary, keep it and bring it out in the early autumn. But I really would like to get it out in the spring, if possible.

It's a *very* good book – honestly it is – and I'm *sure* you needn't worry about it.

Other Golding Projects

I mentioned all your other ideas – Four Enthusiasms (that could be absolutely marvellous), three Novelle (Envoy Extraordinary plus two more) and the book of essays – at our editorial committee yesterday and everybody echoed my own original yes, yes, yes. We would be very happy indeed with any or all of them; and if you would like contracts for any or all of them just let me know.

....

Nafplion–Epidavros! I so much long to be back in Greece that I can hardly bear to think about it – particularly on a grey day like this. I do hope that Greek house comes off.

Love to Ann,
　　　Yours ever,

Charles Monteith to WG   TS

11 November 1963

Dear Bill,

Here's a draft blurb for THE SPIRE. If you think it's absolutely awful just say so and I'll have another shot; or – if there are any particular things about it which you don't like let me know. I'm only too willing to keep on having more goes!

You will let me have the final version by the end of this week, won't you? Unless I have it by then getting it out in the spring really is going to be extremely difficult.

　　　Yours ever,

PS I wonder if you saw this review of Pevsner's WILTSHIRE in last Friday's TLS? Most useful piece of advance publicity don't you think!

Nikolaus Pevsner's *The Buildings of England: Wiltshire* had been reviewed in the *Times Literary Supplement* on 1 November. Despite a positive verdict, the reviewer regretted Pevsner's 'reticence' over 'the whole story of Salisbury's famous spire' and went on to list the architectural problems: the spire is 'well out of true', with 'questionable' foundations so that 'it may be said to "float"'. As if deliberately preparing the way for Golding's novel, the reviewer concluded that the spire is 'a phenomenon to which perhaps only a poet or a novelist could do full justice'.

WG to Charles Monteith   TS

18 November 1963   [Headed Paper: Ebble Thatch]

Monday

Dear Charles,

Herewith the MS of the spire. I've cut something like two thousand words out, and ought to cut the rest, too. But this is all I've the guts to do.

The advance publicity was good; the blurb perfect and *really* let me know what I'd been getting at. As an alternative to authors finding their own novels, how would it be, if publishers sent them blurb to write a novel round? This would surely be the ultimate literary expertise – or better still, the blurb could be fed straight into a novel-writing computer which would do the rest.

The weather down our way is *bloody*. Why did we ever leave Lesbos?

Ann sends her love

Bill

Charles Monteith to WG   TS

20 November 1963

Dear Bill,

Could you possibly bear it if we sent a photographer down to Salisbury to take some more photographs of you with the spire of the Cathedral in the background? I know this sounds the most appallingly ham idea – but I think they would look rather nice; and they would be very useful indeed to us with publicity for THE SPIRE.

Yours ever,

A note on file from Rosemary Goad claims that, after some resistance, Golding did agree to be photographed. Even so, there is no evidence that the photoshoot ever took place. Golding resolved to avoid publicity for his new book whenever possible. He turned down an invitation from the BBC to introduce and read an extract from *The Spire* for the Third Programme, although after a second approach he acquiesced to reading without an introduction or questions.

WG to Peter du Sautoy   TS

29 December 1963   [Headed Paper: Ebble Thatch]

Dear Peter,

    Essays –

    Obviously there are obligations to both firms; and I'm quite unable to weigh one against the other. I think I'd like you to point this out; say I'm leaving it to you to be Solomon (who better?) and that you are therefore left with the onus of deciding the thing on a business basis.

    The Perrys should now be given a timelimit very firmly. I couldnt see them in New York as they'd just left for Los Angeles.

    With regard to Pincher Martin –

    P. Brook and I have a sort of agreement that we will explore the possibility of making Pincher. This is, so to speak, an aesthetic exploration rather than a business one. Since F&F are concerned I suppose I ought to have spoken with you first, but it never occurred to me. I'm sorry. However, if you accept that, de facto, it is surely necessary to say that at the moment, you are unable to discuss the film rights of Pincher Martin (without giving further explanation).

    You'll be annoyed, I think, to hear that some American College Member wants to raise money not only for Pincher, but also for the Inheritors! I'm deflecting him Faberward. As far as I'm concerned he can go ahead with The Inheritors. I never thought I should live to see the day. But I dont think anything will come of it.

    Let's hope we'll all meet somewhere when you come back.

            Ever

                Bill

'obligations to both firms': both Putnam's and Harcourt, Brace wanted to publish Golding's book of essays in the United States. Putnam's owned Coward-McCann, which had published *Lord of the Flies*. Harcourt, Brace had published the subsequent novels.

In 1 Kings 3:16–28, Solomon must decide between the competing claims of two women fighting over the maternity of the same child.

Frank and Eleanor Perry were still interested in filming *Free Fall*, but the delay had caused complications because the BBC was keen to adapt the novel for television.

1964

By recent standards this is a quiet year, made even quieter by Golding's refusal to grant interviews when *The Spire* is published in April. Although reviews are starkly polarised, the novel becomes a bestseller in Britain and the United States. Much of Golding's time is spent assembling the materials for *The Hot Gates*; his writing is limited to the first draft of a novella about predynastic Egypt that eventually becomes the title story of *The Scorpion God* (1971). As for leisure, Golding starts learning modern Greek; he and Ann escape to Thessaloniki in February, and they return with their children to Lesbos in the summer. Around this time, Golding becomes friendly with a new arrival in Bowerchalke, the scientist James Lovelock, and suggests to him that Lovelock's theory of the Earth as a self-regulating organism should be called the Gaia hypothesis.

WG to Charles Monteith   TS

2 January 1964

Dear Charles,

A happy new year and the top of the morning to you. Herewith a more-or-less corrected set of page proofs. I've now crossed off from my list all the questions I asked myself about the book; regarding them as either repaired, or beyond repair. Only one remains, staring me in the face. 'Too much weeping?' For indeed these technicolour, vistavision cutouts are as leaky as an unstaunched wench to quote the disgusting bard. Dont you think? Oughtnt the dustcover to have a handkerchief in it somewhere? And I forgot about holy water damn it.

One other thing. I'm just plain uncertain about the use of capital letters. After twenty year's teaching English, I ought to have them firm as a rock – but I havnt. Nor have I contractions in my head – arnt, doesnt, etc. Have you by any chance, an eager, devoted, aspiring and biddable apprentice with A Level English who would leaf through the book and put me right? My Lord Dean, no, My Lord, My lord, my lord. West end, East End, North west Corner, and all that.

I hope too, that the corrections arnt too heavy for page proof. I'd expected galleys. But if the first few pages seem a bit mucked-about, at least the corrections lighten as the book goes on.

Have the heavenly twins reacted to their copy? I fear a come back more in sorrow than anger; and if Cyprus isnt tidied up soon I shall have to spend April within reach of the reviewers.

I'll get down to my long/shorts now; one, predynastic Egypt, and one about when the spire fell.

Being a publisher must be terrible – when shall we see you again? We are busy living to ourselves at the moment; and a dashed good thing too.

> Ever
> Bill

PS

Can you give me an exact publication date yet?

In the opening storm scene of *The Tempest*, the ship is described as being 'leaky as an unstanched wench' (1.1.41). Scholarship puzzles over whether the 'disgusting bard' is alluding to menstruation or sexual licentiousness.

'more in sorrow than in anger' is proverbial but comes originally from Horatio's description of the ghost of King Hamlet: 'A countenance more in sorrow than in anger' (1.2.231).

'the heavenly twins': Mark Kinkead-Weekes and Ian Gregor.

'if Cyprus isnt tidied up': violence between the Turkish and Greek Cypriots had broken out on 21 December, leaving 166 people dead over the next eleven days.

The 'long/short' about predynastic Egypt later became 'The Scorpion God', the title story of Golding's 1971 collection.

Charles Monteith to WG TS

6 January 1964

Dear Bill,

You couldn't have sent me a better New Year present than the corrected proofs, and they are going straight off to our production people. We will most certainly have them read here – probably by Mrs Hatt, our senior proof reader who will be able to go through all those contractions, worrying capital letters, etc., etc., and put them right where they are wrong. It's the kind of thing I'm very bad indeed at myself!

Publication date. We are aiming at April 24th, but years of bitter experience have taught me never to make any exact and firm predictions about publication dates until the book has been actually printed and bound. If all goes normally, though, I don't see any reason why we shouldn't stick to April 24th.

I think the heavenly twins must be separated for the Christmas holidays – I know that Ian is in Newcastle – and, like you, I haven't heard a word from them for some time, though I have been expecting letters. More importantly, letters about the book on you which they are going to write jointly this year.

All the very best for the New Year to you all.

Yours ever,

PS If you – or you and Ann – are planning a trip to London you will let me know, won't you? It would be very nice to see you again.

Charles Monteith to WG TS

24 January 1964

Dear Bill,

Just a terribly brief note to say that I've been so busy this week – it's partly because of Peter's absence – that I simply haven't had time to settle down and write to you properly about the Essays. I will, I promise you, the first moment I can.

I have heard, incidentally, that THE SPIRE is going to be serialised in America – in three 'shots' – in Show; and that ought to mean quite a nice fat fee. I expect that Peter will tie up all the details in New York – it's very fortunate that he's there at the moment – and that he will let you know about them.

Enormously enjoyed seeing you both last week. I'm certainly going to take you up on that weekend at Ebble Thatch before long.

Yours ever,

The 'nice fat fee' turned out to be $10,000 (£3,580). A schoolteacher's average annual salary in 1964 came to just over £1,200.

WG to Charles Monteith TS

28 January 1964   [Headed Paper: Ebble Thatch]

Dear Charles,

Thanks for your letter of 24th January. I'm sorry you have so much work on your plate, as the enclosure may give you a bit more. But

F&F, to the best of my recollection, are involved in reproduction fees of FLIES, so I have no option but to bother you.

Auntie has slipped up, quite clearly. I feel at once irritated and meanly pleased by it. Every time (twice) I have written for auntie she has waited for the first letter of objection and then issued an abject apology for my work, without consulting me about it at all. My worser nature would like to twist her frail old arm a bit, until she screeches for the cops, or better still, drops her reticule.

The trouble is, of course, that the only people worth pushing are at controller level; and there is a danger of dropping on some pallid clerk in the bowels of Langham Place. It's enough to make me consider switching to ITV. But if you do meet the odd BBC controller in some faded anteroom, stamp on his foot, will you?

Ann and I are delighted to know you propose a visit. Let us know when, and we'll try and drop some trout into the Ebble. We have decided against going away in April and are going to get it in, before Judy breaks up on 20th March. We think of going off the last week in February, greatly daring – and actually going by *train* to Salonika. It's the influence of all those spy-stories.

> Ever
> > Bill

PS

You turned us both into Boulestin fans, and nowadays I would *never* eat sprouts without chestnuts, sorry, châtaignes. 'Cheers,' said the Toff, 'It's Pancake Day! Lets' have Crêpe Suzette!'

'Auntie': the BBC's nickname, often implying a matronly superiority as in the phrase 'Auntie knows best'. By the sound of it, 'Auntie' had been remiss in clearing permissions for its use of *Lord of the Flies*. Langham Place is the location of Broadcasting House.

The Boulestin Restaurant in Covent Garden, founded by the celebrity French chef Marcel Boulestin, was one of Monteith's favourite haunts.

Charles Monteith to WG   TS

30 January 1964

Dear Bill,

Thank you very much for your letter of 28th January and for passing on the letter from the BBC. The position about broadcasting rights seems to be a bit complicated; and, in a recent letter from New York, Peter says that he's had a discussion there with Miss Eleanor Wright of Allen Hodgson (who produced the LORD OF THE FLIES film) about broadcasting rights, etc. He seems to have arranged everything very amicably but since nobody here knows exactly what he's arranged I think we had better keep the BBC letter until he gets back. In the meantime, I'll write an acknowledgment letter to the BBC to let them know that they will be hearing from him within a week or two.

What a super idea to go to Salonika by train. I've still got myself, an old-fashioned thing about enormously long train journeys. One of my favourite fantasies is about doing the whole run on the Trans Siberia express.

Yours ever,

PS I'll enclose with this the typescript of THE SPIRE which you lent to Mark and Ian. So sorry not to have sent it back before now.

'Eleanor Wright of Allen Hodgson': Elinor Wright of Allen-Hodgdon. She was an actor, producer and playwright.

Charles Monteith to WG   TS

4 February 1964

Dear Bill,

Here at last – with renewed apologies for the long delay – is a fearfully schoolmasterish report on the Essays. It's a conflation of the views of Mark, Ian, and myself. When we compared notes we found that we had all reached very similar conclusions.

A word about the classification. 'A' means absolutely first-class and worthy, without any question, of immortality in hard covers. 'B' means certainly worth inclusion but as a minor or supporting item. 'C' means too slight to justify inclusion in a hard cover book.

In brief summary, our conclusions are that there are 17 of these essays which should certainly go into the book, plus three 'doubtfuls'; and there are nine which we think ought to be excluded. We would certainly be perfectly happy to publish a book consisting of the 17 – or the 20 if you decide to keep in the 'doubtfuls' – but I'm sure it would be an excellent idea, as you suggested to me when we lunched together, if it could be 'stiffened up' a little with one or two other major pieces. The San Francisco lecture – which you mentioned – sounds just the job; and I'd be very interested indeed to read it.

There's no reason at all, if you agree, why we shouldn't give you a contract for the book now; and I'll be writing to you again about terms after our editorial committee tomorrow. Peter, I know, has been talking about the Essays to both Putnams and Harcourt Brace – though I don't know yet exactly what he's fixed up. Have you any special feelings, I wonder, about a publication date? Personally, I think we might perhaps leave it until the spring of 1965, leaving THE SPIRE to dominate the 1964 scene in lonely majesty; but if you particularly want to book to come out in the autumn of this year I'm sure we can give it priority.

Any word, I wonder, about the other two books you mentioned to me – Four Enthusiasms and the book of novellas? Looking forward to both enormously.

I'll be writing again in a day or two.   Yours ever,   PTO

PS In a note I've just had from Mark he tells me that he's so busy that he hasn't had time to read THE SPIRE yet – but that he hopes to get down to it next weekend.

Golding's first book of essays and reviews, *The Hot Gates* (1965), was the product of a selection process carried out by Monteith in conjunction with Mark Kinkead-Weekes and Ian Gregor. The three men gave marks to the available material, compared their results, and drew up a proposed list of contents. Kinkead-Weekes and Gregor were not initially persuaded that the book was worth publishing, which may have prompted Monteith to suggest to Golding that it should be 'stiffened up' with the 'San Francisco lecture'. While visiting the United States several months previously in late November and early December, Golding had given a lecture in San Francisco for the National Council for Teachers of English.

Despite having suggested the idea in the first place, Putnam's lost out to Harcourt, Brace, which published the American edition of *The Hot Gates* in 1966.

WG to Charles Monteith   TS

6 February 1964   [Headed Paper: Ebble Thatch]

Dear Charles,

Thanks for your letter, the essays and the examination results. We *do* think you might have used alpha, beta, etcetera; but it was good of you all to take these occasional pieces so seriously. I am struck by the decision with which you distinguish between good and bad. It's just what I wanted; but (though I'm a poor critic) I'd tried to do that myself and I threw out a number of pieces which you never therefore saw. It seems to me that they might be worth just the same steady critical eye as the others, since obviously my marking would have differed from yours. I ought to add, that I accept your marking without any reservation at all.

Now if the book is aimed at Spring '65, there is surely no need for hurry. I have by me five HOLIDAY essays which I threw out but which you havnt seen, and, of course, the San Francisco lecture. That would mean there's another twenty-five thousand words for you to examine. In addition, I'm working on a HOLIDAY essay on EGYPT FROM MY INSIDE which might be B, at least. I'll probably have three more, on DELPHI, OLYMPUS, and THE CATHEDRALS OF SOUTHERN ENGLAND, all of which ought to be finished by the time you'd need the MS. There are also two other HOLIDAY essays which I cant find but which I have somewhere – *

What shall I do? Hold these for you until you can see the lot, or do you want them as they are available? If you want me to hold them, an approximate deadline would be useful. Then there's a BBC thing in Dear To My Heart called THE SHIELD OF ACHILLES. I cant find that either.

There's no denying – at least in private – that writing for HOLIDAY limits one from elaborate language and idea, and frees one into the perilous swamps of outright journalism. I feel this acutely sometimes and try my best to keep interest without sacrificing integrity. But it's a hard row to hoe. Better than teaching, though.

I'm just finishing the first draft of my predynastic Egypt Long/Short. Provisional title, TO KEEP NOW STILL. It's most unsatisfactory, flat as ditchwater and not at all what I intended. I'll have another go. The BARCHESTER long/short is there in my mind and ought to be easier when I get round to it touch wood. I shant touch the FOUR ENTHUSIASMS till I've finished these two.

I had a very nice letter from Forster about THE SPIRE, which almost reconciles me to publishing it and waiting for the boys to operate.

     ever,
      Bill
* PS Plus *another* Holiday piece if I can find it.

Golding has misdated this letter 6 January.

'Egypt from My Inside' is eventually included in *The Hot Gates*, but the articles about Delphi and the cathedrals of southern England (in fact, Winchester and Salisbury only) must wait until Golding's second book of essays, *A Moving Target* (1982).

Dear To My Heart was a radio series on the West of England Home Service in which 'distinguished regional personalities' spoke on a subject about which they felt deeply. Golding's broadcast on 17 December 1956 was titled 'The Shield of Achilles', and in it he describes the shield as 'the poetic perception of our state, half-angel, half-ape, uncertain whether mountains or powers brood over us, ignorant of meaning yet sure of significance'.

E. M. Forster wrote to Golding that *The Spire* was a 'wonderful novel' and singled out its 'sense of weight – stone weight'.

Charles Monteith to WG   TS

6 February 1964

Dear Bill,

Here's the further letter I promised you about terms for the book of essays. We wonder if a straight 15% and an advance of £250 would be OK? (I know you will realise that we can't expect the same sort of sales for a book of essays as we would for a novel – and that this is reflected in the comparative smallness of the advance.) And I wonder when you would like the advance? Should we simply make it payable on publication?

Another, important, point – the title. I wonder what you would like to call it? Perhaps it would be all right simply to use the title of one of the major essays in the book followed by 'And Other Essays' – or something like that. THE LADDER AND THE TREE perhaps?

Yours,

Charles Monteith to WG   TS

7 February 1964

Dear Bill,

Excellent that there's so much more stuff to see – either already finished or to be finished shortly. I think I'd prefer to have it all together; and I wonder if June 30th would suit you as a deadline? Once I have it I'd like, of course, to show it to Mark and Ian and it might take at least a month before we can do our alpha-beta act. If we publish the book in the mid spring of 1965 I ought to get the whole thing off to production in its final form by mid August or so.

Delighted to know that the predynastic Egypt novella exists – at any rate in first draft; and that the Barchester one should go fairly smoothly once it starts. Looking forward to the whole book enormously.

Very pleased – though not surprised I assure you – to know that E.M.F. thinks so well of THE SPIRE.

Yours ever,

PS Everything seems to be sorted out now about the broadcasting rights. I've had a letter from the BBC which clears the situation up.

Charles Monteith to WG   TS

15 April 1964

Dear Bill,

Now that the weekend dust has settled I think one can be reasonably happy. I thought that John Wain in *The Observer* really did write an extremely sympathetic and intelligent review – and one which will, I'm certain, help the book very much indeed. *The Spectator*, too, was excellent; and Dame Rebecca in *The Sunday Telegraph* not at all bad and certainly very well intentioned. The trouble with both Pritchett and Wyndham was, I feel, a sort of temperamental incompatibility. It just wasn't their sort of book – and it was a bit silly, I think, of the two literary editors concerned to send it to them for review. Particularly as both Karl Miller (*New Statesman*) and Jack Lambert (*Sunday Times*), to judge from 'The Critics' on Sunday admired THE SPIRE very much. So far as the unspeakable Allsop and the equally unspeakable Lucie Smith are concerned, neither of them, I assure you, has any importance at all.

The next round should be on us tomorrow . . . and that will include, I know, a 'middle' in the TLS. I gather that Ian's review has already appeared in *The Guardian* – but I haven't read it yet.

It was very nice seeing you and Ann again on Thursday – and to see you both looking so well.

Yours ever,

The Spire had been published on 10 April in a UK edition of 15,000 copies. John Wain in the *Observer* conceded that Golding was 'out of the class of Dostoevsky and Kafka [. . .]. But even to consider him in relation to that class, to have to define what it is that keeps him out – what high praise that is, and how satisfying, in these days, to be able to voice it!' Writing in *The Spectator*, David Lodge was even more adulatory: 'No English novelist has dared – and achieved – so much.' Rebecca West in the *Sunday Telegraph* argued that *The Spire* 'should become a classic', while Ian Gregor's marginally more hesitant *Guardian* review found that 'the spire stands triumphantly and the fable too, but both have been slightly bent in the vastness of the undertaking.' V. S. Pritchett complained in the *New Statesman* of 'obscurity, monotony and strain'; Francis Wyndham felt that Golding's sentences sought 'a state of mystical exultation' unsupported by 'sense'. As for the 'unspeakable' reviewers, Kenneth Allsop in the *Daily Mail* damned *The Spire* as 'pretentious, false-heroic writing, solemn and dull [. . .] a terribly bad book' and Edward Lucie-Smith on the BBC Home Service's *The Critics* found it 'a very, very, very bad book'.

WG to Charles Monteith   TS

26 April 1964   [Headed Paper: Ebble Thatch]

Dear Charles,

Thanks for your letter of 15th April. I've managed to remain a *little* more indifferent to reviews this time – but not entirely. As far as I can judge, the verdict is for, rather than against. I suppose we should leave it at that and concentrate on the future.

I've got a good many other essays sorted out and will send them on when the summer heats up.

Ann and I had three days in Edinburgh with Mark and Ian. We visited the Castle which was shrouded in mist and the Trossacks which were shrouded in mist. Positively heard people saying 'A wee while', and can only believe they were left over from the festival, or the tattoo or something.

I think I told you I wrote my predynastic long/short and was most disappointed in it. Will probably rewrite.

Shall now try for the longest possible period of tranquillity and decision as to what it's all *for*, or something. An anti-portentous book perhaps? Or perhaps an anti-book. See how we pick up these technical scraps!

Student letters seem on the increase, rather than not. It's almost like being back at school. Have you a small, spare secretary? No, I thought not. Sorry for a flat letter. As Lear says, this is a dull sight,

ever
Bill.

'the tattoo': the Royal Edinburgh Military Tattoo is an annual military display, often involving musical performance.

Golding's closing quotation is from *King Lear*, 5.3.256.

Charles Monteith to WG   TS

30 April 1964

Dear Bill,

Peter passed over a bundle of American reviews this morning; and though I haven't had time to read them through yet both he and I thought we ought perhaps to write to *The Reporter* about three small and purely factual points in George Steiner's piece there. (I expect you have your own copy of it – but in case you haven't I'll enclose ours. I'd be very grateful indeed if you could let me have it back.) It isn't true, is it, that THE INHERITORS had been 'written and rewritten' before the publication of LORD OF THE FLIES? I don't think in fact it has ever occurred to me to ask you about this – but I had always assumed that you had settled straight down to THE INHERITORS as soon as LORD OF THE FLIES was out of the way – and, that once it got under weigh, it was finished fairly quickly.

Secondly, it's certainly not true – as Steiner, I think, implies – that we saw and urged you to publish earlier drafts of THE SPIRE. This is my reading of his statement 'Despite the Publisher's excitement over successive versions, Golding held back and reworked.' No one here ever saw any of the earlier versions of THE SPIRE; and you first sent the typescript to us in early May, 1963. All the later corrections and additions you did after that were comparatively minor ones.

Finally, the title. We did of course differ over this – but it wasn't prudery which inspired our objection to *An Erection at Barchester*. We felt that it was much too light weight and 'jokey' for a book like THE SPIRE.

....

I've written a draft letter to the Editor of *The Reporter*; and I'll enclose it with this. I'd be very grateful indeed if you would cast your eye over it; and, of course, I'm very ready to amend or revise it in any way you like. In particular, I would like to say – as I do in my draft – that I've written it with your knowledge and approval. Do please let me know what you think.

Terribly sorry to pester you about this.

Yours ever,

PS The real reason for my letter is that such small inaccuracies, once they get into print, tend to become self-perpetuating errors, passed on by one-writer-about-Golding to another, ad infinitum.

George Steiner's review of *The Spire* appeared in *The Reporter* on 7 May. Having seen a proof copy, du Sautoy forwarded it to Monteith with a note wondering whether they 'ought to do anything' about the claims relating to Faber. Monteith's postscript to Golding repeats almost verbatim du Sautoy's warning that 'it is mainly important for the future, as these things tend to be repeated, perpetuated'. Monteith's rebuttal was published in *The Reporter* on 18 June, along with Steiner's reply, to which Monteith drafted a further elaboration.

WG to Charles Monteith   TS

1 May 1964   [Headed Paper: Ebble Thatch]

Dear Charles.

Your three points.

(I) THE INHERITORS.

I wrote a longhand first draft in a month or less – December 1954; Ian and Mark would know the exact dates as they have the MS which is dated. Then I typed the draft which got published straight from that in another month or less. It was the quickest book I've ever written.

(II)

THE SPIRE.

I certainly had no urging to publish from you. You kept enquiring as I remember; but waited very contentedly until May 1963. The draft you saw then is substantially the one you published.

(III)

THE TITLE.

You thought AN ERECTION AT BARCHESTER was a joke; but if I wanted to use it, you were agreable though loath. The change was made by me (to THE SPIRE) off my own bat. I'm saving AN ERECTION AT BARCHESTER for a long/short.

Harcourt Brace reacted much the same way – except that John McCallum was, I think genuinely shocked, and implied – 'Bill, you are a *one!*'

George Steiner *may* have got it all from Andrew. The Sinclairs were down here last Summer before they went off to America.

Let it be a lesson to me to keep my trap shut. Certainly, though, I've never represented F&F in other than a favourable light. I'm grateful to them, as you must know; and have never seen any reason for concealing that gratitude.

> Ever
> Bill

Of course I officially OK your letter to The Reporter as it stands.
W.G.

WG to Charles Monteith   TS

2 September 1964   [Headed Paper: Ebble Thatch]

Dear Charles,

We're now back in circulation, more or less. Got very brown and did ourselves proud. I believe you'll be back by now, and Peter not.

I dont know who's dealing with the film question of the Spire – Peter, probably. Apparently the time-factor is the important one. Nesta has now finished her play and sent it to be typed. I suppose sometime or other I'll read and OK it. Obviously she doesnt want a film competing; but I wouldn't have thought it would. Surely the film would take something like two years? By when, presumably the play would be all washed up or at least, reduced to Rep. We really ought to have a meeting between all the interested parties to work something out.

Another thing I'm thinking at the moment is to push F&F into a bit of exotic publishing. Have you thought of producing a book or booklet of these Nimbus pictures? They're so exciting and so lovely I cant stop looking at them; and I'm quite sure a book of them would sell like hot cakes. You could even include some SF pictures as predictions, en face with the reality. Admittedly I dont know how you'd get hold of them – but the Europe one in this morning's Times, is one of the most beautiful things I've ever seen – like a Chinese wall painting but full of *thereness*.

So. I expect you've thought of it anyway.

I expect Ann and I will be drifting up to London sometime fairly soon; if only to assure ourselves the place is still there. After Lesvos Athens Naples Assisi Florence Venice it seems a bit unreal. We think of embarking timorously on a bit of culture – Covent Garden and all that.

But nothing's fixed. By the way, Judy got top marks in her A Levels and is all set for Sussex; and refused Oxbridge on the grounds that they make poor girls *work*. Very courageous, very sensible.

Ann sends her love

Bill.

The Golding family had spent a month on Lesbos holidaying and visiting the Greens. They enjoyed a whistlestop cultural tour on the way back: Athens, Naples, Assisi, Florence, Venice.

The Spire, adapted and produced by Nesta Pain and starring Michael Hordern, was broadcast on the BBC's Network Three on 12 May 1965. An internal memo from Monteith to du Sautoy and Rosemary Goad reports an unnamed film company's interest in buying Nesta Pain's script.

The Nimbus 1 Earth-observation satellite was launched by NASA on 24 August. Its images of the Earth from space had a lasting effect on Golding, as apparent in his 1983 Nobel lecture: 'Now we [. . .] have been caught up to see our earth, our mother, Gaia Mater, set like a jewel in space [. . .]. We are the children of that great blue-white jewel. Through our mother we are part of the solar system and part through that of the whole universe. In the blazing poetry of the fact we are children of the stars.'

Judy 'refused Oxbridge' only in the sense that she decided not to apply. After her degree at Sussex, she studied for a BLitt at Oxford.

Charles Monteith to WG   TS

7 September 1964

Dear Bill,

Delighted to get your letter of September 2nd. It reached me almost, but not quite, on the eve of my Greek expedition. On Thursday night I fly to Athens and sometime on Friday morning, God willing, I should be on Thassos. After a week there, Kastoria in Northern Macedonia – said to be very beautiful – and after that I'm not sure. Possibly Crete. It rather depends on the weather and what the people I'm going with want to do. I can't tell you how much I'm looking forward to getting away after a whole summer in Russell Square – excellent summer though it has been.

Peter is due back in the office tomorrow – I'm longing to hear how his Hellenic cruise went – and I'll have a word with him then about the film. I'm sure he'll be getting in touch with you direct himself; and I'm certain that you're right in thinking that a meeting between everyone concerned would be a good idea – if it can be arranged.

I do hope that we're able to meet soon after I get back – I'll be back in the office on October 5th – so that we can swop Hellenic yarns. Perhaps you and Ann will be doing a bit of culture in October.

What excellent news about Judy. Do please give her my warmest congratulations and say how very pleased I am. And Sussex, I'm told on all hands, is infinitely smarter nowadays than Oxbridge!

About the Nimbus pictures. I do agree – they're absolutely marvellous. But this is the sort of book that we're always extremely nervous of. Part of the collective wisdom of publishing is – and I'm pretty certain this is correct – that these sort of big picture books are not only very expensive to produce but, except once in a blue moon, very difficult indeed to sell. They're the sort of book which people pick up in bookshops and rifle through with admiration – but just don't fork out two guineas for. So I think we probably won't pursue Nimbus bookwise – though I'll mention this to Dick de la Mare and see what he thinks.

Much love to Ann – and to all of you.

WG to Charles Monteith TS

3 November 1964   [Headed Paper: Ebble Thatch]

Dear Charles,

Here are the essays back with some others that I threw out because I thought I KNEW BEST. But of course I didnt; and am very happy to push the job on to you and the heavenly twins.

I'm apologising in advance, not only for the tatty state of this lot but also for what I myself regard as their cheapness and sometimes their slickness. They're rank journalism; but the decision is up to you. Some are still missing; notably two of the three EWING lectures which I cant find, and a long notice I did of Fitzgeralds translation of the Odyssy called SURGE AND THUNDER for the Spectator which I cant find either.

Your accounts dept keeps sending us *incredible* quantities of money. I like it so much, and can only hope you'll keep it up.

By the way – your query after the party about whether you could drive my car; yes you could, with the position of the pedals altered – all of which is allowed for in the driving test. Ann now drives her minute car (see para 3) as to the manner born; but has just driven into Salisbury with the handbrake on – which restores my faith in womanliness.

Am waiting to hear in a slavering condition whether that film company is going to come across with a sizable slice of money. Am obsessed with money, money, money. Am very, very vulgar.

Ann sends her love

Bill

PS Essays under separate cover.

PPS Dinner was lovely with you and Rosemary – you must both visit with us soon.

Golding gave his three Ewing lectures at the University of California, Los Angeles, in December 1961. The second of them, 'Fable', appears in *The Hot Gates*; Golding's preface misdates it to 1962. 'Surge and Thunder' is collected in *A Moving Target* (1982).

The '*incredible* quantities of money' being sent to Golding reflected exceptionally strong sales figures. A note from Rosemary Goad to Monteith on 1 October reported that the school edition of *Lord of the Flies* had already sold over 50,000 copies, the film edition 23,000 and *The Spire*, 'despite all the horror stories', nearly 13,000 in hardback.

Monteith would need to alter the position of the pedals on Golding's car because he was a very tall man and Golding was not. The description of Ann driving 'as to the manner born' is another of Golding's habitual Shakespearean allusions, this time to *Hamlet* 1.4.17.

The Goldings had attended a party at Faber on 22 October before going out for dinner with Monteith and Rosemary Goad.

Charles Monteith to WG

TS

5 November 1964

Dear Bill,

Thank you very much indeed for your letter of November 3rd and for the new batch of essays. Of course I'll be absolutely delighted to read them; and so, I know will Ian and Mark. When we've put our heads together about them, as it were, I'll be writing again.

Delighted to know that the money is rolling in so satisfactorily; and I needn't say how much I hope that a film deal doubles or trebles it. We'll do our best for you, I assure you!

Much love to Ann. And love from Rosemary and everyone else here.

Yours ever,

Charles Monteith to WG TS

15 December 1964

Dear Bill,

Here's my 'report' on the second batch of essays – just as horridly schoolmastery as the last one I fear! Do please let me know what you think about it.

I am hanging on to all the essays here – and I've also got the first batch I think. Do you I wonder want me to send them all back to you? We'd very much like to publish the book – as you know – in the Autumn of 1965; and if we're to do that it would be nice if possible to have it in its final shape by the end of January. You will I imagine want to write some sort of introduction for it won't you?

Yours ever,

WG to Charles Monteith TS

18 December 1964   [Headed Paper: Ebble Thatch]

Dear ~~Charles~~ Teacher,

Thanks for sending on my term's report. I'm sorry to have done so badly at Englsih Teachers' Conference Addressing but hope my infant interest in Archaeology and Egyptology make up for it. I'll have another look for the Ewing Lectures but dont hold out much hope. Perhaps the right thing would be to leave this one out, and hope another day to do an essay on the how-why-and wherefore of Lord Of The Flies. (Thinks: *Encounter* would take that one.)

An unforseen catch about Egypt From My Inside is that they have it and have paid for it but havnt published it. It may have seemed a bit esoteric to them; but the question is – would they make a noise about it being published in bookform before their ten million readers had the thing in basic English? (*Holiday*, I mean.)

I'll certainly do some sort of introduction on writing essays and these in particular; but I cant think what to say at the moment; and in any case I suppose it might be quite short.

Yes; you've got the all and only copies. What do I do about this? Do you want me to go to the immense labour of making fair copies? Or can the typesetters work from them as they are? And what do you think about order? How much can I or ought I to amend and alter and cut? After all, this is a proper Lit book, Belle Lettres and the rest and I'm out of my depth.

We're both very sorry to have missed your party; but the fog lay all about and the road was a mirror – and a Family Christmas is approaching with remorseless tread.

Ever
Bill

PS

Ann says 'why dont you get Charles to write the introduction?' What a *good* idea!

With a green biro, Golding has crossed through 'Charles' and written 'Teacher' above it. 'Englsih' may be deliberate or an accidental error allowed to stand.

1965

In search of a new direction for his writing, Golding spends much of the year working on an autobiographical manuscript titled 'Men, Women & Now'. This becomes the basis for his next novel, *The Pyramid* (1967). Royalties, especially from the United States, show no sign of slowing; for the first time in his life, Golding feels wealthy, although he is daunted and distracted by the bureaucracy that his income entails. He and Ann spend early summer in Greece, ending up on Corfu at Monteith's recommendation. *The Hot Gates* is well received when it appears in October.

Charles Monteith to WG   TS

4 January 1965

Dear Bill,

I was absolutely delighted to find your letter of December 18th waiting for me when I got back from Ireland a couple of days ago.

I'll send you with this letter all the essays; and I wonder if I could possibly ask you to let me have all the material which you want to be included – in its absolutely final form – by January 31st? I do hope this isn't too tall an order – but we would like to get the book out, as you know, in the Autumn of 1965 – and I should have thought that the early Autumn i.e. September or early October would be the best sort of time. And to make sure of doing that we must get started on production pretty smartly.

One or two odd points.

a) *Fair copies*   No need to type out fair copies of all these pieces – our printers will, I think, be able to cope with them as they are. I'd be very grateful, though, if you'd keep a specially careful eye out when you are correcting proofs. Things are a little more likely to go wrong if the copy from which the printers are setting is rather bitty.

b) *Order*   Most of the essays fall, don't they, into three or four rather broad and loosely defined categories e.g. autobiography, literary criticism, archaeology, travel etc. Though I've got no very strong views about the order in which these categories should come, I wonder if it might be an idea to start with some of the pieces from *Holiday* – since they'll all be quite unfamiliar – at any rate to British readers. Ian, Mark and I – as you know – were tremendously taken with them.

c) *Editing*   There's no reason at all why you shouldn't amend, alter and cut as you like. If you do that though, I think it might be an idea just to make a brief mention of the fact in your introduction.

d) *Title etc.*   Do you think that the book ought to have a rather catchy title combined with a rather boring sub-title? For example:

ANDROIDS ALL
Essays in Life and Literature

Not that I mean that seriously – but that sort of thing. It might be an idea too, don't you think, to give each main section a sub-title?

e) *Egypt From My Inside*   I think it'll be advisable to clear up the situation with *Holiday* as soon as possible. I don't imagine that they are happy about allowing this essay to appear in book form before they've printed it – but there's no reason, I should have thought, why they shouldn't print it before the book comes out. I imagine you'd like to write to them yourself about this – since I imagine there's someone there with whom you usually correspond. If you'd like me to write officially though, of course I'd be glad to do so.

f) *The Ewing Lectures*   I'd be very sorry, I must confess, to see the one surviving Ewing lecture omitted. It really is most terribly good. But the final decision about this is entirely up to you. I quite appreciate that you feel that its appearance in a book might preclude you from doing another bigger piece on the genesis of Lord of the Flies some time in the future.

A little belatedly, may I wish you, Ann and the whole family an absolutely spiffing 1965? You'll let me know, won't you when you next plan a visit to London? It would be very nice if we could meet.

Yours,

Golding did indeed have a piece titled 'Androids All' – a *Spectator* review of *New Maps of Hell* by Kingsley Amis – but it failed to make the cut for *The Hot Gates*. The 'surviving Ewing Lecture', 'Fable', was included.

2 February 1965   [Headed Paper: Ebble Thatch]

Dear Charles,

Herewith THE HOT GATES. That seems a reasonable title since I've grouped the essays with THE HOT GATES first. However, if you argue with the title or order or anything else, I'm willing to be instructed. I hope in particular you are not going to react strongly to my laisser faire spelling scheme, because if you do so firmly I shant have any preface left!

I wrote off to Schanche at HOLIDAY but havnt heard from him. There's been an almighty upheaval there anyway and the people I once knew have gone. Maybe there aint no more gold in them thar hills. However his silence makes the whole thing difficult; because I dont see how you are to get on unless you know whether we can publish EGYPT FROM MY INSIDE or not.

A further thing is that Curtis Brown arranged my Holiday contact – and I dont know whether they will want a cut. It's all dam' difficult. However, Dhen berazi as doubtless you will agree.

Ann and I leave on Thursday 4th February for Manchester to Pugwash, then to Edinburgh with the Heavenly Twins and return on 9th February. We are going to come up to the smoke for a faintly cultural jaunt 16–19th February I think and will be happy to meet you as and how. At the moment we are only booked for 19th evening. Shall also see Peter Brook about film of PINCHER MARTIN, plans for a script of which have moved on somewhat.

Money is *very difficult* – not because we havnt any but because we have too much. We have now a solicitor, an accountant, and a London wiggery man of awful eminence fighting the Inland Revenue. Once I could just take an exercise book and write. Now three quarters of my mind is in different damned directions. I *ought* to live in Greece and not answer any post except F&F. Moan, moan, moan.

However, some time the heat will be off.

Ann sends her love and we both look forward to seeing you, later on in the month

ever

Bill

The title essay of *The Hot Gates* describes Golding's pilgrimage to Thermopylae to pay homage to Leonidas and the fallen Spartans: 'A little of Leonidas lies in the fact that I can go where I like and write what I like. He contributed to set us free.' Translated literally, Thermopylae means 'hot gates'.

Golding addresses his 'spelling scheme' in the 'Preface' to *The Hot Gates*: 'Where my transatlantic editors altered my spelling to conform with American custom I have let it remain so. Our system and theirs are illogical though reasonable. Why choose between them?'

Don A. Schanche had been the editor at *Holiday* since March 1964.

'my Holiday contact': 'contract' would make much more sense, but 'contact' is just about possible.

'Dhen berazi' – Golding's inaccurate rendition of the Greek δεν πειράζει – means 'never mind'.

Named after the site of its first meeting in Nova Scotia, Pugwash is an international organisation opposed to nuclear weapons; it attempts to find peaceful solutions to security threats.

Golding and Brook worked on a treatment of *Pincher Martin* for several years but could not secure funding to pursue the project. Golding offers his opinion of Brook in a later journal entry: 'I think he is a genius; and what is more, an evolving one so there is no knowing what he may do and achieve' (J, 29 March 1974).

Charles Monteith to WG   TS

10 February 1965

Dear Bill,

I expect you're back in Ebble Thatch by now – and I do hope you had a marvellous time in the North. I much look forward to hearing all about it next week. If the night of February 18th is still free, would you and Ann, I wonder, like to come to the Michael MacLiammoir programme – he's doing his Irish turn that evening which is, I believe, rather good. (I saw the Oscar Wilde turn a month or so ago and it was pretty impressive.) If you could, please let me know and I'll try and get seats, and we could dine together, I hope, either before or after.

THE HOT GATES

1. *Spelling.*   Perfectly happy with your laisser faire – and I'll try to remember to warn the printers *not* to de-Americanise the American bits.
2. *Egypt From My Inside.*   What a nuisance about *Holiday*. Would you like me to write to Holiday or to Curtis Brown about it? It might

be an idea, don't you think, either to ask Curtis Brown's New York office to get on to them or Harcourt Brace? These sort of things are often more easily dealt with on the spot. If Holiday won't publish *Egypt From My Inside* before the Autumn and refuse you permission to include it in the book before their own publication date, I suppose we'll have to drop it which will be an awful pity but wouldn't be an irretrievable disaster, would it?

3. *Curtis Brown's Cut.* CB aren't entitled to any sort of cut on this book since all that they arranged was magazine publication. I've consulted Peter about this and he's as certain as I am!

———————————

Very much looking forward to seeing you both next week.
Yours,

Micheál Mac Liammóir was an English-born actor and impresario who had moved to Ireland as a teenager and adopted an Irish identity. Monteith refers to his one-man show *The Importance of Being Oscar*, which became the biggest success of his career.

It turned out that *Holiday* had no objection to the inclusion of 'Egypt from My Inside' in *The Hot Gates*.

WG to Charles Monteith   TS

26 March 1965   [Headed Paper: Ebble Thatch]

Dear Charles,

A hasty note, written in the discovery that I havnt said anything about G.C.F. Mem: Prize. We shall be glad to come to dinner with Y'all – and I'll even give you herewith a brief glimpse of what I would briefly say, *if* it is absolutely necessary for me to say anything.

Simply two headings, each a para. One, personal debt to firm. Two, impact of early F. impressions on young men who haunted bookshops. Anything more would be out of my knowledge and province. If anyone is to say anything about G.F. as a man it oughtnt to be me, since I hardly knew him.

I hope you think that will be all right. It ought to run to nearly two minutes' playing time. *But I hope you don't think it necessary at all.*
Ever
Bill

The Geoffrey Faber Memorial Prize was established in 1964 in honour of the founding editor of Faber & Faber who had died in 1961. The prize was for authors aged under forty at time of publication and was awarded in alternating years to poetry and fiction. In 1965, Frank Tuohy won it for his novel *The Ice Saints*.

Charles Monteith to WG   TS

26 March 1965

Dear Bill,

Peter has told me your latest piece of tremendously exciting news. I really am absolutely delighted.

Incidentally, I'm hoping to see Mark and Ian in Oxford over the weekend; and we'll be having some preliminary talk about that book on you. Though it's not finished yet, quite a lot has been done.

One small point in connection with the G.C.F. prize on Friday April 2nd. We do, of course, want to pay your and Ann's expenses in connection with coming to London to do this; and do let me have a bill for them when you get back – travelling expenses, hotel expenses etc.

Looking forward very much indeed to seeing you both.

      Yours,

The tremendously exciting news was that Golding was to receive a CBE in the 1966 New Year's Honours List.

    'Mark and Ian': Kinkead-Weekes and Gregor.

WG to Charles Monteith   MS

5 April 1965   [Headed Paper: Ebble Thatch]

                                        Πέμπτη Ἀπρίλιου '65.

Ἀγαπήτε Καρούλι,

    πόσο εὐχάριστο νὰ σάς συναντήσαμε μὲ τοὺς ἄλλους στὸ Λονδίνο τήν ἑβδομάδα τη τελευτάια! Ἡ κύρια Ἄνι συνδέει τάς εὐχαριστιάς της, καὶ θέλει νὰ μάθει πως τὸ λένε αὔτο τὸ ἐστιατόριο ὅπου ἔχομε φάει, γιατὶ ἔτσι νόστιμο ἦταν τὸ φαγητό κι' ἐλύωσε στὸ στόμα.

    Τέλος, σάς ευχαριστούμε πολὺ γιὰ τὸ ὡραίο γεύμα καὶ τὴν εὐχάριστη βραδιά!

    Μπίλ.

    (Γουΐλλιαμ Γκόλνδιγκ.)

251

Ignoring misplaced stresses and misspellings, the translation from modern Greek (which hardly does justice to Golding's playful way with names) is as follows:

Fifth of April '65

Dear Karouli,

How pleasant to meet you with the others in London last week! Mrs Annie relates her thanks, and wants to find out what that restaurant we have eaten in is called, because the food was so tasty and melt in the mouth. Finally, we thank you very much for the lovely meal and the pleasant evening!

Bill.

(William Golding.)

Monteith replied on 8 April – in Greek that was shakier than Golding's – that the restaurant was À l'Ecu de France on Jermyn Street in London.

WG to Charles Monteith   PC

(?) May 1965

Corfu – an enchantment. Her wild strawberries and exciting cheeses! Bookshops stocked *entirely* with L. Durrell. What a good thing. Had lunch with Ann and the gentleman overleaf – Shows you what happens to an island without a National Health.

But –

Ici on parle Linguaphone.

Bill

The postcard is undated and the postmark illegible.

Lawrence Durrell had moved to Corfu with his wife, mother and younger siblings in 1935, and he stayed until 1941 before evacuating as the Germans advanced. His memoir *Prospero's Cell* (1942) has been described as a love letter to Corfu.

The image on the postcard is of a statue of the dying Achilles in the gardens of the Achilleion, Corfu. Golding and Ann had holidayed on Rhodes and toured some of the smaller islands before ending up on Corfu.

Both Golding and Monteith were making a concerted effort to learn modern Greek with the Linguaphone course.

WG to Charles Monteith   TS MONTEITH

14 June 1965   [Headed Paper: Ebble Thatch]

Dear Charles,

What a nuisance these things are – and how difficult it is to believe they're going to be over! Something like the war, which was interminable, but has shut up since so that it seems an episode only.

I dont know how linguaphone progresses – but it seems to me that there's a huge language gap between being able to speak and being able to talk. By now I've got mighty slick at the small change of travel; but what's that, after all? I'm all right so long as the conversation follows predictable lines, since holiday situations tend to repeat themselves. I can even do some car stuff – explain that I have had a *travma* with my *elastike*, *dhexia*, *mprosta*, resulting, I consider, in a *tripa*. But to sit at a table with a real Greek, not a record, and with all the resources of mind on either side, is a sort of linguistic purgatory. The terrible, humiliating thing is, that though I know very little Italian and havnt done any for thirty-five years, I can understand the dam' language better than Greek because I learnt it young and they make accessible noises. If I have a genuine Greek conversation beyond the set bounds of linguaphone it gets more and more Pinteresque and ends in a deadlock.

'I prefer that to this.'

'Yes they do, dont they sometimes?'

It's a kind of shyness. One loses the thread, goes nodding sideways into a sort of uninterpretable oration because one doesnt want to seem so *damn dumb*. They stop, having taken your perfectly Greek gestures of assent as a sign of fluency, then ask a question the answer to which reveals that you've understood nothing. It's some sort of lesson, I suppose – 99% of our humanity resides in speech, in communication; and when you're the one without it you lose cast and become animal or abject or both. I cant think of a solution bar Peter Green's – *have* to do it, rent houses, buy furniture, get things made, argue with the mayor. But there. We're protected men, the two of us. Perhaps if linguaphone included a little man who popped out and chattered away it might help. Or perhaps if one transcribed the discs on to tape and scrambled them so that one didnt know what was coming next there might be some help. It's all the difference between an exercise in the war sense, and being in action. Also one tires, one tires. One cant listen anymore; and then comes the easy but fatal gesture of assent.

I used to think I was bad at languages; and then I thought I was good at them; and now I've come to the most humiliating conclusion of all; I'm low average. It's so odd. There's something easy about them that I just havnt got. Ann and Lalage Green for example, arnt bothered. Is this a sex differentiation I wonder? They have a most marvellous short cut. They are aware of the *whole* person, his or her gesture, intonation, the lot. They *sense* a meaning while I am still listening for tense sequences, jump some sort of hurdle and arrive at a conclusion. They dont mind how they communicate but they do it while I am still trying to think whether a word is M or F or N. They have something of the approach which children have, language as only one aspect of a totality. Damn it I *will* learn Greek, if it takes me the rest of my life.

Corfu – as you told us it would be – was wonderful. In a strange way it was Keatsian. I suppose we all got our first idea of Greece as a separate place, from Keats. But this abundance, this fertility, this lushness; this heat and beauty – It's fashionable, I know, to like the bare austerity of Attica and so forth; I've said that myself. Well then, I – we – have been seduced into enjoying a rich island more than the poor ones. Our house, which gets more and more mythical as the years pass, might very well be there, except that Corfu is nearly as expensive now as, say, Italy. Rhodes was good too but crammed with tourists – other tourists, it might be more reasonable to say. I wonder where you will go in September? We've cased the outer islands now and feel we might see the Cyclades next. I'm *told* if its a consideration that north east Greece (Dhutike Thrake?) is as fertile in its way as Corfu; but it's an awful long way. We recovered from 'flu in Yanina so take a relatively dim view of it. We went for a drive and found ourselves in Dodona by accident, so did some culture without meaning to.

Well, it's pleasant to write you an unbusiness letter; and moreover, one which positively needs no answer. Ann sends her love and best wishes; as do I –

        Until we meet.
           Bill.

'What a nuisance': Monteith was in hospital having an intestinal polyp removed.
   'I have had a *travma* with my *elastike*, *dhexia*, *mprosta*, resulting, I consider, in a *tripa*': the vocabulary and the genders are a little off, but Golding is awkwardly explaining that he has had a puncture in his right front tyre.
   'M or F or N': nouns in modern Greek are masculine, feminine or neuter.
Dhutike Thrake: West Thrace.

Charles Monteith to Ann and WG

MS GOLDING

15 June 1965
Woolavington Wing, Middlesex
Hospital, W1

Tuesday

Dear Ann & Bill,

What an absolutely marvellous letter & absolutely marvellous roses. They both arrived at just the right moment & cheered me up enormously. Thank you very much indeed for them.

I was done on Saturday morning; & now, shaved, washed & de-tubed, feel very chipper & part of everyday life again. The operation, I'm happy to say, was completely successful & satisfactory. A couple of months ago an intestinal polyp – romantic word – was diagnosed in my inside; & though of course I knew, rationally, that the chances of it being anything worse than that were very remote, there was still that persistent irrational worry . . . A worry completely dispelled, along with the polyp, by the operation, I'm very happy to say.

All you say about learning Greek by linguaphone strikes home with horrid precision. It's partly, with me at any rate, a general failing of memory – which extends not only to Greek but to everything else. And this is particularly trying when so much of the vocabulary has to be learned completely from scratch. Though I've been proceeding, deliberately, at an absolute snail's pace I find that I completely forget words which I learned, painfully, only two lessons ago.

I've been thinking of trying to find a Greek – & to find a Greek as opposed to a Cypriot is difficult enough here – for some conversation lessons; but I doubt if I've yet got enough vocabulary to make it worth while.

Indeed, I'm rather resigning myself to becoming the possessor of reasonable tourist's Greek – that seems a possible mark to aim at – rather than someone who can ever really *talk* to a Greek in Greek.

I don't know how long I'll be here – about another week I should think – & after that I've been promised 10 days or a fortnight in Ireland; but I should be back in circulation about mid-July & I do hope we're able to meet sometime after then. – Love, Charles.

Charles Monteith to WG

31 August 1965

Dear Bill,

I thought I ought to show you this exchange of correspondence I've just had with the amiable Professor Biles of Georgia State College – whom I remember meeting six months or so ago. As you'll see, I've been completely non-committal; and of course I won't send him any 'statement' along the lines he suggests, without having shown it to you first and making sure it's got your complete approval. To do it properly I'd have to look back through my old files; and I haven't time to do that now since my annual Greek jaunt is almost on me. But perhaps I'll have a shot when I get back – and have cleared the usual post-holiday pile out of the way.

Tolon this year for a start – I think I remember you and Ann speaking very well of it; after that an island – though I don't know which one yet; and finally Pylos. For the very end I've been promised – or half promised – a lift from Pylos to Milan via Petras and Brindisi. If that comes off it should be rather fun; and I'd fly back from Milan.

It seems absolutely ages since we met. Do let me know, please, if you and Ann plan a visit to London any time after the end of September. Nothing could be nicer than a meal or a drink together.

Yours ever,

Jack Biles had written on 16 August, reporting that Golding had told him about Monteith's role in the editing of *Lord of the Flies*. Biles wanted to know whether Monteith 'would be willing to make any statement at all' about his 'decision to publish this work'. Biles was a scholar of the modern novel. He went on to publish two books on Golding: *Talk: Conversations with William Golding* (1970) was a long series of interviews about his novels, his war experiences and his philosophy; *William Golding: Some Critical Considerations* (1978), which Biles edited with Robert O. Evans, collected essays by fourteen scholars on Golding's fiction.

Charles Monteith to WG

19 October 1965

Dear Bill,

As you may know, a National Library Week is being organized for the week 12th–19th March 1966. During the week a combined effort will be made by the Booksellers' Association, the Library Association, the National Book League and the Publishers' Association to promote and publicise books, authors and reading generally – an excellent cause, as I'm sure you'll agree.

Apart from the Central Committee, a number of Local Committees have been formed to organize National Library Week activities for their own areas. Among the most important of these will be, it is hoped, lectures, talks, readings and demonstrations; and we have been asked to suggest the names of authors who might be willing to take part. Would you, I wonder, be prepared to have your name put forward by us? If you would – as we very much hope you will be – I wonder if you would mind filling in the enclosed form so far as you can (as you'll notice, it has to be signed by someone here) and letting me have it back as soon as possible?

Yours ever,

WG to Charles Monteith MS

26 October 1965   [Headed Paper: Ebble Thatch]

Dear Charles,

Thanks for the Aldiss book – he entertains and depresses in equal proportions.

I'd sooner not do anything for the N. Lib: Wk – we are likely to be away just about then, indeed sometime before. I hope to get in a dollop of work, and flit.

Blood-and-Bones Biles arrives at London AP today – watch out!

ever

Bill

The Brian Aldiss book was probably *Earthworks*, published by Faber in 1965.

Quite what Jack Biles had done to earn his epithet is unclear but it may have been influenced by the corporeal connotations of his surname and a sense that he chewed up his authors. The label seems to have stuck: Golding uses it several times when talking about Biles in his journals during the 1970s. 'AP' stands for 'Airport'.

1966

To his evident delight, Golding is awarded a CBE in the New Year's Honours list. It is a happy and productive time as he works on a series of interlocking novellas provisionally titled 'Stilbourne Stories'. These, he believes, represent a new phase in his writing. By the early summer, he has sent all three to Faber, and under advice from his American publisher he crafts them into what will become his sixth published novel: *The Pyramid*. Even more pleasing is the purchase of a stunning fifty-two-foot Dutch cutter, *Tenace*, as a conspicuous upgrade on *Wild Rose*. In September there is the by now customary holiday to Greece – this time to Athens, where Peter Green has moved from Lesbos. The year ends with another honour: Golding is made Honorary Fellow of his alma mater, Brasenose College, Oxford.

Charles Monteith to WG   TS

6 January 1966

Dear Bill,

I thought you might like to see the carbon of this letter I've just written to Mr Ryan in reply to his letter to me in which he asked me to forward on this note to you. I can't remember if I ever mentioned Taffrail's protest to you way back in 1960 when it was made!

>   Yours ever,

J. S. Ryan had written to Monteith on 4 January claiming that he had found a source for *Pincher Martin*: Taffrail's *Pincher Martin, O.D.* (1916). Taffrail was the pen name of H. Taprell Dorling, who achieved a measure of success as a writer of novels and non-fiction about sailing and the sea. Monteith had first been alerted to the connection in 1956, so Ryan's claim did not come as news. Having spotted an advertisement for Golding's *Pincher Martin* in 1960, Taffrail himself had written to Faber complaining that 'I do not think it fair, or ethical, that an author should use a title virtually the same as that already used by another'. In his expertly emollient reply, Monteith regretted any pain caused, explained that there was 'no copyright in titles', and ended with the compliment that 'the name Taffrail is so very widely known and loved that I don't think any book-buyer, library subscriber or bookseller is likely to mix up a book by yourself with a book by someone else'.

WG to Charles Monteith   MS

13 January 1966   [Headed Paper: Ebble Thatch]

Dear Charles,

Thanks for your congratulations. I feel at once proud and shy like
a girl with illegitimate triplets. Still (as one pillar of the establishment
to another) it's put our credit up, in the valley, and I have even been
invited to join the darts team.

A happy new year from us all to you. Thank God Christmas is over.
ever
Bill.

Monteith's congratulations followed the official announcement of Golding's CBE
in the New Year Honours List. Peter du Sautoy has annotated this letter in the
top-right corner: 'Lord Golding of the Flies?'

WG to Peter du Sautoy   MS

13 January 1966   [Headed Paper: Ebble Thatch]

Dear Peter

Thank's very much for your congratulations. Let *them* say what they
like, an honour is an honour is an honour – and so good for credit!

It would be good if we could all meet again, weather or not. I dont
suppose there's any hope of you both coming this way? If there is, you
know we'd be delighted.

We may both be up for a day trip sometime in January; and would
be happy to eat/drink with you somewhere. If the trip emerges, I'll let
you know.

Good wishes for 1966. Ann sends her love to you both, as do I.
ever   Bill

WG to Charles Monteith   TS

10 March 1966

Dear Charles,

Herewith my *Novella* (!!), INSIDE A PYRAMID. I'm sending it to you, imploring your help. This sort of thing is a new departure for me, and I dont know whether I'm barking up the wrong tree – or indeed, whether there's a tree at all. Ann and I have now written and read three successive versions of the thing, and I still dont know what it's about. It's growed, like Topsy.

Now could you – please – read it or get some inspired and knowledgeable soul to read it and tell me if it's worth anything? I *know* that anything I write nowadays would be printed somewhere; but you *know* that's not the point.

If it's an OK story, I'll set about considering what others could go with it. How many more would make a book? Two? We could call them STILBOURNE STORIES. Or perhaps I wont be able to do the other two; in which case – I dont know in which case. I'm trying the other copy of this on my American Agent on the grounds that it doesnt much matter what gets published over there provided one doesnt go there ones self. The money's so good. But I doubt if any American mag: would take anything so long, vague, and English. Could I have this MS back?

> Sto kalo!
> Bill

'It's growed, like Topsy': Golding quotes a famous passage from chapter 20 of *Uncle Tom's Cabin* by Harriet Beecher Stowe. When asked who made her, the slave girl Topsy replies, 'I spect I grow'd. Don't think nobody never made me.'

Stilbourne was the name that Golding gave to the fictionalised Marlborough, his childhood town. 'Inside a Pyramid' is set there, and becomes, with some revisions, the third and final episode of Golding's next novel, *The Pyramid* (1967).

'Sto kalo!' is Golding's rendition of the modern Greek Στο καλό, meaning 'Goodbye'.

Charles Monteith to WG TS

28 March 1966

Dear Bill,

I've read INSIDE A PYRAMID – as has Peter – and we're both immensely moved and impressed by it. It's an extremely powerful and highly charged piece of work; and I find that, ever since I read it, it keeps reverberating insistently in my memory. *Very* many congratulations on it; we're looking forward immensely to publishing it.

The only problem, in fact – and I know you've been thinking about this – is what is exactly the best way in which to publish it. It wouldn't be advisable, I'm inclined to feel, to do it by itself as a little book or booklet. There's a general prejudice against such things in the trade – among librarians, booksellers, reviewers etc. etc; and they usually start life with several strikes against them, so to speak. Ideally, we'd like to wait until you've another – or, better still, two more – stories of about the same length which we could publish as one book. Do please let me know what you feel about that. But if you didn't want to wait for some time we might think, might we not, about publishing INSIDE A PYRAMID together with, say, MISS PULKINHORN, THE ANGLO-SAXON, and ENVOY EXTRAORDINARY. That would be quite enough, I'd have thought, to make up a book – though it wouldn't, I think, be such a satisfactory whole as a book consisting of STILBOURNE TALES – or some such general title!

All this is very much an initial and off the cuff reaction – which I wanted to pass on to you at once. If you disagree with it completely don't hesitate to say so!

....

Any more word about the PINCHER MARTIN film? That all sounded *very* exciting; and I do hope something comes of it. It would be very nice, too, to see you and Ann again before long. You'll let me know, won't you, when you're going to be in London?

> Yours ever,

WG to Charles Monteith TS

30 March 1966

Dear Charles,

I'm relieved and delighted to find that you and Peter approve of INSIDE A PYRAMID. It's *so* difficult to stand back and see something that's been laboured over as if for the first time.

The publication problem is simpler than it seems. Since sending you the story, I've written another, MIDSUMMER'S EVE (22500) same length as the other – or a first draft at any rate; and have high hopes of it. Quite a lot of the first draft is viable as it stands; so one more push and it'll be done. It's Stilbourne. Oliver, his father and mother, and some others – beautifully sexy and really rather scabrous, I'm glad to say. So for STILBOURNE STORIES we now have APPROXIMATELY 45000 words. Ideally, I suppose, we need four of these stories. I think I see my way to a third, making 65000 words; but I dont know about the fourth.

Now: if you want to publish just the two, you can have MIDSUMMER'S EVE in a matter of weeks – a month perhaps. I could get the third done in the next three months – fourth, tho', is a query. I dont know how you feel about pub; dates. But a dateline would be helpful if you have something in mind. Can work hard – and feel rather happy, as if I'd come through a narrow door, or opened out in some way. It's middle age now securely established or something.

Even have ideas about STILBOURNE jacket – illustrations and end papers.

We dont go to Greece until next September; so I have the summer nicely spread before me.

PINCHER MARTIN film moves on. We managed to be in the same continent together yesterday and inspected this three-screen technique, though without coming to a definite conclusion, since money is involved. We shall now argue, for a bit. Three-screen is *probably* the right medium for Pincher; but against the gains, the defects are many – difficulty of projection in ordinary cinema, danger of gimmickry, and sheer inertia of chaps with money, who have to be lured by the prospect of ten per cent plus. We need someone so filthy rich he wants to lose half a million for purposes of tax avoidance. I dont know anybody like that and have to leave it to the other two; comforting myself every now and then by the thought that after all I did *write* the thing. I'll keep you posted.

To return. I dont think ENVOY EXTRAORDINARY would go at all with STILBOURNE – want to keep it anyway, for a book of the same sort of frivol sometime. The S. STORIES complement and cross-refer; even illuminate each other.

Ann sends her love
    Bill

'Midsummer's Eve' becomes the first part of *The Pyramid*. Golding's plans for 'Envoy Extraordinary' are eventually realised with the publication of *The Scorpion God* in 1971.

An internal memo from Rosemary Goad on 7 December 1966 reported that Golding and Peter Brook had been working on a script for a *Pincher Martin* film for over a year. 'It will be an experimental film told on three levels and using close up documentary techniques taken from e.g. a French medical documentary filmed inside the human body, a film of the steel industry etc.'

Charles Monteith to WG TS

31 March 1966

Dear Bill,

Very many thanks for your letter of March 30th. It's absolutely splendid news that another story is nearly ready; and that you think you could have a third in three months or so. That, I'm certain, is *quite* enough for a book; so there's no need to worry about a fourth. And STILBOURNE STORIES is a super title.

You'll let me see MIDSUMMER'S EVE, won't you, as soon as it's ready? I'm much looking forward to it.

PINCHER MARTIN FILM. There's no chance at all, I suppose, of you and/or Peter Brook extracting a large subsidy from some worthy body such as the Guggenheim Foundation? It would be worth mentioning to Peter Brook, I think – he may know some people in positions of influence there!

Since I'm going to America in October I'm taking my holidays earlier than usual this year; and I'm thinking of taking a house on Samos for July – with some friends. Have you ever been there, I wonder? Any first-hand hard news – or even second-hand – would be warmly welcomed!

Love to you and to Ann,

In a memo to du Sautoy the same day, Monteith writes that 'This all sounds splendid' and that Golding 'seems to be in excellent spirits'. Du Sautoy replies that three stories may be preferable to four, and that it is much better that the stories are interrelated.

Charles Monteith to WG TS

19 April 1966

Dear Bill,

Back in the office after a *very* agreeable long weekend in France – I'd quite forgotten how nice France can be and how good French food is – I've suddenly realized that I've never answered your query about a deadline for STILBOURNE STORIES.

I've now been into this with our production people; and if we were to aim at publication in the autumn of 1967 – as I'd much like to do, I confess – we'd like to have the complete book (i.e. three long shorts) by 30th September 1966. Would that be possible, I wonder? And *of course* if you'd like to have a contract for the book now do just say and we'd be only too happy to give you one.

Love to you all,

WG to Charles Monteith   TS

25 April 1966   [Headed Paper: Ebble Thatch]

Dear Charles,

Thanks for your letters. I havnt replied before because I've been busy writing.

The second draft of MIDSUMMER'S EVE has just run out at 35,000 words. Even if it doesnt carry all that distance and I have to cut, I think it'll still be 30,000 at least. I have one story left to do (Name for now SAOS, standing for Stilbourne Amateur Operatic Society) and it'll probably not be as long but I think I can do it quickly as it contains a *sophisticated character* which will be such a relief!

Now. MIDSUMMER needs tidying, no more. When all three are in being, I shall need to mesh them as to dates and so forth – where who was when and all that – and STILBOURNE STORIES is done.

Is there any possibility since these are coming off so quickly, of getting them out before autumn 1967? I know you like seeing well ahead, but surely autumn 1966 is an early date line for autumn 1967! If it's any help I can promise you the three before the end of May 1966.

Havnt any hard news of your island. But the Ayrtons are turning up on thursday and I believe they've been there. I'll ask about it.

> Ever
> Bill

PS

How's Ian's MS coming on? Havnt seen him or it, for a long time. Stilbourne S's is going to alter my IMAGE! Ian will be *mad*.

The story about the Stilbourne Operatic Society – inviting a more evocative acronym than Stilbourne Amateur Operatic Society would have done – becomes the middle episode of *The Pyramid*.

Michael and Elisabeth Ayrton were friends of the Goldings. Michael completed several portraits of Golding, one of which was reproduced on the front cover of *The Hot Gates*. It is now owned by the National Portrait Gallery.

Ian Gregor had been working with Mark Kinkead-Weekes on their forthcoming study of Golding's fiction.

Charles Monteith to WG   TS

29 April 1966

Dear Bill,

It's absolutely excellent that STILBOURNE STORIES is coming along so splendidly. If you really could let us have them by the end of May 1966 we could certainly get them out sometime in the spring 1967 – but if it's later than the end of May, though spring publication might still be just possible, I couldn't make anything like a firm promise about it. But if we have them by the end of May the chances are, I assure you, rosy!

Would it be a help if we drew up a contract now and put in 31st May 1966 as a completion date? Or a later one, of course, if that would make you feel more comfortable! So far as money is concerned I suggest the same terms as those we agreed on for THE SPIRE i.e. a straight 15% royalty and an advance of £500. Do let me know – and Peter will be only too glad to send you an agreement.

Ian is coming to stay with me at Oxford the weekend after next; and I'll find out all I can then about how the book is coming on. And in the meantime I think I'd better give him some advance warning about STILBOURNE STORIES.

Do please pass on anything you find out from the Ayrtons about Samos. The only adverse point I've heard is *remoteness* – but that, to my mind, isn't an adverse point at all.

Love to you all,

3 May 1966   [Headed Paper: Ebble Thatch]

Dear Charles,

I dont think there's much point in a contract yet. I hoped for publication in the autumn of 66! As that's not to be, there's no need to hurry. I'm in the first draft of 3rd story (now called SOS) and will surface later.

Please dont tell Ian about Stilbourne! Up to the end of The Spire is a period, and apt for criticism. This is a new life, or look or whatnot. I know about the period, because last Sunday (For Reasons Of State) I agreed to be interviewed (and *was*) by Comrade (Mrs) Professor Valentina Ivasheva of Moscow University who told me about it. It was a great pity that before I knew about her I'd turned down an American professor. That would have been A Confrontation. So Ian can be left to roll up all that period like a rug and tuck it away. Nothing personal of course.

Which reminds me; if Ian will be with you next weekend (6, 7, 8 May) and drives to Oxford, would you both feel like driving down here for a meal? It's a pleasant drive, doesnt take all that long and we'd be happy to see you anytime.

Very little information about Samos, except that it is: quiet, fertile, main town an Edwardian sort of watering place on the lines of Rapallo. The other town, smaller, Greeker is the better bet. Sorry to be so little use; but the Ayrton's had only been there in someone else's yacht and that's not the same as staying in a house. Dont forget to 'brush up your Linguaphone'.

> Ever
> Bill

PS It was fun being treated like Tolstoy at his dascha! Comrade Ivasheva was very positive about the chauffeur not eating with us. 'He would not expect it!' Vive something or other.

Golding did not realise that Monteith had already told Ian Gregor about the Stilbourne project in 'a brief warning note' on 27 April.

Valentina Ivasheva got to know Golding a little and visited again in 1973. She wrote about a number of modern English and Irish novelists, including Iris Murdoch and Graham Greene, as well as Golding.

Linguaphone made a series of 'Brush up your . . .' language courses.

Charles Monteith to WG   TS

4 May 1966

Dear Bill,

Very many thanks for your letter of May 3rd. OK – let's not bother about a contract now but wait until the whole thing is complete. Delighted that SOS is under weigh.

Ian knows that there will be a new book next year; and he knows that it's going to be called STILBOURNE STORIES – and will consist of three novelle. But that's *all* he knows about it; and I shan't, I promise you, breathe a further word to him. I can quite see the point about THE SPIRE ending a Period!

If we could manage it, it would be tremendous fun to drive over with Ian and see you next weekend. I'll certainly mention it to Ian as soon as I see him – and we'll give you a ring. I think the only possible time would be Sunday evening since I've arranged a small lunch party for Ian in All Souls – and we wouldn't be able to get away until everybody had dispersed. But if it is a possibility we can discuss times etc. on the telephone. I'd simply adore to hear the full story of the Russian Confrontation.

Many thanks for the Samos information. The village the house is in is *very* remote – so we'll be well away, I've no doubt, from the Rapallo-type town.

　　　　　Love to you all,

WG to Matthew Evans   TS

4 June 1966

Dear Mr Evans,

Thank you for your letter and enclosure of 1st June. It was kind of you to propose a fee for my reading, but I cant accept it. Perhaps you would pass this news on; though I should be happy to get copies of the books when they appear.

Once more, I'm confining my comments to fact rather than interpretation.

THE INHERITORS.

Cap VIII. Since the hunters have not brought back food and the new people are turning against Marlan, he points to the hut where Liku is.

She is killed and eaten, though Fa prevents Lok from seeing this. (Thus homo sapiens exhibits all the beastial behaviour credited to H. neanderthaliensis in the epigraph.)

FREE FALL.

No particular comment, except that I intended the floorcloth to be seen to be left in the broom cupboard by accident.

I dont want to seem to give my personal approval to these books, which seem to me in fact to be the dullest sort of aid to dully passing dull examinations set for dull people by dull people. Since I cant stop it, I have seen that Dr Dewsnap gets his main facts right – and hope for copies of the books to go into my personal museum of the scholastic racket. You'd better not let the Monarch Press read this last paragraph!

       Yours sincerely
       William Golding.

Matthew Evans had joined Faber as Peter du Sautoy's assistant. He became the managing director aged thirty and succeeded Monteith as chairman of the firm in 1981.

    Monarch Press had first written to Faber in February, explaining that it planned to publish a student guide to *Pincher Martin* by Terence Dewsnap. Golding read a draft and made several corrections. Guides to *The Inheritors* and *Free Fall* soon arrived from the same author. Matthew Evans prompted Monarch to offer a reader's fee, which Golding rejected in order to keep his distance. Later in June, Monarch forwarded yet another Dewsnap study, this time focusing on *Lord of the Flies*. Noting that 'our pedestrian friend has done it again', Golding told Evans that he had not read the new guide and that 'this cant go on!'

Charles Monteith to WG   TS

28 June 1966

Dear Bill,

    STILBOURNE STORIES is absolutely super! I read and re-read them over the weekend – and enjoyed and admired them immensely! Very many congratulations on them! I'm looking forward enormously to their appearance in the bookshops next spring.

    I'll return the whole lot with this letter; and I really would be tremendously grateful to you if you could let me have them back in their

A page from the untitled manuscript of what became *Lord of the Flies*.

21 Bourne Avenue
Salisbury.
Wilts.
14th Sept. 1953.

Dear Sir

I sent you the type-script
of my novel
'Strangers from Within'
which might be defined as an
allegorical interpretation of a
stock situation.

I hope you will feel
able to publish it.

Yours faithfully
William Golding

[freelance reader's notes:] True: The Future Absurd + uninteresting fantasy about the atom bomb on the children's exploration of an 'escapee' group of who land in New Guinea. Rubbish & dull. Pointless

The cover letter accompanying 'Strangers from Within', with the freelance
reader's comments in green ink: 'Rubbish & dull. Pointless'.

<u>Alternative titles for William Golding's novel:-</u>

Wyc ?   Island Impact

Hunt the Island

They Came to an Island

AP.   Island Refuge

Offspring of an Island

The Foster Island

Beast in the Jungle

CM.   The Isle is Full of Noises

Fun and Games

Beast on the Island

Trouble Island

The Beast on Coral Island

Island Trouble

AF   Island Story

My Island

Let's Play Islands

Smoke on the Island

New Coral Island

Coral Island Renewed

Suggestions from various Faber editors for the title of Golding's novel.
Monteith reassured WG that 'a perfect title is the sort of thing that
is suddenly revealed rather than thought out'.

Impressed by Peter Brook's film of *Lord of the Flies*, Golding joked to Monteith, 'I must read the book some day which quite clearly is a terrifying piece of work.'

21 Bourne Avenue, Salisbury, where the Goldings rented the middle-floor flat. WG wrote *Lord of the Flies* and *The Inheritors* while living there.

29 The Green, Marlborough, WG's childhood home and lifelong source of nightmares: 'But that garden again, that house again, will it never let me go?' (J, 27 January 1983)

Photographed by Howard Coster for *Vogue*, 1955. 'It makes me look as though I were seated in the police station trying ingratiatingly to explain away my possession of a packet of dirty postcards.'

Left: WG on a family holiday with David and Judy in North Wales around the time that he was writing 'Strangers from Within'.

Right: WG on holiday with Ann, early 1950s.

WG at the helm of *Wild Rose*, having apparently overcome the fear
he had confessed to Monteith: 'I've bought a boat, a huge one, fourteen
tons now lying in Rochester and I'm terrified of her.'

This 1965 portrait by WG's friend Michael Ayrton was reproduced on the hardback cover of *The Hot Gates*.

Left: Ebble Thatch, remembered by Monteith as 'delightful if, when I first went there, slightly cramped with a lethally low-ceilinged passage into the dining room'.

Right: WG at Delphi with Lalage Pulvertaft and Ann, 1967. 'It is beautiful and dead,' he wrote in *Holiday*.

William Golding by Cecil Beaton, 1975.
'It's the nearest I've ever come to looking like Vivien Leigh.'

The Faber Board, 1975. Standing, l to r: John Nichols, Giles de la Mare, Rosemary Goad, Tony Pocock, Matthew Evans, Donald Mitchell, Peter Phillips; sitting, l to r: Peter DuBuisson, Charles Monteith, Tom Faber, Peter du Sautoy, Richard de la Mare.

Above left: Peter du Sautoy, who eventually became Chairman of Faber. 'We feel we have a friend at court,' WG told him.

Bottom left: John Bodley, WG's editor from the mid-1980s, seen here with Valerie Eliot.

Right: Matthew Evans succeeded Monteith as chairman of Faber in 1981 and negotiated several contracts to WG's satisfaction: 'Thank God he's on our side.'

The Nobel Prize ceremony, 1983. L to r: Charles Monteith, Ann Golding, Queen Silvia and King Carl XVI of Sweden, WG. 'It is a great pleasure to meet you, Mr Golding. I had to do *Lord of the Flies* at school.'

Below: Sir William with Lady Golding at Buckingham Palace, 1988. 'As [Her Majesty] was adjusting the ribbon round my neck, with the occasional maternal tuck she said, "Are you still writing?" I replied: "Yes marm." She said "Good.": which I think exhibits a degree of critical insight.' (J, 27 July 1988)

Above: WG and Monteith, 1984. 'Poor Charles, it must be *such* a business jollying authors along.' (J, 18 September 1974)

Tullimaar. 'Charles refers to the move as "your Daphne du Maurier phase", blast him.' (J, 15 January 1985)

WG and Ann at his seventy-fifth birthday party, organised by Faber. 'Everyone was most kind. Happy birthday was sung. I blew out seventy five candles.' (J, 20 September 1986)

Ann and Charles – WG's 'literary parents' – earlier the same day at the Faber offices, with Jacob Epstein's bust of T. S. Eliot lurking in the background.

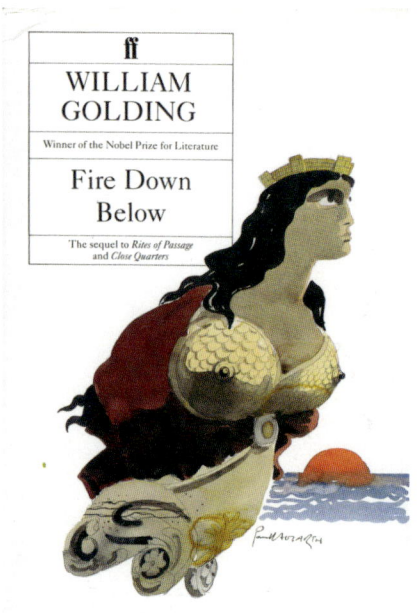

Above left: Paul Hogarth's cover. WG had commented on an earlier sketch, 'The armoured tits arnt big enough. Good God, I could hardly get my own into that indication!'

Above right: Another Paul Hogarth cover, about which Golding complained to John Bodley that the sails were being 'filled with wind arse-backwards'.

Right: WG with Pete Townshend. When asked in interview who had been his most famous guest, Townshend replied, 'William Golding came to dinner with Michael Foot. They were spectacular.'

absolutely final form as soon as you possibly can. I've booked a space for them on the Spring List – but the longer the time goes by without the final manuscript being sent to Production the harder it will be to keep it intact.

The only comments and/or queries I've got arise out of *Midsummer's Eve*. First of all, if the final section – about Colonel Wright – is to be retained then, I think, you ought to retain the opening section as well – which at the moment you've deleted. Without it, it doesn't make very much sense. Personally, I don't myself think that the Colonel Wright frame does very much for the story as a whole – an immensely good story it is – and my vote, given with some hesitation, would be in favour of deleting both the introductory piece and the tail piece.

The second point is about the moment when Ollie realizes the truth about the goings-on between Evie and Wilmot. I'm probably being frightfully crass and stupid about this – but I can't quite see why he should have realized everything at that particular moment. Shouldn't, perhaps, something a little more explicit be either said or done? But I expect I *am* wrong about this – and I mention it with the greatest possible hesitation.

....

What a wonderfully rich mixture the whole book is! I was very moved by it – and also extremely amused – particularly by SOS. And, as you say, it's the beginning of a new Period.

Incidentally, I'm off to Greece on Thursday evening and won't be back in the office until the last week of July. I wonder, therefore, if you'd mind sending the stories back to Rosemary or to Peter; and they'll deal with any queries there may still be.

Much love to you and to Ann,

PS I've suddenly realised that I've been so carried away by STILBOURNE STORIES that I quite forgot to mention money! Would a straight 15% royalty be all right? And an advance of £500 payable as you like? If so do let us know and Peter will send you a contract straight away.

Golding did delete the 'Colonel Wright frame' to which Monteith objected. In the drafts, Colonel Wright is an American soldier temporarily based in England. Chatting to Oliver, he mentions that his late wife came from round these parts. The wife turns out to be Evie, who had died in a car crash in the United States less than a year previously.

What Monteith calls 'SOS' is the untitled middle section about the Stilbourne Operatic Society.

Charles Monteith to WG   TS

29 July 1966

Dear Bill,

I'm back now after three rather spiffing weeks away – two in Samos and one in Turkey. I'll insist on telling you all about them when I see you next.

Any more news, I wonder, about STILBOURNE STORIES? We're much looking forward to getting the final version so that we can get it off to Production; and I wonder, too, if you'd like Peter to send you a contract for it?

Harcourt Brace, incidentally, are delighted to hear that SS is virtually ready; but Julian Muller expresses some misgivings about the title. He thinks, I gather, that a joke title like this might, with some critics, misfire; and I'm inclined to wonder if he mightn't perhaps be right. If a reviewer *wanted* to be nasty it *is* rather handing it to him on a plate! Do please let me know what you think.

       Love to you all,

Julian Muller was Golding's editor at Harcourt, Brace. Monteith reported his own relief in an internal memo that Golding had dropped 'Stilbourne Stories' as a title.

WG to Charles Monteith   TS

23 August 1966

Dear Charles,

Delighted to hear that Samos and Turkey were so good. You must be positively fluent.

We're just back from sea and *Tenace* and am full of horror at work facing me but bracing up. I'll get St–lb–rn– St–r–s to you at the very first moment possible; but irritating mess with Curtis Brown who have Inside A Pyramid and want to sell it to Esquire for next to nothing. Cables flying, Atlantic cables white hot. Damn the lot. Why cant I be a barge master. Also inland revenue blistering my neck with fiery breath. I am thinking more and more seriously of living abroad because I *cant* go on buying the country H bombs.

Perhaps Julian Muller (a cautious type) is right but I dont know. Let's think. Also dont know that Harbrace have lien on stories, what with Curtis Brown holding Pyramid.

I expect we'll be up some time in the Autumn and I'll let you know. It would be good to meet. But we have a half-mind to spend the last bit of Autumn in Greece – when work straight – not having been there for a year. Restless types; and since Tenace has to spend the winter in a yard to be tidied up, we cant immediately set off by boat. (But what a travel book it will be! *Sideways Through Europe in a Racing Hoogaart!*)

'We believe W.G. is moving towards Rome.' *The Tablet.*

Well I cant go on like this. Just putting off work, that's what it is.

    Love from us both

      Bill

Tenace was Golding's new boat, a cutter-rigged Hoogaars that, at fifty-two feet long, was a considerable upgrade on *Wild Rose*. After a conversation with Golding on 25 August, Monteith reported that 'Bill seems in excellent form and obviously the boat (the name is pronounced in the French manner with the accent on the second syllable) is a wow. It's moored at the moment in Beaulieu river and we'll all be invited down for a sail before long.'

'Inside a Pyramid' was published later that year in the 1 December edition of *Esquire*.

Harbrace: Harcourt, Brace.

WG to Charles Monteith

                                      TS

31 August 1966

Dear Charles,

Herewith the stories. I'm afraid the MS is a mess as usual. Will try to do better in future.

Admitting that Julian Muller – in his typical way – has a down to earth point, then I'm stuck for a title. It's about Stilbourne, about women, about Oliver and about – to a lesser extent – music.

    Stilbourne Stories.

    The Music Makers.

Three Women.　　(Three Sisters? Judy O'Grady?)
The Best of British Luck.
The Pyramid.

In a way I like The Pyramid with overtones of weight and deadness and suffocation; we might even have a quotation from the Precepts of Ptah-hotep; 'If thou be among people make for thyself love, the beginning and end of the heart.'

Not much else to say. I've had vague ideas of the next thing. Which reminds me – Ian Gregor makes mysterious mention of September. Does this mean he's finished and we can exchange proof copies? You'll be entertained I hope to hear that I'm collecting a small library of American analyses of me, none very good; or perhaps none very flattering would be more accurate – have even evolved a ballad, some of which goes;

> The boys are back at Flagstaff,
> At Ashcan and at Penn,
> They're rating Full Professor,
> Or even Dean of Men
> Because they wrote a book upon
> The sort of thing I am –
> Now blessings on my Oxbridge
> That doesn't give a damn!

Hope we shall see you down here in your good time

　　　　ever
　　　　Bill

PS Beware. Prof. Biles is lurking in the undergrowth of Grosvenor Square.

Ptahhotep was an ancient Egyptian vizier of the twenty-fifth century BC. His Precepts (more commonly referred to as Maxims or Instructions) were discovered in 1847.
　Grosvenor Square in Westminster was the site of the US Embassy.

Charles Monteith to WG　　　　　　　　　　　　　　TS

9 September 1966

Dear Bill,

The book has gone off to Production this afternoon and a xerox copy is on its way by air to Julian Muller. I'm delighted, too, that Mr

Simmons and your accountant got the contract/tax problem worked out between them – and I'm sure you'll already have got a contract from Peter.

We all like THE PYRAMID (a nice architectural companion piece to THE SPIRE) so may we settle for that; and I've already put in at the right place at the beginning that splendid quotation from Ptah-hotep.

Ian and Mark's book is in Production but we don't expect to have proofs before November. It will probably appear two months or so before THE PYRAMID – which strikes me as the right sort of interval. If they were to appear too near to each other there's a danger, I suspect, that a number of literary editors would have them reviewed together; and that all we'd get about Mark and Ian's study would be a number of concluding paragraphs tacked on at the end of reviews of THE PYRAMID. I'll be fascinated to know what you think of it. I think I can assure you with every confidence that it's *much* better than any of the American books that you have collected.

See you soon, I hope.

Yours,

PS Many thanks for the warning about Prof. Biles. I had forgotten all about him, I confess.

L. R. Simmons was Faber's chief accountant.

WG to Charles Monteith   TS

17 September 1966   [Headed Paper: Ebble Thatch]

Dear Charles,

I'm glad THE PYRAMID has gone to production; and how right you are about the companion piece to the Spire! Visually, it's exact.

Had Boris Ryurikov down here (plus simultaneous translator – but made contact really via my kitchen German, and am very proud of this. Maybe I'm *not* so bad at languages after all? Thinks.) Upshot is, he would like a copy of THE PYRAMID as soon as possible. Seemed rather excited. (*You* know Boris.) I'm not sure of the xerox situation; but *if* there is one about, could you forward it from F&F to the following address:

BORIS RYURIKOV
EDITOR-IN-CHIEF
'FOREIGN LITERATURE' MAGAZINE
41 PYATNITSKAYA STR.
MOSCOW.

I must own that I'm a bit excited too, because it might mean pounds for F&F and roubles for me so that we could come back from Russia next year with Ann swathed in sables and carrying a couple of ikons. Apparently their mean circulation is 170,000; the smallness of which they explained away on the grounds that they are a gigh brow gouse. Apparently wordwise, THE PYRAMID would fit into one issue. Those brows must be high and tough.

Havnt had a contract from Peter yet but am not worried. The fact is we may very well have to leave the country anyway, to break the vicious circle of paying for one Polaris after another.

Took Judy to Agnew's where she was *completely* unable to make up her mind. If it had been me, I'd have bought a sketch of Emma Hamilton by Romney – dead cheap and just the thing for TENACE. (We keep our Romneys in the boat.) But thanks anyway for your help, little use though we made of it.

We both feel a bit buffeted one way and another and shall disappear in the direction of Greece or Dalmatia at the earliest possible moment to catch the end of the autumn. Spend it while you've got it – that's us nowadays.

Ever
Bill

'gigh brow gouse': 'highbrow house' (presumably written here as pronounced).
    Agnews Gallery is an art dealer in London. George Romney was a fashionable eighteenth-century portrait painter.

Charles Monteith to WG   TS

20 September 1966

Dear Bill,

I've been through the final version of THE PYRAMID – and found that I was even more impressed and entertained than I had been before. Those very tiny points which I raised when I last wrote to you about it seem to me to have been dealt with absolutely admirably. One new thing did occur to me however – which, if you agree with it, could certainly be dealt with in proof. It concerns the last of the three stories, *Inside A Pyramid*. It seems to me that this story – which was the one written first, wasn't it? – still retains a few explanatory 'asides' which would clearly be necessary if the story were to stand on its own; but which become redundant when it's positioned as it is now in THE PYRAMID as a whole. The sort of thing I have in mind is that it isn't necessary, surely, in this third story to make it clear that Oliver is the dispenser's son – since we know that already; and I think there are one or two similar short explanatory pieces about other episodes and characters – which anybody who's read the first two stories would know. Do let me know what you think about this.

I've done a draft blurb – of which I'll enclose a copy. Please don't hesitate to make any changes you like – or to rewrite it – or to tell me that I simply must try again and that I've got it all wrong!

Alas, my Dorset weekend has been cancelled – when I hoped to fit in a visit to Ebble Thatch on the way there or back. But it will take place now, I think, when I get back from America in early November – and I'll certainly keep you posted.

Love to you all,

WG to Rosemary Goad   TS

22 September 1966   [Headed Paper: Ebble Thatch]

Dear Rosemary,

Thanks for your letter(s) about POST. But a difficulty rises – and I dont quite know how to phrase this delicately. Am I dealing with them (if I deal with them) through you, or through my American Agents, Curtis Brown? *If* I'm dealing through you – or through myself, they (my agents) will be hurt, wounded, pained, surprised, even.

Is it OK by you if I now waft the affair in their direction? The truth is, I'm a desirable bit of real estate for the time being, and keep wounding people by acting as if I were autonomous. Property, valuable but autonomous, is a very wounding thing in an agent's eyes.

TENACE fulfils all expectation; and is *so* beautiful she had already doubled the influx of tourism to Beaulieu River. As the river trip boats pass, loudspeakers going (and on your right hand you will see a particularly beautiful example of a Dutch Hoogaart's Cutter) I am torn between standing casually on deck, in full possession, or standing on the bank just to look at her.

> Ever
> Bill.

'POST': possibly the *Saturday Evening Post*.

WG to John Oliver   TS

16 November 1966

Dear Mr Oliver,

Yes by all means let there be educational light shed on *Free Fall* <and *Pincher Martin*>. But please give me time to change my mind about *Pincher Martin*, come to think of it – I'm not sure I want that one done.

One proviso about *Free Fall*. I dont want to be asked questions about it. Since I'm being treated as a text book, let me at least claim the privilege of a dead author and be inaccessible to the editor. It's not much to ask, is it?

> yours
> William Golding.

(And wont make audible complaints, but behave just like the Mighty Dead.)

John Oliver oversaw educational editions at Faber. He enlisted Frank McCombie to add an introduction and notes to *Free Fall*; the edition was published in 1968.

The letter in the archive is a copy, so it is not possible to tell whether the original was on headed paper. The angle brackets ('<and *Pincher Martin*>') are Golding's own.

Charles Monteith to WG   TS

5 December 1966

Dear Bill,

How absolutely marvellous about your Honorary Fellowship of BNC. I couldn't have been more delighted when I read about it in the Times this morning. Very many congratulations.

I hope that you'll make frequent visits to Oxford to exercise your rights as a Fellow; and don't forget that there'll always be a warm welcome waiting for you not only in Brasenose but in the College next door as well.

Yours ever,

By 'the College next door' Monteith means All Souls, which is opposite
Brasenose across Radcliffe Square.

WG to Charles Monteith TS

6 December 1966

Dear Charles,

Forgive this faint ribbon – it's frozen or something. I've been working at THE PYRAMID.

It's all very difficult. Julian is right, you are right to agree with him
and so am I. But the plain fact is that these three stories – collops –
cant be made into a pyramid by minor operations. To do that, they'd
have to be chopped up, boiled down, and entirely reconstituted. Even
then they'd make a pyramid so *small* it'd be invisible to the naked eye.
That's not worth the bother.

But of course, they are connected, deeply, inextricably. They have
the relationship to each other that the stories have in *The Slide Area*;
and perhaps even more than that. To extend the metaphor almost
beyond what it'll carry, they are separate blocks of stone, which by
their shape, imply at least *some* of the nature of the whole structure, a
corner, perhaps, a few layers from the bottom. It may be, that in course
of time I shall add other blocks, though never complete the pyramid.

So to my mind, they ought to be published without titles, or numbers
even. Three raw lumps of stone which come to an end, each without
comment, and start without it. So perhaps some day if I get round to
heaving another block into place, it'll lie on, or between the others,
without my having to rebuild the lot. I think that's an honest approach,
tho' it'll be misunderstood as only another attempt at mystification.

Thank you for your kind remark about BNC and standing invitation to ALL SOULS; which I am able to reciprocate, now. The BNC
port was very fair in my time; though I made such a hole in it I'm not
sure it's extant. My Hon; Fellowship touched even my Mao-ist son,
who said – 'Congratters, Pater.'

Ever
Bill

PS Have sent two corrected proofs of *The Pyramid* to David Bland by the same post. B

While in the United States on business, Monteith had met Julian Muller at Harcourt, Brace. After discussions with Monteith, Muller wrote to Golding proposing that *The Pyramid* should be published as a novel rather than a collection of stories or novellas: 'Not only are you dealing with a single narrator, but that narrator is going through an evolution in time, in perspective, and in discovery. This is surely the substance of a novel.' Muller also reminded Golding that novels sell far better and estimated that, as a novel, *The Pyramid* would be 'read by four or five or ten times the number of people'.

Gavin Lambert's *The Slide Area* (1959) comprises seven interlocking stories about Hollywood culture and the Californian coast.

WG to Peter du Sautoy   TS

7 December 1966   [Headed Paper: Ebble Thatch]

Dear Peter,

Thank you for your congratulations. I dont know quite what an Hon; Fellowship entails or brings in its train – but when I look back on my academic career I cant help feeling it's a Turnup For The Book.

We have an enormous boat having bits of wood put into her to keep the water out and are what might be called full of apprehensive enthusiasm.

You must both board her sometime.

Our love to you both,
Yours
Bill

Golding's deeply unhappy 'career' as an undergraduate at Brasenose – where he was the only grammar school boy in his year – included a break in his studies and the racking up of a debt to the college so large that it took him until 1957 to pay it off.

Charles Monteith to WG   TS

8 December 1966

Dear Bill,

Thank you very much indeed for your letter of December 6th. I don't, I assure you, quarrel in the very slightest with what you've done; and I do entirely agree that the three blocks of the PYRAMID do hang together and make an organic whole. I'm sure, too, on reflection, that you're absolutely right about avoiding titles or even numbers.

Julian's suggestions – about which, myself, I felt more or less neutral but felt he should certainly pass along to you if he wanted to – were *only* suggestions; and very tentative ones at that. Whether or not they were worth following up was something that could only be decided by you when you were going through the proofs.

I was delighted to hear from Bertold Wolpe this morning that you may be looking in on Monday or Tuesday; and I look forward very much indeed to seeing you then. I do hope you like the jacket that the jacket designer, Leonard Rosoman, has done – I think, myself, that it's very attractive.

I think you'll be hearing separately, too, from Peter Crawley about the question of whether or not we should renew the Penguin license for LORD OF THE FLIES. I know that Peter would very much appreciate a chance to talk all this over with you; and if you could have a word with him too he'd be very grateful.

I'm beginning to think about my next Greek hol already. It looks as though it will probably be Naxos in June.

Yours ever,

Berthold Wolpe was a typographer who worked in the production department at Faber, and Peter Crawley was sales director. The artist Leonard Rosoman designed the cover for *The Pyramid*: a middle-aged woman, naked except for shoes, hat and gloves, walking out of her house towards her front gate, with only some light foliage in the foreground to protect her modesty from the viewer's gaze.

Charles Monteith to WG   TS

15 December 1966

Dear Bill,

A Christmas present for you. Its authors and publisher will await your verdict with some trepidation! (I ought to point out that the printers have made a boob here and there by not leaving clear spaces between the text and the quotations – for example, at the beginning and the end of the long quotation from LORD OF THE FLIES on pages

16 and 17. I'm assured, though, by all concerned, that this will be put right in the finished books.)

I was terribly sorry to miss you when you called in on Monday afternoon but delighted to hear that all went well. I'm very glad that you agree about the Penguin license – and that you thought the jacket was OK.

In case I shouldn't be writing again before then my very best wishes for Christmas and the new year to you, Ann and the family.

Yours ever,

The Christmas present was a proof copy of *William Golding: A Critical Study* by Mark Kinkead-Weekes and Ian Gregor.

Faber had decided not to renew Penguin's paperback licence for *Lord of the Flies* and to go ahead with its own paperback edition.

WG to Charles Monteith   TS

29 December 1966

Dear Charles,

I've read Ian/Mark's book and enjoyed it. As I told them, they've avoided entombment and kept me as a running target. God knows what they'll make of The Pyramid – or what anyone else will, for that matter. Which reminds me, I've sketched out another story for the pyramid – another block – but as there's no chance of it going in with the other three now I shall take masses of time about it, and even forget it. I had a gay, gaudy idea of using the book as a holdall for Stilbourne Stories, but only now realise it wont work. You cant re-publish just for an additional story. Can you think of any way in which I could add a story from time to time? I could perhaps publish additions as mag; stories – and then, *Ultimately* they could all be put in the one book. I like the idea so much of having something indefinitely extensible, but quite see it's bad economics. Nevertheless I ought to add that I'm happy enough about the book as it stands, an honest, unpretentious job, no matter what the critics think.

If all goes well, we ought to get away in TENACE next April, before publication. Would you like a travel book? SIDEWAYS THROUGH EUROPE IN A HOOGAARTS CUTTER. 'Look, Ann,' I cried. 'Do you see that mountain with smoke coming out of the top? It must be Vesuvius!' (or have I said that before?)

I'm writing to Julian at last by this post to encourage him to send me page proofs and accept British spelling conventions. Quite probably he wont do either.

Ever

Bill

Plus proofs for Miss Brooksbank.

This is another example of a letter by Golding surviving in the archive only as a copy, so it is impossible to tell whether it was written on headed paper.

Golding felt particularly concerned about reactions to *The Pyramid*, as he admitted in his diary a decade after its publication: 'I think it's jolly good! But only for me, a private book of great farcical humour and sorrow. How could anyone else understand it or feel it? The technique of narrative is perfect, but the strategy of writing a book that only I can understand is deplorable. It is self indulgence' (J, 1 October 1977).

1967

A year dominated by catastrophe starts pleasantly enough with trips in the spring to Athens and Tbilisi. Despite Golding's terror of reviewers and his refusal to give interviews, *The Pyramid* is enthusiastically received on its publication in June. The following month, Golding, Ann, Judy and some family friends set off from Shoreham on *Tenace* intending to navigate their way through the French canals to the Mediterranean. They are about ten miles south of Selsey Bill when, in fog at 5 a.m., they are struck and sunk by a huge Japanese freighter; their lives are saved when it turns round to pick them up. There is still time in August for a restorative holiday to Greece, but Golding's confidence is now brittle and he gives up sailing altogether.

Charles Monteith to WG   TS

10 January 1967

Dear Bill,

Very many thanks for your letter of December 29th. I'm fascinated to hear about the further Stilbourne story. It wouldn't be a feasible idea – I'm certain you're right about that – to keep on expanding THE PYRAMID; but there's no reason at all why we shouldn't have another Stilbourne book as soon as you've got enough stories to make one. I'm very much a Stilbourne fan – and I would applaud its appearance enthusiastically.

Lucky old you getting away on the *Tenace* in April. Incidentally, if you do ever seriously think about a travel book – or a Greek book – we'd be delighted.

Yours ever,

Charles Monteith to WG   TS

10 February 1967

Dear Bill,

An odd request! A Mrs Dora Robertson wrote the other day to Dick de la Mare asking him if we might perhaps consider republishing a book she'd written about Salisbury Close many years ago. It was published by Jonathan Cape in 1938; it's been out of print for years but second-hand copies are – according to Mrs Robertson – in demand; but Capes – despite all the hints she's been dropping – have refused to consider reprinting it. She now turns to F&F. Though it's obviously a very long shot indeed Dick de la Mare feels that we ought at any rate to think about it seriously; and he wondered if you could possibly find time to look at the book for us and tell us how it strikes you? If you could we'd be very grateful indeed – and, whatever you feel about it as a book, so to speak, you might perhaps find it of some interest because of the Salisbury associations. The best way of giving you some idea what it covers is, I think, to quote the blurb – so here it is:

> Novels have appeared from time to time about Cathedral Closes, but
> no book has as yet attempted to trace the authentic life-history of a
> close from its first beginnings until the present day. Here, gleaned from
> the archives of the cathedral, is the biography of a community over a
> period of 700 years, with its changing manners and customs, its domestic
> problems, its quarrels – all its strength and its weakness. Running through
> the book, as the main stream of interest, is the history of the daily life
> and education of the Cathedral choristers. Several famous musicians
> had charge of these boys in Elizabethan and Stuart times, and new light
> is thrown on the lives of such men as John Farrant and Michael Wise.
> The close of Salisbury is one of the loveliest and most peaceful corners of
> England: now for the first time its stormy past has come to life.

Of course we'll understand if you feel you couldn't possibly find time to look at this for us; but if you could we'd be very grateful indeed. We would too, of course, be only too willing to pay you a fee – and I wonder if ten guineas would be OK?

....

I've now heard from Peter Crawley – who wrote from New Zealand – about the publication date problem PYRAMID-wise and Mark and Ian-wise. I think everything is going to be OK. Though he's quite definitely against putting THE PYRAMID off to the autumn in view of all the preparations that he's made he would be reconciled, I think, to postponing it until June 15th – which would leave a month's gap between the two books. And Bland now tells me that, after all, it's possible to publish Mark and Ian's book on May 4th. I'm not however passing any of this on to Mark and Ian yet – and I don't think I ought to do so until I'm absolutely certain about what's going to happen. The most likely upshot at the moment seems to me to be publication of Gregor and Kinkead-Weekes on May 4th and of THE PYRAMID on June 15th. That in fact would mean a six weeks gap – which should be more than enough.

Yours ever,

Charles Monteith to WG   TS

13 February 1967

Dear Bill,

A Mrs Helen Rapp who runs the Lively Arts programme on the BBC – I think it used to be Home Service but it's now Third Programme – telephoned me this morning to say that she'd very much like to record an interview with you to be put out about the time of publication of THE PYRAMID. The interviewer, I gather, would be John Bowen.

I told her that I'd simply pass this request on to you – which I'm now doing. From our point of view, of course, all publicity is useful! But don't think for one moment, please, that I'm trying to bring the least pressure on you to say Yes if you'd rather say No. If you would like to do it perhaps you could drop a line direct to Mrs Rapp about it at Broadcasting House.

Yours ever,

WG to Charles Monteith   TS

14 February 1967

Dear Charles,

No interview! I hope that doesnt sound stuffy or haughty but these things build up like a flash – or *did* at any rate. I want to avoid even the very, very slight public Face that the Third Programme would give me. That's mostly on behalf of the books I may write; or so I tell myself. Who knows?

I must declare a faint interest in the Salisbury Close book. I've known Dora Robertson off and on for the last twenty-five years; and

– in confidence – have always been terrified of her. I have slight memories of the book itself and would be entertained to see it again and will do my uttermost to be objective. Only for heaven's sake – no, for *my* sake – let this transaction be wholly betwixt me and thee; for if I were to report adversely who knows what spells would be cast? The spire would probably fall on me. No fee required.

Your request emboldens me to lay a proposal before you. I brought back from Greece, an uncompleted MS of Peter Green's. I've neglected it shamefully, tho' I promised him to undertake what must be a delicate manoeuvre on its behalf.

The story is this.

Years ago his publishers contracted with him for a book on the battle of Syracuse. He got deeply interested and told them that his researches were deepening and going beyond what was suitable for the general public. He got (in writing) an encouragement to go ahead and be as detailed as he wanted to be, and take as long as he liked. Then his publisher died and his successors discovered that the poor man had done all this permissive stuff in the euphoria of his ghastly illness. In a sentence, the MS was useless for their purposes. Peter has, or had, a few weeks in which to do a popular write-up; and I dont know if he has or not.

What I *can* vouch for personally is the amount of dedicated research he put into the MS. Obviously I am not scollard enough – or at all – to assess it. Would you be willing to farm the MS to some equipped person for an opinion on whether anything can be done or not? If you are willing to have a look I'll get the MS to you. In confidence, alas, because P seems to be in a bit of a publishing mess.

There's an awful lot of 'in confidence' about this letter. Am I getting Persecution Mania? Probably.

Judy has been and gone and got herself accepted at St Anne's for a BLit or Phil or something; and provided the U board accepts her and she gets a reasonable degree, next Autumn she will grace the Oxford scene. So now and then you *may* detect bearded author creeping along close to those grey walls.

Am at the moment in a writing slump; and mesmerised by the deathly closing-in of the Income Tax people. Otherwise my eyes are fixed on TENACE – being rebuilt – and April's getaway.

> Ever
> Bill

Judy did get the required degree and started a BLitt at St Anne's College in the autumn.

'U': university.

Charles Monteith to WG   TS

15 February 1967

Dear Bill,

As I think you know, we had a routine request some time ago from St Albans Grammar School for permission to use LORD OF THE FLIES as a basis for a short opera; and we sent the usual routine refusal. As agreed with you, we always refuse permission for any dramatizations of the book.

The Head Master has now written personally to Peter asking him if we'd reconsider; and I'll enclose a copy of his letter with this. In view of what he says I'd rather like – provided you agree of course – to say Yes on the strict understanding that the performance is to be an entirely private one for the school only. If you agree what, I wonder, do you think about the suggestion of paying a fee? Perhaps we ought to let them do it free?

Yours,

Charles Monteith to WG   TS

17 February 1967

Dear Bill,

It's extremely good of you to say that you'll look at Dora Robertson's book; and I'll enclose it with this. Be assured that should your report be an adverse one she'll never hear a word of it; and, indeed, even if it should turn out to be a favourable one she won't hear either without your express permission.

And of course I'd be delighted to consider Peter Green's book on the battle of Syracuse. Though nobody here is competent to judge it if you send it in I'll send it at once, I promise, to some competent expert. Poor Peter! I'm sad to hear that he's in a bit of a mess at the moment. (Incidentally, it would be useful to know whether or not he ever did do a popular write-up of the Syracuse book; and if you should be writing to him I'd be most grateful if you'd ask.)

Not in the least surprised about the interview. Indeed I'd have been very surprised, I confess, if you'd said Yes. I do realize, I assure you, how appallingly rapidly these sort of things can snowball.

What absolutely splendid news about Judy. I couldn't be more delighted. Much looking forward, I assure you, to entertaining her – and, I hope, her parents too – in All Souls next Michaelmas Term.

....

Incidentally, I expect you'll have had a proof of THE PYRAMID jacket by now – Bertold Wolpe showed me one yesterday. I think myself that it's turned out very well indeed.

Yours ever,

WG to Charles Monteith   MS

18 February 1967

Dear Charles,

A hasty note – yes, surely. Let the lads do their operetta type version of *Flies*. Lets not charge them anything, either.

They were one of *six* requests in a month. My Patience Is Exhausted. I shall make my own operetta, using only nursery rimes.

ever
Bill.

'My Patience Is Exhausted': the capital letters indicate that Golding is probably quoting the title of the cartoonist Stephen Roth's book of 1942, which in turn quoted – and mocked – a speech made by Adolf Hitler in 1938.

WG to Charles Monteith   TS

23 February 1967   [Headed Paper: Ebble Thatch]

Dear Charles,

Dora Robertson's book. This is so difficult because it's got virtues. My guess is that its great defect is amateurishness. It misses the general public in one direction and the scholar in the other. Cape's title, SARUM CLOSE must have been a counsel of despair, since the book, which was clearly intended as a history of the Choir School became a holdall for everything Mrs Robertson could find. In fact there are a dozen books here instead of one, and none of them dealt with properly. It would have, I think, a limited local appeal – and it's certainly a useful book for anyone intending to write a novel on the SPIRE; but that, I'm thankful to say, implies an even more restricted circulation.

I have a suggestion to make which would then be up to you. Since, in my time, I've been in every house in the Close, you may believe me when I say they are *fascinating*. Why – you could write a fair-sized book on the plumbing! The saying that they are a compendium of English domestic architecture is literally true. Dora must know them ten times more intimately than I do. (One house with a room where Handel gave his first concert in England and another room decorated in Gothic Revival for a visit by the Prince Regent who Did Not Come! Et cetera.) If you *want* a book from Dora, that's the one.

But SARUM CLOSE as it stands – in my opinion, no. But I hope to goodness you will try it on someone else for confirmation. I'll send the copy back to you.

Havnt had proof copy of the PYRAMID jacket.

> Ever
> Bill.

Charles Monteith to WG TS

28 February 1967

Dear Bill,

Very many thanks for your letter of February 23rd. Everything you say about SARUM CLOSE sounds absolutely convincing – and I'm certain that we'll return it to Dora Robertson with a polite note of regret.

What a fascinating idea about a study 'in depth' – as the phrase seems to be now – of all the houses in the Close. I'll most certainly think about this – and try it out on other people here.

Terribly sorry that Berthold hasn't yet sent you a proof copy of THE PYRAMID jacket – I'll give him a prod about that this morning.

> Yours ever,

WG to Charles Monteith   TS

2 March 1967   [Headed Paper: Ebble Thatch]

Dear Charles,

Herewith, no, sorry, under separate cover, Peter Green's Syracuse thing, and Mrs Robertson's SARUM CLOSE. I dont know if Peter completed his popular treatment. He certainly hadnt done so six months ago. His address, if you should want it, is

10 TSIMISKY STREET
NEAPOLIS LYCABETTUS
ATHENS.

And very nice too. You can see the ACROP and everything – also the noble descendants of Hellenus necking under the olives in every possible combination of the sexes. It's a very classical area.

Two unimportant addenda to my estimate of Dora's book. She has a lovely word picture of a little group of boys in black cloaks and caps marching across the grass to the cathedral. She'd have to alter that now. Shortly after the publication of LORD OF THE FLIES they might be seen strolling in a democratic way and shorts, where they had marched. I believe they still do. When I consider how slowly things change in the close, it makes me feel *massive*. Then again, she has a good deal about the *city*, that outlying wilderness; but nothing on the antics of the City Fathers during our various wars and revolutions. They changed sides with a speed and economy unmatched in Real Politik.

We are off – Ann and I – to Russia next Tuesday, we think, for a fortnight. I've got a lot of spare copies of Own Work as presents for literary chums; but would like any spare proofs you have of THE PYRAMID, that exposé of the Class System. They might very well do it before anything else and then *we*, at least, if not F&F, would have lovely roubles to spend on Furs, Ikons, old, unwanted Czarist junk that would otherwise corrupt the Socialist Sixth.

We have bought a record with two hundred words of Russian and have already learnt four words. I dont believe in Russian at all. Nobody, but nobody could make noises like that.

Ever
Bill.

'Hellenus': the mythical ancestor of the Greeks was Hellen, a Thessalian leader who gave his name to ancient (and modern) Greece: Hellas.

Golding implies that the Salisbury choirboys' dress and behaviour have changed because of his portrayal of the choirboys in *Lord of the Flies*.

The Soviet Union covered one-sixth of the Earth's land surface, a fact that inspired the title of Hewlett Johnson's *The Socialist Sixth of the World* (1939). The book was published by Victor Gollancz, and Golding would have known it from his membership of the Left Book Club in the year prior to the outbreak of war. Golding and Ann met in the spring of 1939 at one of the Left Book Club's events in London.

Charles Monteith to WG   TS

3 March 1967

Dear Bill,

Very many thanks for your letter of March 2nd. Here's the last spare proof I have of THE PYRAMID. Do let me know how the Russkies react to it.

Fascinating about the abandonment of the black cloaks in the Close. The power of the Written Word.

Incidentally, we decided yesterday to say No to the re-issuing of Dora Robertson's book; but we'll certainly think further about your idea of a 'study in depth' of the houses in the Close.

Have a super time in Russia. Terribly sorry that I didn't have the chance, before you went, to introduce you and Ann to our Russian Visiting Fellow at All Souls, Professor Gouber, who has already become a venerable and much loved College Institution.

Yours ever,

PS Peter Green's Syracuse book isn't here yet – but I expect it will arrive by the parcel post later today.

Charles Monteith to WG   TS

20 July 1967

Dear Bill,

You may remember that – back in February – you agreed to allow the boys of St Albans Grammar School to do a private performance of a short opera based on LORD OF THE FLIES. This has now been followed by a request from the Headmaster for permission to make a record of this opera; and he tells us that if this permission were granted copies would be sold only to the boys who took part. Do please let me know what you feel about this. Peter du Sautoy – whom I've consulted – is rather doubtful about the proposal. He points out that once the opera is put on record it becomes permanently available – even though only to a very limited number of people. It could well lead, he feels, to a large number of requests from other schools for similar permission.

Very sorry indeed to bother you about all this.

Yours ever,

Charles Monteith to WG TELEGRAM

19 September 1967

BIRTHDAY GREETINGS AND MANY HAPPY RETURNS – CHARLES

1968

Undeterred by the fact that some notebooks went down with *Tenace* the previous summer, Golding continues working on his next novel, 'Here Be Monsters', early in the year. He does not get far before switching his attention to a collaborative project involving the composer John Barry and the director Anthony Simmons: an experimental film script called 'The Jam'. Golding writes countless versions and hopes that Faber will publish the finished work. In October, he and Ann are in Istanbul, but it only reminds them of their love for Greece. Another benefit of the holiday is to take a break from their struggles with David, whose mental health has deteriorated during the year.

Charles Monteith to WG   TS

5 February 1968

Dear Bill,

I've suddenly realized I never wrote an explanatory note about something rather odd that probably reached you through the post a few days ago – a large poster of W.G. and also a calendar containing W.G. as the picture for January. I saw them advertised in the New York Review of Books and thought that you simply must have them. To be on a calendar really is something I think, don't you?

It was very nice indeed seeing you and Ann again the week before last. We must arrange a lunch together soon.

> Yours ever,

WG to Charles Monteith   TS

19 February 1968   [Headed Paper: Ebble Thatch]

Dear Charles,

I have a notion that this is going to be a mixed-up letter because there are a number of things I ought to say to various members of F&F and I've mislaid the letters with their names. Perhaps you'll know the various people to whom the parts ought to go.

Let me think. Yes.

(1) Some money in Italy. I want it kept there so that I can pick it up on my way through to Greece. As I pay Italian income tax, this is quite proper. The only difficulty is where can the agent put it so that on production of passport Mr W. G. Golding 447605 the said foreign body can carry off the loot in AMERICAN EXPRESS travellers' cheques?

(2) A Hungarian body I met at their legation said I am Top Author there and must have piles of money waiting for me. He said 'You could live like a rajah!' I like the idea of living like a Hungarian rajah but it would be awful to get there and find they were all reading Magnolia Street. Can F&F find out what money would be available to me in Hungary for the purchase of Apes, Ivory and Peacocks?

(3) For your information I have notes towards a book and even a provisional title. HERE BE MONSTERS. I'll keep you posted as to progress. I hope it'll be a big, baggy book as little like the others as possible.

Thanks for the Revue Des Deux Mondes. When lit;crit; is in French, doesnt it seem *perceptive*?

We're both going down to Canterbury for next weekend. Hope you'll be there, but suppose not.

I stumble on each Wednesday/Thursday with M. Greek but honestly, seem to make absolutely no progress. Too late! Too late!

Has THE PYRAMID sold any copies? I shall rebuke Mark & Ian for having the effrontery to write a book about my books that sells more than my books do.

Love from us both

Bill

There was more yet if I could remember.

'Here Be Monsters' is the first glimmering of the novel that will be published in 1979 as *Darkness Visible*.

In its issue of 1 January 1968, *La Revue des Deux Mondes* had published an article by Annie Brierre focusing on Golding, Iris Murdoch and Elizabeth Bowen.

The author of the novel *Magnolia Street* (1932) was Louis Golding – no relation but a potential source of confusion. The mistake had been made at least once before: in 1960, a Danish magazine wrote to du Sautoy requesting permission to publish two stories that it had wrongly attributed to William rather than Louis Golding.

Charles Monteith to WG   TS

20 February 1968

Dear Bill,

Just a line to thank you very much for your letter of 19th February. HERE BE MONSTERS sounds intriguing. *Much* looking forward to it.

I'll get all the right people weaving – either Peter du Sautoy or Simmons or both, I imagine – about your Italian and Hungarian queries; and when they've sorted them out they'll write to you direct.

I'll find out, too, what the present sales figures are for THE PYRAMID and let you know.

Alas, I shan't be in Canterbury next weekend. Do give my love to Ian, Mark and Joan.

Love to you and Ann,
   Yours,

PS I've just discovered that the total sales of the Pyramid so far are nearly but not quite 12,000 – which isn't at all bad, I think.

Ian Gregor and Mark Kinkead-Weekes taught at the University of Kent at Canterbury. Joan was Mark's wife. The Goldings visited them on several occasions, and Golding gave guest lectures there, three of which are collected in his second book of essays and reviews, *A Moving Target* (1982).

WG to Charles Monteith   TS

22 February 1968

Dear Charles,

I knew there was something else! I had a letter from Julian Muller, mainly about Biles; but on the subject of THE PYRAMID he informed me to this effect. They're giving some pocket book company permission to print it on a guarantee of 20,000 dollars. That sounds all right, but apparently the twenty thousand is split equally between us and them! In my reply I've said nothing about this at all; but 50/50 seems rather steep to me. The relevant paragraph is as follows.

> In addition to the revenue on regular sales, we've also leased the
> cheap paperback rights at a guarantee of $20,000. This will make you

$10,000 richer. The terms are half on signing (it's signed!) and half on publication (no earlier than 18 months from our publication). We'll also publish a quality paperback under our own imprint and that should bring you some pleasant income for a number of years. So, with a hasty glance backward, it's been a happy voyage.

As I gather (or know, rather) F&F arranged the agreement with HB & W, you'll obviously know whether or not this comes within the terms. I hope I'm not unnecessarily mean, but repeat that 50/50, merely for arranging for someone else to publish is very, very steep indeed.

> Ever
> Bill

HB & W: Harcourt, Brace & World.
Monteith passed the letter to du Sautoy, who replied to Golding on 28 February explaining that this 50/50 division was standard practice among American publishers.

Ann and WG to Charles Monteith   PC

(?) October 1968   Hotel Pierre Loti, ISTANBUL

We came willing to be fair: have just seen Santa Sophia and are now irrationally, passionately and indignantly philhellene.

It's most amusing when one cools off, to watch how ones hackles automatically rise.

> Love from us both
> Ann & Bill

There is no date on the postcard, but it must be very early in October given that Monteith replies on the 7th.

Hagia Sophia is a Byzantine building from the sixth century, originally a church, with minarets from the fifteenth and sixteenth century when it was converted into a mosque. It was a museum when Golding visited; it reverted to a mosque in 2020.

The writing is in Golding's hand. The postcard is split vertically into two halves. The right half has a photograph of the Selimiye Mosque in Edirne. The left half is divided horizontally in two. Top left is the Uzunköprü Bridge (the longest stone bridge in the world). Bottom left is a group of Turkish wrestlers in traditional costume.

Charles Monteith to WG

7 October 1968

Dear Bill,

I was delighted to get your postcard from Istanbul and to know that the sight of Santa Sophia inspired the same feelings of passionate pro-Hellenism in your breast and in Ann's as it did years ago in mine.

It seems far too long since we last met; and I wondered if by any chance you & Ann were planning an expedition to Oxford any time this term? If you were – and if you could make it at a weekend – I'd simply love to have a lunch party at All Souls for you both. Moreover, Ian Gregor is in Oxford this term and he too, I'm certain, would be delighted to see you again. I think I'll be down virtually every weekend except October 26th/27th and November 16th/17th. A particularly convenient one would be the weekend of November 23rd/24th – but that, I realize, is rather a long way off and autumn may have set well in by then.

If an Oxford plan isn't a practicable one, though, do let me know if you – or you and Ann – are likely to be in London in the near future. It would be great fun to get together for a meal or a drink.

I hope the holiday went very well. I much look forward to hearing all about it.

      Yours,

WG to Charles Monteith

18 October 1968   Ebble Thatch, Bowerchalke

Dear Charles

A hasty note to let you know we're back. We'll certainly be up at Oxford some times this term, what with Judy, and all; but at the moment things are too confused (*ghastly* post et cetera) to make any plans.

Ought to add that at last we took your advice about snorkelling, and bitterly regret not doing it sooner. You were right – how not? – in every particular; a completely new world and we are hooked.

The Greek referendum was wryly funny; NAI *everywhere* at government expense; and now on 23rd October, I believe they'll have to remove them all since that's 'OXI day, when King Paul said '"OXI!' to Mussolini – or turn them into public declarations of 'NAI ΣΤΟ OXI!'

Ann sends love

ever

Bill

'Οχι Day is actually 28 October, a Greek national holiday commemorating the date in 1940 when the prime minister Ioannis Metaxas (not King Paul) refused permission for Mussolini and Axis forces to enter the country. 'Οχι means no; Golding points out the awkward fact that, in the referendum planned for 15 November 1968, the military junta was campaigning for a yes (ναι) vote in favour of its proposed new constitution. *NAI ΣΤΟ OXI!* means *YES TO NO!*

Charles Monteith to WG   TS

12 December 1968

Dear Bill,

I've been conscious for some time that – they're much too nice to press the matter – both Mark and Ian feel that they ought perhaps to have some small share in the royalties of the educational edition of LORD OF THE FLIES – now that it's turned out to be such an established school success.

I brought this up at last week's editorial committee meeting here; and we formulated the very tentative proposal that we might perhaps pay them a 2½% royalty of which, if you are willing, 1¼% would be deducted from your 10% royalty, while we ourselves would make up the remaining 1¼%; i.e. we would be paying on the entire book a royalty of 11¼% of which 8¾% would go to you and 2½% would go to Mark and Ian jointly. If it were economically feasible, we would of course have been very glad to have borne the entire 2½% royalty ourselves – but a total royalty of 12½% on an educational edition simply wouldn't work, since, as I know you'll appreciate, it's absolutely essential to keep everything pared down to the minimum in such a competitive field.

Do please let me know what you think about this; and don't feel, please, that we're putting any pressure at all on you to agree if you feel you'd rather not.

Yours ever,

Charles Monteith

In-house discussion had taken place at Faber over appropriate remuneration for Gregor and Kinkead-Weekes, with some voices arguing that a further flat payment was fine but a royalty for editing an educational edition was wrong in principle. Finally, a precedent was found. T. S. Eliot had agreed a split with Nevill Coghill for Coghill's introduction and notes to *Murder in the Cathedral*: 7.5 per cent to the author and 2.5 per cent to the editor. By agreeing to share the additional cost with Golding, Faber was proposing a better deal than Eliot's.

WG to Charles Monteith   TS

18 December 1968   [Headed Paper: Ebble Thatch]

Dear Charles,

Yes indeed and with the greatest good will not only from me, but Ann too. They're a nice pair, and why not cut them in solely for that reason? A small Christmas present!

I dont know if Rosemary told you, but I've got mixed up in a film script; and rather excitedly so – it feels almost as if some faculty, some muscle were toning up again. Who knows? One day I might even write that book! But the point is, are you ever likely to be interested in *publishing* a film script by me? The only example I can think of is Dylan Thomas's script on the bodysnatchers; and of course, that's different for a number of reasons. But if you were to feel interested of course it would make a difference to the agreement with the film people.

I've missed out what to me is the important part. Right now, (as of now) I've got a concept which seems to me as exciting as anything I've ever done – yet what will happen? I expect that concept to be changed, modified, perhaps for the better but more probably for the worse. Publication (ultimately) of my basic intention in my own words would secure me against that. I'm still expressing myself badly. Can you see what I'm getting at, through all this mishmash of words?

      Ever

       Bill

PS Could your secretary send me a hard cover copy of the Inheritors?

      B

Golding had been collaborating with the composer John Barry and the director Anthony Simmons on a film called 'The Jam' about a huge traffic jam on a motorway outside a city called Megalopolis.

Dylan Thomas's *The Doctor and the Devils*, a film script based on the body snatchers Burke and Hare, was published by New Directions in 1953.

Charles Monteith to WG

19 December 1968

Dear Bill,

Thank you very much for your very exciting letter of December 18th about the film script. Yes, of course we want to publish it. We've already published at least one – John Osborne's script for TOM JONES – and we'd love to publish yours. As soon as you can do please let me know the details; and the moment you'd like a firm contract with us just say. Is it the same idea, I wonder, that Anthony Simmons spoke to Rosemary about earlier this year – the vast traffic jam; or is it something quite different?

All the very best for Christmas and the New Year to you and Ann.

> Yours ever,

PS How extremely generous of you to say that Ian and Mark have a slice of the royalty on the educational edition of LORD OF THE FLIES. I'm writing to them about this now and I know how very grateful indeed they'll be. Indeed, I may see them this evening since I'm going down to Canterbury to a committee meeting about the TSE Memorial Lectures.

PPS A hardcover INHERITORS will go off to you straight away.

Faber had published John Osborne's screenplay of *Tom Jones* in 1964, the year after the film starring Albert Finney was released.

The T. S. Eliot Memorial Lectures at the University of Kent were established in 1967 with W. H. Auden as the inaugural speaker.

1969

As David continues to struggle with mental illness, the toll on Golding's own health is massive and he starts drinking heavily again. Despite successive rewritings of 'The Jam', the project is going nowhere. In July, Golding sets off on a three-month restorative journey with Ann and David to Italy, Turkey and Bulgaria. The only realistic writing plan is for a collection of novellas, of which Golding already has two – 'Envoy Extraordinary' and his rediscovered story of predynastic Egypt.

WG to Charles Monteith   MS

8 March 1969   [Headed Paper: Ebble Thatch]

Dear Charles,

I write to you first as a friend, simply to let you know how we get on.

You may or may not have known that our poor son David has found it increasingly difficult to settle – and later still, for the last 18 months, by contrast, impossible to leave home. All this ended as we ought to have known it would in what as a blanket phrase I will call a severe 'Nervous breakdown'. He has been under treatment for the last six weeks and we begin to dare to hope that he may improve, if slowly, and maintain the improvement. I cannot describe what he has gone through nor what we have gone through. You were kind to him at Oxford; and I think it reasonable for his sake to tell you that his intransigence and 'difficulty' (which you must have noticed) was very probably the signs of his slowly developing sickness. We can hope, but cannot tell what the future will bring.

Now to address you as a publisher! The Jam goes ahead and in a kind of automatic trance I have written a first draft in the shape of a novel from which I and Tony Simmons will ultimately cut a film script. I'm hazy about the agreement situation. But if you're interested, Odgers at Curtis Brown is the man you must contact because obviously this novel and/or film script stands in a different position from any of my other stuff.

I've also turned up a 25,000 word novella about predynastic Egypt which I'd forgotten. Ann says it's good and needs not much more than revising – Would that much and Envoy Extraordinary together make a book?

She sends her love; and, with me, wonders where on earth the Winter went to.

> Ever
>> Bill

David had been committed to hospital against his will in mid-January. After successful treatment, he was now convalescing, albeit with an uncertain prognosis.

The novella about predynastic Egypt had been finished in April 1964, when Golding, feeling dissatisfied, put it to one side, intending to rewrite. As the title story of *The Scorpion God*, it is finally published with 'Envoy Extraordinary' and one additional story, 'Clonk Clonk', in 1971.

Charles Monteith to WG · TS

11 March 1969

My dear Bill,

Thank you very much for your letter of March 8th. I can't tell you how desperately sorry I am to hear about David – though I'm not, I confess, altogether surprised. It must have been a most appalling strain for you and for Ann and I needn't say how much I hope that he does improve under treatment. Do please let me know how he progresses. (Incidentally, I've told Peter du Sautoy and Rosemary, as I imagine you'd have wanted me to. We'll treat it as completely confidential, of course.)

How splendid that THE JAM goes ahead so well. I needn't say how much I long to read 'the first draft in the shape of a novel'. We'll certainly get in touch with Odgers at Curtis Brown; and Peter and I would both very much like to talk over with you personally the whole question of what and when to publish. If you're likely to be in London in the near future do please let me know.

Yes, of course, do send me the novella about pre-dynastic Egypt. I'd very much like to read it and we'd be very glad to think about publishing it together with ENVOY EXTRAORDINARY.

> Very best love to you and to Ann,

Charles Monteith to WG TS

3 April 1969

Dear Bill,

I wonder if by any chance you and Ann would like to come to the buffet supper at Drapers Hall on Tuesday 22nd April when the first Booker Prize for fiction will be awarded? I'd be absolutely delighted if you would. It's at 7.30; but I imagine we could certainly meet for drinks before then and all go on together. Quite a number of people from the firm will be going including, of course, Peter and Molly.

I very much hope that next year there will be a Golding among the candidates! I'm much looking forward to getting that novella from you.

I imagine that you must have been away since I telephoned in vain a couple of times in the hope of arranging a meeting to talk about the film before I made an approach to Curtis Brown. Peter and I would both like to see you and talk it over before we do anything else.

> Yours ever,
> Dictated by Charles Monteith
> and signed in his absence,

The winner of the first Booker Prize was a Faber author, P. H. Newby, for his novel *Something to Answer For*.

Charles Monteith to WG TS

18 April 1969

Dear Bill,

It was very good to see you again last Tuesday; and I'm looking forward immensely both to THE JAM and to the volume of novelle and short stories. I've already written to Graham Watson to make an offer for THE JAM: and I hope that that will all be tied up in the near future.

I do feel, too – as does everyone else here – that it would be a good idea to get the other book tied up as well; and we wouldn't, I assure you, push you or pester you in any way about the completion date. So far as terms are concerned, I suggest the usual straight 15% royalty; and if you'd like an advance – I'm not sure whether or not you want one in view of your present tax situation – should we say £500 payable on demand. I'll ask Peter du Sautoy's dept to send you a contract straight away; but if you've any queries about it don't hesitate, please, to get in touch with me or Peter and I'm sure we can sort things out.

I'll remind you nearer the time about the Chichele Dinner at All Souls on Saturday, May 17th. I'd be absolutely delighted if you could come.

> Yours ever,

Graham Watson worked for Curtis Brown, which was handling the rights for 'The Jam' on Golding's behalf. Golding had written a 65,000-word draft and the first two chapters of a second draft, but there were some copyright complications so opaque that even Faber and the agents struggled to understand them. John Barry's original idea for 'The Jam' was based on a French short story for which he himself had an ownership contract.

The Chichele Dinner at All Souls is an annual event named after the college's founder.

WG to Peter du Sautoy   TS

4 May 1969   [Headed Paper: Ebble Thatch]

Dear Peter,

Thanks for your letter(s). Life has really got a bit out of hand as far as we are concerned down here. I wont go into that, because I believe Charles did as I would wish and passed on the news; but it's difficult to concentrate on anything else, or summon up the energy to do anything. Even a letter seems like a mountain.

I'm leaving the agreement with you for the novellas for the time being; because I cant find the previous one alluded to and to be honest feel the present one like a weight. I've certainly no intention of taking the book elsewhere; and this letter is – partly – to assure you of that.

Can it do two jobs at once? Could you tell Charles that THE JAM *must* go via C. Brown and leave me out of the decision making?

The main thing is, I have to find the energy somewhere to go on writing the thing and dont know where it's to come from. I certainly havnt any to spare.

Oh, and the film (educational) people. The simplest answer is sorry, no.

David convalesces – or that's what we hope it is. Ann's not too good, run down, eyestrain, a floater, whatnot. I'm, I'm, I dont know what.

We'll probably all disappear into Cornwall, if it's still there – they to walk on cliffs and beaches, I, to button down to this damned type-writer – what a machine!

Thine, while this machine is to him

Bill

There is no trace of the 'film (educational) people' in the archive. All we know of them comes from a sentence in du Sautoy's reply: 'I will say no to the film people in America.'

Golding and Ann did not go to Cornwall and – on point of (Ann's) principle – would not go to Greece while the military junta was in power. In early June, they set off with David for a three-month holiday that took them through Italy to Turkey and Bulgaria.

'Thine, while this machine is to him': Golding alludes to the end of Hamlet's letter to Ophelia: 'Thine evermore, most dear lady, whilst this machine is to him, Hamlet' (2.2.121–2).

WG to Charles Monteith MS

10 May 1969　　　　　　　[Headed Paper: Ebble Thatch]

Dear Charles,

By trying to save myself Trouble I seem to have put everybody's back up!

It's perhaps just as well about the Chichele Dinner – I'm trying to stop drinking too much and it's not easy in the circumstances.

I hope you have a good time in Greece – the flowers should still be out, I think.

The enclosure is intended to amuse.

ever

Bill

Negotiations between Faber and Curtis Brown over 'The Jam' were not going smoothly. Among other issues, Monteith's offer of a £500 advance on 15 per cent royalties had been firmly rebuffed. Graham Watson at Curtis Brown insisted that an advance ten times greater, against 17.5 per cent royalties, would be more appropriate.

Golding had been drinking heavily during David's illness, as he acknowledges in his expression of regret that he cannot attend the forthcoming Chichele Dinner.

The 'enclosure' was a letter to Golding from a young American woman who complained that 'Your book *The Spire* was hard for an average person to understand' and that 'you might have sold more had you gotten your point across more quickly'. The vocabulary was 'too deep', there was insufficient action, and the symbolism was too vague. If only Golding had fixed these issues, 'a person wouldn't have to be a genius' to understand the book and 'it might not have been so boring to me'.

Charles Monteith to WG   TS

12 May 1969

Dear Bill,

Thank you very much indeed for your letter of May 10th – and for sending me that marvellous letter from Miss [. . .]. (I'll return it with this.)

You haven't, I assure you, put anybody's back up, at any rate not here! I'm sorting out THE JAM contract with Graham Watson now; and, all being well, everything should be settled before I go to Greece at the end of this week.

We must try to fix up a meeting when I get back – either here or in Oxford.

Yours ever,

Charles Monteith to WG   TS

24 June 1969

Dear Bill,

I was very taken with that splendid drawing by Michael Ayrton which appeared in this morning's Times; and I wonder if it might be possible to get a photograph of it – and also get permission to use it in some of our publicity material? If the drawing doesn't belong to you – as I imagine that it probably does – I wonder if you could let me know who the present owner of it is?

Yours ever,

Accompanying its review of Michael Ayrton's retrospective exhibition at Reading Museum Art Gallery, *The Times* had reproduced one of Ayrton's portraits of Golding. This was, according to the reviewer, perhaps the best of the drawings because it 'seems perfectly to have caught the fierce intelligence of that fixed gaze and the nobility of that almost unbearably wise head'. In reply to this letter,

Golding phoned Monteith to tell him that the drawing was owned by Ayrton. Faber got in touch with the artist and, in due course, the portrait was used on the paperback cover of *The Hot Gates*, replacing another Ayrton portrait from the hardback edition.

WG to Charles Monteith PC

September(?) 1969

We arrived a little botched and bewildered from Turkey; but Bulgaria at last, the peoples paradise! Very fertile, clean, and well organised, from the splendidly amplified band at dinner to the queues for breakfast. The sea does not look good for snorkling, however. Nevertheless, it's good to have got out of the decadent SW Balkans, with their lonely beaches and run down hotels to a forward-looking economy. David is happy to be in a genuinely socialist country at last. I believe tomorrow, we may all visit a collective farm.

Our love and fraternal greetings
Bill

The image on the reverse is of the Slantchev waterfront – a Bulgarian Black Sea resort.

1970

Golding's family problems and heavy drinking finally conspire to put 'The Jam' out of its misery. He returns to other unfinished projects, giving his story about predynastic Egypt a thorough rewriting and a new title ('The Scorpion God') and making a determined but unsuccessful effort, later in the year, to produce a publishable version of 'In Search of My Father'. In July, Golding is awarded an honorary doctorate by the University of Sussex. That same month, Monteith tries to persuade him to dramatise *Lord of the Flies* for the stage – a conversation that continues intermittently for twenty years as Faber's enthusiasm founders against Golding's reluctance.

Charles Monteith to WG   TS

8 January 1970

Dear Bill,

I thought you might be amused at this little exchange which I've had with the Bishop of Liverpool. I don't expect that you heard the talk – it was one of those religious talks which come on every morning at 10 to 8 just before the weather forecast. We'll try to get a copy from the BBC, though, and when we do I'll send it on to you. As the Bishop says in his letter, his references to LORD OF THE FLIES were indeed in friendly terms.

Any chance of seeing you in the near future; and – forgive me please for asking – any more news of THE JAM?

Rather belatedly, warmest good wishes for 1970 to you all.

    Yours,

The Bishop of Liverpool, Stuart Blanch, had referred to *Lord of the Flies* in his guest slot on *Ten to Eight* (the forerunner of 'Thought for the Day'). Judging by Golding's reply to Monteith, Blanch had made a mistake about Golding's nationality.

WG to Charles Monteith   TS

12 January 1970

Dear Charles,

Thank you for your letter and enclosures. I'd already heard from the bishop, and replied amiably to him. In our local (where the news penetrated instantly, like a living example of the Old English Syndrome, Church and Pub) the clientelle was more impressed by the notice taken of me by a genuine bishop than interested in my nationality. Any publicity et cetera! But thank you for taking up the cudgels so quickly.

The JAM goes on, in a time-wasting way. We've now agreed on the story. I wrote two novelish drafts, each about forty thousand words and they were both very very indifferent pieces of work. I *think* now, the next thing will be a screen play; and after rather more than a year, I'm deadly tired of the whole thing.

I realise what an unsatisfactory contributor to your list I am. The truth is, I live a surface-life, because in the circumstances it's less painful that way. I imagine you muttering in an irritated way: 'How much time does the man think he has left?'

I agree. But there it is.

I shall certainly be coming up to London now and then this winter, because I suspect many dreary conferences will ensue over this screen play. It would be pleasant to meet again; so if I, or Ann and I know in advance about a visit I'll write or telephone.

How the days are drawing out!
   Ever
   Bill

'How the days are drawing out!': a Golding family joke, reserved for the days and weeks immediately following the winter solstice.

Charles Monteith to WG   TS

13 January 1970

Dear Bill,

Thank you very much for your letter, I am glad that the episcopal misunderstanding should have sorted itself out so amicably; and I wait eagerly for his Lordships next morning pep-talk in order to see if he manages to incorporate a correction!

Sorry that the JAM is turning into such a bore, let's talk about it when we meet next. It's most excellent news that you – or better still, you and Ann – may be in London before long.

Yours ever,

This letter is not typed by Monteith's usual secretary, which explains the comma splices and the positioning of the valediction.

WG to Peter du Sautoy T S

12 May 1970   [Headed Paper: Ebble Thatch]

Dear Peter,

Meeting. The truth is that we are in a bit of confusion at the moment; and on top of it all Ann's mother is seriously ill and the coping-with falls on Ann. I'm sure she'd like to come up to London but doubt whether she could fix a day. I could come up, I suppose; but I'd really like to stay here while she's having so much to do. Can we leave it that I/we will come up when we can, having arranged a date with you beforehand?

I suppose I ought really to think of dramatising Lord Of The Flies for schools; but I have a distaste for the idea of rereading it. Giles Cooper's radio thing was good, I thought – but more of a variation on the theme of Flies than a straight dramatisation. I dont suppose there'd be any harm in letting you and me see a copy – it's all so long ago. Anyway I wouldnt want to set about it now because there seems to be some possibility that I may be getting back to writing in a fumbling sort of way. What with income tax and the necessity of leaving some sort of post mortem income it's high time I did.

Our love to you both.

Ever
Bill

Ann's mother Nancy Brookfield was in a care home; she died early in 1971.

Charles Monteith to WG

10 July 1970

Dear Bill,

As you know, we've had fairly frequent requests mostly from schools for permission to do dramatized versions of LORD OF THE FLIES; and I think that Peter suggested to you recently that we might perhaps consider publishing – in a slightly edited form – the radio version by Giles Cooper which was first broadcast in 1955.

We've now got a copy of the script from the BBC and it has been read here both by myself and by Phyllis Hunt who looks after our educational books. We both feel that it's on the whole well and intelligently done though of course the need to reduce everything to dialogue involves a certain loss of subtlety; and there's a major loss in the lack of the descriptive passages which build up the paradisal quality of the island at the beginning – and the horrors at the end.

If you find time to read it do please let me know what you think. If in principle you'd be prepared to approve its publication I wonder if there's any chance at all of persuading you to edit it yourself? I'm quite certain you could improve it.

If you would rather not, though, either someone here or some intelligent young schoolmaster could fairly easily 'edit out' the purely radio bits and turn it into something suitable for stage publication.

Any more word, I wonder, either about THE JAM or about TO KEEP NOW STILL? Forgive me please for pestering you about them. I know how difficult things are at the moment.

I'm much looking forward to seeing you – and Ann too, I hope – at Brighton on July 14th. Peter was hoping to come too but, alas, he has an important Publishers Association meeting which he feels he can't cut.

Yours ever,

In the Faber archive, there are countless requests from schools and other organisations for permission to stage *Lord of the Flies*. On several occasions, the performance had already happened without permission, and a teacher had innocently submitted the script in the hope of publication. Having sought legal advice, du Sautoy even sent a letter to the *Times Educational Supplement* in April 1965 stating that Golding was unwilling to agree to any dramatic performance of *Lord of the Flies* 'whether in school or anywhere else'. Nevertheless, the requests and the scripts kept arriving. With Golding showing no sign of doing the job himself, du Sautoy borrowed Giles Cooper's 1955 Third Programme adaptation from the BBC archive in the hope that 'the Cooper version could be made suitable for school productions with a little adjustment'.

The title 'To Keep Now Still' was not jettisoned until very late, when the story finally became 'The Scorpion God'. At this point, Monteith was expecting that the collection of stories would comprise 'To Keep Now Still', 'Envoy Extraordinary' and two as-yet-unwritten stories: one on the fall of Barchester spire, and another on the building of Stonehenge.

Monteith travelled to Brighton to see Golding receive an honorary DLitt from the University of Sussex on 14 July.

WG to Charles Monteith   MS

15 July 1970   [Headed Paper: Ebble Thatch]

Dear Charles

Sorry for holograph (right word?) but typewriter is broken down.

It was so nice to be with you on tuesday, but far, far too brief a meeting. I ought to add that I was a bit dazed and simply didnt connect about transport – I *ought* to have asked Daiches to squeeze you in, but in my gauche way, simply didn't. I hope bussing wasnt too bad.

Ann and I will be in London shortly and I'll ring you at Fabers' before hand.

① The jam is a jam. I believe I am to write the script, either in America, or Malta, or here – I tried twice to make a novel of it, but that turned out to be a load of junk.

② To Keep Now Still – have just completed the 4th draft and am not wholly satisfied – indeed, far from it. I'll have another, and I hope, final look. 22½–25 thousand words.

③ The play on Flies – we must talk I think. Preferably over a meal!
Love from both,
    Bill.

Monteith reassured Golding by reply that he had been perfectly comfortable on the bus because he 'got one of those nice front seats on the top deck'.

The literary scholar David Daiches gave the address at the degree ceremony.

Charles Monteith to WG TS

15 July 1970

Dear Bill,

I thought you looked smashing in that yellow robe! I do hope Ann managed to get a colour photograph.

It was a very great pleasure to see you both again; and I thought the whole ceremony extremely impressive.

Renewed congratulations from us all,

Yours ever,

WG to Peter Crawley MS

15 July 1970

Dear Crawley

Thanks for your letter. No, I'm afraid I dont want to appear at the NBL.

Teenagers oughtn't to be exposed to writers in the flesh. Let's try to leave them one small illusion.

I dont know about the results of switching from Penguin to FPCE – I have no figures. But if you say it has worked out well for us all, then it has!

Yours

William Golding

Peter Crawley had passed on an invitation for Golding to speak at the National Book League (NBL). Several years earlier, he had been in touch about Faber's plans to cancel their licence with Penguin for *Lord of the Flies* and publish their own Faber Paper Covered Edition (FPCE). Following Golding's comment about having 'no figures', Crawley was now able to report that Golding's annual royalties had increased since Faber had started issuing its paperback.

Charles Monteith to WG TS

13 October 1970

Dear Bill,

As I mentioned two or three months ago Peter and I would both very much like to talk to you before too long about the possibility of a dramatisation of LORD OF THE FLIES – either by yourself or someone else. We keep getting requests for this and we really feel that a good dramatisation could be very successful. Do please let me know if you – or, better still, you and Ann – plan a visit to London in the near future. We'd be absolutely delighted if you could lunch with us, not only to talk about the dramatisation – but simply for a general gossip!

Love to you all,

Charles Monteith to WG   TS

29 October 1970

Dear Bill,

It was very nice indeed seeing you and Ann again the other day and finding you both so well. I am *much* looking forward to reading THE SCORPION GOD: and to hearing what you do eventually decide about a possible dramatisation of LORD OF THE FLIES for schools.

In the meantime here is the type script of that novel I mentioned to you – STONEHENGE by Harry Harrison and Leon Stover. I would be fascinated to know what you think of it – but don't hesitate please to stop if you get bored and bung it straight back! It's a bit on the long side I fear.

Yours ever,

Monteith was not the only editor who found *Stonehenge* 'a bit on the long side'. The manuscript was eventually accepted for publication by Peter Davies Ltd, but having failed to find an American partner, they asked the authors to reduce it from 110,000 to 80,000 words. That shortened version appeared in 1972 with Peter Davies in the UK and Scribner in the United States; the full and original version, with the title *Stonehenge: Where Atlantis Died*, was not published until 1983.

WG to Charles Monteith   TS

29 October 1970   [Headed Paper: Ebble Thatch]

Dear Charles,

It was good to see you again – and thank you for our very pleasant lunch.

I've read the radio script of FLIES; and though it's good, it remains a radio script. The job of dramatisation for chapel/gym/open air/assembly hall would be quite another matter. ½i. Damn this typewriter. It's so efficient it punishes every mistake. A Christian sort of machine. To return – I have vague ideas of setting the explosive anarchy of FLIES in a framework of ritual; but first I have to brace myself and read the book!

I enclose a copy of THE SCORPION GOD. You may remember, you were going to be generous and explain to me why I find it so unsatisfactory. Other than this story, ½i, (curses) I have thoughts round several more; but seem to lack self-confidence.

It occurs to me that an educational edition of PINCHER might very well not sell to schools even nowadays, because of the enema. And other things. Oughtnt you and Peter to think twice?

A correspondent tells me that my books are published in Esthonian. It's a great pity that copyright conference never got off the ground. As things are we can only afford a dacha in places we dont particularly want to go. But if you should ever find Ann swathed in sables, you'll know we've gone a progress like medieval kings. Pacific Glory is probably sitting on Tenace.

Ann sends her love

    Bill

Golding has written in pen along the top, 'Also this one which was just being sent when STONEHENG arrived.' He sent this letter and the letter of 3 November in the same packet, together with the manuscripts of 'The Scorpion God' and *Stonehenge*.

Marooned, apparently, on a rock in the mid-Atlantic after his ship is torpedoed and existing on a diet of raw seafood, Christopher Martin is forced to self-administer an enema using his life jacket. Golding suspects that schools will baulk at that and 'other things', no doubt including the novel's sexual violence and its portrayal of God and the afterlife. The educational edition did not go ahead.

The USSR had still not accepted the Universal Copyright Convention. It would finally become a signatory in May 1973.

On 23 October, a collision at sea six miles from the Isle of Wight caused a breach in the fuel tanks of the oil tanker *Pacific Glory*. Thirteen people died in the ensuing explosion. The incident happened near where *Tenace* had been sunk. Although *Pacific Glory* temporarily ran aground, it was successfully refloated on 6 November.

3 November 1970   Ebble Thatch, Bower Chalke, nr.
                                  Salisbury, Wilts.

Dear Charles,

Herewith THE SCORPION GOD and STONEHENGE. The first at least has the merit of being shorter than the second.

I must own, I enjoyed STONEHENGE for the most part, though it was hard to stay with to the end. It's sub-Sinuhe, or sub-Long Ships; in a phrase, not quite a good bad book. I cant put my finger on the defect in the writing. Is it insufficient writing intensity or insufficient imaginative intensity? Or both? God knows, it's an easy enough idiom to slip into, as I know to my cost. Anyway, thank you very much. Incidentally it occurs to me that what so many of these would be historical or pre-historical novels suffer from is a sort of historical reductionism. As Ann said in one of her perceptions, we've had too much Occam's razor and could do with a little tended fertility. Let the plants grow, the people sing, and God be in His heaven.

As for THE SCORPION GOD, I wish I could send it to you in triumph. But having just read STONEHENGE, my doubts multiply. I've cut out tushery and forsoothness, reduced archaeology to the minimum and used history as my humble obedient servant – i.e. bent it where necessary – but what began as a joke has stretched beyond it and become nothing in particular.

Never mind, as from one of the Teuta living under Dun-Ason, what else would you expect? Anyway, thank you (from us both) for a delightful lunch and may we meet again before long – in samain, perhaps, or possibly come next imbolc.

Ann sends her love and I add mine
                    Bill
See letter under this one.

'sub-Sinuhe, or sub-Long Ships': see Golding's letter to Monteith of 17 October 1954. Waltari's *The Egyptian* and Bengtsson's *The Long Ships* seem to have been Golding's benchmark for well-written and popular historical novels.

'one of the Teuta living under Dun-Ason': himself an inhabitant of Salisbury Plain, Golding is adopting the vocabulary of *Stonehenge*, in which 'teuta' are tribes and Dun Ason is a local placename. Samain (or Samhain) and Imbolc are ancient festivals marking the beginning of winter and the beginning of spring respectively.

'See letter under this one': the letter of 29 October, sent in the same packet.

Charles Monteith to WG

6 November 1970

Dear Bill,

I can't tell you how pleased I am to have THE SCORPION GOD. Thank you very much for sending it to me – and for your two letters of October 29th and November 3rd. I'm looking forward immensely to reading it; and when I have I will of course write again straight away.

STONEHENGE. Couldn't agree more about this. I enjoyed the Mycenaen part – though more at a boys' fiction level than on an adult fiction level; but once the narrative moved back to Britain I found my attention wandering.

LORD OF THE FLIES – dramatized version. Do please sometime soon grit your teeth and read the book! I'm absolutely certain that a dramatic version by you with the sort of introduction you mentioned to me and to Peter would be a winner.

PINCHER MARTIN – educational edition. No need to worry, I think, about whether or not this would be used in schools. We were approached quite spontaneously the other day by the London University school examination board who told us that it was short listed as a prescribed book for A level English Literature from 1973 on. They were obviously pleased when we told them that we ourselves were planning to publish an educational edition – and we're keeping our fingers crossed. We should have a definite decision within two months or so.

Very much enjoyed seeing you and Ann the other day – and much looking forward to seeing you both again before too long.

Love to you both,

Charles Monteith to WG

13 November 1970

Dear Bill,

I think THE SCORPION GOD is absolutely tremendous. It passes triumphantly what I consider to be the Golding Test – the minute I'd finished it I turned straight back to the beginning and read it right through again. And all the things that had puzzled me when I read it first – as they were meant to do – clicked beautifully into place. Indeed, the only thing that still puzzles me, I confess – I'm certain I'm being madly stupid here – is the title. THE SCORPION GOD is a splendid title – it arrests the attention beautifully and will look marvellous on the jacket. But I'm still not quite clear exactly what it means. Is it a reference to the fact that a scorpion deliberately kills himself – as the God does here?

If my brief was to make suggestions or to tell you why you yourself found the whole thing slightly unsatisfactory I've failed miserably. I've got no suggestions at all.

We would of course be more than happy to publish this together with ENVOY EXTRAORDINARY. I wonder, too, if this might be the moment to collect between hard Faber covers MISS PULKINGHORN and THE ANGLO-SAXON (which is in the current Macmillan's WINTER'S TALES). Do let me know what you feel about this. Of course, if you'd rather not have the two short stories included we'd be perfectly happy to go ahead with the two novellas only.

There's no reason why we shouldn't have a contract for THE SCORPION GOD now – and Peter would be only too happy to send you one. I suggest we agree on the same royalty that we had for THE PYRAMID i.e. a straight 15%. I'm not sure whether or not you'd like an advance but if you would do please say. In the case of THE PYRAMID we've made it £500 payable 'on demand'.

Congratulations again on an absolutely splendid story.

Yours,

Winter's Tales 16, edited by A. D. Maclean and published in 1970, was the latest in Macmillan's annual anthology of short stories. The volume comprised ten stories, one of which was a reprint of Golding's 'The Anglo-Saxon'.

WG to Charles Monteith   TS

15 November 1970   [Headed Paper: Ebble Thatch]

Dear Charles,

Your letter cheered me no end, as I'm sure it was meant to. Thank you very much.

Title.

One of the vague pharaohs (I can *never* spell that word) of the first dynasty (or just possibly predynastic) was called Scorpion. So in a lordly way, I decided he was the man who tidied up slothful Egypt and set it on the dynastic course. A change of god, in fact; and the title is simply my nasty-minded summation of what I think of chaps who change people into nations. Thin you will say, very. But the title was such a difficulty. At first it was *To Keep Now Still.* Then there were others, but I forget them. If we must stick to *The Scorpion God*, perhaps I might adjust the narrative to give the title more point – but I cant think how to. Yes, I know about Menes. Who doesnt? But just possibly Scorpion is another name for Menes – in which case we're in.

The trouble is, the reader has to know some Egyptology to get a lot of points but not too much, or he'll object, for example, that 'Great House' in writing at least doesn't occur until the Middle Kingdom – and so on. I couldnt care less since I have positive views on history and novels, regarding the one as very much the humble, obedient servant of the other. *Vive Dumas!* Hence the essay or introduction I might write. (The editor of PLAYBOY has just regretfully turned SCORPION down; saying his readers cant tell Osiris from Thoth. Oh my stork and my butter!)

What do you think?

I wouldnt want MISS PULKINHORN and THE ANGLOSAXON published with the other two. They were both written with the right hand while SCORPION and ENVOY were written with the left, if you see what I mean. Also, the left hand might very well write another so that we could publish A TRIVIAL TRILOGY. Just thought of that.

Oddly, since I saw you, I've written twenty thousand words of what might eventuate in another novel. I am going on and hope to get a sizeable draft by Christmas perhaps, then put it away. I cant believe this draft is anything like the final version but have the feeling I've years of work in front of me working towards. It's a great comfort to have *something*. Standing at the back of it is the idea I've had for years called IN SEARCH OF MY FATHER – and it could end as anything. But it *does* put dramatised FLIES back to the New Year. Shall we leave contracts? It's understood the stories go to you, if you want them.

Cant understand £500 on demand. Suppose it means you give me £500 when ever I want it. On the other hand you seem to send me quantities of money anyway. Wish I had thought to ask what the red wine was you gave me in L'Etoile. How about five hundred bottles on demand? Much better than a butt of canary.

> ever
>
> > Bill

PS
  Title.
    'The Great Man.'
    'Our Leader.'
    'Our Hero.'

?

'pharaohs (I can *never* spell that word)': Golding has typed 'pharoahs' and corrected it by hand.

Menes, active sometime around 3000 BC, was the pharaoh credited with having unified Egypt and founded the First Dynasty. Some scholars believe that Menes and King Scorpion (or Scorpion II) were the same individual.

The word 'pharaoh' means 'great house'. Golding freely acknowledges his anachronism: the term was not recorded until the period of the Middle Kingdom, about a thousand years after the setting for his story. Golding invokes the great French novelist Alexandre Dumas, père, whose historical fictions play fast and loose with the facts. The 'essay or introduction' that he 'might write' on this topic waits until his sea trilogy, *To the Ends of the Earth* (1991), when Golding admits that 'the novelist, more allied than the historian to rogues and vagabonds, gets away with what he can'.

Osiris and Thoth were Egyptian gods – Osiris was linked with fertility and the underworld, and Thoth with writing and magic. Golding alludes to the Stork margarine advertising campaign which features an individual who carries out some sort of skilled job but, nevertheless, 'can't tell Stork from butter'.

Golding's joke about 'A TRIVIAL TRILOGY' plays on the etymology of 'trivial' from the Latin 'trivium': the place where three roads meet.

Charles Monteith to WG TS

20 November 1970

Dear Bill,

Thank you very much indeed for your letter of November 15th. I had had a vague notion that the Liar might be the Scorpion God – but I wasn't, I confess, at all sure about it! It's a very good title so let's keep it.

I entirely see the point about MISS PULKINHORN and THE ANGLOSAXON – and the left hand and the right hand. I shan't push this idea any further. I'd be all for another story to go with THE SCORPION

GOD and ENVOY EXTRAORDINARY – but I'm very anxious, too, to publish, if possible, a new Golding sometime in 1971. I'd be perfectly happy to settle for the two we have now – and if you would write that introduction which you mentioned to me over lunch about historical fiction that would be better still. If you could give me some idea of when you'll be able to let me have a final version – or give me a green light to go ahead – I'd be terribly grateful.

Very exciting news that 20,000 words of a new novel – in first draft anyway – are there; and I'm fascinated to hear that it's a version of IN SEARCH OF MY FATHER. I remember reading a chunk of that years and years ago – wasn't there a horrifying bit about pale boys like skins of lard being fattened in cages? I had a vague idea that it was sparked off by something in Xenophon.

Quite happy to wait for the dramatized version of FLIES if you feel you can get down to it – but, again, it's something about which we do get enquiries all the time and I'd be grateful here, too, for some idea of when you think you could let me have it – even if it's only a very provisional one. Terribly sorry to pester you about this and if you'd like me to stop I promise that I will!

        Yours ever,

PTO

PS Would you like me to send back the typescript of THE SCORPION GOD or shall I hang on to it here? It might be an idea, don't you think, if I were to get a fair copy typed? I could easily arrange that if you'd like me to.

The Liar in 'The Scorpion God' is so called because he entertains the pharaoh with what are assumed to be lies about phenomena like ice in distant places beyond the kingdom. At the end of the story, there is the strong implication that the Liar will become the new pharaoh.

    Monteith's anxious enquiries about the next book and the possibility of dramatising *Lord of the Flies* may have been prompted by his awareness of the financial crisis that was threatening Faber's independence at the time.

    Golding continued to spend time rejecting requests for permission to dramatise *Lord of the Flies*. In a journal entry from April 1981, he notes, 'Once more I have refused permission for Lord of the Flies to be staged. That must be the hundredth time, I should think' (J, 1 April 1981).

WG to Charles Monteith

5 December 1970 [Headed Paper: Ebble Thatch]

Dear Charles,

Thanks for your note; and now I'm answering your letter of 20th November.

Introduction to SCORPION and ENVOY, to say nothing of dramatised FLIES depend so much on what happens to this present draft of IN SEARCH OF MY FATHER. Tomorrow I finish the first section (36,000 words) and shall have to have a kind of *brood* on where it's going, size, shape, colour, mode, scope, what have you. This section is twentieth century, and I'm hopeful about it, but wary. Cant quite describe my position – infinite possibilities, and of course infinite dangers of coming unstuck or drying up. But *if* I bring off some sort of complete draft, then there'd likely be a pause during which I c'd do one of the others or both. Perhaps the best thing would be for you to give me a dateline for autumn publication, 1971. First draft of FATHER will take me into the winter, I'm pretty sure; and surely, in the spring I c'd write the intro for SCORPION and ENVOY, so you'd have a book of some sort, anyway. Does this sound too haughty? Not meant to. If things went well of course, I could tackle FLIES too.

Your remark about the MS of SCORPION compunctualises me. I came across some preliminary drafting of it and found the ribbon had got so worn I must have read my own words with the eye of faith. Curtis Brown are probably better off with the carbon. A decent copy would be an act of charity I dont deserve. But I'm quite happy to leave you the original if that's enough.

Ever
Bill

Charles Monteith to WG

11 December 1970

Dear Bill,

Very many thanks for your letter of November 5th. It's splendid news that IN SEARCH OF MY FATHER is progressing so very helpfully. Do please keep in touch with me about how it's getting on.

I've been into the question of a deadline for autumn '71 publication with our Production people; and they tell me that the *absolutely final* one is 28th February 1971. And of course it would help us tremendously if you could let us have the introduction for SCORPION and ENVOY before then if possible. It would be better still, I need hardly add, if you could manage the dramatization of FLIES by then too!

I'm having a fair copy of SCORPION typed – and it shouldn't take very long. As soon as it's ready it will go off to you for checking.

I expect that Wiltshire like London is leading a headily neurotic life because of all these power cuts! I've got a paraffin lamp in my flat which is making my life tolerable. When I shaved this morning I thought I looked remarkably Goyaesque.

Yours ever,

Monteith means December 5th, not November 5th.

This is the last glimpse of 'In Search of My Father' in the correspondence, sixteen years after it was first mentioned. In a journal entry from 1975, Golding recalls that 'the second shot of In Search Of My Father [. . .] died of boredom – my boredom, tho' it had gone to more than sixty thousand words' (J, 12 June 1975).

The Electricians' Union was working to rule, which resulted in national power cuts.

1971

This year is the start of Golding's slow recovery. It begins optimistically, with Judy's marriage in January to Terrell Carver, an American scholar of political philosophy. In March, Golding finishes a new story for *The Scorpion God*, 'Clonk Clonk', and the book attracts respectful reviews when it appears in October. A novel still seems far away but a summer holiday through France, Switzerland, Yugoslavia and Italy results in a breakthrough when Golding, in Rome on 19 August, dreams what he later calls a 'great dream'. He writes 'History of a Crisis' describing his depression, reads Carl Jung with renewed appreciation, and in October (dodging the reviews of *The Scorpion God*) he travels alone to Switzerland on a pilgrimage to Jung's childhood home. Having been prescribed medicines to treat alcoholism and insomnia, he feels invigorated, and determines to keep a daily dream journal in the hope of unlocking his creativity.

Charles Monteith to WG   TS

25 March 1971

Dear Bill,

 'Clonk Clonk' kept me happily dazzled all Monday afternoon; and of course I should have written long before now to say so. It's a brilliant piece of work – William Golding right on form! Fair copies are being typed now and I expect I'll be able to send one to you tomorrow.

 The whole book is en route to our Production Department and unless some major disaster happens we'll certainly be able to publish it in the autumn. We're all very grateful indeed to you for having achieved the deadline!

 Rosemary and I have talked over all you told us about the novel – and we're completely sold on it. I can hardly wait to read it.

     Yours ever,

Having abandoned his plan to write an introduction about historical fiction, Golding had focused instead on finishing a third 'long short'. This was 'Clonk Clonk', which he delivered in person on 22 March, the deadline for Autumn publication. The visit also gave him the chance to inspect the new Faber offices in Queen Square, several hundred metres from their previous headquarters at Russell Square. Golding's private opinion of 'Clonk Clonk' and 'The Scorpion God', as he recorded in 'History of a Crisis' later in 1971, was that 'I did not and do not think much of either as stories' (J, undated).

Charles Monteith to WG TS

29 March 1971

Dear Bill,

'The Scorpion God and other stories'

Clonk Clonk. Enclosed with this is a fair-typed copy of *Clonk Clonk* together with your own original typescript. I'd be very grateful if you'd read the copy through and let me know as soon as possible any mistakes which you spot. I've already sent a copy to our Production Department and another one to Matthew Evans for onward transmission to Harcourt Brace. If you do spot any errors I'll pass a list of them on to Production and Harcourt Brace at once.

Envoy Extraordinary. It would be advisable I think to make absolutely certain that Eyre and Spottiswoode can't at this stage claim any rights in this story. I'll be happy of course to write to them myself about this but before I do I wonder if by any chance you've kept your contract with them – or any relevant correspondence you may have had with them. If so, I'd be most grateful if I could have a look at it so that I can see precisely what rights you granted to them. If the contract has been lost I wonder if you remember whether you were paid a royalty or simply a flat 'once for all' fee? The answer to that question would give some guidance about rights. Terribly sorry to bother you about this.

Warmest congratulations again on Clonk Clonk and on the whole book. We're going full steam ahead now for autumn publication.

Yours ever,

The title proposed by Faber was *The Scorpion God* with the subtitle *And Other Stories*. Golding acquiesced despite wondering whether that would be appropriate for a collection comprising just three stories. The first edition stuck simply to *The Scorpion God* on the cover; the subtitle, where needed, was *Three Short Novels*. This rethink may have been prompted by Julian Muller at Harcourt, Brace, who insisted that short stories simply would not sell in the United States, and suggested, instead, *The Scorpion God: Three Novellas*. Faber disliked the word 'novella', so Harcourt, Brace went ahead with *Three Short Novels* as the subtitle.

10 April 1971

Dear Charles,

Thanks for your letter. I found every contract I've ever had except the one for Envoy Extraordinary! So I rang Juliet O'Hea at Curtis Brown and got photostats. Here they are.

It's worth adding, I think, that Sometime Never (the three stories with Envoy as one) was published in the States by Ballantine Science Fiction Classics, first printed June 1957, Library of Congress Catalog No. 57–11580.

I dont quite understand the situation over mistakes in the typescript. In the event what I had to do was a bit of revising on the type script. I enclose it for you. Is it what you want? I think it's what I would have done with galleys when I got them; and I dont know if it's too late to let the printers have this lot. Otherwise I'll wait till the galleys come; in which case can I have this corrected typescript back?

All very complicated and unprofessional on my part – but I mean well.

Another thought – the dustcover. I gather you'll use one already in being – some pharaoh doing his thing, his *sedheb*. But *my* Great House ought to wear the crown of Upper Egypt, the *hedet* the White Crown, rather than the *desheret* or Red Crown of Lower Egypt. Yours – if it's anything to do with Akhnaten – is likely to wear them both in one – the *shemety* or Double Crown. It doesnt really matter and I find this exhibition of schoolboy learning rather embarrassing; but I thought I'd let you know. The proper crown is a white linen thing, like a dunce's cap with a knob on top. Menes (possibly, just possibly my Liar) would have been the first who could wear the *shemety* though he probably didnt. I seem to remember the only figurine of him (ivory) wears the *hedet*. So. The figurine is almost *too* well known. Might as well have Tut's mortician's outfit.

Our love. It's pleasant to have written again if only a squib.

Bill

'Sedheb' or Heb Sed literally means 'the feast of the tail', and it celebrated the continuing rule of a pharaoh. Originally, it may have involved a test of the leader's vigour, with death the price of failure. 'The Scorpion God' depicts

'Great House' trying to prove his ability to rule by completing a long run in an 'avalanche' of heat – as he must do every seventh year – while wearing a costume with a tail attached.

Akhnaten (or Akhenaton) reigned nearly two thousand years after Menes and wore the double crown of a united Egypt. 'Tut' and the outfits of his period would have been familiar following the Paris exhibition of 1967, Tutankhamun and his Time. Negotiations were underway for the Treasures of Tutankhamun exhibition that opened at the British Museum in March 1972; it remains the most popular museum exhibition in British history.

Charles Monteith to WG

TS

13 April 1971

Dear Bill,

Peter Phillips – the new head of our Production Department – has just told me that galley proofs of THE SCORPION GOD should be here on April 26th. This means that all being well you'll have them the following day. At any rate I think you can certainly depend on having them before the end of April.

I thought I'd let you know about this now since I know you're making plans to go off in early May.

> Yours ever,

PS You may remember that I mentioned when we lunched together A. T. Q. Stewart's THE ULSTER CRISIS which to my mind throws more light on the present situation there than anything else. I'll enclose a copy of it with this and if you do find time to read it I think you'll discover that it's an exciting story as well as an interesting one.

Monteith's postscript about the 'present situation' in his native Ulster refers to the civil violence of February and March 1971, when civilians, IRA members and British soldiers were killed in a number of incidents.

Charles Monteith to WG

TS

16 April 1971

Dear Bill,

Very many thanks for your letter of April 10th. Excellent that everything should be clear about 'Envoy Extraordinary'. I've made a note about it for our file and I'll return the Curtis Brown correspondence to you with this letter.

Many thanks for having revised the typescript. We're sending it off to the printer and our Production people tell me that they think these revisions will just be in time for the galleys. Do please keep an especially careful eye out for them though when you're correcting the proofs.

The dust cover. We'll do our level best, I promise you, to provide a *hedet* rather than a *desheret* or *shemety*!

Yours ever,

Charles Monteith to WG   TS

3 May 1971

Dear Bill,

I do hope you're very much better by now. I was terribly sorry to hear from Ann what a nasty time you'd had.

Proofs have reached you safely, I hope; and I thought you might like to see, too, this transparency of the picture which we'll be using on the jacket. Armed with your letter Shirley Tucker, who's designing it, went to the British Museum where a Mr James – head Egyptologist – was very helpful indeed. Eventually he recommended this particular picture as the nearest thing available to what's wanted. It's from a book called 'Temple of King Sethos I at Abydos', Vol.3. We've had the picture printed – enlarged to the right size – and the colour in it has been slightly strengthened. It's going, I think, to make a most attractive jacket. I do hope you like it.

Yours ever,

PS I wonder if by any chance you and Ann will be back by June 23rd? If you are I'd be absolutely delighted if you could come to the Encaenia luncheon at Oxford then?

Golding had been suffering very badly from bronchitis. The scare was enough to make him give up smoking.

Shirley Tucker worked as a book jacket designer in the production department. Mr James was the esteemed Egyptologist T. G. H. James, who edited *The Journal of Egyptian Archaeology* for a decade.

The Oxford Encaenia takes place every year at the end of Trinity (i.e. summer) term, as university dignitaries process in their robes to the Sheldonian Theatre where honorary degrees are awarded.

4 May 1971

Dear Charles,

Thanks for your letter. My three hairs rose when I read of your Miss Tucker taking my letter along to a genuine egyptologist – that'll teach me to keep my mouth shut!

I can see what he's done – produced number one in the kinglist of (I think) seventy nine pharaohs in what used to be known as the Osireion. It's therefore Seti I's idea of a quite legendary Menes, looking back about thirteen hundred years. Rather like Tennyson's view of King Arthur. Maddeningly, I'd no sooner shot off my mouth to you than I thought of a far, far better thing. Menes is probably three pharaohs rolled up, one of whom was 'Scorpion'. Another was Narmer, whose 'Great Slate Palette' we have; and on the reverse is an absolutely smashing relief of Narmer wearing crown of upper Egypt and about to do a semite with his mace. My Liar, in fact. And utterly contemp. Obverse is even better – first press release ever of Narmer wearing crown of lower Egypt and inspecting rows of decapitated prisoners. History, history! It's the beginning of us all – it's Hitler, Redvers Buller, Stalin, Westmorland, it's where we came in.

Am slightly hysterical. Pay no attention.

God knows when we'll get away now, both feeling rather frail. But I shouldn't think we'd be here for the Encaenia luncheon, and with deep regret, you'd better assume we wont be.

I'm returning proofs to Miss Simmonds by this post.

Ann sends love
        Bill

The 'Great Slate Palette' is better known as the Narmer Palette: it is made of siltstone rather than slate. It dates from roughly 3000 BC and has been called the world's first historical document.

Redvers Buller led the massacre of retreating Zulus at the Battle of Kambula. William Westmoreland was commander of the US forces during the Vietnam War and oversaw the policy of relentless artillery and air bombardment.

Lorna Simmons worked in the production department at Faber.

Charles Monteith to WG TS

6 May 1971

Dear Bill,

I'm stunned! I had no idea that you were such a dab hand at egyptology! Still, since we're rushing the book through we had to go ahead with the jacket straight away and I'm afraid you're stuck with Seti I's idea of a quite legendary Menes!

Too bad about the Encaenia – but I thought that you probably would still be away. Do please, though, let me know when you're back. It would be very nice indeed if we could meet either here or in Oxford.

Lorna Simmons told me that the proofs are back. My very best thanks for having dealt with them so promptly.

Love to you and Ann,

WG to Peter du Sautoy MS

18 May 1971   Ebble Thatch, Bowerchalke

Dear Peter,

Yes, yes of *course* Julian Muller must pay $5000 for *The Scorpion God*. His sky-scraper is much bigger than yours. Moreover, unless the HB paperbacks have collapsed they have no problem there. In any case *The Scorpion God* will do well in USA paperback, not only in the bookshops but also in drugstores et al.

Novellas . . . OK. Make the public think its' getting Reader's Digest three for the price of one.

Emmy Jacobson at CB NY has copy of *The Scorpion God*, but not *Clonk Clonk* which I half designed with PLAYBOY in mind.

Ever

Bill.

PS A thought. Am I becoming contaminated with commercialism? Watch this space!

Blaming a weak market for short stories and a downturn in the economy, Julian Muller at Harcourt Brace Jovanovich (as it was now known) had only offered an advance of $3,500. Golding agreed with du Sautoy that $5,000 was the minimum they would accept and Muller acquiesced. Golding's reference to the skyscraper remembers a passing comment by du Sautoy in January 1962 when he was trying to negotiate a better financial deal for Golding in the United States: 'Harcourt Brace have plenty of money [. . .] they are planning to build their own skyscraper in New York!'

'CB NY': Curtis Brown New York. Golding's consistent underlining of *The Scorpion God* (here marked with italics) disguises the fact that the opening paragraph refers to the volume as a whole and the final paragraph to the title story.

In his reply, du Sautoy singled out 'Clonk, Clonk' for praise, and wondered how Golding managed to 'see these things, so clearly and surely.'

WG to Peter du Sautoy   MS

30 September 1971

Dear Peter

Herewith the signed contract.

Your 'Times' letter – I came across an even unfairer example of USSR publishing what they like – I might even find the letter sometime. I *nagged* to find what roubles I had in USSR in case we should ever want to realise Ann's dream and my nightmare of doing the T. Siberian railway trip. Well – a firm had done *one* of my books; but said foreign payments were held for a year and *if not claimed* then reverted. But the point is, they dont tell the author (unless he's Charlie Snow) what they are publishing. So how the hell can he claim his payment? Admittedly they said they were prepared to 'make the roubles available' if I wanted to visit USSR; but they clearly regarded that as a special favour.

This is for your private information; because I cant back it with the original letter until I've done some excavation; but if you asked around you might get confirmation from other sources.

Had a spotty holiday – operatic weather and poisoned feet.

Our love to you both

Bill

Du Sautoy's letter in *The Times* came in response to C. P. Snow's emollient account of the USSR's cavalier treatment of foreign authors and works. Du Sautoy told Golding privately, 'I really don't think that Snow is doing very much to help us all.'

The Goldings had holidayed in Italy for two months, and it was during the first few weeks at Bracciano that Golding got 'poisoned feet' from (he suspected) walking barefoot at the lake's edge.

WG to Charles Monteith

8 November 1971   Ebble Thatch, Bowerchalke.

Dear Charles,

Thank you for your greetings telegram. I'd gone walking in a remote area to miss the notices: and your message was very reassuring when I got back and read it! Really I've refused to read reviews. I'm getting too old for it, which seems ridiculous – one should be getting indifferent, not more vulnerable. Yesterday evening Ann showed me your advertisement for *The Scorpion God* in the *Sunday Times*; and of course I read it, since it would contain the plums in the cake. And of course, well-intentioned people have murmured this and that. A critical success, I should think! I must reread the stories in the light of the plums, purring gently the while – how's that for a mixed metaphor?

I never thanked you for the terrible, but illuminating Ulster book: tho' I believe Ann told you I'd read it. Really, your personal assessment and prophecy was dreadfully accurate. And what is there for someone like myself to say to someone like yourself who must feel his roots screaming like mandrake? God knows what anyone can say, or do. It's like the fall of the house of Atreus without the resolution at the end.

Ann and I will be at Browns for Friday and Saturday and half Sunday, 19th, 20th, 21st November. If you've the time to spare on any of those days, we might meet: tho' I expect you'll be in Oxford for the week-end in the enclave of etc, etc. etc.

> ever
> Bill Golding.

Monteith's 'greetings telegram' celebrated the publication of *The Scorpion God*, which appeared in an edition of 12,000 copies on 25 October: 'All good wishes on publication day. Warmest congratulations on yesterday's reviews.' For once, Monteith did not need to be careful; the reviews were overwhelmingly positive and respectful despite expressing the occasional regret that Golding had not published a large-scale novel.

Golding's reticence about the identity of the 'remote area' in which he had gone walking is rectified by an unpublished diary entry telling of his gradual recovery from alcoholism at this time: 'I had already declared I would read no reviews of *The Scorpion God*, and that if possible I would be somewhere else when they came out. Now (with Ann's cooperation and encouragement)

I arranged to go off to Switzerland by myself and see the places where Jung was brought up, and lived. [. . .] I left Salisbury on Wednesday 20th October, and came back on the following Wednesday. During that week I had what I believe to be one of the most exciting, fruitful and also happy experiences of my life. [. . .] I moved from Laufen to Bollingen, where I carried out by an inner compulsion a kind of ritual of trespass, theft and admission of discipleship' (J, undated).

In Greek mythology, the House of Atreus is cursed with appalling intrafamilial crimes: murder of fathers, mothers, sons and daughters; incest and adultery; defiance of the gods. Only in the fifth generation, when Orestes pleads his case to the goddess Athena, is the curse lifted.

Brown's Hotel in Mayfair was the Goldings' London hotel of choice.

Charles Monteith to WG   TS

10 November 1971

My dear Bill,

Thank you very much indeed for your letter of November 8th. Good reviews continue to come in, and we're absolutely delighted – 'though not in the least surprised – with the reception which THE SCORPION GOD has had.

I will indeed be in London for part of the weekend of November 19th, 20th and 21st, since on the morning of Saturday 20th I'm going to the confirmation of a godson! That rather knocks out Saturday morning, Saturday lunch and, I suspect, most of Saturday afternoon; but I could manage either Saturday evening, or – perhaps better still – lunch on Sunday. Do please let me know if we can work out something that will be convenient to you and Anne. I'd simply adore to see you both again.

The news from Ulster is really too terrible, isn't it? I can hardly bear to think about it – I simply don't know what's going to happen.

      Yours ever
      Charles Monteith

'The news from Ulster' over the previous months had included the Ballymurphy massacre, widespread riots and internment without trial.

16 November 1971

Dear Charles,

Forgive this ilitterally MS letter – I've taken agin the typewriter for the time being and can only hope you dont too much object to my scrawl. I have an idea for a long/short which might be entitled 'I said: ye are gods.' The point is, that all the problems in which men luxuriate – the nature of man, the nature of the universe, good and evil, and so on – can be rendered irrelevant by the spread of population and pollution. But this version would be shown in the typography.

Now is that possible? bit old hat? Is it prohibitively expensive? Is it silly? I know that Joyce's unpunctuated Molly Bloom's soliloquy – the exact size of the black dot at the end – comes off brilliantly; but Joyce was Joyce and my proposal goes much further. The story, the *personal*, gets edged off, swallowed up, diminished by a rising storm of print, names, what have you: the whole taking place between a totally black page at the beginning and a totally black page at the end. As I see it in my minds eye, the story would open a sort of crack in the blackness of page 2, swallow up the blackness, then when the last page but one has become an illegible mess of the smallest (diamond?) print possible the last page is suddenly black again. It would, perhaps, be madness visible? Or just silly? Alas, madness from the outside is so seldom Shakespearian but so often silly!

      Have you any reactions?

       Bill

The source of the story's proposed title, 'I said: ye are gods', is Psalm 82:6.

Golding misremembers the site of the black dot, which occurs at the end of the penultimate chapter of *Ulysses*, 'Ithaca'.

Golding's plan received a mixed response at Faber. Rosemary Goad, for example, judged that 'it sounds pretentious, but just *might* work.' Monteith took Golding to lunch on 21 November and told him that, although Faber *could* cope with the 'typographical eccentricities', his own instincts were 'pretty much against it'. Monteith reports Golding's assurance that he would not use 'these typographical tricks' unless they proved to be 'the only way to achieve the sort of effect he has in mind'. Golding does not seem to have pursued his idea any further.

Charles Monteith to WG TS

20 December 1971

Dear Bill,

You'll probably hate me for reminding you about this, but you did say, didn't you, that you would think again about the dramatised version of LORD OF THE FLIES sometime this year.

If you have got any ideas about this, I'd be terribly grateful if you could let me know.

Sorry to be a nuisance.

> Yours ever
> Charles Monteith

1972

On the face of it, very little happens this year, so communications with Faber are correspondingly sparse. Golding gives up trying to dramatise *Lord of the Flies* and doubts whether he will ever write another novel. Nevertheless, his journal entries for 1972 – recording dreams as well as daily events – amount to more than 300,000 words. The Goldings' two-month summer holiday begins with a boat trip on the Rhine and a return to Jung country in Switzerland, followed by a journey through Italy to Sicily. The experience inspires part of Golding's ninth novel, *The Paper Men* (1984). With no sign of the Greek junta's rule coming to an end, Golding starts improving his French; France replaces Greece as the usual destination for family holidays in subsequent years.

WG to Charles Monteith   MS

9 January 1972

Dear Charles

Oh dear oh dear oh dear!

Yes. I will read *Lord of the Flies* and so destroy a happy ignorance that has got profounder and profounder over the years.

If the directors of F&F should find themselves gathered together sometime in the future (near future) could they perhaps have a two minutes silence and spare a thought for those in peril on the seas? I *dread* reading the book. That's silly but true.

I'll be in touch

ever

Bill

Golding has misdated the letter 9 December.

Golding's dread was borne out by events. He recorded in his journal that 'during the last three days I've read Lord Of The Flies for the first time in more than ten years. I found it boring and crude. The language is O level stuff' (J, 28 April 1972).

Charles Monteith to WG

13 January 1972

Dear Bill,

Oh dear! I am sorry to have been so insistent about LORD OF THE FLIES. If it really is going to be such a dreadful imposition, do please forget all about it. I do honestly mean that.

> Yours
> Charles Monteith

Although the correspondence goes cold at this point, Golding's journals indicate that he spent considerable time in late April and May 1972 breaking down the novel into scenes and trying to overcome various difficulties with staging. The most striking change comes after Ralph has been captured: 'Proposal by Roger. Pull his shirt up. He takes Jack's spear. Open his trousers' (J, undated). At that point, the 'officer' arrives and the play ends. On 11 May, Golding writes in his journal, 'I have worked out a possible scheme for a play of Lord of the Flies, but dont know if it will work. It's in five scenes, or I suppose acts, and hideously traditional with as much of the action off stage as possible. I'm not enough in touch with the stage, professional or amateur to be able to experiment. I'm sure that someone who had the entrée could do a ritualised version with most things mimed. But for that you have to have either great assurance or a play already of great repute, or the opportunity to experiment. I have none of the three, so must be trad' (J, 11 May 1972). A fortnight later, he admits defeat: 'I am a fool to be wasting my time with Flies. Let someone else dramatise it. I will get down to a novel' (J, 28 May 1972).

Charles Monteith to WG

1 March 1972

Dear Bill,

As you know, we get about three letters from boys a year – they're all in roughly the same age group – pointing out that Piggy couldn't possibly have started a fire with his spectacles! This is by far the most detailed and clearly illustrated one yet! I thought you'd like to see it.

I've simply told Mr [. . .] that I'm passing it on to you.

> Yours
> Charles Monteith

Monteith was not always so restrained. In 1965, he had replied snarkily to one schoolboy correspondent: 'How very clever of you to spot that discrepancy [. . .]. You're only about the third person ever to have done so!'

WG to Charles Monteith

MS

2(?) March 1972

Dear Charles

Sorry you get three enquiries a year about spectacles – I get half a dozen perhaps.

What a horrible little boy. Let's hope he takes up drug-smuggling in Turkey; but alas I'm sure he'll grow and thrive and be a boffin. He reduces me to my final defence – i.e. that I used myopia in the original Greek sense of μύωψ – screwing up the eyes. If he were a bit older I'd descend to the attack direct or retort discourteous – for 'spectacles' read 'testicles' throughout.

What in hell are we to do? Nothing I suppose – I originally thought of the spectacles as those worn by people after a cataract operation when the inside lens is removed as well as the cornea – but little boys seldom have cataracts.

Damn
    Bill.

Golding has misdated the letter 3 March; it is sandwiched between two letters from Monteith dated 1 March and 3 March, so its likely date is 2 March.

Charles Monteith to WG

TS

3 March 1972

Dear Bill,

I don't think I'll pass on your suggestion to Master Whatsisname that he should start selling hash in Turkey! Nor, I think, would his form-master approve of the suggestion that 'spectacles' should be changed to 'testicles' throughout.

Absolutely no need, of course, to do anything about it. I'm sure it gives much innocent pleasure to about a dozen small swots every year.

    Yours
      Charles Monteith

WG to Charles Monteith

18 May 1972   [Headed Paper: Ebble Thatch]

Dear Charles,

It was so kind of you to have me once again among all those many and distinguished souls last weekend. I enjoyed myself and other people! thoroughly. Thank you very much.

Ann joins me in hoping that you'll find the time and the occasion to visit us here; where the ceilings can now accomodate your height!

Στο καλό

Bill.

The distinguished souls at the All Souls dinner included Keith Joseph, Douglas Jay, Richard Wilberforce, A. L. Rowse and John Sparrow.

'Στο καλό': Goodbye (modern Greek).

1973

This year is even more uneventful than the last. Despite a temporary dip in enthusiasm, Golding perseveres with his journal until it becomes a habit: by the end of his life, it amounts to 2.4 million words. He also sets aside two hours each morning to write, hoping that something will turn up; nevertheless, a new novel stubbornly refuses to arrive. There are holidays to the Pyrenees in March and to Switzerland and Yugoslavia in September. Towards the end of the year, Golding's journal starts to contain early hints of *Darkness Visible* (1979).

WG to Charles Monteith   M S

14 April 1973

Dear Charles,

We've just returned from the French Pyraneés (where it was snowing) via the Loire Valley (where it was raining) to subtropical Bowerchalke (where the brightly-plumaged birds utter harsh cries as they flit from palm to palm.)

So I read your two letters backwards and together. I dont think the mistake was material. By the same pile of post I learnt royalty details for 6 months ending 31 Dec 72 and think that *if* (and I only say '*if*') they represent British sales and exclude American receipts then we are all gently in the money.

One thing I should have told you – W.H. Smith & Sons of Salisbury are not selling Faber Paperbacks. I dont know if this is local quirk or widespread; but I thought I would let you know, just in case.

I'm not sure when we'll be in London next, but I'll certainly let you know (or Oxford).

Ann & I send our love
Bill.

Monteith had written briefly to Golding with the news that Faber was going to issue *The Pyramid* in paperback the following spring, and then written again apologising for his 'softening of the brain': *The Pyramid* was already published in Faber paperback.

The six-month 'royalty details' did exclude American sales and came to £4,632.96. The average annual salary for men in 1972 was slightly under £2,000.

Charles Monteith to WG   TS

19 April 1973

Dear Bill,

Thank you very much indeed for your letter of April 14th. I'm delighted you're back – but sorry the weather was so beastly. I'm off to Venice tomorrow morning, for the first time I'm ashamed to say, for a short Easter holiday, or rather a long Easter weekend. Much looking forward to it.

Apologies again for that silly boob of mine about the paperback of THE PYRAMID. I'm very glad that no harm was done. Delighted too that the royalty details for the second half of 1972 seems satisfactory. I'll check about American sales.

I've spoken to John Cornell, our Home Sales manager, about the Salisbury W.H. Smith – and he assured me at once that Faber paperbacks are always well stocked by them. He did, though, in view of your letter, telephone them this afternoon; and the manager confirmed that they carry a full range of Faber paperbacks, including of course all the Golding titles, in their 'serious' paperback department, which I gather is upstairs. Since it is upstairs that may be why you missed it when you were last in. Do try an ascent next time!

Very glad to know you may be in London or Oxford before too long. Much looking forward to seeing you.

Best love to you and to Ann,

Yours ever

> Dictated by Charles Monteith;
> signed on his behalf after
> he had left on holiday.

WG to Charles Monteith   MS

24 April 1973   [Headed Paper: Ebble Thatch]

Dear Charles,

Thank you for your letter. A long week-end in Venice is just about right for the place, I think, unless you are doing the paintings frame by frame. Interesting too and five star is the most expensive coffee in the world – in Pa. San Marco!

Sorry about W.H. Smith of Salisbury – I did indeed go upstairs to the old assembly rooms; and it was there that I had an interview with a singularly wet and bored assistant who told me the F&F paperbacks were not. My apologies all round, except to the assistant.

Hope you are staying in the Danieli. It has something the feeling of taking ones ease by the High Altar at Winchester

> ever
>> Bill

'the F&F paperbacks were not': not in stock.

The Danieli is a five-star hotel roughly a hundred metres east of the Piazza San Marco.

Charles Monteith to WG   TS

8 May 1973

Dear Bill,

Just to say that once more we've been sent in a dramatized version of LORD OF THE FLIES – and this time it has actually been performed at a school somewhere in Hertfordshire. The school didn't of course write to us in advance as they should have done; and if they had, we would have said no.

This prompts me though once more – I know how much you must loathe me for this! – to wonder if you have had any further thoughts about doing your own version. To put things at the very lowest and most commercial, it's something we could certainly sell in a big way.

I had lunch with Howard Newby yesterday – publication day of his new novel – and he was enquiring after you and Ann. He told me how much he had enjoyed meeting you again at the last Booker Prize party.

> Yours
>> Charles Monteith

P. H. Newby's new Faber novel – his first since the Booker triumph in 1969 – was *A Lot to Ask.*

WG to Charles Monteith   MS

14 May 1973   [Headed Paper: Ebble Thatch]

Dear Charles,

Yours of 8th May – Isn't it all vexing? I'll have another look at my abandoned mine-workings after dramatic ore in *Lord Of The Flies*: i.e. I will try to encourage myself once more to try and make a play of it.

Newby was a bright spot in the disasterous Booker thing. I look forward to reading the new book.

> Ever
> Bill.

The Goldings were planning their first trip to Egypt (although they would not get there until 1976), so at the Booker Prize award evening on 23 November 1972 they chatted to the Newbys about their own experiences in Egypt. Golding's journal leaves little doubt that the evening deteriorated after that: 'The speeches were more or less a string of disasters. Roy Jenkins was banal. The Chairman of Bookers incomprehensible, confused and illiterate. And Cyril Connely announced the winner. John Berger [who won for his novel, *G*.] got up, and made a speech explaining how Bookers had exploited the Caribbean – especially a long time ago – and he was going to give the money to the Black Panthers, and also use it to travel with Turkish friends, et al to write a book about immigrant workers – a fine Marxist speech, in fact – what I should call thoroughly lefteous and so boring' (J, 24 November 1972).

Charles Monteith to WG   TS

18 May 1973

Dear Bill,

It's good of you to say you'll have another look at the 'abandoned mine-workings'. When you have do please let me know what you decide.

Incidentally, we've just had a brief letter from Caedmon Records which simply says:

'We would dearly love to get William Golding to that microphone. What shall we do?'

The answer is, I suppose, 'nothing'?

> Love to you and to Ann.

Caedmon Records specialised in spoken-word recordings of writers and actors.

WG to Charles Monteith

3 June 1973   [Headed Paper: Ebble Thatch]

Dear Charles

Thank you for yours of 18th May –

Am still looking at mine-working but am *also* regulating working life. Like the young sailor who applied for permission to cease shaving on the grounds that he was simplifying his life.

Esoteric.

Caedmon. Do they want me to record Anglo-Saxon poetry? Hwaet? The gross answer is 'how much' and 'why not do it here?'

Ann and I will be in London soon looking at 'bathroom suites'. Do you care to know?

ever   Bill

Caedmon Records was named after a seventh-century Anglo-Saxon poet. 'Hwaet' is the first word of *Beowulf*, and it means something like 'Listen!'

Charles Monteith to WG

25 July 1973

Dear Bill,

You may remember that we corresponded fairly recently about the possibility of your doing a recording for Caedmon. They wrote to Liza Wyatt – who looks after permissions here – on July 3rd, and I'll enclose a copy of their letter with this. It struck both Miss Wyatt and myself that the fee they offered was very low – but when we tried to push them higher, they told us that it was their best fee and we found on investigation that this was what they paid T. S. Eliot. So I'd be very grateful if you could let me know what you think. It's entirely up to you – and I wouldn't dream, I assure you, of pressing you about it.

Yours ever

Charles Monteith

Charles Monteith to WG TS

10 August 1973

Dear Bill,

Just a letter to say unofficially that I'd be grateful if you didn't accept that Argo offer for a recording of you reading LORD OF THE FLIES just yet. The reason is – and I'd be grateful if you'd treat this as completely confidential for the moment – that we're thinking seriously of starting another subsidiary firm of our own to manufacture records both of readings and of music – and of course we'd be delighted to have Golding on our opening list. There's nothing definite yet, and there won't be for some months; but if you could at any rate stall competitors I promise to get in touch with you as soon as I've got more definite news.

I'm off to Kythera for three weeks on August 27th and much looking forward to it.

Love to you and Ann,

For 'Argo' read 'Caedmon': Monteith has mixed up two separate spoken-word recording companies.

Charles Monteith to WG TS

23 August 1973

Dear Bill,

Many thanks for your letter. We'll most certainly pass on the news to Caedmon Recordings – and if there's any further news about Faber records of course I'll let you know.

I do envy you getting away until mid October. I go off myself on Monday morning for three weeks on Kythera where I have taken the archaeological dig house. The dig which has gone on for the past six years or so was carried out by an old friend of mine Professor George Huxley. He tells me that Kythera is very beautiful and completely off the tourist track. There are said to be two beaches each of them two minutes walk from the house. So that sounds all right!

Love to you both.

Yours ever,

Charles Monteith.

Golding's letter is lost.

George Huxley, like Monteith, was a Fellow of All Souls. He conducted archaeological digs on Kythera from 1962 onwards and returned regularly to the island.

The Goldings spent nearly eight weeks travelling through France, Belgium, West Germany, Austria and Yugoslavia.

WG to Charles Monteith   MS

1 November 1973   [Headed Paper: Ebble Thatch]

Dear Charles,

We are now back. Thank's for your letter and amusing chart of *The Island*. It ought to have a name. *Kindergarten*?

I believe we were in Austria at time of the obsequies but did not know where. In any case –

Kythera sounds fun. The trick (obviously) is to know the appropriate archaeologist.

We shall be at Brown's Hotel, 5th & 6th November, next Monday and Tuesday nights. Will you be about?

     ever

      Bill.

Golding has misdated his letter 1 October.

Monteith's letter and chart are lost.

The obsequies must have been for W. H. Auden, who had died in Vienna of heart failure on 29 September.

1974

There are holidays to France and Switzerland this year, as well as a three-week trip with David on his canal boat from Pershore to Reading. Golding's publications add up to just a couple of reviews, but as well as his journal he spends two months dutifully writing 2,000 words per day as he attempts to revive 'In Search of My Father'. Having persevered beyond standard novel length, he abandons the manuscript as unpublishable, but emerges with a new confidence that he is still capable of finishing a book if only he can find the right subject.

WG to Charles Monteith   MS

19 April 1974   [Headed Paper: Ebble Thatch]

Dear Charles,

You will readily see that the enclosure is my secret weapon. It was sent to Judy who passed it on to me. God bless Mr, Dr, or Prof: Stern whoever he is and may his entelechy never get further away.

The point is, though, does F&F have a thing for making copies of this: and if they have could they make me a dozen? I get three or four laborious essays a year on Piggy's spectacles. I w'd happily pay out of the next lot of royalties if any.

Judy is now working as 'editor' at Jonathan Cape and claims to enjoy it.

> Ever
> Bill.

The enclosure was page 26 of J. P. Stern's *On Realism* (1973), in which Stern explains in a lengthy footnote the mystery of how Piggy's glasses made fire: 'If Piggy's spectacles are to be used for this purpose [. . .] the lenses must be convex, which means that he must be hypermetropic. That this is the case is confirmed by his inability to see clearly both at a distance (e.g. he doesn't see the tree-tops or the boulder above him) and close up (he complains that without his glasses he sees his hand as a mere blur). Moreover, this hypermetropism [. . .] is part of Piggy's medical history. It goes together with his obesity, asthma, and underdeveloped physique (e.g. his hair hardly grows during the time on the island, so that he always looks civilized and never acquires the savage aspect of the other boys).' Golding elaborates in his journal: 'One never to be too much regarded philosopher, J. P. Stern by name has provided the perfect answer to the mystery of Piggy's spectacles. [. . .] It's clear to me that I must have met the prototype or Ur-Piggy (Urschweinlein?) somewhere in some school or other, as I certainly haven't heard of hypermetropism' (J, 12 April 1974).

Judy had been working as a copy-editor at the Clarendon Press in Oxford since June 1971. She left to take up a new role at Jonathan Cape in March 1974. When she accepted the offer, Golding noted in his journal that it seemed to be 'a step up in interest': 'She has a job with wider implication and more "opportunity to meet authors"! It's odd to find what glamorous creatures we old hacks are' (J, 12 January 1974).

Charles Monteith to WG TS

30 April 1974

Dear Bill,

Terribly sorry not to have replied before now to your letter of 19th April with its fascinating enclosure which at last sets right the whole matter of Piggy's spectacles. I'll be delighted to have some copies made of which I'll send on a batch to you and keep some here. As you know we too get some letters about that damn bonfire several times a year.

Delighted to hear that Judy is enjoying work at Jonathan Cape. It's a very lively firm with a number of extremely interesting authors on its list.

All the very best to you both.
            Yours ever,
            Charles Monteith

Charles Monteith to WG TS

8 October 1974

Dear Bill,

I thought you might be amused by this correspondence from a Toronto newspaper sent to us by our Canadian agents.

Doubtless you will note too that despite the ban on dramatic versions, a play of FLIES has been put on some years ago in Vancouver and that the adapter seems, despite that, to have done reasonably for himself in the world! It was very nice indeed seeing you again last month. I'll most certainly take you up on your offer to drop in when I'm in and around Salisbury.

> Love to you both,
> Charles Monteith

The cutting from the *Toronto Times* discussed a school play that had been adapted from *Lord of the Flies* without permission.

WG to Charles Monteith MS

19 October 1974   [Headed Paper: Ebble Thatch]

Dear Charles

Thanks for your letter and the enclosure from Toronto. I began to read the wrong side first and nearly had heart failure

'—A guard took the children into the building shortly after they arrived and locked them in—'
However I found it didn't apply.

I hope Crete stands where it stood and that you acquired a publisher's normal healthy winter tan.

We'd certainly like to have you down here whenever you can come.

> love from us both
> Bill.

Although the phrase 'stands where it stood' also occurs in Emerson, the more likely source is Byron's *Childe Harold's Pilgrimage*, canto 3, ci: 'and the Wood, / The covert of old trees, with trunks all hoar, / But light leaves, young as joy, stands where it stood'. Golding's enquiry about Crete's stability is no doubt related to Turkey's invasion of Cyprus in July and August.

1975

The highlight this year is a six-week tour of Australia hosted by the Fellowship of Australian Writers. A second canal trip with David, this time on the Thames and the Kennet, exposes ongoing tensions in their relationship. Golding publishes eight reviews in the *Guardian* during the year, several of which will eventually be collected in *A Moving Target* (1982). In October, he settles down to daily stints on a new novel tentatively called 'The Quarry'; this first draft of *Darkness Visible* totals 110,000 words when completed in mid-December.

WG to Charles Monteith   TS

6 February 1975   [Headed Paper: Ebble Thatch]

Dear Charles,

Ann and I are off to Australia – not emigrating as you might expect – but lecturing and so on. We shall be there for the whole of this coming March which we do hope will not be too cold for you in England!

It occurs to me that it might be worth the firm's while to tell whoever represents Faber & Faber in Australia about this. The man who has been organising things is

> Jim Hamilton
> Flat 1, 317 Barker's Road
> Kew, Victoria.

Hamilton is 'in the publications branch of the Ed Dept' and 'secretary of the Victorian Fellowship of Australian Writers'. I am to address them and can only hope they dont bowl too fast.

Financially we hope to break even; but are really going out to interview The Great Barrier Reef.

> Love from us both
> Bill

The Goldings spent six weeks from 1 March to 10 April touring Australia with a programme of lectures, readings and interviews. They were there at the invitation of the Fellowship of Australian Writers and the Australian Society of Authors.

'I am to address them and can only hope they dont bowl too fast': Golding followed test match cricket closely and expressed regret that his trip to Australia would not coincide with the Ashes. In his journal he calls cricket 'the epic among games' (J, 11 August 1972).

Charles Monteith to WG   TS

11 February 1975

Dear Bill,

What exciting news about Australia. The Great Barrier Reef, one of those things I've *always* wanted to see.– it goes right back to all those coloured pictures in the Children's Encyclopaedia. Is there any hope of getting to New Guinea? Of course we'll let our Australian representative know; our books are distributed there by Oxford University Press (Australia) who seem very efficient indeed.

Much love to you both,
Charles Monteith

Monteith enquires about New Guinea because of the setting of *Lord of the Flies*: the manuscript specifies that the aeroplane was heading for New Guinea when it was shot down.

Ann and WG to Charles Monteith   PC

24(?) March 1975

Got stuck here owing to a mistake over plane times. Not very many people include *Gladstone* in their itinerary. As you can see its a bit like *Alice*. Temp: about 100°F humidity 99%. The pic is v. flattering. Green stuff on hill is actually fungus. Am told Queensland gets drier and drier all the way through. People kind, especially to author of the Film of the book.

But my bloody oath, it's hot!

love
Ann & Bill

The postcard is written in Golding's hand, with no date other than the postmark. The image on the reverse is an unenticing photograph of Gladstone's Goondoon Street: a nondescript road with a Woolworths department store on one side.

The Goldings got trapped in Gladstone because the woman who arranged their itinerary forgot that there were no flights out on Saturdays. Golding's journal confirms the impression that he gives to Monteith: 'Gladstone itself is A Town Like Alice; that is, a place which seems to us like the end of the road, though of course compared with some places in the interior it must be the height of civilisation' (J, 22 March 1975).

Ann and WG to Charles Monteith PC

9(?) April 1975

We are now exiting from Australia after six weeks as unofficial salesman for F&F my oath.

We have, or rather Ann had and I appropriated it from her, a marvellous Port Moresby story which I am sure you will appreciate. Tell Rosemary many lamb chops are much in evidence, beginning at 7.30. A.M.

     love   Ann & Bill Golding

The postcard is written in Golding's hand, again with no date other than the postmark. On the reverse is a photograph labelled 'MCLAREN VALE, SA Coriole Winery. Old Slate and Ironstone House built 1860.'

Golding records the Port Moresby story in his journal: 'Apparently among the undergraduates of the university of Port Moresby, New Guinea, the tribal system, customs, ethics, habits, is still strong. There came, we are – [Ann] was – told, a time when a man from Tonga insulted a New Guinea tribesman so profoundly that the insult could only be wiped out by a ritual murder. Fortunately the vicechancellor got to hear of this before it took place and persuaded the tribes to negotiate. At last, after much argument it was agreed that the insult in such civilised parts could be paid for by a ritual feast rather than a ritual murder. So there came the day when on the verandah of the vice-chancellor's office, the two chiefs sat, painted and enthroned, their painted tribesmen around them – paw paw, guava, bananas, fish, fowl, roast sucking pig: the eats, in fact. Just as the beginning of the feast was about to be signalled by the ritual lifting of a spear, one of the roast sucking pigs rolled off a pile of food and came to rest on the verandah: whereupon the New Guinea chief turned to the Tongan chief and said – "Doesn't all this rather remind you of Lord Of The Flies?"' (J, 1 May 1975).

Charles Monteith to WG TS

28 April 1975

Dear Bill,

    Very many thanks for your post card from Australia – I gather from that, and from reports I've heard from our agents there – that it was a wild success. I don't know if you and Ann are back yet; but if you are – or when you are – do please let me know, and let me know too if there's any chance of seeing you both here in London. It's ages since we met and I'd love to hear all your news.

Yours ever,
Charles Monteith

WG to Charles Monteith TS

28 May 1975   [Headed Paper: Ebble Thatch]

Dear Charles

Thanks for your letter of about a month ago! I'm sorry not to have answered it before; but the truth is a trip right across the world proved to be more of an upheaval than I'd supposed and it's taken me a long time to settle down again. It *was* fantastic; and I *think,* successful in the sense that we both enjoyed ourselves and didn't really do the sales of F&F books any positive harm. We also swam on the Great Barrier Reef, or at least on the reef round Heron Island which for floppers-about-in-the-water rather than proper divers is as far as you can get. The underwater stuff was – well, just like all the films of it; as you know after Mombasa. I am meditating tropical waters nearer home & have a notion that if I *could* stay for a bit in Egypt and write my Egypt Book, then I'd nip along the lapis lazuli route (I think that's what it was) to El Quseir for recreational purposes.

I think we might both be coming up some time soon – London, I mean, not Oxford; and if so, will get in touch. Ann has brought back a splendid Port Moresby story. Not that we went there, however.

Love from us both
Bill

Golding's travel book about Egypt, still a decade away, is published as *An Egyptian Journal* in 1985.

El Qoseir, an Egyptian city on the west coast of the Red Sea, is the endpoint of the Wadi Hammamat trail. The Lapis Lazuli corridor links Turkey to Afghanistan.

WG to Rosemary Goad   TS

28 May 1975   [Headed Paper: Ebble Thatch]

Dear Rosemary,

Thank you for your letter and the Keel Boat book which is fascinating. Isn't it extraordinary the way life seems to be being examined at a higher and higher magnification by more and more chaps? I'm sure there's yet to be found the definitive autobiography of a sagger maker's bottom knocker. (This rowdy little book—)

Australia was fun and we avoided lamb chops although they were always on offer. Oddly enough though, the meat wasn't really good, except in top places where it was international cuisine as in all other top places.

I'm glad Jim Walker found us triumphal – we simply thought he was sympatisch or whatever; and Ann found him dishy as well. Actually, here and there we *were* rather big frogs.

We still expect to see you down here some time – at the very least, on your way through; but better, to stay for a bit

Ann sends her love to go with mine

            Bill

Goad had sent Golding a copy of Harry Fletcher's *A Life on the Humber: Keeling to Shipbuilding*, published by Faber that year. A saggar (not 'sagger') is a clay box used to protect delicate ceramics during the firing process; the bottom knocker is the person – usually a boy – who bashes clay into shape to form the bottom of the saggar. As Golding predicted, that book has now been written.

Jim Walker worked in Melbourne for Oxford University Press, which acted as agents for Faber in Australia.

Charles Monteith to WG   TS

3 October 1975

Dear Bill,

A rumour has reached my ears that you've been invited – or, if you haven't been, that you will be invited – to a congress to be held in Rouen next year of people in France who teach English at both a school and university level. Of course I don't want to influence you in any way! But our sales director, Tony Pocock, tells me that if you were to accept we'd almost certainly mount a special exhibition of Faber books; and I needn't add that the works of W.G. would feature prominently. Do please let me know what you've decided to do. If we are going to arrange something, it would be very helpful to arrange something as far in advance as possible.

Any chance at all of you and Ann coming up to London in the near future? If there is, don't fail, please, to let me know. It's far too long since we met.

> Much love to you both,
> Charles Monteith

WG to Charles Monteith TS

13 October 1975   [Headed Paper: Ebble Thatch]

Dear Charles,

Yes it's true I've been invited to Rouen for the burning sorry I mean congressing. I'd have written before this about it to you but the whole thing was unFrenchly imprecise. To be brief, yes I am accepting and subject to acts of God will either lecture on a subject of profound importance to me (say, for example, The Battle Of Maldon) or answer questions or something.

The devil of it is I cant do anything I've done before because I sent my papers, tearoffs, notes, typescripts home by post from Perth and they never got here. The Post Office have compensated me to the tune of three pounds fifty new pence which shows you what the commonalty thinks about it. However, between now and May I'll cook up something for Rouen. How about Joan of Arc and the Two Cultures? Pay no attention whatsoever. I daresay it will be something dull like What Are Novels For? Or even, Where Have All The Flowers gone?

I am feeling dull and dispirited because last Wednesday who sh'd turn up but Zhanya Yevtushenko and we drank wine for twelve hours about, two poor bloody fools that we are.

> Love from us both – Ann and me, I mean!
> Bill

Joan of Arc was executed by burning at Rouen.

Whether or not Golding means it here as a serious suggestion, he had also listed *The Battle of Maldon* as one of his interests in a biographical note for

354

American publishers in the 1950s. In the end he chose to lecture on his own writing processes, and the lecture, 'A Moving Target', becomes the title essay of his second volume of prose pieces, published in 1982.

Golding's throwaway reference to C. P. Snow's 'Two Cultures' may have been prompted by the fact that Snow had hosted an event for the Russian poet Yevgeny Yevtushenko at the Cheltenham Festival the previous month. Yevtushenko and his future wife Jan Butler spent the day with the Goldings in Bowerchalke on 8 October. 'Zhanya' is a near miss for 'Zhenya', the short form of the name Yevgeny.

'Where Have All The Flowers gone?': the title of Pete Seeger's anti-war song, except for some erratic capitalisation.

WG to Charles Monteith   MS

14 October 1975   [Headed Paper: Ebble Thatch]

Dear Charles,

A hasty note to add to yesterdays –

If you will be exhibiting me on a stand in Rouen, Cecil Beaton (who lives one Watercress Bed away from here) has now taken, oh not crude photographs but *studies* of the author living one Watercress Bed away from *him*. He told me when he gave me a batch for sheer love that copies were available for commercial purposes at not more than a few thou.

There's one of me looking through a bead curtain, with back and bottom lighting, that is *echt* Beaton – it's the nearest I've ever come to looking like Vivien Leigh.

Ever

Bill.

Cecil Beaton lived in Broadchalke and Golding knew him socially. After his terrible experience in 1954 with *Vogue*, Golding had done everything in his power to avoid photoshoots for fear of looking foolish. He was also wary about the cost of a Beaton portrait, but finally acquiesced to Beaton's invitation. As he noted in his journal, 'I dont like being photographed, but Beaton is Beaton, and a genius' (J, 30 June 1975). Beaton gave him the photographs for free, and Golding thought that they were 'excellent' (J, 18 July 1975).

Charles Monteith to WG

16 October 1975

Dear Bill,

How absolutely splendid that you *are* going to go to Rouen. I've passed on the glad news to our sales and promotion people and they'll most certainly follow it up with a stand, a Faber display and all the rest of it. Indeed it's just possible that – though in these inflationary times I may find a great deal of difficulty in laying it on! – I might manage to wangle a day or two in Rouen myself.

We all long to see you looking like Vivien Leigh and I've asked John Bodley, our advertising chap, to write to C. Beaton for some prints. Let's keep our fingers crossed about his not overcharging us!

Love to you both,

Charles Monteith

PS Is Yevtushenko *really* nice? I only once met him when he was stepping into the lift at the end of his first and only visit to T.S.E. I stepped to one side politely and opened the lift door for him with a deferential smile. But not only was I not even thanked or smiled at but not even looked at in return. I realized on the spot what it must have felt like to have been a Russian serf and why the revolution happened. 'Some Russians', I said to myself, 'are more equal than others.'

This is the first mention of John Bodley, who joined Faber as a sales clerk aged seventeen and worked in a number of different roles before going on to become Golding's editor at Faber from the mid-1980s.

Charles Monteith to WG

23 October 1975

Dear Bill,

An idea came to me recently – something that, alas, hardly ever happens nowadays. (I now have two black ties, one in London and one in Oxford since I go to so many memorial services in both cities.)

Anyway here's the idea – for what it's worth. As you know we publish a very lively and very successful list of children's books and I wondered if you'd ever thought of writing one – as a kind of light relief, perhaps, from more serious work? Specifically, what I'd thought of was either a piece of complete fiction set in Greece (Ancient Greece I mean) or a retelling of a legend, a group of legends or an historical episode. The sort of age-group I have in mind is 9–13 i.e. a reasonably literate one; and the ideal length would be a short one – something between 30,000 and 40,000 words. I can even – you can see how the imagination runs on – see the book with a Michael Ayrton jacket and perhaps – though this is something no publisher in his senses would commit himself to nowadays! – a few illustrations here and there.

Well there it is . . . Probably an absolutely rotten idea. But I'd be eternally grateful if you'd think about it and let me know, eventually, what you feel.

> Yours,
> Charles Monteith

Monteith had already discussed his idea with the editor of the children's list, Phyllis Hunt. She suggested the 9–13 age group as being 'safest' – 'I suspect that anything Golding writes would tend to be on the difficult side.'

WG to Charles Monteith TS

27 October 1975   [Headed Paper: Ebble Thatch]

Dear Charles,

Thanks for your letter. I know what you mean about Black ties. Last night I lay awake thinking of the people I knew in this village who are now dead and really – I had not thought death had undone so many. So I fell asleep and dreamed that I was looking at a foreshore with yellow weed in the pools where T.S.E. had written a love poem about things passing, particularly hair.

Your ideas are never rotten but may I put the situation as I see it? I am working towards the first draft of a book; or rather I am writing a mess of words to find out if there is a book in there and crossing fingers, believe there may be. The future, at least as far as this 75/76 is concerned would then be something like this. I may well get the mass, the wadge, call it the QUARRY concluded or ended rather than finished by the end of this year. So after a pause to reorganise and so on I might very well be doing a first draft of a book (novel) this winter and spring. Of course, pen to paper is no guarantee of quality but I dont have to stress that except that this may be a *Fata Morgana* even when finished, as I am determined it shall be [finished I mean!]. The will is there. It is a question of judgement and let us hope – an imagination not yet entirely faded.

Add to that, that I have a book on Egypt at the back of my mind to be done when I can get there – but they *will* keep having wars or travel restrictions – or making other places more attractive –

Then I'm always uneasily aware that LORD OF THE FLIES wants me to dramatise it – and I say to myself, why not simply arrange *all* the dialogue in dramatic form, call it a play and let the poor, deluded producer have the trouble? I would even contribute a preface in which I would explain the difficulties. God knows, there are enough of them.

Next September the nineteenth I draw the old age pension – well it's probably called the *Senior Citizen's Retainer* by now – and do in fact feel I hear Time's winged chariot clearly. That's why I'm going to write this book at no matter what cost, while there's time – if there's time! Writing into an inchoate substance does throw up all kinds of unforeseen material and I'm learning new things about what the chaps call the creative process (Shall we all stand?); that is to say, that there's an astonishing lot of it about if you only look.

Sorry for what may seem a distraught letter but it's a tightrope. Yes, I *know* I did it before – but one is only middle-aged once!

Ann sends her love as do I

Bill

'I had not thought death had undone so many': this comes from the opening section of *The Waste Land*, 'The Burial of the Dead': 'A crowd flowed over London Bridge, so many, / I had not thought death had undone so many.' Golding records the dream in his journal: 'Dream ego is examining a piece of foreshore about which Eliot wrote some love poetry. It is to the effect that in this place where her hair was like this yellow weed, now the weed is scanty. The verses are very good, and dream ego knows that he cannot do as well' (J, 27 October 1975).

'The Quarry' is a first draft of what will become *Darkness Visible*.

'*Fata Morgana*': an illusion in which a distant object can become distorted and appear to float (upright or inverted) above the horizon.

'[finished I mean]': Golding has added these words above the line in pen, without the brackets, as a clarification.

'I hear Time's winged chariot': see Andrew Marvell's 'To His Coy Mistress': 'But at my back I always hear / Time's wingèd chariot hurrying near.'

30 October 1975

Dear Bill,

What marvellously exciting news. I can't tell you how pleased I am to know that a new novel is beginning to take shape – though I assure you I've made all the mental foot-notes, reservations, cautions etc. etc. which you adjure me to do. But I'll keep praying that it doesn't turn out to be a Fata Morgana. Do occasionally drop me a line about how things are going.

The Egypt book too sounds a very exciting idea indeed so do please *keep* that in your mind; and of course I'm delighted that the dramatization of LORD OF THE FLIES is still there in your mind – even if only as an occasional irritant. The only way to get rid of the irritation is to do the bloody thing sometime!

I'm rather looking forward in a way to my Senior Citizen's Retainer. If you live in London you get free passes on all buses – provided you don't use them during rush-hour when I'd never want to use them anyway. Just think of being able to go, absolutely free, to all those mysterious places to which buses go and to where one's never been like Old Ford and Homerton. I can see myself spending my days like some minor and mildly dotty character out of an Iris Murdoch novel.

     Much love to you both,
     Charles Monteith

Golding's response in his journal may not have been what Monteith had hoped: 'A letter from Charles in which he is excited both by the prospect of a possible novel and the Egypt book! Dear Charles, he really manages to sound as if he meant it, though living all day and every day among authors and their wretched books he must be hard put to it often enough to keep up even the appearance of lit. enthusiasm' (J, 3 November 1975).

1976

Early in the year, Golding fulfils a lifelong ambition by visiting Egypt. He and Ann tour many of the ancient sites and monuments, but they are often exhausted and ill during the two-month trip. In April he is away again, this time in Rouen where he delivers the lecture 'A Moving Target' about the relationship between authors and critics; it becomes the title piece of his next book of essays. With work paused on the 'Quarry' typescript, during the summer Golding begins what he initially thinks of as a 'long/short'; it grows into his Booker-winning novel *Rites of Passage* (1980). There are worrying health issues for Ann, who finds a lump in her breast and in June undergoes a mastectomy. Three months later, the Goldings become grandparents when Judy gives birth to a baby boy, Nick.

WG to Charles Monteith   M S

26 January 1976   [Headed Paper: Ebble Thatch]

Dear Charles

We are off to Egypt tomorrow and if all goes well shall be away about two months give or take –

This is really a note to tell you I *did* get over a hundred thousand exploratory words towards a novel written by the beginning of 1976: it will need at least two more drafts and might end very long. It's a new departure for me.

I thought you might like to know, therefore that a new novel is factually in the pipeline though a long way down it.

Also there *could* be some sort of travel book out of Egypt tho' obviously I have no certainty. We take a car ferry to Le Havre, drive to Venice and get another car ferry from there to Alexandria.

American Express, Cairo, ought to get us. We hope to drive up as far as Aswan – getting requisite papers from Arabs was a kind of delirium. Anyway, I think we are mad, probably.

Anne sends her terrified love
Bill

Golding's journal records his progress on the next novel: 'I have finished digesting the quarry today and intend to put the whole thing away until we come back from foreign parts. Then I can move towards the shape of a book. Part of the quarry – quite a deal of it – seems vivid to me, but all in fragments' (J, 7 January 1976).

Charles Monteith to WG   TS

28 January 1976

Dear Bill,

I was delighted to get your letter – written the day before you set off for the Egyptian expedition. It's very good indeed of you to let me know how the novel is going – and 100,000 exploratory words sounds immensely impressive I assure you! I shan't, I promise you, pester you about it at all – but if there is some further news, do please let me know. And of course if a travel book came out of Egypt, that would be absolutely splendid.

Can't tell you how much I envy you your Egyptian trip. I simply *must* get there one day.

In the meantime best love to you and Ann,
                    Charles Monteith

Charles Monteith to WG   TS

4 February 1976

Dear Bill,

A brief and very unurgent note to await your return from Egypt. And, incidentally, the warmest of welcomes home – do get in touch won't you? I long to hear all about it.

Our new sales director Tony Pocock – whom I don't think you've met yet – is, like you, a member of the Savile, and he's recently had a letter from Michael Meyer, a member of the Savile Library Committee. I enclose a copy of it. – It's self-explanatory. Perhaps you could – when you're up here – look in and sign a set of your books for the somewhat intimidatingly named Savile Monument? If you would we can arrange to have them all ready for you here – and I suppose they should be charged to you at authors' rates!

Best love to you both,
                    Charles Monteith

The Savile Monument, according to the website of the Savile Club, is 'a collection of books, tapes and discs written, directed, illustrated, edited or translated and presented by members [. . .]. It is a long-standing tradition of the Club that any member who writes, edits or translates a book should present a copy to the Monument with a short dedication.'

Ann and WG to Charles Monteith   PC

3 March 1976

It really *is* as good as they say and better – there is so much to see that one's eyes get burned out with sheer *seeing* and one has to wait for them to get in Trim again
    Ann – Bill
Lovely summer weather!

The postcard is written in Golding's hand. On the reverse is an image of a statue of King Khafre sitting on his throne. It is labelled 'CAIRO – THE EGYPTIAN MUSEUM. King Chephren builder of the 2nd Pyramid 4th Dyn'.

WG to Charles Monteith   MS

4 April 1976

Dear Charles
    Thanks for your note of 4th February. As you can see, we're back after a fantastic period of excitement, strain, enjoyment and suffering. *Nothing* about Egypt is describable and *nothing* is negative, not even the emptinesses. I – we – must tell you more, when possible.
    The *Savile Monument* is like the Pyramids, or better still Ozymandias, 'Gaze on my works ye mighty and despair!' Most of it is missing. However of *course* if the job is painless enough to all concerned I'd be happy to affix my seal (if not cartouche) to the tomb.
    See you soon I hope –
        ever
        Bill

The Goldings had arrived home the previous day.
    Percy Bysshe Shelley's sonnet 'Ozymandias', from which Golding quotes the final line, describes the ruins of a giant statue of Ramses II: 'Two vast and trunkless legs of stone' with a 'shattered visage' lying nearby.

Charles Monteith to WG TS

8 April 1976

Dear Bill,

Delighted to get your letter, to know that you're back and to know that Egypt was such a stunner. I long to go there one day. Would I be right in guessing that THE SERVILE MONUMENT is *about* the pyramids as well as like the pyramids? I long to know more about it and, even more, to read it.

Let me know, won't you, when you, or better still, you and Ann – are going to be in London next.

> Yours ever,
> Charles Monteith

WG to Charles Monteith TS

14 April 1976   [Headed Paper: Ebble Thatch]

Dear Charles,

Thank you for your letter of 8th April. We have got the lines thoroughly crossed. There isn't any SERVILE MONUMENT! That phrase, which in my vile fist you have invented, or created – sheer genius – from SAVILE MONUMENT refers to a collection of works by Savile Club authors! I am supposed to sign a set of my books for the club next time I come up to Queen's Square. Remember?

But SERVILE MONUMENT is so good, one should really write something to fit it – a description of Abu Simbel, perhaps, with a dedication to Ramses II and Charles Monteith.

In terms of writing, I *did* write between forty and fifty thousand words on Egypt in my journal while I was there and also took sheaves of colour photographs. Other than that, before we left I had done rather more than a hundred thousand words towards a new novel; and shall get back on that, to cut, hew, shape, mould a thing out of it later this summer. So you see there are plenty of words about though as ever I have no guarantee as to their standard.

I shall be coming up to London shortly but for the day only and will give due warning, so that you can get someone to put out a set of books. It's Meyer's fault, and your Sales manager's.

Ann sends her love – is very articulate about Egypt, and both enthralled and appalled by it.

>ever
>Bill

Abu Simbel is a historic site in southern Egypt near the border with Sudan. It comprises two huge temples cut out of a solid sandstone cliff during the reign of Ramses II (1279–1213 BC). The Goldings had visited on 9 March; Golding's jaundiced account in his journal concedes that 'the insides of the temples are less tasteless than the outsides: but here again, the hero king is bragging along the walls' (J, 9 March 1976).

Golding's 'forty [to] fifty thousand words on Egypt' remain unpublished but the experience informs his essay 'Egypt from My Outside' which he gives as a lecture in Canterbury in February 1977. It is collected in *A Moving Target* (1982). *An Egyptian Journal* (1985) is based on a second trip to Egypt in 1984.

Charles Monteith to WG   TS

22 April 1976

Dear Bill,

I'm rather proud of THE SERVILE MONUMENT! It *is* rather good isn't it? But I do remember now about *The Savile Monument* – and we'll certainly have a set of books ready for you to sign the next time you're here.

Terrific news that you'll be getting down to work now on shaping the new novel – and terrific news too about the 40–50 thousand words on Egypt. I'm keeping my fingers firmly crossed and hoping for two books before very long.

See you and Ann soon I hope.

>Love to you both,
>Charles Monteith
>(signed in his absence)

WG to Charles Monteith

5 July 1976   [Headed Paper: Ebble Thatch]

Dear Charles,

It was great fun to be with you at the encaenia and allied festivity! I should have written before: but Ann has been in and out of hospital for an operation, and that has been a preoccupation.

But we should both like to thank you most sincerely for an entertaining and delightful day.

Our love.

Bill

Following her discovery of a lump in her breast, Ann underwent a mastectomy at Salisbury Hospital on 29 June. The effect on Golding can be measured by a journal entry four years later in October 1980: 'The diary has no sort of relationship to reality at all – or at most a very tenuous one. I remember how after Ann's operation I spent most of the night sitting on the seat by the pool simply feeling grief-stricken for her – unable in fact to come to terms with her plight and oscillating between grief and sheer rage at blind nature – yet not a word of that emerges in the diary though it was the most miserable experience of my life. I knew then she was *my Ann* which was perhaps a good discovery from my point of view but no cure for her. The diary has not one word of what went on – perhaps it was too painful' (J, 10 October 1980).

Charles Monteith to WG

6 July 1976

Dear Bill,

Terribly sorry to hear that Ann has had an operation. I hope that she's making a complete recovery and do please give her my very best love and good wishes. I'm glad to know that she's back at home again.

Did you realize from the papers, by the way, that the people we joined for tea at the Vice-Chancellor's garden party were our new Warden-elect and his wife? Since, at the time, my lips were sealed I wasn't able to drop any hints!

Best love to you both,

Charles Monteith

The barrister Patrick Neill became Warden of All Souls in 1977.

WG to Peter du Sautoy

MS

(?) October 1976

In so far as I have any report to make on my own writing, I have to admit to being confused. Apart from my journal, my novel writing comprises a vast MS which will need at least one more writing before I can see what it's about; and it might well be two books rather than one. I also broke off a month ago and started on an entirely new tack with a new story which, touch wood, is going well, and going where I can *see* it's going. Now why I tell you this is because between the first draft of this new story and the next draft of it I need to do some research and it dawned on me that the *London Library* will operate by post; but I dont know how to join it. Do you? Or does anyone at F&F? The alternative to post wd be to stay in London or Oxford and that's just not on – at least for any length of time. But it wd be a real help if you could confirm the postal resource and tell me how to join – or get myself elected!

Hope you can make sense of this babble. But there does seem to be a book if not more in this neck of the woods.

> Ever
> Bill

Only this page of the letter has been found. The 'new story' to which Golding refers is provisionally called 'The Sea Passage' before he turns it into a full-length novel and fixes on the title *Rites of Passage*.

Charles Monteith to WG

TS

22 October 1976

Dear Bill,

Peter has showed me your letter which reached him yesterday. Immensely exciting about all the new writing that's going on. You can imagine how eagerly I'll be awaiting further news!

I think the London Library should solve all your problems. They do indeed post books to members who live in the country and are, I believe, remarkably tolerant about the length of time you keep them. I rang them up this morning and they told me that they would send all details on to you straightaway together with an application form to join (The subscription is steepish – but not too steep for these inflationary days. Moreover I'm pretty certain, in your case, that it will be tax-deductible!).

Love to you both,

WG to Charles Monteith MS

29 October 1976 [Headed Paper: Ebble Thatch]

Dear Charles,

Thanks for getting in touch with the London Library. I've joined for a year – or rather *asked to be considered for membership*! for a year which I might renew or not as the thing serves. The big attraction of course is the postal service.

I hope something emerges from the mass of words I've written and continue to write – it's so easy to lay scrawled words to one soul as a kind of flattering unction.

But my hope is better
           ever
           Bill Golding

Golding may have meant 'one's soul' rather than 'one soul'.

1977

Golding starts the year by writing new essays that will end up in *A Moving Target*. In February, he delivers them as lectures in Lille and Canterbury. His practice with the two ongoing novels is to redraft them alternately: *Rites of Passage* gets rewritten in March and *Darkness Visible* in April, although neither is ready to send to Faber. In August, he takes another canal trip with David, this time in Oxfordshire. Towards the end of the year, the Goldings enjoy a seven-week break through France, Spain and Portugal, mixing business with pleasure as Golding gives lectures in Seville and Lisbon.

Charles Monteith to WG   TS

6 January 1977

Dear Bill,

My New Year began well with this letter from [. . .] of Maharastra. He sounds an earnest young man – but one with an excellent overall judgement of the Twentieth Century novel. At the same time I tremble at the thought of trying to explain to him that some English school-boys, underprivileged educationally however intelligent, do sometimes make mistakes in grammar – and that a novelist, for the sake of realism, has to incorporate this into his dialogue.

Then it occurred to me that with your own past pedagogical experience you could probably tackle this problem far far better than I would – I'm certain that a brief note from you would make [. . .]'s year a very happy one! But of course if you're much too busy – or get absolutely inundated with letters like this – please don't bother about it.

All best wishes for 1977 to you and to Ann.

    Yours,

      Charles Monteith

Monteith's young correspondent had been puzzling over Piggy's ungrammatical speech in *Lord of the Flies*, singling out the sentence 'We was scared' and wondering whether the error was the author's or the publisher's. Regardless, he concluded that Golding was the 'greatest novelist' of the century.

WG to Charles Monteith   MS

26 January 1977   [Headed Paper: Ebble Thatch]

Dear Charles,

Thank you – so to speak – for sending on [. . .]'s letter. It occurs to
me that with your service in the Far East you are really rather more
qualified to answer than I – but I will do so.

Best wishes for the new year. Down here we all have the influenza
but otherwise are alive and making feeble movements

ever

Bill

Their correspondent was Indian and not from the Far East, but Monteith served
in India and Burma during the war, so Golding's point stands even though his
geography is wayward.

WG to Charles Monteith   MS

2 March 1977

Dear Charles

Thanks for your letters – Ian Gregor passed on the news that you
were down with 'flu, always a beastly disease, I think, with depression
following it. The one thing is that there *does* come a day when you
suddenly realise you arn't depressed anymore!

The lectures seemed to go well: but on reflection I believe myself to
have been jejune in the first and spent an hour saying nothing in the
second. Still, it's good to have them tucked away for any future occasion. We missed you.

You wanted a copy of my letter to the Indian lad, but alas – I dont
keep copies and cant remember what I said. I believe I was simple and
kind – or hope so.

We shall probably see you at the Peter & Mollie do on 31st March
– but (according to the Financial Times which we read by pure chance)
you are now a frightful swell and will be surrounded by body guards
or something.

Ann is doing well – cheerful and, one might say, happy. As I am too, therefore.

> ever
> > Bill

The two lectures in Canterbury were 'Egypt from My Outside' and 'Rough Magic', both collected in *A Moving Target* (1982).

The 'Peter and Mollie do' was in honour of du Sautoy's retirement; he had been chairman of Faber since 1971 and was now succeeded in the role by Monteith. The party took place at the Travellers Club in Pall Mall, London. Golding describes the scene in his journal: 'It was a gathering of men, mostly, and mostly large, old men, so that with the predominance of dark grey suiting it seemed a bit like a gathering of elephants' (J, 1 April 1977).

Charles Monteith to WG   TS

28 March 1977

Dear Bill,

We've now had a reply from Gallimard about the translation of LORD OF THE FLIES. Here is what they say:

> 'As for William Golding's SA MAJESTE DES MOUCHES, after a fast inquiry, I am in a position to assure you that there are still more than 1.000 copies in stock. If you did not receive any statement since 1972, it is because our Accounting department is having enormous difficulties since we split with Hachette, difficulties that should be solved when we use a computer next year. Anyway, I drew their attention to Golding's book and you should receive the statements very soon.
>
> 'Now, even if we cannot contemplate a reprint for the time being, since we have suffisant stock, at least can we start considering right away the quality of the translation. The original LORD OF THE FLIES desappeared from my archives. Would you kindly send another copy? I shall let you know in due course what we think, now, twenty years later, of this translation.'

So Gallimard, at any rate, are going to consider the possibility of having the book re-translated – but it's very disappointing, I confess, to find that they've still got more than 1,000 copies in stock – and it doesn't appear, from their letter, as if these are moving very fast.

What a lovely surprise to see you and Ann at that most agreeable

Merton Dinner (and, in particular, to see Ann looking so well.) I'm terribly sad that I wasn't able to take you up on your invitation to lunch next day. But perhaps you'll both be able to lunch with me in London before too long?

> Yours ever,
> Charles Monteith

Lord of the Flies had been translated as *Sa Majesté des mouches* by Lola Tranec and published by Gallimard in 1956. Golding and Faber had for a long time felt disgruntled about the quality of the translation and Gallimard's perceived failure to promote the book sufficiently. To date, Gallimard has not commissioned a new translation.

The Goldings attended the Merton College dinner at the invitation of Thomas Braun, Fellow and Tutor in Ancient History.

WG to Charles Monteith   MS

5 April 1977   [Headed Paper: Ebble Thatch]

Dear Charles,

What a splendid party in what a splendid place! Thank you very much.

And what an *annoying* thing about the French! I do really feel that I've been led up the garden path by these French Professors – at least as far as the availability of *Sa Majesté* is concerned: the translation, of course, is another matter. Even *I* can sense that the title is a bit arch and nothing to do with the book.

Incidentally I am having a kind of two-pronged correspondence with you and Miss Fiennes over all this: and suppose that as far as foreign stuff such as translations is concerned I should not be troubling you – which I will now cease to do. But in main line affairs such as possible emergence of another book (draft finished) I will now trust in you and keep my powder dry.

Yes, Merton is good in so many ways – we saw, in the library the actual books used for doing the King James bible. Confounding, dazzling and quite ungraspable, I felt – sort of 'and did those feet', etc

> ever
> Bill.

Judith Fiennes worked in foreign rights at Faber.

'I will now trust in you and keep my powder dry' plays on the maxim often attributed to Oliver Cromwell but derived from William Blacker's poem 'Oliver's Advice', in which Cromwell urges his troops to 'put your trust in God, my boys, and keep your powder dry'.

Blake's 'And did those feet' gives appropriate expression to Golding's awe, which he repeats in his journal with a description of the books as 'legend made manifest' (J, 21 March 1977).

Charles Monteith to WG   TS

15 April 1977

Dear Bill,

I was delighted to see both of you looking so well at the reception for Peter. There was an agreeable little write-up about it in our trade paper, *The Bookseller*; and I'll enclose a copy of it since I thought you might like to see this very jolly photograph of Peter and you having a chat!

I do agree that the French are being extremely tiresome. Judy Fiennes is, however, pursuing this all very actively with Gallimard – people whom she knows reasonably well.

What absolutely marvellous news about the draft being finished of the new book. I needn't tell you how immensely I'm looking forward to reading it.

> Love to you both,

Charles Monteith to WG   TS

3 June 1977

Dear Bill,

Do you remember *The Savile Monument* – which once became, briefly but dramatically, THE SERVILE MONUMENT! Tony Pocock, our Sales Director, has been reminded about it by Michael Meyer of the Savile; and I hope you'll still be willing to inscribe the books the next time you're coming to Queen Square. We'll arrange to have copies here and to take them round to the Savile afterwards.

When you're next planning to visit London perhaps you could write direct to Tony Pocock who'll be in charge of the operation at this end and fix a day and time with him? And of course I hope you and I can have a talk either afterwards or before. I'd love to hear how you're getting on with the re-drafting of the new book.

> Yours,
> pp. Charles Monteith

The file copy is initialled 'H.S.' by Monteith's secretary, Henrietta Smyth.

WG to Charles Monteith   M S

11 June 1977   [Headed Paper: Ebble Thatch]

Dear Charles

Thank you for your letter. I will certainly come to F&F (having previously given you time to assemble the Savile Monument – which ought to be *aere perennius* but in fact gets borrowed with such assiduity you might as well call it *writ in water* –) and sign it all. The only Trouble is I dont see any immediate likelihood of my being in London. I try to do my writing against the odds of distraction & indolence and multifarious interests.

But you wanted to know about it –

I have written the draft of a novel of, I suppose sixty thousand words and put it away to take out again at some future date. I call it *Rites of Passage* and dont think it's all that good.

I have also a sprawling monster, all limbs and no body. God knows how long drawing it all together will take. I call it

Darkness Visible.

So you see there are whole masses of words drifting round the place
> ever   Bill.

This is the first time that the embossed address is positioned to the right.

The line 'exegi monumentum aere perennius' from Horace's Ode 3.30 means 'I have created a monument more lasting than bronze'. Golding contrasts it with Keats's epitaph on his gravestone in Rome: 'Here lies One Whose Name was writ in Water'.

17 June 1977

Dear Bill,

I've been in Spain for a short holiday – I stayed with some friends who have an agreeable little house in the South not on, but near, the coast – and I found your letter of 11th June waiting for me when I got back.

It's immensely exciting news about RITES OF PASSAGE and DARKNESS VISIBLE. There's no need to tell you how very eagerly I'm looking forward to reading them both. Do please let me know as soon as there's any further news about them.

It's very kind indeed of you to say that you'll cope with the Savile Monument. I'll pass on all you say to Tony Pocock, who's also a Savilian – and he'll certainly arrange to have them ready for you. Do please let him or me know when you're going to be in London next.

    Yours ever,
    Charles Monteith

1978

By the end of the year, *Darkness Visible* is almost ready to go. It vies with *The Spire* as the most taxing novel that Golding has written, and after such a long hiatus and so many drafts he is hugely relieved by Monteith's positive verdict. *Rites of Passage* receives less attention, but occasionally Golding tinkers with the typescript and discusses plot details with Ann. He is otherwise busy playing against the latest chess computer and improving his Latin by writing elegiacs. In September, the family – including David, Judy, Terrell and Nick – holidays in the Auvergne. Golding comes back prepared to put the finishing touches to *Darkness Visible*.

WG to Charles Monteith   TS

29 June 1978   [Headed Paper: Ebble Thatch (2)]

Dear Charles,

You will be surprised, I suppose to hear from me after what must be – well, a long time! My memory is that you had conceeded me pur-dah until August which is not yet. This had better be a progress report. (I hope you like the posh writing paper. It was a present and far too expensive for the likes of me.)

I have in front of me a typescript one hundred and thirty thousand words long, give or take a thousand. It is a mess, & is the one for which the *purdah* was designed. It is jumbled, inconsistent, wallowing, and has exhausted me. You'll understand that when I say it is resting on two other previous manuscripts that are of comparable length. The whole pile in fact might well be sold straight away as a basis for those dreary theses that do some, thing, thing, thing and appal the free. But a book in my sense it is not. Ann thinks there is much to it; and I believe in some of it but not all of it. *Honestly, I dont know what to do.*

So this – apart from announcing my return to the light – is a sad admission that if you thought there might be a book for the autumn, well there isn't. I must lay off this thing for a bit and try to get to the point where I can turn round and see it objectively. I might even return to another, shorter MS as a break from this one. (I have given it many titles of which DARKNESS VISIBLE is probably best but sounds presumpteuous. My self I think of it in musical terms as OP 10, op ten.)

Conceivably then if I can ever cut a hard gemlike flame out of OP 10 you'll get something to look at: but obviously by now, not earlier than the spring list. Then again, I may have taken on a book for which I simply am not qualified.

We shall get off to France for most of September (a few miles from VICHY) but otherwise will be in England, I think. Any chance of your coming this way? Ann says August is filling up but any weekend in July is OK and we'd love to have you – a quiet time, perhaps looking at gardens? Wilton, Stourhead? But you know them all! I dont suppose, said he with partly pretended diffidence, you'd want to read the book in its present stage? I think not!

What time I dont spend either in this bloody MS or journalising I spend toiling at our water garden. The only bit that's really successful is the one we call 'the bog garden', though the pool is getting better, bit by bit. My real difficulty is getting the damn thing to hold water. It will come to a plastic lining, I see that creeping up on me. Imagine a pool with a plastic lining hidden beneath dry stone walling – *no one would see it of course, but I should know it was there.* The things that grate on one in ones senility! The other day an American Professor referred to a chat we had in the close as 'Our conversation in the cathedral yard.' It makes you believe that man and his two hundred years.

Ann sends love

    ever

      Bill

The 'posh writing paper' was a Christmas present from Judy and Terrell. Unlike the previous version, the header is printed in ink with no embossing:

Ebble Thatch   Bowerchalke   Salisbury   Wiltshire

Broad Chalke 275

Golding also continues to use the embossed paper at various points.

Golding's anxiety about Monteith's reaction to his new typescript can be gauged from a dream he records in his journal: 'Dream ego is encouraged by Charles Monteith to give him a resumé of the novel he is working at. Dream ego does so, finding it very flat' (J, 26 June 1978).

'The whole pile in fact might well be sold straight away': there may be a missing 'as': 'The whole pile in fact might as well be sold straight away.'

It is not certain how Golding is counting to reach 'OP 10'. He must be including two out of *Poems*, *The Brass Butterfly* and *The Hot Gates*. If he is following the 'by the same author' page of a Faber novel, *Poems* is the text that he misses out.

The American professor was Larry Lee (L. L.) Dickson, whom Golding had agreed to meet near Salisbury Cathedral on 6 June. Dickson went on to publish

The Modern Allegories of William Golding with University of South Florida Press in 1990. The meaning of 'that man and his two hundred years' is unclear.

WG to Charles Monteith TS EXETER

2 July 1978 [Headed Paper: Ebble Thatch]

Dear Charles,
> Herewith the typescript of
> DARKNESS VISIBLE
> With all its imperfections
> on its unkempt head. Ann
>   has just finished reading
>   it and been more complimentary
>   than I would have thought.
>   It's good of you to agree
>   to having a go at it in this
>   state.
>   We look forward very much
>   to seeing you on the 22nd; but
>   alas, I suppose our water-
>   lilies will be over.
>   This is not
>   a
>   prose poem. I dont know
>   why I am typ ng like this
>   ever
>   Bill

Ann says it looks more like a tombstone than a prose poem

Charles Monteith to WG TS

4 July 1978

Dear Bill,

Absolutely delighted to have the typescript of DARKNESS VISIBLE and looking forward immensely to reading it.

Don't think gloomy thoughts if you don't hear from me again for a little while. I'm a bit snowed under at the moment; and I want to clear some space ahead when I can simply go home and read it undistractedly.

Love to you and to Ann,

This letter was slow arriving. Golding notes in his journal, 'No letter from Charles Monteith [. . .] – that makes my teeth ache. Perhaps it will come by the second post' (J, 6 July 1978). (It was delivered on the 7th.) The subsequent wait was just as physically demanding, with Golding recording on the 18th, 'Still no letter from Charles! I had a dreadful night,' and later that day, 'No Charles by second post. My heart is not so much in my boots as down below them and buried' (J, 18 July 1978).

Charles Monteith to Ann and WG MS

25 July 1978

Dear Ann & Bill,

What an immensely enjoyable weekend that was. I loved it all: the company, the food, the drink, the garden. And above all of course it was tremendously exciting to have *Darkness Visible* & to have those long, fascinating talks with you about it.

It really *is* a very powerful book; and, as you know, it impressed Ian & Mark as much as it impressed me.

We're all agreed that some more work remains to be done on it: a little remodelling, reshaping, tying-up of loose ends, general tidying-up. If you *can* let me have it by the end of October I promise you we'll do our best to publish in the autumn of 1979 – though I can't make an absolutely definite promise that we *will* be able to do so.

And then *Rites of Passage* . . . !

Much love to you both,
Charles.

This is the only handwritten letter from Monteith to Golding in the Faber archive.

Monteith spent the weekend of 22–3 July at Ebble Thatch. On the Saturday night, he and the Goldings had dinner at a local restaurant together with the politician and writer Wayland Young and the English-born Australian artist Russell Drysdale and his wife Maisie.

'it impressed Ian & Mark as much as it impressed me': Ian Gregor was not, in fact, impressed. Awkwardly, his report found its way into a bundle of papers that Monteith forwarded to Golding, so Golding would have read that the typescript embodied a 'maldistribution of imaginative energies'; Gregor concluded that it was 'an acrid read'.

WG to Charles Monteith

8 August 1978   [Headed Paper: Ebble Thatch]

Dear Charles,

It was good to have you four here – do it again!

Thanks also for the note and agreement. I've been working on the MS – or MSS – and turned up a good deal for Matty in Australia. I shall, I think, tho' with regret, tauten my girls and do them in fewer and more specific scenes. That is, try to avoid the mixture of psychology – if that's what it is – with terrorism.

This means I dont know what length the final book will be: so I wont do anything about the agreement until I have a definitive MS for you.

> ever
> Bill Golding.

Golding had been perplexed by his readers' judgement of the typescript's strengths and weaknesses: 'They are all much impressed by what I thought was inferior and unimpressed by what I thought was the good part. Charles would publish the book as it stands if I like – but I don't like! I don't know what to do' (J, 22 July 1978). The consensus was that the sections involving Matty were stronger than those that focused on the twin girls Toni and Sophy.

Golding and Monteith agreed a contract during the weekend: an advance of £5,000 against royalties of 15 per cent. The manuscript needed to be delivered by the end of October for publication in the autumn of 1979.

WG to Charles Monteith

26 October 1978   [Headed Paper: Ebble Thatch]

Dear Charles,

Herewith an amended version of DARKNESS VISIBLE, or as I have called it for the moment HERE BE MONSTERS. If the thing, or something like it is to be published we can argue about the title a bit later.

This version answers most of your criticisms though perhaps not all. I have added a good deal more of Matty – you remember? – and toned down and tautened Sophy. I've pushed the organisation of the terrorism into the background and let most of it be inferred. This has meant that the ending has a much smaller pile of corpses and is in consequence duller – However, in the case of Sophy, her decline into someone who imagines a murder without committing it and then when she finds how she's been cheated simply determines to do as much damage to the others as possible (including dad) while at the same time keeping herself in the clear seems psychologically more plausible. However, you may prefer the old bang, smash, Hamletlike pile of corpses and I suppose if you insisted we could lug it back.

The book is also a good deal shorter, so while waiting for your verdict on whether its still a possible publication I'll do nothing about the contract.

You said you wanted to have the thing retyped and copy-edited. I applaud the idea of retyping and hope it takes as long as possible! I hate this book with a profound weariness. The pile of discarded stuff is a foot high. As for copy-editing, please provide me with some kind person who will consider it his or her duty to make helpful suggestions as well as saying now and then 'You cant do that!', and 'The dates dont fit', and 'A gillyflower wouldn't be out in January', and 'Your fire engine is all wrong.'

Really, one of the impulses that made me start this book was to prove I could write about women as well as men. Maybe the copy-editor should be a woman! And one with a daughter young enough to know what young things are saying. I am about twenty years out of date.

Anything else?

Oh yes. The latin quote at the beginning, the epigraph must stay untranslated or be cut altogether.

Hey day, freedom, freedom!   Love from us both.   Bill

PS

I think this version is reduced from the original 140,000 down to about 110,000, which ought to be cheaper to produce. Of course, if you want I can come down some more, or alternatively go up some more!

There are probably showers of literals strewn through this MS but if you *did* want it by the end of October and if you have an office boy he could correct them; or alternatively send the thing back. I'm also in the market for the right title but feel *Monsters* and *darkness* are both reasonable if not perfect.

You'll be entertained I think to hear that I've worked Tassy Drysdale's RAIN MAKER into Matty's adventures, principally to bolster your opinion that the picture was the perfect dust jacket. Can writer's devotion to publisher go further?

This is the only copy of the book.

      B.

'the old bang, smash, Hamletlike pile of corpses': in one draft, both Sophy and the kidnapped child end up dead, along with others.

The novel's epigraph, from Virgil's *Aeneid* 6.266, is 'SIT MIHI FAS AUDITA LOQUI': 'May it be permitted to me to relate what I have heard.' It is Aeneas' plea to the gods to be allowed to recount his experiences of the underworld. As part of his new determination to improve his Latin (which included setting himself the challenge of regularly writing elegiacs), Golding had read the sixth book of the *Aeneid* in September 1977 and again in September 1978, noting in his journal that 'those five words might well stand on the title page of the book' (J, 11 September 1978).

Monteith took up the suggestion of finding a female copy-editor, commissioning Kate Petty to work with Golding. They got along so well that they also collaborated on *A Moving Target* (1982).

'Hey day, freedom, freedom!' Not for the first time, Golding celebrates the completion of a typescript by quoting a drunken Caliban: 'Freedom, high-day, high-day freedom, freedom high-day, freedom' (*The Tempest*, 2.2.162).

Tass (or Tassy) was how Russell Drysdale was known informally. Monteith had met him in Wiltshire in the summer, but Golding had known him longer, having spent an enjoyable day talking about cricket with him during the Australia trip in 1975. Drysdale gave Golding a reproduction of his painting *The Rainmaker*, which Golding already admired when Drysdale's wife Maisie had shown it to him three years earlier: a 'portrait of an aboriginal with an extraordinary mist, or cloud in his face so that he wasnt a modern, sharp or blunt featured man at all' (J, 28 July 1972). This becomes the cover image for *Darkness Visible*.

WG to Charles Monteith   MS

13 November 1978   [Headed Paper: Ebble Thatch (2)]

                                        Monday

Dear Charles

Herewith the agreement for what, for the moment let us agree to call *Darkness Visible*. But we'll find a better title sooner or later – though I'm sorry *Here Be Monsters* didn't appeal.

Have a good break after your 'flu.

      Ever

         Bill Golding

17 November 1978

Dear Bill

Delighted to get your letter and to have the contract. I've passed it on to Giles de la Mare and if he's any queries – I don't imagine he will – he'll be in touch with you.

I've had rather a wretched week, I fear, with 'flu and though I'm back in the office now I still feel a trifle mothy. Moreover I'm filled with guilt since I seem to have given this wretched bug to my secretary who's been battling with it nobley.

So far as the title is concerned do let's by all means settle for DARKNESS VISIBLE at any rate for the time being. If it turns out to be that in the end I think I'd advise dropping the Latin tag at the beginning and substituting for it a short quotation from PARADISE LOST. Presumably the passage quotes in the OXFORD DICTIONARY OF QUOTATIONS (on page 344.9) would do?

I had a very nice letter indeed from Russell Drysdale yesterday together with two excellent transparencies of The Rainmaker. They've aroused great enthusiasm already here, not only with our Jacket Designer, Shirley Tucker but also among our Sales Department. They all agree that it's going to make a splendid jacket. I've written to Russell of course to thank him and I've promised him a copy of the novel when it's ready. Perhaps you'd like to inscribe it for him?

Something quite different. I think that two or three years ago you made a very successful appearence at a congress in France of the Association of Teachers of English as a Foreign Language – in France I think they call themselves Le Congres des Anglicistes. They're having another session in Hamburg in or near Easter week of 1980; and they wonder if you would be willing to appear again. They're very anxious to have you and they'll be delighted if you would. Needless to say we ourselves would very much like you to – and would be only too happy to pay any expenses incurred. I imagine that you and Ann, if you go, would like to go over for a couple of nights. No tremendous hurry about this but it would be a great help if you would let me know reasonably soon whether or not you would like to do it.

       Love to you both.

       Charles Monteith

Monteith proposes for the epigraph the passage from Book 1 of *Paradise Lost* in which the novel's title occurs. After the rebel angels have been flung out of heaven, Satan takes in his new surroundings: 'A Dungeon horrible, on all sides round / As one great Furnace flam'd, yet from those flames / No light, but rather darkness visible / Serv'd onely to discover sights of woe' (1.61–4).

WG to Charles Monteith   MS

21 November 1978   [Headed Paper 2: Ebble Thatch]

Dear Charles,

Thank you for your letters, infos and incs. I am developing a passion for contractions. It saves paper.

I enclose the signed add: to orig: con: for which many thanks. It goes to show what I always really believed – that in almost all circumstances it isn't necessary to read the small print!

As for the *Your MS and Galley Proofs* – my next (well, next but one) shall be a thing of beauty even if the matter of it suffers.

Darkness Vis: – will keep worrying at title. I havnt a copy of the *O. Dict. of Quotes* but suppose you mean *P. Lost* Bk I 61–70. I have Cruden's *Biblical Concordance* and will walk through the ref: *Fire*. It occurs to me ——

And With Fire is just possible. The jacket sounds good. Of course I'll sign a copy for Tassy. Having not read *Darkness. V.* for a few weeks I'm beginning to think quite well of it. Later on I'll screw myself up to another *go*. There must be lots that c'd be improved.

We cant at once reply over *Les Anglicistes* but do note that Hamburg could be considered as on the way to Poland and its zloties. I'll let you know soonish.

We'll be in Brighton for a couple of nights later this month or next. I might nip up, and sign those books from there.

I'm sorry to hear that you and your secretary had a bug – it's beastly. Ann is even now recovering from one. In fact I am the only really healthy, moral, slim character for miles.

y'rs ever
Bill.

The addendum to the contract clarifies the timing of the advance for Golding's new novel: '£5,000 payable half on demand after delivery and half on demand after publication.' The original contract mistakenly mentioned an advance of £2,500.

2 December 1978   [Headed Paper: Ebble Thatch (2)]

Dear Charles,

Word, by a relatively roundabout route has reached me to the
effect that you want the publicity for *Darkness Visible* ready by
Christmas. This puts a different complexion on our combined search
for a title. Brought up short by the prospect of wooing booksellers
and publishers by the title I begin to feel an unholy touch of sheer
expediency which I am too old to feel ashamed of. I take your point
that *Darkness Visible* as a title is OK but only, so to speak as something that will just-about-do. It does have a vanishing, a forgettable
quality about it, a kind of invisible darkness that merges into the
woodwork.

The trouble is I've little better to offer and am wide-open to suggestions. Since there are religious overtones in the book I've searched the
bible. (In despair I even tried the *Sortes Virgilianae* or *sacrae* rather:
but came up with 'Howl ye ships of Tarshish' which was not helpful.)
Cruden's Concordance is easier and I played with: *A Burnt Offering
– A Flame of Fire* (the second Adam, of course) *– A Fire Infolding –
Star from Heaven – Day-Star Arise –* (then from Little Gidding) *– Fire
or Fire – Tongues of Flame – Crowned Knot of Fire –* (also *Tongued
with Fire*) and so on. You takes your pick. *Burning Burning.* (The Fire
Sermon of course)

Ann said the source doesn't matter – why not say what you want?
The trouble is this book is the nearest I shall ever get to a baggy monster and there just *isn't* a comprehensive phrase. Pilgrim's Progress
might have something: but why not a Nursery Rime? That would give
us quite simply: *Fire, Fire.*

As you see I'm doing my best but dont really feel I've got anywhere.

The copy-editor you have provided sounds sympatica and promises
advice on the language of contemporary young things.

I'm sorry you dont like my, or rather Virgil's (he's *in* this semester)
tag. It was meant as a modest disclaimer of any personal knowledge of
spiritual matters.

Ann's not been well but is better now, so we *might* get to Brighton,
but dont know. In any case I'll see you on the ninth. I shall spend most

of Saturday book-hunting and then come along to All Souls – I look forward to it.

> ever
>> our love
>>> Bill.

Ann finds the fire-titles more forgettable than *Darkness Visible*. She just might have something as an addicted title fancier. (She now says she buys books on the strength of the review or the author's name. I suggest WILLIAM GOLDING ⎫
> by   ⎬
> DARKNESS VISIBLE ⎭

The Sortes Vergilianae (Virgilian Lots) was an attempt to foretell one's destiny by opening the *Aeneid* at a random verse. Having followed the same technique with the Bible, Golding has alighted on Isaiah 23:14: 'Howl, ye ships of Tarshish.' It is hard to judge how seriously he took these techniques. In the 1960s, he had used Tarot cards and the Chinese divination text I Ching to make decisions and predict the future; both methods were adopted by David and may have been Golding's way of indulging him.

Alexander Cruden's *Complete Concordance to the Holy Scriptures* (1737) provides Golding with possible titles taken from Leviticus, Hebrews, Ezekiel, Revelation, and the Second Epistle of Peter. T. S. Eliot's 'Little Gidding' (from *Four Quartets*) is another likely trove, partly because it shares with *Darkness Visible* a scene from the London Blitz. Golding also considers '*Fire, Fire*' from the nursery rhyme 'London's Burning'.

Charles Monteith to WG   TS

4 December 1978

Dear Bill,

It would be very nice indeed to see you if you manage to nip up to London from Brighton. I've been down a couple of days there very recently, first arranging for the funeral of an old aunt and then going to it. Being the only mourner at a crematorium is a somewhat depressing experience!

As for the title, let's settle for DARKNESS VISIBLE. I find that it grows on me and my colleagues here, including those very important people, the Sales Directors, are all quite happy with it.

The actual quote from PARADISE LOST is this:

'A dungeon horrible, on all sides round
As one great furnace flam'd; yet from those flames
No light, but rather darkness visible
Serv'd only to discover sights of woe,
Regions of sorrow, doleful shades, where peace
And rest can never dwell, hope never comes
That comes to all.'

Rather suitable for the book, I feel, opening, as it does, with a tremendous fiery furnace effect.

It would be nice if you could manage Les Anglicistes at Hamburg. When you've decided, do please let me know.

> Yours ever,
> pp Charles Monteith
> (Signed in his absence)

The initials at the end are 'H.S.' for Monteith's secretary, Henrietta Smyth. In an internal memo, Monteith reports that he and she like 'Burnt Offering' as a title but that he finds himself 'more and more content with DARKNESS VISIBLE'. His Faber colleagues unanimously agree that 'Darkness Visible' is the best title. Too late to change anything, Golding decides the following March that – as he writes – 'the proper name for Darkness Visible is simply FLAME' (J, 22 March 1979).

WG to Charles Monteith

MS

28 December 1978   [Headed Paper: Ebble Thatch (2)]

Dear Charles,

Kate Petty came down here yesterday and we finished going through *an* MS. However, in the meantime I had rewritten and tautened some bits which she has taken off with her: *Darkness Visible* could now have one of those diagrams on it showing what manuscript is related to which.

However, she will now, I suppose forward her version to F&F. I want to see that MS before it goes to printer as the text-situation is now so complex I cant remember what is which. An alternative suggestion is that I should rely on galleys for corrections: but that w'd be costly. The main thing from my point of view is that I should have *one more* review. After all, the book might very well be about the place for a considerable time!

> Ever – and especially for the new year –
> love from us both
> Bill.

1979

After a long hiatus, this year marks Golding's second coming. *Darkness Visible* is published in October and becomes a great success in Britain and the United States. Golding avoids the attention by taking a long family holiday in France and Spain; he vows never to speak publicly about *Darkness Visible*. During the year, Golding also finishes two more drafts of *Rites of Passage*, and he sends a near-final version to Monteith in December. On the first of that month, his second grandson, Laurie, is born.

WG to Matthew Evans   MS

8 January 1979   [Headed Paper: Ebble Thatch (2)]

Dear Matthew Evans,

Thank you for your kind letter assuring me of the good intentions of Farrar Straus. I daresay I was unduly nervous, cautious and cynical –. I have these flashes of unenlightenment every now and then and they make me feel a PRACTICAL BUSINESS MAN: but they dont last.

Anyway, thank you again.

Yours sincerely
William Golding

Golding was concerned about Evans's executive decision to sell *Darkness Visible* to Farrar, Straus and Giroux rather than to his usual American publisher, Harcourt Brace Jovanovich: 'Giroux was with Harcourt Brace but had a row with Jovanovitch. We had better watch out, I think. What is good for Giroux is not necessarily good for Golding!' (J, 4 December 1978). The tension eased when Golding, Ann and Charles went to lunch in London with Robert Giroux on 14 December and found him 'a pleasant soul' (J, 15 December 1978). The dispute over the right to publish *Darkness Visible* was eventually settled in the American courts in favour of Farrar, Straus and Giroux.

Charles Monteith to WG TS

10 January 1979

Dear Bill,

So sorry to have been such a very long time in replying to your letter of December 20th. I had rather a beastly December – 'flu with complications; and by the time I was back in the office fit and well again the long Christmas/New Year holiday descended – which was, I must say, an extraordinary agreeable successor to everything that had gone before it! I have kept in touch, though, with DARKNESS VISIBLE via Kate Petty and Nicole Foster; and I gather from Nicole Foster that you and she did have that long telephone conversation yesterday afternoon, as a result of which the text now is in its absolutely final form. So we will get it off to Production tomorrow morning.

This leaves one final and difficult problem – the blurb! I expect you guessed that. I suppose I couldn't possibly ask you to have a shot at doing a draft blurb yourself? I know it's the most dreadfully unfair request ever to make to an author – but it's such a big, complex, multi-stratified book that I confess I begin to lose my nerve at the prospect of writing about it with anything approaching conviction in 200 words! But of course, if you would rather not have a go I'll entirely understand. Most certainly it's the publisher's job and not the author's.

Hope to see you both soon. In the meantime, much love and belated good wishes for 1979.

> Yours ever,
> Charles Monteith

PS I enclose a copy of p. 162 which I believe was missing from your xerox copy

Nicole Foster was the firm's chief copy-editor. Golding had alerted her by phone to fifty small changes that he wished to make.

WG to Charles Monteith MS

13 January 1979　　　　　　　[Headed Paper: Ebble Thatch (2)]

Dear Charles,

It's good to know you're back in circulation. I've had a week of 'flu myself and know what it's like. The depression is positively *cosmic*.

Blurb:

Crickey. Golly. My aunt! On the principle of trying everything once I'll have a go: but the basic difficulty is that *I* dont know what the damn thing is about either. I find myself making tiny mental beginnings. This great book. Seldom if ever. When the critics said. This majestic obscurity. Why doesn't he just stop.

You see what I mean: but I will have a go at trying to convey something of the basic orientation of my mind during these too many years. It's what comes of supposing the only good monsters are baggy ones.

But I will try. Then you'll have to give it the plausible air of having been written by someone else –

Unless come to think of it, the blurb is a sort of preface? But I dont want to give myself away.

Oh dear.

I dont know what the fate of blurb is but suppose it to be used first for prepublication publicity – could the fact that I wrote it (wrote *at* it) be concealed? That's not modesty or even egotism, but stems from the fact that over the years I've learnt not to define my own books. The definition always backfires.

and now – *allons*!

Bill

When Nicole Foster murmured over the phone and you wrote in your letter 'its absolutely final form' I felt something coming by the pricking in my thumbs. It must be a publisher's formal phrase like the judge's 'have you anything to say before' et cetera.

I have jotted a few notes of blurb – then found they were two hundred and fifty words already! Now, if I read blurb which says (continued on back page) I shall know the author wrote it.

––––––––––

Here it is at last! I feel that it is larger than you want: and perhaps I have not succeeded perfectly in violating my natural modesty.

Perhaps I can leave the violation of my modesty to you?

Do what you like with this of course – alter, shorten, amplify, throw away or send back.

ever

Bill

This novel races through forty years of our history, for Matty appeared in the terror of the second world war. Who was he? What was he? What was he for? Was he more than human or less? He was maimed in body if not in mind, a jagged, humourless character who devoured his bible syllable by syllable and was crucified by his sexuality. Was the journal he kept madness or inspiration?

The twins were young enough to be his daughters, Sophy, dark, amoral, cruel and Toni, fair, brilliant, empty. They brought a new generation of terror into the world. Perhaps the three were enemies in an ancient war with a child for prize. Yet Matty and Toni never met, and Matty and Sophy for no more than a moment. There was Goodchild too, and Bell, Winnie and Gran, Gerry, Roland, Fido, Bill, the brutal one and Stanhope with his chess. There was Sebastian Pedigree, thought by all to be the wickedest of men but proving in the end less harmful than those who thought they held the one truth firmly in both hands. Perhaps there was witchcraft and piety in combat round a commonplace event of our terrible world. And then again, perhaps it was all in the mind and each character sitting out the time in a separate cell with walls of adamant. The mood is everything, the fact in doubt. 'Entropy', Stanhope called it. But the spirit with the more expensive hat showed that all would be revealed at the appropriate time.

Monteith's request for a blurb prompts further reflection in Golding's journal: 'All I can think of for a moment is a curiosity as to whether I could explain or at least describe female terrorists and if possible from the inside. The other is an interest in those who have or are alleged to have, super sensible experiences. The story began in confusion and perhaps has ended that way. What unity there is in the story is perhaps more one of feeling than event' (J, 12 January 1979).

'I felt something coming by the pricking of my thumbs': for other examples of Golding quoting these lines from *Macbeth*, see Golding's letter to Monteith on 10(?) September 1955 and to John Bodley on 13 September 1980.

Charles Monteith to WG   TS

19 January 1979

Dear Bill,

What a great, good and many-sided genius you are. If you ever feel the need to earn some modest pin-money, let me know and I'll take you on as a resident blurb writer. Seriously, I think that blurb is marvellous. I may play about with it a little bit but it will only be, I'm certain, a very little bit. And I promise you, too, that your anonymity will be most carefully preserved.

Isn't this weather absolute hell?

Yours most gratefully,

Charles Monteith

PS Remember that I said when we last met that our Sales Director, Tony Pocock, would very much like to have a chance to talk to you sometime this Spring about his initial promotion plans for DARKNESS VISIBLE. He's off to India and the Far East – lucky man – at the weekend and won't be back in the office until the end of February; and I'll be in Ireland, both North and South, for the first week in March (not a holiday. Business.). But both Tony and I will be here throughout the second half of March; and if you – or, better still, you and Ann – are planning a visit to London then, do let me know with as much advance notice as possible and I'm sure we can fix up a meeting. Another lunch together would be immensely enjoyable.

Love to you both.

'Isn't this weather absolute hell?': the average temperature in the south of England in January 1979 was below freezing, with heavy snowfalls and hard frost.

WG to Charles Monteith   MS

29 January 1979   [Headed Paper: Ebble Thatch (2)]

Dear Charles

Thanks – many thanks – for your letter. Recognition at last! The secret of my success, though is very simple. I solemnly read all the blurbs I could get hold of, then went and did likewise.

However there *is* one benefit from doing the job. You *do* find out what you meant: or rather, grab at something you may have meant once, then ossify, fossilize that attitude.

I dont know about coming up in March – if this stinking weather goes on we might find somewhere warmer for a bit. But if 'promotion' is a serious intention, well then I must as they say rethink. Only I dont want and you wouldn't want the sort of malarky I endured in New

York after rashly consenting to help push the film of *Flies*!

Nor, come to that, do I want to answer all the questions the blurb asks! In fact, Ann and I were proposing to be out of the country on publication day, because I am no longer able to bear adverse crits. No – that's an exaggeration – but I ask myself, why put up with them?

Your Irish trip, sounds terrifying to a mere Brit. I suppose it's one of the few places where a Brit is safer in the air than on the ground.

But God speed and all that.

Love from us both

    Bill

'the sort of malarky I endured in New York': Golding is probably remembering his disastrous solo trip to New York in February and March 1963, although it was less a publicity drive for Brook's film (which was not yet out) than a lecture tour to promote his own work. See his letter to Monteith, 19 March 1963.

Charles Monteith to WG TS

5 February 1979

Dear Bill,

Very many thanks for your letter. I'll enclose with this the final version of the blurb – slightly shortened from yours but based entirely on it.

We certainly wouldn't dream of subjecting you to any 'promotion' which you found unpalatable; but Tony Pocock would certainly very much like to meet you at any time that's convenient for you and Ann. But do leave it until it really does fit in with any other plans you might have. The idea of getting away from this bloody weather to somewhere warmer strikes me as an extremely sensible one.

    Love to you both,

      Charles Monteith

Kate Petty revised Golding's blurb by shortening it and adding the requisite praise at the end ('William Golding has written a story of our times'). She admitted to Monteith that *Darkness Visible* was a tricky assignment: 'To some of my queries WG gleefully answered, "Let the American PhD students argue about that one."'

WG to Charles Monteith

9 February 1979   [Headed Paper: Ebble Thatch (2)]

Dear Charles,

Thank you for your letter with the reconstituted blurb. (It ought to be a Greek verb dont you think – eblurpsa to begin with and now beblurkamen; or since dose old guys never had no blurb and it's a modern thing, mpemplurkamen.) It all seems OK to me.

In re 'promotion'. Of course I didn't think F&F would do anything in bad taste – it's just as I said, I want to be out of the country when the various hatchets fall.

Two additional points. Take the Latin quote out of the beginning if you think it pretentious when untranslated. It's *no good* with a translation. Also insert the quote from Paradise Lost if you really think it's needed. But cant we rely on what used to be called 'the spread of universal education'? No, probably not. Ah well.

The enclosures and the following paragraph is not really addressed to you but to the right department in the firm which you feel sh'd deal with such a matter. As the correspondence shows it's been all hanging about. Lately I wrote them a thing, then before sending it off I read the letters again and found what looked like *5 grand* for a few paras, was an 'advance'. Advance on what, I asked myself. Are not F&F entitled to a cut as well as I of *any* American copies of Flies? So I suddenly saw the 5 G might be in lieu of *my* cut, F&F not yet informed and suddenly finding I owed them some of it! It is all mixed up in my head and I simply wish to DO THE RIGHT THING DASH IT. My introduction is written (if I can still find it) and I should take the autographing very, very slowly – probably in the south of France or better in the high Valais where we have a couple of friends.

I had supposed the china you had taken from you was the usual spotted dog or two country persons leaning against a treestump – then Ann said she thought you'd lost some Tanagra figurines. Good God! If so, I commiserated far too slightly and should have wept with you for an hour by the clock! I remember two Tanagra dancers in the BM that unaesthetic as I am very nearly encouraged me to break and enter. By the way the Japanese Screen we bought in Brighton continues to please. I have an awful confession to make. The other day my eye fell on it, as it were by accident as if seeing it for the first time and I thought – how elaborate, rich, lovely; and then (as I remembered it was ours) with a slight but beastly salivation – *how costly*!

> our love to you – Bill

Could I have the Franklin guff back?

Golding turns 'blurb' into a Greek verb: 'eblurpsa' ('I blurbed') and beblurkamen ('we blurbed') or, rather, 'mpemplurkamen'. The joke is that modern Greeks transcribe a 'b' sound as 'mp' (μπ).

The enclosures were correspondence from the Franklin Library, a US publisher that produced collector edition leather-bound books. They were proposing to publish *Lord of the Flies* in a luxury edition with every copy signed by Golding. ('5 G' is five grand – 5,000 dollars or pounds.) The project did not go ahead.

Monteith had recently been burgled, although the rumour from Ann that he had lost some Tanagra figurines turned out to be false. Named after the town in Boeotia where many were discovered during excavations, Tanagra are mould-cast terracotta figurines produced from the fourth century BC. The British Museum ('BM') has a small collection of them.

Golding's line about the 'Franklin guff' is written in pen on the reverse of the typed page.

Charles Monteith to WG   TS

13 February 1979

Dear Bill,

Fine. I am delighted the blurb is all right; and I repeat my assurances that F and F won't want you to do anything disagreeable so far as promotion is concerned.

I have told our Production people to leave the Latin quote in and to forget all about the quote from PARADISE LOST. Where did the Latin quote come from, by the way? An ignorant question, I am sure, but I don't know.

I passed all your correspondence with the Franklin Library to Miss Mavis Pindard who looks after rights and permissions here and has had to correspond with these people several times before – last time, I remember, in connection with the Franklin Library edition of the COLLECTED POEMS OF AUDEN. (Incidentally you might say to them, tactfully, that I would quite like a buckshee copy of their posh edition when it is published!) If they simply want to sell their book in the United States excluding Canada then F and F don't come into it at all; but if they want to sell it in any part of our market, which does include Canada, then we certainly must give permission and must, too, get a cut. Mavis Pindard will be writing to them direct about all this and as soon as she has got things sorted out she will get in touch with you again herself direct.

No Tanagra dancers, thank God, just exactly what you say, a spotted dog, country parson, Moody and Sankey, Queen Victoria and all that, but they did look rather nice in a small alcove in my dining room.

Love to you both,
Charles Monteith

PS Since dictating this I have just noticed your own postscript to say that you would like the Franklin letters back. So I'll ask Mavis Pindard to photostat them and send the originals back to you when she has done so.

The Staffordshire figures of the American evangelists Dwight L. Moody and Ira D. Sankey were a favourite with collectors.

WG to Charles Monteith   TS

17 February 1979   [Headed Paper: Ebble Thatch (2)]

Dear Charles,

I'd already decided I'd try to grab a copy of the Franklin Library's posh edition, and will now make it two. They are for the millionaire who has everything and are probably not illustrated but illuminated by hand like the book of Kells.

Thank you for clearing up our mutual situation as to who gets what.

Latin quote – it's from book vi, damn I mean book 6 of the Aeneid. The Hero and the Sybil are about to descend into the underworld carrying the famous Golden Bough (I wonder how she managed all those volumes – six under each arm?) as a sign of entitlement. Vergil is aware that it's all a bit presumptuous, not to say blasphemous, so he says – let me find my Loeb –

'sit mihi fas audita loqui; sit numine vestro
pandere res alta terra et caligine mersas.'
which the man translates as
'Suffer me to tell what I have heard; suffer me of your grace to unfold secrets buried in the depths and darkness of the earth!'

I know that quoting a bit of it sounds rather like cut-price classics; but the first five words *did* seem to me to be what I wanted to have as a disclaimer of any personal knowledge of what goes on in Darkness Visible – it's all made up, quite, quite invented!

I know! The two Latin lines *have the right vibes!*

But dont be too shocked if they vanish in the galleys. Still sorry about the spotted dog and M and S (is there a modern one of Marks and Spencer?)

   Ever
    Bill

The Book of Kells is an illuminated manuscript of the four New Testament Gospels in Latin, dating from around the year 800.

Golding's joke about the 'famous Golden Bough' relies on the fact that the third edition of James George Frazer's classic comparative study of magic and religion, *The Golden Bough* (1911–15), was published in twelve volumes.

Charles Monteith to WG   TS

21 February 1979

Dear Bill,

Many thanks for your letter of February 17th. So it's Book 6 of the *Aeneid*, is it? I did it once for a Higher School Cert and thought I knew it pretty well – but Age has been at its usual work. I was able to do on my own, without help: 'sit mihi fas'; but to be sure about 'audita loqui' I had to consult Giles de la Mare, who's a Greats-man. He, I'm happy to say, coped on the spot!

What about heading the quotation with the words '*Disclaimer*'? (This is *not* a serious suggestion.)

Much love to you and to Ann,

'a Greats-man': the classics degree at Oxford is known as 'literae humaniores' or 'Greats'.

Charles Monteith to WG   TS

5 July 1979

Dear Bill,

I have been asked to send you on this letter from a Ms [. . .]. I know nothing of her at all, I confess; but her agent wrote to me and in a slightly threatening final paragraph said that she will call *me* directly upon her arrival in this country!

All I can say is that The Atlantic Monthly is, as you doubtless know, an entirely reputable and widely read magazine.

Yours ever,
Charles Monteith

WG to Charles Monteith TS

10 July 1979   [Headed Paper: Ebble Thatch (2)]

Dear Charles,

Thank you for your letter and the enclosure. My goodness me. Harvard, a first at Cambridge, one split infinitive and a mis-spelling! (Ms Spelling?) I always did suspect that place when it came to the cruder literary processes rather than lofty criticism.

However. Look –

Judy and Terrell changed houses in Liverpool so we went to help; and on the day they got into the new one Terrell was appointed to a new and improved job at Bristol so they have to up and go again, we, as far as possible, helping. Also I have a sick friend to visit. And I have to do a final draft of RITES OF PASSAGE between now and Christmas. And we are *all* leaving the country in September for a month at least to avoid the publishing high water. And several other things. What I mean is I just havn't time. Moreover DARKNESS VISIBLE is the one book of mine I'm never going to talk about.

God knows why I'm saying all this. The real answer is *of course*, a polite refusal.

I hired a road drill to deepen my pond and am not yet recovered from using it. You've no idea how road men suffer. Tell that to Ruskin!

We both remember with gratitude the evening you gave us at All Souls. I think Ann was specially moved by the beauty and charm of the place, people, ceremony; and so specially grateful to you.

We also have a second grandchild on the way – not sure the news is public but it *does* add to the delightful confusion of everything.

yours ever
Bill

Monteith had already warned the sales department at Faber that Golding would 'probably be out of the country for publication day' and that it would be 'a great

397

mistake to try to persuade him' to take part in activities to promote the book.

The Goldings had dinner with Monteith at All Souls on 20 June.

John Ruskin promoted the virtues of manual labour: 'It is only by labour that thought can be made healthy'.

Charles Monteith to WG TS

20 July 1979

Dear Bill,

Many thanks for your letter of July 10th. It arrived, opportunely, just an hour before Ms [. . .] telephoned; and I passed on your polite refusal and I assure you I was completely firm about it. She was sad – but accepted it with good grace.

Do you remember a Faber novelist called John Hearne? He is a Jamaican whose books were, I thought, pretty good but who hasn't published anything since 1961. He turned up the other day bearing the first half of his new novel – I tremble as I dictate the words – which is set on board ship in the early nineteenth century. It's all about an illegal slaver becalmed in the South Atlantic somewhere between Brazil and the West African coast. *Please* assure me that this isn't what RITES OF PASSAGE is all about! I sometimes toss sleeplessly in my bed at night, thinking that it may be.

Yours ever,
Charles Monteith

John Hearne's novel, *The Sure Salvation*, was published by Faber in 1981.

WG to Charles Monteith MS

25 July 1979   [Headed Paper: Ebble Thatch (2)]

Dear Shipmate O' Mine,

My heart bleeds for all that tossing you do in your bunk. Actually John Hearne's ship is on an East–West course (090°–270°), as we say, while mine is *standing South* (000°–180°). Mine is a ship of the line, though a fourth rate and full of people who are enslaved by nothing but the constraints of the British Social Scene. They *did* sight a strange sail and it *may* have been a slaver – John Hearne's probably. So to cut a short story even shorter you are in the clear and can lie quiet in your bed.

A cutting from USA in which Giroux says 'Golding had already decided to leave Harcourt.' Intuitive, penetrating Giroux! He knows more about me than I know about myself.

> ever
> Bill

The dispute between Harcourt Brace Jovanovich and Farrar, Straus and Giroux over the right to publish *Darkness Visible* in the United States had finally reached the courts. Golding writes in his journal, 'Judy gave me a cutting from the New York Times in which the remark occurs "(Golding) had already decided to leave Harcourt." This is a most extraordinary version of what happened: since Charles assured me that I should leave Harcourt and that was the first I had heard of it. At the lunch with Giroux it seemed to me all sewn up and that I (having [. . .] asked about the morality (!) of the change) was simply following along behind Fabers. However that's all a jungle and I propose to keep out of it' (J, 21 July 1979). See Golding's letter to Matthew Evans, 8 January 1979.

Charles Monteith to WG   TS

31 July 1979

Dear Bill,

What a relief it was to get your letter – particularly as I will in fact be sleeping in a bunk tonight. I'm going to Scotland on the night train. My repose will be as untroubled as a child's.

Yes, indeed, I saw that cutting from the United States about the Harcourt Brace – Farrar Straus affair. What extraordinary intuitive powers these Americans sometimes seem to have.

> Yours ever,
> pp. Charles Monteith
> (dictated by Charles Monteith
> but signed in his absence)

The letter is initialled 'S.B.' by Monteith's secretary, Sarah Biggs.

WG to Charles Monteith   TS

7 August 1979   [Headed Paper: Ebble Thatch (2)]

Dear Charles,

Herewith an address through which I may be reached in September

– or from the seventh to the twentyseventh of it at any rate.

C/O M & Mme A. Roux

Le Pla de Fa

Fa

11260 – Esperaza

Aude FRANCE.

After that I'll drop you a line saying where we are going and when or whatever; but in October failing anything else it might be worth trying our home address because there could be someone (might be someone) who knows where we are.

Of course the whole thing really depends on some vital query needing solution; and the only one I can think of is if some one of the vast film corporations should want to give us a fortune. If it's an Art Film full of integrity with no money attached just tell them not to bother. If on the other hand it is some vast sum of money like six figures then you have power of attorney to accept always provided I get *a percentage of the gross.* That is *essential.*

No other query is likely; and certainly no other is worth interrupting a holiday for. I expect all this sounds a bit early since we dont leave till September anyway; but the posts are all to hell and I cant really be sure when you'll get this. A letter from my bank in Salisbury was posted by them ten days ago and still hasn't arrived, ten miles away.

I hope Scotland stands where it stood and all that

ever

Bill

'stands where it stood': Golding makes the same allusion to Byron's *Childe Harold's Pilgrimage* in his letter to Monteith dated 19 October 1974.

Charles Monteith to WG   TS

24 August 1979

Dear Bill,

Here are the five novels you very kindly said you'd inscribe for my Goddaughter, [. . .]. I am immensely grateful to you – as [. . .] will be, I'm quite certain. She's a tremendous fan. The pile includes, as you see, an advance copy of DARKNESS VISIBLE which looks, I think, very nice. You will, of course, be getting your own six copies very shortly.

I'll enclose a label, stamps etc. for returning them to me here when they are signed.

Have a splendid time in Europe – I promise you my lips are seals about your address. I'm off myself to Greece – Milos, Seriphos and Siphonos on September 10th; and I won't be back again in the office until October 2nd.

> Yours ever,
> Charles Monteith

WG to Charles Monteith MS

30 August 1979   [Headed Paper: Ebble Thatch (2)]

Dear Charles

Herewith books inscribed for your goddaughter. I've put 'best wishes' which seems about right – I'd have put hommage à but I can never remember how many m's the French use.

Have a good time in the isles. We'll probably be passing through there via Corfu, but not Milos, Seriphos or Siphonos! (why, when writing that did I have a mental picture of you squirting soda into a glass?) But in any case, not till mid October.

> ever (or I suppose
> στο καλο!)
> Bill

'στο καλο': 'goodbye'. There is a stress missing on the final syllable.

Charles Monteith to WG TS

5 October 1979

Dear Bill,

I thought you might like to see this first batch of reviews for *Darkness Visible*. Many, many congratulations on them. I am particularly pleased with John Bayley's review in the first issue of The London Review of Books.

The sales picture looks very healthy indeed; and Farrar Straus & Giroux have already ordered a reprint before publication. (They publish on November 5th.)

Roger Straus of FSG will be in London for a week or ten days at the end of November. If you should be back by then I know he'd very much like to meet you and Ann – and, of course, I myself long to see you both again and hear about your European travels.

Much love to you both.

        Yours,

          Charles Monteith

PS Forgive this rushed note dictated as I dash to catch a taxi to Paddington.

The inaugural issue of the *London Review of Books*, dated 25 October, carried a long review by John Bayley claiming that *Darkness Visible* was 'Golding's best book yet'. Golding had, as usual, timed his summer holiday abroad to miss the reviews, but some news did reach him from back home: 'Judy said she knew she wasn't allowed to say anything about the reception of Darkness Visible but the volume looks very handsome. This meant that I spent hours in bed, and for no apparent reason, approving of the book, because I made belief to myself that it had been received well' (J, 13 October 1979).

Darkness Visible had been published on 1 October in an edition of 14,411 copies. Faber required a reprint of 10,000 copies within a month. In the United States, Farrar, Straus and Giroux (FSG) supplemented the first print run of 22,500 copies with 7,500 in late October, 10,000 in November, and another 5,000 in December.

WG to Charles Monteith   TS

22 October 1979   [Headed Paper: Ebble Thatch (2)]

Dear Charles,

We are home early, having run out of weather and unaccountably, energy, let alone money and inclination; but we are keeping as they say, a low profile. Thank you very much for sending a selection of reviews – I have got Ann to acquaint me at a distance with the good bits and hide the rest so at last I am getting a balanced view of my own work! But my goodness, I hope your sales picture remains healthy for we drove and drove, paying much the same price for petrol as for campari and all on credit cards so I expect at any moment to disappear under a whole cascade of demands from everywhere.

One or two things –

When I agreed to the Hamburg and Copenhagen thing, I thought it was one of those disinterested cultural jags (old though I am becoming

I still believe they are possible!) and did not realise that Faber's were viewing it as an opportunity to push (promote) DARKNESS VISIBLE. For one thing it's a book I want *not* to talk about – can't talk about – and for another, my most well received lectures (I believe) were delivered at Kent, the one of which didn't mention me at all and the other of which was an entertainment on the theme of travelling in Egypt.

For that reason, I'm quite willing to give a cloudily impressive general lecture to Germans, allowing them to make the cross-references to FLIES; and then on another occasion answer questions; but I cant *lecture* any more on my own work. After all these years I know less about it rather than more. The same applies, of course about lecturing in Denmark. If these conditions are OK the trip is still on – I hope so, for we both look forward to it, at least the new country aspect, and above all, your company! But if they dont, why then it would be better for me to bow out now, before people feel let-down.

About Roger Straus – I'm not sure what the picture will be towards the end of November – you remember there's RITES OF PASSAGE to be rewritten. (I think that may have encouraged me to get back to the bench.) However, Ann and I have formed the habit of going to Brighton for Christmas shopping for a few days at the backend of November and if we do it this year we might well get to London from there.

But you *were* good to send the reviews – according to Ann and John Bailey I am a magician with words and according to Ann and John Braine I have a daemon – I *like* it! Dont disillusion me if she's making it up.

Judy Terrell and one-and-a-half children are now established in a nineteenth century Bristol semidetached of awesome dimensions and we are very happy for them. The Clifton/Redlands area seems very quiet, secure and civilised – qualities which I have come to value a great deal.

Beyond all the rest, of course you must keep in mind the possibility of repeating your visit here – I know how busy you are, though, so at a suitable time, propose yourself –

> Our love
> Bill

Having already been invited to lecture in Hamburg by Le Congrès des Anglicistes, Golding was now planning to visit Copenhagen as an extension of the same trip, courtesy of the British Council.

John Braine reviewed *Darkness Visible* in the *Sunday Telegraph* on 7 October: 'William Golding, like Kipling, does not have a talent. He is possessed by a daemon. It visits him whenever it has a mind to.'

WG to Charles Monteith   MS

31 October 1979   [Headed Paper: Ebble Thatch (2)]

Dear Charles,

After our telephone conversation, I set to and wrote the letters to Hamburg and the British Council. (Should I put at the head of the letter *we spoke*?)

Here are the copies. I hope you dont find them intolerably pompous – but I think they clear the air.

Lovely sales!

    ever

     Bill

Golding's proposal for both Hamburg and Copenhagen was to give a lecture on a subject to be defined closer to the date and, separately, to have a question-and-answer session in order to create a dialogue with students. Monteith replied briefly that the letters were 'admirable'.

Charles Monteith to WG   TELEGRAM

5 November 1979

WARMEST GOOD WISHES ON AMERICAN PUBLICATION DAY. I'VE SEEN COPIES EARLY AMERICAN REVIEWS. ABSOLUTELY SMASHING. FARRAR STRAUS GIROUX HAVE ALREADY ORDERED THIRD PRINTING. MANY CONGRATULATIONS. CHARLES

WG to Charles Monteith   TS

14 November 1979   [Headed Paper: Ebble Thatch (2)]

Dear Charles,

Things seem to be going very well for us all, both at home and abroad. I've just heard from Miss Fiennes about the various transla-tions already in the pipe line. I dont know what percentage we get from

FSG but *if* it is the fifteen percent then there's money lying about. I welcome it as (privately) we shall turn some of it into bricks and mortar for our immediate descendants.

Which brings me to a point. You remember our accountants told us that we should have money *on call* from you when it came to an advance? They now say with money inflating the way it is, we should claim all money immediately it becomes due. If I have got this right, could you pass the news of the change to your royalties department? I'm a bit confused about it myself; but presumably they will know what to do.

Ann and I are planning a winter break! But it wont happen till in the new year and we dont yet know where we shall go. But you'll have RITES OF PASSAGE in December – (arn't these things getting *splendidly valuable*?) and of course we shall be back for the German/Danish jaunt.

We shall also be in London on the twenty seventh of this month and perhaps a day either side for a lunch and some shopping. Any use? And by the way, do you detect in the mended 'We' that I am now making use of a technological breakthrough in typing?

> Ever
> Bill

'but *if* it is the fifteen percent': Monteith has noted in pencil, 'Yes. 15%'.

It looks like Golding has used a correction ribbon to amend the word 'We' at the start of the final paragraph.

Charles Monteith to WG TS

29 November 1979

Dear Bill,

I'm most appallingly sorry about the mix-up over lunch earlier this week. Just one of those things, I fear. What Kipling referred to as 'life's handicaps' – or, at any rate, perhaps that is what he meant.

I've talked to Tony Pocock; and though we *could* settle things in a telephone conversation, he feels – and I'm pretty certain he's right – that we could arrange things much more satisfactorily if we had a meeting. One day that would be convenient for both Tony and me would be Friday, December 14th; and, if it is convenient for you and Ann, Tony and I would be very happy to come down to Salisbury by train that morning and either come out to Ebble Thatch or give you and Ann lunch in Salisbury – whichever you would prefer. Then we could catch our trains back in the afternoon. I'll be returning to London and Tony has to go to Swansea (of all places).

I'll enclose with this a memo which Tony has drawn up setting out the various points of detail he'd like to discuss with you both; and if you look through it I think you'll see why he feels that we could almost certainly sort things out more satisfactorily at a meeting than we could by telephone. It involves all sorts of little points of detail which it is important to get right if the whole thing is to go smoothly.

A thought has just crept into my head. Perhaps it would be much more prudent not to mention it – but it has just occurred to me that if we come on the 14th I might be able to start *Rites of Passage* on the train back to London!

I do hope the Christmas shopping went well. So far I'm finding it almost impossibly daunting.

    Much love to you and to Ann,
     Charles

PS Matthew tells me that the Americans are reprinting *again*. And what a marvellous German sale!

Golding and Ann thought that they were meeting Monteith for lunch on the 27th, but Monteith did not show up. Golding records in his journal, 'We have rung Charles who was at home and we have both apologised in every direction' (J, 27 November 1979). Rudyard Kipling published a collection of stories titled *Life's Handicap* in 1891.

 The memo from Tony Pocock set out the planned itinerary for Hamburg and Copenhagen.

 Translation rights for *Darkness Visible* in Germany had been sold for £10,000.

WG to Charles Monteith   MS

10 December 1979   [Headed Paper: Ebble Thatch (2)]

Dear Charles,

 Herewith this load of old rope. I hope you can make head or tail of it.

Ann is sitting up in bed with a temperature and reading American reviews and croaking out that they're pretty good on the whole. Greater love hath no woman. I'm sorry about next Friday – lets encounter after Christmas some time.

Ever
Bill

The 'load of old rope' was the typescript of *Rites of Passage*. It was not unusual for Golding to be dismissive or uncertain of his work. The previous April, he had sounded dissatisfied with *Darkness Visible* and *Rites of Passage* in his journal: 'Bits of both are good, but lack the blinding intensity of which I was once capable. More than that I'm not sure Rites of Passage has any weight at all' (J, 4 April 1979). These doubts were often temporary. A fortnight later, he reported re-reading *Rites of Passage* and finding it 'better than I thought' (J, 20 April 1979). In May, 'I have finished reading Darkness Visible. A lot of it is very good but Sim and Edwin are a couple of old bores' (J, 26 May 1979). And just after the publication of *Darkness Visible*, 'I've been reading the book and it's very reasonable from my point of view. But in the fourth quarter of the twentieth century you cant expect much understanding of Matty's life' (J, 19 October 1979).

Charles Monteith to WG
TS

19 December 1979

Dear Bill,

Renewed congratulations on an absolutely stunning book. I shan't say again everything I said about it on the telephone; but I really was exhilarated on re-reading it last night to find everything – or virtually everything – clicking so superbly into place. And now, of course, I simply can't get the book out of my mind. It will stay there, I'm certain, for a long, long time.

Here's the list I promised you of the queries which still baffled me after my re-reading, and which we have already discussed:–

1. Colley in the forecastle. (Infinitely the most important of these points.) As you know, I hadn't got it quite right about what *precisely* had happened to Colley in his cups; and my obtuseness was due, in part at any rate, simply for not knowing the meaning of 'getting a chew off'. (Page 131.) Perhaps this indicates some appalling lack of sophistication on my part! But I suspect that the explanation is a purely nautical one. And it wasn't quite clear to me that it was only Billy's favours he enjoyed. Still, I think I got the general idea!

2. Who was 'Your Sailor Hero' who sent the *billet doux* to Zenobia? I think I'm content with your slightly gnomic answer that it was probably Cumbershum. (Billy?)

3. Wheeler's final disappearance. This puzzled me until you explained it to me. I simply hadn't got the full significance of the Captain's loud denial, (Page 124), of his earlier statement that he had an informant.

4. Anonymity of the ship. You confirmed that this was quite deliberate – as I thought it was. The name of the ship would be, obviously, completely irrelevant.

5. 'The Badger Bag'. I couldn't possibly have guessed that this was somewhat *recherché* and almost certainly obsolete naval slang for 'crossing the Line'. But I think it is probably perfectly all right to leave it as it is – a slight tease to readers.

6. On Page 49 I've deleted a 'cross' which I'm pretty certain wouldn't have been found in an Anglican procession at that date.

Here's the manuscript back. As you know, I've taken three xerox copies of it, one of which will go to Bob Giroux today with a note from me making it quite clear that it is not the final version and mustn't, on any account, be set from or made at all widely available.

It is extremely good of you to say that you will have the absolutely final version back by January 7th together with a short Author's Preface and a sample of Talbot's guardian's Racine translation with instructions about where it should be inserted. And of course I can't say how grateful I am to you for saying that you will let me have a draft blurb.

I was so fascinated by our 'editorial' talk on the telephone that I quite forgot material things. I should, of course, have mentioned terms. For RITES OF PASSAGE I suggest the usual 15% royalty; and an advance of £7500 payable half on demand on signature or at any time thereafter, and half on publication or at any time thereafter. If this is all right I'll ask Giles to go ahead with the contract.

With best wishes again for Christmas and the New Year to you, Ann, Judy, Terrill and the grandchildren.

> Yours ever,
> *Charles*

This copy, on Faber headed paper, reproduces what Golding would probably have seen on the original versions of Monteith's letters from late 1956 onwards: a handwritten signature of '*Charles*', underlined boldly with a rising diagonal line.

1980

This is the year of two prizes: the James Tait Black Memorial Prize for *Darkness Visible* in April and the Booker Prize for *Rites of Passage* in October. The attendant publicity – ramped up by the media's portrayal of the Booker as a heavyweight battle between Golding and Anthony Burgess – sends *Rites of Passage* to the top of the bestseller lists in the weeks before Christmas. Melvyn Bragg's *South Bank Show* helps by dedicating a complete episode to Golding in November. Much of the rest of the year is taken up with travel: a week in Brittany in early February, the trip in April to Hamburg and Copenhagen where Golding delivers his new lecture 'Belief and Creativity', a summer holiday to Switzerland followed by another stay in Brittany, and in November a week in Portugal. Golding worries that he may be lapsing back into a fallow period creatively. Adding to that unease, Charles Monteith announces his intention of stepping down from his role as chairman at Faber but promises that he will continue to act as Golding's editor.

WG to Charles Monteith

TS

3 January 1980 [Headed Paper: Ebble Thatch (2)]

Dear Charles,

Herewith the MS of RITES OF PASSAGE once more. To take the points you raise in your letter of 19th December in your order (and thank you for the welcome praise of the book)!

(1) Please look at the explanation on page 133. I've been as explicit as I can and if the reader doesn't know what 'Fellatio' means, that's his bad luck – so to speak!

(2) The 'Sailor hero' is Billy Rogers. I was in some doubt but you decided me! You'll find the fact stated on page 131.

(3) Wheeler's disappearance – I've tried to enlarge the hint without making it too, too obvious.

(4) Anonymity of ship remains as you agree. After all, there's a great deal of voyage left and who knows? I might need her again? Let her therefore be *adaptable*!

(5) Yes 'badger bag' can stay as an insoluble crux.

(6) Thanks for the information about the cross. Such is always welcome.

You'll find Talbot's godfather's couplet on the last page.

Now that these points are cleared up – or I hope you find they are cleared up, the need for an author's short preface vanishes. Let us drop that idea. It will go much more conveniently into that lecture in Hamburg.

After finishing this letter I'll have a go at a blurb but dont hold out much hope. I havn't an idea in my head. We've mostly been sick or off colour over Christmas and the New Year – Ann's still in bed and full of anti-biotics, the baby has spots and I myself shall probably be the next to go.

I hope you did better – in any case there's a bit of the year left.

I send my love with my good wishes and Ann croaks hers with it.

Bill

Golding was reassured by Monteith's praise, having even started to wonder whether he should publish *Rites of Passage* at all. While waiting for news, he records his worries in his journal: 'No letter from Charles about Rites. I wonder can they be disliking the thing? It's a thing quite unpredictable from the point of view of the William Golding Academic Light Industry, which in a way, makes it extra fun: but perhaps only for me' (J, 18 December 1979).

At the end of (3), after 'too obvious.', someone has written in pencil 'p. 123'.

'the baby': the Goldings' second grandchild, Laurie, had been born on 1 December.

WG to Charles Monteith   TS

13 February 1980

Dear Charles,

You included (I suspect deliberately) my shot at a blurb with the zeroxed MS. I have added a sentence or two; but to tell you the truth I think it's all pretty bad and in any case I'm not at all sure what a blurb's for anyway. The Greeks never had them. (Blurbein, blurbeka, eblurψa).

An ancient ship of the line converted to general purposes was making her way from the South of England to Australia. She carried a few guns, some cargo, some animals, some seamen, some soldiers, some emigrants and a few ladies and gentlemen. There was a clergyman of the Church of England. There was Wilmot Brocklebank, lithographer, marine artist and portrait painter. There was a young army officer.

Representing the higher echelons of administration was young Mr Talbot, who had a good opinion of himself and may very well have been right. He was setting out with the utmost confidence towards a distinguished career. But the voyage taught him some unexpected things. It afforded him more opportunities for observing the ceremonies that mark a progress through life – more chances for a mixture of acute observation and sheer misjudgement – than he could possibly record in his journal; though for his godfather's entertainment, he tried his best. He was mistaken in Deverel, taught some lessons by Mr Summers, shocked several times by Miss Granham and found it unnecessary in the event to keep an eye on Mr Prettiman. Though he drew no inferences from Wheeler's extraordinary lack of balance and never *did* discover the name of the young man whose laughter at his own jests was so infectious it was a sadder and more responsible man who learns from the Reverend Robert James Colley what a bitter taste there is to remorse when it is unavailing.

William Golding, greatest novelist who has ever lived or will ever live has combined in this book the mordant realism of the Old Testament with the vivid spiritual insight of the New. Buy this Authorised Version before it is sold out and you find yourself stuck with the Revised One!

Eithe blurboimen!

Ever

Bill

'Blurbein, blurbeka, eblurψa': if they were not made up by Golding himself, these would be the principal parts of the verb: 'blurbein' would be the infinitive, 'blurbeka' the perfect and 'eblurψa' the aorist. Compare Golding's letter to Monteith of 9 February 1979.

'Eithe blurboimen': Golding plays on Rupert Brooke's 'εἴθε γενοίμην' ('eithe genoimen' – 'would that I were') from 'The Old Vicarage, Grantchester'. Golding's invented Greek therefore means 'Would that I might blurb'.

Someone has deleted in pencil a part of Golding's blurb: 'who had a good opinion of himself and may very well have been right.'

WG to Charles Monteith MS

30 April 1980   [Headed Paper: Ebble Thatch (2)]

Dear Charles,

Well, we have recovered from the excitement, pleasures, delights of the trip – and I personally am able to zip up my pre-Hamburg slacks! So you can see I've gone on short Commons.

I'd like to thank you, though, from us both for the wining, dining, socialising, dancing – and general fun: of which the mostest proved to be, as usual, your own presence throughout!

Prosit!

Arthur Golding (1555–1958)

(Ann says 'skol'.)

Golding had given the lecture 'Belief and Creativity' in Hamburg and Copenhagen earlier that month. It was published in *A Moving Target* (1982).

Prosit is 'Cheers' in German, and 'skol' looks like an attempt at its Danish equivalent: *skål*.

Arthur Golding was a sixteenth-century translator from Latin into English. His real dates were *c.*1536–1606. Golding's joke is explained by his introduction to 'Belief and Creativity': 'It gives me particular pleasure – I might say peculiar pleasure – to address you today in Germany, home of exact scholarship, because it was a German reference book which announced my death in 1957. The announcement was premature but, of course, no more than that.'

Charles Monteith to WG   TS

12 May 1980

Dear Bill,

An All Souls colleague of mine who is a learned Slavonic scholar has sent me this announcement of some forthcoming books from a Moscow publication. The first item, which he has side-lined, announces a Russian translation of *The Spire*, *Lord of the Flies* and *The Inheritors* to be published by Progress in Moscow during the fourth quarter of 1981 in an edition of 100,000 copies. I am not sure whether it is 100,000 copies each or 100,000 copies in all.

Alas, all these books were published before the Russians signed the International Copyright Convention; but Judy Fiennes who deals with translation rights here tells me that this information will strengthen her hand in the negotiations which she is conducting at the moment with the Russians about *Darkness Visible*.

And it may all mean, who knows, a Russian expedition for you and Ann before too long!

Yours ever,

Charles Monteith

WG to Heather Cooper

18 May 1980   [Headed Paper: Ebble Thatch (2)]

TS

Dear Ms Cooper,

Thank you for your letter of 13th May and the enclosure. The cover is quite clearly a splendid piece of work with most conceivable emblems fitted in.

If I have any criticism at all it is this. There is in the book after all a certain element of farce, fun, humour, however it may be described – or I hope so and think so! Isn't any remote suggestion of that wholly absent from the art work?

This may not be a relevant criticism. Perhaps you'd try the point on Charles Monteith. I will abide by what you and he decide between you.

> Yours ever
>
> William Golding

In her role as assistant to the jacket designer Shirley Tucker, Heather Cooper had sent Golding a copy of Cathie Felstead's design for the cover of *Rites of Passage*. Monteith reports in an internal memo dated 21 May that, following a telephone conversation with Golding, it was agreed to go ahead with the jacket as planned: 'He emphasised that he really does like the jacket.'

WG to Charles Monteith

5 July 1980   [Headed Paper: Ebble Thatch (2)]

MS

Dear Charles –

Just off to Switzerland for a week or two. The *Encyclopaedia of Cultivated Orchids* has just turned up in all its splendour.

But what an outrageous bit of cadging on my part it was – I can only plead that I didn't realise what a costly volume I was asking for.

All the more reason for saying a rather humble 'thank you' which I do herewith.

> Ever
>
> Bill

The *Encyclopaedia of Cultivated Orchids* was written by Alex D. Hawkes and cost £30. The Goldings loved orchids, and through the 1980s they spent increasing amounts of time and money cultivating them.

WG to John Bodley

5 July 1980 [Headed Paper: Ebble Thatch (2)]

Dear John,

Thank you very much for your letter. I *did* think at first it was a FEARSOME MS but the truth proved to be even more daunting – It's a wonderful present and all that and I'm very grateful. But I twisted Charles' arm so badly it nearly came away in my hand; only to discover that it's not the comparatively modest volume I had imagined but a thirty pound monster! I am covered with confusion.

All I can do is say thank you very much – and offer to do the whole Danish/German trip all over again.

> Yours
> William Golding

For context, see the letter to Monteith written the same day.

Charles Monteith to WG

21 August 1980

Dear Bill,

I telephoned Ebble Thatch the other day and learned that you and Ann are on holiday – probably not returning until September 7th or 8th. But then I shall be in Greece, en route I suspect from Zacynthos to Cephalonia (a journey which has to be done, maddeningly, via Patras). I won't be back in the office until September 24th.

The reason I rang was to say that we would very much like to give a party to celebrate the publication of RITES OF PASSAGE – the actual date now seems likely to be October 16th. But, of course, we wouldn't dream of pressing this suggestion unless it is totally acceptable to you. If it is – and I very much hope it is – perhaps you could have an initial discussion with Matthew Evans about it before my return? He'll be in touch with you by telephone for I feel it would be unwise to leave all the arrangements until I'm back.

What are your general feelings about giving interviews etc.? We have already had a letter from Roger Straus of Farrar, Straus & Giroux to say that a high level, literate and sympathetic correspondent from the

New York Times would very much like to come and talk to you. We simply said, of course, that we would pass this request on to you and that if you weren't willing we wouldn't press you in any way.

I do hope you had an absolutely marvellous holiday. I long to hear all about it. Whatever happens about the reception I'd be delighted if we could meet for lunch or dinner before too long.

    Yours ever,
     Charles Monteith

The Goldings were holidaying in Brittany with David, Judy, Terrell and their grandchildren.

WG to John Bodley   TS

13 September 1980   [Headed Paper: Ebble Thatch (2)]

Dear John,

Thank you for your letter of the tenth. Thank you too, for the copy of RITES OF PASSAGE. I think it looks and handles well and is altogether handsome. Congratulations to the production department!

As far as hotel expenses are concerned, I dont think F&F should be burdened with them. The point is that Ann and I will be staying for several days, and so working off a number of commitments and of course enjoyments that are nothing to do with my books at all. But it was a generous offer for which we thank you.

We know precious few people who are in any way in the literary swim. The following few are guests we should like to be invited.

———

Lord and Lady Kennet. 100 Bayswater Road.
Miss Jill Tweedie (and friend.) ?
Professor Ian Gregor. 143 Old Dover Road, Dover, Canterbury.
Mr and Mrs Mark Kinkhead-Weekes. South Mystole House, Mystole Park, Chartham Near Canterbury.
Mrs Elizabeth Ayrton. The Maze House. Rockhampton, Berkeley, Glos.
Lord David Cecil and Lady David. Red Lion House. Salisbury Street. Cranbourne, Dorset.

———

I suppose Ian and Mark will receive advance copies of RITES anyway; but I'd be glad if you'd add Professor Herbert Hart and Lord David to that list.

I have got myself a bit scagged between ITV and BBC – thank you for giving SPOKESMAN YOUR opinion. But I begin to feel by the pricking in my thumbs that I was a good deal happier when in purdah!

        Yours ever
        Bill Golding

P. Hart may now have a K: but my Who's Who is out of date. Please check! He sh'd also be in the list of guests. (11 Manor Place, Oxford.)

The party was held in the Faber boardroom on publication day, 16 October. Lord and Lady Kennet were the Goldings' old friends Wayland and Liz Young. Jill Tweedie, the broadcaster and journalist, was a more recent acquaintance. Herbert Hart had been Principal of Brasenose College, Oxford, until 1978; he had not received a 'K' (knighthood). Spokesman was an agency formed within Curtis Brown.

    'scagged': torn.

    'I begin to feel by the pricking in my thumbs': see Golding's letter to Monteith of 10(?) September 1955 and again of 13 January 1979 for earlier examples of this allusion to *Macbeth*.

Charles Monteith to WG   TS

31 October 1980

The more I think about the Booker prize the more delighted and happy I am. It was a wonderfully exciting and entirely enjoyable evening at Stationers' Hall wasn't it? I am only sorry I wasn't able to stay to the very end.

I thought you might like to see this batch of 'promotional material' that we have prepared for RITES OF PASSAGE. The snappy little card in gold and blue is what is known in the trade as a 'crowner'. It is stuck into the top copy of the pile of books on display in the shop or in the window. Incidentally, we have just ordered a substantial reprint and according to last Tuesday's Evening Standard the book is well placed in the London best seller list.

I am taking advantage, if I may, of your very kind offer to inscribe a copy for me – and I hasten to send you one of the first edition before it is exhausted. When you have written in it – and I'd be terribly grateful if you would – I wonder if you could post it back to me? I'll enclose stamps and a label.

Have you and Ann had a chance to talk about visiting Oxford together on December 6th–7th. It would be wonderful if Ann could come with you – and I am only sorry I can't invite her to dinner as well but I am restricted, I fear, to one guest. But I have already provisionally booked a room for lunch on Sunday, December 7th; and I'd like to start inviting guests straight away. Even if Ann can't manage it there will be a lunch of course; but it would be particularly nice if she were there. Are there any Oxford friends that you would especially like me to invite? I'll ask the Bayleys, of course; and perhaps you'd like me to ask the Harts too?

There is one other thing which I'd half meant to mention at the Booker do but I thought it wasn't really an appropriate occasion. Next year I shall be sixty; and, as you know, I have been having a bit of heart trouble over the last two or three years. Because of this I have decided to do a sort of 'half retirement' with effect from 1st April 1981, after which I shall cease to be Chairman – my successor, of course, will be Matthew who will do the job most admirably – and I'll shed all my administrative duties (much to my relief). But I shall, I'm happy to report, continue to be an editorial consultant, with a base here at Queen Square as well as at home, and by far the most important of my duties will be to look after those people whom I still think of fondly as 'my' authors. You, of course, are eminent among them; and if you feel happy about this things can go on more or less as they have up until now – i.e. that you should write direct to me about your books both past, present and future – and I'll pass on to somebody else any points that I can't conveniently deal with myself. When we next meet we can most certainly, if you would like to, talk about this at more length; but I don't think personally that it is going to lead to any difficulties whatsoever.

I am much looking forward to seeing you on December 6th.

PS I seem to have lost that splendidly useful article by some American scholar which explained – and explained away – Piggy's ignition of the bonfire with his specs. I wonder if by any chance you have a copy of it or could give me a reference to it? Queries continue to trickle in. The latest is from a young man called [. . .] who, despite his name, lives in Paisley!

This file copy has no greeting at the start, presumably because Monteith added it by hand.

Golding won the Booker Prize for *Rites of Passage* on 21 October. The ceremony was held at the Stationers' Hall in central London. The novel had been published on 16 October in an edition of 15,000 copies, and its success meant that it immediately required a reprint. *Rites of Passage* topped the *Sunday Times* bestseller list for several weeks in the run-up to Christmas.

The Bayleys were John Bayley and Iris Murdoch. Golding liked Murdoch and admired her fiction. In 1984, the Goldings hosted a lunch for the Bayleys and David Cecil, and Golding's journal gives the briefest snapshot of their friendship: 'Lunch was fun though we drank a lot. Iris tends to plod along not letting me get away with anything frivolous' (J, 29 September 1984).

Monteith's tenure as chairman at Faber had not been successful: he was a much better bookman than businessman. Ill health offered an excuse as well as a reason for his premature retirement. He had first mentioned his health problems to Golding in December 1978: 'Charles rang this evening. His personal news is that he has some kind of fibrillation – a heart condition – which isn't dangerous but gives him dizzy spells' (J, 4 December 1978). When Monteith finally stepped down as Faber's chairman on 1 April 1981, Golding wrote, 'Charles is hanging on to his authors he says and that it will make no difference as far as I am concerned. I imagine they are as careful as they can be about that sort of thing. Authors are a fickle lot' (J, 1 April 1981).

The event on 6 December was the Chichele Dinner at All Souls, and Golding was Monteith's guest.

'some American scholar': Monteith is on the wrong continent. J. P. Stern was born and raised in Czechoslovakia and lived in England after the Second World War until his death in 1991. For context, see Golding's letter to Monteith, 19 April 1974.

The name of the correspondent from Paisley suggests Pakistani descent.

WG to Charles Monteith   TS

2 November 1980   [Headed Paper: Ebble Thatch (2)]

Dear Charles

You can imagine, I believe, what sort of post I've had this last week or two and the floundering efforts I've made to keep up with it! The worst of it is – even with a most liberal or if you like most brutal use of the waste paper basket – the evident trivialities seem to demand to be dealt with first, perhaps because that's easy. Stock answers, stock refusals, stock acknowledgements become mechanical. It's with the genuine letters I want to write that the real trouble begins. By the time you get to them the whole question of correspondence has been devalued to the point where you have to try hard to remember what a simple feeling is and what sort of simple sentence might express it. Perhaps, then, I should have written this one first while I still retained a mite of sensitivity – but I didn't.

418

What I want to say is 'Thank you' not just for recent events and editorial support but for a process that may well – I forget the exact date – have started in 1953. Twenty-seven years, more or less is a long stretch and during it I've always had a feeling of you there, present but not breathing down my neck! In fact I must come out with it. Three people have been of major importance and influence in my life and you are one of them. There is a way in which I am as a writer at least partly your creation.

So there! The embarrassing and unEnglish sentences have been written. You said at the Booker Dinner that it was one of the happiest days of your life. May you have many more of them – and may I continue to contribute to the happiness of my publisher and friend!

Love from me and from another one of the three.

> Bill

Charles Monteith to WG

TS

20 November 1980

Dear Bill,

Here's your invitation card to the Chichele Dinner. No need to reply to it as I've already done so. And Chapel isn't compulsory – though of course you'd be made welcome if you'd like to go.

> Yours,
> Charles Monteith

WG to Charles Monteith

MS

25 November 1980   [Headed Paper: Ebble Thatch (2)]

Dear Charles,

Belatedly thank you for your letter of 20th Nov – Thank you too for the invitation to chapel. I will decline it if you dont mind!

I hope sales of *Rites of Passage* are satisfactory – and the others, of course –

> ever
> Bill

1981

Early this year, Golding starts work on 'The Critic', a project that eventually becomes his next novel, *The Paper Men* (1984). He soon puts it away in order to focus on his second volume of occasional pieces, *A Moving Target* (1982), which he hopes to publish on his seventieth birthday in September. As well as revising old essays and reviews for it, he writes several new pieces, including 'Egypt from My Outside' and 'My First Book'. Holidaying in Brittany with his family in the summer, he starts thinking about a sequel to *Rites of Passage*, and by the end of the year he has a first draft.

WG to Charles Monteith   MS

15 January 1981   Ebble Thatch, Bowerchalke

Dear Charles,

Lovely to hear about the sales – and I can even read the reviews! Nothing succeeds like et cetera.

Enclosed is a photostat you wanted some time (months?) ago. I suddenly remembered when I turned out a copy, looking for essay-stuff. Perhaps the occasion is past – but here the thing is

ever
   Bill

The photostat was of J. P. Stern's explanation about Piggy's glasses and their fire-making capacity. See Golding's letter to Monteith, 19 April 1974, and Monteith's postscript to his letter of 31 October 1980.

Charles Monteith to WG   TS

30 January 1981

Dear Bill,

I'm sorry to remind you of a promise made as long ago as early December (I think it was), but you did say then that you would very kindly sign a copy of RITES OF PASSAGE for my brother and his wife;

and if you would both they and I would be immensely grateful to you. I'll enclose it with this – together with stamps and label for returning it. Their names incidentally are Ted and Rhona Monteith.

I have also had the script of that proposed television play of PINCHER MARTIN which reached me safely yesterday. It is with Mavis Pindard; and when I have had a chance to discuss it with her I'll be in touch with you again.

Love to you and to Ann,
Charles Monteith

There had been at least three proposals to adapt *Pincher Martin* for film or television since Golding and Peter Brook had abandoned their project.

WG to Sarah Biggs   TS

6 February 1981   [Headed Paper: Ebble Thatch (2)]

Dear Miss Biggs,

Herewith the parcel of essays for Charles. I don't know if you'll see him or not; but the point of the extra hard work I'd be obliged if he'd do (appalling typing and some scrambled stuff where the meaning if any has to be divined) is that getting it off for a second opinion is the only way I can possibly leave myself time to correct it before the end of the month. Explain that it's all the fault of this electric typewriter, if I may whisper. The house, a time ago was narrowly missed by some nasty lightning. As the flash struck the typewriter came to and said ?£/*.

It's never been the same since. However, looking at these dotty pages now would be a great help.

Yours sincerely
William Golding.

The 'parcel of essays' comprised potential contributions towards Golding's next volume of occasional pieces.

WG to Charles Monteith   TS

16 February 1981   [Headed Paper: Ebble Thatch (2)]

Dear Charles,

Thank you for your phone-call. I don't know whether my own personal antennae are quivering unduly but I thought I detected some
hesitation in your reply that, yes, the lectures and all that should be
published. I know, or guess, rather, how publishers must tread delicately with writers or some writers at least! So will you take my next
few lines as really *intended*?

So far, I've had a bit of trouble furbishing essays and you've had a bit of
trouble reading them, but no further damage has been done, and no other
work wasted. *If* you feel that this next collection slants away down from
the level of excellence that F&F should maintain as publishers; or that I
am letting myself down in putting out such a bundle, then let us cancel the
whole thing at once with the utmost good will and application of common sense on both sides! There's a looseness in a lecture that is perhaps
proper to the colloquial, a level of humour or wit that can be passed off
with a grin; a high seriousness that is seen to be sincere from the very face
and voice of the man exhibiting it – all these, read rather than listened to
might be a disaster. I say this because I can't, in rereading the lectures, get
away from the occasions and emotions and intonations of their delivery.
I'm very anxious that you shouldn't feel obligated to an old client (rather
than friend in this instance) and do what you otherwise wouldn't.

So. If you want to, change your mind.

I'm sending what I have by me – had meant to make typescripts –
but maybe you'd rather have print!

(If you decide we still go ahead is Kate Petty still available as a bib-
liographer? She would recognise the vagaries of my spelling from of
old; and perhaps feel less put upon by it!) Judy doesn't want to feel the
work she's done for me *would* have been done by Kate – everyone is
good-hearted all round!

                        ever
                        Bill
I'll send on more, as I have them.

With Judy's help, Golding had started collecting his scattered reviews and essays
in September 1980. He was hoping to publish a book of occasional pieces to

coincide with his seventieth birthday in September 1981 and had decided on the title *A Moving Target*. Monteith explained that the deadline would be too soon, and that spring 1982 was more realistic. The clinching argument was that Kate Petty would not be free to copy-edit the book if autumn 1981 were the goal.

Charles Monteith to WG TS

25 February 1981

Dear Bill,

Since the general decrepitude of the national telephone system has got to such a stage that it is proving virtually impossible to make one's meaning clear by telephone I thought I ought to write this time rather than ring you up.

It's to say, first of all, – to eliminate for ever, I hope, that initial telephonic misunderstanding – that I admired and enjoyed immensely the prose pieces you sent me. The only problem that I foresee – and 'problem' isn't the right word for it – is that of making the final selection of material and then putting that material into the most effective and rational order. It's very good indeed of you and Ann to invite me down to Ebble Thatch. I'm looking forward to that very much and I am certain we can get the contents into their final shape then.

Last weekend I read the second batch of material and enjoyed all of it. One or two pieces may prove rather too 'bitty' – your *Langham Diary* for example – though most of the smaller pieces can be preserved, I think, (including, of course, that superb *Gaia Lives OK?*). One or two may be rather difficult to fit in.

I won't begin, though, to start making any tentative suggestions for shaping and sorting out until the final batch comes in about the end of this month.

Once I have had them, and read them through, I hope to be in touch with you again very shortly; and perhaps we can manage the Friday night in Wiltshire before the end of next month. In the meantime, to save time, we are having fair copies made of all the pieces you sent me so that Kate Petty will have easy material to work from. (She will have your originals too, of course, so that she can check any doubtful words or passages).

In the meantime, best love to you and to Ann; and warmest thanks again for the invitation.

> Yours,
> Charles Monteith

Golding had sent the materials in two batches (with a third still to come). The first batch comprised a selection of lectures and essays, and the second batch some shorter pieces accompanied by a handwritten note: 'These smaller reviews total about 6500 words. Could they not *run on*? Or is that inadmissible? I'd like the first, Gaia Lives, OK? to be preserved if it can be – by the way, wouldn't Gaia Lives OK? be a better title?'

'Langham Diary' had been published in *The Listener* on 3 January 1974; it discussed, among other things, the Chinese Exhibition at the British Academy (which Golding visited twice), the prospect of revolution in Britain, and the silence in rural Wiltshire brought about by the global fuel crisis and the consequent reduction in the use of cars and aeroplanes. Unlike 'Langham Diary', 'Gaia Lives, OK?' did make the cut for *A Moving Target*; it was Golding's review for the *Guardian*, in September 1976, of George Gerster's *Grand Design: The Earth From Above*.

WG to Charles Monteith   TS

28 February 1981   [Headed Paper: Ebble Thatch (2)]

Dear Charles,

Thank you for your letter and *eviva* the telephone service which is restoring the lost art of letter-writing! If the same thing would only happen to the typewriter we'd be back in the leisurely days of long hand and our troubles would all slow down.

Yes, the poets do go on about April dont they? February is the better bet. Did you know – but of course you do! – rather than April February is the Roman month of bloody and festive expiation?

Now for the comparatively bad news. By concentrating on the cruellest month I'd forgotten February was the shortest; so you get these bits and pieces on 2nd March and may be warlike about them if you wish. As you are doing some choosing I've simply slung the lot together & include them herewith.

Now for the *really* bad news – they dont include the Holiday pieces. All the libraries have been round in circles and Boston wont play. (Well, I mean, *Boston*!) What will happen is that Judy will storm the BM on Wednesday, March 4th; run these holiday things off on whatever machine they have, cover the distance from the Museum to Queen Square in the shortest time possible and hand them in to Faber's with instructions that they are to be passed on for the personal attention of the chairman; after which she will rush back to her clamorous family.

I'm sorry about all this and shall quite see if you simply hiss through clenched teeth, 'Too late! Too late!' (Well, you couldn't could you) It w'd be all the wrong sounds, you'd have to hiss *shoddy swine*, or *cynical sloth* but you do see what I mean. I am really sorry. It's all a muck.

Some solicitors turn up down here on the 5th. It seems I *may* now be in London on the 9th. We *might* be in London for the 15th. All these are March dates. And you'll be down here sometime in between or after.

>Ever
>Bill

'be warlike about them if you wish': if April is, thanks to *The Waste Land*, the cruellest month, March is the most 'warlike' because it is named after the Roman god of war.

BM: British Museum.

Golding's enigmatic final paragraph alludes to a libel case involving Monteith, Faber & Faber, *Private Eye* and a man named Robin Bryans who had been harassing Monteith for several years. This included exposing Monteith's homosexuality, turning up at the Faber offices and causing a disturbance, and sending semi-coherent allegations about Monteith to prominent people in the judiciary and the arts, Golding among them. Faber had been awarded damages against Bryans in 1979. Golding was preparing to act as a character witness for Monteith in March 1981, but the libel case between Faber and *Private Eye* (which had reported on the incidents with Bryans) was finally settled out of court.

Charles Monteith to WG   TS

10 April 1981

Dear Bill,

Here, belatedly, is the note I promised to send you about the present sales figures of RITES OF PASSAGE. They are, I'm happy to report 50,597 – so we can say, I think, 'well over fifty thousand'!

I do hope you are pleased about this. I think myself, I confess, that it's pretty good. But nothing is too good for a book like RITES OF PASSAGE. The paperback, I'm certain, is going to be a really big seller.

Much looking forward to seeing you in Canterbury in May.

>Yours ever,
>pp. Charles Monteith (signed in Charles
>Monteith's absence)

PS The sales figures I've just quoted to you include March but don't, of course, include April sales.

The letter is signed by Sarah Biggs.

WG to John Bodley   MS

16 June 1981   [Headed Paper: Ebble Thatch (2)]

Dear John,

Thank you for your letter. I am charming, thou art charming, he, she or it –

I've been *very* good during the last six months or so and must now stop. I am, in fact, pulling up the ladder!

There's no need to apologise to Madame Pini: simply explain that like a very sensitive film I react quickly to exposure. If I am ever to write anything more, I need to be Holed Up, and Away From It All.

> Yours
> Bill Golding

PS *Darkness Visible* is permanently off limits, anyway.

Bodley had passed on a message from Madame Pini, his 'charming opposite number at Gallimard', who hoped that Golding would consent to an interview with *L'Express* coinciding with the French translation of *Darkness Visible*. Despite having shown uncharacteristic willingness to publicise *Rites of Passage*, Golding was now reverting to what he called 'purdah'. Even at his most obliging, he steadfastly refused to speak about *Darkness Visible*.

WG to Charles Monteith   MS

7 July 1981   [Headed Paper: Ebble Thatch (2)]

Dear Charles,

This is just a note to say how much Ann & I enjoyed our meal with you and the lovely party!

I hope you will get a bit of rest now, after the fearsome business world you have escaped from. As for me, I am returning as fast as I can to *purdah* or its male equivalent. We've only been away from home for a day or two and the post is ridiculous.

We look forward, though, to seeing you again – perhaps in the autumn?

> Our love
> Bill

Golding and Ann had lunch with Monteith on 2 July and went to a party at the Faber offices in the evening. Golding notes ruefully in his journal, 'Gosh that was a party. We got home round about one o'clock and are spending the day in the recovery ward. Do *all* writers drink to excess?' (J, 3 July 1981).

Charles Monteith to WG   TS

15 July 1981

Dear Bill,

At long last I have a detailed word count for you on the provisional contents of A MOVING TARGET; and I'll enclose it with this.

As you'll see there's absolutely no length problem here at all. The completed pieces which we have already agreed – or provisionally agreed – should be included come in themselves to a total of just over 70,000 words, which is certainly enough, in itself, to form a perfectly satisfactory and manageable book.

I do very much hope, though, that you will let me have 'My First Book' to include in Part Two, *Ideas*. If necessary – or if you wanted to – we could leave out one or two of the shorter pieces in Part Two to make room for it.

So far as Part One, *Places*, is concerned, there is certainly no *need* for you to do another piece to span the gap between Egypt and Planet Earth. Again, though, if you would like to do a piece on, say, Australia or somewhere else fairly remote, I'd be glad to have it. But it's entirely up to you, and I certainly wouldn't dream of pressing you about it.

I'd be most grateful if you could let me have your views about all these points as soon as you possibly can since I'd like to get the book officially into the hands of our copy-editing department which, of course, means in practice the hands of Kate Petty. She will then be in touch with you direct about finalising the text and about incorporating into the existing pieces any changes you want to make – the reference to the Sheldonian sculptures, for example.

There is also, of course, the Preface. Again, I'd be very grateful if you could give me an idea of when you think you will be able to tackle it.

Best love to Ann and to you. I did very much enjoy seeing you on the day of the party; and I hope we're able to meet again before too long.

    Yours,
      Charles Monteith

The contents of *A Moving Target* are divided into two sections: 'PLACES' and 'IDEAS'.

The 'Sheldonian sculptures' were probably the seventeenth-century 'Emperor Heads' on top of stone pillars that mark the northern boundary of the Sheldonian Theatre in Oxford.

WG to Charles Monteith   MS

18 July 1981   [Headed Paper: Ebble Thatch (2)]

Dear Charles,

Herewith the diet sheet – sorry about the delay. May your slim man get out.

About the book – there certainly seem to be words and enough to spare.

① I'll get a copy of *My First Book* back from the Authors' Society. As usual there's only one copy.

② I'll only do a *places* piece if the urge comes.

③ I'll try and get a preface to you 'as soon as possible'.

We leave for France on 1st August. The *party was* fun! I should have sent a thank you letter but believe I didn't.

       ever
        Bill

Golding had been dieting sporadically over recent years. He refers several times in his journal to a 'diet sheet' but never describes or identifies it.

Golding's essay 'My First Book' had just appeared in *The Author*. The title was a tease, because the 'first book' in question was not *Lord of the Flies* but *Poems*, the volume published by Macmillan in 1934.

Charles Monteith to WG   TS

22 July 1981

Dear Bill,

I'm immensely grateful for that diet sheet – though I can't at the moment see when I'll be able first to put it into operation. It will take some advance planning! But I am determined to do it – and of course I'll let you know the result.

Once we have 'My First Book' and the Preface we'll get ahead straight away; and I'll assume there won't be another *Places* piece to come unless you let me know to the contrary.

Have a marvellous time in France. I envy you that trip enormously. It occurred to me only recently that though I have been to France – as everybody has – a number of times I don't really know it at all; and I keep getting a stronger and stronger urge to know it better.

I was in Oxford at the weekend – probably for the last time until the Autumn – and I admired the water garden in the Botanical Gardens which was looking marvellously Rousseau le Douanier. And of course it made me think of you and Ann. I hope your own is flourishing as well.

Yours ever,
Charles Monteith

The Goldings spent August in Brittany along with David, Judy, Terrell and their grandchildren.

The French post-impressionist artist Henri 'Le Douanier' Rousseau is best known for his jungle scenes.

WG to Charles Monteith MS

23 July 1981   [Headed Paper: Ebble Thatch (2)]

Dear Charles,

Herewith a photostat of my bit

'*My First Book.*'

Rereading it, I'm strangely moved by what I can only call its bleak honesty about a trivial matter. I had forgotten so much that came back.

I hope you will 'like it and keep it in'.

ever
Bill

It's also longer than I remember!

'like it and keep it in': when Faber published the facsimile edition of Eliot's *Waste Land* manuscript in 1971, complete with Ezra Pound's marginal annotations, the 19 November issue of *Private Eye* parodied the project by including a review of an imaginary book, 'T. S. Eliot's *Waste Paper Basket*'. The review reproduced a poem draft supposedly salvaged from Eliot's bin and covered in handwritten annotations, one of which read 'I love it. Keep it in. E.P.' The joke made such an impression on Golding and Monteith that they were still quoting it a decade later.

26 July 1981   [Headed Paper: Ebble Thatch (2)]

Dear Charles,

Thank you for your letter of 22nd July. By now you'll have not only the diet sheet but what is I hope easier to stomach, a copy of MY FIRST BOOK. Here is the preface to A MOVING TARGET. It is slightly over a thousand words I think.

I agree absolutely about France. Of late years, what with grandchildren we've tended to spend August there and shall do so once more this year. But it's a fact that it becomes an endurance test as well as a delight when you have to go back to leaping into the cold Atlantic *pour encourager les autres*! Ann and I have a feeling that when it's over we might sneak off somewhere else to recover –

If you feel the preface is too wordy I'll slim it – unless you'd care to wield an editorial axe yourself.

I'm afraid our water garden has got away from me a bit what with one thing and another. I keep telling myself that I'll really put in some work, but I dont. Perhaps this autumn is the one. At the moment though even le Douanier would be hard put to it to sort out the details.

We leave for France on 1st August by a ghastly midnight boat. In case of genuine emergencies like the offer of huge sums of money, I'll leave you my French address which will be –

Ferme du Creac'h, Saint Yvy, Concarneau.

Evidemment on est Breton, as a man said when I complained I couldn't understand him.

     Ever

     William Golding

'*pour encourager les autres*': in Voltaire's *Candide* (1759), a British admiral is publicly executed for cowardice 'to encourage the others'. The account is based on historical events: Admiral John Byng had been executed by firing squad in 1757 for having 'failed to do his utmost' at the Battle of Minorca the previous year.

Charles Monteith to WG TS

3 August 1981

Dear Bill,

By the time you get this Nicole Foster will have telephoned to say that that admirable Preface to A MOVING TARGET and also 'My First Book' – absolutely fascinating, I thought – are safely here. She will, I think, also have told you that she hopes to get ahead with the copy-editing while you are in France. I am quite happy to leave all the arrangements about that side of things to you and her – though of course I'd be very glad to step forward from the side-lines if at any stage you need any help. I don't imagine, though, that there will be.

Have an absolutely super time in France – and I do hope the weather is reasonably good. Certainly, today in London it's almost too hot and close for comfort – but after the summer we've had so far that's very much a fault on the right side.

Much love to you and to Ann.

      Yours,

        Charles Monteith

1982

On holiday in St Ives with Ann in March, Golding learns to ride a horse; he buys an Australian cob called Cobber later in the year and rides him regularly. Between March and May Golding travels alone on lecture trips to Milan, Paris and Greece. Reviewers almost unanimously approve of *A Moving Target* when it appears in late May. Golding's grandson Laurie becomes seriously ill in June and requires ten days in intensive care; Golding, Ann and David take Nick to Brittany so that Judy and Terrell can focus on Laurie's health. All the while, Golding makes limited progress on the next novel, now definitively titled *The Paper Men*. He is intrigued when the publisher Rainbird approaches him with a proposal for a travel book about Egypt.

WG to Charles Monteith   MS

6 April 1982   [Headed Paper: Ebble Thatch (2)]

Dear Charles,

I rang Sarah about the *inc*: today. She will be able to explain any predicament. The correspondence explains itself: tho' I'm sorry to push such a big boring load of business in your direction. If you could shog the lot off on to *your* accountant (or solicitors) he could perhaps deal directly with me, or better still, mine.

Of course I must pay him: but I am being driven up the wall by one thing and another

> ever
> Bill

PS Could I have the INC: back?

The enclosed was a letter to Golding from his accountants asking him to find out from Faber for tax purposes what the monetary value of his 'personal copyright' should be.

WG to Charles Monteith MS

24 May 1982   [Headed Paper: Ebble Thatch (2)]

Dear Charles

Thank you very much for the warm (and decorative) message. The white flower I suppose to be an emblem of a blameless life and the butterfly one of those I ought to have in my turn.

But what an agreable sensation to be shot of those lectures!

Ann and I will be at the East Gate Hotel for the night of 6th June – shall you be in Oxford so that we may take you out to dinner? It would be fun for us.

Ever

Bill

PS Athens was ghastly τὸ νεφος and all that – but it did use up the lectures with a bare week to spare.

Monteith's message was presumably a note congratulating Golding on *A Moving Target*, which was published on 24 May in an edition of 4,000 copies.

Earlier that month, Golding had spent a week in Athens giving lectures under the auspices of the British Council.

'τὸ νεφος': the cloud/fog (modern Greek). The diacritic is inaccurate.

'use up the lectures with a bare week to spare': this was the last time that Golding was able to give these particular lectures as they were about to be collected in *A Moving Target*.

Charles Monteith to WG TS

19 August 1982

Dear Bill,

On Tuesday (17th August) Matthew and I had lunch at Rainbirds with the Chief Editor, David Roberts – very nice, I thought – and the Managing Director Michael O'Mara to talk about Golding and Egypt. (It sounds rather, don't you think, like the title of an opera by some twentieth century German composer?)

At the end of our talk we'd formulated an idea – and I needn't add that it's a completely tentative one and entirely subject to your agreement – of the sort of book with which both Rainbirds and Fabers would be more than happy. The book would be very roughly the same size as

Durrell's GREEK ISLANDS and as lavishly illustrated. The text could be anything between 60,000 and 80,000 words – 70,000 would be ideal – so that it is, so to speak, a real book and not simply a series of captions. The text would be illustrated by about 120 pictures – most, if not all, of which would be colour photographs taken especially for the book in full consultation with you. Needless to say, the photographer would be a first-rate professional. This should produce a book amounting in all to somewhere between 224 and 240 pages.

So far as the travelling is concerned Rainbird would be more than happy to fall in with your own wishes. Full first class travelling expenses for you and Ann would be paid together with all other incidental expenses; and they would be happy to arrange for a competent courier to take care of all your travelling arrangements, as you suggested to me on the telephone. (If only they could produce a David Blow who spoke fluent Egyptian!) Again, it would be up to you and Ann to decide when you wanted to go and how long you wanted to stay in Egypt. The Rainbird people think – and this sounds convincing to me – that the late Autumn and Winter are the best times; and they wonder if the Autumn and Winter of 1983 would possibly suit you.

So far as the financial side of things are concerned, they would be perfectly happy to treat Faber – and in this context Faber means Matthew – as your agent; and I think I can guarantee that he'd produce a satisfactory agreement for you.

When you have had time to digest this I wonder if you would mind dropping me a note or giving me a ring. I'd love to see you and to have a talk about it – and, if it would be more convenient for you if I came down to Salisbury, I'd be delighted to see you, Ann and Ebble Thatch again. And, of course, I can't pretend that I'm not longing to know how the novel is going!

I do hope that the holiday went well – and I long to hear all about it; and I hope, too, that your grandchild is making good progress.

Love and best wishes to you and to Ann,

Rainbird had approached Golding in June to write a travel book about Egypt. The company's modus operandi was unusual: it commissioned the author, agreed the contract, and designed and manufactured the books, but it made deals with established firms to distribute them. This had been the arrangement for Lawrence Durrell's *The Greek Islands* (1978), which was commissioned by Rainbird but published as a Faber book.

David Blow was – in Monteith's words – Faber's 'continental traveller'. He

434

had drawn up the itinerary for Golding's trip to Hamburg and Copenhagen in 1980. Matthew Evans was now Faber's chairman after Monteith's semi-retirement.

WG to Charles Monteith   TS

4 September 1982   [Headed Paper: Ebble Thatch (2)]

Dear Charles,

Thank you for your letter of 19th August which I've now read. We've come back from France absolutely worn out from a month *in loco parentis* for our elder grandson – great fun, really. I'm afraid, the news over the younger boy is not quite so good. He proved to be much iller than anyone thought, was in intensive care for ten days and is recovering bit by bit. Poor little Laurie, in fact had a collapsed lung as well as a hiatus hernia which is a poor start on any count. However he has had splendid care and we hope will get on to a normal life.

You can imagine that with eighteen hours a day child-minding (O for the days of cheap, reliable nannies!) the novel fell somewhat into the back of my mind. I shall resurrect it at any moment, day or week, now and see what I think. It's all based on a remark in Sybil Bedford's life of Aldous Huxley – Mrs Hemingway saying to Mrs Huxley after the demise of both writers – 'Ernest got worse and Aldous better.' I have my own ideas as to what happens to a writer and to his critics – they simply destroy each other. It *could* be *funny* and unpretentious. We shall see.

Now as to EGYPT. We are still attracted to the idea of living there and moving about a bit while I write G in E, or a draft of it or get notes together. After all, I find the Egypt bit in my journal is about fifty thousand words and there's a great deal of the place I *havn't* seen. The time – late autumn or early spring could be chosen later. I have a slight preference for winter/spring on the grounds that after autumn in Egypt one would come back to winter in England and be nipped like a delicate flower.

Of course it all revolves round the money involved. The enormous expenses would have to be in addition to the enormous advance and stupendous percentage on sales; I mean that, *after* F&F have taken their agents ten per cent to which I imagine you and Matthew agree. But before we go any further I'd like to know what sort of sum is envisaged.

We'd love to have you down here! I imagine we'd see you on Wednesday 15th September for Bob Giroux' party. I don't know if Matthew and you would be in a position to be concrete by then – probably not. I suppose it's best left to Matthew, now he's been enthroned. But we would love to have you down here, business or not, when we've become a bit more unnumbed by the Atlantic. It's odd. I bathed dozens of times and the water was as cold as ever. But when you're old you come to a kind of cynical awareness of yourself and throw yourself in jeeringly, saying that hurt didn't it you silly old fool what did you expect?

> love and best wishes from us both.
> Bill

While Laurie was seriously ill, the Goldings – Bill, Ann and David – went on their annual holiday to Brittany taking only Nick with them.

Golding's reference to Sybille Bedford's *Aldous Huxley: A Biography* (1973) mistakes Hemingway's sister-in-law, Virginia Pfeiffer, for her sister (and Hemingway's second wife) Pauline. It was Virginia who told Bedford that 'Aldous was the best man [. . .] she ever knew, getting better and better . . . Ernest: the opposite, he got steadily worse.' The judgement is based on their merits as human beings, not as writers.

WG to Matthew Evans   TS

16 December 1982   [Headed Paper: Ebble Thatch (2)]

Dear Matthew,

Thanks for your letter of 13th December. As Ann said 'Thank God he's on our side.'

Everything in the Egypt Book garden seems lovely, though I think you are right to suggest our approval of any possible 'somebody to look after us'. As luck would have it there's the very word, and appropriate to the proposed country for the sort of bloke we need. He was (as of course you know) called a *Courier* and some description of him is to be found for example in Mark Twain's INNOCENTS ABROAD. I already feel myself to be about to travel in the 19th century way under a pith helmet and with *a length of voile across the neck and shoulders*. However, apart from his 19th century overtones he ought of course to be fluent in Egyptian/Arabic and English; and it would be a bonus if he c'd ride a horse! I have shadowy *plans*. The ideal ways for a benighted

436

Ferhingistani to see Egypt is from a bike or a horse and I bar the bike. Rainbird are going to hire horses (*a son of the desert am I*) though there is no need for them to know that yet. I ought to say at once that we don't know a possible courier/minder but there w'd seem to be plenty of time to find one. In any case I look forward to examining the contract when you send it on.

My next (if any) novel has almost all the keel laid but is still a long way from floating – and may, indeed, sink.

Our love to you and the family and best wishes for Christmas.

      Yours ever

        Bill   William Golding

PS Do we have a photographer with us, do we take our own pics, (I have some smashing Egypt slides if Rainbird could afford them!), or do RAINBIRD send him after they have the MS? Is it possible for us/you to have any say as to who, when, what?

Rainbird had agreed to pay an advance of £30,000 against world rights, with 15 per cent of their receipts on all copies sold as royalties. They also covered all the Goldings' travel expenses and the cost of a travel companion.

'Ferhingistani': Golding may mean 'Farhangestani', Farhangestan being a Persian term for an association of scholars.

'A Son of the Desert am I' is a song from 1889 with an appropriately equestrian opening: 'A son of the desert am I. / The iron clad hoofs of my horse spurn the sand.'

1983

It is a year of public encomiums. In June, Golding is made a Companion of Literature; in July, he is awarded an honorary Doctorate of Letters at Oxford; in November he wins the Nobel Prize. This requires the writing of a 'Nobel Lecture' which he delivers at the ceremony in Stockholm on 7 December. Meanwhile, with *The Paper Men* finally finished after several rewritings, Golding starts to make practical arrangements for the following book: his account of a journey along the Nile. In mid-November, he travels alone to Egypt to choose a boat for the adventure. A few days later, on 20 November, his third grandson, Roger, is born.

WG to Matthew Evans   TS

21 January 1983   [Headed Paper: Ebble Thatch (2)]

Dear Matthew,

Thank you for your letter of 18th January with the enclosures.

Most of the business queries I'm content to leave to you as one instructed in these matters of copyright and all the rest. Nevertheless I have some queries and proposals myself for you to vet and put forward if you think they might carry weight & succeed.

(1) Yes, a courier need have nothing much to do with writing but everything to do with comfort – getting rooms, possibly even arranging for a furnished house or flat, speaking Arabic – and standing in the gate between us and a society from which we are to be protected if I am to *work*.

(2) Clause 5. I shall be photographing and so will Ann; and it is possible some of those photographs will be so close to my individual work they should be used in the book. I dont think I shall use anyone else's pics but if they were *vital* then I think RAINBIRD should stand the expense.

(3) I believe though I may be wrong, that my own alterations in proof have never elicited a penalty from F&F. Unless F&F have simply been being kind – always possible! – it goes to show that I shouldn't need the 10% in 8. stretched to 15%. I mention that to give you a possible concession to swop for a demand from us in some other section.

(4) 11. and 12 b. I am totally opposed to condensation (i.e. *Readers'*
Digest and so forth). So it should require my permission since the
financial insult would have to be colossal in order to overcome my
intransigence.

(5) Paperback percentages are always neuralgic – even from my own
beloved publishers! Can't we, in 11., screw them up to 10%?

(6) To the best of my belief I may have been pulped; but I've never
been remaindered. It w'd feel like, so to say, one of the *grandes hori-*
zontales of the 19th Century working a beat outside the docks. Even
if I overestimate my literary charms, I still think some way should be
found round my finding myself in the January sales among COLLECTING
THIMBLES or WILD BIRDS OF THE HEBRIDES.

I hope this isn't all a bit much; I'm sure you'll do your best for us
all – though of course the ultimate bargaining point is that I dont *have*
to do the book at all.

Eh, voila! By the way, the income tax people, generous hearted
souls, or at least, my accountants who are much the same thing agree
that our horsemanship (acquired at awful physical risk and pain for the
sole object of the Egypt book) shall come off income tax – or I suppose
technically, Corporation tax, may it rot. So I've bought a horse and am
keeping an eye open for one for Ann. Of course in Egypt we'll have
to hire them. But then the book should not be Egypt, but GOLDING'S
EGYPT.

Which brings me to my last point.

(7). 3.(b) must come out or at least be altered radically. If I could
submit a synopsis I shouldn't need to go back to Egypt. Of course
I have many ideas about the book but they need arranging, sorting,
evaluating. What could I tell their editors now? Would it be of any
point to say that I might well write the book backwards, beginning
with Mubarrak and ending with geology and the search for oil in del-
tas that disappeared millions of years ago? Would it help them to talk
about the triads of the gods and the trinity? Or to say that I propose
to assemble the divided body of Osiris? Or to produce a chapter on
dangers – snails, snakes and the water gushing from the apron of the
high dam? Or turn Lake Nasser into Lake Damocles?

I hope you see the difficulty. I believe they must accept me in good
faith.

Who is to find the courier? Have Rainbird or F&F sufficient clout
with the cultural attaché to our Egyptian Embassy? What about the

British Council? I'm thought well enough of there – But he – I don't think a woman would be any good, it w'd have to be a man; he would be the lynchpin of the whole operation.

Has Rainbird considered the possibility of a photographer? Who? When? With us? Parallel with us?

Dear me, I'm confused. I hope all this makes sense; and you'll know what's on and what isn't.

> Ever
> Bill

PS First class hotels – yes of course: but we'll have to stop in places where there *arnt* any and we'll need a house or flat or die of dirt and loathing.

PPS It might be worth exploring the possibility of living on a boat with a crew thus obviating many difficulties.

The '*grandes horizontales*' were high-status demi-monde courtesans who captivated and scandalised Parisian society in the nineteenth century.

Hosni Mubarak was president of Egypt from 1981 to 2011.

There were various 'triads of the gods' in ancient Egypt, often specific to particular cities or regions. The god Osiris was part of one such triad (sometimes referred to as the 'Egyptian trinity') with his wife Isis and his son Horus. After being killed by his brother, Osiris is dismembered and cut into forty-two pieces – one for each of the forty-two Egyptian nomes or provinces. Isis gathers the scattered parts and reassembles his body.

Golding may be renaming Lake Nasser as 'Lake Damocles' because, like the sword in classical literature, it hangs precariously above the heads of its would-be victims who have no way of knowing whether or when catastrophe might strike: Lake Nasser was created by the construction of the Aswan High Dam, and many millions of people would die if ever the dam burst.

WG to Matthew Evans TS

13 February 1983   [Headed Paper: Ebble Thatch (2)]

Dear Matthew,

Thank you for your letters, negotiating efforts and at length, the enclosures which I return, initialled and signed – It's very good news that John Bodley, whom we know and like has appeared (like the angel in the book of Tobit, perhaps) to see about a possible conductor and all that. We most certainly would welcome a visit from him with David Roberts. At my age – (sorry to stress this, as both I and Ann are reasonably tough) – it *is* essential that travel arrangements should be smooth; and the writing of the book thus not impeded.

There's a reasonable amount of time ahead. But if John knows someone who knows someone who could tell us what's possible in the way of *boat*-living and moving it would help. Egypt *ought* to be one of the few places in the world where to be water-borne is not only convenient but comfortable.

However, all that will come out in the wash when John and David Roberts come to us. Ann says would they come to *lunch*? The trains are good – about an hour and a half to Salisbury where I would pick them up at the station and bring them here then taken them back when appropriate.

Ann sends her love
ever
Bill

'angel in the book of Tobit': in the Book of Tobit, the angel Raphael takes on human disguise to become guide and companion to Tobit's son Tobias on a quest to recover money from a relative.

WG to Matthew Evans   TS

4 March 1983   [Headed Paper: Ebble Thatch (2)]

Dear Matthew,

Thank you for your letter and exchanges – things seem to be progressing. As you know we had John Bodley and David Roberts down here yesterday and I believe a valuably good time was had by all.

They both see the force and common sense of our being boat-based rather than dashing hysterically from hotel to hypothetical hotel. We convinced David that we aren't expecting something like Onassis' vast vessel but something small, comfortable and above all, unpretentious. He is setting in train an operation to discover the right riverboat, either converted Egyptian, or modern style. I believe that finding the boat will be our main difficulty.

Oh, and thank you for passing on the cheque – feel free to do the same whenever you like.

Ann and I held off writing to you about an F&F companion as well as an Arab-speaking courier because we wanted to find out whether

John would like the idea, rather than do it as a duty. In the event he seems to envy us and I am sure is eager to come.

The invitation is yours of course: and if you still feel inclined to offer it to John both Ann and I are sure we shall make a cheerful and friendly party – in a sentence, very glad to have him along. Perhaps you'd let us know when, and if, the thing is settled.

You've clearly worked hard on my behalf and I'm very grateful.

ever
Bill

'Onassis' vast vessel': the ninety-nine-metre superyacht *Christina O* owned by the Greek shipping magnate Aristotle Onassis.

WG to Charles Monteith   TS

27 March 1983   [Headed Paper: Ebble Thatch (2)]

Dear Charles,

Herewith, not so much a progress report on PAPER MEN as – well, not quite an 'Alas!' report either! The first draft ran into the sand, mostly I think because of insufficient planning. The second draft has come to a stop but I am starting it again. The truth is I seem to lack energy and am also a bit apprehensive about producing a story in which a novelist and his would-be biographer destroy each other when I know it will be read by those kind of creatures in the real world – novelists and biographers, I mean. So you can see that the date at which I can give you a legible typescript to read must be put back. I shall certainly finish the thing – a book about the length of RITES, I think.

There's little news here. I ride with increasing enjoyment to my astonishment and am discovering long barrows, orchards remaining where the monastery was dissolved, cursūs or cursuses according to taste, and a host of other trivia. The Egypt book is much in our minds.

Anyway I'll keep you posted about PAPER MEN and it will always come in handy for postmortem publication if I don't dare to while on live.

I feel a bit numb; income down, talent down, energy down, weather bad. Hope all this doesn't seem too lenten.

ever
Bill

Golding had been working desultorily on *The Paper Men* for more than a year. This is the first mention of it in the correspondence with Monteith. The idea itself was much older. A journal entry from 1979 records the moment when there 'appeared in the air – I suppose it was in my head, but "in the air" was how it seemed, the idea of a writer watching his biographer coming apart at the seams'; that was coupled with the image of a biographer recording his subject's 'terminal corruption' (J, 20 January 1979).

Golding had bought Cobber, an Australian cob, in November 1982, and rode him regularly.

'cursūs or cursuses': long parallel Neolithic banks with an outside ditch. Their purpose is disputed, but the name comes from the Latin for 'course' because of the belief that they served as racecourses.

WG to Charles Monteith T S

7 May 1983   [Headed Paper: Ebble Thatch (2)]

Dear Charles,

The news on the PAPER MEN front is good and bad. Good, because at least I've done a draft – seventy thousand words by my notional reckoning, you would make it sixty thousand, I think – bad because I dont like it. I find it difficult to tell you why. If I called it The Comedy of the Paper Men, or Black Comedy of the Paper Men you still wouldn't understand what I mean. I'd have to call it Black on Black which isn't what I meant.

Obviously this either destroys or at the least delays the book. Yet there *is* a situation and a book there. I have a variety of choices. One, of course, is to drop this hot potato. Two, is to rewrite entirely. Three is to incorporate into this text some of the White that ought to set off the Black and excise some of the Black.

You see my dilemma – several of them! There *are* bits but there are silly bits, dull bits and gratuitously unpleasant bits. In fact I don't know what to do and I suppose must reread, digest and think about what I've got.

So much dithering ought to put the physical well out of any sort of course. But the fact is both Ann and I are off colour and dont know whether it's 'only age' or other things. Being an author ain't at all what I thought it was when I were a lad.

   Ever Bill

Golding had been even more blunt about *The Paper Men* in his journal several days earlier: 'It is bloody awful and though I have written it in a fortnight it must lack the obsessive qualities of passion, drive and commitment.' Later the same day, he mellows a little: 'I have read the lot it is better than I thought, but certainly not good enough' (J, 2 May 1983). Golding sent the typescript to Monteith on 11 May. His journal records what happened next: 'Charles rang three times getting me at the third attempt. He is coming down for the night next friday and will say what he thinks of the Paper Men. I spend my time gloomily feeling that it's a disaster' (J, 13 May 1983).

Charles Monteith to WG

TS GOLDING

25 May 1983

Dear Bill,

I should have written the moment I got back to say how immensely grateful I am to Ann and to you for all your hospitality on Friday and Saturday. I enjoyed my Ebble Thatch visit enormously and I do hope I will be invited down again before too long. Getting to London via Oxford was absolutely no trouble at all, the trains were exceptionally good both ways and I was able to dump my bags, have lunch in London and be in Oxford in very good time for my committee meeting there.

I'll enclose with this a set of notes (very rough, unpolished and hastily dictated). I'll also enclose the originals of your own notes, of which as you know, I have taken a photostat. ~~PAPERMEN~~* (let's decide on that for a title – it's excellent) is a very powerful and very gripping book so please don't have any doubts or hesitations about it. I think it still needs a bit of tidying up along the lines we discussed, but the book is *there*; and I'm looking forward immensely to its appearance some time in 1984.

Much love to you both
Charles.

* THE PAPER MEN (or PAPER MEN).

A. GENERAL POINTS

1. The Tapes.
The more I think about it the more confident I feel that you don't need the device of having the narrator dictate all the events of the narrative on to tapes for the benefit of some remote descendant. I can see why it

was useful as a device for getting the whole thing going, but it's basically unconvincing. I think you agree about this and I shan't labour the point any further.

2. *Halliday*

Halliday is immensely important; and I think the difficulty here arises from the fact that he's got to be made credible on two levels, first as a sort of deity (second division) and secondly as a human being who is wholly believable as an important figure in the narrative. I'd certainly take out the binding of Wilf's books in human skin which still seems to me to strike exactly the wrong sort of note – it belongs to the whole macabre world of concentration camp horrors or Nazi atrocities; and on reflection I very much like your idea of having Will look him up in some reference book – *Who's Who in America* I suppose would be right – and telling the reader what he finds out.

3. *Time*

It would be a help surely if you were to work out, even if only roughly, how much time various periods in the story take and what ages the characters are during the different episodes. By the time the book opens Wilf is already recognised as a major writer of very considerable literary importance so he must be in his mid or late 40's at the very youngest, so Jake, I suppose would be somewhere in his mid 20's to early 30's. How long does Wilf's 'motorway life' last? (Again roughly). So how much time has elapsed before Jake appears on the scene again? How long was it before Wilf discovered the truth about the appalling fall at Felsenblick? What period of time does the whole narrative cover?

B. DETAILS

1. *Titles of Wilf's books.*

I don't think that KNOCK KNOCK or WINNIE THE POOF (though I like that joke) will do. They've got to be slightly more 'serious'.

2. *Clubs – names*

Though The Greville will do perfectly well for the Savile, I think The Mausoleum is a bit too jokey for the Athenaeum. What about The

Areopagus? Or why shouldn't it simply be left as The Athenaeum (probably the best solution)? As far as I can remember there is nothing even remotely defamatory about it in the text.

3. *Jake's dialogue*
This will be vetted eventually by somebody who can tell whether it rings true or not. I certainly couldn't – it would have to be an American of roughly Jake's age. I'm sure between us we can think of somebody. (A name has just occurred to me – Edward Mendelson a very bright young American who is Auden's literary executor.)

4. *Page 31. Spanish Fly*
I fear one's got to face the truth that this doesn't work, though I hate the thought of losing the Itchyphallic bank clerk. I do hope you are able to think of some way of maintaining him in that state without causing the whole thing by an aphrodisiac pill.

5. *Centre threequarter*
I'm no good at all about Rugger – I managed successfully to chicken out of it at school – but I've an uneasy feeling that there isn't such a position. Doubtless you know more about this than I do and I'll happily bow to your superior knowledge! I certainly remember talk about threequarters but not about centre threequarters. Possibly a confusion here between threequarter and centre forward?

6. *Jiffy Camera*
I think it would be an idea to slip in after the words Jiffy Camera something like a 'sort of proto-Polaroid'. I assumed when I first read the TS that Jiffy Camera was a spoof name for Polaroid – and I think that many readers will think so too unless you make it quite clear that it happened before Polaroids were invented.

7. *Page 40. Monstre Sacre*
I still haven't checked on whether Monstre Sacre is a usual phrase or whether it is Sacre Monstre. I'll talk to some don friend of mine about this; certainly *I'm* not sure.

8. *Page 41 Masefield and Bridges*

At a time when these two poets were established literary figures would Wilf have been old enough and established enough to have corresponded with them – at any rate interestingly? It all depends I suppose on what date it actually is at the beginning of the narrative. I rather feel all this would be much more convincing if you substituted the names of two major writers who were, so to speak, interestingly alive at a much later date. Auden? Eliot? Orwell? Aldous Huxley? There's lots to choose from.

9. *Page 49. University of Astrakhan.*

You ought to make it clearer that Astrakhan is in the US. The first time it is mentioned you should perhaps say Astrakhan, Nebraska or Astrakhan, South Dakota – or something like that. I never got, as you know, the fact that Ole Ashcan is a disrespectful name for Astrakhan. I think that should be explained.

10. *The Stigmata*

I got this right – but I think it ought to be spelt out a little – perhaps by mentioning the word stigmata which would give the reader a clue. (I myself thought it must be the stigmata but I'd have been glad to have authorial confirmation.)

11. *Page 22/29*

I advise taking out the funny names, Jane Fruitcake, Angina Thomas etc. And there actually is a critic called John Hollaway. In the reference to The Great Pageant to English Literature I think a real name would work rather well e.g. from Beowulf to Margaret Drabble (or Iris Murdoch or Kingsley Amis or anyone you like).

Halliday

A further point about Halliday which I forgot to mention. I'd advise taking out the collection of blotting paper and paper clips.

       C.

The first draft that Monteith saw is presented as a transcript of tape recordings made by the main character – the novelist Wilf Barclay – who is about to burn all his papers. In the same draft, the mysterious American millionaire Halliday is keen to establish a foundation which, as well as devoting itself to the study of Barclay's work, would house Halliday's own collection of blotting paper and paper clips. Halliday is rumoured to have his books bound in human skin.

WG to Charles Monteith MS

30 May 1983   [Headed Paper: Ebble Thatch (2)]

Dear Charles,

Thank you for your kind letter. Ann and I agree you are the ideal guest. We're both glad you don't mind having *The Paper Men* dedicated to you. You remember the Victorian Britons who having climbed an hitherto unclimbed peak, 'threw all constraint to the winds and clasped hands warmly'? Perhaps in something the same spirit you'll not mind appearing as 'friend and publisher'.

Thank you too for your very valuable notes. I think at the moment I accept them *nearly in toto*. I ought to say that I hadn't thought of Wilf's index finger and soles as *stigmata* because he is Christ or a saint, he isn't of course: but was transferring the medical *fact* that marks and feelings can appear through psychological intensity 'like the stigmata' which in religion has often happened to hysterics. This is all confused but I know what I mean. Halliday as a good second class god seems fine to me.

Rugger – yes. Wing three, or scrum-half Ann (who was once engaged to a rugby fifteen) tells me. (scream from Ann.)

My *Robert* of which I am quite proud, gives; Par métaph: Les Monstres sacrés: expression appliquée à de grands comédiens (titre d'une pièce de J. Cocteau. 1940). However I've heard it round the place as sacré monstre, I'm certain. The solution, obviously, is that it's *Franglais* – sacré monster in fact, something Liz and Wilf, though perhaps not *Johnny* might well use. I also like the 'itchy'phallic bank clerk and yearn to keep him but at the moment can only think of Spanish fly combined with the same emotional intensity that will one day give him 'stigmata'.

Anyway, directly I've got this off to you I'll begin The Paper Men mark III.

Our love to you
Bill

The dedication to *The Paper Men* reads

For

my friend and publisher

CHARLES MONTEITH.

'Par métaph . . . 1940': 'Figuratively: The Sacred Monsters: expression applied to great actors (title of a play by J. Cocteau. 1940)'. Robert (or Le Robert) publishes French-language dictionaries and reference books.

Golding's reference to the '"itchy"phallic bank clerk' runs with Monteith's misspelling of 'ithyphallic' in the previous letter. The description relates to Wilf's memory of how as a young man he had taken an aphrodisiac pill and ended up with an erection that lasted throughout the next day.

Charles Monteith to WG   TS

8 June 1983

Dear Bill

My secretary has, I know, acknowledged your letter of May 30th which I was immensely glad to get. I'd be delighted – no more than delighted, honoured, pleased, flattered, immensely gratified – to appear as 'a friend and publisher'. Thank you very very much again, I do appreciate it.

Glad the notes were some use and I'm very interested indeed in all your comments on them.

Delighted to know that THE PAPER MEN Mark 3 is underway – and you can imagine how eagerly I'm looking forward to reading it.

Very best love to you both

WG to Charles Monteith   MS

1 July 1983   [Headed Paper: Ebble Thatch (2)]

Dear Charles,

A hasty note – my electric typewriter exploded just when I was on the last chapter of the third draft of *Paper Men*: so alas, I'll be delayed.

Enforcedly idle and reading thru' what I've written has made me very glum. I think a fourth draft or at least *major* revision will be necessary.

ever

Bill

WG to Charles Monteith

14 July 1983   [Headed Paper: Ebble Thatch (2)]

Thursday

Dear Charles,

Herewith what I hope is the penultimate draft of THE PAPER MEN. I'm afraid that as on previous occasions it's the only copy so I'm sending it at awful expense to make sure it reaches you.

I put it on record with this that as you've kindly agreed to accept the dedication, I'll make any changes you feel a good idea for your self protection – or as third-rate contraltos used to write (I'm told and hence Molly Bloom) 'Management's rights respected!'

I'm sorry about the scribbles et al; but the Author (I mean the journal) says you have to spend three thousand five hundred for a word processor and I'd sooner have orcids.

We leave for Santander, Spain, from Plymouth on 1st August. Damn. We leave for Plymouth on 31st July, of course as the boat sails at eight next morning. We get back in England on 31st August.

Our address in France will be: Al Sola, Bld de la Dune, Hossegor. It's about twenty miles north of Biarritz. It doesn't appear to have a 'phone number; but in an emergency I dare say the people who got us the place and who are, Agence Durand, Ave Paul Lahary 40150 Hossegor, FRANCE would pass a message. Their number is

010 33 58 43 50 64

I daresay none of this is necessary. Come to think of it our fellow adventurer John Bodley might be glad of the info.

Ann sends her love and I add mine

Bill

Golding's journal indicates that he was still unhappy with *The Paper Men* even after the latest draft: 'This morning I've just about completed the manuscript of The Paper Men. It's an improvement, I think, from something that wasn't any good and is now only fairish' (J, 14 July 1983).

Golding's enigmatic comments about Molly Bloom and 'Management's rights' are explained by a journal entry from 1977 following a university seminar that he had attended in Canterbury on *Ulysses*: 'My contribution such as it was, was that Molly Bloom as a fourth rate "artiste" would have agreed to the clause "agents' rights respected", which means you sleep with him if he has got you a job, and wants to' (J, 17 February 1977).

Charles Monteith to WG

23 August 1983

Dear Bill

I postponed my second reading of this new version of THE PAPER MEN as long as I could – I wanted to leave a sizeable interval between it and my first reading of it – and I'm more than happy to report to you that this second reading not only confirms but redoubles all the enthusiasm for it which I tried to express when we last talked on the telephone. You've done a superb job in trimming it into what is, in my view, its final shape; and I'm more than happy to treat what I've now got as the final copy. Many many thanks and many congratulations.

You will not be surprised to learn that it will need a vast amount of copy-editing but that, I'm certain, can all be left to our copy-editing department. I'll pass the MS over to Liz Bland (who organises all copy-editing) before I go to Greece and I'm sure she'll be in touch with you direct.

So far as the publication date is concerned, we'll stick, I think, almost certainly to early September 1984. The spring list is already closed & clearly this is something we don't want to rush. More haste does in fact very often mean less speed.

What a marvellous book to have dedicated to one! I'm *immensely* pleased and grateful.

I hope the holiday in France went well and that you and Anne are both feeling very much restored and refreshed. I'm not going away for long myself and will be back in mid-September. Let's meet again as soon after that as we can manage.

Love to you both,
Charles.

PS One very important point: there'll be an editorial committee meeting tomorrow morning when I'll settle our offer of terms. I'll write to you about that straight away and the chances are that both these will be waiting for you when you get back.

PPS One small editorial point which has just occurred to me: Wilfred, referring to his own heavy drinking, says that he could give it up when he likes and adds 'It *is* a good plan. I've stuck to it for nearly half a century.' Does this fit in properly with Wilfred's age which I imagine to be about 70 at the time he is writing. Wouldn't 'nearly a quarter of a century' fit in better?

CM

The challenges of copy-editing Golding's novels are clear from Monteith's note to Liz Bland the same day, warning her that 'it's a terrible MS', 'the whole thing' needs to be retyped, 'the punctuation needs attention throughout', and 'consistency of names also needs checking'. Monteith elaborates with an example: 'A character called Rick used to be called Jake and occasionally Golding forgets to change this.'

Charles Monteith to WG   TS

24 August 1983

Dear Bill

In the pile of post which you'll have found waiting for you when you get back there's another letter from me – perhaps you've read it already – to say how tremendously good the revised version of THE PAPER MEN is and to say, too, that I'm perfectly happy to treat it as a final version.

In the PS to my letter I promised another letter the next day to follow it up – this is it – with a formal offer of financial terms which we'd settle at an editorial meeting this morning.

The meeting's now over and everyone is delighted to know how good the book is and how enthusiastic I am about it. It'll be the highlight of our autumn '84 list. So far as terms are concerned, may we simply agree on the same terms we had for DARKNESS VISIBLE and RITES OF PASSAGE i.e. a total advance of £10,000 payable ½ on publication and ½ on demand, on a royalty of 15% on all copies sold. All the terms etc. to be exactly the same as before. If this is all right I'd be most grateful if you could let my secretary, Fiona McCrae, know and she will ask Giles de la Mare to go straight ahead with a contract.

Yours ever

Charles.

PS A point about the MS which I should have mentioned in my first letter. The original has now been passed to Liz Bland for copy-editing, we also made a photostat which will remain in my room to be used for purposes of reference.

PPS I'll be back in the office on 14th September.

WG to Charles Monteith   TS

25 September 1983   [Headed Paper: Ebble Thatch (2)]

Dear Charles,

I'm sending the MS of THE PAPER MEN off to F&F by this same post and presumably it'll arrive with this letter. I worked with increasing gloom – each advance seemed slighter than the last. However here it is and legible I hope. Perhaps any further copyediting can be done by phone. That worked, I remember with RITES but the list may be longer in this case.

Thank you very much – this is where I should have started! – for your letter of 24th August. Presumably the Liz Bland mentioned in it will now judge as to whether much needs to be done.

There are one or two points about the terms you suggest though. I think the advance has generally been paid, half on *signature* and half on publication. A year or two ago Matthew Evans asked me whether or no I wanted to continue with payment of royalties twice a year or switch. I finally defined my position as 'As much as possible, as soon as possible as often as possible!' He did then agree but the news does not seem to have filtered through to Harlow. That's probably because I neglected to read the print of the last agreement (or two) which still contained the more elaborate (and for my purposes) less satisfactory method of payment. However, be it herein noted that I don't want things on demand but 'as much, as soon, as often'. This is all very clumsy and perhaps I should have an agent for novels but it's never seemed necessary.

Talking of agents, both I and the Society of Authors were going to raise the question of 7½ percent for paperbacks; but I see you've bumped everything to an equal 15 percent and I can't ask better. Agreed, agreed!

I suppose now I have to get stuck into the ground work for this Egypt book – at least the trip ought to be fun. Love from us both. Bill

Golding gives the year as 1083 – here corrected as an obvious slip.
    Faber's accounts department is situated in Harlow.

Charles Monteith to WG TS

28 September 1983

Dear Bill,

Many thanks for your letter of September 25th and the final type-script of THE PAPER MEN. This is simply the briefest of brief notes to let you know that it's here and that I'll read it straight away. After that it will go off – that will be straight away too – to Liz Bland (who is head of our copy-editing department).

So far as the terms are concerned, I'll simply send a xerox of your letter up to Matthew Evans and ask him to sort this out. I was rather taken aback, I confess – though not in the least surprised! – by your enthusiastic agreement to the idea of a 15% royalty on the paper-back edition. On re-reading my own letter of August 24th I see that I expressed myself extraordinarily loosely by saying 'royalty of 15% on all copies sold'. What I should have said, of course, was '15% on all copies sold of the cased edition'. I'll ask Matthew to sort this out when he writes. Clearly my mind's softening very badly at the edges and I'm sure it's far, far better to leave all financial negotiations to him! I'm sure, though, that everything will be sorted out amicably – as it always is. I don't really think, incidentally, that you need an agent for novels – you won't be surprised to hear. Don't forget that it would cost you 10% of all your earnings!

I can't tell you how much I envy the Egypt trip. I do hope we're able to meet again before you both go.

Best love to you both,
Charles

In an internal memo to Matthew Evans that same day, Monteith writes, 'Clearly I made a balls by not making it clear when I talked about a straight 15% royalty I was talking about the cased edition only.' Evans wrote to Golding offering a starting royalty of 10 per cent on the paperback, rising to 12 per cent after the sale of 30,000 copies. *The Paper Men* was published on those terms on 6 February 1984 in an edition just shy of 105,000 copies.

WG to Charles Monteith

(?) October 1983

Dear Charles
    What a blurb! What a book! Let's buy it *at once*!
          ever
          Bill

The card has a printed header as follows:

FROM WILLIAM GOLDING

EBBLE THATCH, BOWERCHALKE, NR. SALISBURY, WILTS. TEL: BROADCHALKE 275

The card is attached to a blurb for *The Paper Men* that Faber had previously sent to Golding. He notes in his journal, 'Charles has written a marvellous blurb for paper men – better by far than I can do. He makes the book sound terrifying' (J, 14 October 1983). The blurb reads as follows:

Fame, success, fortune: a drink problem slipping over the border-line into alcoholism, a dead marriage, the incurable itches of middle-ages [sic] lust. For Wilfred Barclay, novelist, the final, unbearable irritation is Professor Rick L. Tucker, implacable in his determination to become The Barclay Man. Locked in a lethal relationship they stumble half-blindly across Europe, shedding wives, self-respect, illusions. They confront terrifying abysses – physical, emotional, spiritual – continually change roles, change themselves; change the worlds about them. The climax, when it comes, is as inevitable as it is unexpected.

Ferociously powerful, unpredictable, unclassifiable, THE PAPER MEN is as idiosyncratic and original as anything William Golding has yet written.

The 1983 Nobel Prize was the final recognition of Golding's genius, the confirmation of what has already become generally accepted – that of all British novelists now writing, his work is the most likely to survive.

455

1984

Published in February, *The Paper Men* attracts the worst reviews of all Golding's novels to date. Golding is out of the country with Ann on publication day, embarking on the Nile adventure that becomes the basis for his next book, *An Egyptian Journal* (1985). He makes copious notes en route and writes a full draft on his return; after rewritings and revisions the typescript is ready by the end of the year. There are trips to Brittany with the family in August and to Thailand with Ann in October, although a mooted 'Thailand Journal' never transpires. Looking to move west, further away from literary London, the Goldings step up their house-hunting over the summer. In December their offer is accepted for Tullimaar, a Georgian mansion in Perranarworthal, midway between Truro and Falmouth.

Charles Monteith to WG   TS

9 January 1984

Dear Bill

I'm terribly sad that this wretched bronchitis is giving you such a beastly time at the moment. And I'm very sorry indeed to have troubled you. I'll try to keep my calls to an absolute minimum, I promise you.

I got your message from Connie Whittaker and of course I absolutely understand and accept your decision about the Nobel Prize certificate. It doesn't surprise me in the least, I assure you. I was in two minds, I confess, about even passing it on to you.

It's very good of you to say that you'll do a signing session at Blackwell's some time later on in the spring; and again, I promise you, if you change your mind about it later nobody here will press you about it in the very slightest. I'm certain, too, that it would be a big success; and, if nothing else, it would make a marvellous reason for asking you and Anne to come over to Oxford. I needn't say how delighted I'd be if you'd both have a meal with me – either lunch or dinner – at All Souls.

I've reminded John about the big art book for Karen and I gather he's already done a recky of the ground at Hatchards. He'll be in touch with you and Ann about it.

Get well very soon; and in the meantime much love to you both,

> Fiona McCrae
> pp. Charles Monteith
> (dictated by him and signed in his absence)

The proposal was for the Nobel Prize certificate to be temporarily exhibited in Hatchards bookshop.

The Stockholm-based artist Karin Oldfelt had served as a host and guide for the Goldings and Monteith when they came for the Nobel Prize ceremony the previous December. She was sent a 'big art book' – identity now unknown – as a thank you gift.

WG to Charles Monteith PC

(?) March 1984

Home now – and keeping a low profile in view of shot and shell at *The Paper men*.

The enclosed turned up. What do I (we) do? He may do it no matter what. Is the idea of A. Burgess a bad joke or a bit of diagnostic psychology?

> ever
> Bill.

The printed header on this card has the same address and phone number as the card from October 1983. The only difference is that Golding has used one of Ann's cards: it starts, 'FROM ANN GOLDING'.

The reception of *The Paper Men* was lukewarm at best. Having timed their Egypt trip to coincide with its publication, the Goldings arrived back home on 5 March. Awaiting them was a letter from Dr V. P. Varma proposing a multi-author collection of essays dedicated to Golding's work and marking his seventy-fifth birthday. With what must have been accidental irony, Dr Varma suggested recruiting Anthony Burgess as copy-editor. Burgess had not enjoyed the experience of losing the 1980 Booker Prize to Golding and had taken every opportunity since then to make disparaging remarks about his rival. As Golding wrote in his journal after another attack in April, 'Anthony Burgess is on at me again – he has become such a bore!' (J, 22 April 1984).

Monteith put off V. P. Varma by explaining that plans for a birthday volume were already underway.

22 March 1984

I'm immensely grateful to both of you for all your kindness and hospitality on Tuesday – and particularly to Anne for a most memorably delicious game pie. It was very good to see you both back safe and well after what was clearly a pretty harassing as well as very interesting expedition. I can't tell you how much I'm looking forward to the book. From everything you said I feel certain that it's going to be first rate.

I'm sorry to spoil what was meant to be – and I hope is – an entirely 'nice' letter, but Desmond Clarke, our Sales Director, has just reminded me to remind you that you did say some time back that you'd do a signing session in Blackwells. Might it be an idea to fit it in with your dinner at BNC – to be followed, I hope, by a dinner or lunch at All Souls? I know that the date isn't yet settled; but as soon as it is and if you think this could all be fitted in – both Desmond and I would be most grateful if you could let me know.

I'm lunching with John Carey – as I think I mentioned – next Tuesday to talk about the Birthday Book. Either he or I, or quite possibly both of us, will be in touch again after that.

Very many thanks again for a splendid day at Bowerchalke. John Bodley, incidentally, tells me that he sent off the book to Karen today, and I expect we'll all be hearing from her shortly. I do hope she comes over to England this summer. It would be great fun to see her again.

. . . .

Incidentally, you'll be getting a small parcel from me with a Faber label on it, probably some time next week. You'll find that it contains a number of slim volumes, all in paperback, nearly all of them by Seamus Heaney, the Irish poet whom I remember mentioning to you in Stockholm, and whom I think very highly of. Robert Lowell described him as 'the best Irish poet since Yeats'. And I include too, Philip Larkin's other 'canonical' volume, *The Whitsun Weddings*, published by Fabers, to complement *High Windows* which I brought down on Tuesday. (The third canonical collection *The Less Deceived* is published by a very small firm in Hull which refuses to hand it over to us. We are furious, of course, and so is Philip; but I must confess that if I were the small publishers concerned, The Marvell Press, I'd probably behave in exactly the same way.) I also put in Philip's recent volume of miscellaneous pieces, mostly critical, *Required Writing*, which I think you'll enjoy and which recently won the W.H. Smith prize. Of all contemporary poets, I think he is the one I admire and enjoy most.

As becomes increasingly common in the correspondence from Monteith to Golding, the file copy of this letter has no greeting and no farewell.

The lunch on 20 March at Golding's home in Bowerchalke provided the opportunity to discuss *An Egyptian Journal*. Monteith and John Bodley turned up from Faber, and Liz Blair and David Roberts from Rainbird. Golding noted lugubriously in his journal that 'Charles was still keeping Lent so it wasn't a very vinous occasion' (J, 20 March 1984).

'the Birthday Book': Monteith had commissioned John Carey, Merton Professor at Oxford, to edit a Festschrift (although Monteith strongly disliked that word) on the occasion of Golding's seventy-fifth birthday.

WG to Charles Monteith TS

2 April 1984   [Headed Paper: Ebble Thatch (2)]

Dear Charles,

Sorry for this unconscionable delay (a good word that – I wish I knew a bit more about it) in answering your letter. But I've been dug in at the typewriter trying to get enough words on Egypt down before they slipped away. At the moment I'm over thirty thousand which is a critical point; I'm hoping to get to sixty and then use that as a mine for lumps of ore, har har. Thank you very much for Philip Larkin (I suppose actually one should thank the Almighty) who is making me very very jealous though I'm doing my best to disguise my jealousy as admiration. How come he can do what he does do?

Anyway.

Ann says if you say no say no but if you're going to say yes say it graciously. So graciously of course I'll keep my word and gladly do a signing at Blackwell's. You'd better fix up the date with the manager (or is he called director at so august a stall?) and I'll fit in with it. I suppose next weekend is too soon? I'll be on my own from Friday to Monday and now see that Saturday would have done fine but suppose – I've just rung John Bodley who says yes it *w'd* be too short notice so that's that. However the good news is, I repeat that I'll come up and sign books.

I don't know about a meal at All Souls – though I – we – would be delighted to come. The fact is Barry Nicholas hasn't yet fixed up a time when I'm going to give him a medal! I think maybe we're both pussy-footing and *I* think he wants it all ceremonious which I don't wheras *I* think he wants it all ceremonious which he doesn't. I shall have to clear up this situation and will do so and let you know a date or dates when I or we will be in Oxford.

I have a letter from Professor Carey – 28th March – in which he expresses willingness to meet here or there. Of course I'm happy for him to edit my trumpet voluntary and will oblige all concerned by living to be 75. I think I shall acquaint him with the great news that I am fancy free next weekend so there's no reason why we shouldn't meet. Now I see that he's free on the sixth but not then until the ninth. However, never fear; I will fix something.

It was very good to have you down here. You must come again as soon as you feel inclined; or perhaps before that!

Forgive this silly letter; but it's a new experience rewriting a journal and makes me light-headed.

> ~~Yours sincerely~~ and love from us both
> Bill

Barry Nicholas was the Principal of Brasenose College. Golding was lending his Nobel Prize medal for an exhibition in his honour at the college library.

'*I* think he wants it all ceremonious which I don't wheras *I* think he wants it all ceremonious which he doesn't': Golding may have muddled up his pronouns. The meaning is probably that both Golding and Nicholas think that the other 'wants it all ceremonious' when in fact neither of them wants it to be like that.

WG to Charles Monteith   TS

16 April 1984   [Headed Paper: Ebble Thatch (2)]

Dear Charles,

Thank you for your letter and the gift of books. I'm now nearing the point of having P. Larkin OP:OMN. I'm using his occasional pieces as a bedside book but the trouble is they keep me awake. There will have to be another attempt on my part to *get into* Shamus Heaney who so clearly merits it.

I don't know if you heard from Carey. He seems to know what he wants so I at least can lie back and think of the empire. I've given him what addresses I can, and I don't think he has rejected any.

One of the reasons why I am not doing a very solemn investigation of Messrs Larkin and Heaney is that I'm busy and have been busy, try-ing to get down AN EGYPTIAN JOURNAL before I forget the day-to-day events, (even though I have my own journal with me) and impressions dull. All I can say at the moment is that I've got a lot of MS – sixty-six thousand notional words at this morning's stint, which means I'm cer-tainly in the fifties. Rainbird want between fifty and sixty. Of course it's no more than a dreary and rather brutal draft, but next time round I may be able to inject some sweetness and light. I don't really know what they want or expect. It's all so bitty & inconclusive.

Also I have no experience whatsoever of being illustrated or if you like to put it the other way round, serving a set of illustrations. (Sunset at Sakkhara.) Time will shoo½.

> Ever
> Bill

'OP:OMN': opera omnia (complete works).
 Sakkara (or Saqqara), twenty miles south of Cairo, is the site of a complex of pyramids, temples and tombs.
 'next time round I may be able to inject some sweetness and light': Golding had been told by Ann that parts of the latest draft were 'too down-beat', so – as he observes in his journal – he had already begun removing some of the 'subjective gloom' (J, 22 March 1984).
 'Time will shoo½': perhaps Golding means 'time will shoot' – playing on 'time will tell' – because the illustrations are photographic shots.

WG to Charles Monteith

TS MONTEITH

26 April 1984   [Headed Paper: Ebble Thatch (2)]

Dear Charles,

What an awful bore it must have been for you – I've just had a letter from Susannah Foreman putting me more or less in the picture. We're both happy, down here, to know though, that you're out of the wood and convalescing at home.

Karen Oldfeldt rang the other day (I *still* havn't got over the sort of international instant communication which is standard nowadays) and asked – Ann as it happened – to pass on the good news that she is delighted with the book, finds it very beautiful and will we thank all concerned? Lo, I do so, which I suppose, includes me.

As for writing, well I've knocked out a fifty-thousand word draft not notional, but actual. Now it's a question of reorganising. But think of the fun it will give – I was going to call them 'the' but substitute 'My' – critics! I can imagine Jan Morris going to town on travel from the lofty position of an expert, and as for A— B—! Hush, hush, nobody cares, Christopher Golding is saying his prayers.

Needless to say this doesn't need any reply since as a convalescent you are to be coddled, even via the post. I shall unquestionably be on at you, directly you get back to F&F.

> Ann sends good wishes and love
>> as do I
>> Bill

Monteith's secretary Susannah Foreman had written to tell Golding that Monteith was at home recovering from a prostate operation.

Reviewing *A Moving Target* in 1982, Jan Morris had been respectful of the lectures but hostile to the travel pieces. As for Anthony Burgess, he had become Golding's most consistent detractor. Golding adapts J. B. Morton's parody of A. A. Milne to convey his own anxieties about the book's reception.

Charles Monteith to WG   TS

14 June 1984

Here is the third and last canonical book by Philip Larkin – the one I mentioned on the telephone the other day. Unfortunately, at any rate from Fabers point of view, George Hartley, who runs what is left of the Marvell Press, adamantly and perhaps understandably refuses to allow us to take it over – and so we can't, much as we'd like to, publish a Collected Poems. As with all his three major books, there isn't a bad poem in it, I think; and one or two of them are stunningly good – 'Church Going' and 'Lines on a Young Lady's Photograph Album', for example. I do very much hope you enjoy it.

I'm delighted that the Blackwells signing session was such a tremendous success. Everybody here was very pleased indeed with it. And I'll certainly look into Brasenose this coming weekend, or the weekend after, to see the Golding exhibit in the library.

I'm looking forward immensely, of course, to *Egypt*, when it's ready.

I do hope Ann's cold is much better – I know from bitter experience how horrid unseasonable colds can be.

Much love to you both.

Golding rarely agreed to book signings, so the exceptions became significant events. He was in Blackwell's, Oxford, signing copies of *The Paper Men* on 7 June. At that stage, the book had already sold 95,000 copies in hardback.

WG to Charles Monteith   TS

20 June 1984   [Headed Paper: Ebble Thatch (2)]

Dear Charles,

What a *bonne bouche* the Larkin THE LESS DECEIVED is! He certainly ought to be Poet Laureate if he isn't too good for it. Would it be disrespectful to confess that I laughed myself silly over 'the stuff that dreams are made on'?

God knows how he does it. I enjoyed him so much my mind kept on inventing pseudo and/or sub Larkin verses. One was entitled 'Talking about God at dinner' only unfortunately I did it when awake, fell asleep and when I woke up I'd forgotten the rest – no: fortunately. That man from Porlock wasn't wholly bad. Still I hope he makes it to the Butt of Canary. There ought to be one of those lions like (such as) they had in Venice was it? You pop in a note and either your enemy gets his throat cut or elected Doge. Or something. I do find unadulterated, unmasticated, undigested and literal history more and more of a bore and prefer to invent it.

The GOLDING EXHIBITION is a bit of a lark. It did cross my mind that I might have contributed a personal relic or two. Socks, now. After all, the pope –

Egypt goes on. Nagged by my American son-in-law I now count *three* of my beastly typed pages as a thousand words rather than two pages. This present draft is just coming up to forty thousand on that showing and I'm urgent for you to read the whole thing as neither Ann nor I feel competent to assess it. Anyway I'm thumping along at two thousand words (new style) a day so in a fortnight's time I ought to be there, more or less. I don't know if you're off to Cos – to be Cossetted? or elsewhere. We two old things will probably borrow the Nicholas's guest flat in BNC for a few days in July to do research in the Bod.

Ann's better; and painting a deathless masterpiece in the garden.

Love from us both   Bill

'that's the stuff / That dreams are made on' comes from Larkin's 'Toads' and is in turn an allusion to one of Golding's favourite Shakespeare plays: *The Tempest* (4.1.156–7).

'That man from Porlock': a 'person on business from Porlock' interrupted Coleridge while he was writing 'Kubla Khan' inspired by an opium dream. To his 'surprise and mortification', Coleridge found that his vision had vanished when he returned to the poem.

The Poet Laureate traditionally received a butt of canary wine on appointment to the role.

'one of those lions like (such as) they had in Venice': these were the *bocche di leoni* (lions' mouths), the first and most famous of which was at the Doge's Palace. They gave citizens the chance to make secret complaints or accusations which would then be investigated.

Charles Monteith to WG   TS

21 June 1984

Dear Bill,

Philip Larkin asked me to go with him and Monica to Betjeman's Memorial Service in the Abbey on Friday 29th; and I collected the tickets yesterday and noticed they were stamped Deanery Pew. A portent, do you think?

How good would he be as Poet Laureate, do you think? The only evidence I've got so far is, I fear, quite unsuitable for, e.g. The *Times* and even more so for the *Guardian*. In Jubilee Year, when Labour was in power, you remember, he came into my room here one day, saying he'd written a stanza of a Jubilee poem but that it needed several more stanzas both before and after and that he couldn't think of any. Here is the one and only stanza:

[. . .]

(I don't think you ought to show this to Ann, it would upset her very much.)

Do let me know if and when you get the dates fixed for your stay in BNC. If I should be there during your time we must certainly arrange an All Souls meeting.

Excellent that the second draft of *Egypt* is coming along so splendidly. I can hardly wait for it.

Much love to you both,
Charles Monteith.

'Monica': Larkin's partner, Monica Jones. Larkin turned down the opportunity to become Poet Laureate; another Faber poet, Ted Hughes, succeeded John Betjeman in the role.

I have redacted the racist quatrain that Monteith quotes. 'After Healey's trading figures' can be found in Larkin's *Complete Poems*, ed. Archie Burnett, p. 318.

WG to Charles Monteith   TS

4 July 1984   [Headed Paper: Ebble Thatch (2)]

Dear Charles,

Here with the MS (second draft) which you were good enough to say you'd read. It is seventy thousand words at the moment, counting three of these pages to a thousand words and remembering there are interleavings. I propose to get myself one of those type writers which make it all easy.

As the stipulation is a MS from fifty–sixty thousand we *may* get rid of twenty thousand and *must* get rid of ten thousand! The beginning and end are ropey but I hope there are some good things in between. The real trouble is that the only centre to the book is either me or the Nile or both and it has become a bookful of digressions.

Anyway I'll say no more but look forward very much to getting your objective opinion – something neither Ann nor I can give!

I find myself getting old – in the writing sense. After a time I have to stop and two thousand a day of this stuff is really all I can manage.

The joke is that I shall probably have seen you by the time you are reading this, and at the Royal Soc of Lit. Where I shall be limping as Cobber has stepped on my foot and ground my *off big toe* into the cobbles.

I can't understand why my typing is so much worse than usual today¾ – after all, Cobber didn't stand on my hands.

      Love from us both
        Bill

Ann said she enjoyed it and put it down saying she felt she was leaving friends!

Golding is two years out with his dating of the letter, giving the year as 1982.

Golding's journal sets out his worries and describes Faber's modus operandi in Monteith's semi-retirement: 'I rang up Fabers and discovered that they had the manuscript and had sent it to Charles by special messenger so that he c'd read it over the weekend. He has rung back asking them to put it on the agenda for Wednesday. I don't know really what that implies but fear the worst. However I'm quite sure there are good things here and there in the seventy-thousand words' (J, 9 July 1984). The extent of Golding's nervousness is evident the following day: 'Still no word from Charles – it makes me apprehensive' (J, 10 July 1984).

'my *off big toe*': the right side of a horse is the off side and the left is the near side. It follows that the damage is to the big toe on Golding's right foot.

'Ann said she enjoyed it': Ann's true opinion emerges in one of Golding's journal entries from 1988: 'Ann has confessed (after some years) that she doesn't care for An Egyptian Journal. She says it sounds as if I disliked the place. Perhaps I did' (J, 11 July 1988).

Charles Monteith to WG   TS

13 September 1984

Dear Bill,

I was delighted to get you on the telephone this morning. Do please let me repeat what I said when we talked. *Egyptian Journal* is a marvellous book which I enjoyed immensely – even more on the second reading that on the first.

As I told you I've got absolutely no major suggestions to make, only a few (a very few) minor editorial points. I can safely leave to Elizabeth Blair any problems that arise from the 'picture book' side of things. She'd be much more experienced than I am about coping with all that.

First, two general points. (a) Pagination. Since this time I read a photostat copy of which the pages weren't numbered I numbered them myself; and page 1 is the beginning of Chapter 1. (i.e. the title page is *not* numbered; so if, in your copy it is, please add '1' to the page numbers I give.) (b) Copy editing points. I've left all these to be dealt with by Rainbird but there are quite a number of small ones which will need attention – e.g. the positioning of commas and some spellings. 'Molasses' is spelt like that with only one L – you spell it with two (*c.* page 60) and there is some uncertainty throughout about the spelling of 'Libya': sometimes it's correct, sometimes it's 'Lybia' and sometimes it's 'Lybya'. 'Libya' is correct. My impression is, too, that particularly in the early parts of the book, there are rather too many exclamation marks.

Now for my pathetic little bundle of comments.

Page 2 and repeated on page 165. The Duke of Wellington. I fear it *wasn't* – or so the books tell us – about the Apostles' Creed that the Duke was so forthrightly sceptical. This remark was made when a gentleman accosted him in the street saying 'Mr Jones, I believe?' And to this Wellington replied, 'If you believe that, you'll believe anything.' See the *Oxford Dictionary of Quotations* (new edition) page 568.7.

Page 54 *Farony*. This stuck me for a moment and then I got it (or I think I did). Wouldn't it be clearer, though, if it were spelt 'Pharony'? Even if you stick to the spelling 'Farony' throughout perhaps it should be explained on its first appearance.

nobelitis – I got this straight away, you'll not be surprised to hear – though I don't remember any nobelitis – but wouldn't it be easier for most readers if you spelt it and nobelspeak with a capital N – i.e. Nobelitis and Nobelspeak?

Page 74. You ask Alaa what people in general think about you and Ann making this particular voyage. This is the second time you tell of this – but I haven't, I confess, checked back to see where it first occurs. I'd have thought that once would be enough – though it's a splendid story and one which I much enjoyed.

Page 79. Nomes. I was surprised, I confess, to find that in Egypt Governates were once called Nomes. It's such a very Greek word – the number of Nomarchies I've seen there and Nomarchs I've read about there – but I'm sure you're right and I presume this all dates back to the Ptolemaic period?

Pages 108/9. (Which link up with conversation on pages 196/7.) 'Coptic-Catholic Church'. I think this needs a little more explanation. I imagine the 'Coptic-Catholic Church' is a Coptic-Uniate Church which, though it retains the Coptic ritual, is in communion with Rome (and has therefore, presumably, abandoned the Monophysite heresy). Rather like the Uniate Orthodox churches of the East. I'm sure that the main Coptic church to which the vast majority of native Egyptian Christians still belong is not, in any sense, Uniate.

That's the lot, I think.

A house in Cornwall. I can't imagine anything nicer (and you'll have A. L. Rowse as a fairly near neighbour – a mixed blessing, I would say). I'll speak to Raleigh Trevellyan the next time I see him in case he knows of anything that's going.

Best love to you and to Ann,
Charles Monteith

Elizabeth (Liz) Blair at Rainbird had taken over the editing of *An Egyptian Journal* from David Roberts.

Golding revises 'Farony' to 'Pharoni' in the final version. In the book, he describes the word as 'the new Arabic adjective for everything Pharaonic, whether it be a plastic copy of Narmer's slate palette or El Sheik done in wood but only six inches high'. The word 'Nobelitis' comes up in the book's account of a conversation with the Secretary General of Minya: 'The Secretary General and I now began to use *Nobelspeak*, suffering as we both did from *Nobelitis* or inflammation of the membranes of the ego. The Governate of Minya was peculiarly honoured and I was peculiarly honoured.'

The Monophysite heresy believed that Jesus was divine in nature and not divided between the human and the divine.

The Goldings had decided to move house. They looked at houses in several counties, but their preferred option was a property in Cornwall.

Like Golding, the historian A. L. Rowse was born in Cornwall. Monteith knew Rowse well because both men were Fellows of All Souls. His reputation preceded him, but Golding's first mention of Rowse in his journal expresses surprise at the reality: 'The problem with Rowse is – why isn't he a monster? To read some of his books you'd think him impossible, but he is a most kind host: and gets away with outrages – squeezing and patting – and babbling – and name dropping – and suggestiveness – by good-humour and a kind of pixie lightness which doesn't come through in his writing. But it is plain that he is on a very short fuse' (J, 16 August 1985). Golding warmed to Rowse and socialised with him regularly. Raleigh Trevelyan and his partner, Raúl Balín, were friends of Rowse and Monteith and, after the move to Cornwall, of the Goldings as well.

Charles Monteith to WG   TS

10 October 1984

Dear Bill,

Here's a small contribution to the enormous pile of mail that you're bound to find waiting for you when you get back from Thailand – an expedition which I long to hear about.

It's simply to say that on Saturday 8 December we have a Chichele dinner at All Souls and I wondered if by any happy chance you'd like to come to it? I needn't say how absolutely delighted I'd be if you would and could. I can't, alas, ask Ann as well since we are restricted to one guest each; but if you do come and Ann would like to come to Oxford with you I'd love to have a lunch party for you both in College the following day, Sunday 9 December.

I'd be terribly grateful if you could let me know reasonably soon;

and if you do come by yourself of course I can arrange a room in college for you.

Anyway, welcome home to both of you.
Love and best wishes,
Charles Monteith

WG to Charles Monteith PC

(?) October 1984

Marvellous Chichele! Accepted for me with pleasure. May we leave decision over Ann for a week as she's still recovering from the Thailand flight (*ghastly*) and starry-eyed over the place which we found a positive knockout. Promise decision from her next week. Shall talk about trip *endlessly*.

Bill   PS Have F&F a tame Arabic scholar? I want a bit of clout on *my* side in a mild punch-up with our Egyptian minder

B.

PPS Love from Bint Ann.

The card is a duplicate – with the same printed address – of the card sent by Golding to Monteith in October 1983.

The Goldings spent a fortnight in Thailand, and Golding briefly considered writing a 'Thailand Journal' for publication.

The punch-up was not as mild as Golding suggested. Alaa, his minder during the Egypt trip, had withdrawn all cooperation after reading the manuscript of *An Egyptian Journal*. Alaa's sister, the writer Ahdaf Soueif, who features briefly, wrote an angry denunciation of Golding in the *London Review of Books* after the book was published.

'Bint' is a derogatory term in British slang but its Egyptian origins are more respectful: it is the Arabic word for 'girl' or 'daughter'.

Charles Monteith to WG TS

24 October 1984

Dear Bill,

Delighted you can come to the Chichele dinner. I'm looking forward to that immensely. I do hope that Ann feels up to coming to Oxford too, for I'd love to give that lunch party. I'll look forward to hearing from you next week. I'm longing to hear about Thailand – it sounds marvellous.

469

Faber and Faber haven't any fluent Arabic speakers on their staff, I fear, but I'm sure we can contact, if it would help, Albert Hourani, of St Anthony's, who Matthew and I both know.

Love to you both,
Charles Monteith

Albert Hourani was a Fellow of St Antony's College, Oxford, where he established the Middle East Centre.

WG to John Bodley   TS

13 November 1984   [Headed Paper: Ebble Thatch (2)]

Dear John,

The enclosed letters are important in an odd way. Clarence (Gerry) Fry is one of a number of people who knew me when I was young, ignored me as not worth knowing for forty, fifty or even as much as sixty years, then reappeared in my life when it seemed I was worth cultivating. Clarence Fry is a splendid example and with the proposal enclosed herewith has surpassed himself. Could these copies of his letter to me and mine to him be included in what must be by now a kind of Golding archive? For if he goes ahead with his attempt to publish

LADY OF THE THIGHS he may indeed violate copyright and make me look ridiculous into the bargain. So I'd like this and any future letters kept. It all makes our purchase of a house with restricted address even more pressing.

He seems to be in touch with thirdrate people who might be twisters as well and turn nasty with my refusal to have anything to do with this daft suggestion. Or am I contracting a sort of persecution mania?

Ever,
Bill

Jerry Fry had written to Golding on 9 November, explaining that he had completed a 'mirror image' of *Lord of the Flies* titled 'Lady of the Thighs', in which the boys had been replaced by 'a party of harum-scarum girls'. Fry wanted Golding to contribute a foreword in order to increase the chances of publication. Fry went on to promise that, if the book made any profit, his first task would be to repay Golding for money lent in the past. Golding replied that he had long ago written off the money and was 'too old and too busy to be able to spare the time to do anything about the manuscript'. Having received the packet of correspondence, Bodley wrote on it, 'Weird exchange from Bill Golding today . . .' Matthew Evans has added,

'Wonderful letters! Bill is getting a bit paranoid. It reminds me of Henry Root' –
Root being the pseudonym of the satirist William Donaldson who wrote letters to
the great and the good with absurd questions and requests. For the conclusion to the
Fry correspondence, see Golding's letter to Bodley dated 24 September 1986.

Charles Monteith to WG   TS

28 November 1984

Dear Bill,

My secretary, Susannah Foreman, and I were clearing out my office
cupboard this afternoon and among the things I discovered there was
the original typescript of *The Paper Men*. Since this, I imagine, has
probably got considerable value I'll send it back to you separately;*
and I do apologize for the fact that it wasn't returned long before this.

I'm very much looking forward to seeing you and Ann in Oxford.
The Storrs, happily, are able to come to lunch but John and Iris, alas,
were already booked up and have sent a very regretful refusal.

Much love to you both,

* or I'll bring it down to Oxford.

The psychoanalyst Anthony Storr had helped David during his breakdowns, and
he and his wife Catherine were on friendly terms with the Goldings.

WG to Charles Monteith   TS EMORY

11 December 1984   [Headed Paper: Ebble Thatch (2)]

Dear Charles,

As you can see by these present, I have burst right into the technological era and am using a thing called – what irony! – a 'Control
Panel'. It is supposed to produce a clean bit of typing, but its spelling
is still only as good as mine.

You gave us a lovely weekend, arranging even the weather to suit.
I'm terribly sorry that we were so uncouth as to forget our presentation
bottle! I hope you will hold it for another occasion.

We have – or Ann has – finally decided to buy Tullimaar. Of
course I am terrified, but women have that type of natural frivolity,
which enables them to spend huge sums of money as if they were in
government or something. I hope all will be well. Please ensure that

F&F keep us supplied with quantities of money.

On thinking the thing over – did I mention this? – I don't think it's much good searching the alleged Cornish language for the name Tullimaar. Before the creek was so silted up it was used by Norwegian ships for bringing in timber. The pub at the head of the creek is still called the Norway Inn though of course only a rowing boat could get up as far as that now. So 'Tullimaar' may be Norwegian or Swedish or Danish or come to that Dutch. I begin to fantasize that the house is named from a ship, the one which made the fortune of the man who built the house. He owned or he managed a powder factory – gun, not face – and will have been one of the hard-faced men who did well out of the Napoleonic Wars. (Now how did I do that?) His name was Benjamin Sampson and he built the house in 1828 if anyone is interested. We find it all very exciting.

Love from us both
Bill

The visible difference in the letter's layout is that the text is justified.

Golding had been Monteith's guest at All Souls for the Chichele Dinner on 8 December. The following day, Golding and Ann had lunch with Monteith and a small party of friends.

The Goldings paid £200,000 for Tullimaar, a Georgian mansion in the village of Perranarworthal between Truro and Falmouth.

'(Now how did I do that?)': the words 'Napoleonic Wars' are typed half a line lower than what precedes them, for reasons that are evidently not clear to Golding.

Charles Monteith to WG   TS

12 December 1984

I was delighted to get your letter of 11 December and to know that the Tullimaar sale has finally gone through. From all you told me at the weekend it sounds an absolutely wonderful house, and I'm looking forward immensely to seeing it.

Do please tell Ann that the bottle of white burgundy is perfectly safe. I'll certainly look after it – or Quelch will in those cellars which you saw – until the next time I can persuade you to come to Oxford. Perhaps in the Spring?

Quelch was the wine steward at All Souls. Lunch on 9 December had included a tour of the college cellars which, Quelch reported, contained 47,000 bottles.

1985

The early months are spent preparing for the move to Cornwall; the Goldings take possession of their new home, Tullimaar, on 12 April. Several weeks later, Monteith sends Golding his essay 'Strangers from Within' describing his editorial role in the publication of *Lord of the Flies*; this is Monteith's contribution to a book intended to mark Golding's seventy-fifth birthday in September 1986. *An Egyptian Journal* attracts mostly respectful reviews when it appears in July, by which time Golding is making steady progress on a second draft of what he still calls 'Rites (2)' – the sequel to *Rites of Passage*. In October, he and Ann set off on a month-long British Council reading tour of Canada (accompanied by Monteith for some of the time), followed by a trip to Virginia where the Carvers are spending the academic year, and then South Carolina to stay with Terrell's parents. Ann's ill health delays their return but they finally arrive home in mid-December.

WG to Craig Raine   MS

(?) January 1985   [Headed Paper: Ebble Thatch (2)]

Dear Craig,

This work is by an old friend of mine. Is it poetry or has he – as Noel Coward said of your revered predecessor – merely got a narrow typewriter? I can't tell myself, having backed away from the higher reaches of lit: crit. I don't mean read it yourself, but you'll have *people*; and my passing it on to them *via* you w'd make my friend feel he had been taken seriously –

Oh dear, how difficult it all is.

Perhaps, if and when rejected it c'd come back to me?

It was good to have that lunch with you both in *All Souls*. I hope one day you'll see fit to journey into the far West and see us in our new home when we get there.

>   ever
>   Bill

Ann sends love.

Golding's headed paper was now out of date, so he occasionally corrected the defunct telephone number of 'Broad Chalke 275'. This time, he has scribbled it out and written below it 'SALISBURY 780440'.

Craig Raine was poetry editor at Faber; he and his wife, Ann Pasternak Slater, had attended the lunch at All Souls with Monteith, the Goldings and others on 9 December.

The 'revered predecessor' in question was T. S. Eliot. Noël Coward could not understand why Eliot persisted in writing his plays in blank verse when (in Coward's judgement) he lacked the power of the Elizabethan playwrights. One of Coward's friends proposed that the blank verse was an accident caused by Eliot's 'narrow typewriter'.

The work that Golding submitted was 'Return to Crete' by Gilbert Horobin, an old friend who had lived in Greece for many years. Horobin wrote poetry, fiction, plays and travel books. Raine replied regretfully to Golding on 29 January that he 'didn't persevere very far' before rejecting the manuscript.

Charles Monteith to WG   TS

18 April 1985

Dear Bill

Here it is at last. I'm not sure that I would have chosen this as the subject of my first communication to Tulli Maar. You remember, I think, that I confessed to you at an early stage that I was writing a piece for the *Birthday Book* about *Lord of the Flies*; and I said, of course, that I'd send a copy on to you. So here it is in at any rate a penultimate draft; and I've just heard from John Carey that it has his blessing. He has a few suggestions to make – e.g. a slightly fuller account – if I can remember anything more – about our first meeting; of the book's reception by reviewers; the number of foreign translations etc. etc. And I'll see, of course, what can be dug up here.

But – and do let me stress this as emphatically as possible – if there's anything you'd like me to change – and indeed if you'd like the essay to be dropped completely – please don't hesitate to let me know. I only agreed to do it on condition that it was seen and approved of by you.

I do hope that you and Ann are settling comfortably into Tulli Maar. Now that some real Spring weather is with us at last, it must be absolutely marvellous. France – where I spent ten days at Easter, partly in Normandy and partly in Paris – was wet, cold and windy but, as France always is, immensely enjoyable.

I imagine your garden is beginning to reveal its secrets. How easy will Ann find it to reconcile herself to rhododendrons and azaleas? Though I don't actually belong to it, I've sometimes felt some personal sympathy for the British Anti-Rhododendron Society. As I'm sure you know, it is a semi-secret organisation and the only obligation on each member is to destroy one rhododendron a year.

Much love to you both,
Charles Monteith

Monteith's essay is reprinted in the Appendix of this volume.

WG to Charles Monteith   TS

26(?) April 1985   [Headed Paper: Ebble Thatch (2)]

Dear Charles,

Thank you for your letter and enclosure. Alas I was wrong. Our address is TULLIMAAR, PERRANARWORTHAL, which as you see is all one word. I had a couple of hundred cards wrongly printed through sheer ignorance.

What a pity you didn't make your anti-rhododendron feelings known to Ann. She would have exercised her powers as party chairman and proposed you for membership instanter. Yes we do have them and they are awful. For one week they look like the house of the Lord and for the rest of the year like the tents of the ungodly – or do I mean it the other way round? A good question! You could indulge your lust for the destruction of the heart of darkness here to any excess because they have been let go for about thirty years, are mostly blind and very dense. Azaleas are not so bad and we have become the – custodians? – of an awesomely exotic collection. In addition we have primroses, periwinkles, violets, bluebells, pinkbells, wild garlic, magnolias, camelias a vast fern-leaved beech and many other responsibilities. Of course the flowers of all these will have disappeared by 1st May so Ann is rushing round the countryside from garden centre to garden centre buying huge stocks of decent God-fearing lime-tolerant flowers that come out during the summer. The soil here is like fruitcake and probably tastes much the same. It will be fun to find out what you think of it all when you come. At the moment when I suppose most people have the modesty to retire to a bedsit in Knightsbridge and Time-Sharing in

475

the Algarve we have bought this devastatingly beautiful house in the middle of a flowering wilderness. After a fortnight we are even more satisfied with our piece of inspired lunacy.

Of course a fortnight isn't very long. In the deep midwinter we may find we sing a different song. (Walter Pater would *never* have committed that rhyme.)

STRANGERS FROM WITHIN

Lord, Lord, it's a time capsule and you've dug it up from the foundations of the Laureate's monument. What interests me selfishly is the date – so the book was written in 1951 thus only just creeping into the second half of the century! It must have been the rounds for at least a year or more before you saw it. Did I ever tell you that Curtis Brown turned it down as Strangers, but asked obsequiously for my custom when it became Flies, they not knowing both books were the same?

I have to admit that the whole account has its painful side for me. I had fallen desperately sick psychosomatically as I now see. I knew there was something inside me – remember after one rejection, shouting furiously – 'It's Good! I know it's good!' It was a kind of delirium all bottled up in that pursed, bearded, well-conducted schoolmaster.

So.

Seen as objectively as I can, I believe you've written a marvellously accurate account of your hand in the book. I've thanked you as best I could, given you what I could – but not the Praise, Phoebus replied and touched my trembling ears. So now you must have it, out there in public, public praise which is your due.

Mind – I think you're a bit hard on my original opening and I don't entirely agree with you about Simon. He wasn't meant to be a good boy. He was meant to be a saint, prophet, Christ. They arn't good. Jean Vianney, QV and ghastly but Sainte Thérèse of Lisieux. It's a figure I've tried for again and again and I suppose Matty in Darkness Visible is as near as I shall ever get. Sainthood fascinates me for a number of sufficiently bitter reasons. Both Jean and Thérèse as children did exactly what proto-Simon did in the jungle.

A joke – somewhere in Barclay's (The Bank!) vaults is the original MS of Flies when it was not even Strangers – a sprawling ungainly mess with much that never got into the typescript you saw. I don't know whether to get it out and burn it or keep it in the belief that when my heirs and assigns sell it I shall be dead anyway and what does it matter?

This letter has gone *woeful* and I didn't mean it to. I read your article with much rueful enjoyment and now have remembered such things – forgive all this self-pity; and yes, you *may* end your article with my best after-dinner story.

Much love from us both and come down as soon as you can

Bill

PS I'm assuming I can keep this copy?

We have regency *urns*!

Golding carried on using the Ebble Thatch paper for a short time after the move to Cornwall.

'lime-tolerant flowers': this is probably a slip. Cornish soils are, generally speaking, acidic, as borne out by the flowers thriving at Tullimaar – rhododendron, azalea, camellia, and so on. Golding acknowledges that 'lime was one of the reasons we left Wiltshire' (J, 23 May 1986).

Golding gives his first impressions of Monteith's essay in his journal: 'Charles has sent through his factual account for the Birthday Book of how Flies got published and his part in it. It makes rueful reading for me who have taken the praise all these years. Indeed I might complain that he's "got the bridle and the curb all right but where's the bloody horse?"' (J, 25 April 1985).

'but not the Praise, Phoebus replied and touched my trembling ears': for earlier examples of Golding quoting these lines from John Milton's 'Lycidas', see his letter to du Sautoy on 23 November 1962 and his letter to Monteith on 9 January 1963.

Golding is mistaken about the year that he wrote *Lord of the Flies*, the manuscript of which ends by recording the precise moment of its completion: '1600 2nd October 1952'.

'Jean Vianney, QV and ghastly but Sainte Thérèse of Lisieux': Golding had read at least one biography of Jean Vianney, and in 1978 he visited Lisieux where he saw 'the Basilica of Ste Thérèse, her life and miracles in wax, her tomb in the Carmelite convent, and then her statue in the Cathedral. It was all too much' (J, 9 October 1978).

'proto-Simon': the typescript that Monteith saw has not survived, but in the earlier manuscript Simon takes himself off into the forest and there encounters an 'other person' (never named, but evidently a God- or Christ-figure) who 'among the multitudinous simplicity of his being – if being was the word – was merciful. [. . .] The implications of what he was allowed to know, filled Simon with wild delight.' The other person leads Simon in a kind of holy dance. The manuscript is preserved in the William Golding Literary Archive at the University of Exeter.

'Somewhere in Barclay's (The Bank!)': the parenthetical elaboration distinguishes Barclays Bank from Wilf Barclay, the protagonist of *The Paper Men*.

'my best after-dinner story'. This is the story about the great ball on the evening of the Nobel Prize presentation, when Golding was presented to the King of Sweden: '"It is a great pleasure to meet you, Mr Golding," he said. "I had to do *Lord of the Flies* at school."'

Charles Monteith to WG

TS

1 May 1985

I was very glad to get your letter and very glad to have had that conversation with you on the telephone. Of course I entirely see and understand and I'll be only too happy to do a bit of re-drafting. When I've done it I'll send the new version to you and once again I'd be immensely grateful if you'd be completely and absolutely frank with me about it. The more I think about Simon in particular – and since our conversation I've been thinking about him a lot – the more I think that, at any rate, I understand the problem he set. And your mention of Matty is immensely illuminating and helpful. Yes, of course, he's your other great 'numinous' creation. You'll forgive me I hope if – as I may – I pinch this idea, as I pinched your after-dinner story about the King of Sweden!

I'm looking forward immensely to seeing you both in Tullimaar. When I've looked up trains – and I'll also look up planes – I'll be in touch again.

Charles Monteith

Golding's explanation about Simon clearly informs Monteith's revised version of the essay: 'I do not, in fact, think that I fully understood the problem at the time and it is only in the light of Golding's other novels and later discussions with him that I see it more clearly now. Simon is not only a boy, a fully and totally human boy; he is one of those rare people who are in fact – it is impossible to avoid these imprecise and difficult words – "numinous" or "charismatic". Nathaniel in *Pincher Martin* and, most clearly of all, Matty in *Darkness Visible*, are later variations on the same mysterious theme.'

Charles Monteith to WG

TS

15 May 1985

Dear Bill

Here's the redraft of my piece about LORD OF THE FLIES and I would be immensely grateful if, once again, you write or telephone when you have read it to let me know if there are still things which I have got wrong or which you would like to see changed in any way. I have eliminated virtually everything I said about the 'atomic war' passage at the beginning – my memory about all this may very well have been totally at fault since it's well over 30 years since I read it; I've tried to make it clear that the book itself impressed me enormously from the time I first read it and that this admiration grew the better I got to know it; and as a result of your letter and the talk we had on the telephone I think that what I now say about Simon is more sensible and more accurate than what I'd said before. But do please let me know if you still think it needs some further change or alteration. And be as drastic as you like in your comments.

Incidentally I heard from John Carey this morning that he's just had a splendid piece, about 5,000 words, from John Bayley; and as I think you know he's already had a contribution which sounded fascinating from Ted Hughes.

I'm looking forward very much indeed to seeing TulliMaar and of course, even more, to seeing you and Ann again. As you know my train gets to Truro at 4 pm (in fact according to the time table, 3.55 pm, on June 4th). It's very good of you to say that you will meet me there.

'the "atomic war" passage': the manuscript begins with a description of the boys being evacuated out on the last aeroplane; had they been big enough to peer through the windows, they would have seen 'a purple, pustular fist over the horizon, where the bomb had dropped'.
    John Bayley's essay was titled 'The Impersonality of William Golding: Some Implications and Comparisons'; Ted Hughes's was 'Baboons and Neanderthals: A Rereading of *The Inheritors*'.

WG to Charles Monteith   TS MONTEITH

17(?) May 1985   TULLIMAAR, PERRANARWORTHAL,
                                  TRURO

Dear Charles,

This is to place on record my acceptance in full of your piece on STRANGERS FROM WITHIN. You've answered all my objections and at the same time kept your own opinion recorded and spared my blushes. I'm very grateful – yet another debt on top of many years of help I've had from my editor. A thousand thanks.

We look forward very much to having you down here, however sadly short the time you can spare us. I don't know whether there's any bit of Cornwall you havn't seen? Or perhaps you'd prefer a quiet sit round in these curious surroundings? We shall have a tree-surgeon later on and our three-fifths of a gardener is making a difference to the place but you'll still have the doubtful privilege of seeing it as time and the shoe-string living of our immediate predecessors have left it. Yesterday two old friends turned up for tea(!) from Salisbury but apart from them we have had no visitors except people like plumbers, electricians, carpenters and road-restorers: and an odd pair one of whom had a great uncle who used to live here. Living here seems to confer cachet. In my small experience people who have cachet also have bigger bills than hoi polloi so the sooner we get uncacheted the better. At least one – and that the most famous – of the people who lived here strove so hard for that same cachet she made the whole place ridiculous, as we shall demonstrate to you when you come. Mysterious isn't it? But you'll see –

      Love from us both and my grateful thanks once again
         Bill

The letter is written on Ebble Thatch (2) headed paper.

In his journal, Golding reports that 'Charles' amended write-up for the birthday book seems good to me. It describes the inadequacy of the book [*Lord of the Flies*] without making me blush for myself. [. . .] I think perhaps I should tell Charles that he contributed the "in medias res" approach and I leapt on that regarding it as an illumination. He said "after all you know, the people who are going to read this book will be intelligent." Perhaps I should put all this down on paper for him? After all, I owe him a lot' (J, 16 May 1985). The 'in medias res' approach must refer to Monteith's recommendation that the action of *Lord of the Flies* should start on the island, cutting the boys' evacuation and the air battle that take up the first few pages of the manuscript.

The most famous of Tullimaar's residents was Princess Marthe Bibescu (or Bibesco), the Romanian French writer and socialite. Golding refers to her commissioning of a plaque for the hall at Tullimaar which claims that General Eisenhower stayed in the house in 1944 while planning the Normandy invasion.

Charles Monteith to WG   TS

28(?) May 1985

Dear Bill

   Here's a photostat of your submission letter which we talked about on the telephone yesterday afternoon.

   Much looking forward to seeing you and Ann on 4 June.

   Charles Monteith

Monteith sent a photostat of Golding's cover letter of 14 September 1953 (the first letter in this edition) that had accompanied the typescript of 'Strangers from Within'. Having not seen it for more than thirty years, Golding describes his reaction in his journal: 'It is rather manly I think – implied you cant hurt me even if you refuse to publish my manuscript' (J, 29 May 1985).

Charles Monteith to WG   TS

30 May 1985

Dear Bill,

   Here's my re-draft of page one in which the only changes are, as you'll see, to the ends of the first two paragraphs in order to quote both your own covering letter and the ipsissima verba of that unbelievable note by our reader – her name, by the way, is or was Miss Perkins. Nobody here has the faintest idea whether she's alive or dead.

   Much looking forward to seeing you on Tuesday.

   Charles Monteith

'ipsissima verba': 'the precise words'. Polly Perkins was the freelance reader who wrote her judgement in green ink on the cover letter's top left-hand corner: 'Absurd & uninteresting fantasy [. . .]. Rubbish & dull. Pointless.'

WG to Charles Monteith   TS MONTEITH

10 June 1985   [Headed Paper: Ebble Thatch (2)]

                                                              Monday.

Dear Charles,

   A hasty note bashed out on this inscrutable machine immediately on receipt of your letter. It was lovely to have you here and extra-lovely to hear how much you like the place. It made us feel we were neither mad nor rational when we bought it but inspired. Yes of course come again as soon as you like.

Now for the point of the haste. We'd love to have you in a menage a trois once again! How can we help? It seems to me that with your long acquaintance with such legendary figures as Eliot and Auden to say nothing of Durrell and save the mark, you are in a strong position to be a candidate for talking, lecturing and answering intimate, not to say embarrassing questions! The only problem I see over this is in persuading Greg Gatenby of this great truth. You may have taken a note but he is (in case you havn't) at the Cambridge Poetry Festival from June 14–16th and in London C/O the British Council meanwhile. Can I do anything? If I can, ring me here to save time and I'll lay my neck on the block if necessary. I need the phone call because there's so little time left.

Ann joins with me in what I've written. You'll be interested to hear that we went back to Trerice a couple of days ago, found that the 'Tree Mallow' (my mistake) is of course an abutilon and managed to contact the gardener who sold us a slightly darker specimen together with a few other plants.

Today we identified a pleasant country pub with food and real beer – it's in Frogpool!

Love from us both – anyway we'd love to have you for yourself lecture or no lecture

In haste

Bill

Greg Gatenby, the Founding Director of the International Festival of Authors in Toronto, had invited Golding to Canada and arranged an itinerary of readings and lectures across the country. Golding and Ann flew out to Montreal on 14 October. The campaign to include Monteith must have been successful because he joined them a few days later.

'save the mark': a mild and usually ironic oath to ward off an evil omen. Here it is presumably warding off a mention of Golding's own name.

Golding explains the muddle over tree mallow and abutilon in his journal: 'We went out looking for what I had called a Tree Mallow. It was, as I think both Ann and Charles knew, an Abutylon. We went to two garden centres and did not get what we wanted and finished up all over again at Trerice, where we got a somewhat darker abutylon, an orange honeysuckle a geranium and two fuchsias' (J, 6 June 1985). Trerice is a National Trust Tudor manor house a mile or two south of Newquay.

The pub in Frogpool, about a mile from Perranarworthal, is the Cornish Arms.

WG to Rosemary Goad   MS

4 August 1985   Tullimaar, Perranarworthal, Truro

Dear Rosemary,

Thank you for your letter. I'm afraid my opinion hasn't changed over dramatisation of *Lord of the Flies*. A camera can move in and so magnify them till they are equated with adults. On the stage they remain a mob of unruly kids.

I'm glad we are of a good report! Certainly people seem to like the place. It would be fun to show you the house and grounds. Are you going to be in these parts? Ann says if you are touring – friend (Eliza?) – and all we sh'd be happy to put you up for a day or two. The area is mildly interesting and really somehow the whole Cornish holiday thing doesn't seem to touch us here.

> Ever
> Bill Golding

The letter is written on Ebble Thatch (2) headed paper. Golding has crossed through the old Ebble Thatch header.

Goad had forwarded to Golding yet another unsolicited dramatisation of *Lord of the Flies* and, separately, reported having heard 'glowing reports' of the new house and garden.

WG to John Bodley   PC

3(?) October 1985   Tullimaar, Perranarworthal, Truro

Dear John,

My God yes. What a book. If we buy a boat down here we'll use it as an anchor – if not build it into the rockery.

Anyway thanks ruefully much

> Bill.

In preparation for their imminent trip to Canada, John Bodley had sent the Goldings a copy of *The Oxford Companion to Canadian Literature* (1983), edited by Eugene Benson and William Toye. Golding confessed in his journal, 'I dont suppose either of us will look at it' (J, 3 October 1985).

1986

The Goldings start French conversation classes in January and are promoted to the advanced French group in August. This is one manifestation of a busy social life in Cornwall, which incorporates new friends as different from each other as A. L. Rowse and Pete Townshend. There is the usual family holiday to Brittany in the summer. On his return to Tullimaar, Golding adds the finishing touches to *Close Quarters* and starts work almost immediately on the third volume of his sea trilogy. *William Golding: The Man and his Books*, edited by John Carey, is published in September as a tribute on Golding's seventy-fifth birthday; it contains contributions from friends and fellow writers, including Monteith, Peter Green, Seamus Heaney, Ted Hughes and Ian McEwan.

WG to Charles Monteith   TS MONTEITH

(?) January 1986   [Headed Paper: Tullimaar]

Dear Charles

I ought to have written to you, I suppose, a good time ago; but did'nt really know what to say. It's so facile to come offering ignorant sympathy and wearing hobnailed boots. We never knew or met Phillip Larkin so that it seemed an impertinence to say anything about what must be a great grief to you. All I can say, then is that we are truly sorry that immediately after our combined adventure you found your mixed satisfaction, exhilaration and relief suddenly pushed into the background and a grim, wearying, inevitable desolation taking its place.

Enough of clumsiness! What of life down here? Well – the other day we had Raleigh Trevelyan and Raúl, Colin and Joy Wilson, the Evanses and Leslie Rowse to lunch and you were unanimously remembered with affection. Sorry – I can't answer for Colin who must be the only person in England you don't know. Well, there he was, taking an unaccustomed lunch and by the waste of a couple of hours, presumably set back at least one volume and probably many more. Leslie was in splendid form and even conducted a party round the house, expatiating as he went. We are really growing fond of him.

When shall we have you here? Spring is probably our best time when our flowers have to be seen to be believed. William is working wonders among the rhodos (the right, rather contemptuous name for them) and we have had a few trees which were dying removed by proper tree surgeons; and feel that we are doing right by the ESTATE. Perhaps you will like (when you come) to be taken round places you remember to see if they are still there.

We are gradually recovering from Canada. Apparently we flew out of Victoria half an hour before the great blizzard struck and shut the continent or at least the top half of it down. I wonder if we would all three have found – say – Siberia a better bet? Ann had blood-pressure and a frightening nose bleed. I acquired gout of all things – officially! It's the result I suppose of giving up alcohol. The temptation to undertake the logical cure is severe. The local doctor took one look at me wearing bedroom slippers and said 'gout'. Apparently it's one of those recognised symptoms, like the 'petit papier' for hypochondria. However, the pills I have to take seem to work; and painful feet encourage me to get back onto a horse or into a boat except that both Ann and I are now getting so forgetful that anything with a degree of physical risk attached is getting what one might call questionable. Have I told you how bad my memory is getting?

Writing. I have in prospect the further adventures of young Mr Talbot and quite a lot of them written but need a push to complete the job. I am in process of girding up my loins – well I'm not Lawrence and don't write with my loins but something a bit higher up. Well then, I am in process of girding up my surloins, for the plunge.

Much love from us both.
    Bill

Golding's new headed paper for Tullimaar mistakenly divides 'Perranarworthal' into three words:

Tullimaar
Perran Ar Worthal
Truro
Cornwall. TR3 7NT

Philip Larkin died on 2 December. Monteith had flown back to England from his 'combined adventure' with the Goldings in Canada on 17 November.

Colin Wilson was the prolific author of about thirty novels and a hundred works of non-fiction, hence Golding's crack about his having wasted the opportunity of writing another volume by spending two hours over lunch.

The Evanses – Matthew and his wife Liz – had recently bought a house on the Roseland Peninsula.

William: the gardener at Tullimaar.

'one of those recognised symptoms, like the "petit papier" for hypochondria': *la maladie du petit papier* is the French term diagnosing a patient who provides a written list of symptoms. It is strongly associated with hypochondria.

'the further adventures of young Mr Talbot': the novel published in 1987 as *Close Quarters*, the second instalment of Golding's sea trilogy.

Charles Monteith to WG   TS

15 January 1986

I did indeed hear about your lunch party, not only from Matthew but also from Raleigh and Raul. But not yet from Leslie Rowse! They all seem to have enjoyed it immensely.

Yes please, I'd love to come down and stay in spring when your flowers are at their best. Do please keep me posted about this and suggest suitable dates.

I can't tell you how much I admire your resolution about alcohol. My own annual abstention starts on Ash Wednesday – Easter and therfore Lent is appallingly early this year – but I always have the marvellous prospect of opening a particularly good bottle of wine on Easter Sunday. (I don't remember how many years I've stuck to this by now, but it must be well over ten and I've acquired a certain number of followers who imitate me – which helps to swell my spiritual pride).

Of course you can imagine how delighted I am to know that the novel's under weigh.

It is indeed very sad about Philip. If by any remote chance you and Ann should be in London on Friday 14 February do come to the Memorial Service in the Abbey at 12 noon (if you are able to come let me know as far in advance as you can and I'll make sure you get tickets). There'll be no address but quite a lot of poetry and jazz.

Much love to you and Ann.

Charles

WG to Charles Monteith   TS

20 June 1986   [Headed Paper: Tullimaar]

Dear Charles,

If you find this MS a bit much and decline to plough through it I shall understand – and might well applaud, since I'm very much aware of what a mess it is. If on the other hand you are willing to do a majestic job – either or: no, no Mr Golding a very pretty concept but you must not call it a novel; I'd be glad. I can even put my finger on the two principal questions which need to be decided.

(1) Is the material of a novel here?

(2) If the answer to that is 'yes' – to whom is Talbot writing? For the rather entertaining pose of the first volume was the result of Talbot projecting himself as he hoped his god father would see him, intelligent, responsible, man of the world and all that and fundamentally *political*. But if he is really writing a journal in the sense that I keep mine, then it wont be a pose and the conscious wit and pose will go – as it has done. *If* he is writing to a girl, well it's different again. It's a big decision if it has to be made. Does it have to be made? Might we divide things up? A letter to his mother perhaps, one to his god father – and so on; so that the whole thing would become a slice of The Talbot Papers, shades of Wilfred Barclay whom you may have forgotten!

(3) Who is the hero, or centre piece? The focus seems to shift from one person to another. Does that matter? I hope that over all the focus focusses more and more finely on the ship.

So. We both look forward to seeing you down here when you can manage it – though the weather remains unpleasant. Could you waft the MS back first if (as I think you said) you wont be down until some time in July? A confused letter. Well – I *am* confused and perhaps ought to retire. You can tell me what it feels like.

The trouble with writing of course is that you can't tell whether you've retired or not. I suppose one dribbles on into drivel and ends by writing saliva.

ever

Bill

What a nauseating letter! Of *course* you'll plough through it – you always have! We can cut it down by a quarter anyway. What I need is an enforced period away from it!

Yesterday I shot a 'rhodo' as we call them locally in our vulgar way: but rescued a pretty flowering shrub from under it which we cant name. It has hanging red bells and no, it isnt a fuchsia!

ever.

There is a line running from 'Bill' down around the text in the left margin. It ends under the final 'ever', possibly indicating that the word 'Bill' needs to be moved to there. The last section, beginning 'What a nauseating letter!', has been added in pen.

As Golding's own hesitation suggests, the question of who was now responsible for editing his novels was only informally settled. On 8 April, Golding and Ann had dined at the Groucho with various Faber bigwigs to celebrate Monteith's retirement (more precisely, his retirement from semi-retirement). Golding reports in his journal that 'he is keeping me on, however, and all I do is send manuscripts to him via Matthew' (J, 8 April 1986).

WG to John Bodley   TS

24 June 1986   [Headed Paper: Tullimaar]

Dear John,

Thanks for your letter. Herewith information to be passed to the French translator of An Egyptian Journal.

(1). Ceramicus is a district of Athens. It's where the potters used to work, hence the name. An alternative spelling, which would be a direct transliteration from the Greek, would be Kerameikos, but either will do.

(2) Cocking-troop is more complex. When the Angles, Saxons and Jutes invaded the British Isles after the Roman Legions were withdrawn they gave various names to Roman sites. Some, were no more than heaps of shards or 'crocks' which are fragments of crockery. Thorp is – Jutish I think – for an inhabited place, a ham, ton, or what have you. So a place with heaps of crocks (a ceramicus in fact) they called a crocking thorp; which in our ignorant way we have turned into Cocking-Troop. The same phenomenon will have occurred in France and affected place names. A local archaeologist or historian could probably provide French examples.

      Voila, M. Bodley!
   Avec mes sentiments les plus respectueux –
      Bill

The French translator was Marie-Lise Marlière. Her enquiry, conveyed via John Bodley, refers to a passage in chapter 9 of An Egyptian Journal in which Golding visits the site of a huge kiln: 'We saw the ancient hill constructed of pot fragments, so that remembering "Cocking-troop" and "Ceramicus" I asked if it had a special name but as usual, Arabic was not all that forthcoming. It was called in Arabic "The Heap".'

WG to Charles Monteith

MS

7 July 1986   [Headed Paper: Tullimaar]

Dear Charles,

Herewith a suggested postscriptum. Perhaps you c'd add it to your copy of

The
Entertainment.

and even ponder a bit. By the way of course the title is a working thing and dull.

> ever
> Bill

In his journal entry for 25 June, Golding reports that 'Charles rang this morning. He thinks the MS is frightfully good but feels left up in the air! So we have to provide some sort of a coda to assure the reader that everybody makes out, though I'm sure I dont know how to do it' (J, 25 June 1986). The new 'postscriptum' is the solution because it establishes a crucial fact about Edmund Talbot's journey to Australia: 'I have openly said or allowed Edmund to say that he survived' (J, 6 July 1986). This was still not the final version: Golding rewrote the postscript in November.

A note at the bottom of this letter, added in pen by Rosemary Goad and dated '18/7/86', records that the novel's working title is being replaced at Monteith's suggestion: '"Close Quarters" (?) Sugg'd by C.M. to W.G. who apparently likes it.'

Charles Monteith to Ann and WG

MS GOLDING

17 July 1986

Dear Ann and Bill,

What an absolutely splendid three days in Cornwall. I'm tremendously grateful for your hospitality. Tullimaar is not only a very beautiful house, it's an immensely nice, welcoming, friendly house – exactly the right house for its owners. And a wonderful house for its guests.

By a coincidence I found a letter from David Treffry waiting for me when I got back last night. He hopes to get to Cornwall sometime next month but it's going to take him some time to move in, get the old house disposed of & all that. So my Fowey visit will probably be in mid or late October, which in Cornwall should be marvellous. So we'll meet again in the Duchy then tho' in London of course long before.

Tomorrow morning I'll be seeing John Bodley & briefing him about the novel. So you'll certainly be hearing from him very shortly.

With, again, my warmest thanks & best love,
Charles.

Monteith stayed at Tullimaar from 14 to 16 July. The letter is on headed paper: 10 WELLINGTON ROAD NW8 9SP.

David Treffry was an old friend of Monteith. After a distinguished career as a colonial servant and international financier, he settled in his family home: Place House in Fowey. Golding met him in 1986 and they became friends.

WG to John Bodley   TS

24 September 1986

Dear John,

Many thanks for your work on the party – we had the whale of a time!

The monstrous Clarence (Jerry) Fry (whom you will have forgotten) has returned to the attack! As you will see from the enclosures, he is beginning to shout aloud to the press who are helping him to make a fool of himself. I don't propose to answer him: but could you add the enclosures to the file?

Perhaps one of your little girls could put them on the copying machine and send me the result? I dont see how he can damage me: but he is moving to the slimey as well as silly so a record ought to be kept.

Novelists can't invent real people! They havn't a hope in competition with the Almighty or perhaps the All-lowest.

Ever
Bill

The header gives Faber's address rather than Golding's own:

c/o Faber and Faber Ltd.
3 Queen Square
London WC1N 3AU

The party the previous week had celebrated Golding's seventy-fifth birthday.

For Clarence Fry, see the letter to Bodley dated 13 November 1984. Fry's latest letter to Golding had included – and apologised for – an article in a local newspaper beginning 'Budding author Clarence Fry is still smarting after an unexpected snub from Nobel Prizewinner, and old school pal William Golding'. Fry is quoted as stating that his manuscript, now called 'Girl of the Thighs', is in some ways superior to *Lord of the Flies*.

WG to John Bodley   TS

5 November 1986   [Headed Paper: Tullimaar]

Dear John,

Herewith what is now THE MASTER COPY of volume two – CLOSE QUARTERS!.

I've had to retype about a dozen pages, including the POST SCRIPTUM. Could you send the MS round to Charles's new address if he is there? Age is making me very anxious and I can imagine the whole thing going missing so that I have to do it all again.

I've tidied up the queries. The art work for the cover might be a bit mucked up by my present realisation that only *some* ships had one great stern lantern – the most common arrangement was sometimes two lanterns, one at each after corner of the quarterdeck or poop. But let's not drive ourselves into a decline worrying.

I'm including a note for Charles to go with this MS. It's a bit difficult for now he is retired I don't know whether or no he is willing to go all the way with the MS or whether his first reading was all he wanted to do. However, I shall be – we will be – spending next week (9th to the 15th November) in London and may well see him then.

    Yours ever

        Bill

PS What I *meant* to say – silly old me! – is that all copies must now be taken from this MS as it differs from the earlier one in a number of ways

        Bill.

Monteith read this version and wrote to Bodley from All Souls on 9 November with his verdict that it was 'splendid'. He reported having brought to Golding's attention only two or three minor points, among them the anachronism that at one stage Talbot seems to quote Kipling. According to Golding's journal entry for 7 November, Bodley also read the manuscript 'and did a "how to keep authors happy in one short lesson", he thinks it's all marvellous!' (J, 7 November 1986).

Golding had initially proposed that the cover should depict the stern of an eighteenth-century wooden warship with two or three great lanterns. Later, he elaborated that the artist (Paul Hogarth) should think of the stern lantern of HMS *Victory*. The final cover image depicts – as Golding puts it – 'one great stern lantern'.

The Goldings did visit Monteith in his new flat in Randolph Avenue, and Golding was suitably impressed: 'He has a sitting room, small dining room, big kitchen, bath, loo, two quite big bedrooms – and projecting from the rear of the house a well built Victorian style conservatory! Really it is the height of luxury' (J, 11 November 1986).

1987

In January, the Goldings set off for a two-month lecture tour of India. On their return, Golding continues work on the final volume of the sea trilogy and completes the second draft by the summer. *Close Quarters* is published in June to reviews so overwhelmingly positive that Golding is prepared to read them himself. After the family holiday in Brittany, he finishes a third – but still not final – draft in November. Golding is delighted when Judy's first novel is accepted by Duckworth, but not all the news is good: David is again struggling with his mental health.

WG to John Bodley   MS

6 January 1987   [Headed Paper: Tullimaar]

Dear John,

Herewith the proofs. I must apologise for the mess. My hand does not seem as steady as it was when I was a lad of seventy four.

     Ever
      Bill

The proofs were for *Close Quarters*.

John Bodley to WG   TS

24 April 1987

Dear Bill,

Matthew has just been in my room crowing that he has had in his hands the third volume of *Talbot's Journal*. I'm green with envy. He also said that you would like to see how Durrell's four-hander looks in one volume. Perhaps you would like your omnibus done on India paper . . .

     Yours

Evans and Faber's publicity director, Joanna Mackle, had turned up on 21 April for lunch and a business meeting with Golding at Tullimaar. It must have been there that Evans held a draft of the third (and still unnamed) book in the sea trilogy.

Even before completing the novel that became *Fire Down Below*, Golding seems to have been planning the publication of the sea trilogy in a single volume – a project for which Lawrence Durrell's *Alexandria Quartet* (1962) served as touchstone.

WG to Matthew Evans   MS

14 June 1987

Dear Matthew,

It may have been the general blueness of the election charts which overflowed into every bosom left of centre and left us all well-nigh wordless on parting. Alternatively it may have been the booze. In either case I am sending our belated thanks, not just to the chairman of F&F for our nostalgic visit to Browns: but to you, for conveying us about so devotedly. I dont know why you do it and am reduced to crediting you with a good nature with which you would not credit yourself! Grateful thanks –

The notices keep on being good – yesterdays Guardian was fine and included a portrait of yours truly, to go into my rogues gallery.

Love and kisses also to Liz. I can't think how the two of you manage to withstand the high life.

    Bill

The general election on 11 June resulted in another comfortable majority for Margaret Thatcher's Conservatives, albeit twenty-one seats down on the landslide of 1983. Golding's evening had begun with a party at Faber to celebrate the publication of *Close Quarters*, followed by dinner at his usual London hotel (Brown's in Mayfair), and afterwards an election party at Melvyn Bragg's home. A Labour voter all his life, Golding had already predicted in his journal that the latter would be 'a wake rather than a party' (J, 11 June 1987).

Close Quarters had been published on 8 June in an edition of just over 41,000 copies. Reviewing it in the *Guardian* on 12 June, Ronald Blythe argued that 'Golding's trilogy is turning out to be a great sentimental journey of the naval kind'. The review was accompanied by a large cartoon of Golding by David Smith.

Charles Monteith to Ann and WG MS GOLDING

29 July 1987   [Headed Paper: Randolph Avenue]

Dear Bill & Ann,

I enjoyed my stay in Tullimaar so much that I simply don't know how to begin thanking you for it. It's rare for any house to combine so much beauty with so much space & comfort as Tullimaar does; the garden (or gardens) already a notable triumph of order, reason & beauty over blind Nature; & the meals, the wine (a lot of it, I fear) & the expeditions, especially Trengwainton, all superb. Thank you very much. I did enjoy being with you both.

I do hope the Brittany holiday is a great success – I'm sure it will be – & of course I'm looking forward more than I can say to the final version of the novel.

Finis, I've no doubt, coronabit opus. (Hope I've got that right.)

Much love,   Charles.

The printed header for Monteith's new home reads:

FLAT G 38 RANDOLPH AVENUE

W9 1BE

Telephone 01289 2276

Trengwainton Gardens, owned by the National Trust, is a mile or so from Penzance. Monteith stayed with the Goldings for four days from 22 July, and they visited Trengwainton together on the 24th.

The Goldings spent August in Brittany.

'Finis [. . .] coronabit opus': 'the end will crown the work'. The phrase normally occurs in the present tense ('coronat') and is attributed to Ovid. Monteith is referring to volume three of the sea trilogy, *Fire Down Below*, which Golding was writing at the time.

Charles Monteith to WG MS GOLDING

12 October 1987   [Headed Paper: Randolph Avenue]

Dear Bill,

I've just got my All Souls 'fixture card' for this term & I see there's to be a Chichele Dinner on Saturday, Dec. 5th. Is there any chance of persuading you to come to it? It's a long way from Cornwall, I know, but if you could make it I'd be immensely pleased.

Alas, I'm only allowed one guest so I can't invite Ann as well; but if

495

she were to come with you to Oxford I'd be delighted if both of you could have lunch with me next day (Sunday, Dec. 6th)? Perhaps it could be fitted in with a last-minute Christmas shopping trip to London?

I'll not pester you with enquiries about the new novel; but I think you said you hoped to have it ready by the end of the year. I'm *much* looking forward to reading it.

Love to you & to Ann.   Charles.

Charles Monteith to WG MS GOLDING

23 October 1987   [Headed Paper: Randolph Avenue]

Dear Bill,

Your letter arrived this morning as you predicted it probably would when we talked last night on the telephone. I'm most terribly sorry to hear that David's going through a bad patch. It's bound to be the most appalling worry & you & Ann have all my sympathy.

Apart from that – & all the discomforts of winter travel – an Oxford visit in the Spring or early Summer would be much more enjoyable & I promise to renew the invitation then,

Love to you both.
Charles

There is no trace of the letter to which Monteith is replying.

WG to John Bodley MS

12 December 1987   [Headed Paper: Tullimaar]

Dear John,

Thank you for your letter. Golly, I didn't know *volume III* was causing such a stir.

To repeat what I said to Charles the other day: I hope to get volume III finished by the end of 87. However I have to own there's more to do to this third draft than I'd thought. Ann read it word by word and we agree in our fault-finding by about ninety per cent. Slightly less than half needs skimming. The lot totals 75–80,000, so I can if necessary ditch 15–20,000. The second half and rather more is OK. When the skimming is done I'll try it on Charles for size.

① I havn't a title – or rather I have too many.

UTMOST DESPATCH. (Charles liked that though it isn't very applicable to the text – but what the hell?)

SALT WATER SOAP. (My idea – tongue only a little way in cheek.)

THE BEST OF FRIENDS. (A bit dull, but with a certain relevance.)

② I certainly think next autumn is on: tho' it w'd be good to know the absolute, absolute, absolute last date for delivery of MS in that case. After all, with luck the main work is done. Of course that has a drawback in a way since what's left is dull work – cutting – and needs something inspirational, like for example, money. But I go on.

③ Advance blurb? I havn't thought – 'Mr Talbot makes new friends and enemies, becomes even more closely acquainted with water – celebrates another *rite* and becomes an involuntary disciple of Aesculapius.'

Not very good I'm afraid. Could you use your advanced technology to give Charles a copy of this and then drop it down to Matthew in his foxhole?

> Ever
>
> Bill

PS If I died tomorrow, a competent editor could cut VOLUME THREE out of this MS I – or rather we – am, are, working on

> B

Golding noted in his journal the previous day that Ann 'thinks the second part of the book is good but the first unauthoritative. I'm sorry to say she confirms my worst suspicions. It means a lot more work – but at least the book can be rescued and the work will be negative, that is, cutting rather than "creating"' (J, 11 December 1987).

Aesculapius: the Greek god of medicine, here spelt the Roman way.

1988

The Goldings' advancing years – and Ann's regular bouts of ill health – do little to diminish their love of travel. In January, they attend a conference of Nobel laureates in Paris, before setting off at the end of the month on a fortnight's trip to Singapore and Malaysia. Back in Paris in April, Golding lectures at the Sorbonne, then Hamburg a week later, Spain in September and Japan in November. August is devoted to the annual family holiday in France. Amidst all these journeys, Golding completes a final draft of *Fire Down Below*. In June, he hears that he has been awarded a knighthood: he and Ann are now Sir William and Lady Golding.

WG to Charles Monteith

TS MONTEITH

1 January 1988   [Headed Paper: Tullimaar]

Dear Charles,

A happy new year to you from the milling throngs of Tullimaar wherever you are, England, Ireland, All Souls (a separate country) or just your own delightful flat!

As for me, I come like a *ghost to trouble joy*, as you will have guessed from the weight of the package. It is *a* MS rather than what it ought to be which is *the* MS. The fact is I have reached a point where I can't at the moment improve this load of cod's wallop. It is as far as I can see publishable in the last resort. But I dont know if it's too long or too short – if dull, where it's dull – if muddled – if in the last resort it's worthless! You won't believe the contrivances I've been at even to get this far.

Are you unretired enough to have a look? I'm afraid the chances of publishing the thing in the summer are off and the possibility of doing so in the autumn slight. It looks like early 89, curse it. I havn't even found a decent title.

Anyway, here it is.
                    Bill

'I come like a *ghost to trouble joy*': Golding quotes from Alfred Tennyson's 'The Lotos-Eaters', at the point when the mariners who have eaten the lotos find reasons for abandoning the world and never returning: 'For surely now our household hearths are cold, / Our sons inherit us: our looks are strange: / And we should come like ghosts to trouble joy' (117–19).

This was the fourth draft of what became *Fire Down Below*, provisionally titled 'The Best of Friends'. On New Year's Eve, Golding writes in his journal that 'I am getting to a kind of shuddering distaste for this draft of the book. I feel incompetent' (J, 31 December 1987).

Charles Monteith to Ann and WG MS GOLDING

13 January 1988 [Headed Paper: Randolph Avenue]

Dear Bill & Ann,

Many, many thanks again for an immensely enjoyable visit to Tullimaar. It was all very happy: the meals, the conversations, the garden, the greenhouse, those enviably superb orchids & there was even something authentically & typically Cornish – or Western – about the rainy drives to & from Tregenna Castle. Most important of all, I felt that our talks about *Fire Down Below* were useful – or I hope they were – that the last volume of the great trilogy is settling triumphantly down into its final shape.

The journey back to London was comfortable & uneventful; & the sandwiches & carrot wine provided by Lord Sieff – that great & good man – were very sustaining.

I do hope the Paris junketings go well; & I'm sure that you'll have a marvellous time in Singapore & KL (as I'm told it's always referred to by Old Malaysian Hands). I long to hear all about it when you get back.

Many thanks again,
Love,
Charles.

PS: –

A tentative idea that has occurred to me about the *Epilogue* (or whatever.)

Talbot, thirty years or so on & by now, say, a Minister of State (First Lord??) rereads his journals. He adds a shortish postscript – Benét & his bridge (if bridge it be), the Prettimans & the Ideal City etc. It could perhaps be sparked off, (as I think I may have suggested) by a chance meeting with Benét – perhaps sitting side by side at a City livery dinner. And then, that night, he has *The Dream*.

Monteith visited the Goldings from 8 to 10 January. They had lunch together on the 9th at the Tregenna Castle Hotel in St Ives.

This is the first time that the title *Fire Down Below* has been used. Although Golding's own suggestion, it does not appear in his journal until 1 March.

'Lord Sieff': Marcus Sieff, chairman of Marks & Spencer (where Monteith must have bought his sandwiches and carrot wine).

The Goldings went to a conference of Nobel laureates in Paris on 17 January. At the end of the month, they flew to Singapore on a tour sponsored by the British Council, then on to Malaysia, and were back in Tullimaar on 14 February. 'KL' is Kuala Lumpur, the capital of Malaysia.

Golding follows the outline of Monteith's suggestion about the epilogue but not the detail. In the published version of *Fire Down Below*, Talbot is glimpsed, many years after his journey, working at the Foreign Office and enjoying a glittering career. He receives a letter from Oldmeadow and resolves *not* to reread his journals but casts his mind back over all the characters described during his voyage to Australia. That night he has '*The Dream*' that brings the sea trilogy to a close.

Charles Monteith to WG MS GOLDING

24 March 1988   [Headed Paper: Randolph Avenue]

Dear Bill,

Here's a draft blurb for *Fire Down Below* – very short & 'unspecific' about details I'm afraid but I thought that would be better than an attempt at a précis. But if you don't agree *please* don't hesitate to say so – or to make any changes or alterations that you'd like.

I do hope that Ann's 'flu has at last disappeared. All my sympathies are with her for I caught the same, or a very similar, bug myself & it took me a fortnight to get over it. Indeed I'm just beginning to feel normal & reasonably cheerful again.

Isn't it lovely to have the Spring starting?

> Love to you both,
> Charles.

WG to Charles Monteith TS MONTEITH

30 March 1988   [Headed Paper: Tullimaar]

> thirtieth I thiujnk.

Dear Charles

Thanks for your letter and enc. We have joined the reciprocal club! You have edited and improved my MSS. Now I am returning the compliment.

This typewriter has a mind of its own. Where I meant 'females of one kind or another' it wrote 'females of one kink or another.' It's like being led by rime.

The book is taking a weary time and seems to get worse rather than better. At least I think a few corners have ironed themselves out.

Do you remember CHU CHIN CHOW and the Cobbler's Song? 'I cobble all night and I cobble all day.' That's what I feel like and would I were a shepherd and kept sheep. Have you read THE FATAL SHORE? I find it helpful. If you haven't, *do* look at a tear jerker to end all tear jerkers on pages 601/602. But you have to be strong to read it and preferably in the early morning. I read it in bed and burst into tears.

'The boy has far more sensibility than he knows.'

> Ever
> Bill

Golding was 'returning the compliment' by revising the blurb for *Fire Down Below* that Monteith had written: 'I've spent the morning on the manuscript and got somewhere. I've also sent off a blurb, an emended version of the one that Charles thought up' (J, 31 March 1988).

Chu Chin Chow (1916) is a musical comedy by Oscar Asche; 'The Cobbler's Song' appears in Act 2. Golding had been reminiscing in his journal: 'Work all day "I cobble all night and cobble all day" as I think the cobbler says in Chu Chin Chow, which I saw with my mother when I was as small a boy as you could get into a theatre – a moonlit scene. I was very impressed to see moonlight on the stage. Was it at Swindon? Or Newquay? Or Truro? Or Falmouth? I remember a long journey to get there and back' (J, 15 January 1988).

The previous January, Golding had bought a copy of Robert Hughes's *The Fatal Shore* for information about the England to Australia route in 1814; he was writing *Fire Down Below*, in which the ship finally reaches Australia.

'The boy has far more sensibility than he knows': Golding quotes from his own novel, *Close Quarters*. Talbot faints after witnessing a suicide. Sometime later, as he comes round, he hears Miss Granham's voice: 'Poor boy. He has far more sensibility than he knows.'

Charles Monteith to WG   MS GOLDING

8 April 1988   [Headed Paper: Randolph Avenue]

Dear Bill,

Very many thanks for your letter and (*much* improved) blurb which I found on my return from France yesterday evening. I'll pass the blurb on to John Bodley today.

I'm going to cut out my phrase (which I was rather pleased with) about a 'roman fleuve'. 'Fleuve' is a *river*; and, according to my French dictionary (Penguin. v. good) there isn't, as I'd hoped, a verb 'fleuver' meaning 'to flow'.   Alas.

Much looking forward to reading the final version of the novel when you finally top it out.

> Lots of love to you both,
> *Charles.*

WG to John Bodley MS

11 April 1988   [Headed Paper: Tullimaar]

Dear John,

Are you able to square yr conscience with helping to maintain my low profile?

You see from the enclosed document that there is a lit: festival rising like a genie just over the garden wall – ours, I mean!

The enclosed letter explains that I shall be *out of the county during that week*.

Could you bear to slip it in with Fabers' post? If it's postmarked Cornwall they'll come straight over the garden wall –

Sorry to be paranoid.

> ever
> Bill

PS The enclosed is a joyous read otherwise

> yrs. Literato

Golding had been invited to participate in 'the first International Literature Festival to be held in Cornwall'.

Charles Monteith to WG MS GOLDING

29 April 1988   [Headed Paper: Randolph Avenue]

Dear Bill,

Here's an official invitation card to the Chichele Dinner on 14 May. No need to reply to it – I've already said you'd be coming.

I'm *very* much looking forward to seeing you & Ann in Oxford then. On Sunday 15th I'll try to arrange a small lunch – tho' it won't, I fear, be in College since the servants can't cope with private entertaining on the day after any big 'do'. They're too busy clearing up the debris of the night before.

(I'll also enclose a list of new Phalaenopses sent to me the other day. One or two of them seem to me to verge on the vulgar – though perhaps, when it comes to orchids, thin-blooded good taste should be discarded at once.)

> Love to you both,
> *Charles*

'Phalaenopses' are moth orchids. See Golding's letter to Monteith of 4 May for an acknowledgement of the difficulty of pluralising 'Phalaenopsis'.

WG to Charles Monteith

MS MONTEITH

4 May 1988   [Headed Paper: Tullimaar]

Dear Charles,

Thanks for the official invitation – how *nice* to be able to ignore one! – we are much looking forward to our Oxford visit, I, sitting above the Chichele salt! Did you see the Cellini 'Salt' on *Connoisseur* last night? Marvellous. No home sh'd be without one.

The revolt of All Souls' servants gives us the opportunity of dining – or lunching *you* in Oxford! Please be our guest –

Only we dont know the present chefs – what Classical chaps w'd call 'οἳ νῦν –' or what eateries are in and deservedly so. Could you bear therefore to book us a table at your favourite place and consider yourself a guest there? Or is that too much to ask? *Yes!* But please do it if you can.

Judy's Book is out and we are biting our nails waiting for reviews which have not yet appeared. What are Duckworth *doing*?

The catalogue is fun. Nothing can outdo Mad Hatter x Mad Lips x Mouchette. It must be what a pornographer keeps in his bedside commode, or somewhere. The plural of phalaenopsis is a problem.

– MS of *Fire Down Below* not yet returned – a very restful situation

> Ever
> Bill

The Goldings were in Oxford from 13 to 16 May, and dined with Monteith at Le Petit Blanc on the 14th. The usual one-guest rule meant that Golding attended the Chichele Dinner with Monteith but without Ann at All Souls on the 13th.

Connoisseur was a BBC2 arts quiz presented by Bamber Gascoigne. Its latest episode must have featured the Cellini Salt Cellar, a gold cellar lavishly designed and sculpted by Benvenuto Cellini for Francis I of France in 1543.

'οἵ νῦν': the people of today (ancient Greek). There is a superfluous diacritic on the iota (ί).

Judy's novel *Moving Pictures*, written under her married name Judy Carver, had been published by Duckworth the previous week.

'Mad Hatter x Mad Lips x Mouchette': cultivars of *Cymbidium* orchids.

WG to John Bodley   MS

12 May 1988   [Headed Paper: Tullimaar]

Dear John,

Thanks for roughs. But the figure head sh'd not have free arms or a trident – they would be carried away by the first big sea. The arms should be down by the sides and disappearing at the waist which would be hidden by scroll work. The *stance* in profile should be that of a woman projecting out of the woodwork and then bent up so that she is staring ahead. (As the Chinese fishermen say – if boat have no eyes how see where go?) She can be draped over the shoulders with a cloak if that makes things easier. Gold crown, perhaps dark red cloak?

The armoured tits arnt big enough. Good God I could hardly get my own into that indication! If the whole figurehead is wave-worn and weathered, so much the better.

Hope you are having fun with the letters.

     ever

     Bill

Bodley had sent along Paul Hogarth's roughs of the ship's figurehead for the jacket of *Fire Down Below*. Golding and Bodley had already discussed the jacket image at length, as Bodley's Editor's Brief made clear: 'I've had a long conversation with Golding. We've decided to have a ship's figurehead, a strong woman with a battlemented crown, wearing a metal breastplate that emphasises her BOOZOOM – the metal must be "plastic" enough to permit her powerful nipples to show through. She has a *dusky* complexion, with rather staring eyes. Golding says she is a fun lady. It is important, he says, for the colour of the metal breastplate to contrast with her dusky skin.' There is a secret about the figurehead's identity (and, relatedly, the name of the ship) that Golding never reveals, even in his journal: 'Charles rang, giving me the usual line about how good it all is. I dont really know these days how seriously to take the general attitude. I suggested a figure-head – a woman with a turretted crown. I haven't told him yet but it should be a brown woman. Shall I ever let on what the name is? I dont know' (J, 10 March 1988). In 1981, while plotting *Close Quarters* in his journal, he had confessed that 'the real joke is that I dont know the ships name myself: though if the series goes to three volumes I might invent a name myself at the very end' (J, 2 October 1981).

WG to John Bodley   MS

6 July 1988

Dear John,

It was kind of you to welcome our inception in the calm world of publishing and to crown it all with the gift of Paul Hogarths painting which is very pretty and decorative. I like it.

Mature consideration however, has revealed to me the root of a profound misunderstanding between us. When I said 'tits' you thought – living in the real world as you do – that I meant breasts, boobs, boozies, or knockers. Living in the ideal world as I do – it is where Nobel Lit. laureates must live to qualify by evidence, like cricketers – I thought that tits = teats, or nipples. So as the lady's bosom has waxed fuller her tits have nigh on disappeared! Not, I hasten to add, that it matters – the joke is a private one anyway and only to be disinterred or unravelled by profound research in the navy lists.

Also I w'd have the dear girl one tone darker in her glowering face –

But all this is out of the ideal world and if you leave her as she is I shall be quite, quite happy.

> ever
> Bill

The Goldings were in London for a garden party at Buckingham Palace, and the letter is on Brown's Hotel headed paper. John Bodley has written on the envelope, '*Mr Evans* Another insight into WG's mind!' Golding notes in his journal, 'John Bodley has given me the latest version of the dust cover of Fire down below. It is pretty but not exactly what I meant' (J, 6 July 1988). On 2 November, Bodley sent a revised image of the figurehead 'with bigger nipples.' As he was about to depart for Japan to give a lecture on ecological conservation, Golding replied hurriedly, 'Yes sure, OK nipples We are off to nippon.'

WG to John Bodley

16 July 1988   [Headed Paper: Tullimaar]

Dear John

Herewith the corrections. The only difficulty is altering the name
Captain Phillips to Captain Phillip. We have McQuarie as governor
and Capt: *Phillip* as deputy – this is historical. It is to 'give verisimilitude to an otherwise bald and unconvincing story'. But I havnt the
MS. Could your kind copy-editor do the job? The servant (or steward) remains as 'Phillips'. The deputy governor, whenever he occurs
becomes 'Captain Phillip' without the S.

That should actually make enough difference – I hope.

     Bill

Names proved a problem several times through the trilogy. Benêt sometimes lost
his circumflex in manuscript and Pike in *Close Quarters* very nearly became Pyke
in *Fire Down Below*.

Golding quotes from Act II of *The Mikado* by Gilbert and Sullivan: 'Merely
corroborative detail, intended to give artistic verisimilitude to an otherwise bald
and unconvincing narrative.'

1989

Like the previous volumes in the sea trilogy, *Fire Down Below* is enthusiastically reviewed on its publication in March. Sales are boosted by a new *South Bank Show* episode dedicated to Golding's work, nine years after the last. Golding is already casting around for the next novel without much luck, but he does finish a new story, 'Caveat Emptor', for an anthology of writings by Booker Prize winners. There are lecture trips to Berlin in October and Mexico in November. After two decades of polite but pressing enquiry from Faber, Golding finally agrees that *Lord of the Flies* should be dramatised for the stage, and Nigel Williams is recruited to do the job. Golding feels increasingly helpless watching David's mental health deteriorate during the year.

WG to John Bodley   TS

11 February 1989   [Headed Paper: Tullimaar]

Dear John,

Thank you for your letter of 2/2/89. I've got myself into a state of confusion (chasis) about what has, is and will happen to EGYPTIAN JOURNAL. But don't try to explain for heaven's sake. My mind is clear as well water. The essential bit of any operation is so that I earn the advance which I didn't heretofore, thus stabbing RAINBOW in the ultraviolet and ensuring its collapse.

I don't like the cover! What's Akhnaten doing on *my* journal? If you *want Akhnaten's* journal I'll write it for you but not him trespassing on mine! Now I see you're taking him off anyway. Sorry. Yes, I suppose a boat or boats is the thing. Somewhere – ask an Egyptologist – there's a picture of an Egyptian war ship returning from the Middle East with prisoners and the King of Akkad or someone hung upside down from the bow. That would do marvellously I think. I've got some smashing closeups of beautifully cut hieroglyphs (taken on our first visit but what of that?) and I would have thought the label containing the title could well be one of them. The picture of Ann and me and the crew is funny enough to stay as it is.

> ever
> Bill

'(chasis)': Golding had a story about an officer in the Second World War who, criticising his men, complained of 'chasis' when he meant 'chaos'.

'RAINBOW' is a slip for Rainbird, although Golding's joke about the 'ultraviolet' would not work if it were corrected. The contractual situation over *An Egyptian Journal* was so complex that Golding's confusion was merited.

After visiting the senior Egyptologist at the British Museum, Bodley relayed the news that the museum had no modern photograph of the image that Golding wanted. The edition went ahead with the colour photograph of Ann and Golding and the crew, along with a photograph of a sandal boat on the Nile.

WG to Matthew Evans   TS

11 February 1989   [Headed Paper: Tullimaar]

Dear Matthew,

Nice to hear from you – but I wasn't suggesting that writing an India book from here would save F&F money! I was only wondering if it was possible! The whole situation is confused because I still have vague feelings about writing a thunderously illustrated book but have only the wildest ideas how I should go about it. It had best simmer (back burner) for a bit.

I also seem to have confused myself, let alone you as to what I suppose happened over the EGYPTIAN JOURNAL. I have memories of not actually earning the advance from Rainbird in a sum of £500 or whatever. Since Penguin seem now to have a finger in the pie I supposed it is they who are trying to get some money back. This is wondrously confused by the fact that John has just sent me a markup of the cover of the paperback sent *him* by Pentagram whoever those quintet are or is. If it would be helpful I have scads of lovely Egypt photographs I've never shown anyone as they date from our first visit there.

LWT have just spent five days with us and we both feel a bit wrung-out though they are one and all a nice bunch. I am trying to think up a short story for Martyn Goff but shall probably have to send him BILLY THE KID anyway. I'm also earning (or alternatively robbing the OUP of) the 2nd Edition of the OED.

                    ever
                    Bill

Golding and Ann had spent two months in India from January 1987 on a trip sponsored by the British Council. The experience inspired Golding to formulate plans for a coffee-table book titled 'In Praise of India'. Evans was supportive but wondered whether Golding could write it without returning there.

Pentagram is a design consultancy firm that, from 1981, designed the jackets and paperback covers for Faber books.

LWT: London Weekend Television. They were filming a *South Bank Show* episode dedicated to Golding; it aired on 24 March.

Martyn Goff was editing an anthology called *Prize Writing: An Original Collection of Writings by Past Winners to Celebrate 21 Years of The Booker Prize*. Despite assuming that he would end up offering 'Billy the Kid' (his childhood memoir already published in *The Hot Gates*), Golding finally surprised himself by delivering the goods: a new story titled 'Caveat Emptor'.

Golding's review of the second edition of the *Oxford English Dictionary* appeared in the *Evening Standard* on 16 March. As he observed in his journal, it was a good deal: 'The cloth bound edition is fifteen hundred pounds and I get a fee of seven hundred and fifty pounds. It seems a reasonable return for fifteen hundred to two thousand words' (J, 25 January 1989).

WG to Charles Monteith
MS MONTEITH

1 April 1989   [Headed Paper: Tullimaar]

Dear Charles,

What a lovely party! I think it was the best bit of our London foray – but perhaps I shouldn't say that –

I'm half-persuaded to break my long prejudice (*can* one break a prejudice?) and start reading Phyllis as a matter of acquaintance. But this letter is getting a *bit off*.

We look forward very much to y'r visit with us here. I have a couple of *ozmundae regales* but they are neither more than three inches high!

ever

Bill (Ann sends her love.)

Phyllis: P. D. James, the detective novelist recruited as a Faber author by Monteith and Rosemary Goad in 1961.

The *Osmunda regalis* is commonly known as royal fern.

WG to John Bodley
PC

11(?) July 1989

Dear John,

Thank you for sending on the books – what a *slob* Baudelaire was!

Sales figures a bit depressing I think – I must try to make people love me.

ever   Bill

The card is postmarked 11 July and its printed header reads, 'From Sir William Golding, Faber & Faber Ltd, 3 Queen Square, WC1N 3AU'. Golding has crossed out everything after his name.

The Baudelaire book may have been a copy of Enid Starkie's biography, first published by Faber in 1957. Golding admitted in his journal that 'Reading a life of Baudelaire at night gives me the willies I mean I get a positively eerie feeling from the man, shut the book and try to think happy thoughts' (J, 10 July 1989). As for sales of his latest novel, Golding had been dissatisfied for several months: 'Sales of Fire Down Below in the first fortnight were sixteen thousand. I dont regard this as good' (J, 4 May 1989).

WG to Charles Monteith

TS MONTEITH

1 November 1989   [Headed Paper: Tullimaar]

Dear Charles,

This is a laborious and perhaps unnecessary letter – but I shall send it nevertheless. You probably know that there has been another film made of *Flies*. I havn't seen it, have dissociated myself from it and propose to stay that way!

But it occurred to me that my recourse, small as it may seem, was to have a play made of the book, preserving its British-ness et al. I put this up to Matthew as he's a Royal Court man. He has got Nigel Williams working on the thing.

Only now and grossly late has it occurred to me that as you have always been intimately and lengthily associated with the story, that you should have been in from the start. I'm sure you would have agreed – but I should have told you. My sincere apologies for this really obtuse neglect.

When shall you come our way again so that I can be sure I am forgiven

Ann sends her love

Ever

Bill

The new film of *Lord of the Flies*, directed by Harry Hook, was released in March 1990. It bombed at the box office and was criticised for its deviations from the novel – not the least of which being the shearing away of its 'British-ness' in favour of an American cast.

Matthew Evans was for many years chairman of the Royal Court Theatre, where Nigel Williams's plays had been performed. Williams's novels were published by Faber between 1985 and 1995.

WG to Matthew Evans   MS

16 November 1989   [Headed Paper: Tullimaar]

Dear Matthew,

Thanks for your letter(s). There's absolutely no need to worry about
the Booker affair – Ann and I were very tired and I more shaken than
I had thought by cracking my head. (It's as good now as it ever is.
I'm sorry about the hangover you all got at the Groucho.) We left a
message but it never got through apparently – it was a simple plea for
understanding that we couldn't make it to the Groucho.

Biography. Yes: I have thought about it off and on but each time
with a more and more *tight* feeling that it could be no more than factual. I'd also thought of ways round that, amorphous, nonsensical,
vaticinatory, a lump of writing – financial!

Would Faber be interested? It w'd at least allow you to say to
would-be biographers 'He's doing it himself but God knows when he'll
finish it—'

      ever
      Bill

PS Shall we see you in Mexico? They have a bookfair!

Golding liked Kazuo Ishiguro and admired the 'quite seductive newness' of his
work (J, 13 January 1989). Ishiguro's latest novel, *The Remains of the Day*,
had been shortlisted for the Booker Prize, so the Goldings went to London for
the prizegiving ceremony in support of a fellow Faber author. Golding gives his
account of the sorry events of 26 October in his journal: 'I left my briefcase in the
train. I rang up from Brown's and the briefcase was already in the lost property
office. I arranged to pick it up this morning. Then, straightening up from bending
down to reach the phone books which were on the floor I struck my head sharply
on the corner of the overmantel and bled, as they say, profusely. [. . .] We ended
by calling in the hotel who staunched the flow but the delay made us so late that
we missed the drinks in the library of the guildhall and almost at once went into
dinner. We sat majestically at what would have been a high table except that it
was on the same level as all the others. Ishiguro won the prize as we had forseen.
I kept my drinking to a minimum and feel the better for it. We were going on to
the Groucho but felt very tired so cut it, which I regret as it looks like indifference
to Ishi and to Matthew and I shall have to write notes. We were back here, I
suppose, by half past eleven' (J, 27 October 1989).

Monteith had broached the subject of a biography to Golding on his visit to
Tullimaar in early August: 'To my surprise and I must say, irritation Charles had
a session talking about "biography". I thought he meant autobiography but he

knew in fact that I refuse to contemplate one. He began talking about John Carey doing one and when I said I didn't want a biography either, he said in a matter-of-fact way "There will be one." He means if I dont authorise a biography there will be an unauthorised one' (J, 6 August 1989). As the letter to Matthew Evans suggests, Golding subsequently hatched a plan of starting an autobiography – or at least telling everyone that he had started an autobiography – to stymie would-be biographers.

The Goldings spent twelve days in Mexico from 22 November on a trip sponsored by the British Council.

1990

Golding begins to suspect that he has written his last novel. He decides with some relief that he has definitely written his last lecture: 'Aspects of Narration', which he delivers at Oxford in February. A few days later, having been commissioned by the *Sunday Times* to write a long travel article, he and Ann set off for a cruise from Bali to Malaysia and Singapore. This is the year's biggest foreign adventure, but the Goldings also visit Rome on a British Council trip in May and spend August in Brittany. David is absent, having been hospitalised in May after another breakdown. The treatment works, and on his release he seems much happier. Hoping to deter potential biographers, Golding makes slow progress on an autobiography provisionally titled 'Scenes from a Life'. His priority for the last months of the year is to revise the sea trilogy and write an introduction for its publication as a single volume under the title *To the Ends of the Earth*.

John Bodley to WG   TS

30 March 1990

Dear Bill,

I was so sorry to hear that you had been burgled – fellow feeling, since the Bodleys have been turned over at least three times over the years.

The enclosed may interest or annoy you. In any event I thought you should see it. It opened to mixed reviews at the National this week.

Yours

The Goldings were in Bali when their Tullimaar home was burgled in early March. Golding records the inventory of loss in his journal: 'Our house has been broken into and all the obvious pictures stolen to say nothing of our French clock. Some of the oils, the De Faux and the Williams are gone. It may be the two little hunting pictures have gone as well. We are giving what information we can: but with pictures one doesn't really have much hope. They could be abroad already' (J, 6 March 1990).

The enclosure was a copy of Tony Harrison's verse play *The Trackers of Oxyrhynchus*, which opened at the National Theatre in March and was published by Faber at the same time. The play combines one of Golding's long-held interests – the excavations by Grenfell and Hunt at Oxyrhynchus in

Egypt – with an imaginative rewriting of one of their most important discoveries: Sophocles' satyr play, *Ichneutae*. *Ichneutae* is the Greek for 'trackers'.

WG to John Bodley

2(?) April 1990

Thanks for *The Trackers*! I imagine it's huge fun – A penalty of living down here, of course is that one's only connection with the modern world is being turned over. Sorry to hear it happens to you regularly though (interested to see that even ff can't guarantee accurate Greek text – 'Μαρσυασ' should be 'Μαρσυας!')

I won't tell, though. Thanks again

Bill

The printed header is the same as for Golding's card to Bodley dated 11(?) July 1989 – Golding's name with Faber's address.

ff: Faber & Faber.

'"Μαρσυασ" should be "Μαρσυας!"': the satyr's name is Marsyas, and Golding is pointing out that the name should end with a final sigma, not a mid-word sigma. Golding spent a lot of time correcting the Greek in *An Egyptian Journal* and his sea trilogy, at one point suggesting with a hint of exasperation that Faber might want to consider finding someone competent in Greek to set and proofread the Greek expressions.

John Bodley to WG

22 October 1990

Dear Bill

About trilogy titles . . . Isn't there one that stares us in the face, so to speak? Why not quote Talbot himself and call the three-in-one *To the Ends of the Earth*? Then you could run the title page and the jacket panel like this:–

TO THE ENDS OF THE EARTH
A sea trilogy comprising
Rites of Passage
Close Quarters
Fire Down Below.

Well, just a thought to throw in with all the brilliant ones you are having yourself. I haven't tried this on the others, so you can ignore it. They may think it is a dud anyway!

Yours

Golding and Bodley had agreed to publish the sea trilogy in one volume to mark Golding's eightieth birthday. They had been mulling over possible titles for several months, with Golding having proposed what Bodley described in-house as 'two non-starters': 'Farewell and Adieu' and 'There WAS a Ship'. (Golding's journal lists another possibility: 'The Endless Waves'.) Golding readily accepted Bodley's latest idea: 'John Bodley has suggested To the Ends of the Earth for the Trilogy and I approve of it. So that's one thing out of the way' (J, 23 October 1990).

John Bodley to WG TS

29 October 1990

Dear Bill

I thought you would be pleased to know that everyone here likes *To the Ends of the Earth* as the title for the Trilogy. I've sent photostats of your alterations to New York for them to evaluate, and I hope to hear this week that FSG can incorporate them into the original typesetting without too much difficulty.

Did you have any further thoughts about the jacket? You told me that it must be of the ship itself, and I remember that you were thinking of going to Greenwich to look for inspiration among the paintings. Are you happy for us to use Paul Hogarth again? Is there a ship profile of the correct specifications (even a famous painting) that would guide the illustrator if he chose to depict a ship at sea? Knowing Hogarth he will try to condense this into a single image – he loved doing the figurehead! Any guidance welcome, since I have to brief the design team this Wednesday.

If you have finished with Masefield's anthology of sea poems I will return it to the London Library . . .

Yours

In the search for a title, Bodley had borrowed and sent to Golding a copy of John Masefield's sea anthology, *A Sailor's Garland* (1906).

One complication for *To the Ends of the Earth*, as for the individual volumes in the trilogy, was that the typesetting was being carried out by Golding's

American publisher, Farrar, Straus and Giroux. The potential for error as Golding made revisions and corrections and sent them to Faber was much higher than usual.

Explaining why Golding wanted a ship for the jacket, in an internal memo Bodley quoted Golding saying that 'the ship itself is the main character in the books'.

'the figurehead': the image on the cover of *Fire Down Below*.

WG to John Bodley   MS

31 October 1990   [Headed Paper: Tullimaar]

Dear John,

The enc: is self-explanatory I think. If its too long I'll think again – *and* if it's too short!

Your Sailor's Garland entertained me: but I think your title is better than any I found.

We *did* get to Greenwich & were overwhelmed. If Hogarth wants a ship (74) he sh'd look at the ship models, *not* pictures – there was no specific one which w'd do as a template!

Perhaps old Byron's dark blue rolling ocean sh'd be an element?

      ever

      Bill

y'r Sailors Garland is coming

   B

Golding enclosed his draft of the foreword for the trilogy.

The Goldings visited the National Maritime Museum at Greenwich on 18 October, with Golding recording that 'of the lot I think that the ship models are the most astonishing and beautiful. But I have to admit that I found nothing which would help me to a trilogy title' (J, 18 October 1990). See Bodley's letter to Golding of 22 January 1991 for the resolution.

'74' (or seventy-four) was a two-decked sailing ship of the line, first designed by the French in the eighteenth century and then adopted by the British navy. It took its name from the number of guns it carried.

'Byron's dark blue rolling ocean' is an allusion to Byron's *Childe Harold's Pilgrimage*, canto 4, clxxix: 'Roll on, thou deep and dark blue Ocean – roll!' It appears twice in *Close Quarters*. The first reference comes in slightly disguised form when Talbot records: 'The present weather is sharply defining our horizon for us in a dense blue which obeys Lord Byron's famous injunction and continues to roll on endlessly – such is the power of verse!' On the second occasion, Lady Somerset, described as a 'devotee' of Byron, quotes the line verbatim and is stopped by her husband from going any further.

John Bodley to WG TS

1 November 1990

Dear Bill

Your Foreword is absolutely perfect for the Trilogy – thanks so much for writing it so promptly. Thanks also for your advice about the ship and the jacket. I'll pass on what you say straight to Hogarth. I'm advertising in the rare book trade for a copy of the Masefield anthology. If I find one you shall have it!

Yours

Returning the book via Bodley to the London Library, Golding had decided that he would like his own copy of *A Sailor's Garland* and enclosed a note accordingly: 'Worth begging, borrowing or stealing?'

1991

Golding's work on a new novel about Herakles ('The Curtain') peters out after a few months, but he continues to tinker with 'Scenes from a Life'. As well as his annual holiday to Brittany, he has two overseas trips with the British Council: to Czechoslovakia in May and Paris in November. In December he attends a gathering of Nobel laureates in Stockholm. *To the Ends of the Earth* – the sea trilogy published in a single volume – appears in September to coincide with Golding's eightieth birthday.

WG to John Bodley   MS

7 January 1991   [Headed Paper: Tullimaar]

Dear John,

Here is the intro to *To the ends of the Earth* back again. It's grown a bit I'm afraid and hope that doesn't matter.

I tried to make you a fair copy – tried three times but kept making my usual mistakes. I give up and simply hope the thing is legible. I must be sickening for something.

I'll deal with the artwork as soon as I can.

     ever
      Bill

WG to John Bodley   TS

17 January 1991   [Headed Paper: Tullimaar]

Dear John,

It's a bit difficult to begin talking about the rig of the ship, HMS Dustcover. *If* Mr Hogarth is giving an accurate representation of what he found at Greenwich I bow my head and withdraw all objections – but I can't believe it! As I interpret what is before my eyes on the paper, both the sails on the mainmast *and* on the foremast are on the wrong side (aft) of the mast! If this is supposed to represent a ship taken aback, all those sails will have had to pass through a positive thicket of taut ropes without affecting them. Is the ship by any chance supposed to be 'hove to'? In that case, her sails would be shortened and balanced one against the other in a way which might vary in detail from one ship to another but which wouldn't result in all the sails on the main and fore being filled with wind arse-backwards. The artist could get away (I think) with this rig if he allowed both those masts to appear as I have indicated by my adjustment to his sketch. He'd have also to shade the sails on the main as he has those on the fore or the thing still makes no sense. I'm sorry to be so niggly. But if (for example) he had drawn a stage coach with two of the horses facing forward and two facing the driver it would occasion comment. I quite see that a nominal, indeed, an emblematic, or even symbolic ship on a symbolic sea would be appropriate but this sketch seems to me to fall between two stools or waves – it isn't a real ship or a symbolic one. In fact it's what the navy with what Kipling called its capacity for having the right words for everything, what the navy calls 'a bunch of buggers'. I ought to add that I very much like Mr Hogarth's sea.

I hope this isn't too severe. I'll try to finalise the intro as soon as I can but think this Jeremiad about the ship should reach you as soon as possible. Ever.
Bill

WG to Matthew Evans MS

18 January 1991   [Headed Paper: Tullimaar]

Dear Matthew,

Thank you for your letter. What shocking news about MacArthur! We will do what we can do – a letter I suppose: there's little else.

I enclose a letter which might be worth following up. They have put a finger on what I've always thought – music (the choir) the Beast (bass – if possible double-bass!) and the naval officer (high tenor).

What do you think? I'd want to retain the possibility of doing the libretto (book) myself.
Ever
Bill

Norman MacArthur was senior book rep at Faber; he occasionally dropped in on Golding to deliver parcels of the latest publications. Evans had passed on the news that MacArthur was dying of cancer, with only months to live. 'Matthew asks me to write him a cheery note! [. . .] I don't think a "cheery" note is possible. I must ring Matthew tomorrow and find out what he means' (J, 20 January 1991).

Over the decades, Golding received many requests to adapt *Lord of the Flies* for opera. He does not record the identity of the latest enquirer and the proposal does not seem to have progressed, but after all the previous rejections his mild approval is unexpected.

John Bodley to WG TS

22 January 1991

Dear Bill,

Thanks for your amusing letter about the work of the landlubber Hogarth. Your observations have gone on to him today. We've also decided to reset the whole trilogy here in England, rather than get the printing film patched with your alterations in America. After talks with Farrar Straus we could all see the advantage of a fresh piece of setting, not least the cost and convenience of proofing. One thing I've taken for granted is that when the revised texts have been published in *To the Ends of the Earth* we shall have to replace the old paperback readings with the revised ones. A matter of phasing out rather than doing it overnight. I assume that you wouldn't want discrepant editions available. If you *do* fancy having two version running to dazzle the passengers (like Auden with his pre- and post-1939 versions of poems) please put me straight.

Yours

WG to John Bodley TS

25 January 1991   [Headed Paper: Tullimaar]

Dear John

Thanks for your letter of the 22nd. I've been messing about with the foreword and think I should now send it to you before it gets any longer. It's about two thousand words I think. I made desperate efforts to get you a clean copy but found I invariably made mistakes though their number is reduced a bit.

You mention resetting. I take it that means you will have a choice of 'founts' if I have the right word. Would it be possible to retain the pleasantly large type you used before, without making too unhandy a volume? I have wondered whether or not my feelings about Durrell's omnibus Alexandria(?) wasn't an unconscious reaction to the small print. But I can't lay my hands on it at the moment so can't settle the question. Perhaps we could have even thinner paper and even larger print! I hope you will cellophane-wrap the volume for publication otherwise we shall have people standing in Blackwells, reading the introduction then putting the book back. Also, come to think of it, cellophane wrapping would mean I couldn't do my signing. You see it would have advantages all the way round. Your note about the *revised text* – yes, I suppose we must let the old paperbacks wither away and only come out with new ones when they are gone. I take it that's what you mean. Or do you mean you wont publish in separate paperbacks? To answer your question, *I* dont mind discrepant editions if you don't – or do I? I think I'd better leave that to you as a delicate publishing question and one on which I havn't really a *financial* opinion. One day, too, you must explain to me the 'cost and convenience of proofing'! This is a wandering letter. I suppose I'm writing it to find out what I mean; and conclude I dont mean anything. Did I tell you one of my eyes is getting longer sighted while the other one is getting shorter sighted? Ideally I should have one fount on the sinister page and a different one en face.

ever

Bill

Golding is probably referring to Faber's 1962 omnibus edition of *The Alexandria Quartet*, for which Durrell made revisions and added an introductory note. The question mark in parentheses is his own.

Charles Monteith to Ann and WG

MS GOLDING

22 February 1991   [Headed Paper: Randolph Avenue]

My dear Ann & Bill,

My very warmest thanks for that enchanting little box. It's an absolute gem which reposes, at the moment, on my dressing table where I admire it at least twice a day. What shall I put in it? Too beautiful, surely, for pills?

I'm delighted you were able to come to my birthday party. Quite a jolly occasion, I thought. – & an immense pleasure to see so many old friends.

If I may, I'll descend on Cornwall when the weather is rather more clement & I very much look forward to seeing you again then.

Love,
Charles.

The Goldings attended Monteith's party in London on 20 February. The birthday gift was a small tortoiseshell box.

WG to John Bodley   TS

25 February 1991   [Headed Paper: Tullimaar]

Dear John,

This business of the dust jacket is pretty much hell. A ship is an incredibly subtle shape yet it must have a rigid bilateral symmetry! From the point of view of the *illustrator* rather than fancy-free artist, it's the worst of all worlds. The fact remains that this ship simply wont do. I'm afraid it's really a job for a computer – a solid shape which has to be seen tilted, veered, turned-turtle, in fact rotated in every dimension until you or he has that shape in his mind or wherever as a solid thing. I dont know what to do. Does it help to point out the following? (1) The masts are distributed at approximately equal intervals along the length of the ship.
(2) The masts are stepped on the keel and rise vertically in the central plane of the bilateral symmetry.
(3) The shrouds (the strings which hold the sticks up!) would therefore make ~~equilateral~~ isosceles triangles bisected by the mast.

Well there. This is all silly. Either you feel the shipness of a ship or you dont. I dont know the technical means by which all this three-dimensional stuff can be made plain or at least not violated by the drawing. It's possible of course that Mr Hogarth is quite legitimately laying some picture at Greenwich under contribution. In that case I bow out, only pleading that the name of the original illustrator may be included in the acknowledgements. By the way, the masts wouldn't be the enormously thick sticks as shown – that was my scribbled indication.

I pass.
Bill

'~~equilateral~~ isosceles triangles': the revision is made in pen, presumably by someone at Faber because there is a marginal note in the same hand: 'WG phoned!'

John Bodley to WG   TS

21 March 1991

Dear Bill

I took the saga of the Trilogy jacket picture to the Pentagram design meeting, with the sales director present, and I read them all (and sent Hogarth) your letter. After hours of toing and froing we decided to take advantage of the sentiment in your letter that if we insisted on the jacket for commercial reasons you would allow it so long as Paul Hogarth showed where his 'inspiration' had come from. I'm sorry to have run out of time to start again, as I had hoped, but the sales troops need a jacket desperately to start selling around the world. Shall I be keel-hauled for this? I'm sure you feel I've failed you.

Hogarth's elaborate justification for his picture is as follows: 'the cover is based on the seascape *"Resolution" in a Gale* by Willem van de Velde and on various ships' models in the National Maritime Museum, Greenwich'. We'll put that somewhere on the jacket.

I enclose a draft blurb for your consideration. It has gone into an advance catalogue but you can alter it completely if you wish for the jacket itself. I liked the quote from your Foreword very much.

Yours

Bodley expressed his misgivings in an internal memo written the next day: 'Just as I feared, [Hogarth] has used as his model the work of a marine painter a hundred years too early for the period of Golding's ship. Why do I write briefs when no-one takes any notice of them? I have loyally written to Golding saying that you all preferred the jacket as it stood for commercial reasons [. . .]. I hope he will agree to let us use this unsatisfactory picture, but be prepared for a broadside nevertheless.'

WG to John Bodley   MS

23 March 1991   [Headed Paper: Tullimaar]

Dear John,

Thank you for your letter and enc: I agree with everything. (I have just been done over by the Vatman & *dare* not disagree with anything!)

I'm impressed by the research which went into the carefully selected quotes from my many admirers. I had not met them before and do not propose to examine the surrounding prose.

Please pass my apologies along to the wounded mr Hogarth – tell him I'm not really all that ugly

ever

Bill

Tax had become a particularly stressful issue for Golding ever since (in 1988) his long-standing accountants had been found responsible for not keeping up-to-date records, costing him a five-figure sum in back taxes. His experience with the firm was so traumatic that – as he acknowledged in his journal – 'the whole thing has become a phobia' (J, 19 March 1991).

WG to John Bodley   PC

14 October 1991

Dear John,

Herewith *The Salt of Life* by Chaman Nahal. I was quite taken with a lot of it – including the clear-eyed view of Gandhi.

ever

Bill

The card has a printed header with Golding's name and Faber's address.

Chaman Nahal had published *The Salt of Life* in India in 1990 and sent it to Golding in the hope that he would recommend it to a British publisher. The day before posting it on to Bodley, Golding wrote in his journal, 'I've read Nahal's The Salt of Life and am rather tired but impressed – five hundred odd pages: and that's only one of a tetralogy' (J, 13 October 1991).

Golding followed up this letter with a further note of explanation to Bodley, having discovered in the meantime that the novel had already been turned down once by Faber.

WG to Matthew Evans   MS

23 October 1991   [Headed Paper: Tullimaar]

Dear Matthew,

Last night I sat up suddenly like the way they do in novels, remembering. I never thanked you properly for the splendid spread, company, *expensive* volumes and huge hurrah of my eightieth birthday celebration!

I do so now in affectionate gratitude for a mark of friendship and respect such as seldom falls to the lot of man, as they also say in novels – bad novels. I suppose this ought really to be a kind of shotgun letter to be passed on to all those who had the uneven tenor of publishing life made even more than usually effortful, exhausting and *expensive*! Well that is all in the past, the fascinating print now decorates our walls, the trilogy is admired as an *object* by all who see it and make fruitless guesses at the price. I myself am realising but not very deeply that yes, I am old.

Please pass on this handout of gratitude, however *inexpensive* a reply – you will know to whom it should be offered

      ever
      Bill

Sorry about the naked revelation of what is nearest to my heart. (Ann sends love as do I.)

    B

The letter is written in green ink with the addition after 'Bill' in black ink. Also in black ink, and therefore explaining that postscript comment, is Golding's underlining of 'expensive' (twice) and 'inexpensive'.

Faber had organised a party on 18 September to celebrate Golding's eightieth birthday the following day: the palindromic 19 9 91, as he noted in his journal. The event also marked the publication of *To the Ends of the Earth*, so Golding was presented with a suitably nautical gift: 'an engraving of – I think – Victory' (J, 19 September 1991).

John Bodley to WG

TS

29 October 1991

Dear Bill

This is a belated response to your letters and postcards about the Indian novelist Professor Nahal. Before your second letter arrived I had been reading his book for a bit, and found myself put off by the wooden naturalism and the cargo of indigestible historical matter. Also, the prof isn't exactly a facile writer. But I am fascinated by anything to do with Gandhi, having looked after Erikson's wonderful biography of him, and so I was predisposed to be very intrigued by the main characters in the story. Then your second letter arrived with the surprising news that my colleague Robert McCrum had already turned the book down for more or less the reasons that were forming in my mind. Robert reads masses of contemporary fiction, has visited India several times, and has brought on to the list a number of Indian writers (Mistry and Seth for example). The fact that his judgement and mine were so similar warns me to respect our publishing instincts here – totally different readers reaching more or less the same conclusions about whether we could publish and sell an old-fashioned writer like Nahal. Robert is away this week but I will talk to him about the professor when he comes back. I think that it is very unlikely that we can reverse our opinion about Mr Nahal's chances with us. I'll read some more of his book, out of fairness, and of course we'll write to him ourselves in due course.

No offence to you, I trust?

Yours

Erik H. Erikson's *Gandhi's Truth: On the Origins of Militant Nonviolence* was published by Faber in 1970.

Robert McCrum was editor-in-chief at Faber from 1990.

Faber published Vikram Seth's *The Golden Gate* in 1986 and Rohinton Mistry's *Such a Long Journey* in 1991.

WG to John Bodley   TS

3 November 1991   [Headed Paper: Tullimaar]

Dear John

A belated reply to your belated reply of 29/10/91 – I don't agree with 'wooden naturalism' but 'the indigestible historical matter' certainly sinks Nahal's book. However, the same could be said of Tolstoy's War and Peace except of course that few people ever reach the last part where the excruciation is. But before I knew that F&F had seen Nahal's book I supposed you might agree that he needs an editor as much as a publisher, preferably one armed with a sharp pair of scissors.

I don't know Mistry and Seth but when you talk about 'an old-fashioned writer like Nahal' I begin to be nervous on my own behalf and wonder whether I shouldn't start hawking my wares round the Trollope Society! But there's no offence to me, certainly, rather the reverse in that I'm sorry to have wasted your time in a naive and silly attempt to pass on a problem. Apologies

ever

Bill

Golding finally rectified his ignorance of Vikram Seth's work by reading an advance copy of *A Suitable Boy* at the end of 1992. On New Year's Eve he writes in his journal, 'What a way to finish the year. Seth's book has distinct merits beyond the obvious one of exoticism from our point of view. In it he talks about a novel like the Ganges and indeed the image is just for this one. It wanders, changes course and receives a number of tributaries. Yet all is lightness, a panorama of India [in] variety, complexity, gentleness and instant ferocity. It has humour' (J, 31 December 1992).

1992

There is still no sign of a new novel. Intending to visit Spain rather than Brittany for their summer holidays, the Goldings start to learn Spanish. In May, Golding is awarded an honorary doctorate at Oviedo, and he and Ann travel on to Salamanca and Madrid for question-and-answer sessions. They are back in Spain with the family in July, then in Toronto in October and Portugal (courtesy of the British Council) the following month. At the end of the year, Golding has an operation to remove cancerous cells from his nose; he is given the all-clear several weeks later.

WG to Matthew Evans   MS

13 January 1992   [Headed Paper: Tullimaar]

Dear Matthew,

Thanks for your letter of 9/1/92 – It's good news to hear that the theatrical undergrowth is stirring: or should it be the palms, waving aloft?

[. . .]

In any case, after forty years (since writing) the original, many translations, a pyramid of lit: crit: two films and two prizes, I am left cynically caring for *money* and must leave loftier aspects in the capable hands of my publishers!

I've just heard from Yannick Guillou of Gallimard that they're reprinting *Fire Down Below*. I'd be more impressed if I knew what the first run was. It will be good to see you both if we get a moment, at Peter's party. But what an antediluvian lot we are!

ever
Bill

Evans had written on 9 January to tell Golding that Richard Eyre, artistic director at the National Theatre, was 'keen on' Nigel Williams's stage adaptation of *Lord of the Flies*, and was hoping to produce it in late 1992 or early 1993.

Gallimard had published *Fire Down Below* as *La Cuirasse de feu*, translated by Marie-Lise Marlière, in 1991.

Peter du Sautoy's eightieth birthday party took place on 19 February, prompting a burst of melancholia on Golding's part: 'Golly, what a party. Donald Mitchell who started Faber music, said as we went in, "It's like the last pages of Proust." Ann wishes she had said that. We really were a crumbling crew. Peter was said by everybody to look the same as ever. I didn't think so' (J, 20 February 1992).

WG to Matthew Evans   MS

25 March 1992   [Headed Paper: Tullimaar]

Dear Matthew,

① Thanks for the information – if any of these three possibilities gets through it may be the crock of gold!

② I wrote to Curtis Brown really to find out what the situation was between me and them. It was mainly a matter of royalties on magazine stuff (*Thinking as a hobby*).

I'm sending you sheaf of incomprehensibility – at the very least you'll know which dept of F&F to send it to, if any!

The 'three possibilities' were Richard Eyre's theatrical production of *Lord of the Flies*, a film of *The Spire* (recently placed under option by the actor Miranda Richardson) and a film of *To the Ends of the Earth* that had already been under option for several years with the producer William P. Cartlidge. The filming of *The Spire* did not go ahead; nor did Cartlidge's project, but *To the Ends of the Earth* eventually became a three-part BBC miniseries in 2005 starring Benedict Cumberbatch, Jared Harris, Sam Neill, Daniel Evans and Victoria Hamilton. Richard Eyre withdrew from *Lord of the Flies*; the first professional production was directed by Elijah Moshinsky for the Royal Shakespeare Company.

Golding's essay 'Thinking as a Hobby', first published in *Holiday* magazine in 1961, is still uncollected. It has been reprinted several times in the United States.

The 'sheaf of incomprehensibility' has proven untraceable.

1993

Golding finds his subject at last: in January he starts a novel about the Delphic oracle. Writing 2,000 words each day, he has a first draft by the start of February. A second draft takes him from March to early June. The book will be published posthumously as *The Double Tongue* (1995). In the early hours of 19 June, after a party at Tullimaar for friends and relatives the previous evening, Golding dies of heart failure. Two days later, Ann suffers a stroke; she survives but with severely limited mobility. Golding is buried at Bowerchalke on Midsummer's Day, and on 20 November a Memorial Service is held in his honour at Salisbury Cathedral.

WG to Matthew Evans   MS

19 May 1993   [Headed Paper: Tullimaar]

Dear Matthew,

Thank you for your letter which I have mislaid but remember fairly well.

We sh'd be glad to come to London for a couple of nights but are so free that it w'd be better if you were to set the dates rather than I.

We have a party here on June 18th for which I enclose an invite, though I dont suppose you & Caroline want to come that far as we can't offer a bed, what with family and attachments.

I've done 40,000 *first* draft of a story and think it will go to 60,000 about. Of course, most of this draft is unspeakably silly and jejune.

When are the awful claws of the recession going to close on me? I live in yearly terror of it.

> ever
> Bill

The literary agent Caroline Michel was Evans's second wife.

Replying on 2 June, Evans apologised for not being able to attend the party. He reassured Golding that publishers thrive in a recession because books are a relatively cheap form of entertainment.

Charles Monteith to Ann Golding

MS GOLDING

19 June 1993   [Headed Paper: Randolph Avenue]

My dear Ann,

A tiny note to send you all my love and all my sympathy. Bill was a great man whom I loved dearly and I shall miss him more – far more – than I can begin to say.

Much, much love,
Charles

Golding had died suddenly at Tullimaar early in the morning of 19 June.

1994

Charles Monteith to Ann Golding MS GOLDING

3 November 1994   [Headed Paper: Randolph Avenue]

Dear Ann,

John Bodley has sent me a copy of the dedication to Bill's last novel. & I'm simply writing to say how immensely grateful I am to you and to all the family. Nothing in the world could have given me more pleasure. My friendship & association with Bill – and through him with you & Judy & David – has been one of the really great things in my life. Bower Chalke and Tullimaar will always be very important & very happy parts of my memories.

I'm sorry to hear from Judy that you haven't been terribly well recently but you're *much* better now, I'm told. – and I look forward immensely to seeing you again in the spring of 1995 when David Treffry has invited me to stay at Fowey.

Again, my warmest & most grateful thanks & all my love
         Charles

Ann died on New Year's Day, 1995. Monteith died of a heart attack later that year on 9 May. The following month, *The Double Tongue* was published by Faber with the following dedication:

The author's family
wish to dedicate his last work
to all those at Faber
who helped, encouraged and cared for
him and his writing
over the past forty years.
Above all, this book is for
CHARLES

Appendix

Strangers from Within

CHARLES MONTEITH

The typescript was unenticing. Bound between two pieces of cardboard, the sheets had a dog-eared, shop-soiled, down-at-heel look. The edges of the first dozen or so were yellowish, evidence that they, and they alone, had been read a number of times; the remainder were whiter but not pristine. Though I had been a publisher for less than a month, I could already spot a manuscript that had been the rounds and this was an obvious example. A short submission letter, written from Salisbury, was attached: 'I send you the typescript of my novel *Strangers from Within* which might be defined as an allegorical interpretation of a stock situation. I hope you will feel able to publish it.' It was signed 'William Golding'.

A Tuesday afternoon in late September 1953. As usually happened on Tuesday afternoons, three or four editors were weeding out the week's haul of manuscripts in preparation for Wednesday's weekly editorial committee, appropriately, if somewhat quaintly, called the Book Committee, at which decisions were made. *Strangers from Within* was in the pile pushed in my direction. Our professional reader – she read for a number of other publishers as well as Faber and also for a leading literary agency – had already given it one of her 'quick looks' and her verdict was in green ink at the top of the author's letter: 'Time: The Future. Absurd and uninteresting fantasy about the explosion of an atomic bomb on the colonies and a group of children who land in jungle country near New Guinea. Rubbish and dull. Pointless.' This was followed by a capital R enclosed in a circle, the symbol for 'reject'.

I opened it expecting nothing and after the first dozen or so pages was inclined, like so many readers before me, to abandon it at that point. They described a nuclear war. Remembering them now, more than thirty years later, my impression is that they were powerful, if occasionally over-written, and that they contained, initially, no characters at all. Later the focus shifted earthwards and to a hurriedly organized evacuation of schoolchildren destined, presumably, for the Antipodes. The planes in which they flew had detachable cabins, 'passenger tubes', which could be released by the pilot *in toto* to float to earth beneath giant parachutes. The focus altered once again to one particular plane, to a fierce air battle over the Pacific, to the release of the 'passenger tube', to the island and, at last, to some human beings. They were all boys.

As I read on I found that, reluctantly, I was becoming not merely interested but totally gripped. The island was vividly, brilliantly real and the boys were real boys: despite his half promise, Ralph's betrayal of the secret of Piggy's nickname; the appalling sycophantic laughter of the crowd; Jack's authority over his choir. A fat, spectacled boy at school myself, I squirmed for Piggy. I said that I would take the manuscript home to read properly and when I had finished it I found it unforgettable. Indeed, to anticipate a little, as I read and reread it over the next month or two, thought about it, discussed it with colleagues and with the author, it came to dominate my imagination completely. I found that, increasingly, I kept talking about it until friends began to hint that I was becoming a Golding bore.

But I realized that the novel had flaws which seriously weakened it and might, for some readers, make it a partial or total failure. Some were superficial – commas which studded the pages as thickly as currants in a fruit loaf, Piggy's 'common' speech – his 'ass-mar', 'them fruit' – laid on with too heavy a hand; but these could easily be put right. Two others were more serious.

The first was structural. In addition to the long description of atomic war at the beginning, there were two further occasions on which the scene shifted from the island to what was happening in the world outside: an 'interlude' occurring about halfway through and describing an air battle many miles above the island which culminated in the body of the dead airman, the 'Beast from Air', drifting down by parachute; and, at the very end, an outline of the lethal manoeuvres in which the 'trim cruiser', the whole fleet of which it formed part and the enemy fleet opposing it, were engaged – rather too clearly placed there, I thought, to show that what had happened on the island was a fable, reflecting in miniature what was happening in the adult world. These passages needed severe pruning.

The second flaw, more fundamental and much more difficult, was Simon. Simon was Christ; or, too obviously, a Christ figure. At times

536

he would retire to a secret place in the jungle hidden behind a mat of creepers, where a Voice spoke to him from the green candle-buds as they opened in the scented dusk to reveal their white flowers; a vision assured him with prophetic certainty and he assured Ralph, at a moment of appalling doubt, that Ralph would get home safely; when the boys' fragile society began to fall apart and Jack and his blood-smeared hunters began their murderous dances, Simon led the boys, or some of them, on Good Dances on the beach. Alone and terrified he confronted and was not vanquished by the Lord of the Flies – a literal translation of Beelzebub, as Golding later told me. Simon alone, despite his weakness, the threat of epilepsy, taunts that he was 'batty', seemed untainted by an otherwise universal stain. In the end he was murdered.

To put it crudely and insensitively, Simon was not to me, and would not be, I suspected, to most readers wholly credible. I do not, in fact, think that I fully understood the problem at the time and it is only in the light of Golding's other novels and later discussions with him that I see it more clearly now. Simon is not only a boy, a fully and totally human boy; he is one of those rare people who are in fact – it is impossible to avoid these imprecise and difficult words – 'numinous' or 'charismatic'. Nathaniel in *Pincher Martin* and, most clearly of all, Matty in *Darkness Visible*, are later variations on the same mysterious theme. But Simon, as he first appeared, was not entirely successful. For the reader – or at any rate for me – the suspension of disbelief was a very unwilling one and the only idea I had was that any purely mirac-ulous events in the narrative must be made ambivalent, eliminated or 'toned down' in such a way as to make Simon explicable in purely rational terms. At the same time his importance, indeed his centrality, must be preserved.

At the next Book Committee I reported that the novel was odd, imperfect but potentially very powerful and that I would like to dis-cuss it with the author. There was general doubt, not unnaturally in view of the description I had given of it and the reservations I had expressed; and it was decided that it should have several more readings before any contact was made. Two editorial colleagues agreed with my verdict; Geoffrey Faber took it and was also prepared, though with doubts, to support me. The final hurdle was the Sales Director who, like our 'reader', was regarded as a real professional who could tell by instinct whether or not a book would sell. He kept it for a week or two but eventually brought it to a Book Committee meeting where we all waited for his verdict which he gave – he was a kind-hearted man – with a ruefully apologetic glance at me. The book, he said, was unpublishable. This led to a heated discussion at the end of which it was decided – this was chiefly due to Geoffrey who was unwilling to dampen too abruptly a young editor's enthusiasm – that I could meet the author and discuss the changes I thought would improve the book, but that I must make it clear that the firm was in no way committed to publishing it.

Golding and I first met in early December. I was nervous and so, I suspect, was he: he was the first of 'my' authors. In advance I had speculated a good deal about him and had decided that he was almost certainly a young, or youngish, clergyman, for the more I thought about the novel the more its theological sub-structure became apparent. Brought up a Presbyterian as I had been, with parts of the Shorter Catechism immovably embedded in my mind, I could recognize Original Sin when I saw it: 'the guilt of Adam's first sin, the want of original righteousness and the corruption of man's whole nature, together with all the actual transgressions which proceed from it'.

So the neatly trimmed beard – clerical beards were not as common then as they are now – the grey flannel trousers and tweed jacket surprised me; but when Golding told me he was a schoolmaster I realized that I had been stupid. Only a schoolmaster would know so intimately, and with such precision of detail, how awful boys could be. We talked at length and at the end I felt that a cautious trust and even liking had established themselves between us. I made my suggestions, rather nervously, and Golding, to my relief, promised to take the typescript back with him and, in the light of a rereading, consider them.

About ten days later he sent me

> . . . some bits of the emended version of my novel – the beginning, the
> middle and the end. I've done away with the separate bits, Prologue,
> Interlude, Epilogue, and as you'll see, merged them into the body of
> the text. Furthermore, Chapter One now begins with the meeting of
> Piggy and Ralph and I'm allowing the story of how they got there – or
> all that is necessary of it – to come out in conversation. Simon is the
> next job, and a more difficult one. I suppose you agree that I must
> convey a theophany of some sort or else he won't be as big a figure as
> he ought. I'm going to cut down the elaborate description of it, though,

and try to get the same effect by reticence. Then I'm distributing odd
bits and pieces of 'Simonry' throughout the text, to build him up . . .
I'm making Piggy's speech ungrammatical but not misspelling it . . .
Rereading the novel as a stranger to it, I'm bound to agree with almost
all your criticism and am full of enthusiasm and energy for the cleaning
up process. In fact I'm right back on the island.

The changes were even better than I had hoped for. All that I had
suggested was a drastic shortening of the 'nuclear war' passages but
Golding's solution was more radical and totally successful. They had
disappeared completely and the novel's new opening could not have
been bettered. In my reply I congratulated him and suggested a few
other, fairly superficial changes which he accepted in a letter a few days
later with which he enclosed the redrafted 'Simon' passages. It is clear
from my reply – which rereads, I fear, rather pompously – that I was
still not completely satisfied.

> Here are the 'Simon' bits back again, with my tentative emendations
> pencilled in. I think you have hit on the right approach to this most
> tricky of all the problems in the novel; and my emendations are again
> simply 'toning down' of emphasis. I think the danger to be guarded
> against now is turning Simon into a prig, a self-righteous infant who
> insists on saying his prayers in the dorm while the naughty boys
> throw pillows at him. In the early stages I feel it is enough simply
> to indicate that he is in some way odd, different, withdrawn; and
> therefore capable of the lonely, rarified courage of facing the pig's
> head and climbing the mountain top. The allegory, the theophany,
> is the imaginative foundation and like all foundations is there to be
> concealed and built on.

Before long, Golding returned the typescript in what was to be, by and
large, its final form. He had been ill, running a very high temperature
which was partly due to tonsillitis and partly to 'the effort of patching – so much more wearing than bashing straight ahead at a story'.
With this version I was, by and large, satisfied, though I thought a few
small changes might be made with advantage; and when I reported all
this to the Book Committee it was decided, at long last, to accept the
book for publication. I suggested we offer Golding what was then our
usual advance for a first novel, £50, but in view of the author's patience
Geoffrey Faber made it sixty. And so it was settled.

The next problem was the title. In our earliest exchange of letters I had said that *Strangers from Within* didn't seem to me right – both too abstract and too explicit – and Golding did not demur. Indeed, he began at once to suggest alternatives, 'A Cry of Children', 'Nightmare Island', 'To Find an Island'. Both I and my editorial colleagues offered suggestions – my own favourite hunting ground was *The Tempest* which is set on an island – but it was Alan Pringle, an editor rightly reputed to be good at titles, who eventually thought of *Lord of the Flies*. It has turned out to be probably the most memorable title given to any book since the end of the Second World War. Chapter titles were the next problem. Our Production and Design department was adamant that a decent-looking novel must have chapter titles to be used as running heads; and Golding, though he said his instinct was slightly against them, accepted without further protest a list of suggestions I sent him.

The book went into 'page on galley' proofs, which looked like galleys but were half the length, and it was only then that I carried out a final editorial operation – cutting Ralph's hair. In the desperate chase at the end, when Ralph is being hunted down by Jack and his pack, his long, unshorn locks keep falling blindingly over his eyes, symbolizing effectively but perhaps too heavily the descent of irrationality, instinct, panic, over reason and intelligence. Golding was as patient as ever: 'By all means cut Ralph's hair for him. I had some doubts of it myself.' So I simply took out every other reference to it. The Production department completed its work and Sales took over.

Before publication we made various efforts to whip up some advance publicity but with only modest success. *John O'London's Weekly*, that forgotten literary periodical, was to make it 'Novel of the Month' but ceased publication a week before the accolade was to be conferred; a committee set up by the first Cheltenham Festival did not even short-list it for their First Novel award – nor did it have any better luck with the Authors' Club's annual Silver Quill. The Book Society, then a very powerful body, promised a reference to it, though no more, in their monthly magazine.

On 17 September 1954 *Lord of the Flies* was at last published, by a curious coincidence exactly a year after it was first submitted. Its early reception by reviewers was usually good, and even, on occasions, enthusiastic. E. M. Forster and C. S. Lewis both praised it. Eliot, who had not read it before, was told by a friend at the Garrick that Faber had published an unpleasant novel about small boys behaving unspeakably on a desert island. In some mild alarm, he took a copy home and told me the next day that he had found it not only a splendid novel but morally and theologically impeccable. The book began not only to be talked about but to sell and before very long we had to order a reprint. In the United States, where we had great difficulty in placing it, it made little impression at first, but after a year or two, a paperback edition began to spread like forest fire through university campuses, at first on the West Coast and then in the rest of the country. Personally, I was first alerted to what was happening when an article on Golding appeared in the *Hudson Review*. And finally the book began to be 'set' at university level, at A level, finally at O level, in Great Britain and then at equivalent levels abroad. By now there are translations of it into twenty-six languages, including Russian, Thai, Japanese, Slovak, Serbo-Croat, Catalan, Icelandic and Persian; and versions in Indonesian and Malayalam are in preparation. Sales of Faber editions alone total over three million copies but there is no record, so far as I know, of total sales throughout the world. They must be astronomical.

In December 1983 Golding invited me to accompany him and his wife to Stockholm for the Nobel ceremonies; and on the evening of the presentation there was a great ball at which the laureates and their entourages were presented to the King and Queen. Carl XVI Gustaf – a spectacled, serious-looking young man – shook Golding's hand warmly. 'It is a great pleasure to meet you, Mr Golding,' he said. 'I had to do *Lord of the Flies* at school.'

The version of 'Strangers from Within' published in *William Golding: The Man and his Books* (1986) ends at this point. What follows was written sometime between Golding's death in June 1993 and February 1994.

But when *Lord of the Flies* was first published all that – the astronomical sales, the translations, the ever-increasing swatch of honorary doctorates, the Nobel Prize, the knighthood – lay unforeseeably far in the future. *Flies*, as we had begun to refer to it in Fabers, was starting to sell, there was talk of a reprint, the reviews had been encouraging. What was beginning to occupy my mind more and more was the question of what would come next. Bill – we had by now dropped the 'Mr Golding' and 'Mr Monteith' and, after a brief, old-fashioned spell of 'Dear Golding' and 'Dear Monteith', had become Bill and Charles to each other – told me that he was at work on a successor and I waited for it with a mixture of expectancy and apprehension. *Lord of the*

Flies, after all, might turn out to be what is sometimes dismissively referred to as a 'one-off', a single brilliant idea – boys totally isolated from any form of adult control – which had produced a single, brilliant book. But that idea was unrepeatable. What could possibly follow?

When one morning a heavy, foolscap envelope lay waiting for me on my desk, addressed in handwriting which by then I knew well, I opened it, took a quick look, saw that it was called *The Inheritors*, and decided to take it home. That evening I started to read it and after two pages put it down, filled with intense and utter dismay. 'O God,' I said to myself, 'first it was schoolboys, now it's cavemen. Bloody *cavemen*.' (For me, as for most of us, 'cavemen' tends to be a generic term for all prehistoric peoples.) But I took it up again and, apart from a hurried supper, didn't put it down until I'd finished it. It was another masterpiece. It was a masterpiece as original, as compelling, as powerful – perhaps even more original and more powerful – than *Lord of the Flies*. And I realised, to my surprise, after at least two re-readings. that I had no changes whatever to suggest. It was perfect as it stood.

The Inheritors was published the following year, 1955, and got some magnificently enthusiastic reviews: 'an earthquake in the petrified forests of the English novel' Arthur Koestler wrote in the *Sunday Times*. And yet it has never sold even fractionally so well – or been read by fractionally as many people – as *Lord of the Flies*. Most people's reactions, I imagine, are very much like my own initial one: who, for entertainment, would want to read a novel about cavemen?

From *The Inheritors* I realised, too, how masterfully Golding could use the device of the altered viewpoint, of suddenly making his readers see, from a totally different angle and a totally different light, people and situations they had been living with cheek by jowl and thought they knew intimately. In *Lord of the Flies* the arrival of the naval officer at the very end transforms in a moment a yelling, murderous, evil mob into a crowd of dirty, over-excited small boys. In *The Inheritors*, about two-thirds of the way through, we – the new people, *homines sapientes*, humans – suddenly see ourselves through Neanderthal eyes and realise how very strange we look.

> The new people did not move like anything he had ever seen before. They were balanced on top of their legs, their waists were so wasp-thin that when they moved their bodies swayed backwards and forwards. They did not look at the earth but straight ahead. And they were not

merely hungry. Lot knew famine when he saw it. The new people were dying. The flesh was sunken to their bones as Mal's flesh had sunken. Their movements, though they had in their bodies the bending grace of a young bough, were dream-slow. They walked upright and they should be dead. It was as though something that Lok could not see were supporting them, holding up their heads, thrusting them slowly and irresistibly forward. Lok knew that if he were as thin as they, he would be dead already.

In *Rites of Passage* Golding does it again when Talbot's discovery of Colley's diary suddenly transforms the shy, awkward, self-righteous, rather ridiculous young clergyman into a tormented, suffering creature at the mercy of terrible forces which he can neither understand nor control. The most brilliant example of all, perhaps, is in *Pincher Martin* when Christopher Martin's seaboots, which he kicks off on the fourth page, are still on his drowned corpse when it is retrieved at the very end of the story. We suddenly realise that, for three hundred or so pages, we have been not on Rockall but in Purgatory.

After *The Inheritors* the novels continued to appear. There were occasional gaps – most notably between *The Scorpion God* (1971) and *Darkness Visible* (1979), when Golding seemed to run into a blind alley – but usually the flow continued steadily.

The years as they passed transformed Bill's neat, brown, naval beard into white, prophetic splendour and transformed Bill himself more and more firmly from an 'author' into a friend. Fairly soon after *Lord of the Flies* was published the Goldings left their flat in Salisbury – Bill taught English at Bishop Wordsworth's School for boys. His wife, Ann, was a Mathematics mistress at a boys' preparatory school and they had two children, Judy and David – and bought a cottage in Bower Chalke, a small, quiet village a few miles west of the city. Ebble Thatch – their cottage was named after the little river which flows behind it – was delightful if, when I first went there, slightly cramped with a lethally low-ceilinged passage into the dining-room and with occasional piles of belongings, mostly books – Bill's, Ann's, the children's. David, I remember, had a particularly splendid collection of science fiction – a taste which I and, as I soon discovered, Bill himself half-surreptitiously shared. As the years passed and Golding's literary income began to swell, Ebble Thatch expanded. Rooms were added, the back became rather a grand front, the garden grew bigger; on the riverbank Bill established a water-garden which he tended lovingly.

Travel, too, became a considerable pleasure. Fame – for he had become beyond question famous – brought invitations from all over the world, Europe, America, Asia, Australia, Africa. The Nobel Prize presentation in Stockholm was a crowning honour.

Some years before he died Golding left Wiltshire – a bitterly cold, wind-swept county in winter – for the more clement Cornwall where he had been born and had spent most of his boyhood holidays. Tullimaar, about halfway between Truro and Falmouth, is a graceful Regency house surrounded by woods and gardens, where Kilvert had been a visitor and where Eisenhower had lived during the Allies' invasion of Europe. In Tullimaar Golding wrote his final books and re-established his Cornish roots. The last time I stayed there, early in 1993, he told me about the new novel he had started to work on. It became *The Double Tongue*. In the summer I was invited to Cornwall again for the big summer garden-party which was becoming an annual event, but to my infinite regret I was already committed to being elsewhere. Since then I have heard about that day from so many people that I feel almost as though I had been there. Children and grandchildren were staying in Tullimaar, Cornish neighbours were there and friends from London, from the country, from abroad. The weather was perfect, the air full of garden scents and in the evening, after the party, Bill sat up for hours, talking.

Next morning he was late coming down to breakfast and his son-in-law, Terrell Carver, took a cup of tea to his bedroom. He found Bill there, still partly dressed, lying on the floor. The heart attack had been massive and instantaneous.

His body was buried in the churchyard at Bower Chalke in a grave which looks out over green, unspoilt countryside. At the funeral there were only his family and a few close friends. But for the memorial service Salisbury Cathedral, beneath the soaring spire that had inspired one of his greatest novels, was packed. A boy from Bishop Wordsworth's School read the account of Simon's death from *Lord of the Flies* and the Poet Laureate, Ted Hughes, unforgettably declaimed passages from *The Inheritors*. As the great Gothic arches reverberated to his triumphal shouts I remembered, sharply and suddenly, the dog-eared pile of typescript pages I had first seen forty years before.

Acknowledgements

Editions are collaborations, and I have been fortunate to work with countless people who have generously shared their time and expertise.

My first debt is to William Golding's daughter and son-in-law, Judy and Terrell Carver. They encouraged me from the start, provided access to Golding's unpublished writings, answered an endless stream of questions, and saved me from innumerable mistakes. I have been the grateful beneficiary of their cooking and their proofreading. Between them, they turned what might otherwise have felt like a long slog into a pleasure.

The copyright of Golding's writings is controlled by William Golding Limited, and I thank all the directors for granting permission to publish this volume and to quote freely from Golding's journals. The Monteith family has also supported the project throughout. Ted and John Monteith kindly made available Charles Monteith's post-Faber correspondence and permitted its inclusion.

Faber & Faber is in the strange position of being both publisher and, in a roundabout way, the co-subject of this volume. I was privileged to have the freedom of their archive, which I could only navigate thanks to the knowledge and patience of Robert Brown and Leigh Haddix. Some of the correspondence published here had not been seen since it was first filed away; it would have evaded me, too, were it not for Leigh's indefatigable determination to help me track it down. Henry Eliot, Alex Bowler, Ella Griffiths, Rachel Alexander, Rachael Williamson, Emmie Francis, Aisling Brennan, Alex Bradshaw and Stephen Page have also contributed in various ways to the making of this volume, and I thank them and everyone at Faber. Sam Matthews performed the unenviable task of copy-editing and typesetting the book, deftly discriminating between Golding's errors and my own. Melanie Gee did a superb job with the index and Sarah Fish rescued me from another batch of errors at proofreading stage.

My institution, the University of Exeter, is home to the William Golding Archive, and my colleagues in Special Collections have been unfailingly kind and encouraging throughout my research. I am grateful to the entire team, past and present: Caroline Walter, Christine

545

Faunch, Angela Mandrioli, Sarah-Jayne Ainsworth, Annie Price, Lisa Wills, Hollie Piff, James Downs, Harriet Calver, Beth Mills, Anna Harding, Sue Inskip, Gemma Poulton, Matt Lee and Mike Rickard. Gary Stringer in Digital Humanities made the high-quality photograph of the page from the *Lord of the Flies* manuscript. Arabella Currie and Bradley Osborne know more about William Golding's fiction than almost anyone else; our conversations have enriched my understanding of his work. Nick McDowell, Philip Schwyzer and Ellen McWilliams have spurred me on with the right advice at the right moment. My students Molly Thatcher, Lucy Allen, Anna Chafer, Brian White and Sebastian Lewis contributed to the mammoth task of transcribing the letters. The University of Exeter granted me a perfectly timed period of research leave in the final stages of the project.

At school I chose German over Greek and have regretted it ever since. Kyriaki Hadjiafxendi, Henry Power and Arabella Currie came to my rescue and advised about the Greek ancient and modern in this volume. For answering my queries about E. M. Forster, Lawrence Durrell, Anthony Burgess and H. Rider Haggard, I am grateful to Lawrence Jones, Charles Sligh, Andrew Biswell and Shirley Addy respectively. I have benefitted immensely from Toby Faber's knowledge of who was who at Faber & Faber from the 1950s to the 1990s. Heather Cooper clarified her role at the firm and Karin Oldfelt Hjertonsson shared with me her memories of Golding and Monteith on their visit to Sweden for the Nobel Prize ceremony. Christine Davies in Special Collections at the University of Kent at Canterbury cleared up my confusion over the T. S. Eliot Memorial Lectures. Kathy Shoemaker of the Stuart A. Rose Manuscript, Archives, and Rare Book Library in Emory University promptly sent me a digital image of a letter from Golding to Monteith, thereby sparing me a transatlantic flight. Philip Lancaster, Peter McDonald, John Haffenden, John Lee, Nicola Presley, John Carey and Christopher Reid have provided wise words and guided me by example.

I have started and ended this project fit and healthy. What came between – cancer, chemotherapy and a serious cardiological issue – made me doubt at times that I would ever be able to see it to completion. To my friends and family whose love kept me sane and steady even in the grimmest moments, thank you, thank you, thank you.

Index

Abbreviations: CM = Charles Monteith; WG = William Golding. William Golding's wife and children are referred to in the index as Ann, David and Judy. All works are by William Golding unless otherwise indicated.

stroke 530; surgery for cyst on breast 127, 133–4, 135–6, 142
- HOMES *see* Golding, William: HOMES
- INTERESTS: as 'an addicted title fancier' 385; French language learning 484; gardening 146, 475; membership of Left Book Club 290; Spanish language learning 528
- OPINIONS/QUOTED: on accepting Blackwell's book signing graciously 459; *Darkness Visible* 375, 377, 384, 385; Egypt ('enthralled and appalled' by) 364; *An Egyptian Journal* 461, 465, 466; *Fire Down Below* 496, 497; *The Hot Gates* 245; on military junta in Greece 304; on 'pirates' trying to lure WG away from Faber 149; *The Spire* 178, 211, 213; on 'tombstone' letter 377; on Walker ('dishy') 353
- SKILLS/EXPERTISE: communication in Greece 253–4; cookery 458; 'perceptions' 315; rugby 448
- WORK: analytical chemist 152; reads 'Chemistry for Beginners' for Faber 151, 152, 153; teaching 79, 543
Golding, Arthur (no relation) 412
Golding, David (WG's son): birth 3; book gifts from CM 108, 113, 114, 159; canal boat 346, 349, 368; as director of William Golding Limited 175; education 116, 130–1, 140, 145, 152, 159–60, 192; 'ghastly' Oxford digs 192; interest in Japanese prints 107, 108; interest in science fiction 159, 181, 543; left-leanings 277, 306; mental health problems 142, 292, 300, 301, 304, 471, 493, 496, 507, 513; predicting the future 385; socialises with CM in Oxford 159, 181; visits Oxford for 'preview' 91
Golding, Eileen (WG's cousin/adopted sister) 146
Golding, Louis (no relation): *Magnolia Street* 293
Golding, Mildred (WG's mother) 140, 145, 146
Golding, William: birth 17–18; Book Society panel member 127, 136–7, 141, 148, 186; childhood 8, 501; death and funeral 530, 544; death very prematurely announced in German reference book 412; discussions about editing Faber poetry anthology 185–6, 190, 192–3, 208–9, 210–11, 212; education xiii, 17, 131, 278; eightieth birthday 515, 518, 525; journals *see*

dream journal (WG); journal entries (WG); marriage 17; meets Ann 290; naval career 17, 126; reaches pensionable age 358; refuses recording offers 189, 342–4; rejects CM's children's book suggestion 357; sense of inadequacy xiv (*see also* journal entries; *under specific* works); seventy-fifth birthday 458, 459, 490
- AWARDS/PRIZES/HONOURS: Booker Prize 409, 416, 417–18; CBE 251, 258, 259; Companion of Literature 438; honorary doctorate at University of Oviedo, Spain 528; honorary doctorate at University of Oxford 438; honorary doctorate at University of Sussex 307, 311, 312; Honorary Fellowship of Brasenose College, Oxford 258, 276–7; James Tait Black Memorial Prize 409; knighthood 498; Nobel Prize 438, 455; shortlisted for Prix International 161–2, 163–4; Society of Authors travel grant 124, 125
- FAMILY MATTERS: births of grandsons 38, 360, 410; cares for Nick during Laurie's illness (grandsons) 432, 434, 435; children *see* Carver, Judy; Golding, David; death of father 117, 181, 182; death of mother 140; illness and death of Ann's mother 309; mother moves into Ebble Thatch 145–6
- FINANCIAL MATTERS: arrangements while WG is in US 170; BBC fees for radio adaptations 56; contracts, advances and royalties *see under specific works*; decides to claim advances as soon as they are due 405, 453; dissatisfaction with writing income 85–6; establishes William Golding Limited 175; Faber's payment on account of accrued royalties 59; income from film rights to *Lord of the Flies* 191–2; income from reviewing *Oxford English Dictionary* 508, 509; Italian account 293; plans to purchase properties for children 405; preoccupation with money xiv; Rainbird contract and advance for Egypt travel book 437, 508; receiving 'incredible' quantities of money from royalties 242, 243; rent increase 57; royalties for US paperbacks 174, 175, 196, 197; school fees 36, 170; *Show* magazine fee for *The Spire* serialisation 230; six-monthly royalty income 339–40; supporting David through university 145; talks of moving abroad for tax reasons 271, 274;

Golding, William, FINANCIAL MATTERS (*cont.*): taxation 75, 248, 271, 285, 309, 432, 439, 524; thoughts about 'post mortem income' 309; thoughts on fees for films after *Lord of the Flies* 195; wealth management 246, 248

- HEALTH: alcohol problem 204, 300, 304, 307, 323, 331; Asian flu during US lecture tour 209–10; bronchitis 327, 456; emergency appendicectomy 124, 125; eyesight 521; flu 67, 69, 133, 142, 369, 388–9; gout 485; horse injures toe 465, 466; insomnia 323; 'poisoned feet' 330; poor memory/confusion 485, 487; skin cancer 528; tonsillitis 10, 11

- HOLIDAYS AND TRAVEL *see under* Australia; Austria; Belgium; Canada; Czechoslovakia; Egypt; France; Germany; Greece; India; Italy; Japan; Malaysia; Mexico; Portugal; Russia and USSR; sailing and boats; Singapore; Spain; St Ives; Sweden; Switzerland; Thailand; Turkey; United States; Yugoslavia

- HOMES: childhood home, Marlborough 8; 21 Bourne Avenue, Salisbury (council flat) 3, 57; Flat 2, St Mark's House, St Mark's Avenue, Salisbury 49, 61, 69; building work at Ebble Thatch 200, 202–3, 205; Ebble Thatch, Bowerchalke 117, 130, 543; garden at Ebble Thatch 376, 397, 430, 543–4; garden at Tullimaar 475, 477, 480, 482, 484–5, 487, 495, 499; planning move to Cornwall 467; Tullimaar home address is kept private 490, 502, 510, 524; Tullimaar home is burgled 513, 514; Tullimaar, Perranarworthal 456, 471–2, 473, 474–5, 480, 484, 489, 495, 544

- IMAGES OF: cartoon by Smith 494; photograph of WG, Ann and crew used for *An Egyptian Journal* 507–8; photograph on poster and as 'January' in calendar 292; photographed by Beaton 355, 356; photographed for *Vogue* 41, 43, 54, 74, 75, 78, 79, 82; portraits by Ayrton 265, 305–6

- INTERESTS: *The Battle of Maldon* 354–5; cricket 350, 381; Egyptian archaeology 513–14; 'four enthusiasms' (Greek, sailing, music, archaeology) 222; French language learning 335, 484; gardening 397, 430, 475, 476, 482, 487,

509, 543–4; Greece and Greek *see under* Greece; Greek, ancient and modern; horse riding *see* horse riding (WG); Latin learning 381; membership of Left Book Club 290; orchid cultivation 413, 499, 503, 504; piano playing 156; sailing *see* sailing and boats (WG); science fiction 51–2, 53, 57, 543; snorkelling 296, 306, 352; Spanish language learning 528

- INTERVIEWS: *Herald Tribune* 141, 196–7; with Ivasheva (Moscow University) 266; *Monitor* (TV arts programme) 138, 139; Q&As in Spain 528; refuses interviews/Q&As 166, 226, 228, 284, 287, 396–8, 426; *South Bank Show* (TV arts programme) 409, 507, 508, 509; *Talk: Conversations with William Golding* (Biles) 256

- RADIO/TELEVISION APPEARANCES: BBC Third Programme (radio) 235; BBC West of England Home Service (radio) 234, 235; *The Brains Trust* (TV panel show) 110, 111, 137; *Monitor* (TV arts programme) 127, 138, 139; *South Bank Show* (TV arts programme) 409, 507, 508, 509

- REFLECTIONS ON WRITING: appeal of writing (with novel-writing computer?) from the blurb 225; being an 'unsatisfactory contributor' to Faber's list 308; being overworked 114; composing at the typewriter 52; desire to 'write a funny or poetry' 123; dislike of revisions ('patching') 10; dislike of writing plays 114; experience of writing *Lord of the Flies* 17; experiences 'creative impotence' 165–6; feeling strain of 'doing two full time jobs' 103, 123; feelings about 'tea-cup novels' 84; glowing reviews for *Lord of the Flies* causing doubts about later writing 35, 52, 53; lack of time 150–1, 166; learning about 'what the chaps call the creative process' 358; perils of travel writing 234; on poetry 17, 117, 463; poor grasp of capital letters 228; poor grasp of contractions 228; poor handwriting 24, 45–6, 493; poor punctuation 8, 10, 13, 22; poor spelling 58; reduced stamina in older age 465; relaxed attitude towards historical accuracy 318, 319; sanguinity over 'succession of near-misses' 66; 'shapeless books' 136; stories settling 'like flying saucers' 64; vowing never to 'try

to be portentous again' after *The Spire*
222; writing out of himself rather than a
persona 170; writing own blurb 389, 410;
writing with integrity 171, 234
- RELATIONSHIP WITH CHARLES
MONTEITH: address each other as
'Charles' and 'Bill' 81, 541; attend
first night of *The Brass Butterfly*
together 119–21; birthday present
from WG to CM 521, 522; book/play
recommendations and gifts 17, 18, 19,
23, 25, 26, 51, 53, 55, 87–9, 94, 99, 100,
101, 107, 110–11, 113–14, 117, 118,
124–5, 134, 135, 136, 326, 331, 413–14,
458–9, 460–1, 501; CM addresses letter
to 'my dear Golding' 25; CM as one of
three people 'of major importance and
influence' in WG's life 419; CM as WG's
'literary godfather' 118; CM hosts WG
at All Souls College 152–3, 154, 198,
199, 200, 201, 202, 303, 304, 338, 397,
398, 417, 418, 419, 468–9, 471, 472,
495–6, 502–3, 504; CM invites WG and
Ann to attend *The Importance of Being
Oscar* 249, 250; CM invites WG and
Ann to cocktail party and lunch 73, 74,
76, 77, 78–82; CM invites WG and Ann
to Encaenia luncheon 327, 328, 329;
CM joins WG in Canada reading tour
482; CM keeps WG on after retirement
from Faber 488; CM misses lunch date
with WG and Ann 405, 406; CM on (in
'Strangers from Within') 538, 541, 543;
CM responds to WG's death 531; CM
sees WG receive honorary degree from
University of Sussex 311, 312; CM sends
flowers to Ann after surgery 156; CM
signs off 'love, Charles' 255; early power
relations xi; first letters and meeting
3–5, 6, 538; private jokes 130, 166; WG
attends CM's birthday party 521–2; WG
dedicates *The Paper Men* to CM xv–xvi,
448, 449, 450, 451; WG has lunch with
CM at Travellers Club, London 106, 107;
WG hosts CM at Ebble Thatch 131, 132,
148, 150, 221, 378, 444, 448; WG hosts
CM at Tullimaar xv, 481–2, 489, 490,
495, 499, 500; WG offers to host CM
at Ebble Thatch 69, 70; WG sends CM
flowers in hospital 255; WG signs books
for CM's goddaughter and brother 400–1,
416–17, 420–1; WG signs off 'our love

and fraternal greetings' 306; WG's family
dedicate *The Double Tongue* to xvi, 532
- REVIEWS OF OTHERS' WORKS: *Eton*
(Hollis) 154; *Grand Design: The Earth
from Above* (Gerster) 423, 424; *The
Luck of Ginger Coffey* (Moore) 148;
makes misattribution in review 148;
New Maps of Hell (Amis) 247; *Oxford
English Dictionary* 509; reads 'The
Lyrical Existentialists' (Hanna) for Faber
155; reads *Sarum Close* (Robertson) for
Faber 282–3, 284–5, 286, 287–8, 289,
290; reads 'Schoolmaster into Farmer'
(Heckstall-Smith) for Faber 151, 152,
153; reads *Stonehenge* (Harrison and
Stover) for Faber 313, 315, 316
- SCHOLARSHIP ON: *The Art of William
Golding* (Oldsey and Weintraub) 196;
'The Impersonality of William Golding:
Some Implications and Comparisons'
(essay) (Bayley) 479; *The Modern
Allegories of William Golding* (Dickson)
377; *Talk: Conversations with William
Golding* (Biles) 256; *William Golding:
A Critical Study* (Kinkead-Weekes
and Gregor) 143, 211, 230, 251, 264,
265, 266, 272, 273, 279–80, 283–4,
293; *William Golding: Some Critical
Considerations* (ed. Biles and Evans) 256
see also Carey, John, *William Golding:
The Man and his Books* (ed.)
- TEACHING, TALKS AND LECTURES:
ad hoc talks and classes for WEA and
WI 36; declines participation in National
Library Week 257; Ewing lectures at
University of California, Los Angeles
242, 243, 247; gives 'A Moving Target'
lecture at Rouen 353–6, 360; gives
'Aspects of Narration' lecture in Oxford
513; gives 'Belief and Creativity' lecture
in Hamburg and Copenhagen 382, 383,
386, 402–3, 404, 409, 412; gives 'Egypt
from My Outside' lecture in Canterbury
364, 369, 370, 403; gives 'Rough Magic'
lecture in Canterbury 369, 370, 403;
guest lectures at University of Kent at
Canterbury 294; lecture for National
Council for Teachers of English in San
Francisco 233; lecture tour of Australia
349–52, 353, 354; lecture tour of India
493, 508; lecture tours of US 171–2, 176,
179, 181, 204, 205, 209, 210, 392;

Tullimaar home 513; on cricket ('epic')
350; on dieting 428; on 'disastrous'
Booker Prize award evening 342; on
eightieth birthday gift from Faber 525;
extent of 335, 339; on first trip to
Egypt 363, 364; on garden acquisitions
482; on Gladstone, Australia ('the end
of the road') 351; on head injury and
early departure from Booker Prize
party 511; on likely general election
outcome 494; on loyalty to Faber xii;
on meeting an Ur-Piggy somewhere
347; on misinformation about place of
birth 18; on Molly Bloom contribution
to seminar on *Ulysses* 450; on not
attending too closely to dates of letters
94; on pilgrimage to Jung's childhood
home 331–2; on 'Port Moresby story'
351; on seeing *Chu Chin Chow* with his
mother 501; on ship models at National
Maritime Museum 516; on soil at Ebble
Thatch 477; on suitability of 'a cheery
note' for colleague 519–20; on taxation
('a phobia') 524; on unlikelihood of
letters being published xix
– on own works: 'Clonk Clonk' and
'The Scorpion God' (feelings about)
324; *Close Quarters* (Bodley's feedback)
491; *Close Quarters* (postscript)
489; *Darkness Visible* (avoiding
early reviews) 402; *Darkness Visible*
(epigraph) 381; *Darkness Visible*
(feelings about) 379, 390, 407; *Darkness
Visible* (keeping out of dispute over
rights to publish in US) 399; *Darkness
Visible* (title) 386; *An Egyptian Journal*
(Ann's opinion of) 466; *An Egyptian
Journal* (removing some of the subjective
gloom) 461; *To the Ends of the Earth*
trilogy (title) 515; *Fire Down Below*
(Ann's opinion of) 497; *Fire Down
Below* (blurb) 501; *Fire Down Below*
(feelings about) 499; *Fire Down Below*
(sales) 510; *Fire Down Below* (ship
and figurehead in jacket design) 504–5;
Free Fall (shortcomings) 139; *Lord of
the Flies* (seeing submission letter to
Faber after many years) 481; *Lord of
the Flies* (staging) 320, 335, 336; *The
Paper Men* (blurb) 455; *The Paper Men*
(feelings about) 443–4, 450; *The Paper
Men* (initial ideas appearing 'in the air')

443; *The Pyramid* ('self indulgence')
281; 'The Quarry' (pausing work on)
360–1; *Rites of Passage* (feelings about)
407; 'In Search of My Father' ('dying
of boredom') 322; waiting for CM's
responses to manuscripts 378, 466
– on other people/their works:
('Blood-and-Bones') Biles 257; Ann
and CM as 'literary parents' xii; Ann
and CM watching *Neighbours* xv;
Ann's mastectomy ('the most miserable
experience of my life') 365; Auden
('Meeting him at a party was enough')
212; Beaton's photography ('a genius')
355; Bodley (unsolicited book gift from)
483; Burgess ('such a bore!') 457; CM
stepping down from chairman at Faber
418; CM's (appearance of?) enthusiasm
about 'authors and their wretched
books' 359; CM's heart problems 418;
CM's Lenten abstemiousness 459; CM's
missed lunch date 406; CM's Randolph
Avenue flat ('the height of luxury') 492;
CM's stance on (auto)biography of WG
511–12; CM's 'Strangers from Within'
477, 480; du Sautoy's eightieth birthday
party 529; du Sautoy's retirement
party ('a gathering of elephants') 370;
Duggan's novels 131; Eliot ('the silly
old twit') 81; Giroux ('a pleasant soul')
387; Judy's work at Jonathan Cape
347; Murdoch's friendship 418; Peter
Brook ('a genius') 249; *The Rainmaker*
(portrait by Drysdale) 381; Rowse ('a
most kind host' but 'on a very short
fuse') 468; *The Salt of Life* (Nahal)
524; Starkie's biography of Baudelaire
('gives me the willies') 510; *A Suitable
Boy* (Seth) 527; *see also* dream journal
(WG)
Journey into Space (BBC radio drama) 56,
57, 84
Joyce, James: *Ulysses* 333, 450
Jung, Carl 323, 332, 335

Keats, John: gravestone epigraph 179, 373
Kennerley, Morley 132
Kennet, Lord *see* Young, Wayland
Kermode, Frank 105, 106, 107, 157, 158;
International Literary Annual article on
WG 143, 144
Khrushchev, Nikita: WG meets 204
Kidnappers, The (film) 40, 41